A HISTORY OF JAPANESE LITERATURE

VOLUME THREE

The High Middle Ages

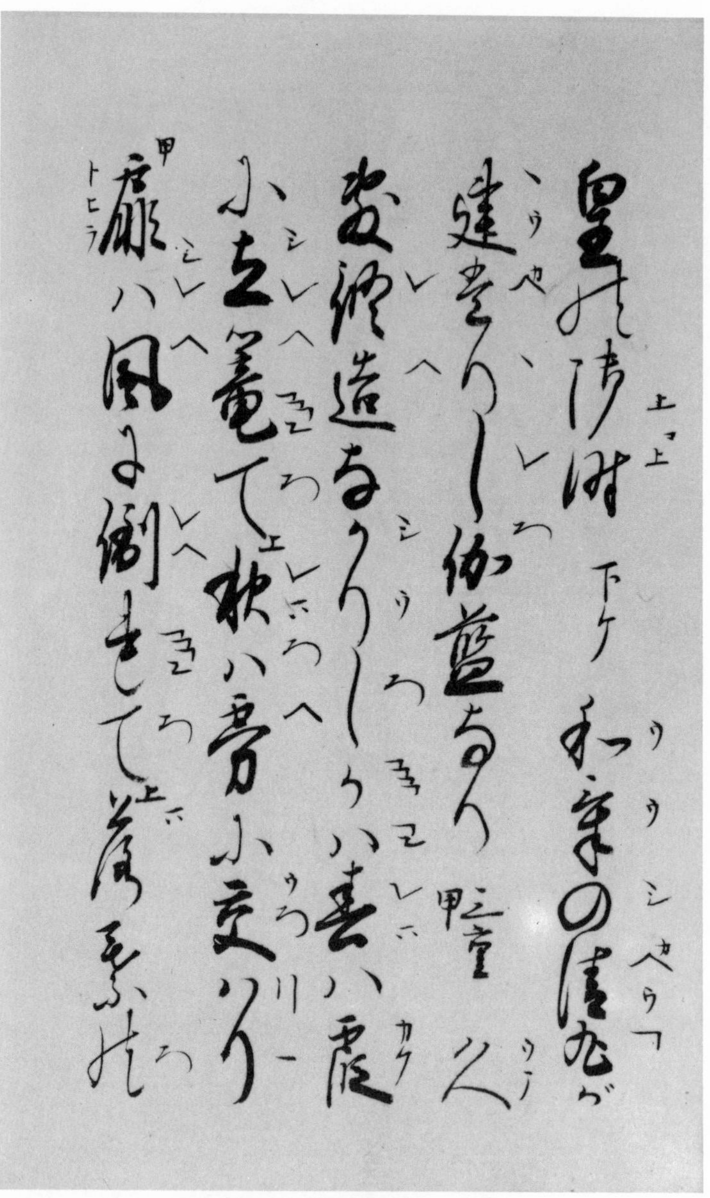

Heike Mabushi
Scorebook of the *Heike Monogatari*
Compiled by Ogino Kengyō (1731-1801); copied ca. 1900.
In the possession of the Library of Congress.

A History of Japanese Literature

VOLUME THREE

THE HIGH MIDDLE AGES

By Jin'ichi Konishi

TRANSLATED BY

Aileen Gatten AND

Mark Harbison

EDITED BY

Earl Miner

PRINCETON UNIVERSITY PRESS

Published by Princeton University Press, 41 William Street,
Princeton, New Jersey 08540
In the United Kingdom: Princeton University Press, Oxford

Library of Congress Cataloging-in-Publication Data
(Revised for volume 3)

Konishi, Jin'ichi, 1915–
A history of Japanese literature.
Vol. 3 translated by Aileen Gatten and Mark Harbison.
Includes bibliographies and indexes.
Contents. v. 1. The archaic and ancient ages —
v. 2. The early Middle Ages — v. 3. The high Middle Ages.
1. Japanese literature—History and criticism.
I. Miner, Earl Roy. II. Title.
PL716.K64813 1984 895.6'09 83-43082
ISBN 0-691-06592-6 (v. 1 : alk. paper)
ISBN 0-691-10146-9 (v. 1 : pbk.)

The publisher and author wish to thank
The Japan Foundation for its support

This book has been composed in Linotron Sabon

Princeton University Press books are printed on acid-free paper,
and meet the guidelines for permanence and durability
of the Committee on Production Guidelines for
Book Longevity of the Council on Library Resources

Printed in the United States of America by
Princeton University Press,
Princeton, New Jersey

1 3 5 7 9 10 8 6 4 2

(Pbk.)
1 3 5 7 9 10 8 6 4 2

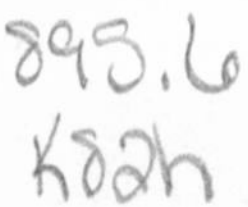

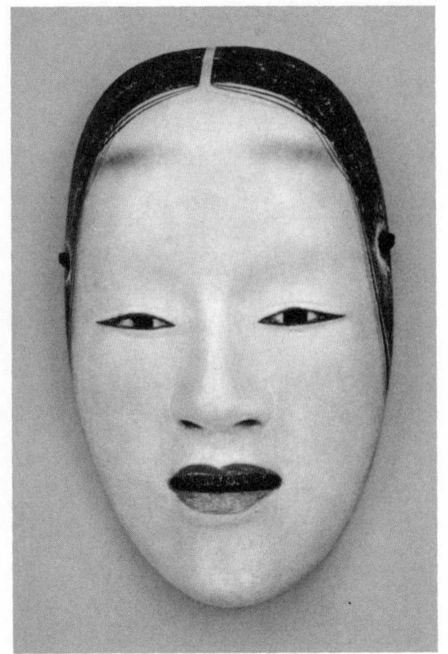

1. "Zō." By Zōami (14th-15th c.). Kanze Collection.

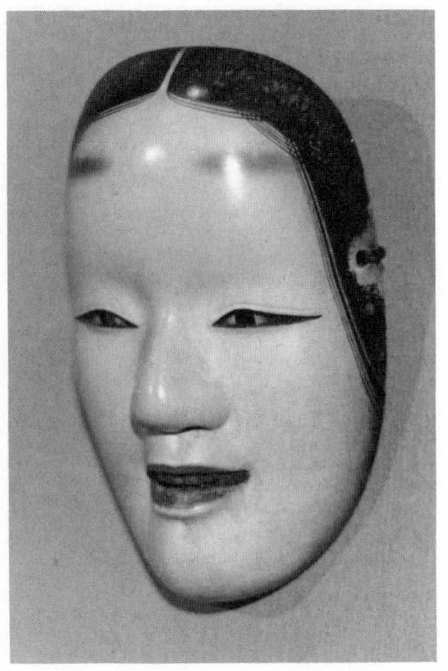

2. "Wakaonna." Maker unknown. Kanze Collection.

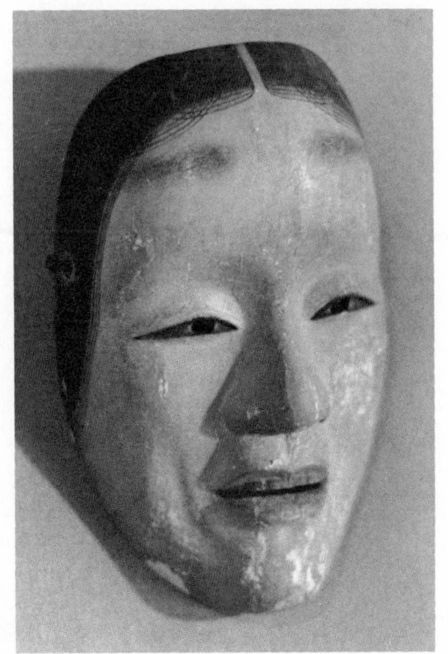

3. "Fukai." By Ochi (14th c.). Kanze Collection.

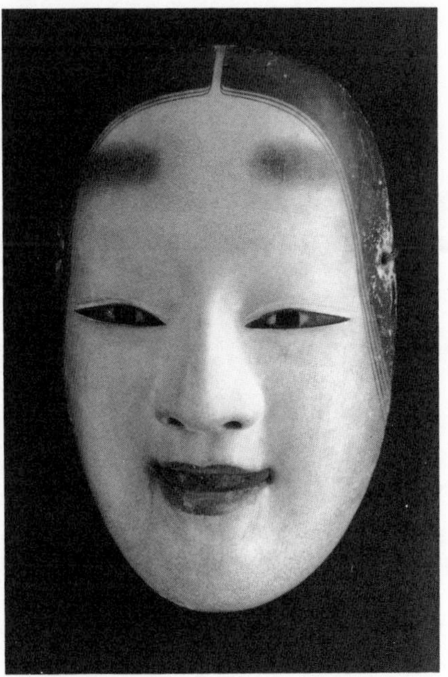

4. "Magojirō." By Kauchi (d. 1657). Kongō Collection.

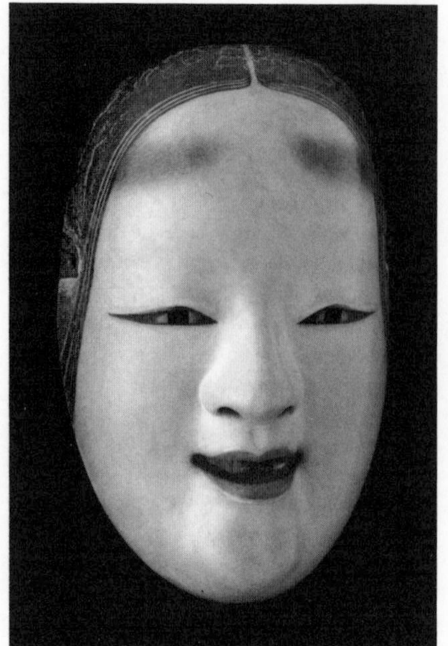

5. "Koomote." By Yasha (14th c.). Kanze Collection.

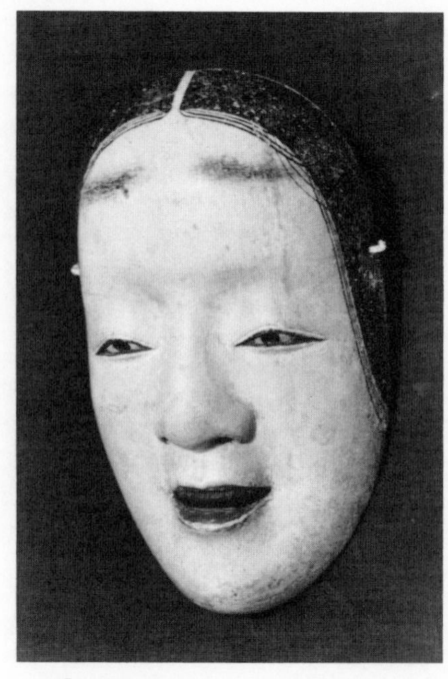

6. "Ōmionna." By Yasha (14th c.). Kanze Collection.

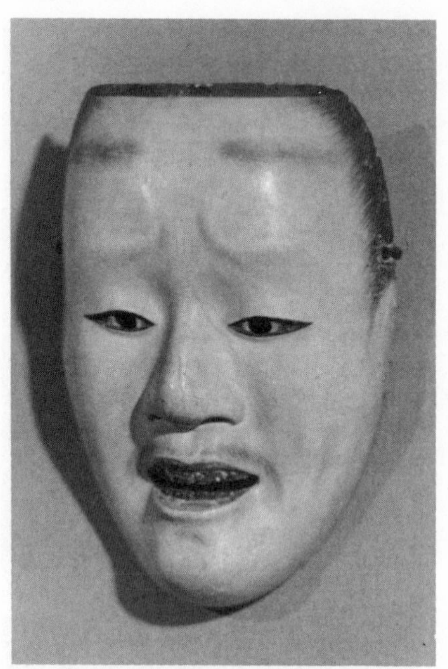

7. "Imawaka." By Yasha (14th c.). Kanze Collection.

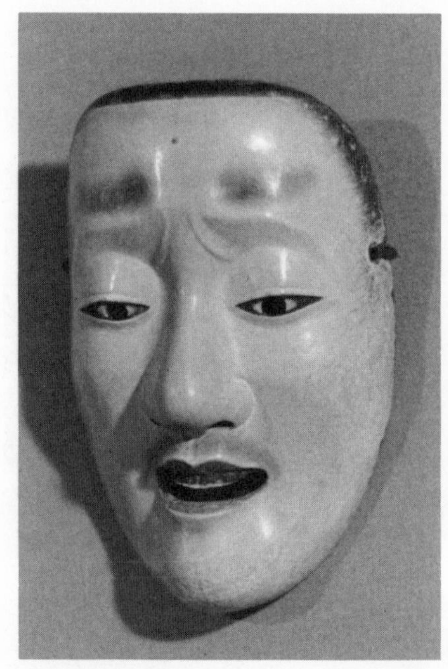

8. "Chūjō." By Kauchi (d. 1657). Kanze Collection.

IN MEMORIAM

Nose Asaji

CONTENTS

Part Three
The Formation of the High Middle Ages

Part Four
The Achievement of the High Middle Ages

LIST OF ILLUSTRATIONS

EDITOR'S FOREWORD

This is the third of the five volumes of Jin'ichi Konishi's *History of Japanese Literature*. His career has been unusual among modern Japanese scholar-critics in that his work ranges from earliest times to poetry in his own lifetime. (In fact he is a published poet himself and makes a brief renga sequence in this volume.) It is also true that if one were required to specify a period of literature in which he has seemed most at home, it would be that represented by this volume. That fact no doubt explains why this will be the longest of the five pre-modern volumes.

The first writer quoted here is Nakahara Hirotoshi (fl. ca. 1130-50), who wrote Chinese verse. The last is Komparu Zenchiku (1405-70), an actor, dramatist, and theorist of nō. They and the other writers treated certainly do not monopolize important Japanese literature. Much that is great has been treated in the two preceding volumes, and much that is great will be discussed in the ensuing two. But this volume deals with writers whom Japanese think their most profound. The author does not so much agree with that belief as give grounds for it.

A reader opening this volume without knowledge of the preceding ones may have some questions. Given certain unorthodox features of this *History*, such a reader may well wonder how the author construes "literature," "Japanese," and "history." Other questions might well be asked. What are the author's principles of periodizing? What kinds of ideology does he presume to be at work? Literary historians seldom deign to discuss these matters, and they are not discussed in this volume. Professor Konishi has, however, discussed them in the "General Introduction" that leads off the first volume of this *History*, and readers owe it to themselves to ponder that unusual essay on method. I do not promise that a reader will find that introduction entirely new in its principles or that everything in it may achieve total consent. But I do believe wholeheartedly that it is a remarkable statement of method, that it makes the author's enterprise intelligible, and that it is a model—an unprecedentedly explicit model—for a *literary history*.

Response to the first volumes in Japan has been highly enthusiastic. Our reviews come out more slowly, but what might be termed high gossip about the first volume has involved admiration with the opinion that this *History* may be above the heads of all but specialists. As a condemned generalist, I find that response somewhat surprising, although on reflection it does occur to me that certain articles on Japanese literature by James T. Araki and Howard Hibbett were ahead of their time. Even Robert H. Brower's and my *Japanese Court Poetry* seemed on appearance to have only Donald Keene as an "understander" (opposed by Ben Jonson to the "mere reader"). It is, however, one thing to desire and another thing to do. If this *History* is in advance of the state of our art, I can imagine our successors saying in another thirty years: "Yes, that seems very true" (or "needs alteration now") and, especially, "Did people really require such things explained then?" In short, I thoroughly believe that if this *History* is in advance of the state of our art, it will bring that state to par in five or ten years. What more could be hoped for?

There are other matters that my responsibility to the author and his readers requires to be made plain. For one thing, this English version departs in some ways from the Japanese. Some matter has been deleted. Some things have been transferred from notes to the main narrative. And things have been added by the translators or myself. Where possible, these are signaled by information supplied in square brackets or otherwise. Such is the author's care that he has supplied detailed "References" for us. From time to time notes will be signaled "Auth., Trans." or "Auth., Ed." These involve a kind of dialogue by the translator or myself with the author, either by adjusting his references into notes or by offering comments based on correspondence with Professor Konishi. Of course the aim in all this is to indicate those instances where the author is not entirely responsible for what appears here.

Another major change involves our reduction of the heavy cross-referencing in the Japanese version. The reason for the cross-references in the original is that there is no index to each volume but only a single index planned to appear in the last. This English version, however, is being published in our usual fashion—volume by volume. We therefore supply detailed indexes to each volume.

The readers of this *History* will include specialists along with those for whom this five-volume account will be the first history of Japanese literature they will read. Specialists may wonder about a period of Japanese literature termed "The High Middle Ages." (The Japanese, "chūsei dainiki," means something rather more like "the second medieval period.") The explanation of the author's division is to be found in the "General Introduction" referred to, and certain matters concerning our usages will be found in the "Editor's Foreword" to the first volume. In particular, our usages are explained there for matters such as names, titles, and terms. (As will already have been clear, we do not italicize Japanese terms unless they would be italicized if they were English words. Anything else would needlessly clutter the pages, and nobody is likely to think that "yūgen" unitalicized or unquoted is an English term.) In leaving numerous terms "as they are" (such as waka, renga, hon'i, en), we do supply translations, definitions, or descriptions. Strictly speaking, however, there are no English equivalents, any more than there is a Japanese equivalent of "sestina" or "the sublime." True understanding—or at least familiarity—

comes only empirically. It is also true that Professor Konishi often attaches his own meaning to terms, and in those cases we have tried to signal his usage. A reader who forgets what is meant by hon'i, for example, can most easily find some account by consulting the index. The entry for "hon'i, defined" may not lead to a true definition, but it will assist in clarification.

Jin'ichi Konishi is well known for the strength, independence, and innovation of his thought. These qualities are sometimes esteemed more in theory than in practice (other than our own). The function of the translators and myself is to present in clear fashion what our author thinks, not to second-guess him. At times, however, he assumes knowledge that may be possessed by Japanese readers but that cannot be assumed by non-Japanese readers. In these instances, we have tried to supply necessary information.

Even specialists will be surprised by some things. There are two notable poets who appear in this volume, Kyōgoku Tamekanu and Saionji Sanekanu. At first I thought the translator was wool-gathering in mentioning them, but a look at the Japanese manuscript beside the English on my desk showed that Mark Harbison had got things right. Curious about the demise of my old acquaintances, Tamekane and Sanekane, I asked Professor Konishi why he designated them Tamekanu and Sanekanu. He replied that, in reading a facsimile of an old, trustworthy edition of Gofukakusa In Nijō's *Towazugatari*, he found that she consistently writes (in kana syllabary) "Tamekanu" and "Sanekanu." Since she knew them both, she knew how their names were pronounced.

A few other matters can be clarified. The age represented in the second volume of this *History* was no doubt the most creative of new kinds of writing of any age of Japanese literature. Specialists and novices alike will do well to consult (perhaps by its index) that volume for Professor Konishi's definitions of terms that apply to literary phenomena first appearing in the period of that volume. In particular I recommend attention to his discussions and definitions there of monogatari, nikki, and zuihitsu. In this volume, new kinds of literary practice emerge: for example, imayō, nō, and renga. To consider the last, Professor Konishi is one of but two or three living people to have composed renga. (His renga master, Yamada Yoshio, came from a family that practiced Satomura-school renga as an art.) His personal library is rich in old manuscripts of renga sequences and renga treatises. As he says in one of his books, his knowledge of renga and his criteria for judging that form of linked poetry are those he was taught. He says in effect that there may be other conceptions, but he does not know them. Because there is a little debate in the United States whether the dominant unit in renga is the stanza or the entire sequence, I have taken some pains to get the author's ideas clear, taking particular care over chapter 15, and consulting Professor Konishi about details of presenting renga in English. I have also added an appendix to help nonspecialists gain a minimum idea of that kind of linked poetry.

In mentioning such matters, I owe it to the translators to thank them for their ardent care with the original. The three of us are well aware that we have had many peaks to cross, numerous shoals to ford. Getting across—the end of translation—is something we do not do clearly and gracefully without work, without luck. The translators have been not only devoted to the original but patient with my editing. Since I have been the last to lay hands on the volume, and since I have often retranslated, especially in the case of literary examples and passages, any faultfinding with the translation should begin with me.

To compare great things to small, this volume does not simply represent a momentous period in the history of Japanese literature. It also is the end of one stage in the English version. Aileen Gatten, the main translator of the first three volumes, ends her work with chapter 12 here, and I end my work with this third volume. I can say for both of us that we feel something of the pangs of ending that Gibbon felt for more authoritative reasons on completing his *Decline and Fall of the Roman Empire*. But each of us feels that it is the time for fresh minds to deal with the fourth and fifth volumes. In order to smooth the transition, we have sought and acquired the skills of Mark Harbison, who has translated chapters 13 through 18. Henceforth the editor is expected to be J. T. Rimer, whose qualifications are well known.

As with its two predecessors, this volume will be seen through press by Aileen Gatten and me. The acknowledgments will recount various kinds of aid we have received. And I speak for both of us in saying that if the first three volumes of this *History* mean as much to others as they have to us, readers will find this volume in particular no ordinary experience.

My apologies are due the author, the translators, and the readers of this volume for the delay of its appearance. The problems encountered were but two. For a time the material simply sat in the office of the editor to whom it had been assigned, with nothing happening till it had been moved to readier hands. The more serious cause of delay has been the nature of the "material." The two translators decided to speed matters by using word processors. Unfortunately, in spite of strenuous efforts, it proved impossible to coordinate the software of three different word-processing systems, including that of Princeton University Press. As a result, the very long manuscript had to be typed and proofread in the old way.

Princeton
Spring 1985, Summer 1987

THE TRANSLATORS

AILEEN GATTEN has been chief translator of the first three volumes of this *History*. She is Research Associate at the Center for Japanese Studies, University of Michigan, and has taught at the University of California, Berkeley, and at the University of Michigan. Her interests and publications center on the *Genji Monogatari* and later eleventh-century vernacular fiction.

MARK HARBISON, translator of the last six chapters of this volume, resides in Tokyo. His interests include classical poetry, modern prose narrative, and activities of The Society for Study of Monogatari. He is the designated translator for the remaining volumes of this *History*.

ACKNOWLEDGMENTS

Aileen Gatten wishes to express her gratitude to the Center for Japanese Studies, University of Michigan—especially to its former director, Professor John Campbell, and to Ms. Elsie Orb—and to Mr. Weiying Wan, Mr. Masaei Saitō, and Ms. Choo-won Suh of the Asia Library, University of Michigan, for their valuable advice and assistance.

As editor, I wish to offer thanks to Walter Lippincott, Director of the Princeton University Press, for cutting the Gordian or computer knot that bound fast this volume. His payment for retyping in the old-fashioned manner enabled me to engage the services of Helen Wright, who has done excellent typing for me over a period of many years.

Cathie Brettschneider, the copyeditor of the previous volume, taught Aileen Gatten and me a good deal about copyediting then and has given assistance to the present volume. To Margaret Case we owe the benefits of faith, intelligence, and good humor in this volume's vicissitudes. One of the two readers of the manuscript of this volume, Marian Ury, identified herself, so enabling me to thank her on behalf of the author, the translators, and myself for an extraordinarily meticulous reading that has led to greater accuracy in numerous details.

Since my editorial responsibilities end with this lengthy, rich, and rewarding volume, it is altogether decorous to thank Nicholas Teele, who translated part of the first volume; Mark Harbison, who has begun with this volume; and Aileen Gatten, who has been the main translator of the first and third volumes and the sole translator of the second. I cannot imagine a more responsible or cheerful colleague than Aileen. Her voice returns in my memory as I read pages here and there. Although I have revised, changed, and retranslated, particularly the literary examples, and although I recognize that final responsibility for the English version of these first three volumes rests with me, I cannot thank her enough. She has also assisted greatly by making the index to this volume.

The manuscript of this volume consists of almost thirteen hundred pages. Fortunately, two skilled pilots helped bring it to port. Siobhán A. Roder of Princeton University Press has been unfailingly cheerful, helping not only on this large undertaking but also on additional navigational tasks. Of our copyeditor, Nancy Moore, I can offer no higher praise for that demanding task than this: she has the intelligent art of distinguishing at one end the essential from the important and, at the other, the small from the irrelevant. Would it were always so.

Of course, as Japanese say, the original is the original. I lack words to describe the satisfaction of working about a decade on these first three volumes of Jin'ichi Konishi's *History of Japanese Literature*. The privilege is a rare one, as has been learning about waka and renga from close discussions with him begun over thirty years ago and now continued through the very end of reading copyedited manuscript on this segment of medieval Japanese literature. "Kyō ni nosuru gin."

PART ONE

Between the Early and High Middle Ages

CHAPTER 1

The Afterglow of Prose and Poetry in Chinese

The Late T'ang Style and the Shift toward Plainness for Verse in Chinese

We begin with Japanese shih (poetry in Chinese). During the eleventh century this poetry was characterized by simplicity and increasing conventionalization, and it displayed no significant change with the beginning of the twelfth century. The shih flourished in quantity but was lackluster in quality. Yet the equally lackluster work of the twelfth century saw the rise of new trends.

The first of these was a broadening of subject matter. Eleventh-century Japanese shih unquestionably gravitate toward the safety of conventional subjects. A glance at any shih collection from this period will reveal a succession of subjects: "A Sketch of a Spring Day," "A Fu Composed on Peonies," "Delighting in the Moon at the Hosshōji Temple," or "At the Hearthside, Refined Conversation." They demonstrate that the shih constituted a Japanese version of the ga (refined, high-art) ideal from the eleventh to the twelfth century. In China this was the time of the middle of the Northern Sung dynasty (960-1126), which fostered a new, colorful shih style. Japanese shih, on the other hand, moved toward ever more homogeneous expression.

Chinese shih display various styles from the T'ang period (618-906) on. If we include the yüeh-fu (ballad) among the forms of Chinese poetry, their subject matter touches every aspect of life in society (see vol. two, ch. 6). Japan followed an opposite course, essentially because official relations had broken off between the two countries. The thirteenth Japanese embassy to the T'ang court, departing in 838, was the last official mission for centuries, and the consequent severing of government-sponsored exchange with China had a great effect on Japanese culture.[1] Private commerce by merchant ships, combined with many instances of Japanese monks traveling to China aboard these ships (Mori, 1948, 174-88), ensured that new Chinese books would continue to reach Japan. But books and information were imported only sporadically with this non-

[1] [Official relations with China recommenced in the latter half of the fourteenth century, at the behest of the shōgun Ashikaga Yoshimitsu.—Trans.]

governmental procedure and could not raise a cultural momentum great enough to affect the whole of Japan. There is no sign, after the tenth century, of literary activity equal to that engendered by the earlier overwhelming influence of Po Chü-i's (772-846) shih style on Japanese rulers and the court intelligentsia. For this reason, the situation of Japan in the eleventh and twelfth centuries resembles its self-imposed isolation from the seventeenth through the mid-nineteenth centuries. The varied stylistic currents within Chinese poetic circles were not reflected in the shih of Japanese poets, whose fixed critical standards consisted only of those widely applied in Japan. In this respect the period may be considered an extension of the Early Middle Ages.

The Japanese who wrote shih in the twelfth century constituted a self-contained group. They adopted little in the way of new poetic styles from China, not because the Japanese had developed their own styles, but due to certain preferences. Of all the poetic subjects deemed appropriate for the literati in China, the Japanese chose one category—called "leisure and tranquility" (hsien-shih) by Po Chü-i—and the stereotyped stance associated with it. The speaker of a poem composed in this style would employ lofty sentiments in praising the tranquil beauty of a suburban villa, a fisherman's thatched cottage, a renowned temple, or a similar place he has visited. A Japanese shih composed "On Visiting the ——— Temple on an Autumn Day" might be concerned with the temple of Chōrakuji, Ryōzenji, or Hōrinji, but the poem bears no relation to the subject of the title. The treatment is virtually identical regardless of the temple's or the poet's identity. Modern readers tend to dismiss such stereotyping out of hand. But before we force our own critical views—which stem from European Romanticism—on twelfth-century shih, we should consider why their authors were content to use the same approach repeatedly. Where we moderns find only uniform expression, they discovered a subtle, deeply resonant freshness. Moreover, a poet repeatedly composing on the same subject using the same treatment would be drawn to characteristic aspects of that subject. The poet's approach was, then, to strive to grasp the most typical element of the subject, its essence. It is highly significant that this approach was applied to shih at roughly the same time as waka poets were concerning themselves with the principle of hon'i (essential nature; see ch. 2).

Occasionally atypical shih subjects appear. They are few, but well worth our notice. Several shih, for example, are concerned with kugutsu, itinerant female performers commonly doubling as prostitutes.[2] Ōe no

[2] There are, so far as I can tell, seven such poems in the extant corpus of twelfth-century Japanese shih. Burton Watson has translated one, Fujiwara Tadamichi's "The Puppeteers" (*Hosshōji Shū*, 406; Watson, 1975, 69).

Masafusa (1041-1111) treats this subject in prose in his "Kugutsuki" ("An Account of the Kugutsu"; see vol. two, ch. 9). It seems to have been a rather popular subject. Our concern is with its treatment. "The Kugutsu," by Nakahara Hirotoshi (fl. ca. 1130-50), contains these lines (*Honchō Mudaishi* [=*HMDS*], 2:239):

They peddle love in Tamba, unaware of their ugliness;
In notorious Akasaka, many sport moustaches.
Faces powdered and daubed with rouge, they flirt constantly,
Always praying that the gods and buddhas will grant
them favor.

Hirotoshi appends commentary to his shih: he wrote the first line, he says, "because every kugutsu in Tamba is ugly"; and the second line was written "because a great many kugutsu from Akasaka, in Mikawa province, have moustaches. They are called the Moustachioed Misses." It is a shameful scene—the notoriously homely Tamba kugutsu and their Akasaka counterparts, known for their moustaches, making coquettish approaches through heavy make-up—but it also communicates a sense of pathos.

Let us consider another shih, "On Seeing a Peddler Woman," by Fujiwara Tadamichi (1097-1164; *HMDS*, 2:240).

A sorry sight, this downcast woman in her shabby clothes
Who goes about peddling until the sun has set:
Raising the price for undue profit, she stands before a door,
Or cries her name outside the gate, lingering there awhile.
A poor household offers custom, but she pays no heed,
Forcing herself unbidden onto one of greater wealth.
"The autumn moon" and "spring blossoms" struck me as passé,
But this topic came to me very naturally.

This is the entire poem. Tadamichi occupied the supreme court offices of regent and chancellor. We do not know how he came to be so well informed about life in the city streets, but he gives a vivid description of the peddler woman. That is, modern readers find the poem vivid: other twelfth-century shih writers probably deemed it unacceptable. What is more, "On Seeing a Peddler Woman" clearly outdoes Hirotoshi's "Kugutsu" in the frequent use of expressions that would puzzle a native Chinese. It goes far beyond the usual degree of linguistic distortion practiced by Japanese shih poets and yields a sense of unnaturalness in disregarding

Chinese poetic concepts. This is not simply a matter of diction. In the last two lines, the speaker takes the part of the composer to explain why the poem was written, a technique corresponding to the authorial intrusion (sōshiji) in fictional monogatari. Such expression is anomalous in regulated verse (lü-shih). Tadamichi probably intended his poem as a light piece, but the existence of several similar twelfth-century shih can only mean that they represent a contemporary poetic trend.[3]

Twelfth-century shih poets found value, then, in repeating established subject matter and styles, but its members also composed on the humblest of topics, using unprecedented approaches. A corresponding movement was taking place with waka during this period. There were two trends: to discover a subtle freshness in poems observing established expression and to seek out unprecedented subjects and styles (see ch. 2). Essentially, then, two literary positions coexisted during the twelfth century, one advocating retention of the formal ga aesthetic, and the other seeking to find freshness in the realm of zoku (nonstandard, lower art). We can only conclude that an identical literary consciousness functioned in both shih and waka and that this is one of the hallmarks of the twelfth century.

A second trend in the twelfth-century Japanese shih is a limited revival of the ornate (Ch. ch'i-li, J. kirei). Ornate features are also present in eleventh-century shih, but it is a Six Dynasties (400-618) style of ornateness—familiar to Japanese shih poets from the ninth century on—that becomes less striking through Po Chü-i's impact on Japanese shih. The ornateness in eleventh-century shih therefore suggests a possible return to the Six Dynasties style (see vol. two, ch. 6). By contrast, twelfth-century shih (though relatively few in number) abandon a muted ornateness to display something denser. This trend approximates the Late T'ang style more than that of the Six Dynasties. Po's style reigned in China during the Middle T'ang period (766-835), after which it swiftly declined.

During the Late T'ang period (863-906), poets like Tu Mu (803-52), Li Shang-yin (812-58), and Wen T'ing-yün (812-70?) reinstated the ornate style. The Six Dynasties ornate style is inclined toward beautiful diction, and overelaboration is more striking than the poetic concept. The Late T'ang emphasis, on the other hand, is on beauty emanating from the concept itself. The beauty of Late T'ang shih is underscored by a sense of

[3] "On Seeing a Woman Peddling Charcoal" (*HMDS*, 2:240), by Prince Sukehito, describes a vendor from the northern suburbs of the capital. Subject matter for other shih includes: farmers, salt merchants, prostitutes, fortune-tellers, greengrocers, patent medicines, rice cakes, dogs, mice, flies, and colloquial speech. Gamblers appear in "One Hundred Couplets Composed in Reminiscence on a Day in Early Winter" (*Honchō Zokumonzui* [=*HZM*], 1:15-18), by Fujiwara Atsumitsu (1063-1144), which depicts ordinary urban affairs.

extreme delicacy, the ethereal attraction (yōen), say, of a flower at the last moment before it begins to fade. The beauty suggested by Six Dynasties poetry is youthful, while the Late T'ang sense verges on the emptiness of imminent decline. The High T'ang period (710-65), the most accomplished in the long history of China, began its downward course after An Lu-shan's revolt (755-63). After the Late T'ang period proper, there came a new, unsettled time, the Five Dynasties (907-59), an age of constant political upheaval. Late T'ang poetry charms one with its beauty, but leaves a sense of emptiness. This alluring, empty beauty reappears, albeit rarely, in twelfth-century Japanese shih.

The Late T'ang style has many facets. Its shared features with the twelfth-century Japanese shih are perhaps best seen in nature poetry. One example is "View from a Farmhouse on an Autumn Day," by Minamoto Tsunenobu (1016-97; *HMDS*, 7:283).

> I visit a farmhouse at dusk; then, about to leave, I hesitate.
> Pressed to stay, I linger awhile, to gaze at the scenery.
> On the way through the suburbs, the last flowers were fading;
> At my lodge, near the water's edge, bent willows show autumn
> colors.
> Clouds darken the thatched eaves, rain comes from the mountain;
> A gale opens the pine door on fields veiled in mist.
> Reeds on the strand shine tonight with the moon bright on the
> waves.
> Oh, to row off angling with an aged fisherman!

There is no sign of the sumptuous diction characteristic of Six Dynasties poetry. The subject matter is similarly austere: autumnal growth is depicted as it fades rather than at the height of its beauty. This calls up a vision in the speaker's mind of the flowers as they had been at their peak, and because it is idealized, the envisioned beauty of the flowers exceeds their past beauty in reality. Focusing on fading reality while evoking an underlying beauty superior to that of reality is a technique redolent of Late T'ang poetry. The other subjects treated in Tsunenobu's shih are equally lacking in splendor. The autumnal willow, dark clouds, thatched eaves, the pine door, mist-wrapped fields, and reeds are all images of desolation. But because the scene is bathed in moonlight, the tone of the poem as a whole is one of tranquil beauty. The nature poetry of the High T'ang poet Wang Wei (699?-761) is justly celebrated, and it is not impossible that his collected works had reached Japan by this time. Wang's nature poetry certainly deals with rural scenes and phenomena, but the keynote is the vigor and vitality of nature. There are no scenes of emptiness. In other words, Tsunenobu's shih bear closer affinities to Late T'ang poetry.

Of course, the Late T'ang style was oriented toward more than tranquil beauty, and many Late T'ang poems are brighter in tone. A corresponding example from the Japanese shih corpus is by Ōe no Masafusa: "Gazing at the Snow and Serving Wine" (*Chūyū Shihai*, 43).

> My face peach colored, I am drunk: petals seem to dance;
> A tea branch cracks, my eyes open: the sound of bamboo breaking.
> The frigid moon is held captive by the indigo waters at dawn.
> White clouds fill the clear sky over jade mountains.

An evening's entertainment of snow-viewing and drinking continues through the night, and then the day begins to dawn. One is struck by the fresh, lovely colors—crimson peach blossoms, indigo waters, white clouds at dawn—and by the auditory image of bamboo branches snapping in the cold. This is a more affirmative poem than Tsunenobu's. Yet its beauty is sustained only by minute observations, a feature shared with Late T'ang poetry. Minute observation is an important element of the Late T'ang style, and it yields a beauty particularly characteristic of the period when verse is in the descriptive mode.

Subtly depicted scenes also appear to some extent in twelfth-century Japanese shih. There are several examples in *Honchō Mudaishi*.[4]

> Glimpsed through a grove of scarlet leaves, the huts of fishermen;
> Mountain peaks pierce blue sky, the birds' path is secluded.
> (1:229; Minamoto Tsunenobu, "The Royal Progress to the Temple Byōdōin")

> Their fragrance reaches my shutter; bedecked with dew, how charming they are!
> Stamens blow in an oblong course under the bamboo blinds.
> (2:233; Fujiwara Atsumitsu, "On Gazing at Blossoms in the Garden")

> Slender leaves blow in the wind, a sound heralding autumn's chill;
> Glimpsed through delicate branches, one moon is bright despite the dawn.
> (2:237; Koremune Takatoki, "On Gazing at the Bamboo at My Window")

[4] *SGRJ* ("Bumpitsubu," 7).

Forest blossoms scatter like snow on a gently breezy evening;
Riverbank willows are wreathed in mist, a pleasant daytime sight.
(4:257; Fujiwara Atsumoto, "A Reluctant Farewell to Spring")

Mist enfolds the dewy bamboo, as on the banks autumn deepens.
The wind brings a cicada's song, chill as the forest darkens.
(5:271; Fujiwara Michinori, "Composed Alone and at Leisure")

Leaves scatter scarlet, covering my guests' path;
A stretch of moss, still green, will make them splendid seats.
(9:298; Fujiwara Shigeaki, "On a Scene Before Me, One Autumn Day at the Zenrinji Temple")

An indigo stream, colored by leaves, seems aflame in autumn;
From a grand hall, a bell's tolling comes in snatches on the dawn wind.
(9:299; Fujiwara Mototoshi, "On a Scene Before Me, One Autumn Day at the Zenrinji Temple")

The sunset light beneath the eaves comes filtered through the trees;
A sound at dawn, bamboo leaves rustling at the window.
(10:316; Fujiwara Chikamitsu, "On a Scene Before Me, at a Monastery in Higashiyama")

Observation this minute does not easily accord with the fabricated logic characteristic of the Six Dynasties style.[5] All the verses given above are in a purely descriptive mode, a feature also common to the Late T'ang style.

In absolute numbers, twelfth-century Japanese shih do not contain great quantities of expression in the Late T'ang style, but then again it is not a rare occurrence. What circumstances would account for this? As has been said, merchant ships continued to travel between Japan and the continent after the Japanese discontinued their embassies, suggesting that collections of Late T'ang shih may have entered Japan by such means. We know that Fujiwara Michinori (d. 1159) had poetry collections by Lo Yin (833-909) and Tu Hsün-ho (846-904) in his library.[6] It follows that other Late T'ang collections were probably brought to Japan. A passage from Ōe no Masafusa's "Shikyōki" ("An Account of the Stages of Shih")

[5] Fabricated logic is discussed in connection with the Early Middle Ages (see vol. two, ch. 1).

[6] *Michinori Shomoku*, 548, 553.

reads: "In recent times, Po Chü-i and Yüan Wei-chih [Yüan Chen] changed the fashion. . . . The result came to be called the Yüan-ho style. It was practiced by everyone, including Chang Hsiao-piao, Hsü Hun, Tu Hsün-ho, and Wen T'ing-yün" (*Chōya Gunsai* [=*CG*], 3:64-65). We may correctly conclude that Masafusa mentions Chang Hsiao-piao and the other Late T'ang poets not simply as names known to him, but because he had read their shih collections.

Nevertheless, there was no effort made on official levels to adopt Late T'ang culture, an indication that the poetic styles of the Late T'ang period did not revolutionize Japanese shih. Typical Japanese shih remained focused on the traditional Po style. We have seen, however, that some twelfth-century Japanese shih contain expression in common with Late T'ang poetry: can this be satisfactorily explained by the sporadic importings of Late T'ang poetry collections? I would like to consider one more factor, the role played by Korean shih. Because few survive from the tenth and earlier centuries, their stylistic hallmarks are difficult to discuss. Ch'oe Ch'i-wŏn, an exemplary Korean shih poet during the late ninth through early tenth centuries, has left us examples written in the Late T'ang style, however (see vol. two, ch. 1). The many extant twelfth-century Korean shih are also written principally in the Late T'ang style, and so the same was probably true for the centuries immediately preceding. One example, drawn from the *Tong Munsŏn* (*Korean Selections of Refined Literature*), is the work of the renowned twelfth-century Korean poet Kim Pu-sik (1075-1151) and is titled, "Worshipping at the Temple of Anhŭasa" (19:224).[7]

Though autumn nears its end, the shade is dense from garden trees;
The night still, I hear clean sounds of water coursing stones.
I waken to a chilly morning, as though rain might fall,
And recollect a night spent in a fishing boat among the reeds.

Kim's poem, like Tsunenobu's, captures a tranquil beauty through the minute description of scenery. This style appears frequently in twelfth-century Korean shih, although a brighter beauty is also to be found. "The West Capital," by Chong Ch'i-sang (d. 1135), is a good example of the latter (*Tong Munsŏn*, 19:226).

A spring breeze sweeps misty rain through the grand avenues;
Dust lies undisturbed, willow branches bend.

[7] The *Tong Munsŏn* is an anthology of traditional poetry and prose written in Chinese by Koreans and is patterned after the Chinese anthology *Wen Hsüan*. The *Tong Munsŏn*, in 154 units, was compiled by royal command during the Yi dynasty, between the reigns of Sŏngjong (r. 1470-94) through Chungjong (r. 1506-44). The editors include So Kŏ-jŏng and Sin Yong-gae.

Green window-frames, vermilion shutters, sad songs to the music
of pipes:
Each house belongs to a professional entertainer.

The lively imagery of the poem harks back to the ornate Six Dynasties style, but its detailed observation is truly characteristic of Late T'ang shih. "After Drinking," by the same poet, also has a Late T'ang beauty (*Tong Munsŏn*, 19:226).

In rain made crimson by peach blossoms, birds twitter and chirp;
The blue mountains ringing my house are dimmed by green mist.
My black silk cap is crooked; too much trouble to adjust it;
Drunk, I sleep on a flowery bank and dream of Chiang-nan.[8]

This poem and Masafusa's "Gazing at the Snow and Serving Wine" share a similar tone.

It is unclear whether such similarities do indeed stem from the influence of Korean shih. So far as I know, we have no information indicating whether Korean shih reached twelfth-century Japan in any quantity or how deeply they affected Japanese shih circles. On the other hand, during the twelfth century, both Korea and Japan undeniably slighted High T'ang poetry, preferring to compose in the Late T'ang style. If we discount direct influence, we must conclude that common features evolved in Korean and Japanese shih for some specific reason. That reason remains obscure. Nevertheless, both Korea and Japan made the Late T'ang style an object of enthusiasm during the twelfth century, a hundred years after its decline in China. This demonstrates that the cultural proximity between Japan and Korea was greater than that with China.

Ga in Parallel Prose and Zoku in Plain Prose

Parallel prose (Ch. p'ien-wen; J. bembun) was the principal style of prose written in Chinese during the tenth and eleventh centuries in Japan, while the plain prose (Ch. san-wen; J. sambun) style was only beginning to emerge. The advance of plain prose becomes more marked in the twelfth century. Not that parallel prose went into retreat: it continued to be used frequently in Japan for formal documents. Despite the vast quantity of parallel prose works generated during this period, however, hardly a one deserves enthusiastic judgment. This may be because the Japanese were not exposed to the innovative plain prose styles of Han Yü (768-824) and

[8] Chiang-nan, a region in southeast China centering on the Yangtze River, is famous for its scenery. Its rose plum blossoms, willows, and bamboo are often celebrated in shih. [Auth., Trans.]

Liu Tsung-yüan (773-819; see vol. two, ch. 6). Han and Liu advocated plain prose in reaction to the tired parallel prose style. As the plain prose style became more subtle, however, the writers of parallel prose were also obliged to strive for a more refined style. In fact, Late T'ang parallel prose, reinvigorated after the collapse of Han's and Liu's plain prose movement, displays expression even more finely rendered than that found in Early T'ang parallel prose, an indication of the Late T'ang desire that parallel prose not lose to plain prose in delicacy of treatment.[9]

Japanese plain prose, by contrast, simply employs freer expression than that used in parallel prose. It has none of the pleasing, compact structure and other features that are hallmarks of Chinese plain prose. Instead it might be described as a headlong rush toward lax expression. Deprived of the stimulating discipline that knowledge of true plain prose would have brought, Japanese parallel prose quite predictably lacks polish.

Although Japanese shih share some stylistic points with Late T'ang poetry, twelfth-century Japanese parallel prose is not at all like its Late T'ang counterpart. The reason may be that parallel prose was chiefly used for practical purposes in Japan. For example, *Honchō Zokumonzui* (*Continued Superlative Literature of Japan*), an anthology in thirteen parts, contains fu and shih in Part One and shih prefaces in Parts Eight through Ten. But the rest of the text is given over to various public documents such as royal edicts (sho), royal responses (chokutō), certificates of court rank (iki), formal responses (saku), official requests (hyō), memorials to the throne (sōjō), official letters (shojō), and to practical writings like encomia (san), disputations (ron), poetic inscriptions (mei), interbureau notices (chō), statements for sponsoring Buddhist services (hyōbyaku), and formal Buddhist prayers (gammon).[10] The trend is more marked still in another work, *Chōya Gunsai* (*Anthology of Public and Private Documents*), extant in twenty-one parts.[11] Although Parts One through Three are entitled "Rhymed and Unrhymed Verse and Prose," there are not many works in such acknowledged literary genres as fu, shih, shih prefaces, waka prefaces [written in Chinese prose], prose on emotional themes (ji), and prose accounts (ki).

More than half these books consists of practical documents: poetic inscriptions, prose encomia, expositions to the throne (kei), formal Buddhist prayers, sponsors' statements, explanations of the origin of a cere-

[9] Li Shang-yin and Wen T'ing-yün are exemplary composers in this style. Books on parallel prose composition appeared in great numbers earlier, during the Middle T'ang period, in response to growing technical subtleties (Kuo S., 1934, 273-81).

[10] *Honchō Zokumonzui* contains works composed between 1018 and 1140. It is attributed, without firm evidence, to Fujiwara Suetsuna.

[11] *Chōya Gunsai*, originally made up of thirty parts, was compiled by Miyoshi Tameyasu (1049-1139).

mony or a religious institution (engi), explications of rules and customs (shiki), royal edicts (sho), pledges (kishō), state declarations to gods and buddhas (kokubun), and petitions to gods and buddhas (saimon). The twenty-five sections beginning with Part Four are given over entirely to public documents: royal decrees (choku) and edicts, informal royal messages (senji), state directives (kampu), certificates of court rank, official documents of resignation (jihyō), monthly court duty rosters (gassō), official requests (seisō), applications (mōshibumi), and internal memoranda (chōjō). The most utilitarian official documents were written in plain prose, but parallel prose was used in formal circumstances. Practical documents like formal Buddhist prayers and sponsors' statements were also written in parallel prose as a rule. Whether ceremonial or official, the circumstances in which parallel prose was employed were governed by the situation at hand, so rendering highly decorative language infeasible.

There are four essential conditions for parallel prose: (1) it must consist primarily of lines of four and six characters; (2) the main section must utilize parallelism; (3) the principal diction must follow evident prior example; and (4) a given one-line unit must follow an established pattern of level and deflected tones (see vol. two, ch. 1). But the matters dealt with in bureaucratic or everyday documents are of a different temporal nature from the subjects of the ancient Chinese classics, and appropriate literary precedents are not easily discovered. Japanese parallel prose in the twelfth century was therefore inevitably poor in literary allusions and not at all lovely by Chinese critical standards.

T'ang parallel prose is thought to have reached its zenith with the work of the Middle T'ang writer Lu Chih (754-805; Liu Lin-sheng, 1936, 88-94), but two somewhat later figures, Li Shang-yin and Wen T'ing-yün, also wrote beautiful parallel prose during the Late T'ang. Because of their abundant classical allusions, their works in practical prose kinds are quite lovely. Apparently, dealing with one's own national classics made it less difficult for the Chinese to express contemporary practical matters in precedented language. Further, the use of tonal patterns to differentiate one line of parallel prose from another was in effect no more than an intellectual, conceptual convention to the Japanese, who were unable to appreciate the beauty created by Chinese tonal patterns (see vol. two, ch. 1). So long as a work consisted basically of four- and six-character lines and used parallelism in its main section, Japanese considered it parallel prose.

Japanese parallel prose may be criticized from two perspectives: its failure to fulfill half the requirements of parallel prose (conditions 3 and 4 above) makes it rather dull literature, and its formal restrictions, which inhibit an author from stating his ideas freely, kept the genre from developing. Neither criticism hits home, however. Both are negated by a single fact: parallel prose was composed in great quantities from the thirteenth century on. The volume reaches particularly impressive proportions with the fifteenth century and Gosan literature.[12] If parallel prose had been an uninteresting or an extremely difficult style, compositions employing it would not have appeared in such number.

Japanese parallel prose is lackluster when measured by Chinese criteria, but medieval Japanese, who did not take such criteria into account, undoubtedly found it quite interesting. Its fascination lay in the basic structure of parallel prose, which effectuates logical thought processes. Although the Japanese have not often shown talent for writing orderly, reasoned prose, an external framework can enable them to compose in a logical style. The more inept one is at writing logically, the greater one's satisfaction at finally being able to do so. It may seem bothersome to write prose entirely by the rules. On the other hand, one has only to keep the parallel prose form in mind and shape everything else to fit it, and one will achieve, fairly effortlessly, a decent prose style. This method will not yield a great style, but then neither will it be poor. This can be deduced from the sōrōbun style, the standard Japanese epistolary form up to the 1920s.[13]

It follows that parallel prose composition demands above all that form be kept in mind. Not surprisingly, the growing popularity of parallel prose during the twelfth century was accompanied by a demand for handbooks on parallel prose composition. *Sakumon Daitai* (*Basics of Composition*), compiled by Nakamikado Munetada (1062-1141), is an excellent example. One of its chapters, "Hitsu Daitai" ("Basics of Formal Prose"), gives a very clear picture of parallel prose structure.[14] It mentions the following kinds of parallelism, used in the principal sections of a parallel prose piece (*Sakumon Daitai*, 68-69).

> Decorative couplet (shōku): 3 characters per line (appears after the hokku, or opening phrase).[15]

[12] ["Gosan" or "five mountains" refers to three sets of five temples from the early fourteenth through the late sixteenth centuries: five of Zen monks in Kyoto, five of Zen monks in Kamakura, and five of nuns. Since little is presently known of the five convents, the expression refers principally to the monasteries. The identity of the five in Kyoto and Kamakura was not always the same, and there were not always five in one or the other place.—Ed.]

[13] Sōrōbun originated from thirteenth- and fourteenth-century colloquial Japanese that was later polished into a literary language. It became a fixed form from the seventeenth century. Only a primary school education was necessary to compose a correct letter in sōrōbun, so long as it formed part of the curriculum. Writers usually followed a set pattern that could be varied to include the correct proper nouns, season, and location relevant to each letter.

[14] The chapter probably predates Munetada's time (see vol. two, ch. 1, n. 61).

[15] "Syllables" might be employed in this passage in place of "characters," since a Chinese character is monosyllabic.

Short couplet (kinku): 4 characters per line.

Long couplet (chōku): from 5 to 9 characters per line and occasionally exceeding 10.

Alternating couplets (kakku; a reference to alternating parallelism. Subdivisions follow).[16]

Light alternating couplets (keikakku): 4 characters per line in the first couplet, 6 per line in the second.

Heavy alternating couplets (jūkakku): 6 characters per line in the first couplet, 4 per line in the second.

Sparse alternating couplets (sokakku): 3 characters per line in the first couplet, any number in the second.

Dense alternating couplets (mikkakku): 5 or more characters per line in the first couplet, 6 or more per line in the second.

Equivalent alternating couplets (heikakku): both couplets have either 4 or 5 characters per line.

Mixed alternating couplets (zakkakku): 4 characters per line in the first couplet and from 5 to 8 per line in the second. Or, from 5 to 8 characters per line in the first couplet and 4 per line in the second.

In all cases, couplet lines end in an alternating tonal pattern. Parallel prose elements other than couplets include the following, none of which requires attention to tonal patterns.

Opening line (hokku): generally 1 or 2 characters but sometimes 3 or 4. Used to begin a work.

Free-form line (manku): from 4 to 8 characters and occasionally exceeding 10.

Concluding line (sōku): 1 or 2 characters. Indicates the end of a sentence.

Interjection (bōji): the wording is similar in nature to that used in the opening phrase. Interjections appear well into the work.

Correctly arranged, these lines produce prose that is beautiful in form and lively despite the predominance of four- and six-character couplets. *Basics of Composition* quotes Ki no Haseo's "Prayer on the Occasion of Dedicating the Round Hall at Temple Ninnaji" as an example of parallel prose (*Sakumon Daitai*, 70-71). An excerpt may be diagrammed with certain symbols: "L" indicates a level tone, "D" a deflected tone, and "X" the acceptability of either tone.[17]

[16] In alternating parallelism, lines 1 and 3 and lines 2 and 4 form antitheses (see vol. one, ch. 7).

[17] Varying the tone only at the end of a line is an abbreviated form, but this became standard in Japan (see vol. two, ch. 1).

(interjection)
X X
(mixed alternating couplets)
X X X X X L
X X X X X X D
X X X X X D
X X X X X X L
(interjection)
X X
(decorative couplet)
X X D
X X L
(long couplet)
X X X X X L
X X X X X D
(interjection)
X X
(free-form line)
X X X X X X X X X X
(short couplets)
X X X L
X X X D
X X X D
X X X L
(light alternating couplets)
X X X L
X X X X D
X X X D
X X X X L

Such prose did not always meet the Chinese criteria for truly beautiful writing. Nevertheless, the Japanese must have been amazed to find that they could turn speculative or nonlyrical subjects into orderly, cadenced prose if they followed the parallel prose form. And such disciplined prose had considerable charm for Japanese in the twelfth century. Without the element of this appeal, we cannot explain why so much parallel prose was composed, or why it was included with shih and fu in collections of literary prose and poetry in Chinese.

Twelfth-century Japanese parallel prose certainly has no appeal for twentieth-century readers. But this is because our scant knowledge of, and experience with, parallel prose keeps us from enjoying the same ga perspective as did the twelfth-century Japanese. We can have no reason to doubt their preference for parallel prose. The *Heike Monogatari* (*The*

Tale of the Heike) bears this out by quoting on nine occasions internal memoranda, solicitations for ecclesiastical contributions (kanjinchō), formal Buddhist prayers, and supplications to gods and buddhas (ganjo)—all parallel prose forms.[18] In the widely circulated version (rufubon) of the *Heike*, these documents are transcribed in Chinese characters interspersed with kana, but the original versions of the parallel prose texts can easily be demonstrated. The documents are quoted in their entirety in the *Heike* because audiences enjoyed hearing them read aloud. The presence of nō plays like *Kiso*, *Ataka*, and *Shōzon*—where the important scene is one in which an official document is read aloud—gives further support to my statement.[19] The musical techniques of reading a work out loud are emphasized in nō; but why was this particular style of document recitation incorporated into nō plays? Such documents had been objects of literary appreciation since the twelfth century, and their later role as artistic recitations served to enhance the original appeal that parallel prose had for Japanese.

The original parallel prose text (written in Chinese) retained its appeal when mingled with Japanese. When parallel prose is read aloud in Chinese, the long and short syllables, tempo, cadence, and tonal patterns are a symphony of vocalic contrasts, but this beauty vanishes when parallel prose is read in Japanese. Appeal nevertheless remains in the significance of the work, specifically in its parallel couplets.

The Japanese interest in parallel couplets originated in the tenth century. One of the chief motives for compiling anthologies like the *Wakan Rōeishū* (*Collection of Japanese and Chinese Songs*, 1013) was to revel in parallelism (see vol. two, ch. 6). Admiration was limited to individual parallel couplets, however. When parallel prose is read in Japanese, antithetical couplets are intermixed with non-antithetical ones, making the parallelism in the text stand out more than in the original. There is no monotony in its variety of long and short parallel couplets. Japanese prose dominated by parallelism had been attempted in the Japanese Pref-

[18] *Heike Monogatari* [=*HM*] (Kakuichi manuscript), 4:297-98, 299-300, and 300-302; 5:357-58 and 369-70; 7:70-71, 85-87, 88-89, and 89-91. If Yasuyori's norito [text for Shinto rites] is counted as equivalent to parallel prose, there are ten instances (2:200-201). Royal commands by former tennō (10:251-53 and 11:364-66) are not counted.

[19] Reciting the document texts in these three plays has become a focal art in modern nō. *Kiso* is based on an episode in the *Heike* in which Kiso Yoshinaka, a commander of the Genji forces, has his secretary Kakumei compose a prayer (ganjo) to Hachiman, tutelary deity of the Genji clan, beseeching him to grant Yoshinaka's forces victory over the Heike army in a coming battle. The recitation of the prayer and Kakumei's dance before the shrine form the core of the play. One of the high points in *Ataka* is Benkei's impromptu recital of the contents of a make-believe subscription list for rebuilding the temple Tōdaiji in Nara. In *Shōzon*, the warrior-monk Shōzon, sent by the shogun Yoritomo to assassinate Yoshitsune, writes a pledge (kishō) before Yoshitsune attesting that he has not in fact come to kill him. [Auth., Trans.]

ace (kanajo) to the *Kokinshū* (the first royally commissioned collection of Japanese poetry, ordered in 905). But that was an exception.

By the twelfth century, on the other hand, the popularity of reading prose in Chinese by means of a Japanese transcription was joined by the practice of appreciating parallel prose in this form too. The apparent result was the rise of Japanese prose in the mixed style (wakan konkōbun), influenced by parallel prose.[20] Nakatada, one of the heroes of the *Utsuho Monogatari* (*The Hollow Tree*), is commanded to read aloud a work written by his grandfather Toshikage. He does so, "once in Japanese pronunciation [kun] and once in Chinese [koe]" (*Utsuho Monogatari*, "Kurabiraki," Pt. 2: 268/1062).[21] This was the tenth-century method of reading. By the twelfth century, however, Chinese prose seems hardly ever to have been read in its original word order and according to Sino-Japanese pronunciation. My surmise is supported by the rapid increase, from the twelfth century on, of manuscripts of works in Chinese with detailed kunten annotations [supplementary kana and marks indicating Japanese word order; see n. 21]. Prose in the mixed style, influenced by parallel prose, arose from these conditions. They provide important points of reference in considering the *Hōjōki* (*An Account of My Hut*) and *The Tale of the Heike* (see ch. 11).

Twelfth-century Japanese prose in Chinese is noted for its breadth of subject matter. Japanese were taking an interest in the matter of their writing as early as the tenth and eleventh centuries (see vol. two, ch. 6), and by the twelfth, many essays had appeared on events occurring in Japan and on matters of private import. Up to this time, writers of prose in Chinese had selected such subjects as could be expressed in the classical literary language and had made no attempt to write about things that could not be elegantly expressed. By contrast, twelfth-century writers made no effort to avoid previously eschewed subjects. The reasons are of a reciprocal nature. First, Japanese writers had become more advanced in composing prose in Chinese. They were now able to write about matters that did not demand attention to proper diction and parallelism. Second, Japanese prose in Chinese began to take on a more indigenous cast as

[20] Passages in the *Eiga Monogatari* appear to be parallel prose transcribed into Japanese, indicating that prose in the mixed form originated in the eleventh century (see vol. two, ch. 8). The practice of reading parallel prose in Japanese did not become popular until the twelfth century, however. [Wakan konkōbun, mingling of Sinified and Japanese readings of characters, designates a practice that developed over the centuries, becoming in effect the standard way of writing and speaking and so the basis of modern Japanese.—Ed.]

[21] ["Kun" refers, in one meaning, to reading Chinese prose or poetry in Japanese word order (which differs significantly from the Chinese) and with Japanese particles and verb endings. Special marks (known as kaeriten) inserted between characters indicate how the Chinese text is to be reordered in its Japanese reading. "Koe" (now "on") refers to reading the Chinese text in its original form, and pronouncing the characters in a Japanese approximation of the original Chinese sounds.—Trans.]

Japanese tolerance increased toward writers using language that would appear odd to Chinese readers. This is why subjects previously left untouched now begin to appear. Needless to say, plain prose was the only feasible style for such subjects. Parallel prose would have been virtually a technical impossibility.

A good example of a nontraditional subject is *Mutsu Waki* (*Account of the Mutsu Rebellion*), which describes the suppression, from 1051 to 1062, of a rebellion in Mutsu province.[22] It is written in fairly proper Chinese prose. I say "fairly proper" because the diction and couplet structure in *The Mutsu Rebellion* are relatively free of Japanese usages, and its author is familiar with parallel techniques. Since *The Mutsu Rebellion* is written in plain prose, it contains only two instances of alternating parallelism [requiring two couplets], but several skillfully composed single couplets appear in the work.[23] It also contains many classical allusions. Composing such a work demands considerable erudition, a fact that has led, probably correctly, to the conjecture that the author was a Confucian official gifted in prose composition (Ōsone, 1964, 45-51). There are indeed many allusions to the Chinese classics, but the quantity is striking only in a twelfth-century Japanese context. There are also qualitative problems. A contemporary Chinese intellectual had access to far more classical texts than his Japanese counterpart and memorized them from childhood. He could therefore choose the allusion that would most effectively express a given matter in his composition. But Japanese writers, who were far less conversant with the Chinese classics, had enough to do applying their meager store of allusions as aptly as possible. Inevitably, incorrect allusions occurred. The author of *The Mutsu Rebellion* embellishes several accounts of events with information gleaned from Chinese classics (Ōsone, 48-50). This is less fiction or invention than a sign that the author, limited in his knowledge, was unable to choose the most appropriate literary authority.

Attempts to write on Japanese subjects in Chinese prose increased rapidly during the twelfth century. Some examples are Ōe no Masafusa's "Yūjoki" ("An Account of Courtesans"), "Kugutsuki" ("An Account of the Kugutsu"), and "Rakuyō Dengakuki" ("An Account of Dengaku in the Capital"), all of which are concerned with popular matters of the day.[24] Masafusa's "accounts" (ki) deal with subjects unbefitting a genre

[22] *Fusō Ryakuki* (XII.1062) quotes a section from a work called *Ōshū Kassenki* (*Record of the Civil War in Mutsu*; *Fusō Ryakuki*, 29:298-99) that very nearly matches part of the *Mutsu Waki* text. Variants unique to each text suggest that *Ōshū Kassenki* is an early draft of the extant *Mutsu Waki*. The older text is assumed to date from the end of the eleventh century, and so *Mutsu Waki* was probably written in the early twelfth century.

[23] *Mutsu Waki*, 36 and 46.

[24] "Yūjoki" (*CG*, 3:66-67); "Kugutsuki" (*CG*, 67); "Rakuyō Dengakuki" (*CG*, 68-69).

ranked as the literary equal of poetic inscriptions, prefaces, official requests, and prose encomia.

In the ninth century Po Chü-i wrote a great deal on the popular society of his time, but his medium was always the shih, not prose. Subjects like Masafusa's do not appear in the extant twenty-four prose accounts by Po. Aside from a difference of scale, Masafusa's accounts are essentially similar to Yang Hsüan-chih's (fl. 528-50) *Lo-yang Ch'ieh-lan Chi* (*Account of the Monasteries of Loyang*).[25] Yang's work is a record of what he saw and heard in the former capital of the Northern Wei dynasty, Loyang—its scenery, culture, customs, and history. Despite his humble subject, Yang's style is far above base writing. It differs in nature from the ornate mainstream style of the Six Dynasties period, but Yang's sorrow at the lost glory of Loyang is vividly expressed by this emotionally controlled work. By comparison—and setting aside the question of thematic weight—Masafusa's accounts have nothing in their style that moves us. But rather than lament that a Joseph Conrad did not happen to be born in twelfth-century Japan, I would like to discuss the abundance of varied subjects treated by writers of prose in Chinese during this time. Their interest in popular subject matter proved to be highly useful in strengthening the bond between the intelligentsia and setsuwa [here, as in "setsuwa bungaku," setsuwa are stories originating in the past or present (usually the past) and presented as if actual or true].

Masafusa was apparently fond of local gossip and stories; his *Gōdanshō* (*The Ōe Conversations*) contains several such entries. A fondness for gossip is not limited to Masafusa. *Fukegatari* (*Lord Fuke's Stories*) and *Chūgaishō* (*Notes on Matters Inside and Outside the Capital*) are similar works that also display the contemporary intellectuals' strong interest in stories about society.[26] Masafusa's *Honchō Shinsenden* (*Accounts of Japanese Immortals*) provides further evidence of his interest in local tales. It recasts setsuwa from conventional documents into the Chinese biographical sketch (chuan) genre. But Masafusa relied on more than written setsuwa. There are clear signs that he incorporated oral folk transmissions

[25] [A translation of this work appears in W.J.F. Jenner, *Memories of Loyang: Yang Hsüan-chih and the Lost Capital (493-534)* (Oxford: Oxford University Press, 1981).—Trans.] The Chinese capital was moved to Loyang by Emperor Hsiao-wen in 493, during the Northern Wei dynasty. Loyang flourished until 534, when civil war forced Emperor Hsiao-wu to move the capital to Yeh, and subsequent wars reduced Loyang to ruins. In 547, during the reign of the Eastern Wei dynasty, Yang Hsüan-chih visited Loyang on official business, was pained to see its sorry state, and re-created its past glory in his prose account. Little is known of Yang's life.

[26] *Fukegatari* is Takashina Nakayuki's (1121-79) record of some of Fujiwara Tadazane's (1078-1162) conversations. Tadazane was known as Lord Fuke (Masuda, 1960b, 42-67). *Chūgaishō* is another collection of Tadazane's conversations, recorded by Nakahara Hiromoto (dates unknown). The first part is missing its opening passage, but the second survives intact.

to embellish his stories. The anonymous author of *The Mutsu Rebellion* writes, "This book is composed of excerpts from reports sent from the provincial seat to the central government, combined with what I gathered from conversation among the populace" (*Mutsu Waki*, 57).

There seems to have been a contemporary tendency to make use of oral folk transmissions. One of these is Masafusa's "Kobi Ki" ("A Record of Fox Magic"), an example of unusual events set down in Chinese prose.[27] "Fox Magic" records how foxes bewitched people in Japan and China and includes an instance of a Japanese bewitched in 1101. The Chinese have written from antiquity about foxes that take human form and bewitch people. Masafusa writes: "The Chinese histories record many instances of foxes bewitching people to mysterious effect. Consort Ta of Yin was in fact a fox with nine tails who had taken human form. Miss Jen became a man's concubine, but when she went to Ma-wei she was killed by a dog" (*HZM*, 11:192).[28] Stories of humans bewitched by foxes were probably transmitted from China and disseminated among the people through the agency of intellectuals, an instance of an elite subject "descending" to a lowlier plane. On the other hand, after such stories became popular among the common people, they reappeared in prose in Chinese. Here the opposite phenomenon occurs: a subject of lowly origin "ascends" to a higher literary plane. (For further details, see vol. one, General Introduction.) In both cases, an intelligentsia well grounded in the Chinese curriculum (kangaku) played an instrumental role. The phenomenon of intellectuals mediating between lowly and refined subjects first shows signs of life in the eighth century and by the twelfth had made marked advances. One facet of this phenomenon was the tendency of twelfth-century literary figures—including writers of prose in vernacular Japanese and in the mixed form—to deal with subjects centering on society. Then again, the interest taken in such subjects by Masafusa and other kangaku specialists would have given the trend considerable impetus.

[27] *HZM*, 11:191-92.

[28] There are episodes in *Sou-shen Chi* (18:219-20) and *Lo-yang Ch'ieh-lan Chi* (4:204-205) concerning foxes that take human form. Such stories therefore seem to date from the Six Dynasties period. Masafusa's allusion to Consort Ta is obscure, but we may assume that the writer mentions Miss Jen in reference to the T'ang story "Jen-shih Chuan" ("The Story of Miss Jen") by Shen Chi-chi. The latter story appears in *T'ang-Sung Ch'uan-ch'i Chi* (*Ch'uan-ch'i*, 1:33-42), and is translated by H. C. Chang in *Chinese Literature, Volume 3: Tales of the Supernatural* (New York: Columbia University Press, 1984). A man named Cheng falls in love with a beautiful woman, Jen, who is in fact a fox in human form. Cheng eventually discovers this, but his love for her remains unchanged, and the two continue to live happily together. Then Cheng is posted to a remote area in the west, and he asks Jen to accompany him. She refuses, saying that a sorceress warned her not to go west that year. Cheng mocks her superstition and forces her to go with him. When they reach a place called Ma-wei, a hunting dog bounds out of a thicket. Jen falls from her horse, takes her true form, and runs away, but the dog catches and kills her. The fox is buried with great ceremony by the grief-stricken Cheng. [Auth., Trans.]

The situation differed considerably in the field of Chinese prose written by Koreans. Under the leadership of Kim Pu-sik in the early twelfth century, plain prose had begun its rise, while parallel prose was excluded from formal composition. A Korean approach to plain prose composition, modeled on precepts of the Chinese ku-wen (ancient prose) style, first manifested itself in Yejong's reign (1106-23), but became fixed during the reign of Injong (1123-47). The Koryŏ dynasty (918-1392) established official relations with Sung China in the late tenth century, and Sung literature entered the country in great quantity. In 1080, Pu-sik's father, Kim Kŭn (dates unknown), was dispatched as a government envoy to China. This proved to be the direct impetus for the Korean adoption of the plain prose style systematized by Su Shih (Tung-p'o, 1037-1101). Kim Kŭn, a devotee of Tung-p'o's school of plain prose, taught his children the style upon his return to Korea.[29]

To be sure, little survives from the twelfth-century corpus of Korean prose in Chinese. The few pieces contained in such anthologies as *Tong Munsŏn* (*Korean Selections of Refined Literature*) provide insufficient data for any general observations (Yi, 1961, 102), but Pu-sik's *Samguk Sagi* (*History of the Three Kingdoms*), in fifty parts, indicates the level attained by contemporary Korean plain prose. Because Pu-sik naturally relied on already extant documents in writing his history, we cannot tell how much of the text reflects his own style. Nevertheless, Pu-sik's orderly narration of a wide range of events displays a command of advanced plain prose techniques, and his faithful observance of Chinese vocabulary and grammar is very likely a tendency shared by Korean intellectuals of the time.

There are obvious differences between the *The History of the Three Kingdoms* and a Japanese historical work like Fujiwara Michinori's *Honchō Seiki* (*The Annals of Japan*). Michinori, one of the best known kangaku scholars of the twelfth century, wrote his *Annals* in a Chinese prose style heavily laced with Japanese usages. This is due to the author's small inclination to reproduce faithfully accurate Chinese; it does not indicate that Michinori was less proficient in Chinese than Kim Pu-sik. *The History of the Three Kingdoms* and *The Annals of Japan* underwent similar formative processes, since both are amalgams of earlier records. But where Pu-sik seems to have corrected texts with erroneous or unnatural

[29] Kim Kŭn had four sons, Pu-p'il, Pu-ch'ŏl, Pu-sik, and Pu-ŭi. The eldest son was named after Fu Pi (1004-83) ["Pu-p'il" is the Korean pronunciation for characters read "Fu Pi" in Chinese], a famous government minister of the Northern Sung dynasty; the second son was named after Su Che (1039-1112) ["ch'ŏl" and "Che" are written with the same character], and the third son after Su Shih ["sik" and "Shih" are written with the same character]. Pu-ch'ŏl used the pseudonym Tzu-yu (also employed by Su Che) and later changed his name to Pu-il. Kim Kŭn probably chose such names out of a wish to make Sung culture, which he greatly admired, take root in Koryŏ Korea (Kim S., 1973, 173-74).

Chinese usages, Michinori evidently left the Japanese usages in his sources untouched. Their procedures reflect the difference between Korean and Japanese attitudes toward Chinese culture, rather than individual differences between Kim Pu-sik and Michinori.

Twelfth-century Japanese intellectuals revered Chinese culture and worked hard to absorb it, but they did not fret if aberrant features appeared in their writing. Accordingly, from the thirteenth century on, Japanese produced great quantities of prose in Chinese that would have struck a Chinese as incomprehensible. This corpus has been subjected to criticism and reexamination by Japanese scholars of Chinese in more recent times. In ideal terms, study of a foreign culture should yield the ability to express oneself as correctly as a native of that country. But the ideal is rarely attained. Once one realizes the infeasibility of speaking and writing like a native, there are two paths from which to choose. With the first, one gives up trying to express anything that cannot be phrased correctly in the foreign language, limiting oneself instead to what *can* be expressed. The second approach is to say whatever one wishes, regardless of the result.

The Japanese intellectuals of the twelfth century took the latter path. Their choice invites criticism on purely rational grounds, but its consequences were not all pernicious. Prose from the twelfth century on was greatly enriched by its authors' attempts to express—in something resembling Chinese prose—content that could never have been accurately presented in proper Chinese. A Koryŏ literatus would have found works like the *Azuma Kagami* (*The Mirror of the East Country*) acutely discomfiting and would not have wished to write anything of the sort. And yet I need not stress how vividly *The Mirror of the East Country* communicates a sense of thirteenth-century Japan. Since most of the Koryŏ literary corpus was destroyed by war and rebellion, we cannot assert that Koryŏ never possessed literature on various aspects of society. On the other hand, Japanese written records also suffered severe damage during the wars of the fifteenth and sixteenth centuries, and yet even the most inconsequential works of prose in Chinese happen to survive. We may conclude that the Koryŏ intelligentsia composed and transmitted only works written in correct Chinese. It depends on a country's criteria whether or not Chinese culture is adopted in its purest, most faithful form. The opposing positions taken by Japan and Korea unquestionably guaranteed that the two countries would produce differing literatures in versions of Chinese from the thirteenth century onward.

CHAPTER 2

Old and New Styles in Waka

Innovation and Conservation

Once the subjective *Kokinshū* style was consolidated in the *Shūishū* (1005-1008) period, the only literary phenomenon worth remarking in waka (poetry in Japanese) until the compilation of the *Goshūishū* in 1086 is an enormous output. That year also marked the initiating of indirect rule by the strongly individualist abdicated sovereign Shirakawa (r. 1072-86), and the commencement of a period of rule by cloistered sovereigns (insei).[1] The political trend was not immediately reflected by poetry, however, which continued to keep to established styles. The first clear indication of a new style appears in the Kōwa era (1099-1104) with the *Horikawa In no Ōntoki Hyakushu Waka* [=*Horikawa Hyakushu*] (*Hundred-poem Sequences from Horikawa's Reign*). The new style can hardly have sprung up in those five years. Poets had clearly been moving toward the new style for some time, although lack of external evidence makes it impossible to arrive at precise dating. If we adopt the reasonable assumption that the formation of the innovative style required at least ten years, we may conclude that the first developments occurred around 1090.

The *Shinkokinshū* period (in the wide sense, ca. 1190-1232) marks the formation of another revolutionary style, and that collection offers the quintessential literature of the High Middle Ages. Needless to say, the age did not suddenly come into being when this, the eighth royally commissioned waka collection, was submitted to the throne in 1205. As with the new waka style of the eleventh century, we must go back some years to find the origin of the *Shinkokinshū* style, and again there is no clearly discernable date. The *Shinkokinshū* was immediately preceded by the

[1] [In 1086 Shirakawa abdicated in favor of his son Taruhito, who reigned as Horikawa Tennō. Horikawa was eight years old at the time of his enthronement. Because he had no Fujiwara connections on his mother's side, the new tennō was not controlled by a Fujiwara maternal relative—as had long been the practice—but by his abdicated father. Shirakawa thus continued to rule indirectly through his son. The insei system [indirect rule by a retired monarch] continued—with varying degrees of actual power—until the establishment of the Kamakura shogunate in 1185. For further information on Shirakawa and insei, see G. Cameron Hurst III, *Insei: Abdicated Sovereigns in the Politics of Late Heian Japan, 1086-1185* (New York: Columbia University Press, 1976), 3-9 and 130-47.—Trans.]

Senzaishū, submitted in 1187. In 1193, the famous *Poetry Match in Six Hundred Rounds* (*Roppyakuban Utaawase*) was convened. The *Shinkokinshū* style of profound beauty is a strong presence in the *Match*, and proved so overwhelming that even Fujiwara Shunzei (1114-1204), the Grand Old Man of Waka, could not suppress it. Thus even the most conservative estimate would place the emergence of the *Shinkokinshū* style no later than 1190, the year of the poet Saigyō's death.

Taken cumulatively, these points indicate that there are clear signs of transition from the *Kokinshū* style to the *Shinkokinshū* style during the hundred years from 1090 to 1190. The transitional period ends about ten years before the start of the twelfth century proper. For purposes of convenience, however, I shall term the innovative poetry twelfth-century waka, since its chronological boundaries can only be vaguely delineated.

One obvious fact aiding us in determining the nature of twelfth-century waka is a fifty-percent reduction in the scale of the royal collections of this period. There are various explanations why the fifth and sixth anthologies, the *Kin'yōshū* (ca. 1124-27) and the *Shikashū* (ca. 1151-54), are the only ones to consist of ten rather than twenty books. Whatever the reason for the reduction, both anthologies were compiled by royal command, so that the change of scale would have required the concurrence of their sponsors, a tennō or former tennō. The fancy titles—*Kin'yōshū* (*Collection of Golden Leaves*) and *Shikashū* (*Collection of Verbal Flowers*)—must have been equally surprising for twelfth-century readers. The titles of preceding anthologies—*Gosenshū* (*Later Collection*; 936-66), *Shūishū* (*Collection of Gleanings*), and *Goshūishū* (*Later Collection of Gleanings*)—all signify the transmitting and supplementing of material bequeathed by earlier ages. This was essentially true for the poems and their subjects. But in keeping with its revolutionary name, the *Kin'yōshū* includes innovative categories like renga.[2] Such radical departures could not have been achieved without the strong concurrence of the *Kin'yōshū* sponsor, the cloistered Shirakawa.

Shirakawa named Minamoto Shunrai (i.e., Toshiyori; 1055?-1129?) editor of the *Kin'yōshū*. Shirakawa did not act in the usual way of sponsors, however, and passively certify the results of the editor's labors. Quite the contrary: the first draft of the *Kin'yōshū*, probably submitted between the Twelfth Month of 1124 and the First Month of 1125, was rejected by Shirakawa as "too old-fashioned."[3] Shunrai thereupon took the drastic step of omitting most of the works by poets already repre-

[2] [The renga involved is not that of sequences as usually thought of but tanrenga (short renga), a capping of the first three lines of a waka form with the last two by another poet. See *Kin'yōshū*, 10:692-710. See also "From Waka to Linked Poetry" in this chapter.—Ed.]

[3] Ikeda Tomizō has deduced the probable date of submission (Ikeda, 1973, 88-91). Shirakawa's opinion is quoted in *Imakagami*, 7 ("Musashino no Kusa"):313.

sented in the first three royal waka anthologies, among them at least thirteen poems by Ki no Tsurayuki (884-946) that had appeared in the first draft.[4] But the second draft, "representing none but poets favored by His Majesty," was also rejected.[5] The third draft, which Shirakawa finally accepted, included several more poems by Fujiwara Nagayoshi, Minamoto Michinari (fl. ca. 1020), and Sone no Yoshitada (fl. ca. 985), and borrowed considerably from Nōin's *Gengenshū*.[6]

The favor accorded waka composed by Yoshitada—who had been labeled a "crazy, addled fellow" during his lifetime—is a further indication that new literary conceptions were coming into being. These events are frequently interpreted politically, as signifying Shirakawa's extending into the realm of waka his determination to overthrow the Fujiwara regency and return the country to royal rule. This process may well have occurred. But explanations linking a literary phenomenon to a single source tend to present difficulties. It is difficult to see the connection between the ideal of a royal restoration and the wildly fluctuating editorial decisions made in the three drafts of the *Kin'yōshū*, other than as fluctuations clearly occasioned by Shirakawa's strongly held opinions. The impress of royal opinion is one of the hallmarks of twelfth-century waka.

Poetic styles also exemplify individuality. Unless one remembers the poet's name, tenth- and eleventh-century waka are difficult to distinguish by style alone. Then contemporary readers would have found subtle differences among such poems, but even those by the most famous poets of the period—Tsurayuki, Ki no Tomonori (d. ca. 905), Ōshikōchi Mitsune (dates uncertain), and Mibu no Tadamine (d. ca. 920), for example—all seem alike to modern readers. Only Yoshitada and Izumi Shikibu (b. 976?) have distinct poetic styles, and neither received much recognition from contemporaries. From the twelfth century on, their waka came to be valued highly. Two prominent twelfth-century waka poet-critics, Shunrai and Fujiwara Mototoshi (1056-1142), have very distinct waka styles. There are equally clear differences between Saigyō's (1118-90) and Shunzei's poems. Individual poetic styles become still more pronounced in the *Shinkokinshū* period, when the poetic scene presents a grand spectacle of many different flowers abloom all at once.

[4] The only extant manuscript of the first draft, in the Seikadō Bunko collection, is in a hand attributed to Fujiwara Tamesuke (Matsuda Takeo, 1956, 186). It is, unfortunately, incomplete, reproducing only the first five books. Thirteen of Tsurayuki's waka appear in this section, and there may have been more in Books 6-10. That is why I say "at least thirteen" of his waka were omitted.

[5] *Imakagami*, 7:313. The second draft was submitted to Shirakawa in IV.1125. This has been the widely circulated version (rufubon). The third draft is a relatively recent discovery.

[6] "The monk Nōin lived not long ago. He determined to follow in Kisen's footsteps, and his poetry was famous. Selecting waka by every poet he had ever known, Nōin called his collection the *Gengenshū*" (*Goshūishū*, Preface, 426). [Further information on Nōin appears in the next section of this chapter.—Trans.]

An antecedent phenomenon occurs during the twelfth century, that is, in the Japanese shift in shih poetry from the Six Dynasties style to the T'ang style, which took place about four hundred years after the original Chinese trend. The Chinese were able to distinguish among individual Six Dynasties poetic styles: "Yü Hsin's style is clear and fresh, / And Pao Chao's elegant and free." They strike one, however, as about as distinct as Tomonori's style is from Tsurayuki's. Yet even I can make some distinctions among poems by Li Po (701-62), Tu Fu (712-70), Han Yü, Po Chü-i, Li Shang-yin, and Wen T'ing-yün. Increasing individuality proves to be an important indicator in differentiating the waka of the High Middle Ages from that of the Early Middle Ages.

In the judgments handed down at waka matches (utaawase) we also find a growing individuality. Mototoshi and Shunrai are important twelfth-century poetic arbiters; Fujiwara Akisuke (1090-1155) and his son Kiyosuke (1104-77) were also influential. But Shunzei was the supreme authority. These judges were instrumental in altering the nature of the waka match. A judge's opinion, which evaluated each waka submitted for competition, naturally differed according to the individual judge. Depending on who pronounced on the poems matched, the results would vary considerably. The variance reflects a twelfth-century change in the attitudes on which judgments were based. In the tenth and eleventh centuries, waka matches were essentially elegant diversions for highborn nobles, who revelled in presenting formal waka amid splendid settings (see vol. two, ch. 7). Victory was less important. But by the twelfth century, winning a waka match meant great glory for a poet, and conversely, defeat brought deep shame. The thought of giving one's life for a single superlative waka, an idea nonexistent in the eleventh century, was a widely held view from the twelfth century on (see ch. 5). Moreover, when the waka match changed from refined rivalry over achieving the utmost luxury of the setting and instead focused on the quality of the poetry itself, the importance of the judge also increased.

This important shift stimulated the development of waka poetics. Through the eleventh century, when victory in a waka match was of less than supreme interest, Fujiwara Kintō (966-1041) and a few others produced some works on poetics. Their authors were well aware of Chinese treatises, and they consciously strove to formulate an authoritative critical account of waka so that it might achieve equality with shih as a premier art. Many of their treatises are theoretical (and occasionally pedantic), rarely having much bearing on actual composition.

Works on waka poetics not only increased markedly during the twelfth century but also are clearly different in quality. Rather than offer pure theory, these treatises incessantly address the practicalities of winning at waka matches. Modern Japanese scholars of their country's literature tend to perceive waka treatises as works on aesthetics. They are correct insofar as waka is an art; analyzing the principles set forth in waka treatises will therefore yield aesthetic thought. On the other hand, it is difficult, at least with twelfth-century waka treatises, to discern a conscious drive to state aesthetic thoughts in a logical, systematic fashion. Their authors were concerned instead with what they perceived as the most important matter: offering their readers, as amply and accurately as possible, information necessary for victory in a waka match.

Not surprisingly, Shunrai and Mototoshi, both eminent scholar-poets, wrote treatises. Shunrai's *Shumpishō* (*Secret Notes by Shunrai*) strikingly reveals the concerns of his fellow poets.[7] *Secret Notes*, a far longer work than earlier waka treatises, both demonstrates that such information was sought after and illustrates how copious data were amassed in order to respond to this need. Although somewhat disorganized, the contents of *Secret Notes* may be classified into three categories: (1) ancient customs and precedents; (2) waka interpretation; and (3) distinctions among poetic styles. Shunrai has been taken as the leader of an innovative group of poets. His style certainly takes a new direction, but it is very dubious whether an innovative *group* was centered around Shunrai. The information in his *Secret Notes* is based on an awareness of poetic models: present practice should follow that of the past. No recognizable innovations are asserted here. He produced innovative waka only in informal circumstances, never on such formal occasions as waka matches, and in his *Secret Notes* he gives the reader information necessary for winning a waka match. Of course it contains no innovative assertions, since waka fine enough to sacrifice one's life for were never recited in informal circumstances. He displays little difference in this respect from Mototoshi, who has been branded a conservative.

Mototoshi wrote a waka treatise, *Etsumokushō* (*Notes to Gladden a Reader*), that does not survive. Its theoretical approach probably resembled Fujiwara Kiyosuke's in his *Ōgishō* (*Notes on Innermost Meaning*) and *Fukurozōshi*. Both works are partially concerned with matters akin to those in Shunrai's *Secret Notes*, although Kiyosuke devotes little space to stylistic distinctions. On the other hand, he goes into far greater detail on matters of ancient custom and precedent and on interpreting waka from the past. Kiyosuke's interpretations are not personal opinions. They reflect a retrospective view, maintaining that poetic tradition dictates the meaning of a given waka. Kiyosuke stresses that the past is the foundation for both composition and interpretation. Retrospection, one of the hallmarks of the High Middle Ages (see ch. 5), was already an established

[7] *Shumpishō*, also known by the titles *Shunrai Zuinō* (*Shunrai's Essentials*) and *Shunrai Kuden* (*Shunrai's Oral Transmissions*), was probably compiled between X.1114 and I.1115 (*Nihon Kagaku Taikei* [= *NKGT*], 1 ["Kaisetsu"]:48).

principle by the middle of the twelfth century. All twelfth-century waka poets might be called conservative in this sense.

Shunrai, Mototoshi, and Kiyosuke are alike in basing their composition and interpretation on precedents. There was no confrontation between innovators and conservatives where waka matches and other formal events were concerned, although their opinions sometimes differed when they judged waka matches. Shunrai and Mototoshi certainly had different approaches to judging a match. The clearest instances appear in the *Naidaijin Ke Utaawase* (*Waka Match Held at the Palace Minister's Residence*), convened in the Tenth Month of 1118. Both men served as judges. As a good example of their differences, here is the ninth round of the match, on the topic "Love."

The Left [declared the winner by Mototoshi]: By Lord Michitsune

Au koto no	Our love meetings
Ima wa Katano to	Now are, like Katano, hard;
Narinureba	And that is why
Kari ni toikoshi	He who used sometimes to hunt here
Hito mo toikozu.	Comes to visit me no more.[8]

The Right [declared the winner by Shunrai]: By Lord Tadataka

Osōreba	Hands cannot check
Amaru namida wa	The overflow of tears that seep
Moruyama no	Down Moruyama,
Nageki ni ataru	Where each sorrowing tree is laden
Shizuku narikeri.	With the teardrops of my grief.[9]

Shunrai remarks: "The first poem uses the place name, 'Katano,' and so it ought also to have 'comes hunting / comes but seldom' [kari ni ku]. To have the lover 'come no more' [kozu] is at odds with precedent.[10] The

[8] "Kata" means "difficult and hard" and also functions as part of the place name "Katano." "Kari" can mean both "hunting" and "occasionally," "seldom." The *Ise Monogatari* (*Tales of Ise*) and other sources reveal that Katano was conventionally linked with hunting in waka. The poem alludes to *Kokinshū*, 18:972; see n. 10.

[9] "Moru" means "to seep, leak through," and also serves as the first part of a place name, Moruyama (Moru Mountain). Similarly, the "-ki" of "nageki" (grief) can also mean "tree." These pivot words effect a metaphor for the speaker's plight: the flood of tears, matching the speaker's depth of grief, is as abundant as the many trees covering Moru Mountain. [Auth., Trans.]

[10] The "precedent" mentioned by Shunrai is a waka from the *Kokinshū* (18:972), a variant of which appears in dan (section) 123 of *Ise Monogatari*. The poem is in reply to one that plays on the place name Fukakusa (deep grasses), the (grammatical) subject of the first line: No to naraba / Uzura to nakite / Toshi wa hen / Kari ni dani ya wa / Kimi wa kozaran. (If it turns to fields, / Like the quails I shall cry on / As the long years pass; / Surely you will come sometimes / To hunt them and to seek me out?) [Auth., Trans.]

second poem shows deep sensitivity with its 'overflow of tears that seep / Down Moruyama.' My response was such that I find it reasonable to declare the latter poem the winner."

Mototoshi says, "Neither poem has outstanding faults, nor is either particularly striking. But the first poet displays greater delicacy when his speaker laments that she does not even hear 'sometimes' [kari ni] from her lover" (*Heianchō Utaawase Taisei* [=*HCUT*], 6:1772).

Mototoshi finds the Left's poem free of "outstanding faults," but Shunrai criticizes the impropriety of linking "-kozu" ("does not come") with Katano, a place name celebrated in waka. Instead, he says, the positive verb "ku" ("come") should have appeared together with the pivot word "kari." He is a greater stickler for precedent here than is Mototoshi. Their different approaches are visible in Shunrai's praising Tadataka for directly stating his speaker's emotions, as contrasted with Mototoshi's response to the obliquely presented emotions in the Left's poem. Michitsune, whose speaker wishes in vain that her lover might give her some comfort by visiting her openly, expresses what is "kokorobososhi" (delicacy, subtlety of import).

By praising a poem in which the speaker gives free expression to her feelings, Shunrai pits himself not only against Mototoshi, but against the *Kokinshū* style itself. The hallmark of that style is obliqueness. Rather than directly express the poet's sentiments, a work in the style is curvilinear, making detours through the use of fabricated logic (see vol. two, ch. 1). Shunrai rejects that indirection, favoring instead Po Chü-i's poetry, characterized by an unfettered expression of the poet's sentiments. This concept came to dominate Japanese shih and, approximately a century and a half later, that Chinese style was absorbed by waka (see vol. two, ch. 7). Mototoshi, on the other hand, emphasizes the significance of "sometimes" in the second poem. He discovers and praises a delicate, peculiarly feminine thought process in the speaker's lament: her lover's rare past visits were clearly halfhearted acts, but now he does not even bother to come. The poet is unmistakably using a form of logic—but it is not the fabricated logic of the Six Dynasties period. What Mototoshi is praising is the subtlety inherent in what might be called true logic, a logic characteristic of Late T'ang poetry and linked to the poet's or speaker's thought processes.

There were no opposing groups among twelfth-century waka poets, only individually diverging positions and opinions. They were uniformly conservative, and yet opinions like Shunrai's and Mototoshi's were aired at a formal waka match convened by a minister of state. This indicates how greatly individuality was prized. The appearance of individual stylistic and critical differences represents the new style of twelfth-century waka. Even Mototoshi, heretofore considered a typical conservative, must be thought a new-style poet in this sense, because his Late T'ang orientation does not appear in earlier waka.

The twelfth-century acceptance and approval of individual differences was connected with another contemporary concept, the worth of individual existence itself. Although neither held public office, Mototoshi and Shunrai were often asked to judge formal waka matches, a sign that they commanded respect as waka poets.[11] Similarly, the low-ranking Tsurayuki and his colleagues were probably appointed editors of the *Kokinshū* because people proficient in waka were relied upon and respected in the tenth century. And yet Tsurayuki and his circle, renowned poets all, were in principle forbidden to attend waka matches even when their own poems were entered into competition (see vol. two, ch. 7). It would have been unthinkable for any of them to act as a judge. That twelfth-century people no longer considered such participation unthinkable manifests, I believe, an altered social awareness: now anyone proficient in an art was worthy of respect, regardless of court rank or position.

Respect for those accomplished in an art, regardless of rank, was not limited to waka, and this attitude was a great break with the past. Through the eleventh century, the only accomplishments considered to be premier arts were those performed between composer and audience within a closed circle. Arts that required training beyond the grasp of the usual member of the group were looked down upon as "crafts" (see vol. two, ch. 3). This mentality endured into the twelfth century, undergoing considerable internal change. High-ranking nobles began trying their hand at arts so specialized as to have been regarded previously as skilled crafts. Their actions stemmed from an awareness that artistic specialization was worthy of respect. Horikawa (r. 1086-1107) presents an excellent example. He often performed as a flutist at royal concerts, and his retinue included several virtuosi in various instruments (Hashimoto, 1966, 138-39). The Sung emperor Hui-tsung (r. 1101-26) was an accomplished painter, but his example probably occurs too late to have influenced twelfth-century Japan. The developing Japanese reverence for artistic specialization was apparently an independent phenomenon. Within each artistic field, individual talents came to be acknowledged and prized. The respect accorded artistic specialization was vital in shaping the high medieval ideal of michi (artistic vocation; see ch. 5).

Medieval respect for individual waka talents differed from earlier varieties in one essential feature: a medieval poet's abilities were always to be displayed under the aegis of a hereditary school or family (ie). Of

[11] Mototoshi was assistant commander of the Left Gate Guards from 1077 to 1081; he held no other official posts (Hashimoto, 1966, 107). Shunrai's earliest recognition came as a musical virtuoso. He became an acknowledged waka poet only when he held no public office (ibid., 145).

course, waka talent also ran in families during the tenth and eleventh centuries. Ki no Tsurayuki (ca. 872-945) and his son Tokifumi offer one such example. Usually, however, these were simply cases of there being more than one poet in the family. There was little sense of responsibility to perpetuate and refine waka as the family art. Fujiwara Akisue (1055-1123) was the first to feel this responsibility. A middle-ranking courtier, Akisue was a confidant of Shirakawa, consequently becoming influential among waka poets as well as in government affairs. Akisue bequeathed his political power to his two oldest sons, Nagazane and Ieyasu, while training his third son Akisuke in waka traditions, composition, and reliable textual transmission (Hashimoto, 1966, 321). Akisue's action is clearly a deliberate effort to transmit the art of waka within a family. This marks the beginning of poetic families or schools. Akisuke named his patrimony the Rokujō Fujiwara School (Rokujō Tōke; abbreviated as Rokujōke, or the Rokujō School). Kiyosuke, the monk Kenjō (fl. 1161-1207), Fujiwara Ariie (1155-1216), and other influential poets active during the *Shinkokinshū* period were members of this school.[12]

Another school of waka, founded somewhat later than the Rokujō, was the Mikohidari. Although its founder was Fujiwara Michinaga's (966-1027) sixth son Nagaie, its reputation as a waka school dates from the time of Toshitada (1073-1123), Nagaie's grandson. Of course, the

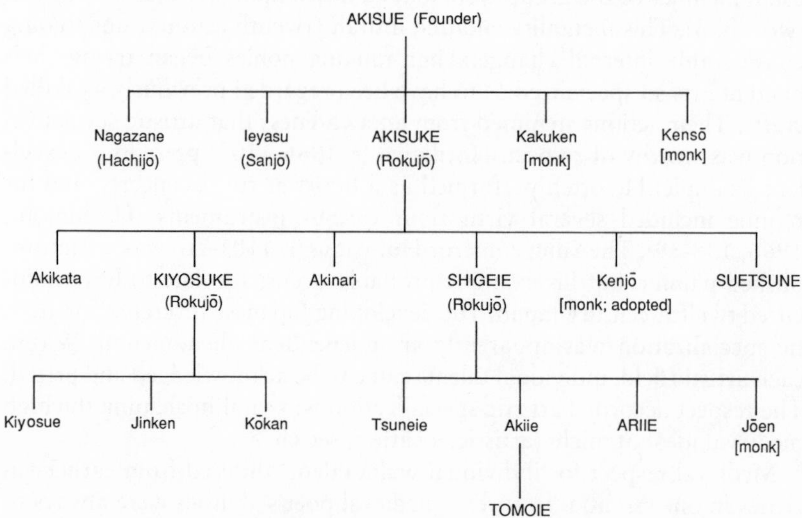

FIGURE 2.1 The Rokujō School (Surnames are "Fujiwara" unless otherwise indicated)

[12] Names given in capital letters in the Rokujō school genealogy denote important poets of the school. The same is true for the Mikohidari school genealogy, given below.

greatest achievements of the Mikohidari school were yet to come. Its fame was truly established in 1138, when Toshitada's son Shunzei became Mototoshi's pupil. On the fifteenth day of the Eighth Month, 1138, Shunzei called on Mototoshi and made "a covenant between master and pupil" with him.[13] The actual significance of this relationship is unclear. There may be some possibility that Shunzei submitted his waka drafts to Mototoshi for criticism and correction, but we have no evidence of such teaching methods existing in the twelfth century. There are quotations from Mototoshi's oral transmissions, known as "Kingo Osetsu" ("Teachings of the Gate Guardsman") in Mikohidari waka treatises.[14] Also, Shunzei and his son Teika (i.e., Sadaie, 1162-1241) each used Mototoshi's manuscript of the *Kokinshū* as the copytext for their versions.

Such evidence suggests that Mototoshi's relationship with Shunzei was chiefly one of transmitting ancient waka traditions, composition methods, and knowledge of reliable manuscripts.[15] Guided by the belief that the best is to be found in the past, the medieval poetic schools took on the duty of transmitting ancient teachings and important materials. Why did not Mototoshi pass on his knowledge to his own descendants? Probably because none had the proper talent. The idea of transmitting an art within a family notwithstanding, a blood descendant who lacked genius could not gain the status of a member. Zeami (1363?-1443?) writes, "A school is not in fact a school unless it properly transmits its art; a man is not in fact a man unless he masters his art" (*Fūshi Kaden*, 7:65). The spirit of Zeami's words seems already present in Mototoshi's teaching.

Mototoshi could not form his own school because his family lacked poetic talent. Much the same occurred with Shunrai: his father, the gifted poet Minamoto Tsunenobu (1016-97), bequeathed him the requisite blood line and poetic achievements for founding an important school. And his own son, Shun'e (dates unknown), had a salon called the Garden of Poets (Karin'en), where accomplished poets assembled for occasional waka gatherings (Yanase, 1977, 29-43). But Shunrai's line did not form a school to rival the Rokujō and the Mikohidari. Transmission was the lifeblood of such schools, and it could only be effected by talented individuals. Neither Mototoshi nor Shunrai was blessed with such descendants. With its marked individuality, the twelfth-century waka world differs from the strongly homogeneous poetic circles of the tenth and eleventh centuries.

[13] Kamo no Chōmei recorded Shunzei's words in his *Mumyōshō* (56). Shunzei was twenty-five years old at the time, and Mototoshi eighty-five.

[14] "Kingo" is the Sinified pronunciation of the T'ang term for a palace-gate guardsman. Mototoshi once served as assistant commander of the palace guard (see n. 11).

[15] According to a statement dated Eiryaku 2 (1161), which appears in Shunzei's copy of the *Kokinshū* (Royal Library coll.), Shunzei had earlier made a copy of the *Kokinshū* version in Mototoshi's possession (Kyūsojin, 1961, 35).

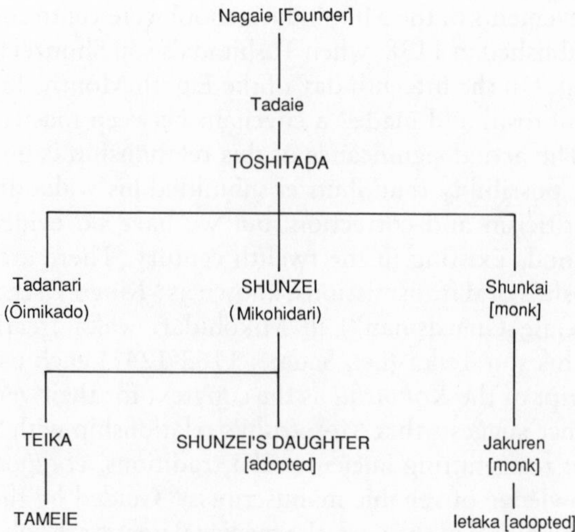

FIGURE 2.2 The Mikohidari School (Parentheses designate branches of the Fujiwara)

THE NEW STYLE MOVES TOWARD THE REFINED

To judge from what has been said so far, one might conclude that twelfth-century waka was thoroughly imbued with the new style. The facts are otherwise, however. The "old style"—in effect since the *Shūishū* period [early eleventh century]—continued to flourish into the late twelfth century and was the dominant style in terms of volume. By contrast, the "new style of waka," inaugurated in the twelfth century, displays a marked individuality. The nature of this "new-style waka" will be considered later. First I would like to discuss its orientation toward the ga ideal.

Poetic Adornments and Composition on Set Topics

One trend among twelfth-century waka poets was a growing interest in utamakura (poetic adornments). Originally signifying any subject frequently appearing in waka, utamakura later came principally to mean place names often used in waka. Eventually the term was confined exclusively to poetic place names. The first documented appearances of the term "utamakura" occur in the early eleventh century.[16] Place names

[16] Examples appear in the *Genji Monogatari* ("Tamakazura," 373) and in Fujiwara Kintō's *Shinsen Zuinō* (1:66). [Utamakura (poetic pillows, convenient adornments) originally included various kinds of matter. For example, the longer version of *Nōin Utamakura* (*NKGT*, 1:73-107) begins with pillow words (makurakotoba). It has a section on famous places, province by province (pp. 91-101), but most of the treatise is taken up with explanations, associations, and related concepts for individual words and images. For example,

seem to have made up much of the utamakura corpus by that time. Sei Shōnagon (fl. ca. 1000) probably reflects this when she lists evocative place names in her *Makura no Sōshi* (*The Pillow Book*; see vol. two, ch. 8).

Place names became synonymous with utamakura, because certain locations were thought to possess spiritual properties capable of evoking emotion, and so they served as guide phrases (dōshi) during the Archaic Age (to ca. 604) and Ancient Age (ca. 604-905).[17] Examples are Niibari (*Kojiki* [=*KJK*], 25); Ichijishima (*KJK*, 42); Honda (*KJK*, 47); Kusakae (*KJK*, 95); Ōmi no Mi (*Nihon Shoki* [=*NSK*], 95); Hasa no Yama (*NSK*, 71); and Mieshino (*NSK*, 126). Because their spiritual properties invigorated literary expression, their names were used in poetry. Spiritual elements also shaped the medieval concept of poetic place names. Consequently, not all place names were considered utamakura. An utamakura is a place prominent in history or legend, whose rich associations invigorate a waka. The stories associated with utamakura were well known and could easily be told to anyone unfamiliar with them. Poetic place names in the Middle Ages were, so to speak, condensed myths.

The spiritually active guide phrase was transformed in the Early Middle Ages (ca. 850ff.) into two rhetorical devices, the preface (jokotoba) and the pillow word (makurakotoba). Place names became essential components of waka composition during this time, performing a vital function as poetic material. A comprehensive knowledge of poetic place names was considered important for medieval waka poets, who were urged to learn as many as possible, together with their related legends. *Nōin Utamakura* (*Utamakura Compiled by Nōin*) ministered to this need.[18] Although no clear evidence indicates that the work is really by Nōin (987-1058?), Kenjō quotes from it in his glossary of poetic diction, the *Shūchūshō* (*Pocket Notes*; comp. late twelfth century), and it was regarded as Nōin's collection from that time. Extant manuscripts of *Utamakura Compiled by Nōin* have substantial textual variants, suggesting that the text was augmented and revised around the twelfth century. The manuscript line with the most entries has 718 locations listed under the heading "Place Names of the Provinces" ("Kuniguni no Tokorodokoro

---

"wasuregai (shell of forgetfulness) means a shell from the sea" (not a river), p. 85. For poetic place names, see Miner-Odagiri-Morrell, 1985, 433-41.—Ed.]

[17] The guide phrase (dōshi) is the progenitor of the pillow word (makurakotoba) and preface (jokotoba; see vol. one). The transformation from guide phrase to pillow word/preface occurred toward the close of the second half of the Ancient Age (see vol. two, ch. 7).

[18] "Utamakura" in the title refers to the broad sense of the term. The work is a compendium of words and phrases—including place names—necessary for waka composition. *Nōin Utamakura* is found in *NKGT*, 1. [See n. 16. "Place names" were "nadokoro" and later "meisho"; the terms are normative, unlike the descriptive modern "chimei."—Ed.]

[no] Na"). Such lists tended to grow longer as time passed. *Utamakura Nayose* (*Place Names with Poetic Associations*), probably compiled at the start of the fourteenth century, contains 2,624 place names.[19]

A passion for accumulating information is highly characteristic of the twelfth century. A similar consciousness produced the gigantic *Ruiju Utaawase Maki* (*Classified Scrolls of Waka Matches*).[20] Collecting such information in writing surely meant that it was considered knowledge worth sharing among all waka poets. Unless a composition was based on shared information, the audience would have difficulty responding to or understanding the work. Only when both poet and audience shared information would successful literary activity occur. This is the sphere of ga, as defined in the second volume of this *History*.

The tenth century saw a rising awareness of ga by waka poets, centering around Ki no Tsurayuki. The twelfth-century orientation toward ga proved stronger and—at least so far as poetic output can reflect—far more striking than the earlier movement. Once again, however, an intense focusing on ga was accompanied by a wish to come into contact with something predating ga: zoku, the low or commonplace. The wish was manifested in the twelfth century by the concept of the journey (tabi). Poets turned from mere memorizing of poetic place names to traveling to those places, in the hope of gaining direct personal experience of a locale long celebrated in poetry.

Nōin traveled frequently, but we must question whether his motives were exclusively those just described. His principal purpose for traveling was probably horse trading.[21] But the poet was not likely to have been unaffected by traveling to locales long celebrated in waka. With each visit, Nōin seems to have gained a greater understanding of the importance of his activity. The same is true for Saigyō. His many journeys did not always have clear objectives. One purpose was probably to solicit contributions for temples, and he may well have had other more business-oriented goals as well.[22]

[19] *Utamakura Nayose* was compiled shortly before the thirteenth royal waka anthology, the *Shingosenshū* (submitted to the throne in 1303; *Utamakura Nayose*, "Kaisetsu," 101-107).

[20] *Ruiju Utaawase Maki* is an augmented version of *Waka Gasshō*, compiled around 1096. It was discontinued ca. 1106-1108, during the time the *Kokin Utaawase* was compiled. Plans to expand the *Ruiju Utaawase* to twenty books were never realized (Horibe, 1945, 84-101).

[21] *Nōin Shū*, Nōin's personal waka collection, contains an unusually large number of poems on horses. Some have been interpreted as stemming from Nōin's transporting horses from Michinoku province in northern Japan. Other poems, dating from 1040-45, describe Nōin as owning and lending horses. This suggests that horse-trading was on the poet's mind when he wrote, "On going to Michinoku on pressing business" (*Nōin Shū*, 104, Forenote; Mezaki, 1959, 330-36).

[22] There is much to Gorai Shigeru's theory that Saigyō solicited contributions for temples

The concept of a waka poet wandering at will out of longing for the beauties of the seasons was probably first envisioned around the fourteenth century. Such journeys were unimaginable in the twelfth century, when travel was both difficult and dangerous. Saigyō would nevertheless have found the same meaning as Nōin in personally visiting places celebrated in waka of the past. Their desire—to discover something there with one's own eyes—can only be an orientation toward zoku, defined earlier as "a world without precedents" (see vol. one, p. 59). The presence of zoku as an entity separate from the intensely cultivated ga is a matter of great significance to twelfth-century assumptions and practice.

Much the same might be said for daiei, poetry composition on assigned topics. Daiei are present as early as the ninth century, but begin to flourish only with the twelfth. Waka on assigned topics are rare in the *Shūishū* (ca. 985). There are considerably more in the *Goshūishū* (comp. 1086), and the three *Kin'yōshū* drafts show a still more dramatic increase.[23] We find a twelfth-century manifestation of this phenomenon in the contemporary preference for waka with assigned topics over waka composed on actual scenes or situations. There is a likely connection between this preference and the transformation undergone by waka matches. As we saw above, twelfth-century poets strove to emerge victorious in strictly judged waka matches. Detailed, accurate judgments on the quality of a poem were most effectively made when the topic was a narrow one. Rather than have a general topic like "Love," for example, more specific categories—such as "Falling in Love" or "Concealed Love"—provided more accessible grounds for a judgment. If a topic was made still more specific, as in "Love When He Visits but Does Not Stay the Night," the judgment could be based on the poet's ability to express the nature of the topic. The results were a marked proliferation of categories and subcategories within a given topic, with further encouragement for the already growing popularity of assigned topics in waka.

The practice of composing waka sequences in a fixed number of poems also had a considerable influence on the popularity of assigned topics. I define "waka composed in a fixed number" as a waka sequence made

---

(Gorai, 1965, 159). This was hardly his only motive for travelling on foot across the country, however (Mezaki, 1978, 261-93).

[23] Waka composed on assigned topics are determined as follows. (1) Cases in which these phrases appear in a fore- or afternote: (a) "Composed on the Topic 'X'," (b) "Composed on the spirit [kokoro] of 'X'," (c) "Composed on 'X'." (2) Cases in which the topic is directly stated as a title to a waka, as in "Trees by the Water Make a Splendid Scene." (3) Entries in waka matches, where the topics are clearly stated in the match. I exclude eighth-century and earlier waka entitled "Composed on 'X'." Fifteen of 1,351 waka in the *Shūishū* are on assigned topics, while the next royal waka anthology, the *Goshūishū*, has 150 poems out of 1,220 on assigned topics. The total number of waka in the *Kin'yōshū*, considering all three drafts but excluding repeated waka, is 1,033; there are 563 waka on assigned topics. [Another implication is that waka was becoming increasingly fictional.—Ed.]

up of a number of waka generally acknowledged as appropriate. The most common number of poems in a sequence is fifty or one hundred. The two earliest surviving examples of hundred-poem sequences were composed by Sone no Yoshitada and Minamoto Shitagō (911-83), each of whom dedicated his sequence to the other. The next oldest instance is by Minamoto Shigeyuki (d. 1000).[24] In all cases, the text is divided into large, general categories like "Spring," "Summer," "Autumn," "Winter," "Love," and "Miscellaneous," and none contains more specific topics within the categories.

By the twelfth century, highly specific topics appear in hundred-poem sequences. Exemplary sequences from this period are included in the *Horikawa In no Ōntoki Hyakushu Waka* (or simply *Horikawa Hyakushu*), the *Hundred-poem Sequences from Horikawa's Reign*, composed between 1099 and 1104, and the *Horikawa In Godo Hyakushu* (*Later Hundred-poem Sequences from Horikawa's Reign*, commonly called the *Eikyū Hyakushu*, or *Hundred-poem Sequences of the Eikyū Era*, composed in 1116. Poets probably developed a corpus of increasingly specific waka topics in the course of collecting and systematizing earlier works, particularly categorized waka anthologies like the *Kokin Waka Rokujō* (*The Six-book Anthology of Old and New Waka*) and the *Wakan Rōeishū* (*Collection of Japanese and Chinese Songs*), with its section headings (Hashimoto-Takizawa, 1976, 337-41).

The topics in early hundred-poem sequences served as models for later generations and determined their course of study. The incorporation of the hundred-poem sequential form into waka matches deserves special attention. The *Waka Match in Six Hundred Rounds* of 1193 experiments with very specialized topics indeed, but many of them are taken from the *Hundred-poem Sequences of the Eikyū Era*. The *Waka Match in Six Hundred Rounds* (although displaying originality in its subdividing of love topics) must be recognized as a structure based on the hundred-poem sequence form.

The subdividing of waka topics is not itself a matter of great import, but it did lead to the evolution of a noteworthy concept, hon'i, born from the poets' concern with *how* to approach a given topic. The following waka provides an illustration. It was composed for the *Kampaku Naidaijin Utaawase* (*Waka Match Held by the Chancellor and Palace Minister*), held on the twelfth day of the Ninth Month, 1121. The poem was presented in the first round by the Left, and the topic was "Mountain Moon."

[24] The first two sequences appear in *Sōtanshū*, 369-470 and 484-583 (compiled ca. 959-61). Shigeyuki's sequence, in *Shigeyuki Shū*, 221-323, was possibly written in the poet's twenties, between the years 958 and 967 (Mezaki, 1960, 274).

By a Court Lady[25]

Ko no ma yori	So great is my delight
Izuru wa tsuki no	To see the moon emerging
Ureshiki ni	From among the trees,
Nishi naru yama no	That I wish to make my dwelling
Nishi ni sumabaya.	Westward of the western mountains.

Acting as judge, Mototoshi commented: "It is well known that the moon *emerges* [izuru] from behind a mountain rim [implied: to the east]. What sort of scene does the Left suggest in having the moon emerge instead from among a stand of trees? I have read a good many waka from the past in which moonlight 'comes filtering [morikuru] through the trees' " (*HCUT*, 6:1847). If "moon" appears in connection with a "mountain rim" (yama no ha), the correct verb is "emerge" (izu). Similarly, traditional waka usage demands that the phrase "among the trees" (ko no ma) be employed with the verb "to filter" (moru). Mototoshi's point, therefore, is that Tadamichi's use of the word "emerge" is not appropriate to the topic of his waka, "Mountain Moon." The comment should not lead us to conclude hastily that Mototoshi's citing of ancient waka is a sign of his conservatism.

The *Yōen Narabō Utaawase* (*Waka Match Held at Yōen's Nara Residence*), convened in the spring of 1124, contains a poem by the postulant Ushigimi, a member of the Right side. It appears in the second round, on the topic "The Moon."

Aki no yo wa	This autumn night
Tanomuru hito mo	Is not one when my beloved
Naki yado mo	Will visit here,
Ariake no tsuki wa	And it is the faint dawn moon
Nao zo machiizuru.	That I wait for with such hope.

The judge, Minamoto Shunrai (1055?-1129?), remarked, " 'The dawn moon' [ariake no tsuki] is a phrase conveying a sensitive, delicate import. But I wonder whether it should appear in a waka match under the topic 'The Moon.' If so, we need an earlier waka to provide a precedent" (*HCUT*, 6:1887). Shunrai's judgment holds that each further condition added to a general topic demands special treatment. In this case, for example, "dawn moon" should be treated differently from "hazy moon," "midnight moon," or other subdivisions in the "Moon" topic category.

[25] Custom dictated that tennō, former tennō, regents, chancellors, and other eminent participants compete under a pseudonym, such as "court lady." The custom was an expression of the highest respect. In this case, the "court lady" is Fujiwara Tadamichi (1097-1164).

The judgment is not unique to this poem; it is an observation based on contemporary standards. Shunrai's *Secret Notes* details the art of composing on assigned topics.[26] His position is no different from Mototoshi's, since both assert that following the right form will produce esteemed results. Shunrai's classicism is also evident in his reliance on established precedents whenever a poetic decision is in doubt.

The fixed, determined interpretation of each waka topic is called its "hon'i" (essential nature) by twelfth-century waka poets. Consider the following poem, written on the topic "The Moon" and presented by the Right on the thirteenth of the Ninth Month, 1134, in the first round of the *Chūgū no Suke Akisuke Ke Utaawase* (*Waka Match Held at the Residence of Akisuke, Assistant Master of Her Majesty's Household*).

Yomosugara	Throughout the night
Fuji no takane ni	On the lofty peak of Fuji
Kumo kiete	The clouds dissolve,
Kiyomigaseki ni	And at Kiyomi Barrier
Sumeru tsukikage.	The moonlight shines unsullied.

The poem is by Akisuke himself. Mototoshi, the judge, declares it the loser for two reasons. First, clouds conventionally vanish quickly in shih and waka, and Mototoshi finds it odd for these clouds to dissipate gradually over the course of a night. Second, the use of the topic "Fuji" requires a poet also to mention smoke in the waka. Akisuke's substituting clouds for smoke flouts this convention. Mototoshi cites a precedent. "Lady Sagami once composed this poem for a waka match":

Yo to tomo ni	Our relationship
Kokoro sora naru	Floats uncertainly in the sky
Waga koi ya	That is our love—
Fuji no takane ni	On the lofty peak of Fuji
Kakaru shirakumo.	The white clouds gather thickly.

Yet the judge criticized the poet for writing of clouds in place of smoke and for failing therefore to evoke the essential nature [hon'i] of Mount Fuji. It was declared the loser. (*HCUT*, 7:1976)

"The essential nature of Mount Fuji" can only signify the most characteristic aspect of the topic "Mount Fuji," as it became fixed in waka. That, broadly speaking, is the hon'i of a topic. Examples appear in the *Taikō no Suke Taira Tsunemori Ason Ke no Utaawase* (*Waka Match*

[26] *Shumpishō*, 137-40. The concepts date back to the *Utsuho Monogatari* (see vol. two, ch. 7).

Held at the Residence of Lord Taira Tsunemori, Assistant Master of the Dowager's Household). This was convened in the Eighth Month of 1167, and its topic for the eighth round was "Autumn Leaves."

The Left: Koreyuki

Momijiba wa	Although the leaves
Kurenai fukaku	On the maple trees become
Nariyukedo	Even redder,
Hitori sametaru	The pine that stands by itself
Matsu no iro kana.	Retains its sober color.[27]

The Right: Kojijū

Hahasohara	When drizzle falls
Shigururu mama ni	Turning red the woods of oak trees,
Tokiwagi no	Then I do perceive
Mare narikeru mo	How sparsely there grow the trees
Ima zo miekeru.	Whose leaves are forever green.

The judge, Fujiwara Kiyosuke, commented: "Both sides ignore the topic, 'autumn leaves,' to celebrate evergreens. Neither captures the hon'i of the topic" (*HCUT*, 7:2126). Conforming to a predetermined stance was considered an approach "having hon'i." Another, more general name for the essential nature of a topic is "the spirit [kokoro]" of a given topic. An example appears in the seventh round of the *Naidaijin Ke Utaawase* (*Waka Match at the Residence of the Palace Minister* [Fujiwara Tadamichi]), held on the thirteenth day of the Seventh Month, 1118. The topic is "In Search of an Absent Beloved."

The Left: His Lordship [Tadamichi]

Tazunuredo	I have searched for you
Kimi ni au se mo	In vain without some shallows
Namidagawa	In the Stream of Tears—
Nagarete tsui ni	That flow that you have made me weep,
Shizumu beki kana.	Where I shall sink into the depths.

The Right: Sadanobu

Yuku kata o	Where has he gone?
Toedomo sara ni	I ask about but no one says—

[27] Koreyuki implies that the redness is like that which comes to the face of many East Asian people after a certain amount of drink. By contrast, the evergreen is sober. [Auth., Ed.]

Iwashimizu	Iwashimizu Shrine
Soko ni sumu to mo	Seems nearby his dwelling place—
Shiranu koi kana.	What a fragile love is this![28]

Fujiwara Akisue, the judge, commented, "The Left does not grasp the spirit (kokoro) of the topic. The Right does, and should thus be declared the winner" (*HCUT*, 6:1815). The topic is concerned with searching for an absent lover. But Tadamichi, acting for the Left, presents a poem concerned with an earlier stage in a love affair and communicates no sense of a mistress' absence. Sadanobu, on the Right, suggests absence with the words "yuku kata" (destination) and "shiranu" (fragile, lit. unknown), as well as communicating a sense of searching with the word "toedomo" ("I ask about it"). His poem indeed grasps "the heart of the topic" and is therefore declared the winner of the round. In later periods, a waka lacking the spirit of its topic was described as a rakudai, or "lost topic" poem.[29]

A poet including in a poem all the meanings implied by a given topic had reason to expect praise. This, as we noted earlier, resulted from a demand for objective standards in judging, which in turn stemmed from the strongly competitive nature of waka matches. But we must also consider the influence exerted by Chinese treatises on poetics. During his stay in China, Kūkai (774-835) acquired Wang Ch'ang-ling's *Shih-ke* (*Poetics*), which explains a phenomenon called "lo-chieh ping," a poetic "disease of lost focus."[30] Ch'ang-ling's example is a shih on the topic, "The Moon."

A jade hook hangs ten thousand feet high;
Waves of gold stretch ten thousand leagues around.
When the pearl wanes, the lunar disc grows smaller;
As the ming leaves drop, the laurel loses shade.[31]

[28] [The speaker is a woman trying to ascertain her lover's identity, so far with few results. Since most romantic meetings took place at night and ended before daybreak, and since lovers saw each other's faces only when the affair was fairly well advanced, the situation described in the poem would have been familiar to the audience. An excellent example of such an affair is found in the "Yūgao" ("Evening Faces") chapter of *The Tale of Genji*. Genji goes to great lengths to conceal his identity from the lady of the evening faces, and though the lady has his messengers followed to discover his address—and thereby his identity—she meets with no success.—Trans. Both poems invoke verbal plays: pivot words (kakekotoba).—Ed.]

[29] "When treating the topic, 'Concealed Love,' the secrecy of the affair should of course be evoked. If a poet unduly emphasizes the element of secrecy, so that the speaker's excessive caution might draw attention to his affair, the topic may resemble 'Concealed Love,' but it is in fact a lost topic [rakudai]" (*Chikuenshō*, 420).

[30] "Wang Ch'ang-ling, *Shih-ke*, 1 fasc.: I obtained this book in China from an associate of the author" (*Seireishū*, 4:231).

[31] The Chinese believed pearls waxed and waned within their oyster shells, in correspondence with the phases of the moon. The ming plant and the laurel tree are also associated

The blossoms' fragrance comes blended with the wind,
And graceful birdsong filters from the trees.
A wife, left alone in her stately mansion,
And oblivious to the beauty, passes a sad night.

Only the first two couplets deal with the moon, while the rest tend to focus more on blossoms, birds, and human concerns. This evidently means that the poet has lost the "essential nature" (hon'i) of the topic (Konishi, 1953e, 100-105). "Hon'i" was first used in waka match judgments during the *Gosenshū* period (921-81), but only in the ordinary sense of "a longstanding expectation" or "a condition to be satisfied."[32] "Hon'i" in the special usage discussed above does not appear until the twelfth century. The "essential nature" discussed in Wang Ch'ang-ling's *Poetics* conforms to the twelfth-century sense of hon'i as a specific critical term. Nor can we easily conclude that the use of the word "lost" (J. raku, Ch. lo) in "lost focus" (lo-chieh) and "lost topic" (rakudai) is purely accidental. Because Chinese shih treatises were imported in considerable quantities during the twelfth century, Wang Ch'ang-ling's *Poetics* cannot be declared the direct source of this concept.[33] Middle T'ang shih treatises nevertheless contributed to the development of the concept of hon'i in the twelfth century.

Centuries of accumulated precedent led to a standardized treatment of each waka topic. Composition on assigned topics was therefore based on an awareness of the ga ideal, according to which already existing expression was a valued model. Exclusive concentration on waka form would quickly degenerate into predictable, hackneyed poetry. For this reason, conforming to the predetermined "spirit" of a topic had also to include the poet's original contribution. This can only reflect an orientation toward the zoku ideal, an individual search for freshness. Another hallmark of the twelfth century is this orientation toward freshness, manifested even by the formal waka in royal anthologies. A growing respect for set forms was accompanied by a corresponding increase in original poetic concepts. When a poet's original concept ceased to be concerned with an externally visible freshness and instead sought a level of consciousness so deep that the poet himself was unaware of it, the idea of hon'i became the most characteristic focal point of the

---

with the moon in Chinese lore. The legendary ming plant grew a leaf every day for the first fifteen days of the lunar month and shed a leaf every day for the last fifteen days. This was said to have inspired Emperor Yao to invent the lunar calendar. A great laurel tree was believed to grow on the moon. [Auth., Trans.]

32 "Although the poem seems well devised, the kerria [in the waka] must be of the double variety or the requisites [hon'i] will not be satisfied" (*Tentoku*, 82).

33 Works like *Sakumon Daitai* refer frequently to various Chinese books on shih composition.

Middle Ages (see ch. 5). But that is a matter pertaining to the thirteenth century.

Nature and the Emotions

The popularity of assigned topics brought about a noteworthy phenomenon, the further development of waka that were descriptive of nature. There had been no dearth of poems on nature from the *Kokinshū* period on, but their conceptual foci always had a logical cast. Although there are of course differences of degree, all are oblique.[34] The marked increase in the volume of nature poetry written in the twelfth century was accompanied by qualitative changes. Minamoto Tsunenobu (1016-97) was a forerunner in this new style. Not that this style appears in the royal anthologies: only six of Tsunenobu's poems were chosen for the *Goshūishū*, and all follow the traditional *Kokinshū* style. Only one is a nature poem, and it is not cast in a purely descriptive mode: this is "Okitsukaze" ("The wind of the offing"), quoted below. Sone no Yoshitada has nine poems in the *Goshūishū*, all cast in the *Kokinshū* style. Tsunenobu nevertheless did write poems consisting wholly of natural description. A few appear in his personal waka collection, *Dainagon Tsunenobu Shū* (=*DTS; Collected Waka of the Major Counselor Tsunenobu*). Examples follow.

Composed at Fushimi on the topic "Autumn at a Cottage in the Mountains."

Onozukara	Unexpectedly,
Aki wa kinikeri	The autumn has fully come.
Yamazato no	In a mountain village
Kuzu haikakaru	The arrowroot vines entangle
Maki no fuseya ni.	My little hut's brushwood walls.
	(*DTS*, 97)

Composed at Katsura: "Wind on the Rice Blossoms."

Hita haete	Bird-clappers hang
Moru shimenawa no	And the stout ropes that support them
Tawan made	Are brought to sway
Akikaze zo fuku	As the autumn wind blows in gusts
Oyamada no ine.	On rice plants in small mountain fields.
	(*DTS*, 102)

[34] Examples from Book 1 of the *Kokinshū* are numbers 6, 9, 12, 15, 22, 24, 26, 27, 39, 41, 43, 56, 59, and 60. See also vol. two, chs. 1 and 7. [The "oblique" quality involves elegant confusions of features and in general a clear rational control rather than a pretense to present things as they are.—Ed.]

"Autumn Winds in a Farmhouse"

Yū sareba	As evening falls,
Kadota no inaba	It comes to visit rice plants
Otozurete	In fields by my gate,
Ashi no maroya ni	And to my reed-thatched cottage
Akikaze zo fuku.	The autumn wind has blown its way.
	(*DTS*, 103)

"Looking at an Autumn Ricefield"

Kiri haruru	The mists arise
Kadota no ue no	From the fields before my gate,
Inaka no	And their sheaves of rice
Arawarewataru	Are distinctly visible
Aki no yūgure.	In the autumn twilight.
	(*DTS*, 104)

Composed when Yorinaka, governor of Tosa,
spent a night at my house in Nagaoka:
"A Winter's Night in a Mountain Cottage."

Yamazato wa	In a mountain village,
Yodoko saetsutsu	I toss and turn in my cold bed
Akenu rashi	Till dawn seems to come:
Tokata zo kane no	From afar there is the sound
Koe kikoyu nari.	Of what seems a temple bell.
	(*DTS*, 167)

On "The Feeling of Travel"

Tabine shite	I sleep upon my way,
Akatsukigata no	And just as dawn is about to break,
Shinobine ni	Along with stifled cries
Inaba no sue ni	There is the sound of rice leaves
Akikaze zo fuku.	Blown over by the autumn wind.
	(*DTS*, 275)

Thus presented, these waka may easily convince a reader that Tsunenobu's forte was descriptive nature poetry. In fact, however, these six are the only ones of their kind in the 277 poems comprising Tsunenobu's *Collected Waka*. The rest have the oblique reasoning characteristic of the orthodox *Kokinshū* style. Tsunenobu was particularly proud of one such poem:[35]

[35] Manuscript A of *Dainagon Tsunenobu Shū* (Royal Collection) contains 277 waka.

Composed while accompanying Gosanjō In to the Sumiyoshi Shrine.

Okitsukaze	The wind of the offing
Fukinikerashi na	Must indeed have blown full force!
Sumiyoshi no	For at Sumiyoshi
Matsu no shizue o	The lower branches of the pines
Arau shiranami.	Are washed over by the whitecaps.
	(*DTS*, 189)

Waves rising to the bottommost pine branches are conventionally said to "wash" the branches.[36] The reason given in Tsunenobu's poem for the phenomenon—that the waves presumably are rising because a strong wind has been blowing in the offing—is firmly in the oblique tradition. Tsunenobu's own pride in the poem indicates that his poems quoted earlier—poetry of natural description—were no more than occasional experiments. They may have been few and wholly experimental, but the very existence at this time of descriptive waka is a notable herald of twelfth-century poetry.

The *Kokinshū* style was still at its height at the close of the eleventh century. Then why did poets experiment with the description? To answer this, we must realize that Tsunenobu was also a shih poet. The shih circle of his time, though dominated by the style of Po Chü-i, did produce some nature poetry in the style of the Late T'ang period. Tsunenobu wrote such shih (see ch. 1). Verse-topics (kudai) and composite topics (ketsudai) were being used in waka composition during this period.[37] The practice was very likely based on a shared awareness of the role played by verse-topics in shih. When Tsunenobu composed "Yū sareba" ("As evening falls," quoted above) on the topic, "Autumn Winds in a Farmhouse," it would

Manuscript B (also of the Royal Collection) has 231. Both manuscripts are acknowledged twelfth-century compilations. Manuscript B includes all of Tsunenobu's waka that appear in A. The rufubon version (131 poems) postdates the mid-fifteenth century (*DTS*, "Kaisetsu," 15-17). As for Tsunenobu's pride, Gotoba remarked of such matters, "The great poets of the past did not always determine their best waka [jisanka] by quality, but according to whether its subject was elegant and impressively delivered" (*Gotoba In*, 148).

[36] The expression seems to have evolved from contact with T'ang shih. For example: "The Silver River [Milky Way] crests, and waves *wash* the sky" (Shen Pin, "Eulogy for Ma Yin," *Ch'üan T'ang-shih* [= *CTS*], 743:8458) and "Night rains *wash* the Milky Way" (Ch'i Chi, "In Early Autumn, After a Rain," *CTS*, 838:9445).

[37] Strictly speaking, a verse-topic [kudai] is a title [in this case for waka, though they were of course also used for shih] consisting of a line from a famous Chinese shih. I use the term here in a broader sense, to define a verse-topic as any line having a predicate and serving as a topic. (Example: "At Dawn I Hear Plovers.") A verse-topic in this sense is not necessarily limited to a line from an already existing shih. A composite topic [ketsudai] combines several subjects. It has no predicate, only nouns and particles, and participial modifiers are also not elements of a composite topic. (For example, "Accumulated dew" is not a composite topic.)

almost unavoidably have had conceptual and rhetorical points in common with one of his shih, "View from a Farmhouse on an Autumn Day" (*HMDS*, 7:283; see ch. 1). Not only are both descriptive; the subject in both works is a lonely landscape, portrayed in a tranquil tone. The reader's sense is of encountering twin works in differing genres. This phenomenon also appears in the work of Ōe no Masafusa, another writer adept in both Japanese and Chinese. Although few of the 523 waka in his *Gō Sochi Shū* (*Collected Waka of the Ōe Governor-General*) are descriptive, those that are may testify to the influence of shih. Two examples follow.

Composed at the Toba Palace, on the topic "Snow at a Traveler's Lodging."

Kusamakura	Grasses for pillow,
Mabara ni fukeru	I spend the night in a hut
Ashi no ya wa	Rudely thatched of reeds,
Hiroi mo aezu	Where too deep to brush away
Yuki zo tsumoreru.	The snow grows ever deeper!

(*Gō Sochi Shū*, 139)

Composed at the Harbor of Naniwa, on the topic "Cries of Plovers Heard at Dawn."

Yo o samumi	So cold the night
Naniwa no ura no	At the Bay of Naniwa
Irishio ni	With its rising tide,
Yukima o wakete	The plovers seem to cry out
Chidori naku nari.	As they make their way through snow.

(Ibid., 165)

During the twelfth century there was a further increase in the volume of poems of natural description. Mototoshi and Shunrai are the outstanding waka poets of this period, and, of the two, Shunrai wrote more descriptive poems. Mototoshi's work includes the following.

"Mosquito smudge burns in a mountain hut."

Natsu no yo o	Through the summer night
Shitamoeakasu	It smolders on until dawn breaks—
Kayaribi no	The mosquito smudge
Keburi kebutaki	Whose smoke hangs thickly over
Ochi no yamazato.	To the village on the peak beyond.

(*Mototoshi Shū*, 26)

"I await the moon by the water."

Natsu no yo no	On a summer's night
Tsuki matsu hodo no	Waiting for the moon to rise,
Tesusabi ni	I beguile the time
Iwa moru shimizu	Scooping handful after handful
Ikumusubishitsu.	Of water trickling from the crags.
	(Ibid., 30)

"Daybreak at a Mountain Village"

Yamazato no	My mountain village
Obana sakayuku	Has plumegrass in full bloom
No no ma yori	Across the fields,
Ariake no tsuki wa	Where it frames the pallid moon
Sashiidenikeri.	As it emerges in the dawning sky.
	(Ibid., 44)

Although the description is certainly not a frequent feature of Mototoshi's waka, his vocation as a shih poet surely indicates that waka like these are evidence of the influence of shih. Let us consider one of Mototoshi's shih, "An Excursion to a Temple on a Spring Day" (*HMDS*, 10:310). It consists almost entirely of natural description, except for some interweaving of the speaker's feelings.

There is a temple in the Eastern Mountains, so high it touches the clouds:
Pine pillars, brushwood gate, bamboo rails are old too.
Moss grows deep on stone-paved paths, softening the way in spring;
The incense halls and chapels may be cramped, but the evening sky is vast.
The vales are still; birds sing in concert near the windows.
Blossoms open and are viewed by monks concluding meditation.
I had thought to worship the Buddha and then take my leave;
Enraptured by the bells' toll, I linger here awhile.

The first and seventh lines contain expository language. Late T'ang poetic criteria would mark the poem as scarcely better than average. It is even somewhat inferior to Tsunenobu's "View from a Farmhouse on an Autumn Day." "An Excursion to a Temple on a Spring Day" nevertheless provides evidence that Mototoshi and others proficient in both waka and shih played a major role in increasing the amount of descriptive nature waka written during the twelfth century.

Of course, a literary phenomenon need not originate from one source alone. The marked proliferation of descriptive nature poetry mode cannot be entirely explained by postulating the influence of poets proficient in both shih and waka. Shunrai's waka corpus contains more descriptive nature poetry than Mototoshi's, and yet Shunrai left no shih. His poems include writing like that in the following.

"Scattering Blossoms Follow the Breeze."

Ato taete	No human foot
Kewashiki taki no	Steps on the rocks of the high crag
Iwa no ue ni	Whence the water falls,
Hana kokiorosu	And there the cherry blossoms drift,
Haru no yamakaze.	Scattered by spring mountain winds.
	(*Samboku Kikashū* [=*SBS*], 1:124)

Composed at the Hachijō residence of Morotoki, Provisional Master of Her Majesty's Household, on the topic "The Lakeside Breeze Grows Cool at Eventide."

Kaze fukeba	As breezes blow,
Hasu no ukiha ni	On the floating lotus leaves,
Tama koete	The jewels are stirred,
Suzushiku narinu	And as the coolness comes—
Higurashi no koe.	The cicadas join their cries.
	(*SBS*, 2:312)

During Horikawa's reign, his majesty had the courtiers compose waka on allotted topics, all concerning autumn flowers. I drew the topic "Plumegrass," and submitted this poem.

Uzura naku	The quails cry out
Mano no irie no	In the rough fields by the bay
Hamakaze ni	And in the beach wind
Obana nami yoru	The plumegrass ripples like waves
Aki no yūgure.	The twilight of an autumn day.
	(*SBS*, 3:414)

"All Night I Hear Leaves Falling"

Hitori nuru	Where I lie alone,
Fuseya no hima no	Gaps in the walls of the hut

Shiran made	Grow white with dawn,
Ogi no kareba ni	And on the withered leaves of reeds
Konoha chiru nari.	The tree leaves seem to be falling.
	(*SBS*, 4:597)

These poems were all written on assigned topics, mostly of the verse-topic or composite-topic variety. Because verse-topics were originally confined to shih [see vol. two, index], waka poets composing with verse-topics were probably well aware of the kinds of expression used in shih on a given topic. The same would apply to composite topics, which are an extension of the verse-topic.

The twelfth-century shih poets were much involved in composing nature poetry in the Late T'ang style, and the natural consequence was for waka poets to follow suit and experiment with similarly descriptive styles. The results are indeed best described as experimental. Even Shunrai does not have many poems of natural description. If we also consider that verse-topic and composite-topic waka proliferated rapidly after the compilation of the *Goshūishū*, this suggests that twelfth-century waka poets were affected by something more than the work of poets proficient in both shih and waka: most wished to experiment with expression like that used in Late T'ang nature poetry. For example, among its 1,220 poems, the *Goshūishū* has forty-nine on verse-topics and twenty-nine on composite topics.

Their new inclination is reflected in the selections for royal waka anthologies. The new critical preference undoubtedly accounts for the inclusion of waka by earlier poets unacclaimed during their lifetimes. Sone no Yoshitada's work comes to mind.

Topic Unknown

Yamashiro no	As I gaze afar
Tobata no omo o	Upon the Toba paddies
Miwataseba	In Yamashiro,
Honoka ni kesa zo	This morning it is so gentle!
Akikaze wa fuku.	The autumn breeze that stirs.
	(*Shikashū* [=*SKS*], 3:82)

Yamazato wa	The mountain village:
Yukiki no michi no	The little road that leads by it
Mienu made	Has disappeared—
Aki no konoha ni	In the autumn, leaves from trees
Uzumorenikeri.	Have buried its whole length.
	(*SKS*, 3:133)

Requiring logic as a medium in nature poetry, the *Kokinshū* style is also necessarily oblique in waka dealing with a speaker's emotions. When Shunrai compiled the *Kin'yōshū*, he accorded high value to witty expression, even applying the criterion to his own contributions.

Composed in despair when a minor courtier was promoted to a position higher than his own.
By Minamoto Shunrai

Seki mo aenu	Impossible to stem,
Namida no kawa wa	The swollen river of my tears
Hayakeredo	Flows in swift current,
Mi no ukigusa wa	Yet I, a wretched waterplant,
Nagarezarikeri.	Advance no farther with its flow.
	(*Kin'yōshū* [=*KYS*], 10:599)

Although the subject is chagrin over a personal event, the technique employed is that of *Kokinshū*-style waka. The speaker's weeping is evoked by the familiar conceit of a river of tears, and the water imagery is carried on when the poet's situation is represented by a waterplant. "Uki," a pivot word, links the poet's wretched (uki) state to the floating waterplant (ukigusa). This is typical of the style of the twelfth century, at least for royal waka anthologies. But in a few cases, the poet revealed deeply felt matters without elegant logic. For example:

"Parting," from a hundred-poem sequence.
By Kuninobu, Provisional Middle Counselor

Kyō wa sa wa	So, today, then,
Tachiwakaru to mo	We go on our separate ways,
Tayori araba	But should chance arise,
Ari ya nashi ya no	Be kind enough to write, if just
Nasake wasuru na.	"How do things get on with you?"
	(*KYS*, 6:355)

Composed at a waka match held at the residence of Akisuke, Master of the Left Capital.
By Narimichi, Major Counselor

Yoso nagara	Rather than receive
Aware to iwan	Messages of fond concern,
Koto yori mo	I would much prefer

Hitozute narade	Being told right to my face
Itoe to zo omou.	"You are one I cannot stand!"
	(*SKS*, 7:196)

Personal waka collections contain a far greater incidence of non-oblique expression. Several poems like the following appear in Shunrai's personal collection, *Samboku Kikashū* (=*SBS*; *Strange Poems by a Useless Fellow*).[38]

Composed in despair when a minor courtier was promoted to a position higher than mine.

Uki koto wa	Bitter treatment
Mezurashikaranu	Affords no novelty at all
Mi naredomo	To this life of mine.
Tabi ni mo sode no	Yet, even if I were traveling,
Nuremasaru kana.	Would my sleeves be more drenched than now?
	(*SBS*, 9:1136)

From a hundred-poem sequence on regret for my inadequacies and shame at my bad fortune. Presented by the acolyte Nōton[39]

Nanigoto mo	No matter what,
Omoiitaranu	Nothing turns out as one would wish
Yo no naka ni	In this sorry world,
Mi wa amarinuru	But it seems that I alone
Mono ni zo arikeru.	Am counted worse than useless.
	(*SBS*, 9:1497)

The former poem was probably composed in the same circumstances as "Seki mo aenu" ("Impossible to stem"; *KYS*, 10:599, quoted above), but here witty expression has quite vanished. The two poems ably illustrate the decisive role of fabricated logic in Shunrai's critical apparatus: the witty, rational poem was selected for a royal anthology while the unadorned statement of emotions was omitted.

This tendency also appears when earlier poets' works are selected for royal anthologies. Izumi Shikibu, for example, is frequently represented

[38] ["Samboku" literally means "useless wood products." The title plays on the poet's official position as Director of the Carpentry Bureau.—Trans. The author's preceding note on topics for *Goshūishū* was put by me into the main text.—Ed.]

[39] Nōton ("Talent for Avarice") is a fictitious name used by Shunrai. The name is of course ironical, since a monk is supposed to be free of avaricious tendencies. [Auth., Trans.]

in the *Goshūishū* and later anthologies.[40] Few of the waka chosen depart from the traditional style, but some possess no oblique expression at all:

Composed when Koshikibu no Naishi died and I was left with my grandchildren.[41]

Todomeokite	She has left us,
Tare o aware to	And who is it that she wishes
Omou ran	To have most of all?
Ko wa masaru ran	Her children must be the ones—
Ko wa masarikeri.	My child is the one I yearn for.
	(*Goshūishū* [= *GSIS*], 10:568)

After Koshikibu no Naishi died, the Dowager Shōtō Mon'in continued to send clothing as in the past.[42] Izumi Shikibu composed this on seeing "For Koshikibu no Naishi" written on the bundle.

Morotomo ni	I remain alive
Koke no shita ni wa	Instead of joining her to molder
Kuchizu shite	Beneath the moss;
Uzumarenu na o	Only her name survives unburied—
Kiku zo kanashiki.	How sad to hear it spoken!
	(*KYS*, 10:611)

Topic Unknown

Yūgure ni	In the evening gloom
Mono omou koto wa	The things I feel most deeply
Masaru ya to	Seem to multiply:
Ware narazaran	I would like to ask of someone
Hito ni towabaya.	If this is not true for all.
	(*SKS*, 8:249)

A few other non-oblique waka by Izumi Shikibu also appear in the *Goshūishū*, demonstrating that by the twelfth century the ga aesthetic in

[40] The *Shūishū* has not one waka by Izumi Shikibu, but the *Goshūishū* contains sixty-seven. The *Kin'yōshū* has only eight, and the *Shikashū* sixteen.

[41] [Koshikibu no Naishi was Izumi Shikibu's daughter, and a poet in her own right.—Trans.]

[42] Shōtō Mon'in [or Jōtō Mon'in] is the name taken by Akiko (992-1074), consort of Ichijō Tennō and daughter of Fujiwara Michinaga, when she became Dowager. Koshikibu was one of her ladies-in-waiting, and the clothing represents her salary. (Since money was not used during this period, purchase and payment were conducted according to a barter system.) The Dowager's great affection for Koshikibu probably lies behind her unusual gesture of continuing payment after the lady's death. [Auth., Trans.]

waka was not restricted to the *Kokinshū* style.[43] The following may be given as examples.

Kurokami no	I do not even know
Midare mo shirazu	If my long hair is tangled.
Uchifuseba	As I lie beside you,
Mazu kakiyarishi	You, my darling, are so dear
Hito zo koishiki.	To begin by stroking it aside.
	(*GSIS*, 13:755)

Arazaran	Soon to be no more!
Kono yo no hoka no	As a memory of this world
Omoide ni	Taken to the next,
Ima hitotabi no	I wish now for one more time
Au koto mo gana.	When you come for love with me.
	(*GSIS*, 13:763)

Mono omoeba	Distressed in thought,
Sawa no hotaru o	I take a firefly in the marsh
Waga mi yori	To be my soul,
Akugareizuru	Somehow flown from my body,
Tama ka to zo miru.	Flickering off into the dark.
	(*GSIS*, 20:1164)

The presence of these poems in a royal collection signifies general recognition of their status as honka—"foundation poems" whose words could be used for new poems by allusion or as precedent. In other words, slightly anomalous writing was now one of the features of ga.

Refined Charm and Tranquility

Waka styles remained largely unchanged in the twelfth century, although the *Senzaishū* period (1158-1218), when Shunzei and Saigyō were active, presents some departures. Kamo no Chōmei (1153?-1216) remarks that the *Senzaishū* follows in the footsteps of the *Goshūishū*.[44] This is basically sound, since both works offer a little non-oblique expression in their poems on nature and the emotions while retaining the *Kokinshū* style as

[43] [The author does not present the following three poems in his text. I have put them there to join them with the preceding poems by Izumi Shikibu and to avoid a lengthy note.—Ed. For further discussion of the poet and these three poems see vol. two, ch. 7.—Trans.]

[44] "The *Shikashū* and the *Senzaishū* are generally in the style of the *Goshūishū*" (*Mumyōshō*, 83).

their keynote. But the *Senzaishū* period is novel in its tonal emphasis on refined charm (yūen) and tranquility (kanjaku).

En, or refined beauty, is linked to the fūryū (elegant) life. The vital significance of en for early medieval literature and aesthetics is discussed in the second volume of this *History*. Because everyday aristocratic life was oriented toward fūryū in the Early Middle Ages, the en ideal tended to appear in their nikki [personal accounts in the present tense] and in their monogatari [prose narratives written in the past tense]. But it is not necessarily a dominant ideal in waka.[45] Beginning with Shunzei, however, poets deliberately stipulated yūen, refined charm, as the supreme aesthetic in waka. Their judgment was generally accepted up to the fifteenth or sixteenth century. Shunzei's positive rulings at waka matches are most often characterized by the phrase "yū nari" (polished), which is used 279 times. This is followed by "en nari" (refined), which Shunzei uses ninety-six times.[46] The early medieval usage of "en" denotes something more implicit than the meaning conveyed by its Chinese counterpart, yen (see vol. two, ch. 5). Nevertheless, since yen/en originally signified the kind of beauty possessed by female immortals, the term has an alluring, positive quality. "Yū," by contrast, refers to a polished beauty. The finer the polish, the more "yū" possessed by a poem. The concept of yū may strike one as slightly more subtle than en, but there is no substantial difference in meaning between the two. Thus they can be combined to form a new aesthetic concept, refined charm.

Three points must be discussed in connection with the bringing forward of yūen as the principal tone in waka during Shunzei's day. First, "yūen" expresses only one kind of beauty, but its components apparently had differing connotations. "Yū," which receives little mention in earlier centuries, eventually came to be used more frequently than the once popular "en." Although both have essentially the same meaning, "yū," a term distinguished by degrees of refinement, is a more intense version of the beauty represented by "en." Shunzei's emphasis on yū probably manifests both a respect for the en of the past along with his drive to achieve greater refinement than that of bygone days. By the late twelfth century, the nobility was no longer able to maintain the old fūryū life. En, an aesthetic rooted in fūryū, now existed only as an ideal beauty sought after when a

[45] The *Wakatei Jisshu* (45-49), attributed to Mibu no Tadamine, Kintō's *Shinsen Zuinō* (26-27), and *Waka Kubon* (32-33), and the judgments made at contemporary poetry matches attach no specific importance to en. [For the author's definitions of nikki and monogatari—briefly stated in brackets in the preceding sentence—see vol. two, ch. 8.—Ed.]

[46] The figures are based on Taniyama Shigeru's research (Taniyama, 1951, 255). They are not absolute, owing to the presence of textual variants. In addition to "yū" and "en," Shunzei uses the related term "yasashi" thirty-one times. I do not mention this in the text because "yasashi" differs somewhat in nature from the other terms.

poem treated longing for past glory. A profound longing for things past can evoke an imagined beauty surpassing that of the present. The beauty Shunzei sought was the en aesthetic of earlier centuries; but his en, heightened by a longing for the past, evolved into yūen, a subtle, even lovelier version of en.

A second point involves the relationship between the yūen tone and monogatari. A good example of the yūen ideal in an actual composition is a famous waka which its composer considered his finest work.

A waka on autumn, composed upon submitting a hundred-poem sequence.
By Shunzei, Master of the Dowager's Household

Yū sareba	As evening falls,
Nobe no akikaze	Along the fields the autumn wind
Mi ni shimite	Pierces to my heart,
Uzura naku nari	And the quails can be heard to cry
Fukakusa no sato.	At Fukakusa lost in deep plants.[47]

(*Senzaishū* [=*SZS*], 4:258)

Modern readers might be hard pressed to comprehend how this poem embodies refined charm. In fact, most readers would discover in it a sense of tranquility, and yūen is precisely that, a tranquil beauty. Unless one knows, however, that Shunzei's poem is based on a scene from the following tenth-century oral waka story (utagatari), its refined charm will not be communicated.

Once a man gave this poem to a lady at Fukakusa—someone in whom, it seems, he had been gradually losing interest.

Toshi o hete	These many years,
Sumikoshi sato o	I made this place my home;
Idete inaba	Were I to leave,
Itodo Fukakusa	Might Fukakusa's deep grasses
No to ya narinan.	Become still more tangled fields?

The lady's reply:

No to naraba	If it turns to fields,
Uzura to narite	Like the quail I shall cry on
Nakioran	As the long years pass;

[47] [Adapted from Brower-Miner, 1961, 17.—Trans.]

Kari ni dani ya wa	Surely you will come sometime,
Kimi wa kozaran.	To hunt them and to seek me out?

The man, deeply moved, no longer felt inclined to leave.

(*IM*, dan 123:180)[48]

Shunzei's poem acquires a refined charm when read with this story from the fūryū world as a backdrop. Without the utagatari episode from the *Ise Monogatari* (*The Tales of Ise*), Shunzei's waka would not be the acknowledged masterpiece it is. The difference can be perceived by comparing Shunzei's poem with the following waka, which depicts a similar scene [but lacks the affective depth and literary resonance of Shunzei's conception].

Topic Unknown
By Minamoto Tokitsuna

Kimi nakute	Lacking your visits,
Aretaru yado no	My neglected house grows rampant
Asajifu ni	With wild plumereeds
Uzura naku nari	Where the quails seem to cry:
Aki no yūgure.	Evening of an autumn day.

(*GSIS*, 4:302)

By combining the subject of quails with the poetic place name Fukakusa, Shunzei had evoked the aura of an utagatari and *The Tales of Ise*. This is the source of the refined charm in his poem. Some of Shunzei's waka judgments corroborate this, including one from the *Waka Match in Six Hundred Rounds*. The topic is "Typhoon."

The Left: [Nakayama] Kanemune [1163-1242]

Momokusa no	The lovely blossoms
Hana mo ika ni ka	Of the many plants in bloom
Omou ran	Must resent it:
Ana nasake na no	"Oh, typhoon, you have no pity,
Kesa no nowaki ya.	To wreck the fields this morning!"

[48] [Adapted from Helen Craig McCullough, trans., *Tales of Ise: Lyrical Episodes from Tenth-Century Japan* (Stanford: Stanford University Press, 1968), 148-49.—Trans. In the author's terms (see vol. two, ch. 8), the poems and their prose constitute an utagatari in the *Kokinshū* (18:971 and 972). In the *Ise Monogatari* they constitute one dan or episode in an utamonogatari.—Ed.]

The Right: Provisional Master of the Consort's Household [Fujiwara Iefusa (1167-96)] (Winner)

Fukimidaru	Blown in a tangle
Nowaki no kaze no	By the typhoon gales in fields
Arakereba	Where it shows its rage,
Yasuki sora naki	None among the various flowers
Hana no iroiro.	Is allowed a moment's peace.

It was said that neither the Left nor the Right poem is particularly distinguished. The judge remarks: " 'Oh, heartless!' [Ana nasake na] is apparently intended as a clever device. The Right's use of 'Blown in a tangle' [fukimidaru] calls to mind Tamakazura's plight in the 'Typhoon' ['Nowaki'] chapter of the *Genji*, and so evokes refined beauty [en]." (*Roppyakuban Utaawase* [=*RU*], "Autumn, 1" 131) It is agreed that neither poem is an impressive work. But the Right's undistinguished contribution is declared the winner over the no less commonplace poem of the Left because the former has acquired refined beauty by a connection to one of Tamakazura's poems in the *Genji Monogatari* (*The Tale of Genji* [=*GM*]; "Nowaki," 59):

Fukimidaru	Blown in a tangle
Kaze no keshiki ni	As the wind sweeps across the scene,
Ominaeshi	The maidenflower
Shioreshinu beki	Is filled with the conviction
Kokochi koso sure.	That she will fade away and die.

The episode describes how Genji comes to Tamakazura's quarters, ostensibly to learn how she fared in the recent storm. He finds her behind a pillar, as though she is trying to hide. She is turned slightly away from him. As he approaches to embrace her, her hair falls to one side, hiding her face. Inwardly annoyed, she nevertheless leans calmly against him ("Nowaki," 58). The "maidenflower" of the poem is a metaphor for Tamakazura herself. By evoking *The Tale of Genji*, the Right's "Blown in a tangle" performs the same function as Shunzei's use of "Fukakusa" in suggesting *The Tales of Ise* to his audience. But the Right's victory is due even more to the refined charm of its waka. Shunzei's famous dictum supports this: "Murasaki Shikibu was a better writer than a waka poet. Her 'Festival of the Cherry Blossoms' ['Hana no En'] is especially refined [yū]. A poet who has not read the *Genji* is to be deplored" (*RU*, "Winter, 1" 188).[49]

[49] ["Hana no En," the eighth chapter of the *Genji*, describes elegant spring pastimes along with amours at court and at residences of the nobility.—Trans.]

Shunzei praises waka with monogatari referents. Waka using other waka for referents presented no problem in this period, since waka was a premier art, but until the early twelfth century the status of monogatari was definitely not equal to waka. The reason why monogatari were eventually invoked as allusive grounds for waka can only be that the monogatari came to be perceived as another premier art. Not that this was a wholly established attitude in the late twelfth century. It was probably no more than an opinion held by Shunzei and a few like-minded colleagues. Indeed, the *Waka Match in Six Hundred Rounds* also records diverging views among the participants on the question of whether the *Genji* had sufficient literary status to serve waka suitably for allusion.[50] By the thirteenth century the concept of monogatari as a premier art becomes dominant. This tendency is reflected in the *Shinkokinshū*, which contains fourteen poems clearly alluding to the *Genji*, as compared to the somewhat earlier *Kin'yōshū* and *Senzaishū*, each containing only one such poem (Konishi, 1974a, 24-25). Monogatari now held a status equal to waka because both genres were sources of refined charm. Poets revered only those monogatari that were deeply imbued with refined charm, and other monogatari were not welcome to poets. We may conclude that *The Tale of Genji* and *The Tales of Ise* epitomized monogatari up to the fifteenth or sixteenth century because the keynote of each was yūen, refined charm.

A third point concerns understatement. Modern readers do not easily perceive Shunzei's "As evening falls" ("Yū sareba," *SZS*, 4:258) as an example of yūen. It is easy for us to consider yūen only that which *we* feel to be yūen. But while refined charm in the eleventh and twelfth centuries was the same kind of beauty as that perceived as yūen by a modern reader, it manifested itself in far subtler ways.[51] Too obvious a manifestation loses its refined charm. This is the case for waka, as Shunzei states in his judgments of *Jichin Kashō Jikaawase* (*Master Jien's Waka Match*; "Postscript to the Sequence on Jūzenji Shrine").

> A poem need not always employ witty devices or clearly express its content. A poem is generally recited rhythmically, and in such a case, as also when it is simply read aloud, it should communicate a sense of charm [en] and profundity [yūgen]. This is what is meant by a fine

[50] The question is raised in the thirteenth round (topic: "Evening Faces") apropos the Right's poem: "The *Genji Monogatari* is employed here as the sole authority. I wonder if it should be acknowledged as a locus of authentic precedent?" (*RU*, "Summer, 2" 100). Shunzei's reply is equivocal: "The poem is indeed based on the *Genji Monogatari*, but would you not call its style refined?"

[51] Murasaki Shikibu describes as "very en" a scene in which Genji visits the Rokujō lady in Sagano during the autumn. All the flowers are fading, the reeds are withered, and the hoarse songs of insects blend with the wind in the pines; from afar Genji hears the faint sound of music (see vol. two, ch. 5).

poem. It will have not only diction and form, but carry with it an ineffable vision. (*Utaawase Shū* [= *UAS*], 472).

Shunzei holds, then, that a superlative waka must have yūgen—profundity—as well as en and that its audience will sense a visionary scene underlying the language of the poem. Writing that states all the intended meaning of a poem squanders the aesthetic potential of en. Paradoxically, the refined charm of a subject is most effectively perceived when it is incompletely expressed. The missing parts are intended to be supplemented by the audience, in the affective-expressive manner; but that does not mean we can add whatever we please. The poet leaves things unsaid in the belief that his audience will supplement the poem within a Gestalt anticipated by the poet. This presupposes an audience whose cultural background is homogeneous with the poet's. Beauty expressed by understatement, in other words, can be appreciated because it appears within a ga sphere (see vol. two, ch. 3). The absorption of Western late Romantic expressivism in early modern Japan resulted in a nearly complete loss of the medieval ga aesthetic, however. That is why the tones that struck Shunzei and his colleagues as yūen do not affect us in the same way.

The adoption by waka of refined charm seems to have developed fairly naturally from the tenth or eleventh century on. We must also acknowledge, of course, the role played in its *development* by the delicate, ornate style of Late T'ang poetry as communicated through twelfth-century Japanese shih. The influence of shih amplified an already continuing process, that of waka refining the en of earlier centuries into an even subtler yūen, but the yūen aesthetic did not owe its *creation* to the Japanese reception of Late T'ang poetry.

A contrasting aesthetic does appear in late twelfth-century waka, that of tranquility (kanjaku)—although it certainly cannot be called one of the principal tones of the age. Probably the tranquil tone did not evolve naturally among twelfth-century waka poets. The influence of Chinese shih seems to have played a greater role in its case than in that of yūen. "Tranquility" is used to designate the kind of tone found in the following poem.

Topic Unknown
By [Ōe no] Masafusa, Treasury Minister

Okuyama no	Deep in the mountains
Iwagaki momiji	By sheer cliffs the red foliage
Chirihatete	Has wholly scattered,
Kuchiba ga ue ni	And upon the moldering leaves
Yuki zo tsumoreru.	The snow grows ever deeper.

(*SKS*, 4:156)

Snow piling up on fallen leaves makes a lonely winter landscape, and yet the speaker does not respond in a gloomy manner, choosing instead to appreciate the scene as possessing a kind of beauty. Although all the leaves have fallen, the mention of "red foliage" (momiji) implies a memory of the scene as it was not long before, that of autumn at its most resplendent. This too reflects the poet's admiration of his setting. Typically, the many waka depicting winter—both preceding and following Masafusa's chronologically—tend to abhor its desolation. For example, here is the poem alluded to by Masafusa:

Okuyama no	Deep in the mountains
Iwagaki momiji	By sheer cliffs the red foliage
Chirinu beshi	Must be all fallen;
Teru hi no hikari	The radiance of unclouded sun
Miru toki nakute.	Is never to be seen these days.[52]
	(*KKS*, 5:282)

Here is another, from a time closer to the *Shinkokinshū*:

Topic Unknown
By Sone no Yoshitada

Toyama naru	On nearby hills
Shiba no tachie ni	The upstretched leaves of brushwood
Fuku kaze no	Agitate with wind,
Oto kiku ori zo	And whenever I hear the sound
Fuyu wa mono uki.	Winter is a hateful thing!
	(*SKS*, 4:147)

Desolation is rarely praised. The *Senzaishū*, however, contains quite a few waka whose tone is one of admiration for a lonely scene. Some examples follow.

On the topic "Deer."
By the monk Jakuren

Onoe yori	From the hilltops
Kadota ni kayou	To the field before my gate

[52] [This poem by Fujiwara Sekio has been taken by me from the author's running commentary and inserted in the text with some prose as well before and after.—Ed.]

Akikaze ni	Comes the autumn wind,
Inaba o wataru	And with it the crying of a stag
Saoshika no koe.	Passes across the sheaves of rice.[53]

(*SZS*, 5:324)

Topic Unknown
By Fujiwara Mototoshi

Shimo saete	Chilled by frost,
Kareyuku ono no	The withered grasses of a field
Okabe naru	Stand upon a hill,
Nara no hiroba ni	Where broad leaves of the oak trees
Shigure furu nari.	Sound in the autumn drizzle.[54]

(*SZS*, 6:400)

Composed on the topic "Autumn Rain at a Mountain Dwelling."
By Minamoto Nakayori

Minegoe ni	Crossing the peaks,
Nara no ha zutai	Its visit rustles into sound
Otozurete	Leaves still upon the oaks,
Yagate nokiba ni	And soon the edges of my eaves
Shigure kinikeri.	Give voice to the autumn drizzle.

(*SZS*, 6:415)

Naturally we cannot be completely sure that these poets composed their works out of conscious admiration for a desolate landscape. There are instances, however, of waka in a similar tone that are praised for their "sabitari" (lonely, sere) qualities, an indication that the compiler, Shunzei, was probably well aware of the tone of these three poems in selecting them for the *Senzaishū*. I refer to a round in the *Waka Match in Six Hundred Rounds* (Topic: "In Search of the Beloved").

[53] Although Jakuren considered this his best poem, Shunzei rejected it for inclusion in the *Senzaishū* [*SZS*] with the comment, "It is an interesting poem, and not wholly implausible, but it might have a bad influence on future waka." It appeared in the *SZS* only at Teika's urging (*Kyōgoku Sōgo*, 334). Despite its problems, the poem was acknowledged by Shunzei, Teika, and Jakuren to have "goodness."

[54] This poem appears at a match given by Fujiwara Tadamichi, the Palace Minister, on X.1118 (judged by Shunrai and Mototoshi). Shunrai judged the round a draw, but Mototoshi found this waka the winner, commenting that it "used slightly more familiar expression" (*HCUT*, 6:1763). Again, such expression presented problems, but was acknowledged by both judges to have a certain "goodness."

Judgment: Draw

The Left: A Court Lady

Tazunetsuru	I sought her in vain
Michi ni koyoi wa	On this path where the nighttime
Fukenikeri	Has grown very late.
Sugi no kozue ni	Then, on tips of cedar branches,
Ariake no tsuki.	Here it is—the moon at dawn.[55]

The Right: Nobusada

Kokoro koso	Indeed, my heart
Yukue mo shirane	Has flown I know not where!
Miwa no yama	Here at Miwa Mountain,
Sugi no kozue no	The tips of cedar branches
Yūgure no sora.	Show against the evening sky.[56]

Neither side voices any criticism. The judge remarks, "The Left's 'Then, on tips of cedar branches, / Here it is—the moon at dawn' [Sugi no kozue ni / Ariake no tsuki] and the Right's 'The tips of cedar branches / Show against the evening sky' [Sugi no kozue no / Yūgure no sora] are both very clever indeed. The Left does not mention Miwa Mountain, which makes it all the wittier. 'Here it is—the moon at dawn' has a particularly lonely tone [sabite] and so improves the waka, but the Right's 'evening sky' is not its inferior. Thus I declare the round a draw." (*RU*, "Love, 1" 242) The speaker in the Left's poem is on his way to visit his lover. He encounters some sort of difficulty and, finding that the night is nearly over, gazes up at the dawn moon there beyond the cedar branches and makes his way through the dark grove of trees. Shunzei praises the second half of the poem as having a "particularly lonely tone"; his criteria for selecting waka for the *Senzaishū* were probably of this kind.

Praise for a "lonely" poetic scene did not always stem from criteria

[55] The poet is Gokyōgoku Yoshitsune (1169-1206) using a pseudonym. "Ariake" is a pivot word: the dawn (ariake) moon reveals the cedar(s) marking the lady's house that the speaker has been seeking (see n. 56), and he exclaims, "Here it is!" (ari). But he has taken too long to find it; dawn is breaking, and he must wait until night comes again to pay her another visit. [Auth., Trans.]

[56] The poet is Jien (1155-1225) writing under the pseudonym and alluding to a well-known poem in the *Kokinshū* (18:982): Waga io wa / Miwa no yamamoto / Koishiku wa / Toburaikimase / Sugi tateru kado. (My dwelling lies / At the foot of Miwa Mountain; / When you long for me, / Come, come pay me a visit— / It's the gate where the cedar stands.) The speaker of Jien's poem has journeyed to the foot of Miwa Mountain in response to this invitation, only to find his mind a blank on reaching the lady's house. His great longing and his eager search for her paradoxically result in his standing vacantly under the cedar, wondering where his heart has flown. [Auth., Trans.]

typical of the *Senzaishū* period.[57] Although the "lonely" tone was emphasized from the thirteenth century on, we should also note that it had gained a certain recognition by Shunzei's time. As was mentioned earlier, the belief that there is beauty in a desolate landscape was probably not a natural product of tenth- and eleventh-century waka practice. Considerable credit must instead be given to the influence exerted by Chinese shih. I say this because the "lonely" tone first appears in waka by poets proficient in Chinese as well as in Japanese. One example is Masafusa's "Deep in the Mountains" ("Okuyama no"; *SKS*, 4:156). Another is

Topic Unknown
By Ōe no Yoshitoki

Yama fukami	Deep are the mountains
Ochite tsumoreru	Where fall and gather into mounds
Momijiba no	The autumn leaves,
Kawakeru ue ni	On which, now grown curled and sere,
Shigure furu nari.	The cold drizzle is heard to fall.
	(*SKS*, 4:144)

Both waka have much the same concept or were inspired by similar T'ang poems.[58]

Composed for submitting a hundred-poem sequence during Horikawa's reign.
By [Ōe no] Masafusa, Former Middle Counselor

Takasago no	At Takasago
Onoe no kane no	The temple bell upon the hill
Oto su nari	Seems to have sounded.
Akatsuki kakete	As the day begins to dawn
Shimo ya oku ran.	Does not the frost cover all?
	(*SZS*, 6:397)

By Fujiwara Mototoshi

Hisagi ouru	Where catalpa grows
Ono no asaji ni	In little fields of sparse reeds

[57] Some assume that the aesthetic of loneliness was widely accepted in Shunzei's time, but this runs counter to fact. There are instances of Shunzei himself commenting that a poem "sounds lonely" (*RU*, "Spring, 1" 14; "Winter, 1" 197) and then ruling it the loser or a match a draw.

[58] [The poems by Ōe no Masafusa and Ōe no Yoshitoki are by individuals whose family was long distinguished for Chinese learning.—Ed.]

Oku shimo no	Covered with the frost,
Shiroki o mireba	I can tell from the whiteness
Yo ya fukenu ran.	That night must be near its end.
	(*SZS*, 6:398)

This pair of poets is also proficient in shih composition. Both find interest in the concept of a tranquil, frosty night, but such poems were rarely selected for royal anthologies. Shunzei did include thirty-six of his own compositions in the *Senzaishū*; yet none resembles the tonality of these poems. Only one can approximate it:

A poem on summer rain, composed upon presenting a hundred-poem sequence to Sutoku In.
By Shunzei, Master of the Dowager's Household

Samidare wa	The summer rains
Taku mo no keburi	Sprinkle the smoke that rises
Uchishimeri	From burning seaweed,
Shiotaremasaru	Dampening more than usual
Suma no urabito.	The people of the Suma shore.
	(*SZS*, 3:183)

In this case, however, the shore people are "dampened" in spirit because their physical "dampening" makes it difficult to extract much salt from the seaweed. The poem communicates dislike, not approbation, for the depressing summer rains. Saigyō has eighteen poems in the *Senzaishū*, but only one takes a positive approach toward a "lonely" scene.

Composed on the topic "A Cold Night's Moon."
By the monk En'i

Shimo sayuru	Oh, that someone
Niwa no konoha o	Might come to ask—through the garden
Fumiwakete	Where the tree leaves
Tsuki wa miru ya to	Have been taken by the chill of frost—
Tou hito mogana.	"Are you too here to see the moon?"[59]
	(*SZS*, 16:1006)

A few other poets also employ a tranquil tone.[60] But their number is negligible through the twelfth century, making it unlikely that they engen-

[59] "En'i" was a name used earlier by Saigyō. [Auth., Trans.]

[60] Including Tsunenobu (*KYS*, 3:164), Shunrai (*KYS*, 3:233), Kanemasa (*SKS*, 3:112), Kakuen (*SZS*, 16:1016), and very few others.

dered the aesthetic of tranquility. If we consider that (1) tranquility was not a favorite tone among waka poets, and (2) that most waka on tranquility were written by men proficient in both shih and waka, our best conclusion might be that the aesthetic of tranquility entered waka through Chinese shih.

The Chinese love of nature does not date from antiquity.[61] Nature became a subject for poetry from the Six Dynasties period on, probably because of Buddhist influence and the spread of Taoism, with T'ao Ch'ien (365-427) and Hsieh Ling-yün (385-433) pioneering in the development. Hsieh in particular sought out the Taoist world of immortals in actual fields and mountains and was learned in Buddhism.[62] But when nature is sought within the conceptual boundaries of Taoism and Buddhism, it tends to become a vast entity, thus discouraging the promotion of a tranquil tone. An example will suffice. When Hsieh Ling-yün made an excursion to enjoy the beauties of nature, he was accompanied by several hundred attendants. He had trees felled to blaze a trail through the trackless forest, and he forded raging rivers.[63] Nothing here suggests "loneliness."

T'ao Ch'ien differed, seeking to live quietly and at peace within the natural world. His work was neglected until the T'ang period, however, when Wang Wei (699?-761) recognized his fresh approach and put it to use in developing his own new style of nature poetry. T'ao Ch'ien bequeathed him the practice of living in seclusion among fields and gardens, and Wang Wei learned from Hsieh objective descriptive techniques in order to perfect his highly individual nature poetry. But the world of seclusion created by Wang Wei is a fantasy, a utopia built on his own conceptions. Thus the nature Wang depicts could not conquer his real-life suffering or conflicts. Nature manifests itself instead as an entity communicating sadness and cold (Iriya, 1976, 577).

If twelfth-century Japanese poets had indeed known of such shih, we would have a truly appropriate occasion for the aesthetic of tranquility to appear in waka. But there is no clear evidence that Wang Wei's shih collection had reached Japan by this time—then, again, there is no clear evidence that it had *not*. We simply cannot say there is proof sufficient to conclude that Wang Wei's influence accounts for the recognition by certain waka poets of the aesthetic of tranquility. On the other hand, shih written from seclusion and describing the pleasures of leisure also appear after Wang Wei's time. The Middle T'ang period contains not a few in-

[61] I follow Aoki Masaru (see vol. one, 383).

[62] Hsieh was a friend of Hui-yüan (334-416?). Hsieh's collaboration in translating the Southern Version of the *Nirvāna Sūtra* means that he was familiar with Sanskrit. His ideas on Sanskrit grammar are quoted by the Japanese monk Annen (b. 841) in his *Shittanzō* (2:21).

[63] *Sung Shu*, "Hsieh Ling-yün Chuan" (67:1775).

stances, including the poetry classified under the rubric "Tranquility" in Po Chü-i's *Ch'ang-ch'ing Chi.* Many of Po's "tranquil" poems resemble Wang Wei's compositions in their quiet tone—allowing for Po's tendency to look at a subject from a social point of view. Po's works were, of course, well known in twelfth-century Japan. Since contemporary waka poets could only become aware of the aesthetic of tranquility through books imported from the continent, the most likely means of contact was with those subjects and expressions—in Po's poetry—that resembled Wang Wei's. Some Late T'ang poetry also celebrates tranquility; the delicate expression of these poems more closely approximates the "lonely" waka of the *Senzaishū* period. We might therefore best seek the source of "tranquility" in Late T'ang shih.

Late T'ang poetry is characterized by an ethereal charm underlying its subtle perceptions. Its charm, that of a flower about to fade, is directly linked to the emptiness communicated by the flower's imminent decay (see ch. 1). When emphasis is placed on this emptiness, a poet seeks beauty in a lonely scene. One example is Cheng Ch'ao's "On Staying at a Lodge by Miracle Stream" (*CTS*, 504:5734).

> I sing alone, and autumn rains stop;
> The desolate lodge is circled by ranged peaks.
> At dawn, herons roost on sheer crags;
> Autumn waterweed gathers in sunken boats.
> The stream drops from Flowery Summit;
> Trees go on to the Red Fortress.
> Having long sought after quiet,
> I look to meet you again in our old age.[64]

The scene is Miracle Stream (Ling-hsi) on Mount T'ien-t'ai, where the speaker stays the night at a lonely travelers' lodge. In the early morning, he sees herons building nests in the crags by the river and, near the banks, he finds half-submerged boats overgrown by waterplants. Just then an autumn drizzle begins falling. But the speaker of the poem praises the scene. Wishing to live a secluded life, he promises the innkeeper that he will surely return to the area when they are both old. This is indeed a poem written in admiration of a "lonely" landscape, and its tone does not differ from that of tranquil waka.

I noted earlier that the tranquil tone also appears in twelfth-century Korean shih and that a similar attitude is to be found in Tsunenobu's poetry in Chinese (see ch. 1). From the late eleventh through twelfth cen-

[64] Few details are known of Cheng Ch'ao's life. He is thought to have passed the civil service examination between 847 and 860. He is taken as a Late T'ang poet, since that period is defined as beginning in 863.

turies, Korea clearly adopted Late T'ang shih styles on a fairly advanced level. Japan did so too, although to a lesser degree. Consequently, both facets of Late T'ang poetry—ethereal charm and tranquility—were diffused in Korean and Japanese shih, as also in waka, by Japanese literati proficient in both waka and shih composition. The early medieval waka tradition dictated that ethereal charm not be adopted for what it was, but perceived instead, temporarily, as an expressive principle on the scale of yūen, refined charm, and the aesthetic of ethereal charm does not flourish in waka until the beginning of the thirteenth century. The same holds for tranquility. It only begins to gain importance in the twelfth century and becomes acknowledged as an independent aesthetic from the thirteenth century on. When we consider the great importance accorded to the concept of tranquility, not only throughout the High Middle Ages but also as a central feature of the sabi ideal in Bashō's haikai, it becomes vital that we note the evolving poetic cognition of this aesthetic, even in its embryonic form.

The New Style Moves Toward the Low

Another important characteristic of twelfth-century waka is a limited assertion of zoku (low) expression, a style that had been neglected earlier. Because the advance of zoku is predicated on the development of a suitable affective presumption, we shall begin by considering this latter factor.

The ga (high, polished) approach seeks to harmonize with already existing expression. Thus the composer of a ga poem concentrates on discovering subtle differences of import within well-established terms. The ga poet does not express personal opinions or sentiments, displaying individuality only by finding a previously unknown freshness, by perceiving a well-worn subject from a slightly different angle. Little freshness may in fact emerge, but the audience, being thoroughly familiar with precedented expression, will think it considerable. Waka of this kind are frequently evaluated as "well wrought" (kokoro okashi). Modern readers no longer inhabit the same ga sphere as the twelfth-century poets, and, unable to make fine distinctions among the various expressive choices once available to waka poets, we find their poems much the same, lacking in individuality.

In the twelfth century, however, there first appears an attitude permitting the poet to express individual, personal opinions or feelings. Significantly, such poems came increasingly to be valued. When twelfth-century poets responded to a given scene with emphatic statements of their own feelings, rather than by resorting to well-worn, anticipated emotions, their waka were praised as "moving" (kokoro fukashi; earlier I used the term "emotive"). By this I mean the kind of poetry that expresses a poet's individual sentiments.

"Moving" though they were, such poems were composed in a literary context still dominated by poets who retained an essentially ga approach. A modern reader will, therefore, probably find it impossible to discover what is strikingly "moving" about many such waka, and yet twelfth-century critics regarded the advent of emotive poetry as a noteworthy phenomenon. Fujiwara Shunzei and the monk Saigyō are perhaps the outstanding exponents of emotive waka.

> I recall Shakua's poetry as gentle and evocative, infused with deep feeling and moving in its sensitivity.[65] His style particularly appeals to my humble taste. Saigyō's poetry is interesting and gives expression to unusually deep feeling combined with rare qualities of originality—a born poet, I feel. But his poems are not suitable for imitation by those who are still uncertain of their art. His is a skill that cannot be explained in words. (*Gotoba In*, 145)[66]

Gotoba's (1180-1239) famous critique acknowledges depth of feeling in both poets.[67] Shunzei and Saigyō probably enjoyed a similar reputation in the twelfth century. Of course, neither wrote poetry so expressive of emotions as to approximate the modern reader's conception of "emotive." Consider, for example, a poem by the thirty-seven-year old Shunzei in the *Kyūan Hyakushu* (*Hundred-Poem Sequence of the Kyūan Era*).[68]

Yamazakura	Mountain cherry trees—
Saku yori sora ni	Since they bloomed the sky has been
Akugaruru	Where my thoughts have roamed;
Hito no kokoro ya	Why will you not know one's mind,
Mine no shirakumo.	White clouds upon the mountain top?
	(*Chōshū Eisō* [=*CE*], 1:9)

Looking at the clouds covering the mountaintops, the speaker imagines that, far off in the distance, the late mountain cherry blossoms should be opening; full of longing for the sight of the blossoms, his heart wanders to the mountains. The cloud-like cherry blossoms are a radiant vision

[65] "Shakua" is Shunzei's name in religion.

[66] [The translation is taken from Brower, 1972, 35-36.—Trans.]

[67] [Gotoba's *Secret Teachings* were probably written in the 1230s, toward the end of the former tennō's life.—Trans.]

[68] Properly called *His Majesty's Hundred-Poem Sequence of Kyūan* 6 [1150]. This was a sequence on a grand scale: fourteen famous poets participated in producing a work patterned after a famous multi-topic sequence dating from Horikawa's reign. Chiefly because of the Kyūan sequence, the hundred-poem sequence form was acknowledged to rank in literary eminence with the royal anthologies (Matsuno, 1973, 166-67).

before the speaker's eyes. In fact, the beauty of the cherry blossoms is enhanced because they are not actually seen, only envisioned.

Shunzei probably had similar scenes in mind when he wrote that a superlative waka has "both en and yūgen" (in the *Jichin Kashō Jikaawase*, quoted above). Instead of having a refined, charming scene before his eyes, the poet imagines the clouds of cherry blossoms in the mountains at this season of the year, simultaneously feeling a desire to go and view them. Shunzei's use of the third person in "hito no kokoro ya" ("one's mind") suggests that everyone is in agreement on this matter, while superimposing the speaker's first-person perspective: I wish to see the blossoms more than anyone else. Shunzei's technique, which emphasizes the refined charm in the speaker's roaming thoughts, is precisely what I mean by the emotive stance.

Chōmei's waka master, Shun'e, might have criticized Shunzei's poem for taking a scene of perfectly refined charm and weakening its impact by using a term lacking in depth, "akugaruru" (roaming), to express the speaker's desire to view the blossoms.[69] But another of Shunzei's waka, with the same motif, was enough of an accomplishment to have been publicly acknowledged by the poet as his masterwork.

Composed when Sutoku In, during a progress to the Konoe Mansion, commanded us to compose on the topic "Seeking Blossoms in Distant Mountains."

Omokage ni	I set the vision
Hana no sugata o	Of the flowers' configuration
Sakidatete	Before me as I go;
Ikue koekinu	How many mountains have I crossed,
Mine no shirakumo.	Oh, white clouds that wreath the peaks?[70]
	(*CE*, 2:207)

Drawn on by a vision of beautiful blossoms, the speaker wonders how many mountain peaks wreathed in trailing white clouds he has crossed in his search. But the speaker's longing to see the blossoms is not stated openly. The poet has the speaker instead *led on* by a vision of cherry blossoms, thus producing a more suggestive work than the earlier "Yamazakura" ("Mountain cherry trees"). Moreover, in the earlier poem the speaker is merely gazing at far mountains, whereas in the latter the

[69] *Mumyōshō*, 73.

[70] The Konoe Mansion was the residence of the chancellor, Fujiwara Tadamichi. The poetic gathering was apparently held in the Third Month of 1143, although it may have taken place as late as 1155 (Matsuno, 1973, 617-20).

speaker actually crosses untold peaks in the desire to view mountain cherry blossoms. The exaggerated attachment to cherry blossoms well illustrates Shunzei's emotive bent. Surely the former tennō Gotoba refers to expression such as this when he praises Shunzei's style as "gentle and evocative, infused with deep feeling."

Saigyō shares this tendency. He is well known for his enormous output of poems on cherry blossoms. The formal poems among them—those selected for inclusion in royal anthologies—have expression similar to that in Shunzei's poem just given. For example,

A poem on cherry blossoms
By the monk Saigyō

Yoshinoyama	On Mount Yoshino
Kozo no shiori no	I change from the path marked last year
Michi kaete	By breaking branch tips,
Mada minu kata no	In order that I might seek out
Hana o tazunen.	Other blossoms yet unseen.
	(*SKKS*, 1:86)

The speaker deliberately chooses a path different from last year's, in order to see blossoms where he has not yet been.[71] The poem is underscored by an intense desire to see *all* the cherry blossoms of Yoshino. Saigyō's attachment surely embodies the twelfth-century concept of "kokoro fukashi" (moving, impressive). Compared to Shunzei's waka on crossing untold peaks, Saigyō's offers a somewhat subdued impression of the blossoms' refined charm. Yet Saigyō is witty in having his speaker choose a path other than the one he marked last year. Gotoba probably refers to such aspects of Saigyō's poetry in commenting that it is "interesting and gives expression to unusually deep feeling."

Waka designated as displaying "deep feeling" present a problem: whose "feelings" are expressed? I mentioned earlier that Shunzei's poem on mountain cherry blossoms (*CE*, 1:9) uses a third-person expression, "hito no kokoro" ("one's mind"), that simultaneously signifies the first person. In waka collections arranged by season, all poetic speakers inhabit the sphere of ga; consequently all respond in the same way. The "feeling" expressed in such poetry therefore does not differ, regardless of the poet. But if a poet expresses emotions attributable to no one else, the

[71] "Shiori" originally meant breaking branches to mark an unfamiliar mountain path. Saigyō, however, more likely intends to say that he left marks to remind him of good blossom-viewing locales. [The dictionary *Kōjien*, ed. Shimmura Izuru et al., 2nd ed. (Iwanami, 1969), quotes the poem for the former meaning; the one the author suggests is, however, more tastefully poetic (kokoro ari).—Ed.]

poem veers away from the sphere of ga—shaped by common response—to set foot in the zoku world. "Depth of feeling" means that a poem's "depth," or degree of emphasis, is unusually pronounced. The nature of the "feeling" remains unchanged, however. Waka poets share a homogeneous "feeling" of admiration for cherry blossoms, but Shunzei and Saigyō have an unusually strong response to them. All the waka quoted above therefore belong to the sphere of ga. Now, a strong response can also affect the quality of the "feeling," which is easily transformed from a communal sentiment to an expression of personal emotions. This, the zoku stance, appears frequently in waka that are not arranged according to season.

In principle, the first half of a royal waka anthology is dominated by seasonal waka, and the second by love poems.[72] The *Kokinshū*, the structural prototype, was probably planned to contain formal poetry in its first half and informal poetry in the second (see vol. two, ch. 7). The *Senzaishū* perpetuates this structure. Even its informal poetry leans heavily toward the ga aesthetic, however, because of the dramatically increased incidence of waka composed on assigned topics. On the other hand, personal waka collections contain love poetry in its original state—that is, expressing individual [non-fictional] emotions. Consequently, zoku writing frequently appears in personal collections. The zoku approach is consciously proclaimed in Shunzei's famous poem:

A poem on love, written upon learning that I was to submit poems for a match at the residence of the Commander of the Left Guards.[73]

Koisezu wa	Never to have loved—
Hito wa kokoro mo	Such a person can but be one
Nakaramashi	Lacking real heart,
Mono no aware mo	For the deep pathos of our lives
Kore yori zo shiru.	Can be only known from that!
	(*CE*, 2:352)

The poem asserts Shunzei's own opinion of love; in syntax and moralistic generalizing his expression verges on prose. Many more love poems endorsing this opinion appear in Shunzei's personal collection, *Chōshū Eisō*, demonstrating the high degree of toleration for the zoku aesthetic in personal waka collections.[74]

[72] Exceptions are the *Kin'yōshū* and the *Shikashū* (in ten rather than twenty books each): both are deliberately arranged to contain formal poetry in the first half of the collection and informal poetry in the second.

[73] The guards officer is Gotokudaiji Sanesada (1139-91).

[74] Examples in *CE* include poems numbered 63, 77, 325, 340, and 351.

Waka on miscellaneous subjects are second only to love poetry in their informality. Shunzei has left waka like the following among his miscellaneous works.

Composed after reading deeply moving waka by poets of the past, at a time when I was compiling an anthology of sorts.[75]

Yukusue wa	Off in the future
Ware o mo shinobu	Will there be anyone to prize
Hito ya aran	What I have done?
Mukashi o omou	Longing for the days of old
Kokoronarai ni.	Is human nature, after all.
	(*CE*, 3:476)

Again, both content and expression are very close to prose.

Shunzei's personal waka collection was not the first in which informal waka—love poems and those on miscellaneous subjects—tended to employ zoku expression. Minamoto Shunrai provides an obvious precedent. Shunrai has frequently been misinterpreted as the leader of a group of innovative poets, a man who composed waka only in new styles. All his innovative poems, however, are to be found in the informal waka sections in *Strange Poems by a Useless Fellow* (*Samboku Kikashū*, his personal collection). When he composed in formal circumstances, on the other hand, his expression hardly differed from the traditional *Kokinshū* style. Shunrai was not an innovator, at least in his formal waka.

Much the same might be said for Saigyō. His waka have been praised for their clear, direct enunciation of spontaneous thoughts and emotions. Although this assessment is not wrong, it surfaced only anachronistically with the advent of modern standards of criticism and the poetic approaches advocated by the *Araragi* school. It is not the only perspective. Saigyō's waka were evaluated much differently in the twelfth through thirteenth centuries. Saigyō has ninety-four waka in the *Shinkokinshū*, the highest number of any poet represented there; but the honor is not due to the plainness and clarity of his waka. Saigyō is so well represented because his poetry is both emotive and skillfully refracted in intent. One good example, "Yoshinoyama" ("On Mount Yoshino"; *SKKS*, 1:86), is quoted above. Another, belonging to the miscellaneous category, appears in the second half of the *Shinkokinshū* and is therefore highly informal.

[75] Shunzei compiled an unofficial anthology prior to 1177. It apparently formed the basis for the *Senzaishū* (Taniyama, 1961, 65-70).

Topic Unknown
By Priest Saigyō

Yoshinoyama	I do not intend
Yagate ideji to	To take leave for quite a while
Omou mi o	From Mount Yoshino,
Hana chirinaba to	But some may be expecting me,
Hito ya matsu ran.	"Now that the blossoms are no more."

(*SKKS*, 17:1617)

This is certainly more than a clear, simple poem. Its intent is: those who know the speaker's attachment to cherry blossoms might be thinking (or saying) that he will leave Mount Yoshino once the blossoms have fallen. But the speaker has no desire to leave then, because he can still see the blossoms' beauty in his mind and remains spellbound by a vision transcending the actual cherry blossoms. The poet underscores an ordinary conception with a statement of purpose: "I shall not leave the mountains." The speaker's reason: his envisioned blossoms are more enchanting than any to be seen by human eyes.

Saigyō's mental refraction is a version of the *Kokinshū* obliqueness made much more subtle. That was probably what Gotoba had in mind when he praised Saigyō's poetry as "interesting." The sense of being lured on by a vision of cherry blossoms is not unique to Saigyō: it also appears in Shunzei's "Omokage ni" ("I set the vision"; *CE*, 2:207). But a longing for envisioned blossoms so intense as this—in which the speaker remains on Yoshino after the blossoms are gone—indicates an extraordinary attachment to cherry blossoms. This may well be why Saigyō is said to have written poetry of "unusually deep feeling." Such criteria determined why Saigyō is the best represented poet in the *Shinkokinshū*. It appears that no poem was selected that had distanced itself from the ga aesthetic.

A very different situation presents itself in Saigyō's personal waka collections, or, more precisely, in the informal poems within his collections. Love poetry is usually a highly informal genre; yet Saigyō's poems on love are formal, displaying little zoku expression.[76] His poems on miscellaneous subjects, on the other hand, deal with various worldly matters.

I came by way of Hibi and Shibukawa, intending to cross to Shikoku; but the wind was bad, and so I stayed a while. At a place called Shibukawa Bay, children were gathering a great many objects. Upon

[76] Perhaps because they were composed on assigned topics, nearly all the love poems in the *Sankashū* (578-615, 653-711, 1241-1350) have manipulated concepts. [The obliqueness of the so-called *Kokinshū* style.—Ed.] Zoku expression appears only in poems numbered 678, 679, 682, 710, and 1321.

inquiry, I learned that they were gathering a kind of snail called "tsumi."[77]

Oritachite	Fishermen's children,
Urata ni hirou	They have come to gather things
Ama no ko wa	From the tidal flats;
Tsumi yori tsumi o	They seem to have learned to sin
Narau narikeri.	From the tsumi snails they take.
	(*Sankashū* [=*SK*], 2:1373)

On the island of Manabe, merchants from the capital came to deal in all manner of items. Composed on hearing that the merchants would then cross to Shiwaku Island to sell their wares.

Manabe yori	From Manabe
Shiwaku e kayou	Onward to Shiwaku go
Akibito wa	The peddlars by ship;
Tsumi o kai nite	Their eager oars seem to expect
Wataru narikeri.	Profit from a sinful cargo.[78]
	(*SK*, 2:1374)

Composed on seeing food for sale on skewers, and being told they were dried clams.

Onajiku wa	If sell you must
Kaki o zo sashite	Be good enough to skewer instead
Hoshi mo su beki	Oysters that are dried;
Hamaguri yori wa	Their "kaki" name is sweeter far
Na mo tayori ari.	Than that of "hamaguri" clams.[79]
	(*SK*, 2:1375)

These are subjects never before treated in waka. Saigyō's decision to compose on them clearly reflects a zoku attitude. To be sure, the expressive focus in all three poems is on pivot words, a witty technique forming part of Saigyō's "interesting" style.

Other poems by Saigyō are even more concerned with worldly matters,

[77] "Tsumi" also means "sin." Saigyō, a Buddhist monk, uses the homonym in his poem to suggest the sinfulness of taking life. [Auth., Trans.]

[78] Saigyō uses two pivot words (kakekotoba): "tsumi" (bundle/sin) and "kai" (expectation [of profit]/oar).

[79] The copy text reads "kani" for "kaki"; the corrections are made from the *Kokkashū* text. The pivot is on "kaki," a homonym for "oyster" and "persimmon." [Presumably Saigyō would rather hear the food-sellers cry "dried kaki" because the item for sale could be either dried persimmons or dried oysters. The priestly poet (who of course practices vegetarianism in observance of his vow not to take life) is again protesting the practice of eating marine life.—Trans.]

including the battles between the Minamoto and Taira clans that came to be known as the Gempei War (1180-85).

> War has broken out, and there is no place, be it north, south, east, or west, where there is not a battle. It is frightful to hear how many people are being killed each day. The numbers are so large that they hardly seem real. What purpose does all this fighting serve? How pitiful it all is!
>
> | | |
> |---|---|
> | Shide no yama | How can there be |
> | Koyuru taema wa | Pauses in the traffic crossing |
> | Arajikashi | On the Hill of Death? |
> | Naku naru hito no | Those whose lives have been taken |
> | Kazu tsuzukitsutsu. | Keep going there in multitudes.[80] |
>
> (*Kikigaki Shū* [= *KGS*], 225)
>
> I imagine soldiers crossing the Hill of Death in troops and battalions. Were they in this world, their great number would free them from fear of highway robbers. I recalled having heard that, at the battle of Uji, the Taira forces crossed the river on horses tied together.[81]
>
> | | |
> |---|---|
> | Shizumu naru | So many drown |
> | Shide no yamagawa | That the river swells with them |
> | Minagirite | At the hill of death; |
> | Umaikada mo ya | And there is no hope for crossing |
> | Kanawazaru ran. | Even on living rafts of horses. |
>
> (*KGS*, 226)
>
> The warrior Kiso is indeed dead!
>
> | | |
> |---|---|
> | Kisobito wa | That fellow Kiso |
> | Umi no ikari o | Could hardly quell the furious sea |
> | Shizumekanete | To drop his anchor, |
> | Shide no yama ni mo | And he as well has entered on |
> | Irinikeru kana. | The journey of the Hill of Death.[82] |
>
> (*KGS*, 227)

[80] [According to *The Sutra of the Ten Kings* (*Jūōgyō*), the first seven days after death were spent crossing this hill (or mountain). The agony of death is compared to the ordeal of a hill. This fitted perfectly with pre-Buddhist Japanese thought, which tended to spatialize and even localize the time "between" life and death. See Nakanishi Susumu, "The Spatial Structure of Japanese Myth: The Contact Point between Life and Death," ch. 3 of *Principles of Classical Japanese Literature*, ed. by Earl Miner (Miner, 1985)—Ed.]

[81] The implication is that the troops of soldiers, fearless of bandits' depredations in the world of men, have much to fear once they have crossed the Hill of Death and descended into hell. [Auth., Trans.] Saigyō recalls an event later recorded in the *Heike Monogatari* (4:312).

[82] There is a pivot word, "ikari," meaning both "fury" and "anchor."

Saigyō's subject is the tragedy of civil war, but his stance is playful. One waka suggests that the recent rise in mortality rates has led to congested traffic on the road of the Hill of Death. Saigyō also jokes that the presence of so many warriors on the routes of death frees them from the usual fear of highwaymen, making their paths safer than those used by the living. There is no sentimentality here. Another poem experiments with hyperbole: the river running down the Hill of Death, swollen to flood stage with drowned warriors, cannot be crossed even by men riding horses lashed together. The third poem, a cheerful account of the death of the hero Kiso no Yoshinaka, displays substantial distance from its tragic subject. In these three poems Saigyō develops the "interesting" techniques of his seasonal waka. Yet we observe that, in his reflection on the wars, his techniques produce scathing criticism. By laughing at tragedy instead of proclaiming its horror, Saigyō informs us with cruel clarity of the futility of a world in which people kill one another. The extreme contradiction between tragic subject matter and playful expression may be termed irony. It is probably the first instance of irony in traditional waka and was undoubtedly perceived as appallingly zoku by the inhabitants of the ga sphere, accustomed as they were to an aesthetic based on shared, traditional concepts and responses.

Shunzei had already experimented actively with zoku writing, but only in his informal waka. Saigyō followed his lead. Just what this meant at the time is not as simple as might be thought. In the twelfth century there was no single, clearcut criterion for reception of waka, and it is always necessary to consider the circumstances in which a poem was presented. The advances made in the twelfth century by zoku poetry are attributable to the growing variety of circumstances in which poems might be composed, since some of the new circumstances tolerated waka and zoku language and subject matter. Unlike the highly formal poetic gatherings and matches of the tenth and eleventh centuries, some in the twelfth century were regarded as "very private affairs" (*Denryaku* [8.VI.1102], 134), and a mere recluse like Shun'e could host a waka salon called the Garden of Poets (Karin'en; Yanase, 1977, 29-43). The new informality was good tidings indeed for zoku poetry. which had not previously been blessed with the right circumstances for composition. Similarly, personal waka collections, previously compiled only by royal request, increased dramatically in number during the twelfth century—at least so far as can be told from surviving texts. The increase may have been stimulated by knowledge that the Chinese were avid compilers of personal shih collections. More fundamentally, however, it resulted from the literary activity of a succession of influential waka poets appearing from the middle- and lower-ranking literati among the nobility. Now that personal collections were being compiled with little ceremony, influential poets could freely include their favorite poems. That may be another reason why so many zoku poems are extant from the twelfth century.

This discussion has been intended to explain why the criteria that entitled Saigyō to ninety-four poems in the *Shinkokinshū* cannot be applied to the zoku poems in his personal collections. We must employ different criteria for the latter corpus. But even Saigyō wrote waka that must be judged inferior, whether by modern or by twelfth-century literary criteria.

Written after composing several poems on cherry blossoms.

Tagui naki	They have no rival,
Hana o shi eda ni	The blossoms flowering
Sakasureba	On its branches:
Sakura ni narabu	That is why no tree at all
Ki zo nakarikeru.	Compares with the cherry.
	(*SK*, 1:73)

Written after composing fifteen poems on cherry blossoms.

Hana to kiku wa	To hear "blossoms"—
Tare mo sa koso wa	Anyone quite naturally
Ureshikere	Is filled with delight!
Omoishizumenu	And the longings do not cease
Waga kokoro kana.	In my agitated heart!
	(*SK*, 1:147)

The Moon

Ureshi to ya	Are they not happy,
Matsu hitogoto ni	Every one of them who waits
Omou ran	In longing?
Yama no ha izuru	On the mountain rim emerges
Aki no yo no tsuki.	The moon on this autumn night.
	(*SK*, 1:308)

Composed at a travelers' lodging.

Akazu nomi	Never did I tire
Miyako nite mishi	Of gazing on its brilliant light
Kage yori mo	While in the city;

Tabi koso tsuki wa
Aware narikere!

But the moon of travelers
Affects me even more!
(*SK*, 1:411)

Sent from Mount Kōya to someone in the capital.

Sumu koto wa
Tokorogara zo to
Iinagara
Takano wa mono no
Aware naru kana.

Well may people say
That anywhere one inhabits
Has its special charm:
Kōya is indeed
A most impressive place!
(*SK*, 2:913)

On the topic "Personal Grievances."

Harahara to
Otsuru namida zo
Aware naru
Tamarazu mono no
Kanashikaru beshi.

Pitter-patter,
The tears fall on and on,
Moving me to ponder
The unbearable things
That seem to cause such sorrow.
(*SK*, 2:1032)

Similar waka appear frequently in Saigyō's verse on cherry blossoms and the moon. One may reasonably designate them as inferior poetry from a literary standpoint. Even a great poet like Saigyō cannot be expected to produce only superlative poetry. But these poems are *so* poor that one wonders why they were included at all in a personal collection of Saigyō's. A religious perspective is necessary to solve the problem.

I have noted that "inferior" expression occurs frequently in Saigyō's poems on cherry blossoms and the moon. It is well known that Saigyō's waka corpus contains an enormous output on these subjects. In other words, cherry blossoms and the moon hold a special meaning for Saigyō. The following waka may explain their attraction. The first two begin a sequence on the twenty-eight chapters of the *Lotus Sūtra*.

Introduction
"Mañjūṣaka flowers," "Fragrant breeze of sandalwood"

Tsubomu yori
Nabete ni mo ninu
Hana nareba
Kozue ni kanete
Kaoru harukaze.

Since coming into bud,
The flowers were quite unlike
Any of this world;
Therefore the spring breeze has blown
So long fragrant from the branches.
(*KGS*, 1)

This will be clearer from the passage Saigyō alludes to. The Introduction to the *Lotus Sūtra* contains a gāthā (verse composition), recited by the bodhisattva Maitreya to the bodhisattva Mañjuṣrī, after the Buddha has delivered a sermon and entered into samādhi incarnation before preaching further. The gāthā begins,

> Mañjuṣrī
> Why from the leader's
> Tuft of white hair does a great
> Ray shine in all directions
> Raining down māndārava and
> Mañjūṣaka flowers,
> And with a breeze of sandalwood scent
> Gladden many hearts?
> For this reason
> The earth is wholly purified.[83]

Expedient Devices

"Those Buddhas who receive the world's veneration manifest themselves in this world to fulfill a single great objective."

Ama no hara	Without a wind
Kumo fukiharau	To sweep clear the Heavenly Plain
Kaze naku wa	Of blocking clouds,
Idede ya yaman	Will not the moon be unable
Yama no ha no tsuki.	To rise above the mountain rim?[84]
	(*KGS*, 2)

The first poem corresponds to that part of the sutra in which Shakyamuni is about to preach the Dharma: mañjūṣaka flowers fall from heaven, and the air is filled with the scent of sandalwood.[85] The splendor of the Buddha's sermon is symbolized by the heavenly flowers and fragrance, which Saigyō represents by cherry blossoms and spring breezes. The second poem states in waka form the gist of a passage from the sutra. The Buddha comes into the world to perform the sublime duty of eliminating

[83] Hurvitz, 1976, 5. Saigyō's waka is an allegory of the splendor to be anticipated when the Buddha begins to preach the Dharma. [Auth., Trans.] [I have moved most of this note into the main text.—Ed.]

[84] "Expedient Devices" (Hurvitz's translation) is the second chapter of the *Lotus Sūtra*. Upāya (J. hōben; lit. "approach" or "reach") are the various means the Buddha offers all humanity that it may gain, by some means or another, a correct understanding of the truth. As will be seen below, Saigyō's waka uses natural metaphors to illustrate the workings of the "devices." [Auth., Trans.] [Here, as not seldom in poems on Buddhist subjects, the moon is a figural image for the Buddha or his teaching and the enlightenment it brings.—Ed.]

[85] Mañjūṣaka is a flower of paradise.

evil passions (bonnō, delusions stemming from an ignorance of the truth). The clouds of Saigyō's poem symbolize evil passions, and the moon is the Buddha, the embodiment of truth.

The following poems further clarify Saigyō's conception that cherry blossoms and the moon symbolize the Buddhist world of truth.

Belief and Understanding

"At this time the poor son, hearing his father's words, straightway rejoiced greatly, having gained something he had never had before."[86]

Yoshinoyama	Blessed I am
Ureshikarikeru	That such a guide should take me
Shirube kana	Over Mount Yoshino!
Sarade wa oku no	For had he not been with me
Hana o mimashi ya.	Would I have seen the farthest blooms?
	(*KGS*, 4)

Comfortable Conduct

"Deeply entering into dhyāna-concentration / And seeing Buddhas in all ten quarters."[87]

Fukaki yama ni	When in mountain depths
Kokoro no tsuki shi	The moon that is my human heart
Suminureba	Is cleared of spots,
Kagami ni yomo no	As if with mirrors on all sides
Satori o zo miru.	I behold enlightenment!
	(*KGS*, 15)

The first poem is based on the parable of a prodigal son who leaves his father's house, unable to comprehend his father's merciful nature. Over the years the son becomes a beggar who roams the country. The father then disguises himself as a vagrant, makes the acquaintance of his unknowing son, gradually wins his heart, and in the end brings him back into the household.[88] The quotation that forms the forenote is taken from the passage in which the son grasps the supreme truth of his father's instructions. Superficially, the speaker of Saigyō's poem rejoices that his knowledgeable guide has made it possible for him to penetrate the usually

[86] [Hurvitz, 1976, 88. "Belief and Understanding" (Hurvitz's translation; J. "Shingebon") is the fourth chapter of the *Lotus Sūtra*.—Trans.]

[87] [Hurvitz, p. 223. "Comfortable Conduct" (also Hurvitz's translation; J. "Anrakugyōbon") is the fourteenth chapter of the *Lotus Sūtra*.—Trans. The author explains "dhyāna" below—Ed.]

[88] *Lotus Sūtra*, "Shingebon," 16-17. [Hurvitz, 1976, 84-100.—Trans.]

inaccessible depths of Yoshino and that he delights in being able to see splendid blossoms there. But the waka is in fact an allegory: the guide corresponds to the father (the Buddha) in "Belief and Understanding," the speaker is the wandering son (sentient beings), and the rare Yoshino blossoms represent enlightenment (the comprehending of Truth).

Saigyō's second poem employs unusual imagery: the ascetic practice of dhyāna (meditation), the seeking of truth by mental concentration. The deep mountains and the moon are metaphors for meditation and truth, respectively. The sutra text has "ten quarters" instead of the "four directions" (yomo, translated above as "on all sides") of the waka, because there is no native Japanese equivalent for the scriptural expression, but much the same concept is of course intended. Imagine a one-room octagonal building. Add a ceiling and floor to the room, and one has ten directions. Now imagine that the ten surfaces are covered with mirrors, so that each mirrored surface reflects all the others. If a light is placed in the middle of the room, its reflection in the ten mirrored surfaces will be reflected over and over again, becoming endless light. The image of infinite light symbolizes the boundless beauty of truth. Saigyō's poem does not explain why moonlight is shining into a room covered with mirrors. Nevertheless, modern Japanese and Westerners can probably sense the beauty of truth symbolized by moonlight and inhabiting a mirror-lined world.[89]

For Saigyō, the world of truth is symbolized by images of blossoms and the moon, a concept that may originate from his practicing esoteric Buddhism. After his thirtieth year, Saigyō resided chiefly on Mount Kōya, and he was evidently adept in Shingon esotericism. Esoteric Buddhism regards the Buddha as the truth that is present in all the beings of the universe. Although this truth is omnipresent and constantly manifest, ordinary human beings cannot perceive it.

Shakyamuni was the first of many incarnate Buddhas entrusted to reveal the truth in human language. The Kegon, Tendai, and Sanron schools of Buddhism, among others, evolved from the belief that eternal truth is accessible through language. The esoteric position, on the other hand, maintains that human language, being imperfect, is necessarily limited in expressive capacities and that therefore language cannot articulate all the significance of the Buddha's truth. The part that cannot be expressed is hidden—esoteric—to those incapable of perceiving it. Yet truth, which remains hidden when pursued by the language of intellect, is in fact apparent everywhere. Its all-too-apparent presence paradoxically renders it unperceivable. The rustling of leaves in the wind and the glitter of dewdrops in the morning light, for example, are manifestations of

[89] The mirrors, flowers, and moon in Saigyō's "Fukaki yama" ("When in mountain depths"; *KGS*, 15) have been interpreted as symbols of enlightenment (LaFleur, 1978, xxv).

truth and consequently of the Buddha. One can only perceive this through insight, which transcends intellect. Insight, enabling one to pursue Buddhist truth, must be obtained through strict discipline. Various forms serve as mediums for insight in the disciplinary process. Forms that symbolize truth are called mandala.

Pictorial mandalas, such as the Diamond (Kongō) and Matrix (Taizō), come first to mind, but mandalas are not confined to already existing or fixed objects.[90] Any form that possesses order can be a mandala. For instance, the configuration and movement of stars in the night sky, having a systematized order, manifest the truth and may thus be called a star mandala. Nor need the shape be limited to static objects. An ordered action can also be a mandala: a karma-mandala. Saigyō perceived cherry blossoms and the moon as mandalas. Empowered by his esoteric training to perceive the Buddhist truth in the moon and cherry blossoms, Saigyō responds in waka form. Readers who do not perceive the mandala nature of cherry blossoms and the moon cannot understand Saigyō's response; their only possible conclusion is that the poems are mediocre or worse.

Why was Saigyō drawn only toward the mandalas of cherry blossoms and the moon when any form can be a mandala? Here, in addition to the religious perspective, we must consider the special significance that cherry blossoms and the moon have for the Japanese. In waka and linked poetry (renga and haikai), "hana" (flower, blossom) conventionally means cherry blossoms. To such an extent do Japanese think the cherry blossom the preeminent flower. The Japanese admire the sight of branches covered with cherry blossoms; only rarely are they attracted to the peculiar splendor of blossoms about to fall (Yamada Y., 1938, 377-88). Cherry blossoms in full bloom are more than beautiful. They were thought to exude a vitality that invigorates and strengthens human beings and to possess spiritual properties that drive away evil. The ceremony called Yasuraibana (evil-averting cherry blossoms) is a prime example.[91]

[90] [A mandala (J. mandara) is described as "a geometric disposition of symbolic attributes, germ syllables (Sk. bīja, J. shuji), or images endowed with magic power. It is the point of departure for a system of specific meditation, which aims at assuring the ultimate, mystic union with the Supreme Unity (in Japan, Dainichi Nyorai; Sk. Vairocana). . . . It can assume a number of forms according to the use for which it is intended. . . . The best-known form is the one which is permanently fixed on paper, silk, linen, etc. and is meant to be used as the object of successive meditations" (E. Dale Saunders, *Mūdra: A Study of Symbolic Gestures in Japanese Buddhist Sculpture* [New York: Pantheon Books, 1960], 24-25).—Trans.] The Diamond Mandala is a pictorial representation of the Diamond World (Kongōkai), which in turn symbolizes the adamantine wisdom of Vairocana, the central object of worship in Shingon Buddhism. The Matrix (or Womb) Mandala represents the sentient world: all states of existence are embraced by the infinite compassion of Vairocana, of whom all sentient beings are a manifestation. [Auth., Trans.]

[91] [The ceremony, also known as Chinkasai (same meaning as "Yasuraibana"), takes place at the Murasakino Imamiya Shrine in Kyoto, presently on 10 April of each year. There

Saigyō was able to sense the vitality inherent in cherry blossoms, and this ability combined with his esoteric vision to make him a devotee of cherry blossoms.

One practice employed in esoteric meditation is called lotus contemplation.[92] In this devotional act, one looks at the picture of a lotus blossom, concentrating the mind so as to become one being with the flower. Only one flower appears in the picture. But the Japanese find it easier to meditate on a host of cherry blossoms rather than on a single lotus blossom, a preference probably incomprehensible to the Indian masters who originated the practice. The moon presents no such cultural gap. A prerequisite to practicing the lotus contemplation is meditating on the moon's orb (gachirinkan). This involves concentrating on and achieving unity with the moon instead of a flower. The Japanese easily linked their long-standing affinity with the moon to the contemplative methods of esoteric Buddhism.

The concept of cherry blossom and moon mandalas is not meant to lend Saigyō's waka an air of esoteric allegory, however. In his poems on cherry blossoms, Saigyō celebrates blossoms; in his poems on the moon, he celebrates the moon. And yet a reader or audience familiar with the esoteric sense would understand why Saigyō is deeply moved by simple phenomena and would join him in his response. This view can also be extended to waka on miscellaneous worldly matters. Human actions and social events, complex and strange though they are, all possess order. The order is imperceptible to most of us because it is concealed beneath so many varied surfaces. To perceive the hidden order is to see human acts and events in society as karma-mandala that, like cherry blossoms and the moon, are deeply affecting phenomena. Let us reconsider a waka quoted earlier, "Sumu koto wa" ("Well may people say"; *SK*, 2:913). It is a simple statement: living on Mount Kōya is wonderful, although any place has its good and bad points. The intent of the poem contains Saigyō's perception of the order inherent in inhabiting a location. Another of his poems, "Harahara to" ("Pitter-patter"; *SK*, 2:1032), expresses a

---

is traditional music and dancing in a circle to the chant "Yasuraibana yo." The evil the blossoms are enjoined to avert is illness, particularly epidemics.—Trans.]

[92] The practitioner may face a picture of a circle representing the full moon, sitting quietly, regulating breathing, and concentrating until gaining a sense of unity with the moon. This, known as moon contemplation, is relatively basic. Another method is to meditate on the picture of an eight-petaled lotus blossom superimposed on the orb of the moon. In addition to achieving a sense of unity with the flower, the practitioner concentrates on unity with the symbol of wisdom, the Sanskrit syllable "van." This is called the lotus contemplation. The most advanced meditative practice is the contemplation of the letter "a." The practitioner is to achieve unity with the Sanskrit letter "a" (expressing non-being) that is written above the lotus blossom. By doing so, one comprehends that aspect of all existence that is neither generated nor extinguished. Mastery of these three methods signifies enlightenment in the esoteric sense.

humdrum fact: when sadness comes, tears fall. But Saigyō, perceiving this ordering of body and soul in a mandala-like sense, tells how it moves him. Despite the extreme simplicity of its surface meaning, the poem springs from deep emotions.

A reader or listener who does not share Saigyō's esoteric experience will be unable to understand or respond adequately to such poems. But it is unreasonable to require or expect that everyone be acquainted with esoteric contemplative practice. Anyone who shares Saigyō's perceptions can grasp the sense of the poems without having to undergo esoteric training. Such people are exceedingly rare in modern Japan, however, and probably even harder to find in the West. The poems just given are therefore properly judged to be poor compositions, so long as they are evaluated as literature. On the other hand, we must give full consideration to how many people in the twelfth century would have been deeply moved by these poems. They would have thought the poems to be low (zoku) because they did not form part of the shared sphere of high art (ga). But Saigyō's "low" poetry would be taken as zoku of an impressive kind, since the poems are, after all, concerned with the two mandala worlds. The usual view of zoku at the time—that it deals with humble subject matter—does not apply in Saigyō's case. From the thirteenth century on, this unconventional sense of zoku gradually grew in strength.

From Waka to Linked Poetry: The Development of Mixed Tones

A genre mingling the tones of ga and zoku is another noteworthy literary creation of the twelfth century. This new kind, which became fixed in the thirteenth century, is perhaps best exemplified by the derivation of linked poetry (renga) from waka. Linked poetry predating the thirteenth century differs significantly from renga produced after that point, although the two groups are known by the same name. Early linked poetry consists of a witty dialogue: the first part of a waka (kami no ku, the first three lines—seventeen syllables) is composed by one person, and the second part (shimo no ku, the last two lines—fourteen syllables) is composed by another. The earliest examples appear in the middle of the ninth century. The oldest preserved instance may be this, from the *Shūishū* (18:1184).[93]

[93] Ōtomo Yakamochi's poem in the *Man'yōshū* (*MYS*, 8:1635), which has been regarded as the first example of linked verse (Shimazu, 1969, 6-14), is actually no more than a single tanka, albeit amoebic (composed by two people). It may signal the genesis of linked poetry, but the poem itself is hardly the first example of the form. [Both the *Shūishū* and *Man'yōshū* examples are examples of what is usually termed short renga (tanrenga). The author distinguishes the first *Shūishū* example (rather than the *Man'yōshū* one) as the oldest instance of renga because he sets stricter criteria for renga than joint composition. Those criteria will shortly be identified.—Ed.]

He had a rendezvous with a court lady one night. But he was late to arrive, and the lady, hearing the watchman announce "Three-quarters past the Hour of the Ox" [2:30 a.m.], sent her lover a message:

Hitogokoro	That heart of yours—
Ushimitsu ima wa	Now at three-quarters past the Ox—
Tanomaji yo.	I shall not trust it.

[His reply]:

Yume ni miyu to ya	Hoping to see you in my dreams,
Ne zo suginikeru.	I have overslept the Rat.
	By Yoshimine Munesada[94]

The lady plays on the meaning of "ushi mitsu" ("three-quarters past the Ox" and "felt your cruelty"). The first half of the waka is her message: having waited in vain till half-past two for Munesada to arrive, she now realizes how cruel he actually is. She vows no longer to trust him. Munesada in turn plays on the word "ne," which can mean both "sleep" and the hour designation "Rat" [the period between 11 p.m. and 1 a.m.]. His poem replies that he went to sleep hoping to dream of her; but he overslept and woke to discover that it was past one o'clock.

The distinct grammatical break between the two halves of the poem, as well as the individual positions taken by each speaker, indicate that this is the earliest extant example of linked poetry. Its appearance is probably fortuitous, however. A great many similar amoebic poems survive; in all cases, however, they are unified waka divided between two poets. Almost all can be read as single, conventional waka if the reader is unaware (or ignores the fact) that it was actually composed by two poets. A basic element of linked poetry is that each poetic unit must have a meaning complete in itself, that the seventeen- or fourteen-syllable units be able to stand on their own. Since amoebic waka can be read as single poems, their composition period is probably not the formative period for linked verse, despite the occasional appearance of freestanding units within a waka.

The idea of composing freestanding waka units became a principle by the twelfth century, the formative period of linked poetry. In the twelfth century, the first half of a waka was regarded as independent of the second half. This conception was reflected in the development of an inverted waka form: the second half of a waka (fourteen syllables) precedes the first half (seventeen syllables). An early example appears in the eleventh century.

94 The secular name of Bishop Henjō (816-90). The poem must have been composed before 850, when he became a monk.

> One moonlit night in spring, many gentlemen were in attendance and performing music when a royal command was announced. The court was to go into retreat. "How very strict of them," said the controller Michikata, adding,
>
> | | |
> |---|---|
> | Izuru sora naki | I do not wish to leave your sky, |
> | Haru no yo no tsuki. | O moon of this spring night. |
>
> I responded with,
>
> | | |
> |---|---|
> | Furusato ni | As it is longing |
> | Matsu ran hito o | For one who is also waiting |
> | Omoitsutsu. | Where I once lived. |
>
> (*Akazome*, 138)

The fourteen-syllable portion comes first because of a perceived distance between it and the seventeen-syllable part; but the two are not yet freestanding in terms of meaning. When rearranged to fit the conventional waka form, the poems differ little from an ordinary waka:

Furusato ni	As it is longing
Matsuran hito o	For one who is also waiting
Omoitsutsu	Where I once lived,
Izuru sora naki	I do not wish to leave your sky,
Haru no yo no tsuki.	O moon of this spring night.

By the twelfth century, stress is placed on the autonomy of individual parts. Shunrai writes,

> One might also mention linked poetry. A unit consists of one part of a waka. A sequence may commence with either the first or the second part. Everything one wishes to say should be said in a single part. It is bad form to leave something unsaid, since it obliges the poet composing the next link to finish your poem for you. (*Shumpishō*, 124)

Note that the poet is advised to say everything that needs to be said within the bounds of his link. Shunrai did not advocate this solely on theoretical grounds. All fifty-five renga in his *Strange Poems by a Useless Fellow* (*SBS*, 10:1568-1622) end with a sharp grammatical break, and each has complete significance in and of itself.

When the two parts of a waka become distinct stanzas, independent of each other, they lack integrae, complete meaning when joined. They are freestanding entities not easily recast into a single waka whole. This distinct division of given waka represents the evolution of real linked verse, although the genre becomes still better defined with the appearance of "chain renga" (kusari renga)—linked poetry consisting of three or more stanzas. The term appears in the *Imakagami* (*The New Mirror*, ca. 1180).

> The household contained some famous poets among the ladies in attendance, including Kodaishin and the wetnurse Echigo. Whenever gentlemen came to call, the group composed a kind of poetry called chain renga. (*Imakagami*, 8:324)[95]

Chain renga probably became popular in the mid-twelfth century.[96] *The New Mirror* also contains examples of the chain renga produced by the group of poets mentioned above (8:325).

Nara no miyako o Omoi koso yare.	Nara, ancient capital, Oh, how my heart yearns for you! *Fujiwara Kiminori*
Yaezakura Aki no momiji ya Ika naran.	Its double cherries, Its scarlet leaves in autumn— Are they not splendid? *Minamoto Arihito*
Shigururu tabi ni Iro ya kasanaru.	Every time that drizzle falls, Do their colors grow still deeper? *Echigo*

We should note that this is not merely an instance of two stanzas expanding into three: the sequence possesses the requisites of linked poetry. Of course, all three stanzas end with a clearcut grammatical break, and all are mutually independent in meaning. But there is more: the first and third stanzas do not connect in meaning. This is a defining feature of renga. Mutually independent stanzas are a requisite of linked poetry, but that feature alone does not qualify stanzas as renga. Any two-stanza sequence should also correspond in meaning. In the sequence above, the first stanza expresses longing for the ancient capital, Nara, and the second stanza gives two concrete instances of the speaker's longing. Similarly (in connection with the first) the second stanza expresses uncertainty as to what the autumn leaves must look like in Nara. The third stanza's reply

[95] [The *Imakagami*, an anonymous factual monogatari in ten books, seems to have been intended as a sequel to the *Ōkagami* (*Great Mirror*, probably early twelfth century, discussed in vol. two, ch. 8). The *Imakagami* is an account of events at court and in the capital from 1025 to 1170.—Trans.]

[96] It is known that Minamoto Arihito (1103-47) attended a chain renga session. Echigo, Kodaishin, and Fujiwara Kiminori, all contemporaries of Arihito, are represented in the *Kin'yōshū*.

(to the second's inquiry about the leaves)—that the color of the leaves deepens each time it rains—again provides tangible content, this time to the interrogative "Ika naran" ("Are they not splendid?") of the preceding stanza.[97]

In other words, the first and second stanzas connect in meaning, as do the second and third stanzas. But stanzas one and three are completely unconnected. These two features—the presence of semantically connected adjacent stanzas and the lack of semantic correlation between stanzas separated by another stanza—are basic to the unique genre of linked poetry. "Chain renga," the twelfth-century term for linked poetry, is a very clever name indeed [in that each link "touches" only the one before and after it]. Chain renga sequences gradually expanded into tens of stanzas and eventually into the hundred-stanza sequence, a set form in renga. Regardless of size, however, the two cardinal elements remain unchanged and deserve to be stressed again:

1. Each stanza is both semantically and grammatically freestanding.
2. Adjacent stanzas connect in meaning, while those separated by one stanza [or more] are unconnected in meaning.

These are the formal hallmarks of early linked poetry. Let us now examine its expressive features in the twelfth century. Colloquial language, one such aspect, appears frequently in Shunrai's linked verse. The establishment of the *Kokinshū* style originally produced an unwritten rule that—special cases excepted—waka were to employ only ga language, that is, the precedented language used in formal circumstances. But Shunrai often experimented with colloquialisms:

Tagasa kite	That old man
Hatake ni kayou	Wears a paddy-farmer's hat—
Okina kana.	Walking to dry fields!
Ushi ni mumakuwa	An ox that pulls a horse-plow
Kaketaru mo ayashi.	Is another curious sight!
	(*SBS*, 10:1605)

"Hatake" (dry field) is a colloquial word; the ga equivalent is "hata." Similarly, "tagasa" (paddy-farmer's hat) and "mumakuwa" (horse-plow) do not belong to the vocabulary of ga, since they do not appear in waka.

[97] [Given the principles the author is setting forth, the translation of the second stanza should be changed in connection with the third. The two "Its" referring to Nara in the first stanza should now be thought of as "The." That is why collections of renga stanzas give the preceding stanza (maeku) with the exemplary one. The absence of singular and plural, the disuse of the abundant personal nouns in Japanese, and the frequent omission of grammatical topics and subjects—all assist the changing flow of renga.—Ed.]

Colloquial diction can be found in renga early on, but the frequent use of colloquialisms becomes current only from Shunrai's time.[98]

Another characteristic of linked poetry is the use of Sinified words.

Naishi koso	The Waiting Lady,
Shitaku no uchi o	Who should properly be in,
Idenikere.	Is at present out.
Geki wa omoi no	But the external secretary
Hoka ni mairedo.	Comes to court out of the blue.
	(*SBS*, 10:1617)

"Naishi" ("The Waiting Lady" at the inner palace), "shitaku" (expectations), and "geki" (secretary for external affairs) are all Sinified words. Again, there are earlier examples, but the incidence increases rapidly by Shunrai's time.[99] The *Kokinshū* style dictated that only the Yamato language be used in waka (see vol. two, ch. 7). Sinified words were employed only in specifically exempted cases, so that they and colloquialisms were regarded as zoku language to be excluded from the sphere of ga. Their approved presence in linked poetry signals the advent of a literary aesthetic inhabited by ga and zoku alike.

Linked poetry employed zoku diction (colloquialisms and Sinified words) because it matched the content of the genre. As we have seen with Yakamochi's poem, linked poetry was originally witty poetic repartee cast in the form of the first and second parts of an amoebic tanka. A humorous effect is always anticipated in early linked poetry, although degrees of humor differ. Humor is present in Yoshimine Munesada's poem, quoted at the beginning of this section, and it becomes even more pronounced in the twelfth century. Shunrai's "Tagasa kite" ("That old man") states a paradox: anyone who wears a rice-planting hat should be on his way to a paddy, but this old man, oddly enough, is going to the dry fields. The next stanza responds: isn't it also strange for an ox to pull a horse-plow? Humor is the primary objective of these poems. Again, the sequence that begins "Naishi koso" ("The Waiting Lady") aims at achieving a similar humor. Contrary to the expectations (shitaku) that one forms from her title, the inner-palace handmaid (naishi) does not stay indoors (nai): she has gone out. The second stanza replies: the secretary for external affairs (geki) arrives *out* of the blue (omoi no hoka), a paradoxically logical surprise, because "out" (ge, hoka) modifies both the secretary and his action. Humor based on wordplay often appears in impromptu poetry.

[98] Henjō's "ushi mitsu" and "nesugu" are colloquial expressions (see the beginning of this section).

[99] The *Shūishū* (18:1179) has instances of Chinese loanwords: "ryūshoku" ("vulgar") and "chinchō" ("making much of").

A friend of mine, the middle counselor Mototsuna, asked Kintoshi, governor of Noto, to invite me to a party. On receiving the invitation, I accepted, and found carp being prepared in a reception room. I composed this upon watching a cook named Master Grand [Chō Daibu]:

Kono michi no Hōchō Daibu Chōshitari.	Master Grand himself, The Grand Master of cuisine, Grandly wields the knife.
	Chōsai, Master of Discipline

An old man was cooking across from Master Grand. "Who is he?" I asked. "Miyoshi, the assistant," was the reply.

Mireba miyoshi no Sukeru ryōri mo.	Behold the beauty to behold, Miyoshi as assistant cook.
	(*SBS*, 10:1571)

The stanzas use colloquial words: "miyoshi" ("beauty to behold"), "sukeru" (assist); as also Chinese loanwords: "hōchō" (knife), "Daibu" ("Master"), "chō" (grand), and "ryōri" (cooking). The primary objective of the poems is to find extemporaneous humor in subjects supplied by a given scene, situation, or participant. Only those involved in the situation can understand the humor, however. That is why the forenotes contain detailed explanations. Interest stemming from a sense of participation evolved into a valued element of linked poetry (see ch. 9 below).[100]

Tolerating colloquial language in the diction of linked poetry, like the parading of impromptu humor in its content, meant that renga retained a few ga elements along with a great many zoku ones. The founding of a new literary aesthetic, ga-zoku, is one of the more important phenomena of the twelfth century, particularly as concerns genre. The presence of a renga section in the *Kin'yōshū* is evidence of the phenomenon. We cannot understand why it occurred in the twelfth century, however, unless we turn our attention to the question of the influence exerted by lien-chü, linked Chinese verse.[101]

A lien-chü is a poem in Chinese (shih) that is jointly composed by several poets, each of whom contributes a line. Such a poem looks like an ordinary shih so long as the reader remains unaware of its multiple au-

[100] "Sense of participation" translates the author's "tōzasei," literally "being present at the event itself." This sense is peculiar to insiders and initiates, who will recognize and fully appreciate the situation described in verse and will understand the language used to express it. [Auth., Trans.]

[101] [Lien-chü is pronounced "rengu" or "renku" in Japanese. The character for "lien" ("ren") is not that (Nelson 4702) used for "renga" but the very different one (Nelson 3713).—Ed.]

thorship. Although linked verses were composed as far back as the Six Dynasties period, the lien-chü was not an influential genre in China. It achieved a certain popularity during the Middle T'ang period when Han Yü, Po Chü-i, and Yen Chen-ch'ing (709-84?) wrote lien-chü. Although most linked Chinese verses keep to the established ga expression, lien-chü composed in part by Yen are chiefly aimed at achieving a humorous effect. An example is "Silly Talk: Linked Verses" (*CTS*, 788:8886).

He clutches a rice cake, never stopping to lick his fingers;
—E

He craves grilled food, standing nearby drooling heartily.
—Chen-ch'ing

The butchershop just passed, his jaws work shamelessly;
—Chou

Outside the restaurant gates, he staunchly stands his ground.
—Chien[102]

The poem, a verbal gallery of gluttons, shows that a shih may permissibly differ from the norm by ignoring the rules of shih composition [introduction, development, reversal, conclusion]. The many colloquialisms and the choice of a humorous subject stem from this latitude. Another lien-chü employs similar expression, but its humor is concentrated in the final line (*CTS*, 788:8885).

Words of Joy: Linked Verses

Having crossed the River of Suffering, the enlightened monk rejoices;[103]
—E

New friends fill the room, smiling and greeting one another.
—Chen-ch'ing

Warriors, returning home, join their wives and children;
—Chou

Students out on vacation sneak off to the fair. —Chien

Lien-chü apparently entered Japan at a fairly early date: the genre was quite popular by the beginning of the eleventh century. Fujiwara Michi-

[102] "E" is Li E; "Chen-ch'ing" is Yen Chen-ch'ing; "Chou" is a nickname for the monk Chiao-jan; "Chien" is Chang Chien.

[103] "Suffering" (J. ku, Skt. duḥkha) is the Buddhist term for the human condition, which inevitably involves birth, old age, sickness, and death. Our human misconceptions of suffering are compared to a great river that is difficult to cross. The enlightened monk has achieved his "crossing" by realizing that suffering is in fact devoid of substance. [Auth., Trans.]

naga (966-1027) mentions linked Chinese verses three times in his diary, the *Midō Kampaku Ki*. In all three cases, lien-chü were composed on the way to Uji, during a boating excursion that was further enlivened by music. Linked Chinese verses, apparently, were treated less seriously than shih, as entertainment rather than art.[104] Lien-chü composition also served to divert participants during waka gatherings in the mid-eleventh century. One such instance is mentioned in *Unshū Shōsoku* (*Izumo Correspondence*), by Fujiwara Akihira (989-1066).

> One day they held a waka gathering at Korokujō. The topics were "Blossoms that Resemble Snow" and "Warblers Emerge from the Valleys." The preface to the sequence was written by the assistant commander of the Right Gate Guards. He recited it at dawn. All night long we composed linked Chinese verse [lien-chü] and sang Chinese couplets. (4:532-33)

Akihira's "all night long" suggests that the participants amused themselves during intermissions in the formal waka presentation by trying their hand at lien-chü composition. Regarded solely as a diversion, lien-chü were probably not intended to achieve the polish of a ga genre. Because few lien-chü by Japanese survive from this period, little can be said of its actual state as literature. The most widely circulated text of Masafusa's *Conversations* contains some lien-chü, which enable us to make limited conjectures (6:627).[105]

> My mouth foams whenever I see bitter medicine swallowed.
> —Yasuyoshi
>
> Shouldering the God of Poverty, poor sickly Yasuyoshi!
> —Tadana

Humor is not the only objective here. Ki no Tadana also tries to evoke a sense of participation by putting Yasuyoshi's name into his verse. Their composition shares some features with the linked verses written by Yen Chen-ch'ing and his colleagues. The *Conversations* records another exchange in the same section (6:627).

> The "double-blue" was worn a single summer. —Kan
>
> But the "fallen leaf" has lasted several autumns![106] —Ki

[104] "We left for Uji in early morning. The women went with us in the boat, along with the inspector. We viewed autumn foliage. Linked Chinese verses were composed during this time" (*Midō Kampaku Ki* [25.X.1017], 122).

[105] The Daigoji, Kanda, and Maeda manuscripts, as well as other members of the Kohon line, do not have the lien-chü entries.

[106] ["Double-blue" (futaai) and "fallen leaf" (kuchiba) are the names of clothing colors. A "double-blue" robe gets its name from the twofold dyeing process that produces its pur-

The first line contrasts "*double*-blue," the color of a robe, with the *single* summer that it has been worn; the second line responds that a "fallen leaf"-colored robe might be expected to last only one autumn (since a fallen leaf lasts only that long), but this one has been worn for several seasons. The exchange is noteworthy for its *Kokinshū* style of wordplay and its use of Japanese diction for the two robe colors, "futaai" (double-blue) and "kuchiba" (fallen leaf). The presence of Japanese words in Chinese verses can only mean that the poets, aware that lien-chü was a less than premier art, intentionally experimented with nonstandard expression. If Japanese words were perceived as permissible in lien-chü, then Chinese loanwords would have been equally welcome in another secondary art, renga.

Once it had evolved into chain renga, Japanese linked poetry no longer bore a resemblance to lien-chü that were composed by dividing shih of ordinary length among several poets. The two-line lien-chü in Masafusa's *Conversations*, on the other hand, do have the same form as early renga. Japanese linked poetry might well have incorporated the humor and sense of participation conveyed by lien-chü. Although we cannot be certain that renga composers drew the humor and participatory sense in their work directly from linked verses by Yen and his fellow poets, twelfth-century Japanese were probably aware of the kinds of expression used in Chinese linked verse. Lien-chü is not always an expression of humor and shared participation: in China, at least, the mainstream observed the ga aesthetic. In Japan, where few surviving lien-chü predate the twelfth century, the mainstream is not so easily distinguished. We can be sure, however, that ga and zoku elements coexisted in it. Similar circumstances obtained for linked poetry in Japanese. By the thirteenth century, renga observing the ga aesthetic had come to be known as ushin (standard, serious) renga, while those that experimented with zoku expression were called mushin (nonstandard, humorous) renga (see ch. 9).

Renga adopted both ga and zoku attitudes, but it was openly denied status as a ga genre because it possessed zoku elements. A renga composition might employ ga expression, but this did not make it purely ga. Rather, it was a ga-zoku work that aspired to ga expression. Renga became an independent kind in the twelfth century by its new birth as a ga-zoku genre. Once established as such a genre, renga pushed waka into a sphere devoted exclusively to ga, an event discussed below (see ch. 8).

plish-blue color: it is dyed first with indigo, then with safflower. A "fallen leaf" robe is orange, produced by a red warp and yellow weft.—Trans.]

CHAPTER 3

The Transformation of Prose in Japanese

The coexistence of the elegant and polished (ga) with the low or common (zoku), that hallmark of twelfth-century Japanese literature, is manifested not only in poetry but in prose written in Japanese (wabun). Although monogatari [prose narratives written in the past tense] gravitate strongly toward zoku, a marked countershift toward ga developed in both fictional and factual monogatari by the thirteenth century. In nikki [prose narratives written in the present tense], only the factual variety remains by the twelfth century, the fictional nikki having ceased to exist with the *Izumi Shikibu Nikki* (early eleventh century). The zoku element increased in factual nikki from the twelfth century on.

Ga and Zoku in Monogatari

Weighty and Light Aspects of Fictional Monogatari

The *Genji Monogatari (The Tale of Genji)*, the greatest fictional monogatari [tsukurimonogatari], appeared in the early eleventh century. The high standard set by the *Genji* raised readers' expectations and put fiction writers on their mettle. The authors' response took one of two directions. For the precedented, ga approach they followed the course laid out by the redoubtable predecessor, depicting much the same world and introducing a few, subtle differences guaranteed to affect an attentive audience. For the second approach, they sought to achieve a novel effect by presenting interesting subjects and situations not found in the *Genji*. Both approaches appear in eleventh-century fictional monogatari and sometimes coexist in a single work (see vol. two, ch. 8). By the twelfth century, however, fictional monogatari tend definitely toward either the ga or the zoku, a characteristic that becomes further pronounced in the thirteenth century.

Torikaebaya Monogatari (The Changelings), *Ariake no Wakare (Parting at Dawn)*, and *Matsura no Miya Monogatari (The Tale of the Matsura Shrine)* are the only fictional monogatari to survive from the twelfth century.[1] A short monogatari, "Mushi Mezuru Himegimi" ("The

[1] I use the title *Torikaebaya Monogatari (The Changelings)* to refer both to the original, nonextant version and to the rewritten text. [The work deals with a half-brother and a half-

Lady Who Loved Insects"), may also date from this time.[2] A detailed study of twelfth-century fiction is clearly impossible, given so few surviving examples. The content of these works suggests that much of twelfth-century fictional monogatari was fantasy; and yet some fiction from this period, no longer extant, was probably concerned with more realistic, polished presentations of elegant (fūryū) court life. The marked increase in short, almost oppressively ga stories that begins in the thirteenth century is a sign of the twelfth-century movement toward elegant narratives, since the presence of so many such works in the thirteenth century is very likely founded on the existence of earlier works in the same vein. The *Mumyō Sōshi (An Untitled Book*, ca. 1200) provides further evidence that ga fiction existed in the twelfth century. Some of its critiques of lost monogatari from this period suggest that the stories did not differ significantly from eleventh-century counterparts in plot, characterization, or style. Many twelfth-century examples probably disappeared in the fifteenth and later centuries, when readers began to lose interest in such stories. In any case, twelfth-century fiction writers retained a strong orientation toward the ga aesthetic.

Certainly, extant twelfth-century monogatari show a growing tendency toward fantasy. *The Changelings*, which centers on the motif of exchanged sexual identities, strikes at least us modern readers as a work sustained by fantastic elements. *Parting at Dawn* relies even more heavily on fantasy for its effects. Like the female Chūnagon in *The Changelings*, the protagonist of *Parting at Dawn* is a woman who has been brought up as a man. In the course of the story she holds various high court offices restricted to men, including provisional middle counselor, commander of the right guards, and provisional major counselor, before resuming a conventional female identity. She then enters the tennō's household and eventually becomes the mother of a prince. Although *Parting at Dawn* and *The Changelings* share the same motif, the former is given a more fantastic cast by its heroine's uncanny ability to disappear at will with the aid of a magic cloak.[3]

The twelfth-century taste for fantasy is usually dismissed as yet another manifestation of an aristocratic society in decline. *The Changelings* has

---

sister brought up as if as of the other sex well into adulthood, offering a very interesting examination of just what sexual identity means.—Ed.]

[2] *Asaji ga Tsuyu* (Tenri Library coll., fourteenth-century manuscript) has also been thought to date from the twelfth century. But it is apparently a different work from *Asaji ga Hara no Naishi no Kami*, mentioned in *Mumyō Sōshi* (98), and it is probably a thirteenth-century work.

[3] The author of *Ariake no Wakare* may have borrowed this motif from an older fictional monogatari, *Kakuremino* (*The Magic Cloak*; Matsuo, 1939, 14-17; see vol. two, ch. 8). [Curiously enough, a magic cloak was the stage prop for demonstrating invisibility in English performances as late as Milton's *Comus*.—Ed.]

consequently been characterized as a work of fin-de-siècle decadence and described as "sordid," "bizarre," "lewd," "perverted," "sensual," and "shocking." Yet the theme of exchanging sexual identities, though certainly perceived as fantasy, was not an object of particular censure in the twelfth century. *An Untitled Book* finds the rewritten version of *The Changelings* to be "not at all displeasing, with many fine points" (*Mumyō Sōshi* [=*MMSS*], 84) precisely because it shares the role-reversal motif of the earlier version. It was probably the narrative style of the earlier, nonextant version of *The Changelings*, rather than its focus on sexual roles, that moved the author of *An Untitled Book* to call it "frightful and alarming" (*MMSS*, 81).

Assuming that the original version of *The Changelings* differed little in motif, subject, or plot from the rewritten, surviving story, we may conclude that a hallmark of this monogatari is its treatment of the varieties of human love. While parental and sibling love are well illustrated, love between spouses claims the greater proportion of the author's attention. Homosexual love, as it is depicted in *The Changelings*, is not drastically abnormal behavior or a problem requiring excuse (Suzuki H., 1968, 307-40). Authorial interest in the many, varied aspects of humankind seems to have been a general twelfth-century trend. It appears somewhat earlier in Japanese shih, which concern all manner of worldly subjects (see ch. 1). Much the same is true for prose written in Chinese: Ōe no Masafusa's *Yūjoki* (*An Account of Courtesans*), for example, describes ordinary urban events (vol. 2, ch. 9). Waka from this period also take up a new subject: war (see ch. 2). The author's multifaceted depiction of love in *The Changelings*, although seemingly unrelated to these larger events, is in fact part of a general twelfth-century movement.

The contemporary interest in variety had another effect on fictional monogatari. The vogue for fantasy tended to transform fiction into colorful narratives with little connection to actual human concerns. A good example is Fujiwara Teika's *Matsura no Miya Monogatari*: while unique among wabun monogatari for its detailed battle scenes, their description produces virtually no tension.[4] The protagonist, a Japanese holding the joint posts of controller and lieutenant in the royal guard (ben no shōshō) is en route to China when the Chinese emperor dies. The Prince of Yen, the emperor's younger brother, brings on civil war by struggling to take the throne from the crown prince. The forces of the Prince of Yen are commanded by the valiant Yü-wen Hui, and prospects are bleak indeed for the crown prince. But the Japanese lieutenant joins the crown prince's

[4] The *Mumyō Sōshi* mentions *Matsura no Miya* in a passage that begins: "Lieutenant [Fujiwara] Teika seems to have written a good many stories, including . . ." (*MMSS*, 98). If this statement is reliable, Teika wrote *Matsura no Miya* before 1202, when he was promoted from lieutenant to captain.

side, and as the loyalist army waits in the mountains for the enemy's approach, he invokes the Japanese gods and the buddhas. The decisive battle unfolds:

> Prince Yen's pursuing forces moved along the shore as day was breaking. As they were passing, the crown prince's army, in two camps lying about ten miles apart in the far foothills, simultaneously lit bonfires. The enemy looked in the dark sky, baffled; when from behind, a great shout went up and the crown prince's army rushed down upon them. The enemy forces, taken by surprise, lost all desire for battle. Cries came in concert both before and behind the enemy who, thinking themselves surrounded, were driven panic-stricken toward the shore. Like mountain stags fleeing pursuit, the enemy ran: not one soldier stood firm against the volleys of arrows.
>
> Yü-wen Hui, commander-in-chief of Yen's forces, was a peerless warrior. His prowess and endurance surpassed ordinary bounds; the mere mention of his name struck fear and trembling into every heart. Though attacked from the rear, he showed neither surprise nor fright. He advanced at the head of his troops as they met the opposing army. Espying Tu-ku Jung [one of the crown prince's generals], Yü-wen descended upon him and, pulling Tu-ku Jung close, without a word cut off his head and let it fall. None who saw this dared to do battle with Yü-wen Hui.

Later in the battle, as Yü-wen Hui pursues the Japanese lieutenant, nine horsemen come to the rescue. They are mirror images of the lieutenant, identical in face, dress, horses, and saddles. They cleave Yü-wen Hui and his men in two like so many stalks of bamboo, and then vanish.[5] The Prince of Yen's army, thirty thousand strong, flees, and the crown prince triumphs (*Matsura no Miya*, 51-52).

The earlier *Shōmon Ki (An Account of Masakado)*, contains battle scenes, but they are not in the descriptive mode employed by Teika in the *Matsura no Miya*.[6] The *Shih Chi (Records of the Historian)* and other Chinese histories may have inspired Teika's descriptive passages.[7] Unlike the battles described in the *Records*, however, Teika's martial scenes lack

[5] The *Suwa Sha Engie* (*Illustrated Scroll of the History of Suwa Shrine*, 1356) depicts gods and buddhas who manifest themselves as mirror images of the hero and vanquish an enemy general (19-24). Legends employing the same motif probably predate the twelfth century. The author of *Matsura no Miya* may also have borrowed from temple and shrine legends in making his hero a celestial page in a previous life and in creating similar backgrounds for other characters.

[6] Examples of battle scenes in *Shōmon Ki* include those on pp. 61, 83, and 123.

[7] Examples appear in "The Biography of T'ien Tan" (*Shih Chi*, 22:2455), "The Biography of the Marquis of Huai-yin" (ibid., 32:2612), and "The Biography of General Li [Kuang]" (ibid., 49:2868-69).

intensity. One reason may be that his work is written in pure Japanese prose, not Chinese. But another, more basic reason is that the blessings bequeathed by the gods and buddhas are the deciding favor in the crown prince's victory. The vivid battle scenes in the *Heike Monogatari (The Tale of the Heike)* result from depicting real human beings fighting with all the wit and courage at their command. The writing style used in the *Heike*—the mixed style (wakan konkōbun)—is only a minor factor in achieving such intensity. The realistic impact of *Matsura no Miya* is further diminished by the main characters being presented as reincarnations of divine beings: the Japanese lieutenant was a celestial pageboy in his previous life, his lover Empress Teng dwelt in the Trāyastriṃśa Heaven, and Yü-wen Hui has been an asura.[8] The more detailed their descriptions, the more transparent these characters become. Like *Hamamatsu Chūnagon Monogatari (The Nostalgic Counselor)*, *Matsura no Miya* widens its scope to include foreign settings, but its fantastic elements diverge from the bizarre but plausible mainstream of eleventh-century fantasy. The result is reminiscent of the old version of the *Utsuho Monogatari (The Hollow Tree)*.

The interest in the manifold aspects of society displayed by Masafusa's *Account of Courtesans* also appears in short fiction of the twelfth century. "The Lady Who Loved Insects," though not indisputably a twelfth-century work, also manifests such an interest (*Tsutsumi*, 376-84). This in itself suggests that "The Lady Who Loved Insects" is most appropriately considered along with twelfth-century works of fiction. The special quality of the story stems from the character of its protagonist, an extraordinary young woman. Although born into a good family, she is uninterested in such typical ladylike accomplishments as music and poetry. She is instead absorbed in a curious hobby: collecting, keeping, and examining insects and larvae. The inspiration for the heroine may have been an actual woman who suffered from chlorosis.[9] There is an obvious orientation to fantasy in this story of an eccentric woman. On the other hand, the heroine of "The Lady Who Loved Insects" is unquestionably a creature of this world, unlike the gods and buddhas who annihilate the enemy general in *Matsura no Miya*, and her story treats its fantastic elements in much the same manner as *Konjaku Monogatari (Tales of Times Now*

[8] The Trāyastriṃśa heaven (J. Tōriten) is located in Buddhist cosmology at the summit of Mt. Sumeru, the center of the universe. It is reigned over by Indra (Taishakuten); its inhabitants have thousand-year life spans. Asura are warlike beings that battle with Indra to destroy the Buddhist dharma. [Auth., Trans.]

[9] Chlorosis, the result of faulty ovarian function and consequent anemia, occurs in women between the ages of thirteen and twenty. The lady's love for insects and larvae is probably a fetish brought on by a related blood disorder (Yamagishi, 1954, 51-53). [This sounds like what was termed green-sickness in the Renaissance.—Ed.]

Past), that lively collection of bizarre stories. [See the next chapter.] In such fashion narrative moves closer to the zoku aesthetic.

Ga and zoku are also reflected in the textual transmission of fictional monogatari. *The Tale of Genji*, already a classic in the twelfth century, has few textual variants that significantly affect the content of the work, despite the many manuscript copies that survive (Morris, 1964, 279). A monogatari like the *Genji* demanded careful copying, since the reception of its subtle, polished style would be greatly affected by a few altered words or sentences. Consequently, the variants that do emerge are fairly limited in both number and degree. Prior to the twelfth century, royal waka anthologies were not copied faithfully; conscientiously transcribed texts do not become the rule until Teika's time (see ch. 6). Nevertheless, the texts are far more stable for waka manuscripts than for monogatari and nikki.

Because monogatari did not originally form part of the ga sphere, they were not copied as carefully as waka collections, even in the twelfth century. Sesonji Koreyuki (d. 1175), poet and literary scholar, advised his daughter: "You are better off not copying monogatari. People may press you, but you must excuse yourself, since you are not to do so" (*Yakaku Teikinshō*, 892). Famous calligraphers often copied royal waka anthologies, the *Wakan Rōeishū (Collection of Japanese and Chinese Songs)*, and other well-known poetry collections. Recopying such manuscripts was considered a valuable means of improving one's handwriting. Monogatari, on the other hand, were usually copied by ladies-in-waiting, some of whom were poor calligraphers. So it was thought that copying a monogatari might worsen one's hand, which is no doubt why Koreyuki warns his daughter against doing so. His comment bears on contemporary attitudes toward textual transmission as well: monogatari, copied by unqualified people, were not likely to have been reproduced so carefully as were waka anthologies.

The *Genji* was the exception. Koreyuki compiled the oldest surviving commentary on *The Tale of Genji*, his *Genji Monogatari Shaku*. In China, commentaries were a sign of respect for a written work. A similar mentality was transmitted to Japan, and Koreyuki's *Genji* commentary was an acknowledgement of its classic status. A general awareness of its high literary position probably prompted Fujiwara Shunzei to state that "a poet who has not read the *Genji* is to be deplored" (p. 58). The *Genji* is also exceptional in the relatively small incidence of variants in its text. This would have been only natural, given the attitudes described. Conversely, the very frequent incidence of variants in the *Sagoromo Monogatari (The Tale of Sagoromo)* reflects the treatment accorded the work: its copyists considered it permissible to alter the text. Variants cluster in dramatic passages involving Lady Asukai, the heroine. In such loci the text may be doubled or be condensed to a third of its original length, depending on the copyist's taste. Probably inspired by a copyist's intense interest in, and involvement with, the plot, the variants are more appositely termed rewriting (Mitani, 1952, 268-89). The act of copying becomes more than a receptive process in this case: the copyist-reader also serves to some extent as author. The three processes of composition, reception, and transmission occur simultaneously, performed by one person.

Although they are particularly conspicuous in *Sagoromo*, extreme variants also appear in differing degrees in other fictional monogatari. It was apparently fairly common practice for a recipient to become so involved in the act of copying that personal responses became confused with the author's position, resulting in a rewritten text. Even massive recastings seem to have met with little opposition, especially when the copyist was a close relative or descendant of the author. This was unavoidable, to be sure, in the absence of anything resembling a modern copyright. Carried a bit further, the practice resulted in completely rewritten stories and supplementary narratives. The *Sumiyoshi Monogatari (The Tale of Sumiyoshi)* and *Yowa no Nezame (The Tale of Nezame)* are two of the many works of prose fiction rewritten in the thirteenth and later centuries. The surviving version of *The Changelings* is evidence that some monogatari underwent complete rewriting in the twelfth century as well.[10]

The best examples of supplementary narratives are "Sakurabito" ("Cherry-blossom Girl"), "Kagayuku Hi no Miya" ("The Radiant Princess Consort"), and other imputed chapters of the *Genji* that are known to have existed in the twelfth century and that were not, with any likelihood, the work of Murasaki Shikibu (see vol. two, ch. 8). The supplementary chapters did not, however, alter the original text of the *Genji*: that is the difference between supplements and rewritten monogatari. *Nezame* provides an excellent example of a rewritten text, since most of the original work survives along with the later version. In the rewritten *Nezame*, the section corresponding to the original chapters 1 and 2 has much the same content, but the text is condensed by one-half; the rest of the ancient text to survive (now known as Chapters 3 through 5) is reduced to one-fifth of its original length in the rewritten version. The dominant tone of melancholy in the original is also alloyed, and the plot is changed to accommodate a happy ending (Nagai K., 1962, 103-12). Needless to say, such phenomena do not appear in supplementary narratives.

The distinctions mentioned are signs of the different attitudes shown in transmitting ga and zoku monogatari. Writers of precedented, ga mono-

[10] The *Mumyō Sōshi* was written between 1200 and 1201 (*MMSS*, "Kaisetsu," 135); the rewritten *Torikaebaya* mentioned in it is therefore probably a work of the late twelfth century. The original version is also generally given a twelfth-century date.

gatari sought to create worthy literature by following the examples set by existing works. They rejected the zoku practice of making a novel impression with material and plots never used in earlier masterpieces. But the tie to already existing expression weakened once new subjects and plots, including fantastic material, began to receive critical approval. The weakening of precedent produced a recognizable distance between the transmitting recipient and the original text. Thus the recipient came to resemble the copyist who alters or rewrites a work with a favorite motif—say, an exchange of sexual roles—to suit his personal mood and taste at the time. In the Archaic Age, differentiation already existed between certain setsuwa (stories) that were to be preserved intact and others that did not require transmission in their original form (see vol. one, pp. 165-70). The two courses taken in transmitting monogatari during the twelfth century apparently corresponded to the archaic distinction. We would do well to question why the correspondence exists.

During the Archaic Age, those setsuwa requiring faithful transmission (the slightest variation from the text was not tolerated) dealt with the land of Japan and the nation's illustrious forebears. The great significance such setsuwa held for the nation or group gave them particular gravity: that is why I have called them "weighty setsuwa." Despite the advent of writing, weighty setsuwa continued to be orally transmitted—without a single variant—by people with powers of memorizing now beyond our grasp. "Light" setsuwa, on the other hand, existed to entertain. Minor details might be altered at will, so long as the central motif remained unchanged. The transmitters of light setsuwa clearly shared some attitudes with twelfth-century fiction copyists, since the latter thought nothing of altering or wholly rewriting a text.

What was it about *The Tale of Genji*, then, that gave it the "weight" to be transmitted virtually intact? Twelfth-century society did not of course consider the *Genji* worthy of comparison with weighty setsuwa: it had, after all, been misread as a compendium of lewd stories. Yet the extreme care taken in transmitting the *Genji* must indicate that its audience recognized a certain weightiness in the work. Although its subjects are light, the *Genji* also depicts people as they really are. This quality may have struck readers as a kind of weightiness unlike that of archaic setsuwa. Another acknowledged "weighty" composition, *Records of the Historian*, states unchanging truths about human individuals and society by narrating historical events. The twelfth-century *Genji* audience recognized that this monogatari possessed a weightiness similar to that of the *Records*.[11] A far larger audience, however, continued to prefer "light" fiction that could be altered or rewritten at will.

[11] [Interestingly enough, Murasaki Shikibu records in her *Nikki* that on perusing some

The Elegant and the Commonplace in Factual Monogatari

Like its fictional counterpart, the factual monogatari developed an affinity for both the ga and the zoku aesthetics in the twelfth century. Where fiction tended to diverge into subgenres defined by ga or zoku, however, the factual monogatari developed into something best regarded as ga-zoku, a synthesis of ga and zoku. This would be a logical result for a genre based on fact. Ga-zoku factual monogatari are, however, not homogeneous: some tend more toward ga, others toward zoku. An example of the former is the ten-chapter sequel to *Eiga Monogatari (A Tale of Flowering Fortunes)*; the *Imakagami (The New Mirror)* exemplifies the latter trend.

Flowering Fortunes has long been known to consist of two disparate parts, known as the main section and the sequel. Consider the role played by waka in the two parts. In the main section, waka blend with the prose context so well as to suggest a poetry collection. The sequel, on the other hand, quotes waka out of context so that no lyrical effect is produced (Matsumura, 1960, 56-63). The different uses to which waka are put indicate different authors. Both sections, however, share the view that glory is a thing of the past, and both admire the splendor and refinement characteristic of formal aristocratic life. That both sections of *Flowering Fortunes* should adopt the same stance toward past glory is only natural, given their shared title. The basic method used throughout the work is to give a faithful account of the grand events of the past, so that they may serve as exempla for the future.

Despite their common stance and method, the sequel is considered inferior to the main section. A difference in the two authors' temperaments partially accounts for this evaluation. Another reason for the difference in style is the differing nature of the nikki employed by each section as source material. The main section of *Flowering Fortunes* draws on sources of considerable literary merit, such as the *Murasaki Shikibu Nikki.* The result is a work whose excellence of expression approaches that of its sources. There are no surviving twelfth-century factual nikki that are based principally on court events (as is the *Murasaki Shikibu Nikki*), but extant court nikki from the thirteenth century suggest that the lively accounts of characters and scenes characteristic of eleventh-century nikki tended to give way to prosaic description in later works (see ch. 10).

Similarly, factual nikki concerned with private and informal matters, like the *Sanuki no Suke Nikki*, emphasize the writer's own emotions, and they would thus have been quite inappropriate sources for any account of formal events related in a historical fashion. Murasaki Shikibu is able

---

portion of the *Genji Monogatari*, Ichijō Tennō said that its author must have read the *Nihongi (Nihon Shoki)*.—Ed.]

to hint at her own feelings in the course of describing formal events. The author of the *Flowering Fortunes*' sequel was not so gifted. Nothing of the caliber of Murasaki Shikibu's *Nikki* is thought to have existed in the twelfth century.

The sequel to *Flowering Fortunes* uses the same title as the main section. *The New Mirror*, patterned after the earlier *Ōkagami* (*The Great Mirror*; 1041-51), also adopts a structure appropriate to a sequel. Both *Mirrors* have the same chapter arrangement, patterned after the "basic annals" and "biography" format of the Chinese histories. The framework of *The New Mirror* also resembles that of its predecessor: its narrator tells his story while resting during a pilgrimage to the temple Hasedera. Moreover, courtly chapter titles like "Kumoi" ("The Sky") and "Nenobi" ("Excursion on the First Day of the Rat") indicate that the author of *The New Mirror* intended to carry on the tradition of *Flowering Fortunes* to some extent. Consequently, *The New Mirror* is more markedly retrospective than *The Great Mirror*. It seeks to recapture the glory of the past in the present. *The Great Mirror*, which traces the history of the Fujiwara regency at the height of its power, describes Michinaga's life of luxury in the most glowing terms. Despite the hyperbole, however, there are never any contradictions between fact and style in *The Great Mirror*. *The New Mirror* is a history of the period spanned by the reigns of Goichijō (r. 1016-36) through Takakura (r. 1168-80). Insei—rule by a retired, nominally cloistered tennō—was the form of government for about seventy percent of this period. During that time, the Fujiwara regental government was dismantled and in the latter part of the period the Heike seized power. Yet the author of *The New Mirror* describes this time as if the courtly, elegant life of the past still exists.

The New Mirror is almost exclusively concerned with fūryū events. There, gentlemen compete to compose the cleverest, most beautiful waka, shih, and Chinese prose; they play fine music and delight in feminine companionship. The Hōgen and Heiji Wars, and other momentous events that brought down the Fujiwara regency, merit only the briefest mention.

Descriptions of the fūryū life in *The New Mirror* stress the value of the past. Carrying on the practices of the past is clearly perceived as enhancing the elegance of present life as well. That is what is meant by statements like these:

> An informal banquet was held. Practices that had died out over a century ago were performed to the delight of everyone. (3:141)

> The poetry composed at the royal festivities was fully worthy of that time in the past when the great poets had assembled at Prince Kaya's waka match. (4:180)

People were respected for their ability to perform the fūryū arts. An aristocrat was required to excel in at least one such "accomplishment" (nō), as these arts were called. The chancellor Fujiwara Moromichi (1062-99) is praised for being "spirited, and superior both in looks and accomplishments" (4:183). By contrast, the adopted sons of Minamoto Masasada (1094-1162) are criticized: "All attained high rank; unfortunately, none carried on his father's accomplishments" (7:307). A passage about Fujiwara Kin'yoshi (1115-61) gives concrete examples of the contemporary meaning of "accomplishment."[12]

> This minister was known for his aptitude for music and matters of the intellect. Although his father and grandfather had not been of a scholarly bent, he composed poetry in Chinese. He was a most superior person in temperament as well as appearance. Having served as middle counselor and general, he became minister of the right. He also possessed a fine voice. In his youth, when he was a chamberlain and guards lieutenant, he once sang gongen songs. This was during an imayō performance held at the court banquet that followed the Gosechi dances. (6:270-71)[13]

The same standards applied to women. Consider this entry for Kin'yoshi's third daughter, Ōiko, who was the principal consort of two tennō:

> Her Majesty is attractive in every respect, and most sensitive. She writes a beautiful hand. Even her drawings are said to be unlike ordinary sketches. Although I have not had the privilege of hearing her play the koto and biwa—her principal accomplishments—I understand that she rivals the best musicians and has a discriminating ear. (6:274)[14]

Possessing such accomplishments was the highest ideal for twelfth-century nobility—in the opinion of the author of *The New Mirror*, at least. Accomplishments were displayed to best advantage at banquets and other gatherings. *The New Mirror* contains detailed accounts of cherry-blossom-viewing parties given by the retired sovereigns Shirakawa and Toba (2:111-15). As described in these passages, the participants' splendid clothing and accessories impress one as having been even more luxurious than those enjoyed by the nobility of the past when they attended grand

[12] The term "nō" is the origin of the later usages connected with drama: "sarugaku no nō" and "dengaku no nō" (Konishi, 1983c, 10-13). "Nō" is mentioned many times in the *Imakagami* to signify "accomplishment" (for example: pp. 179, 252, 267, 307, 321, and 352).

[13] "Gongen" is a kind of ashigara song; the ashigara is a variety of imayō (i.e., kinds of song popular in the eleventh century; see ch. 12, below).

[14] Ōiko was the consort of Konoe and Nijō (*HM*, 1:107-11).

events.[15] Are the descriptions accurate? Probably not. They were probably written out of a desire to make contemporary events seem more splendid than anything preceding them. If "sentimental" may be used to designate a response in excess of that expected from a given phenomenon, then the description in *The New Mirror* can be sentimental indeed.

Although *The New Mirror* embraces the ga aesthetic to the point of sentimentality, deliberately or not, the author provided considerable zoku for much of the work. There is more here than a longing for the past. The story is also sustained by a strong interest in contemporary people and society. One example is this anecdote about the chancellor Fujiwara Morozane (1042-1101).

> One day as he was viewing a game of kickball, Morozane lauded the skill of one of the players, Morinaga, governor of Awaji. This annoyed Yukitsuna, governor of Shinano, who felt that his playing was every bit as good. While Morozane's legs were being washed, Yukitsuna pinched them from time to time. "Why are you doing that?" Morozane enquired. Yukitsuna replied, "The kickball is unknown to these legs," and he washed them himself. Morozane then remarked that Yukitsuna was also skilled at kickball. Yukitsuna responded by gently massaging Morozane's legs. (4:181)

The passage illustrates Morozane's generosity and refinement, manifested in both word and deed. These are virtues befitting a member of the regental house. There is some conscious admiration for past glory in this passage, although the stronger element is a delight in the interest generated by the story itself. Because the subject is everyday aristocratic society, the story is concerned with routine, small matters rather than with bizarre or miraculous events. Yet the author's intentional search for interesting elements is no different from the folk-tale predilection for strange and marvelous events. The Morozane anecdote does not describe an elegant event within the framework of a polished, precedented world. It treats a commonplace, zoku subject, a part of daily life free from models and precedents. Narrating such a story might be termed creating setsuwa about aristocratic society. *The New Mirror* has certain features of the setsuwa, in this sense of the word.[16]

Unlike the earlier utagatari (oral waka stories), the setsuwa transmitted

[15] *The New Mirror* is noted for its detailed descriptions of ancient court customs, including the clothing and accessories appropriate to various occasions (Yamauchi, 1980, 279-93).

[16] [The author's general meaning for "setsuwa" involves stories that are mythic, legendary, or folk in nature—or in a special sense lore involving temple and shrine recountings (engi), or even poems. Setsuwa are generally zoku in the author's classification, so that introduction of zoku elements into accounts of aristocratic life gives *The New Mirror* "certain features of setsuwa."—Ed.]

orally throughout twelfth-century aristocratic society emphasize their factual qualities. Oral waka stories, set in an indeterminate past, often commence with "In the past" ("Mukashi"). Twelfth-century social anecdotes—aristocratic setsuwa—are narrated within actual time. There is a strong desire shown in them, moreover, to elucidate the process of transmission. *The New Mirror*, for example, often names the sources of its stories:

> I gather that Morimichi, son of Morishige, told this story. (7:287)
>
> This was told, I understand, by a member of the school who was both learned and eminent. (7:287)
>
> The story was apparently told by Nakamasa, the man's son. (10:369)

The point of such conclusions is to stress the factual nature of the story. Similar statements are routinely used to conclude stories in *Konjaku Monogatari Shū (Tales of Times Now Past)*. They may be considered a formulaic element in twelfth-century anecdotes about society. Another sign of a factual orientation is the use of recent events for subject matter. One example is the story of the principal handmaid who served Nijō Tennō (*Imakagami*, 7:314-15). Because the events in the story occurred between 1158 and 1165, the author probably witnessed them personally. The presence of zoku stories about aristocrats in *The New Mirror* is best regarded, however, as another indication of the ga-zoku nature of the monogatari genre, rather than as a radical departure from the ga aesthetic.

Anecdotes about society seem to have been popular among twelfth-century aristocrats. The stories were recorded in various documents, including *The New Mirror*. For example, the story of the monk Ryōsen in *The New Mirror* (1:80) appears in somewhat longer form in *Shumpishō* (*Secret Notes by Shunrai*, 219-20). The story of the diviner Abe no Ariyuki (*Imakagami*, 9:362) is also included in a later work, *Kokon Chomonjū* (7:240). Similar kinds of anecdotes furnished much of the material for *Chūgaishō (Notes on Matters Inside and Outside the Capital), Fukegatari (Lord Fuke's Stories)*, and *Gōdanshō* (*The Ōe Conversations*; see ch. 1). The contemporary nobility were enthusiastic compilers of anecdotes. The narrative style of such stories resembles the zoku style of certain anecdotes in *The New Mirror*. As oral transmissions, the stories followed a format; they retain their original oral-narrative style even after being transcribed (Masuda, 1960a, 195-200).

A medieval anecdote about society has several characteristics: (1) an element of surprise; (2) a combination of several small events; (3) no delineation of a character's thought processes; (4) no focus on a single protagonist; and (5) emphasis on factualness. The last characteristic is the most noticeable.

Thus endings follow a set form, as, for example, in Masafusa's *Conversations* (Kanda manuscript):

> This was told by my grandfather. Later, apparently, Hirotoshi and his father Toshisada also told this story, saying it was told by the people of that province. (*Kohon Gōdanshō*, 330)

Masafusa's format resembles that of *The New Mirror*. Factualness is further stressed by frequent use of description, as in this passage from Shunrai's *Secret Notes*:

> During the tenure of the Kamo high priestess known as the Great Priestess, a chamberlain, Nobunori, came secretly to her precincts one night to court a certain lady-in-waiting. He was discovered by the guards, who, suspecting something, demanded that he identify himself. Instead he tried to hide, and could not speak. The guards locked the gate and arrested Nobunori; whereupon his ladyfriend put his dilemma before the high priestess. "What a shame—is he not a waka poet? Let him go immediately!" said the priestess. Nobunori was thereupon released. Before he left, he composed this poem.

Kamigaki wa	These holy precincts
Ki no marodono ni	Are not the Round Wooden Hall
Aranedomo	Of Asakura,
Nanori o seneba	And yet if one withholds his name,
Hito togamekeri.	He will indeed be censured![17]
	(*Shumpishō*, 176-77)

Like the utagatari, this story is focused around a waka (see vol. two, ch. 8). Unlike the utagatari, it speaks in the language of the social anecdote: the scene is so graphically described as to be almost visible. A story based on similar material appears in *Tales of Times Now Past.*[18] It comes close to the shōdō tradition (see next chapter), however, by its use of exposi-

[17] Nobunori alludes to a kagura, "Asakura" (*KR*, 79): Asakura ya / Ki no marodono ni / Waga oreba / Waga oreba / Nanori o shitsutsu / Yuku wa tare. (Oh, Asakura, / It has a round wooden hall— / That is where I dwell, / That is where I dwell; / Who do you think that you are, / Calling out your name?)

[18] *Konjaku Monogatari Shū* [=*KMS*] 24 (story 57):357. Fujiwara Nobunori (d. 1011) was the older brother of Murasaki Shikibu. In her *Nikki*, Murasaki Shikibu describes how their father Tametoki lamented the fact that she was learning the *Shih Chi* from him more quickly than her brother was (*MSN*, 500).

tion. The story of Nobunori narrated in Toshiyori's *Secret Notes* resembles *The New Mirror* in narrative style.

The growing interest in depicting real people and society in monogatari corresponds to the increasingly popular tone taken in shih and waka. Both are characteristic twelfth-century phenomena. The decline of oral waka stories may be connected to the new interest in facts. The disappearance of the waka narrative (utamonogatari) as a genre after the appearance of the *Yamato Monogatari (Tales of Yamato)* is very likely due to the decline of its basic building block, the oral waka story. Heightened interest in facts and reality led to a shift in literary preferences: the ga method of appreciating waka within a framework situated vaguely in the past was abandoned for the ga-zoku approach, which emphasizes the people and circumstances connected to a waka. The latter approach yields not a waka story, but a society-centered anecdote that happens to have a waka for its subject. *Tales of Times Now Past* and *Kokon Chomonjū* contain many stories concerning waka, but they are not waka stories.[19] Rather, they are written versions of society-centered oral anecdotes that deal with waka.

Ga and Zoku in Nikki

During the twelfth century two kinds of writing that had flourished earlier cease to be practiced. One is monogatari centered on waka (utagoto no monogatari), and the other the fictional nikki. Only factual nikki survive from the twelfth century. Although the extreme scarcity of these works makes it difficult to determine contemporary trends in this kind, representative works like *Sanuki no Suke Nikki (The Nikki of Lady Sanuki)* suggest that informality was becoming an increasingly dominant element. As we have seen, formal court nikki, no longer extant, were the likely sources for *The New Mirror* and the sequel to *A Tale of Flowering Fortunes*, but inferences from what no longer exists are difficult to draw. Several thirteenth-century nikki are chiefly concerned with court events, including *Kenshunmon'in Chūnagon Nikki, Ben no Naishi Nikki*, and *Nakatsukasa Naishi Nikki.* Court nikki of this kind very likely had twelfth-century predecessors. Many nonextant fictional monogatari seem to have dealt with the elegant life at court (p. 96); we may surmise the same about nikki from this period.

Nevertheless, the twelfth-century factual nikki displays an increasingly informal quality. A late eleventh-century work, *Jōjin Azari Haha no Shū* (=*JAHS*; *The Waka Collection of Master Jōjin's Mother*) is a very early

[19] *KMS* has twelve stories about waka in Book 30, and one in Book 31. *Kokon Chomonjū* has eighty-eight such stories in Book 5.

instance of the informal nikki. This idiosyncratic narrative does not of course exemplify contemporary literary trends; it is discussed here because its strikingly informal tone is shared by similar works of the twelfth and later centuries.

In 1072 the monk Jōjin (1011-81) journeyed to Sung China aboard a Chinese merchant vessel. He was sixty-two years old at the time, and his mother was eighty-five. Book One of the nikki begins with waka composed by the narrator, Jōjin's Mother, in 1071. This was the year in which she moved from the temple of Daiunji in Iwakura, where she lived with Jōjin, to the Ninnaji temple in Omuro. Jōjin has made arrangements for a younger brother, a master of discipline at the Ninnaji, to look after their mother in his absence.[20] Jōjin immediately sets off for Tsukushi [Kyushu] to begin his journey. In Book Two of *Master Jōjin's Mother*, the narrator and her younger son move from the Ninnaji to the capital; she suffers from ague in their new surroundings. Waka predominate up to this point, as suggested by the title of the work. But monthly entries begin thereafter: the first, dated the last part of the Eighth Month, 1071, records that the mother has heard that Jōjin is arranging to obtain passage aboard a ship. *Master Jōjin's Mother* takes on the attributes of a nikki from this point. On the thirteenth day of the Tenth Month, Jōjin unexpectedly returns to the capital; the following day, he sets off for the province of Bitchū [now Okayama Prefecture]. Hereafter both the day and the month are recorded. Jōjin succeeds in leaving for China in the Third Month of 1072, but his letter to this effect does not reach his mother until the Sixth Month. Another letter from Jōjin, now living in China, arrives the following year. His mother's health is deteriorating: in the Fifth Month of 1073, she is afflicted with dropsy. Though distracted by pain, the author prays that she will achieve the Pure Land now. The nikki ends here.

Master Jōjin's Mother focuses unusually closely on its author, perhaps because parting is the primary theme of the work. The tenth-century *Kagerō Nikki (The Gossamer Years)* describes love and its attendant problems solely from the wife's viewpoint; yet the author maintains a distance between her actual feelings at the time and the heroine's emotions in the nikki. In several passages, the author actually observes herself as a character in the work: the heroine appears not as "I," but as "she." In the later work, Jōjin's Mother, unable to distinguish herself from the speaker of her nikki, becomes its narrator. One sign of this is the ubiquitous presence of the humble verb, "haberi." A fairly short work, *Master Jōjin's Mother* contains ninety-one instances of "haberi." Of the ninety-one, sixteen appear in conversation—a natural occurrence in medieval litera-

[20] The younger brother is probably Jōson (1012-74), a monk famous for his knowledge of esoteric Buddhism (Nagai Y., 1967, 241-84). See *Genkō Shakusho* (13:140).

ture—but the remainder are to be found in narrative passages. For this reason, *Master Jōjin's Mother* has been termed a soliloquy (Hirabayashi F., 1977, 22-26). The tone of the work, however, might better be perceived as conversational. Jōjin, the other member of the conversation, is absent, but his image is always before his mother's eyes.

Master Jōjin's Mother begins in the style of a waka collection, and so "haberi" is not an unnatural element in its narrative passages. "Haberi" is conveniently used in forenotes to waka, both in royal anthologies and personal collections. An example appears somewhat later in *Master Jōjin's Mother*:

I read [mihaberu] in a letter to his highness the Holy Teacher:[21]

Kawa to kiku	River-like in sound,
Namida ni ukabu	The tears upon whose stream I float
Kanashisa ni	Betray a misery
Oritatsu mi o ba	So profound I cannot keep
Seki zo kanetsuru.	Myself from being swept away.[22]
	(*JAHS*, 1:59)

The author's use of "haberi" here may be interpreted either as expressing respect for Jōjin or as common usage in a waka forenote.[23] Somewhat later in the text, however, expressions appear that clearly signify the author is addressing Jōjin. Not only does "haberi" continue to appear in the author's references to herself, but honorific verbs like "owasu" (to be) and "mitamau" (to see) are also employed to express respect for the addressee of her work. An example appears in a prose passage following several of the author's waka: "None of these poems deserves writing down; but I would like you to see [mitamae] them, should you return [owashi; lit. 'be here'], so that you will know how I have felt" (*JAHS*, 1:65). The object of her honorific verbs can only be Jōjin.

[21] Miya Azari, a reference to the Holy Teacher Eikaku, Abbot of Tennōji. Eikaku was the son of Prince Atsumichi and the poet Izumi Shikibu.

[22] "Kawa to kiku" ("They sound like a river") responds to "Namida no kawa" ("river of tears"), a phrase used in a waka to the author from the Holy Teacher.

[23] Classical Japanese has three modes of address: the polite, the honorific, and the humble. In conversation or written correspondence, when the addressee is directly perceived, the polite (self-lowering) form expresses the speaker's formal stance. The speaker employs the auxiliary verbs "haberi" and/or "sōrō." The honorific form places the addressee on a higher plane than that of the speaker. The auxiliary verbs employed with this form include "-su," "-sasu," "-shimu," "-tamau," and their compound forms, as well as honorific synonyms (such as "notamau," used in place of "iu," "to speak"). The humble form places the speaker on a plane lower than that of the addressee. This form is often used to express respect, since humility on the speaker's part automatically exalts the addressee. Humble synonyms are often employed; for example, "kikoyu" or "mōsu" in place of "iu," "to speak."

Imagining her son's presence, the author addresses him from the nikki. An entry dated the thirteenth of the Tenth Month, 1071, records her impressions following a brief visit from her busy son:

> You said to me, "If we do not meet again while you live, we shall surely be reunited atop the same lotus." How I regret my speechlessness then, my surrendering to tears and grief as I bade you farewell! There can be no greater joy in store for me than a speedy death. Surely anyone would agree who knows something of my feelings. I too believe that we shall be together in Paradise: how then can I doubt your words? (*JAHS*, 2:84)

In the original, the honorific verb "notamau" (to speak, say) is used in reference to Jōjin's speech, whereas "idashiyarikikoyu," a humble verb meaning "to bid farewell, see someone off," is used to describe the mother's action, as is the humble "omoihaberu" (to think, believe). The choice of verbs stems from the mother's perception that Jōjin is the direct recipient of her writing. The nikki character Jōjin is unified with Jōjin the recipient.

A composite character-recipient and narrator-author appear in *Master Jōjin's Mother* because the author maintains little distance between herself and the events she describes. In this sense, the work centers on the author. The waka in *Master Jōjin's Mother* share this assumption. Many are unadorned statements of the author's emotions.

Oshimiwabi	Regret and suffering
Ne nomi nakaruru	Left me with no resources but weeping
Wakareji wa	Where we said farewell;
Namida mo e koso	Yet your going, like my tears,
Todomezarikere.	Was not within our power to halt.
	(*JAHS*, 1:57)

Nageku ni mo	To voice complaint
Iu ni mo kai no	Is something wholly pointless
Naki mi ni wa	For one like me,
Ideiru iki no	Rather, I await the moment
Tayuru o zo matsu.	When I draw my final breath.
	(*JAHS*, 1:64)

Needless to say, these waka employ zoku expression. Another then unusual element of *Master Jōjin's Mother* is its audience of one: the author has a single recipient in mind, and she addresses him alone. In her nikki Jōjin's mother therefore veers sharply away from the ga standard, for the author of a ga work of literature anticipates many recipients sharing a homogeneous background. Yet, evaluating the extent of zoku in this work is not easily done, since one's conclusions will vary greatly depending on the criteria used. Let us rather note the growing presence of an important literary trend, that of linking an author to the facts recorded in the work composed. Narratives like *Master Jōjin's Mother*, which mingle speaker with author, are forerunners of the modern watakushi shōsetsu [more or less factual, autobiographical prose narratives].

A somewhat later work, *Sanuki no Suke Nikki* (*The Nikki of Lady Sanuki* [= *SN*]), is another example of an informal factual nikki, but unlike *Master Jōjin's Mother*, *Sanuki* maintains a certain formality.[24] The nikki is divided into two books. Book One relates the events surrounding the death of Horikawa Tennō (1079-1107); Book Two tells how the author returns to court to serve Toba Tennō (r. 1107-23). Despite the change of reigns, Sanuki continues to long for her dead sovereign in Book Two. Thus *Sanuki* is essentially an elegy for Horikawa.

Book One records how Sanuki nurses the bedridden tennō until his death and describes her grief thereafter. Although the work is essentially a memoir, it is written in the present tense in accordance with the conventions of the nikki genre (see vol. two, ch. 8). The author's use of the present tense creates noteworthy expression: her descriptions of Horikawa's illness and suffering, for example, are vivid in the extreme. The twenty-eight-year old Horikawa is presented as a human being rather than as a sovereign as he lies on his deathbed. He is in pain from various ailments; he frequently becomes irritable, and although strongly attached to life, he knows he ought to place his hopes on peace in the world to come. He is aware that his condition is hopeless, and he is forced to endure a slow death. This is not the image of the sovereign evoked in the *Man'yōshū*: "Because our ruler / Is indeed divine" (*MYS*, 3:235). Rather, it is the picture of a human being dying in agony, a death scene not unlike that of the Meiji poet Masaoka Shiki. One example of Horikawa's character as an invalid occurs in the following passage, in which Sanuki has just spent the night caring for him.

> It is morning, and I decide to sleep a bit as soon as other attendants are up and ready to take my place. The shutters are opened and the lamps taken away. I lie down to rest, covering myself with a singlet; whereupon his majesty, seeing this, draws away my covering. I get up again, for it does not seem his wish that I sleep. (*SN*, 1:121)

Horikawa behaves like a small child who wants its mother to be always awake: he will not let the exhausted Sanuki rest. Such selfishness is nota-

[24] "Sanuki no Suke" (Lady Sanuki) is a court lady's sobriquet. The author is thought to be Fujiwara Nagako, the daughter of Akitsuna (d. 1101). She was born ca. 1079; the year of her death is not known (*SN*, "Kaisetsu," 18-30).

ble in invalids. And yet, although driven to behave so objectionably, Horikawa is also capable of much thoughtfulness. The chancellor, Fujiwara Tadazane, comes to consult the bedridden Horikawa about certain prayers being commissioned for the tennō's recovery. Horikawa bends his knees under the bedclothes, making a tent behind which Sanuki, on the other side of the bed from the chancellor, might hide from the gentleman's gaze. She crouches behind the bulk formed by Horikawa's raised knees and covers her head and face with a singlet. She emerges from the singlet only after the chancellor withdraws, his business completed. A noblewoman's face was not normally revealed to men other than her father, husband, lover, or son (Morris, 1964, 211). The prospect of being seen by Tadazane, a man with no close relationship to Sanuki, would have been highly embarrassing. Horikawa, although clearly in pain, shows deep consideration for Sanuki, who in turn seems to have responded with the utmost respect and gratitude.[25] Sanuki devotes herself to nursing him, but his condition worsens.

Bedrest eventually becomes painful for Horikawa, whose body is swollen with edema. He puts one arm around a lady-in-waiting's neck while she helps him to sit up. His feet, held in place by another lady-in-waiting, rest on a small platform. He sucks pieces of ice; perspiration is repeatedly wiped from his body.[26] "How very painful it is! Surely I must be dying," he exclaims as he invokes Amitābha. As his suffering grows more acute, Horikawa calls on Shinto deities and buddhas alike: "I am dying! Succor me, divinities of Ise! Hail, O wonderful *Lotus Sūtra*, preached by the compassionate Embodiment of Wisdom!" (*SN*, 1:135-37).[27] In extremis, he probably has no notion whether he is praying to be restored to health or to be born in the Buddhist paradise.

We cannot know whether *The Nikki of Lady Sanuki* is true to fact, since there are no corroborating data. It is of course unwise to assume that a nikki is by definition an accurate record of historical events. What we are concerned with here is not its faithfulness to fact, but the individuality of *Sanuki.* It narrates facts as those are understood by feelings unique to Sanuki herself. The descriptive method employed by the author of *Sanuki* is not common to most nikki written in Japanese prose. It represents a departure from the ga aesthetic, which is based on the expecta-

[25] We may surmise this because Sanuki recalls the incident several times in later passages (*SN*, 2:163, 178).

[26] Ice was harvested in winter and stored in icehouses (himuro), thick-walled buildings located in cool, shaded locales. Ice was available in summer only to royalty and members of the high aristocracy.

[27] [The "divinities of Ise" (daijingū) are the gods and goddesses enshrined in the Inner and Outer Shrines of Ise, two hereditary shrines of the royal house. Most likely, Horikawa is addressing the chief occupants of the shrines, Amaterasu and Toyoukehime, respectively. "Embodiment of Wisdom" refers to the Buddha.—Trans.]

tion of similar responses shared by a homogeneous circle. That is why *Sanuki* can impress with its urgency and immediacy modern readers unable to comprehend the medieval ga aesthetic. It possesses a power possibly attributable to zoku elements; but zoku is less pervasive in it than in *Master Jōjin's Mother*. In the latter, the sadness of parting is emphatically reinforced throughout the narrative, although the author-narrator makes little effort to explain the circumstances of her own sadness. Sanuki, on the other hand, works hard to communicate the grief of a bereaved woman: she describes the tragic course of events as well as her own feelings. Her intent is manifested in the orderly structure of Part One, which depicts Horikawa's illness from its onset through his last moments. The author also takes considerable care to demonstrate the duration of her grief by describing the yearly memorial ceremonies held for Horikawa, maintaining a certain distance by focusing on her subject matter rather than herself.

The Nikki of Lady Sanuki is in part oriented toward the ga aesthetic. Its opening passage, with its highly stylized language, is strongly suggestive of a Chinese prose preface. Parallelism, though rarely found in prose in Japanese, is employed in this passage, and poetic allusions are embedded in the text. The prose of *Sanuki* even contains pillow words; for example: "I recall things from the past, events as old as Isonokami" (*SN*, 1:114). ["Isonokami" is a pillow-word for various expressions beginning, "furu-," which is homophonous with "furu" meaning "old."] Such ornamentation suggests that the author had an audience in mind. Her audience was a limited one, however, not the indeterminately large readership anticipated by modern writers. *Sanuki* concludes with a passage strongly reminiscent of a postscript:

> I have thought of going over this account with others who yearn for his majesty as I do; yet, on second thought, who indeed does not yearn for him? Then again, problems might arise should I show my book to people who are unfavorably disposed toward me, for they would spread unpleasant rumors about its content. Even those favorably disposed may have too small an acquaintance to generate much interest in the book. If only there were someone suitable to hear the story of his majesty! Then I remembered Lady Hitachi, the only person worthy to know of my story. I invited her to my rooms, where she proved herself as friendly and concerned as I had hoped. We spoke of the matter until late into the evening. . . . (*SN*, 2:197)

The author-speaker apparently wished to limit her audience substantially. She required that her audience be favorably disposed toward herself, have friends who were also favorably disposed, and know Horikawa well. Unless her audience sympathized with Horikawa and his relationship with Sanuki, it might misinterpret the motives behind her detailed descriptions of the sovereign's sufferings. This in turn would reflect unfavorably on Horikawa's character. The author deliberately assumes a limited audience. Sanuki needs a primary recipient who will help to ensure her of a fairly large, favorably disposed audience, and she finds an excellent candidate in Lady Hitachi.[28] The author may have purposely recorded Lady Hitachi's name at the end of the nikki as a reminder to her friend: should the nikki be shown to the wrong sort of people, Lady Hitachi must bear the blame for any subsequent unpleasant repercussions.

Whatever the author's motives, *The Nikki of Lady Sanuki* apparently gained a rather large readership by the time *The New Mirror* was written (ca. 1180):

> Our sovereign [Horikawa] did not live to see his thirtieth year; his death was a severe blow to the court. Evidently his majesty's last days were recorded in detail by an Assistant Handmaid known as Sanuki. I once heard her account read aloud. Have you come across it, by any chance? (*Imakagami*, 2:108)

Clearly, Sanuki did not write in vain. But her audience was probably not composed of as many sympathetic people as she would have wished.

The Nikki of Lady Sanuki is a hybrid, or ga-zoku, work: its essentially informal nature is combined with a fairly formal, mannered style. Nikki tend to be ga-zoku when the subject concerns an individual. This had been true from the earliest period of the genre, as demonstrated by the *Tosa Nikki* (*The Tosa Diary*; see vol. two, ch. 8). Although nikki possessing ga-zoku expression are not necessarily guaranteed masterpiece status, the harmonious blend of formality and informality in *Sanuki* may well have accounted for the favorable response accorded it by late twelfth-century readers. Modern readers, bereft of the medieval ga aesthetic, are likely to evaluate the work on the basis of its zoku elements alone. There is nothing wrong in doing so; but we must not forget that other criteria also exist.

[28] The *Chūyūki* (entry for 5.V.1093) describes an iris root-matching contest in which a Lady Hitachi, in the retinue of the former sovereign Shirakawa, is a member of the Right team, and another Lady Hitachi, in attendance on Horikawa Tennō, is a member of the Left. The "Lady Hitachi" mentioned by Sanuki is probably one of these ladies (*SN*, "Kaisetsu," 64-65).

CHAPTER 4

Prose in the Mixed Style: First Glimmerings

As prose in Chinese became increasingly adapted to conform to Japanese lexical and syntactic tastes, a new prose style evolved consisting of a mixture of Chinese and Japanese elements. The new development was only a style, not a genre. This prose in the mixed style (wakan konkōbun [the basis of modern Japanese]) might rather be seen as an offshoot of prose in Japanese (wabun) that created new expressive forms by incorporating various features of Chinese prose. Before this stage was reached, however, writers and audiences alike had to accustom themselves to reading Chinese prose in Japanese grammatical order. One determining factor in achieving this ability was the public Buddhist religious service (shōdō), a popular feature of medieval Japanese life.

Setsuwa and Public Buddhist Services: The Early Period

The eleventh century marks the first stage in the transformation of Chinese prose into a Japanized amalgam. This was the period in which the *Ōjō Yōshū* of Genshin (942-1017) was recast into an approximation of Japanese prose (see vol. two, ch. 5). The rephrasing of Buddhist scriptures, treatises, and other writings into a kind of Japanese prose was an influential force in the early developmental stages of the mixed style. This practice occurred in various circumstances: scholastic monks, for example, seem to have read their lecture and research texts, customarily written in Chinese, in a kind of Japanese.

The most significant application of this practice, however, was in the public Buddhist service, and especially in the sermon that was its focal point. When a preacher addressed a large, mixed congregation, he knew that most of its members would be unfamiliar with the difficult Chinese texts that form the basis of Japanese Buddhism. The preacher thus felt obliged to rephrase his scriptural quotations in language intelligible to the average Japanese. But certain facts and concepts, inexpressible in pure Japanese, had to be communicated by means of Chinese loanwords, by Sinified language. Accurate expression of complex facts and subjects often strained the capacities of the indigenous Japanese language. For example, the grand metaphysical speculations made by Dōgen (1200-53), the founder of Sōtō Zen, could be expressed in his native language only by employing Chinese loanwords and other expressions typical of Chinese prose. The incorporation of Sinified language and vocabulary into Japanese prose was, therefore, more than a stylistic event: it substantially altered Japanese mental processes as well. Not that anyone anticipated such a result. The momentous process was set in motion by a practical motive, to communicate a sermon on a Chinese Buddhist text to a lay audience.

Public Buddhist services were probably first celebrated in Japan soon after the introduction of Buddhism to the country, but little is known of their form until the twelfth century. The earliest extant instance is a record of a series of sermons on the *Lotus Sūtra*, held over a three-hundred-day period in 1109. The record survives only in a fragment describing twenty of the three hundred days.[1] The following passage appears there:

> Discussion on this chapter will include comments on its connection to earlier parts of the sutra, an explanation of the meaning of the chapter title, explication of the text, and several other matters. Since these follow the set form for sermons, I need not elaborate further. (*Hokke Hyakuza* [12.III.1109], 42)

In other words, a preacher began by linking the sutra chapter under discussion with sections dealt with earlier in the series of sermons. He then explicated the chapter title and analyzed important parts of the text, breaking them down into small sections. The sermon also included a goodly number of stories [setsuwa] introduced in connection with a given subject to aid in communicating a point. The stories were probably the most interesting part of a sermon, and they had been a vital component of Buddhist sermons in China from the late Six Dynasties period, if not before.[2] The recorder of the sermons given in 1109 may have shared the Chinese fondness for such stories, since he devotes considerable space to

[1] Known variously as *Hokke Hyakuza Hōdan Kikigaki Shō, Hokke Suhō Ippyakuza Kikigaki Shō*, and *Tennin Hyakuza Hōdan*, although the original work is untitled. The single extant manuscript, a late twelfth-century copy, is owned by Hōryūji. Tsukudo Reikan has explained the value of the document as a source of data on medieval sermons (Tsukudo, 1932, 255-69).

[2] The *Kao-seng Chuan (Biographies of Eminent Clerics)*, compiled by the monk Hui-chiao in the Liang dynasty, contains this passage: "Sermons: . . . The preacher seats himself at a high pulpit and discourses on the Dharma. In the course of his sermon he will discuss various subjects connected to the temple and to the appointed scripture, or will tell stories with moral content" (*Kōsōden*, 13:417). A preacher might enliven his sermon, for example, by telling a story connected with the founder of the temple at which the service is taking place or describe the earlier incarnations of buddhas and bodhisattvas mentioned in the scriptural text under discussion. [Auth., Trans. The author defines "setsuwa" as used here to be folk, legendary, or mythic stories. In nature and function they resemble the exempla used by medieval Western preachers.—Ed.]

recording the setsuwa employed in the sermons. Each day of the series concluded with a speech praising the virtues of the sponsor, a member of the royal family.[3]

The document of 1109 does not provide fully detailed descriptions of the content and form of contemporary sermons and services. Fortunately, further information survives in a thirteenth-century work, the *Hossokushū*, compiled by the monk Shinshō.[4] His descriptions do not significantly contradict the outline in the 1109 account, and we may therefore assume that twelfth-century services followed much the same form. A public Buddhist service, as described by Shinshō, may be outlined as follows.

1. The congregation enters and is seated. The sponsor or a representative announces a desire that the service begin.
2. A chevron-shaped stone gong (kei) is struck to signal the beginning of worship. Celebrants and congregation perform three prostrations before the principal cult image.
3. The *Heart Sūtra* (J. *Hannya Shingyō*) is recited as an offering to local Shinto deities.
4. There is a reading of the hyōbyaku, which announces the sponsor's purpose in commissioning the service.
5. A formal prayer (gammon) is read on behalf of the sponsor. The prayer is recited in a soft tone, with some musical decoration being given to the most important parts of the text.
6. The title of the scripture for the day is intoned.
7. The hotsugan (a prayer that the Buddha grant the above requests) and the offertory are recited.
8. The scriptural text for the day is recited.
9. Psalms (kyōge) are chanted.
10. The sermon is preached in this order: the scriptural text for the day is placed in its context in the sutra, the meaning of the relevant chapter title is given, and the text is explicated.
11. The prayer for the sponsor (seshudan, beseeching the Buddha to grant merit to the sponsor of the service) is recited.[5]
12. A requiem is said for the deceased, in whose memory the service is given, and for all those who have died.

[3] The sponsor may have been Princess Toshiko, the second daughter of Gosanjō Tennō (Satō R., 1963, 161-68).

[4] Shinshō was a great-grandchild of Fujiwara Michinori (d. 1159). The *Hossokushū* is thought to have been compiled in the late thirteenth century.

[5] The *Hossokushū* (67) stresses the importance of this prayer: "It is said that a preacher's skill and training—or his lack of same—is revealed when he recites the seshudan. Unless he gives careful thought to it, and conducts himself accordingly, even an experienced priest may commit unimaginable blunders."

13. The stone gong is struck to signal the conclusion of the service, and the name of Shakyamuni Buddha is intoned.

The procedure appears rather complex at first sight. If, however, formalistic events are omitted—such as the recitation of the *Heart Sūtra* for local deities—the service can be reduced to a tripartite structure consisting of (1) petitions (including the sponsor's formal prayer and the offertory), (2) sermon (explication of title and text of the scripture for the day), and (3) prayers on behalf of the sponsor (including the requiem).[6] Other thirteenth-century accounts of Buddhist services describe their structure similarly.[7] The *Hossokushū* mentions musical notation, names of melodies (such as "Sashikoe" and "Yuru"), and tonic markers ("level," "rising," and "falling") to be used in parts of the service.[8] The sections sung were chiefly psalms and parallel prose couplets. Discursive sections, principally the explication of scripture, were probably spoken and unaccompanied by music.

Public Buddhist services (su-chiang) in T'ang China also had a liturgy with both musical and nonmusical sections.[9] Only fragmentary data survived on T'ang Buddhist services until the discovery of several pien-wen works in the Tun-huang Caves.[10] These have supplemented the previously scanty store of knowledge on T'ang Buddhist ceremonies and sermons and provide a fairly accurate view of how T'ang services were performed. A typical public Buddhist service adhered to the following order.[11]

1. Assembly and Seating of the Congregation. The bell is struck and the congregation assembles. Both sexes, all social classes, clergy,

[6] "A service is usually divided into three parts: petitions, explication of the scripture, and prayers on behalf of the sponsor" (*Hossokushū*, 64).

[7] An example is the account of a series of sermons on the *Konkōmyō Saishōōkyō (Suvarna-prabhāsottama-sūtra)* presented at court during the thirteenth century. The account appears at the beginning of the *Gonsenshū* (13-26), a compendium of formal liturgical elements including sponsors' statements and prayers. The *Gonsenshū* is thought to date from the late thirteenth century (*Gosenshū*, "Kaisetsu," 1972, 471-75).

[8] The tonic terms are identical to those used to designate the Chinese tones, but the tonal values differ greatly. Small differences exist between the Tendai and Shingon chanting traditions.

[9] During the Six Dynasties period, a public Buddhist service was called "ch'ang-tao" (J. shōdō); essentially the same ceremony was called "su-chiang" (J. zokō) in the T'ang period.

[10] [Pien-wen has been defined recently as a prosimetric script usually recited while an illustrated scroll of a story was displayed. The content was not necessarily Buddhist. See Pai Hua-wen, "What Is '*Pien-wen*'?" trans. Victor H. Mair, *Harvard Journal of Asiastic Studies* 44, no. 2 (Dec. 1984), 493-514.—Trans.]

[11] Hsiang Ta was the first to conduct substantial research on public Buddhist services during the T'ang period (Hsiang, 1934). The services are described in detail by Sun K'ai-ti (Sun, 1937). Sun's research needs some revision in the light of recent discoveries, but his work remains generally useful. The outline that follows is based on Sun's research, with amplifications and revisions taken from work by Lo Tsung-t'ao (Lo, 1972, 872-960).

and laity are represented. The preacher and the lector mount their platforms and seat themselves.[12] The preacher is seated to the right of the principal cult image, and the lector is seated to its left.

2. Commencement of the Service. Celebrants begin the service by singing Sanskrit verses, followed by psalms in Chinese. The intended effect is to quiet the congregation.
3. Introduction of the Topic. The lector intones the title of the scripture to be preached on that day, and the congregation joins in. The preacher explains the significance of the title.
4. Lauds. The glory of the Buddha and the emperor's consummate virtue are praised, and the congregation is pronounced to be a righteous gathering. Lauds may be repeated or be followed by a confession of sin.
5. Explication of the Scripture. The lector chants a short section from the sutra reading for the day. The section is explicated and amplified (through allusions to history, legend, anecdotes, and the like) by the preacher. The procedure of recitation, explication, and amplification is repeated until the reading for the day has been explained. The preacher's discourse is essentially a speech in plain prose, accompanied by chanted psalms and possibly enlivened by pictorial illustrations. The same preacher was generally charged with both the explication and the chanting of psalms.
6. Benediction. The Hymn to Amitābha is chanted by celebrants and congregation. Prayers are intoned asking that the sponsor of the service be blessed by the Buddha's benevolence and that this benevolence be extended to all sentient beings.
7. Dismissal. The congregation withdraws, and the celebrating clergy—the preacher, lector, and attendant monks—prostrate themselves before the main cult image.

"Chuan-pien" is another term used to designate the preacher's explications and general applications. His text would follow the pien-wen form. Documents called piao-pai (J. hyōbyaku) were recited at the service. "Piao-pai" signifies a variety of texts, including lauds, the confession, prayers on behalf of the sponsor, and prayers for all sentient beings; hence the term is used in a more general sense than the Japanese equivalent, "hyōbyaku," which refers solely to the sponsor's statement of purpose in commissioning the service.

The Japanese monk Ennin (794-864) attended public Buddhist services during his stay in T'ang China, and he mentions them in his *Nittō Guhō*

[12] The term "fa-shih" is used in a special sense to designate the preacher at a public Buddhist service. He was also called "tso-chu." The lector was charged with reading the sutra passage appointed for that day. He was known as the "tu-chiang" or "tu-kung."

Junrei Kōki (Record of a Pilgrimage to China in Search of the Dharma).[13] Ennin's accounts of such services indicate that they conformed to the procedure outlined above. In all likelihood, Ennin and the Japanese monks who came after him to study in China introduced the practice of the public Buddhist service to Japan on their return. The service apparently evolved into the ceremony described in the *Hossokushū*. Ennin's entries do not mention the Chinese practice of dividing the liturgy into sung and spoken parts; we may nevertheless assume that this feature too was transmitted to Japan. Its origin apparently lies in Indian Buddhist services, in which a text was first spoken and then repeated as a chant. Chinese Buddhists incorporated the practice into their services; from there, it was brought to Japan. The concept of including both sung and spoken sections in a Buddhist service took on great literary significance in the thirteenth century. Its impact on the development of nō drama and heikyoku [the recitation of passages from *The Tale of the Heike*] will be discussed later.

Public Buddhist services contributed significantly to the development of Japanese literature in another way: by generating, transmitting, and disseminating setsuwa. It was noted earlier that the most interesting part of a service, from the viewpoint of the congregation, was that part of the sermon in which the preacher explained his scriptural text by means of practical applications. Chinese and Indian congregations probably responded similarly. The ancient, rich storytelling tradition of India is reflected in its Buddhist canon, which gave rise in turn to a large number of popular stories centered around Buddhist themes. These stories became virtually indispensable elements of Six Dynasties and T'ang Buddhist services. A Buddhist story essentially retells something from the Buddhist canon in simple language. Later stories are based on Buddhist-connected events in China; still later stories deal with secular matters. Even a secular subject was considered potential material for a sermon, so long as it might be interpreted as a Buddhist allegory or as a vehicle for making a moral or religious point. Secular stories on light subjects were easily lost in the course of oral transmission; but if a story was thought important for the propagation of Buddhism, it would immediately be prized. It would be transmitted with few variants and might even be written down. The stories compiled in the *Ming-pao Chi* and *Fa-hua Hung-tsan Chuan* demonstrate the T'ang view that light stories were to be transcribed with no stinting of labor or expense, so long as they served the Buddhist cause.[14]

[13] *Nittō Guhō Junrei Kōki*, 3:120-22.

[14] The *Ming-pao Chi* was compiled by T'ang Lin (600-59). Although it has long been nonextant in China, several ancient manuscript copies survive in Japan. The *Fa-hua Hung-tsan Chuan*, in ten fascicles, was compiled by Hui-hsiang during the T'ang period. It is a collection of exemplary tales about people who performed one of eight virtuous acts in

A similar phenomenon occurred in Japan. The earliest Japanese setsuwa collection, *Nihon Ryōiki* [ca. 823; see vol. one, ch. 11], was compiled by a Buddhist monk, Keikai, and its content stresses karmic retribution. Keikai probably believed that his compiling the *Nihon Ryōiki* would help to propagate Buddhism. This does not mean that the collection was linked directly to contemporary Buddhist sermons. Even staunch Buddhist discourses like Yoshishige Yasutane's (934?-97) *Nihon Ōjō Gokuraku Ki (Japanese Accounts of Birth in Paradise)* and Minamoto Tamenori's (d. 1013) *Sambōe (The Three Jewels)* were not considered particularly apt works to mine for sermons. On the other hand, the popularity of public Buddhist services in Japan led to a belief that Buddhist-related stories were worth transcribing. Moreover, the stories told in the course of sermons were a vital ingredient of setsuwa collections.

Once Buddhist setsuwa began to be written down, interest in the stories increased, and several setsuwa collections appeared. Their number began to increase rapidly by the twelfth century. Setsuwa collections can be divided into two general categories: those focusing on Buddhist stories and those concentrating on secular tales. Secular setsuwa collections contain both tales of everyday, ordinary matters and fantastic tales. Twelfth-century Buddhist setsuwa collections include *Shūi Ōjōden*, by Miyoshi Tameyasu (1049-1139), as well as *Jizō Bosatsu Reigenki* and *Uchigiki Shū*.[15] Secular setsuwa collections may be compared to other twelfth-century collections, especially the *Gōdanshō*, the *Chūgaishō (Notes on Matters Inside and Outside the Capital)*, and *Fukegatari (Lord Fuke's Stories)*. The latter group draws on anecdotes about aristocratic society and focuses on matters familiar to potential readers. By contrast, one secular setsuwa collection, *Kohon Setsuwa Shū*, consists chiefly of tales situated in a time and place removed from our everyday world. The two groups are very different in nature. The *Konjaku Monogatari Shū (Tales of Times Now Past)* includes a wide variety of setsuwa, both Buddhist and secular. This great setsuwa compendium reflects a growing critical belief that tales of any kind are worth putting down in writing.

Even the eclectic *Tales of Times Now Past*, however, begins with Indian tales on exclusively Buddhist themes. Precedence is given to Buddhist

---

connection with the *Lotus Sūtra*—translating it, preaching about it, copying it, etc. The earliest Japanese copy of the work was made in 1120 by a monk of the temple Tōdaiji in Nara; hence its original would have been brought to Japan before the early twelfth century (Katayose, 1943, 112-14).

[15] *Shūi Ōjōden*, in three fascicles, was compiled in 1123. It concentrates on biographies of eminent clerics. *Jizō Reigenki* was compiled by the monk Jitsuei of the temple Miidera. He is evidently an early- or mid-twelfth-century figure. The text survives in fourteen fascicles rewritten in the High Middle Ages. The original text apparently consisted of three fascicles (thirty-nine tales). The *Uchigiki Shū* is an anonymous work. Only the second half of the text survives, in a manuscript dated ca. 1134; it was probably compiled only slightly earlier.

tales in the collection, a reminder that the critical judgment that setsuwa are worthy of transcription was originally linked to the goal of propagating Buddhism. Buddhist tales also dominate the sections devoted to Chinese and Japanese setsuwa; all the secular tales in these sections are accorded secondary placement. The popularity of Buddhist services, a social phenomenon of the twelfth century, probably inspired the compilation of the massive *Tales of Times Now Past*. The phenomenal popularity of Buddhist services also affected the way that people read and responded to the *Tales*. While praising its Japanese secular stories, modern scholars have produced virtually no impressive studies of the Buddhist stories in this section. The twelfth-century readers of the *Tales* would have regarded the collection differently. Their knowledge of the techniques used to narrate setsuwa during sermons probably enabled them to re-create a storytelling style when they encountered the tales in written form.

Setsuwa were originally intended for aural reception. A storyteller adjusted the narrative style to suit his purposes and taste: he varied tempo and rhythm at will and occasionally embellished his story with gestures and vivid facial expressions. A congregation, enthralled by his masterful presentation, would revel in the strong emotions evoked by the storyteller. To achieve a similar impact through writing and visual reception, an author would have to give substantial consideration to setting, as well as to linguistic nuance, plot development, and characterization. Literary craft is barely distinguishable in *Tales of Times Now Past*, however. Its stories do not have any specific design, a fact indicated by the formulaic manner in which each tale begins ("Ima wa mukashi," "At a time now past") and ends ("to nan kataritsutaetaru to ka ya," "so the tale's been told, and so it's been handed down").[16]

Lack of design may seem like an evasion of literary responsibility on the part of a compiler more interested in preserving stories than in polishing their expression. The truth is otherwise, however. The spare, formulaic style of the stories reflects a belief that the audience of the *Tales*, thoroughly familiar with clerical storytelling techniques, would have been satisfied by the amount of narrative presented in the collection. The remainder of the text could be supplemented by each reader, according to taste. The compiler anticipated a fairly homogeneous readership, one whose familiarity with certain narrative conventions rendered elaborate designs unnecessary. The receptive stance of this readership undoubtedly belongs to the ga sphere. It would be better described as ga-zoku, however, since setsuwa embody a ga aesthetic unlike that associated with shih and waka.

One reason for placing setsuwa literature in the ga-zoku sphere is style:

[16] [These are Marian Ury's translations of the formulas. See Ury, 1979.—Trans.]

setsuwa are written in a style based on Chinese prose.[17] By contrast, Chinese loanwords were not to be used in any but special kinds of waka. Monogatari and nikki, written in Japanese prose, use a fair number of Chinese loanwords. In most cases, however, these words formed part of the writers' daily vocabulary and were probably only vaguely perceived as words of foreign provenance. More importantly, there is a fundamental difference between the prose style found in monogatari and nikki and the style created when Chinese prose is read in Japanese syntactical order. *Tales of Times Now Past* uses many of the idioms customarily employed in converting Chinese prose into an approximation of Japanese. Many Chinese loanwords appear in its text. The style of the tales is zoku, then, since it departs from the ga aesthetic applied to waka and to prose in Japanese. On the other hand, ga is clearly present when a circle of setsuwa cognoscenti responds homogeneously to tales told in the "zoku" style. The ga-zoku designation for setsuwa is derived by combining its zoku style with the ga response accorded setsuwa by its audience.

There is a second reason why setsuwa literature belongs to the ga-zoku sphere: the content is far less specific than that of ga works. Monogatari and nikki, written by people connected with the court, are formal or informal accounts of matters concerned directly or indirectly with court life. Some of these works attempt to portray exotic settings, as is the case with *Hamamatsu Chūnagon Monogatari* (*The Nostalgic Counselor* [see vol. two, ch. 8]). The China depicted there, however, is no more than an image projected by the Japanese court. *Tales of Times Now Past*, on the other hand, presents its readers not only with tales set in China but with stories from the even more remote land of India. Moreover, many of the varied stories in the *Tales* are completely unconnected with Japanese court life. Japanese prose had heretofore been concerned exclusively with court-related subjects; if judged by preexisting literary standards, the *Tales* would appear to be a collection of zoku stories. But when its zoku content is considered together with the special kind of ga described above, the *Tales* becomes a ga-zoku work. Its wide-ranging content could not be expressed adequately in the old court prose style, which relies chiefly on native Japanese vocabulary. This is an excellent example of the enormous expressive potential exhibited by Chinese loanwords. The massive infusion of them into the Japanese language broadened the scope and increased the precision of narrative prose, while performing this feat with unusual speed, taking approximately one century for their incorporation.

A prose style that employs a large proportion of Chinese loanwords will not spread rapidly unless the potential readership adapts itself to the

[17] I define setsuwa literature [as opposed to setsuwa pure and simple] as written setsuwa that were intentionally collected into an anthology. Setsuwa literature can be written in Chinese, "pure" Japanese (wabun), or the mixed style.

new style. In fact, the mixed style made remarkable advances during the twelfth century, apparently as a result of the popularity of public Buddhist services. Their congregations were all-inclusive: both sexes, all social classes, and laity as well as clergy were in attendance. Women, even those from the aristocracy, tended to have little familiarity with Chinese prose and would therefore have had difficulty understanding unfamiliar Chinese loanwords. The lower classes probably found such vocabulary even more bewildering. But the preacher, tutored in the scriptures from boyhood, had to use Chinese loanwords in sermons that were invariably based on sutra passages. Female and lower-class members of a congregation were thus confronted with a great many unknown Chinese loanwords. Of course, repeated use of a given loanword in the course of the sermon would have provided the less educated with contextual referents from which to deduce a meaning. The sermon, after all, was intended as a means of explaining a difficult scriptural text to a general audience. So the preacher probably approached a difficult word or phrase from various directions to help his flock understand its meaning.

This practice created a class of audience that understood and responded to words homogeneously—it created an untraditional ga circle, in other words. Sarugaku and dengaku plays, extremely popular events during the Early Middle Ages, were performed only on rare occasions. Entertainment was a scarce commodity. Public Buddhist services provided the people with one form of entertainment during this period.[18] Buddhist temples, open to the public for such services, became rather like city colleges where people learned new Chinese loanwords and characters in the course of being entertained. Without the sustaining presence of these "city colleges," *Tales of Times Now Past* might never have come into being.

Ga and Zoku in Setsuwa

In China, most of the surviving pien-wen tales have Buddhist subjects. Typical examples include the "Miao-fa Lien-hua-ching Chiang-ching-wen" ("Stories from the *Lotus Sūtra*"), the "Ta-Mu-kan-lien Ming-chien Chiu-mu Pien-wen" ("How the Great Maudgalyāyana Rescued His Mother from Hell"), and "Ti-yü Pien-wen" ("Tales of Damnation"). But some pien-wen are concerned with secular matters, as, for example, "Wu

[18] Sei Shōnagon's famous comment that "a preacher should be handsome" (*Makura no Sōshi*, dan 33:73-74) suggests that noblewomen thought of Buddhist services as a form of entertainment. Preachers also seem to have endeavored to entertain their congregations. The *Ōkagami* (6:271) describes the oratory powers of two eminent preachers, Seishō and Seihan. [One example of Seihan's formidable talents is his memorial sermon for a dog. See Helen Craig McCullough, *Ōkagami: The Great Mirror* (Princeton: Princeton University Press, 1980), 231.—Trans.]

Tzu-hsü Pien-wen" ("The Tale of Wu Tzu-hsü"), "Han-chian Wang Ling Pien-wen" ("The Tale of Wang Ling, General of the Han"), and "Wang Chao-chün Pien-wen" ("The Tale of Wang Chao-chün").[19] According to Cheng Chen-to, the secular stories developed when Chinese audiences grew tired of Buddhist tales and demanded something different. Moreover, the secular pien-wen tales are of two kinds: those based on historical fact (such as "The Tale of Wu Tzu-hsü"), and those constructed around current events (as is the case for "Hsi-cheng Chi" ["Subjugation of the Western Barbarians"], also known as "Chang I-ch'ao Pien-wen" ["The Tale of Chang I-ch'ao"], Cheng, 1938, 252-68).[20]

A similar evolution seems to have occurred in twelfth-century Japanese setsuwa. A discussion earlier in this chapter dealt in part with the first twenty chapters of *Tales of Times Now Past*, all of which are devoted to Buddhist subjects. Chapter 21 is nonextant [as are Chapters 8 and 18]; the remaining chapters of the *Tales*, 22 through 31, are secular setsuwa with no overt Buddhist moralizing. One might think it natural that *Tales of Times Now Past*, the first major Japanese collection of setsuwa, would contain both Buddhist and secular tales; but the concept of "balanced" collections is a modern creation. Twelfth-century readers probably perceived the arrangement differently. Secular Japanese setsuwa, like the secular pien-wen tales, are divided into two kinds. The first consists of old stories like "How a Poor Man Left His Wife and How She Became the Wife of the Governor of Settsu" (*Konjaku Monogatari Shū* [=*KMS*], 30 [story 5]:224-26).[21] The second kind involves stories drawn from incidents that occurred shortly before the *Tales* were compiled; an example is "How Minamoto Akiie, Director of the Bureau of Grounds, Took the Lives of Animals" (*KMS*, 29 [story 27]:183-85). The first kind of secular story probably found its way into the *Tales* with little resistance; but the compiler was surely aware that some readers would question the choice of stories from the second group, which tends to contain very quotidian tales indeed.

Minamoto Akiie is known to have been governor of Higo province in

[19] ["Wu Tzu-hsü was a famous warrior and statesman of the late sixth and early fifth centuries B.C. whose biography is the subject of *Shih Chi* 66." Burton Watson, trans., *Records of the Grand Historian of China* (New York: Columbia University Press, 1961), 2:373n.—Trans.] Wang Ling (dates unknown) served Kao Tsu (r. 206-195 B.C.), the founder of the Han dynasty. Wang Chao-chün, a concubine of Emperor Yüan of the Han (r. 48-32 B.C.), is the sad heroine of a story in which she is sent to the frontier to become the bride of the Hsiung-nu king. [Auth., Trans.]

[20] The story is based on accounts of a Chinese campaign against Tibet in 856, during the reign of Hsüan-tsung of the T'ang. Chang I-ch'ao commanded the Chinese forces. [Auth., Trans.]

[21] [For a translation of this story, see Ury, 1979, 192-94.—Trans.] This famous legend also appears in the *Yamato Monogatari* (dan 148), and is the basis for the nō play *Ashikari (The Reed Cutter)*. [Auth., Trans.] [Versions are discussed below.—Ed.]

the Tenth Month of 1106, and his tenure probably lasted for several years during this period (*KMS*, 1, "Kaisetsu," 10). Thus the story of "How Minamoto Akiie . . . Took the Lives of Animals" was written not long after the actual events took place. Why were stories like these—more or less accurate accounts of recent happenings—thought to be worth transcribing? The story of Akiie is not completely unconnected to Buddhism, of course, since its topic is the taking of life, one of the five great Buddhist prohibitions. The nature of Akiie's transgression might have guaranteed the inclusion of the tale, even though its content is not at all Buddhist. But there are other stories in *Tales of Times Now Past* that cannot possibly be construed as Buddhist setsuwa. "How the Vassal of Fujiwara Akiie, Governor of Chikuzen, Displayed Bad Manners" (*KMS*, 28 [story 34]:109-10) is one example.[22] The story tells of Yorikata, a warrior, whose bad table manners ruined his reputation. We should note, however, how the story ends:

> Now, Yoritaka may have been valiant, but he was also childish and unwise. No matter what you may encounter, then, think well and carefully before you act. So the tale's been told, and so it's been handed down. (*KMS*, 28 [story 34]:110)

By itself, the story is merely a tale of failure among the middling classes; but the whole is encompassed by the moral.

Similar matters are recounted in secular anecdotes that cannot be dated. These are in fact the most valued and renowned stories in *Tales of Times Now Past*.[23] They have been praised long and often for their vivid portraits of warriors, commoners, and other members of society whose daily lives were rarely portrayed in monogatari and nikki. Modern readers are invariably struck by the realism and the insight into human character in the secular stories. This is a just response. One modern perspective enables us to discern vital questions raised by the matter of these tales. Yet we should also observe that our perspective differs from that of twelfth-century readers. One sign of this is the moral that appears at the end of virtually every tale.

Consider, for example, the story entitled "How a Monk on Pilgrimage to Ōmine Came to a Village Where Wine Flowed from a Mountain Freshet" (*KMS*, 31 [story 13]:270-72). On his way back from practicing

[22] Fujiwara Akiie is to be distinguished from Minamoto Akiie, the protagonist of the story on taking life. Fujiwara Akiie served as governor of Chikuzen from 1072 to ca. 1080 (*KMS*, suppl. notes, 132). This is another instance of a story based on a historical event that occurred shortly before the compilation of *Konjaku*.

[23] So highly esteemed are they that the *Nihon Koten Bungaku Zenshū* ed. of *Konjaku* (Shōgakukan) omits the section of Indian tales [which deal exclusively with Buddhist subjects], while the *Shinchō Nihon Koten Shūsei* ed. (Shinchōsha) has only the Japanese secular stories.

austerities on sacred Mount Ōmine, a monk loses his way and finds himself at an unknown village. He finds the local spring bubbling with wine instead of water. The villagers move to kill the monk; they tell him that all travelers who wander to the village are killed, so that the secret of the miraculous spring will not be revealed to outsiders. The monk pleads with them to spare his life. He vows on his honor as an ascetic that he will never speak of the matter. The villagers release him, but the monk, a talkative fellow, does indeed tell others about the village. Some sturdy young men who hear his tale decide they can easily take possession of the marvelous wine spring, since the villagers are neither demons nor deities. Arming themselves, they set off for the village with the monk as their guide. None of them returns. The narrator concludes by stating that one must constantly resist the temptation to be indiscreet or to break a promise and that the young men who rushed to the village upon hearing the monk's story were complete fools.

The narrator's opinions are not based on lofty Buddhist precepts or Confucian ethics. They convey instead a worldly wisdom. The commonsensical, practical principles—mundane principles, if you will—on which this homely wisdom is based maintain that certain actions will no doubt yield appropriate results. Although such principles are philosophically humble, they are at once easily understood and applicable to people's lives when glossed by simple morals. Buddhist morality is based on the concept of an elemental, universal Principle, and the morals of the *Tales* seem very lowly indeed by comparison. Yet they are morals all the same. Properly considered, Buddhist morality is an extremely abstruse, subtle subject, whereas the secular stories of the *Tales* present ideals within the grasp of ordinary intellects. The morals of these tales can be summed up simply: try to live a better life. Despite their rudimentary nature, the morals ultimately serve a purpose identical to that of the higher morality propounded by Buddhist scriptures. Both, after all, are intended to aid people in improving themselves. Twelfth-century readers must have read the secular stories in such terms. That perspective is reflected in *Tales of Times Now Past*, a melange of secular and Buddhist setsuwa.

These mundane principles won wide recognition shortly before the beginning of the twelfth century. Opinions based on mundane principles had constituted one of the hallmarks of the *Ōkagami (The Great Mirror)* (see vol. two, ch. 8), and *Tales of Times Now Past* does not differ. This fact leads us to another important matter. Given the recognition of such mundane principles in twelfth-century Japan and their use as standards for action and judgment, it follows that a mutual understanding of such principles existed within that society. If there had been no such understanding, the compiler of *Tales of Times Now Past* could not reasonably have hoped to communicate the point of a story by a short, simple moral.

To create mutual understanding without recourse to elaborate detail may be characterized as ga in matters of behavior. The stimuli of behavioral ga differ from those that elicited mutual responses from members of waka and shih circles. What is more, behavioral ga is linked to a far greater range and variety of phenomena. Nevertheless, both kinds of ga have the same intent: to effect the proper disposition of their charges. The vast range and variety of subjects in the *Tales* signifies zoku in social matters. But ga is present in the readers' shared response, based on preexisting criteria. The combination of the two aesthetic principles produces ga-zoku. Its nature is probably much the same as that of the ga-zoku created for the congregations of public Buddhist services. Medieval congregations, fully cognizant of conventional preaching techniques, could respond easily and positively to sermons presented in a fixed format (as discussed in the first section of this chapter). The compiler of *Tales of Times Now Past* would have included the many secular setsuwa with just such an audience in mind.

On the other hand, not all the secular setsuwa of the *Tales* end with morals. What might that mean? One example is the story recounting "How a Thief Climbed to the Upper Story of Rashō Gate and Saw a Corpse" (*KMS*, 29 [story 18]:169-70).[24] A thief climbs to the second story of the gate in order to conceal himself. He sees a faint light coming from the lattices that enclose the inner room on this floor; upon investigation, he finds that the light comes from a torch placed near the head of a corpse, a young woman. Her hair is being plucked from her head by an old crone. The thief rushes into the room, threatening the crone with his sword, whereupon the old woman explains why she is there with the corpse. The young woman was her mistress; there was no money to pay for the funeral, and so her body has been brought to the gate. The crone is pulling out the young woman's hair for a wig, since she thinks it a shame for such long, lovely tresses to go to waste. After robbing the crone and her dead mistress of their clothing, the thief leaves. The modern writer Akutagawa Ryūnosuke (1892-1927) proved conclusively that this tale could succeed as a short story if given a modern theme.[25]

[24] [For a translation of this story, see Ury, 1979, 183-84. The Rashō Gate (or Rashōmon) was a large, two-story roofed edifice that stood at the southern entrance to the capital.—Trans.]

[25] Akutagawa's short story "Rashōmon" first appeared in *Teikoku Bungaku* (vol. 21, no. 11; Nov. 1915). I refer to the text in *Akutagawa Ryūnosuke Zenshū*, vol. 1 (Iwanami Shoten, Jul. 1977), 127-36. Akutagawa wrote other short stories using material from *Konjaku*, including "Hana" (*Shin Shichō*, Feb. 1916), "Imogayu" (*Shinshōsetsu*, Sept. 1916), "Un" (*Bunshō Sekai*, Jan. 1917), "Chūtō" (*Chūō Kōron*, Apr.-Jul. 1917), "Ōjō Emaki" (*Kokusui*, Apr. 1921), "Kōshoku" (*Kaizō*, Oct. 1921), "Yabu no Naka" (*Shinchō*, Jan. 1922), and "Roku no Miya no Himegimi" (*Hyōgen*, Aug. 1922). He also wrote an essay on the collection, "*Konjaku Monogatari Shū* Kanshō" (Shinchōsha, *Nihon Bungaku Kōza*, 14 [May 1927]: 29-34).

The success of Akutagawa's experiment has motivated others to try similar recastings of secular setsuwa. Although the aim is wholly acceptable, we might keep in mind that twelfth-century readers would probably not have understood or been moved by the modernized versions. The moral may be unstated in the story of the thief and the old woman, but twelfth-century readers were well aware, by the end of the tale, that they were being enjoined to refrain from evil deeds. For the theft that you may commit may make you the victim of a thief more heartless than yourself. The ga-zoku of these setsuwa was so stable an aesthetic that the morals of stories could be left unsaid. Each reader could be counted on to discover a meaning shared by other readers.

Despite their newfound stability, twelfth-century ga-zoku works remained different from shih and waka in their envisioned audience. The large size and unspecific nature of the ga-zoku readership meant that secular setsuwa were generally written in expository fashion. This choice of narrative style may have been related to the medieval preacher's technique of telling stories in an explanatory way during his sermon: by focusing thus on the less educated members of his congregation, the preacher ensured that the entire congregation would comprehend more and respond accordingly.

We may consider a setsuwa mentioned previously in this section, "How a Poor Man Left His Wife and How She Became the Wife of the Governor of Settsu." An earlier version of the story appears in the *Yamato Monogatari* (*Tales of Yamato*; dan 148), where it is called "The Reed Cutter" ("Ashikari"). If the styles of the two stories are compared, however, the *Yamato* version appears to be the later work, because it is told with the newer technique of limited narrative point of view.

The plot of "The Reed Cutter" may be summarized as follows. An impoverished couple decides to part company in the hope that each, acting independently, will find a way to solve their financial difficulties. The woman goes to the capital, where she becomes employed as an attendant in the household of the governor of Settsu. The governor's principal wife dies, and the governor, who has long been fond of the woman, makes her his new principal wife. Unable to forget her first husband, the woman returns to their old home in Naniwa under the pretext of undergoing a purification. There she encounters a miserably poor man selling reeds. The woman recognizes him as her first husband, despite his tragically altered appearance. She gives the man a generous sum for his reeds; meanwhile, he catches a glimpse of the lady through the carriage curtains. Realizing that the lady is his wife, he throws down his reeds and runs away. An attendant is sent after him. The man borrows an inkstone and writing materials from the attendant and writes a waka:

Kimi nakute	Without you by me
Ashikarikeri to	My reed cutter's life is hard,
Omou ni mo	As well I know;
Itodo Naniwa no	But life will now seem even worse
Ura zo sumiuki.	Spent by the Bay of Naniwa.

He asks the attendant to deliver the poem to the woman. She returns in tears to the capital. "The Reed Cutter" in the *Tales of Yamato* version is told from the woman's point of view. Of course, it would be too much to expect "The Reed Cutter" to possess the completely limited point of view found in modern novels. The narrator occasionally enters into the man's feelings, as in this passage:

> Looking through an opening in the carriage curtains, the man saw that the lady resembled his wife. Surprised, he looked more carefully: the face and voice were hers indeed. Then there was her kindness to him—it must be she. How wretched his appearance had grown over the years! Filled with shame, he threw down his reeds and ran away. (*Yamato Monogatari*, dan 148:319)

With this one exception, "The Reed Cutter" is narrated entirely from the woman's point of view, while the man's thoughts are left for the reader to surmise.

By contrast, "How a Poor Man Left His Wife," in *Tales of Times Now Past*, often describes the man's innermost feelings. In this version of the legend, the woman gives the reed cutter a robe with a piece of paper attached to it. A poem from the lady is written on the paper. Reading it, the man thinks, " 'Why, this is my former wife!' How sad and shameful was his destiny, he now realized."[26] The narrator of "The Reed Cutter" had not told the reader what happened to the man once he and his wife decided to separate. Instead, the story was narrated to maximize the woman's sense of shock on discovering her former husband's wretched state.

"How a Poor Man Left His Wife," on the other hand, traces the man's ruin in detail:

> [The woman's] original husband had thought his luck might improve if he were separated from her, but instead he fell on even harder times. In the end he was unable to remain in the capital and in the course of his wanderings went to Settsu Province. He became a mere farmhand whom others hired, [. . .] doing peasants' work, tilling the fields and cutting wood. But he couldn't get used to the idea, couldn't do the work at all. (*KMS*, 30:224-25)[27]

[26] [Ury, 1979, 194.—Trans.]

[27] [Ibid., 192-93. The bracketed phrase has been added to Ury's translation. [. . .] signifies a lacuna in the manuscript.—Trans.]

The description of the man's appearance had been restrained in "The Reed Cutter": "She looked long on the man's face, and saw that it was he." The account in *Tales of Times Now Past* gives a more detailed account:

> Observing him from close by, she knew that it truly was he. He wore a hemp shirt, black with filth and without sleeves, that scarcely reached his knees. A shabby cloth cap covered his head. Earth clung to his face, to his hands and feet: he was utterly filthy. Leeches were sucking at the backs of his knees and his shanks, exposing the raw flesh. Appalled, the governor's lady had one of her people give him food and wine. She examined his face as he squatted in front of her carriage eating and was shocked indeed. (*KMS*, 30:225)[28]

The great stylistic differences displayed by these two versions have less to do with narrative dexterity than with the different audiences at which each story was aimed. Comparison of the counterpart passages suggests that one audience group was expected to be more impressed by the man's downfall if his unfortunate career and appearance were *not* described in detail, whereas the other group of readers was thought to respond most sympathetically when the man's ruined state *was* depicted as meticulously as possible. Works that are orally transmitted and aurally received benefit greatly from minute, concrete narration; compare, for example, Homer's *Iliad* (battle scenes) and *Odyssey* (the Cyclops) and *The Tale of the Heike* (battle scenes).

The narrative hallmarks of *Tales of Times Now Past* do not indicate that it was a source of oral or sermon anecdotes, however. The *Tales* were intended instead to be read by the same sort of people who came to hear public Buddhist sermons. The sermon audience wanted to know how a story was resolved; there was less interest in discovering the general meaning inherent in a given character's situation. The most effective narrative style for the *Tales*, as for the sermon anecdotes, was therefore a detailed, concrete exposition of facts. Because the readers of a setsuwa did not attempt to discover its unstated meaning for themselves, the narrator was entrusted with revealing its general relevance. "How a Poor Man Left His Wife" concludes with the statement: "Everything is reward or retribution for the deeds of our previous lives; it is ignorance that makes one resent one's fate."[29] This doubtless met the expectations of twelfth-century readers.

The audience for a medieval sermon included members of the upper aristocracy, among them intelligent women like Sei Shōnagon. The act of listening to a sermon, however, is a passive process in which the preacher

[28] [Ibid., 193, with minor changes.—Trans.]
[29] [Ibid., 194.—Trans.]

instructs his flock: members of the congregation tend to eschew more active spiritual responses, such as seeking out meanings unelucidated by the preacher. Moreover, the presence of less educated listeners lowers the collective mentality of the entire audience. The twelfth-century Japanese preacher related his facts in detail, placed them in realistic settings, and appended a moral in order to inform and direct his listeners' passive spiritual responses. A similar phenomenon appears in secular setsuwa of the time.

Detailed, concrete narration is a zoku component in the ga-zoku aesthetic. The zoku element in literature possesses endless possibilities and constantly renewable vitality (see vol. one, p. 59). The zoku present in secular setsuwa consequently evokes responses from modern readers, who inhabit a zoku world. The secular setsuwa of the *Tales* are highly esteemed today precisely because of their zoku essence. We should, however, reconsider the standard modern approach to these tales, understanding that their detailed, concrete narrative style is a form of realism and that the realistic depictions are what attracts us. The realism that dominated nineteenth-century Western literature is not necessarily identical to the narrative detail found in medieval Japanese sermons, and yet the zoku component of secular setsuwa remains a vital force. This very vitality is a principal reason why the secular setsuwa of the *Tales*, as retold by Akutagawa, are regarded as masterpieces by readers accustomed to modern realism.

Ga-zoku elements are present throughout the *Tales of Times Now Past*. If we move away from our study of individual tales to consider how the collection is assembled, we will note that the compiler was also attentive to ga aesthetics. The individual stories are arranged according to principles of organization. *Tales of Times Now Past* is now understood to be an ordered, classified collection of setsuwa, thanks largely to Kunisaki Fumimaro's discovery of a pattern of thematic links between any given two contiguous stories. The patterning method present in the *Tales* resembles the principles used to order waka within a collection; it has also been compared to the linking processes of renga.[30]

Chapters 1 through 3 of the *Tales*, for example, contain setsuwa about the life of the Buddha; they are arranged chronologically, from his birth to his entering nirvana. This is equivalent to the principle of progression employed in structuring a waka collection (see vol. two, ch. 7). Of course these three chapters are not wholly devoted to accounts of Shakyamuni; stories of the Buddha are interspersed with tales about his more eminent

[30] Kunisaki, 1962; *KMS*, 2, "Kaisetsu," 11. This introduction includes a section on "Organization and Structure" that details how each story is arranged according to a variety of principles. [The preceding note by the author has been incorporated into the text, with slight revisions and omissions.—Ed.]

disciples. Chapter 3, moreover, begins with two stories featuring the bodhisattva Mañjuśrī; the third through sixth stories tell of Maudgalyāyana, Śāriputra, and other disciples; and the seventh through eleventh stories are about dragons.

Such groupings resemble the categories used to create waka sequences in the royal anthologies. An anthology begins with a sequence on early spring, followed by poems chronicling the gradual progression of the season: waka on young herbs give way to others on greening willows, plum blossoms, cherry blossoms, and so on. Connections between sequences in the *Tales* may be rather subtle. The subject of Story 6 in Chapter 3, "How Śāriputra Ridiculed Ānanda," is unconnected to that in Story 7, "How the New Dragon Defeated the Resident Dragon." Story 6 does mention an ox, however; the connection between Stories 6 and 7 is based on the fact that both the ox and the dragon are animals (*KMS*, 1, "Kaisetsu," 14). For example, three successive stories in *Tales* may mention the following things:

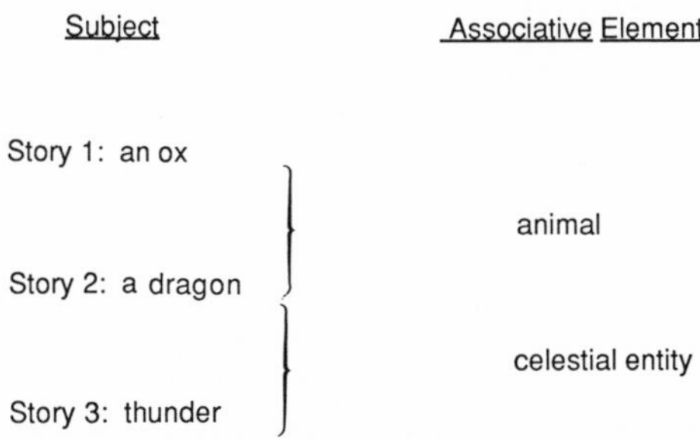

FIGURE 4.1 Association of Subjects in *Tales of Times Now Past*

Thematic links between two successive stories produce an associative focus (Kunisaki, 1962, 1-29), and occasionally three contiguous stories contain common elements.

The stories are, then, arranged according to principles similar to those found in royal waka collections. Perhaps the compiler of the *Tales* chose such a configuration on the assumption that some readers would be sufficiently familiar with waka collections to recognize the principles at work in the *Tales*. Readers with no knowledge of waka collections would remain unaware of the design. The compiler of *Tales of Times Now Past* may thus have expected that certain readers of the entire work would be proficient with ga principles. Twelfth-century compilers were more strongly drawn to the ga aesthetic than their tenth- and eleventh-century counterparts, but—unlike their predecessors—they were also active in pursuit of the various forms of zoku. This phenomenon is equally applicable to the genres of shih, waka, and prose in Chinese or Japanese. The aesthetic interests dominating twelfth-century intellectual life motivated the compiler of the *Tales* to classify the stories according to an acceptable order, as well as to adopt the striking narrative devices used by preachers in their sermons. Clearly, a certain kind of twelfth-century audience valued this ga-zoku approach to literature.

PART TWO

The High Middle Ages: The Michi Ideal

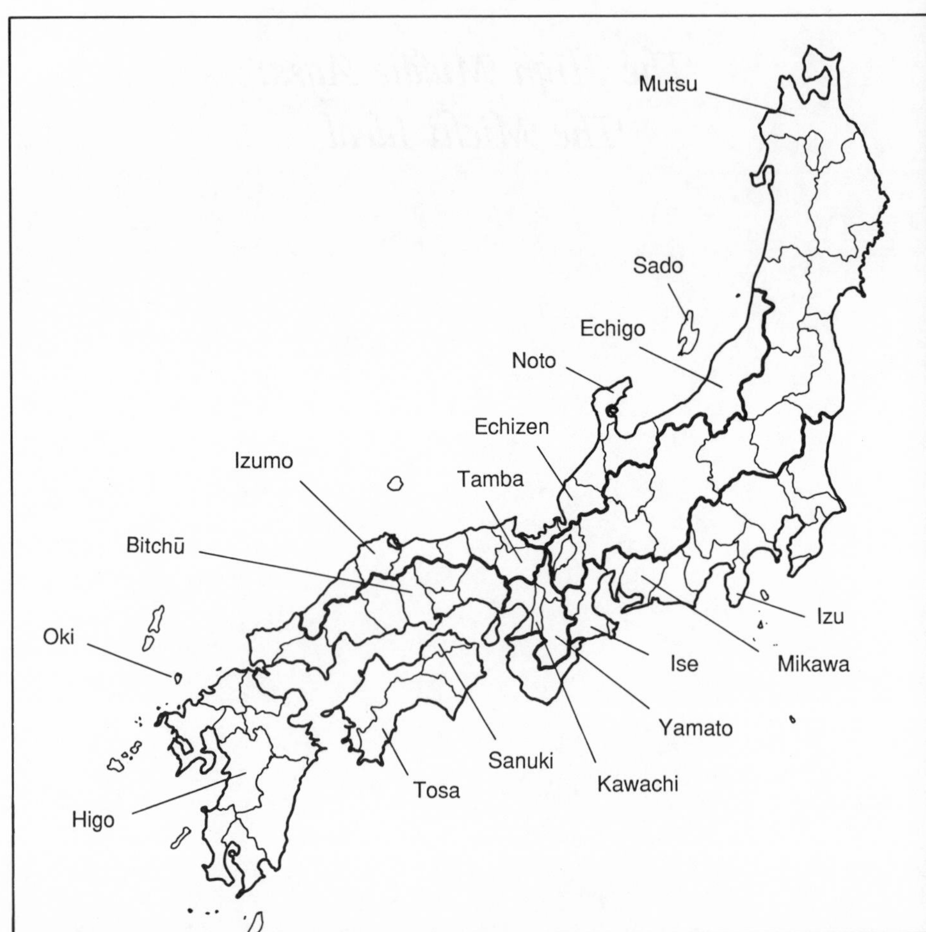

Map 1: Japan in the Middle Ages

CHAPTER 5

The Nature of the High Middle Ages

The twelfth century marks a transitional period in Japanese literature. The High Middle Ages begin with the thirteenth century and end approximately in the late fifteenth century. The sixteenth century is another period of transition. The early seventeenth century represents the beginning of the Late Middle Ages. The symbolic starting point for the High Middle Ages is 1205, the year in which the *Shinkokinshū* was compiled. The Late Middle Ages symbolically begin in 1597 with the establishing of the Keichō Royal Printer.

From Fūryū to Michi

High medieval literature is characterized primarily by its neoclassicism. Classicism seeks its models in the past and strives to attain perfection through close emulation of those models. The Japanese approach to classicism created the sphere of ga, an aesthetic founded on the concept that all members of the literary circle combine the roles of composer and recipient. Pseudoclassicism and neoclassicism are two other ways of approaching the models of the past. Pseudoclassicism faithfully perpetuates the ideals represented by past models and esteems most highly those works that best approximate the model.[1] Neoclassicism also draws on past models, but it enjoins an artist to capture a personal view of the model. Neoclassical works, consequently, are not always faithful to their models.[2]

Neoclassicism and pseudoclassicism existed in the Early Middle Ages. Neoclassicism was still in an immature stage, however, because Japanese

[1] There are various concepts of pseudoclassicism. The French pseudo-classicisme refers to a movement by the inheritors of seventeenth-century French classical literature. The German Pseudoklassizismus, a movement in the latter half of the eighteenth century, preceded true German classicism and endeavored to adopt ancient literary standards. In England, pseudoclassicism designates the eighteenth-century movement that followed in the footsteps of English classicism. My usage follows the more English concept of pseudoclassicism. [As this and the next note show, the view here is German. The English would hold that the Renaissance or humanism was followed in the eighteenth century by neoclassicism or the Augustan.—Ed.]

[2] The Germans refer to their neoclassical movement as Klassizismus rather than Neoklassizismus: they believe that real classicism (in the German sense) signifies imbuing the Greek and Roman classics with the German spirit.

literature did not yet offer the necessary models. Ki no Tsurayuki and his fellow *Kokinshū* compilers shaped a ga aesthetic for waka by focusing on the shared characteristics of Six Dynasties shih and the Japanese concept of "sama" (style, expressive technique). In other words, Tsurayuki's models were Chinese. Tsurayuki's wish—to establish a style of waka drawing on aspects of Six Dynasties poetry—may indeed be termed neoclassical. But we must observe that his chosen model was Chinese poetry rather than the waka of the *Man'yōshū*. This is not to say that the Japanese classical scope should be limited to Japanese works. Both the *Wen Hsüan (Selections of Refined Literature)* and Po Chü-i's poetry collection, the *Po-shih Ch'ang-ch'ing Chi*, were considered classics in Japan up to the nineteenth century. But neoclassicism is not perfected within a country until its own literature is perceived as a source of models. The first waka classic was created when Fujiwara Shunzei declared the *Kokinshū* worthy of deep respect (see ch. 8). It follows that neoclassicism was not yet fully established in the Early Middle Ages.

Classicism requires that a work be patterned on past models. Neoclassicism does the same: "neo-" does not signify a departure from the practice of using past models for inspiration. Japanese neoclassicism, from the thirteenth century on, sought to achieve fresh effect through amplifying preexisting aesthetic images. Fūryū (elegance), an early medieval ideal, is based on the aesthetic principle of en (refined beauty; see vol. two, ch. 5). Another aesthetic ideal, yū (polish), evolved during the twelfth century. Yū was in fact an amplified, more polished version of the earlier en. The absence of major differences between the two ideals enables us to combine them into a single term, yūen (refined charm; see ch. 2).

Refined charm is the keynote of the High Middle Ages. All the principal genres of this period—waka, linked poetry, prose in Japanese, and nō—gradually became more polished according to the standards set by refined charm. Another aesthetic ideal, ethereal beauty (yōen), also commanded the attention of the principal waka poets of the High Middle Ages. Ethereal beauty emphasizes the loveliness to be found in the world of immortals, a loveliness that forms the essence of the early medieval ideal of en. Both new ideals, refined charm and ethereal beauty, thus perpetuate an earlier ideal, en.

They do so by amplifying it. Although the older ideal retained its eminence in high medieval aesthetics, the beauty that appears in compositions from this period—their refined charm and ethereal beauty—in fact surpasses that of en in early medieval literature. The High Middle Ages perceived en as the beauty evoked by a vanished or vanishing world. En was a creation of the fūryū or elegant world, which in turn owed its existence to aristocratic society. The elegant world could exist only so long as aristocratic society remained stable and prosperous.

The heyday of fūryū life coincided with Fujiwara Michinaga's career, gradually fading away thereafter. By the twelfth century, splendor and glory had come to be seen as things of the past. General opinion became incontrovertible fact when political power passed into the hands of the military aristocracy in the late twelfth through the thirteenth centuries. Although Michinaga's glories were now beyond their grasp, the court nobility felt it their duty to emulate the old, elegant life in their own subdued way. They did so by consolidating and emphasizing their authority over the past. One manifestation of an aristocratic turn toward the past is the twelfth-century penchant for compiling old documents. The results ranged from shih and waka collections to compendia of rules and ancient customs.[3] Those who lived according to this attenuated code of elegance tended to idealize and magnify the vanished beauty of the past. Both refined charm and ethereal beauty are ideals signifying an unapproachable, longed-for beauty. Consequently, the beauty communicated by these ideals surpasses that of the early medieval en.

The Early Middle Ages were thought an age of glory by high medieval literati. The glory (eiga) did not encompass the entire early medieval period, however: only one part of it was the object of their longings and encomia: "nakagoro." A term often found in twelfth-century documents, "nakagoro" signifies "an intermediate past," as compared to the distant past ("furuki yo" [ancient times] or "kamitsuyo" [the age of the gods]) or the recent past ("chikaki yo" or "chikagoro"). The concept of an intermediate past being relative, any point in time might conceivably serve as a marker, and anything occurring between the distant and the recent past might reasonably be designated part of that intermediate glory. In fact, however, twelfth-century writers used "nakagoro" most frequently to refer to a period beginning with Daigo's reign (897-930) and ending with that of Ichijō (986-1011). In other words, the intermediate past was thought of as a defined period. Specific dates are difficult to assign to the intermediate period, since perceptions of it varied somewhat in the twelfth century. We would do well to extend the period by fifty years in each direction, so that the intermediate past may commence with Montoku's reign (r. 850-58) and conclude with the reign of Goreizei (r. 1045-68). Twelfth-century usage, however, indicates that the hundred-year period between Daigo's and Ichijō's reigns was considered most typical of

[3] Shih collections compiled in the twelfth century include *Honchō Monzui, Honchō Shoku Monzui, Honchō Reisō*, and *Chōya Gunsai*. The massive *Ruiju Utaawase Maki* is a waka collection. *Shumpishō, Kigoshō, Waka Dōmōshō*, and *Ōgishō* are works on poetics that also include various information about waka. The *Ryōjin Hishō* is a compendium of songs. *Hōsō Ruirin, Gōke Shidai*, and *Untoshō* are compilations of rules and etiquette, and *Konjaku Monogatari Shū* is a setsuwa collection. Works like *Waka Genzaisho Mokuroku* and *Michinori Nyūdō Zōsho Mokuroku* may also reflect the contemporary tendency to compile information from the past.

the glorious era. Its literature is epitomized by the *Kokinshū* and *The Tale of Genji.*

Thirteenth-century and later neoclassical writers modeled their work on the best literature produced during this glorious century. The models remained unchanged up to the middle of the nineteenth century and are still emulated today. One example is the modern Japanese conception of classical grammar. The grammar now termed classical is based on the waka and wabun corpus produced during this hundred-year period; even if we extend the age of glory by fifty years in each direction, the grammatical basis still encompasses a mere two hundred years of literature.

Literary style always followed the foremost works of the age of glory. Writers opposed to classicism did not reject these works; instead, they set up other works from the same period as their models. Such perceptions were nonexistent in the Early Middle Ages, because Chinese literature was then considered to be the sole source of the classics. The concept of classics existing within Japanese literature was established during the High Middle Ages. Twelfth-century aristocrats longed for the glorious century or two delineated above, because that period marked the apogee of elegant aristocratic life. It was also the classical age of composition and reception; this applies only to waka and prose in Japanese, however. None of the prose and poetry written in Chinese during the age of glory is worthy to be called a classic. After the twelfth century, consequently, Japanese literature written in Chinese produced nothing equivalent to neoclassicism.

Neoclassicism was clearly the preeminent literary movement from the thirteenth century on. The significance of all other contemporary literary movements might therefore logically depend on their relation to neoclassicism. One style of high medieval literature defies such pigeonholing, however: this was the anticlassical style, highly esteemed in the High Middle Ages. The highly valued *Maigetsushō*, a waka treatise from this period, predictably stresses the various expressive forms associated with refined charm and ethereal beauty. But it also observes that the poet who has mastered these techniques may experiment with the "demon-quelling" style—coarse expression usually avoided in waka (p. 394). It does not endorse the use of coarse expression: it is deemed permissible, but it is not recommended. Yet the poet-monk Kōben (1173-1232) filled his informal waka with diction so unrestrained that the ordinary poetic standards of his day could not possibly deal with it (pp. 266-67). Fujiwara Tamekanu (1254-1332) made similar experiments (pp. 271-73). Zeami (1363-1443) emphasizes an actor's attaining profundity (yūgen) in his art (profundity signifies refined charm for Zeami); but he also states that an actor who has mastered his art will act in a "pure and orthodox style" (zefū) even when he imbues his acting with "improper elements" (hifū; p.

541). Many of Ikkyū Sōjun's (1394-1481) shih also repudiate contemporary critical standards. Tamekanu, Kōben, Zeami, and Ikkyū all maintain that ga expression, centering on refined charm, is essential to their art. Even Ikkyū does not reject ga. Although his shih corpus seems to have been devoted to zoku expression, his poems are predicated on the supposition that a grand ga aesthetic exists. Ikkyū believed that perfect expression could be achieved only at the moment when different or conflicting concepts interact.

Although there was great respect for ga during the High Middle Ages, the kind of expression produced and applauded by literati of this period would have been inconceivable to their early medieval predecessors. The fūryū spirit alone could not provide a basis for understanding and responding to such literature. The High Middle Ages embody a different spirit, created possibly by the adoption of cultural and Buddhist elements from Sung China, a matter of some complexity. During the Early Middle Ages, the culture of Six Dynasties and T'ang China was imported and modified to suit Japanese tastes. Although the Sung dynasty was established by the middle of the tenth century, official cultural exchange between Japan and China had been terminated in 839. Japanese monks interested in studying abroad travelled to China as private individuals aboard merchant ships, but the information and goods they brought back had little effect on Japanese culture. With what seems an improvement in Chinese shipbuilding techniques in the thirteenth century, merchant ships from the continent began to appear more frequently at Japanese ports, and student monks began traveling to China in greater numbers. Thereupon, Sung culture was evidently introduced to Japan rather smoothly.

The advent of Ch'an (J. Zen), the most influential school of Buddhism in Sung China, had a revolutionary impact on high medieval Japanese culture. In addition to their own religious doctrines, Ch'an monks brought Neoconfucianism to Japan (Sansom, 1961, 2:160-63). T'ang and earlier Confucianism was centered on textual explications of the Confucian canon; Neoconfucianism, by contrast, attempted to build a system of metaphysics. The basic concepts and logical approach of Neoconfucianism were drawn largely from Buddhism, perhaps because the Han Chinese do not excel in systemic conceptualization. Ch'an interest in Neoconfucianism stems from this metaphysical connection.

More significantly, the Zen monks of Japan had a deep interest in, and understanding of, Sung literature. Strictly—or formally—speaking, Ch'an frowned on literary pursuits. In fact, however, Ch'an temples produced a great outpouring of prose and poetry during the Sung and Yüan periods. Prose and poetry exchanges between monks were popular means of socializing. Their literary bent was probably strengthened by contact with lay literati like Su Shih (or Su Tung-p'o; 1037-1101), committed men with a considerable knowledge of Ch'an.[4]

The monks probably originated a new literary direction taken during the Sung period: the veneration of the simple (p'u) and the rough or clumsy (cho). "Simple" signifies a lack of design or ornamentation. The trend toward external simplicity is found throughout Sung literature. The ornate beauty characteristic of Late T'ang poetry was eschewed in favor of expressing the thoughts underlying a poem. A potential drawback to this approach was summed up by Ming critics, who found some Sung poetry to be "overly explanatory." Roughness (cho) was an even more influential literary concept. Roughness or clumsiness, ordinarily perceived as a negative quality, was not esteemed prior to the Sung period. The Zen monks of Japan probably experienced some initial shock on learning of "simplicity" and "roughness" as literary ideals. Such concepts were reasonable enough from the Ch'an/Zen perspective, however, and the Japanese monks seem eventually to have propagated them. These anomalous literary ideals, so antithetical to the concept of refined charm, made great advances in Japan during the thirteenth and subsequent centuries. The emissary role played by Zen monks strongly influenced this process.

Non-being (Ch. wu, J. mu), the central concept of Ch'an/Zen, is very difficult to explain. Taoist thought, as recorded in the *Lao Tzu* and the *Chuang Tzu*, occasionally expresses an idea of non-being similar to that signified by "wu." Zen is thus effectively explained by borrowing Lao Tzu's or Chuang Tzu's explanatory methods of philosophical intent. Both Taoist sages in fact stress "simplicity" and "roughness." Lao Tzu denies that wisdom is based on judgment or action. Instead, the true Tao, the way of reason, lies in inaction. Beauty produced by human actions is, then, a sham and an illusion, while true beauty rests in that which people perceive as rough and clumsy.[5] The ideals of simplicity and roughness were adopted in Japan with revolutionary results, not only for literature but for all of high medieval art. Consider the optimum surroundings and accoutrements of the tea ceremony, for example: a plain, pristine hut is preferred to an ornate mansion, and the best tea vessels and equipment evoke natural forms. The atmosphere created by a tea ceremony is described as sabi (desolation) or wabi (misery); taken literally, both words

[4] Tu Sung-pai details how Sung poetry was permeated by Ch'an thought (Tu, 1976, 299-363). The connection between Ch'an and Chinese poetry began in the Middle T'ang period, but that early stage did not affect Japanese literature.

[5] "What is most straight appears to bend; what is most skillful seems rough" (*Lao Tzu* [section 45], 12). Aoki Masaru has discussed the relationship between artistic expression and the ideals of simplicity and roughness (Aoki, 1929, 195-99).

have negative connotations.[6] Their transformation into aesthetic norms was very likely the result of Taoist thought conveyed through the medium of Zen.

Taoism values simplicity and roughness for themselves. The Japanese "desolation" and "misery" therefore differ somewhat from the Taoist ideals, probably because of Zen influence. Desolation (the opposite of superficial splendor) and misery (the opposite of wealth) do not achieve their value through negating or excluding splendor and wealth. In acknowledging and encompassing the value of splendor and wealth, desolation and misery acquire the hidden facets of their opposites. Splendor and wealth, in other words, exist within desolation and misery, but they cannot be seen. The concept is based on the Zen view that all existence, be it humble or magnificent, depends on the same universal, vital principle; thus all beings are considered equal.[7] At the beginning of this *History*, I stated that Japanese literature is characterized by implicitness, a quality opposed to splendor and wealth (see vol. one, pp. 16-17). Implicitness was not developed within a Japanese cultural vacuum, however: it was effected through the medium of a foreign force, Zen.

Excessive emphasis on the aesthetics of desolation and misery might lead us to suppose that implicitness is the sole aesthetic standard of the High Middle Ages. This is an obvious mistake. Refined charm was as respected an aesthetic as desolation and misery during this period. Not only did they coexist, they incorporated parts of each other: refined charm sometimes communicates a sense of quietude, while desolation and misery have a touch of refined charm. The high medieval aesthetic ideal therefore involved a dialectic of opposed ideals. A similar phenomenon appears in Sung art. Sung-dynasty painting, exemplified by the ink paintings of Su Tung-p'o, is monochromatic and rather abstract. Undeniably, these paintings have the same import as does Tung-p'o's poetry: his lofty thoughts are presented in fairly undecorated language. The muted approach, however, is not true for all of Sung art; some painters moved in an opposite direction. Richly decorative, colorful paintings, such as those of Emperor Hui-tsung (r. 1101-26), were also much in vogue at this time. Sung-period shih were not given to opulent expression, but tz'u lyrics have a delicate beauty similar to that evoked by Hui-tsung's paintings. As performed by members of the T'ang-period Singers' Guilds, tz'u were known for their beautiful language (see vol. two, ch. 1). Their

[6] If "sabu" (to be desolate or lonely) is taken to have ambiguous connotations, "wabu"—to be miserable or impoverished—could only have had a negative meaning originally.

[7] This concept first appears in the Tendai doctrine of Ten Worlds Concurrent. Tendai was no longer a major influence in Japanese society after the fourteenth century; thus I treat the concept in connection with Zen, which inherited the doctrine and gave it further amplification (see the next section of this chapter).

lyrics underwent further refinement during the course of the Sung and eventually came to embody delicate, elegant expression. Perhaps in response, shih moved increasingly toward undecorated diction.

In Sung China as in high medieval Japan, splendor and plainness did more than coexist. Sung poetic treatises do not assign value to simplicity and roughness in and of themselves; the poetic ideal was instead perceived as external simplicity or clumsiness enclosing a rich beauty. By the Southern Sung period (1127-1279) this ideal had become generally acknowledged (see ch. 15). There is no mutual opposition or exclusivity between the Japanese concept of refined beauty on the one hand and the stark ideals of misery and desolation on the other: each contains part of the other. Such conceptualization is feasible only when based on the view that all things contain the Buddha-nature, the universal vital principle. To restate this in Zen form, "Dogs also have the Buddha-nature." From all this, we can see that certain aspects of high medieval literature can only be understood in connection with Zen. There is a mapping correspondence between Sung China and high medieval Japan—despite a three-century time difference—in their respective creations: a Ch'an/Zen-mediated movement to attain an aesthetic dimension higher than that of either element in the coexisting beauty and nonbeauty.[8] In this respect the High Middle Ages clearly differ from the early medieval period (which has a similar mapping correspondence to the Six Dynasties and T'ang periods in China). The Early Middle Ages are distinguished from the High Middle Ages for this reason.

The High Middle Ages accord great significance to the ga aesthetic and to emulating models from the past, but they also accord equal status to zoku, an aesthetic without models. This position is founded on strong, conceptually insoluble contradictions. Its existence as an active, unified force depended on its being practiced so intensely as to overwhelm all the contradictions. The hallmark of the High Middle Ages is the concept underlying this practice: michi, or artistic vocation. The complex significance of michi will be explained in the following section.

Michi and Medieval Literature

The Formation of the Michi Ideal

Michi, or artistic vocation, is generally regarded as one of the most significant ideals of the Japanese Middle Ages, but it has not always been well defined. Before examining the interrelationship between medieval lit-

[8] The time difference between the Sung creation of a new aesthetic and its development in Japan would be approximately 340 years, if we base our calculations on the death years of Su Tung-p'o (1101) and Zeami (1443). See vol. one, p. 65.

erature and artistic vocation, I shall investigate the nature and formative process of michi. Artistic vocation consists of the following components: specialization, transmission, a conformist ethic, universality, and authority.[9] These are not parallel elements, nor do they manifest themselves simultaneously. They are best considered, therefore, in order of appearance.

"Michi" originally signified a special skill. For example, "carpenter" is the modern English equivalent for "ki no michi no takumi" (lit. "one skilled in the michi of wood"; *Genji Monogatari* [= *GM*], "Hahakigi," 68). The intended meaning of the phrase is "a technician of carpentry." Another expression from *The Tale of Genji*, "koto fue no michi" ("the michi of zither and flute"; *GM*, "Azumaya," 132), indicates that music was an acknowledged field of specialization. The very presence of specialized fields means that the knowledge or skills necessary to become a specialist can come only from particularly trained individuals. Such people were called "michi no hito," literally "michi people" or "skilled people" (*Utsuho Monogatari* [= *UM*], "Fukiage," Pt. 2:138/541).[10] Specialization is the element most basic to michi, and michi cannot exist without it. Moreover, the specialization was necessarily one a house transmitted from generation to generation. No matter how outstanding, a line of endeavor that died with its practitioner was not subsequently considered a michi. We should also note that the transmission of michi characteristically took place through units called "ie" ("family," "house," and eventually "school"). Hereditary houses had not always controlled the transmission of specialties. At least in principle, family transmission would have been preceded by transmission from master to disciple, a method of instruction still used in Buddhist training. The chief means of transmission was nevertheless via the house unit, as is illustrated by a famous maxim: "One is not human until one knows a skill; a family is not a family until it transmits tradition" (*Soga*, Daisenji manuscript, 8:210).[11]

To agree that michi is found in the act of transmission is to assume the presence of already existing material: michi is rooted in retrospectivity. The condition is not limited to michi, however. Throughout the Middle Ages, the past was mined as the proper locus of ga models. What is truly characteristic of michi is its intensely restrictive focus. Michi required that transmission from earlier ages communicate a conformist ethic to future generations, so that a transmission might be received exactly as it was handed down. Today people assume that an individual's specialized

[9] Initially I defined michi in terms of specialization, universality, transmission, restriction, and practicality (Konishi, 1956b, 15-24); these were later revised (Konishi, 1975a, 13-15).

[10] "Michi no hito" refers to a specialist in Chinese studies (kangaku) in the *Utsuho* passage cited here.

[11] The maxim is quoted by both Zeami (*Kaden*, 7:65) and Shinkei (*Sasamegoto*, sue:194).

knowledge or skills will improve if creativity is given free rein. This is not an incorrect belief, but neither is it the only truth.

The denial of creativity also yields improvement, albeit of a different kind. Anyone who undergoes training in nō drama, for example, will find that performance is deemed competent only when it conforms precisely to that of the teacher. A student whose performance deviates even minutely from the teacher's will be considered a novice practitioner of nō. True, many of the nō actors instructed in this fashion produce trite, stereotyped performances; but a master actor whose skills have been tempered by such training has an individuality far stronger than that of any actor whose creativity has been freely exercised since youth. The master actor performs with a freshness that makes even the most seasoned nō devotee feel, "This is the first performance I have seen!"

The conformist ethic, which was of course linked to the perception of "houses," had a negative side as well: it led to the practice of secret, orally transmitted traditions. But even this closed system had its positive features. Medieval students and masters did not perceive the system as a means of fettering creativity: rather, it signified the strict denial of one's own insignificant ideas in order to attain a higher dimension of freedom.

Until fairly recently, Japan claimed many recognized proficients in the medieval arts. They belonged to various artistic spheres—nō or calligraphy, for example—but all shared one trait, so far as I know. Although each adhered faithfully to traditional form, none gave the slightest impression of being bound by that form. In other words, various kinds of artists, each highly accomplished in a certain field, seem always to have attained proficiency under similar circumstances—and this despite a total ignorance of any field except their own. The specialization or concentration that characterizes michi, a seemingly closed concept, gives it a higher significance, a universality applicable to all artistic fields. My intent here is not to state my own experience of this truth, for it has been well known since antiquity. My experience is only one more instance confirming its validity.

A field of expertise may be widely respected in society (as is waka), or it may be concerned with practical technique (as in equestrian sport), or it may be a game (like chess). Yet all are michi and as such possess a universality as advanced achievement. Yoshida Kenkō (ca. 1283-ca. 1352) believed that a master of even the humblest skill—such as tree climbing—will experience truths identical to those realized by masters of more artistic spheres, and his pronouncements will necessarily be apposite to society in general. Thus Kenkō remarks of a master tree climber, "This man belonged to the lowest class, but his behavior was in perfect accord with the precepts of the sages" (*Tzurezuregusa*, dan 109:167).[12]

[12] [The translation is from Keene, 1967, 93.—Trans.]

Universality is vital to artistic vocation, and concentrated specialization in a given art is not true michi unless the practitioner ultimately attains universal truth.[13]

According to this view, although some specialized arts prove to be of little use to society, complete mastery of even a trivial pastime can yield truths like those found in more highly respected kinds of specialization. All expertise therefore possesses a common authority, artistic vocation. The extremely rigorous practice and training demanded of students of a given michi surely stemmed from the authority inherent in artistic vocation. We can perhaps respond sympathetically to the setsuwa of a man who sacrifices years of his life in return for composing a single superlative waka, because his specialization is a premier art.[14] Modern readers may be caught between wonder and scorn, however, when confronted with another medieval story: a man is willing to die if he can first excel at horsemanship, a mere utilitarian diversion.[15]

Specialization apparently existed in embryonic form during or prior to the Ancient Age. When the god Hōri persecutes his older brother, the latter shows his submission by vowing that he and all his descendants will serve Hōri as his "wazaoki."[16] The wazaoki was evidently an occupational group, related by blood, that performed an art similar to mime. Here, perhaps, is an early awareness of something approximating specialization. The older brother's promise to have his descendants serve Hōri as wazaoki performers also signifies that this specialized art included transmission.

The specialization and transmission operative at this stage were not elements of michi, however, because they were not yet linked to authority. Becoming a wazaoki was a sign of submission. The art of wazaoki was thus practiced by people of the lowest social class. In China, the wives and daughters of captives were usually assigned to the performing staff of the Music Bureau; professional singers (kwandae) in Korea were also of lowly origin.[17] Relegating professional musicians and actors to the

[13] Attaining universal truth through specialization is also a goal of natural science. The natural scientist differs from the "michi person" in two respects, however: (1) michi, a strongly ethical ideal, maintains that its truths elevate and perfect individual human character; and (2) the "michi person" grasps truth through immediate experience rather than through induction based on protracted research.

[14] Yorizane, a minor official of the Left Gate Guards, prays to the god of Sumiyoshi, "If I compose a waka that makes me famous, I will give you five years of my life." The god enables him to compose a masterpiece, and in return Yorizane dies five years before his time (*Imakagami*, 10:368-69). The anecdote reflects the contemporary belief that a superlative waka was worth part of one's life.

[15] Suketomo of Shimotsuke, eager to win a horse race, commissions incantations on his own behalf. They are performed on the condition that he be willing to forfeit his life. Suketomo wins the race, and thereupon dies (*Chomonjū*, 15:385). There are several other setsuwa in this vein.

[16] *Jindaiki*, 2:183-84.

[17] Kishibe, 1960, 190-93; Kim T., 1974, 209-10. See vol. two, ch. 2.

plebeian or lower classes is a phenomenon common to East Asia from antiquity. Japan was no exception. Under such circumstances, specialization and transmission could not possibly evolve into artistic vocation. Certain tasks were performed by specific families on a hereditary basis in ancient Japan. The Nakatomi and Imbe clans, for example, were entrusted with performing Shinto ceremonies.[18] There are several other instances of families (J. be) engaging in specific occupations, including the Storytellers (Kataribe), the Interpreters (Osabe), the Potters (Hajibe), and the Saddlemakers (Kuratsukuribe).

The first step toward capturing social respect for transmitted professional occupations is to have one such occupation be admired. Kangaku, scholarship along Chinese lines, was the first transmitted profession to achieve this status. The Japanese Court School (Daigaku), patterned along T'ang Chinese lines, focused on specialized curricula: Confucianism (Myōgyōdō), Law (Myōhōdō), History (Kidendō, later Monjōdō, a more or less literary curriculum for court secretaries and other officials), and Mathematics (Sandō). The suffix "dō" [the Sino-Japanese reading of the character for "michi"] in the curricular titles signifies the sphere of a given specialization, which might or might not be identified with the michi ideal. Divided though it was into specialized spheres, kangaku was perceived in toto as a highly valuable pursuit. This perception was an early factor in forming the medieval ideal of artistic vocation.

The link between specialization and transmission was also strengthened by assigning value to kangaku studies. The Sugawara, Kiyowara, and Ōe families, all acknowledged specialists, instructed students in the same kind of knowledge, but the content of each family's transmission was distinctly, if subtly, different. These nearly imperceptible differences, which emphasized the value of the specialization monopolized by a given family, came to acquire great significance. Today, a scholar whose findings are superior to those of others will explain why his findings are better. A medieval kangaku scholar, on the other hand, would wish to give his school greater authority by putting his superior findings under its exclusive control. Okototen, a code consisting of specially placed marks (whether dots or short lines) surrounding a given Chinese character, were employed in making interlinear notes during lectures on Chinese works (see vol. two).[19] Each school used a different code as its marking system. As secrecy became more vital to medieval scholarship, students were forbidden to reveal the teachings of their school to outsiders. This closed

[18] ["Imbe" means "Family of worshippers."—Trans.]

[19] The okototen system was apparently invented by monks. Each major temple had its own marking code. The Confucian scholarly families seem to have followed the ecclesiastical example: the Sugawara and the Ōe each had a characteristic marking code, known respectively as Kanketen ("the Sugawara family code") and Gōketen ("the Ōe family code").

system is the source of a high medieval institution, the secret oral tradition. A more significant development is an awareness of the conformist ethic: both instructor and pupil were expected to follow a teaching faithfully, because it had been transmitted to them in exactly that form from ancient times.

If specialization, transmission, and the conformistic ethic had embraced other, less respected spheres at this point, the formative stage of the michi ideal would have been soon to follow. But this had yet to occur. One more element was needed to establish the concept that the lowliest sphere is ultimately as valuable as kangaku. That element is universality, the cosmic view that an all-encompassing, universal truth dwells in even the tiniest, humblest of entities. Once this stage was attained, the specialized occupation gained an entirely different kind of authority. The formative order of the components of michi was specialization, transmission, a conformistic ethic, and universality. Specialization, the most basic element, was joined through derivation or accretion by successive elements and gained in authority with each stage. The formative process can be shown in a diagram.

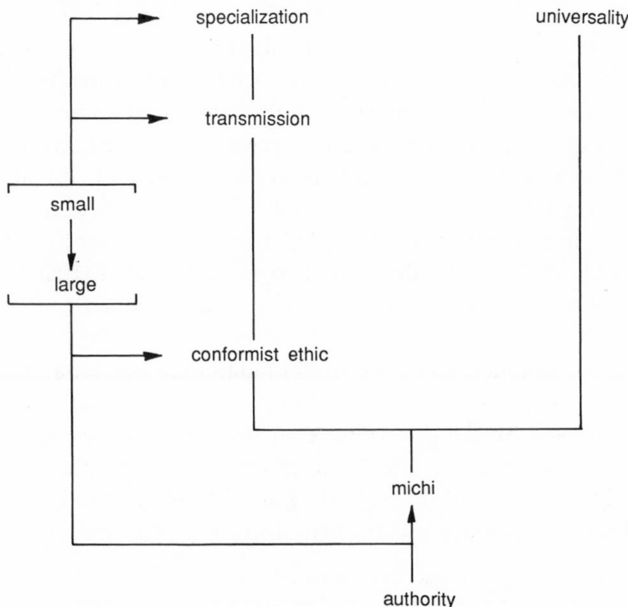

FIGURE 5.1 The Formative Process of the Michi Ideal

No single element alone comprises michi. Michi becomes an operative concept only when all the above elements are considered together.

The Background for Michi

The medieval concept of michi was slow to develop, despite an ancient tradition of transmitting specializations within specific families or occupational kinship groups. The prominence of Sinified ideas in noble society may account for the tardy development of michi as a concept. A governing principle in the Chinese bureaucracy was that literati should have a broad range of knowledge. Specialized work, consequently, was not respected, and those performing it belonged to social classes beneath that of the literati.[20] Once a similar perception had come to dominate Japanese attitudes, specialists probably had difficulty summoning up a life-or-death passion for their chosen vocation.

The sole exception was kangaku, the study of the Chinese literati curriculum: the Confucian classics (ching), the Philosophers (tzu), the Histories (shih), and the Anthologies (chi). The importance accorded these subjects in China convinced Japanese noblemen that they should be approached with respect. The *Utsuho Monogatari* (*The Hollow Tree*, mid-tenth-century?) gives a candid portrayal of a Court School student with the Sinified name Tō Ei, a diligent worker despite crushing poverty ("Matsuri no Tsukai," 110/431-114/447), who nevertheless was accorded respect because of his knowledge. This fictional account may well reflect tenth-century reality. Aristocratic society in early medieval Japan differed from its Chinese counterpart in the absence of a connection between education and high government service. A Chinese literatus might win appointment to ministerial rank upon passing the higher civil service examination, whereas family status usually determined the bureaucratic careers of the high Japanese nobility.[21] Consequently, the sons of powerful families displayed little dedication to the Chinese curriculum. The Court School professors who appear in *The Tale of Genji* are very nearly caricatures ("Otome," 278-80).

Kangaku commanded less authority in Japan than in China. What authority it possessed in Japan weakened in direct proportion to the degree of success enjoyed by the governing system known as the Fujiwara regency (ca. 858-ca. 1158), in which learning was no qualification. Yet the minor nobility of this period was well aware that an acknowledged command of kangaku could be instrumental in obtaining one of a limited

[20] See vol. two, ch. 3, and vol. one, General Introduction.

[21] From their debut as government officials, sons of powerful houses were treated preferentially, in keeping with their family standing. They began their careers with a higher official rank than that of the average appointee. This practice was called "on'i," "ranking by indebtedness" (i.e., obligation felt toward the young appointee's influential forebears). Professional advancement in later life was also frequently determined by family status. [These matters are important throughout the *Genji Monogatari*, where "names" are commonly titles that alter in the course of the story.—Ed.]

number of good government posts. Moreover, Japanese intellectuals of all ranks were devoted to kangaku; thus Tō Ei and his kind, middle- and low-ranking nobles specializing in Chinese curricula, were granted considerable respect and social standing. The Sugawara and Ōe families established themselves as kangaku schools under just such circumstances.

After Chinese studies, waka was no doubt the next specialized pursuit to gain esteem. Thanks to the extraordinary efforts of Ki no Tsurayuki (d. 945) and his circle, waka attained a literary position equivalent to that of Chinese poetry. This must have taken considerable time, however, since waka schools do not appear before the end of the twelfth century. Naturally Tsurayuki and his colleagues regarded waka as a worthy specialized activity, but their opinion was not generally held. The high nobility of the time seem to have regarded even a poet of Tsurayuki's genius as a purveyor of poetry, someone who could be counted on to write good-quality waka for folding screens and deliver them promptly. Sone no Yoshitada (fl. ca. 985), a somewhat later figure, considered himself the best waka poet of his day and felt that no poetic gathering worthy of the name should be without him. He invited himself to one such affair only to find that it was closed to people of his relatively low status. He was ejected and thoroughly humiliated (see vol. two, ch. 7). If michi had been an operative ideal at this time, low-ranking waka poets would have been welcomed at formal gatherings.

This situation began to change in the twelfth century. Two noblemen of middling rank, Minamoto Shunrai and Fujiwara Mototoshi, were leading figures of twelfth-century waka and were constantly invited to waka gatherings given by members of the high nobility. We should recall here that Fujiwara Shunzei was one of Mototoshi's pupils (*Mumyōshō*, 56). By the twelfth century, in other words, transmission through "houses" consisting exclusively of blood relatives had been supplemented by transmission from master to pupil. At this point Fujiwara Akisuke's waka "house," the Rokujō, became a true school (see chs. 2, 8). Not long afterwards, Shunzei's Mikohidari school began to evolve into the dominant waka "house" (see ibid.). The establishment of the michi ideal was close at hand.

Other arts besides the authoritative kangaku and waka were perceived as worthy occupations in the twelfth century. The *Kokon Chomonjū*, a setsuwa collection compiled in 1254, has sections on music, divination, military arts, equestrian skills, kickball, and graphic arts. The arts are described as remarkable when practiced by masters and adepts, whose training demanded enormous sacrifice before yielding a command of marvelous skills. These sections reflect a contemporary esteem for any skill possessing excellent practitioners. Many of the masters and adepts who appear in these setsuwa, moreover, lived during the twelfth century. A general respect for all kinds of art may thus have evolved by this period.

Although the esteem did not come entirely from the lower classes, they would have been the segments of society most likely to benefit from specialization. Unable to rise in rank like the nobility, the lower classes could gain glory for themselves only through specializing in a vocation. But the most exalted members of society also respected specialization. From his youth, no less a personage than the cloistered sovereign Goshirakawa (1127-92) labored to master the popular songs known as imayō, so that he might transmit the proper performance method to future generations.[22] His efforts are understandable only when we realize that they originate in an esteem for the act of specialized artistic transmission. Now, the art of imayō was practiced mainly by waterfront prostitutes (asobime) and itinerant female entertainers (kugutsu, kugutsume; see pp. 19-20 above, vol. two, ch. 9). Performing imayō was thus a far more lowly occupation than was instrumental music performance, and yet a cloistered sovereign dedicated himself to the songs.

Goshirakawa's compilation of the *Ryōjin Hishō* (*The Secret Store of Marvelous Song*) is indicative of a growing tendency, beginning in the twelfth century, to codify knowledge transmitted from the past (see p. 141). This trend was further fostered by the contemporary conviction that single-minded pursuit of an art, even one held in low esteem, would lead to personal enlightenment. Goshirakawa wrote his "Unique Instructions in Imayō Performance" (*Ryōjin Hishō*, "Kudenshū," 10:122) because he believed that "when secular literature is transformed [i.e., comprehended in a different way], it too becomes a factor extolling the Dharma and a link to the preaching of the Buddha's Word." Goshirakawa's statement is based on a passage from Po Chü-i's "Postscript to My Loyang Anthology, Presented to the Hsiang-shan Monastery" (Waley, 1949, 200):

> I have long cherished one desire, that the secular literature I have written in this life and the faults occasioned by my wild words and fancy language be transformed, for worlds to come, into a factor extolling the Dharma and a link to the preaching of the Buddha's Word. (*Po-shih Ch'ang-ch'ing Chi*, 71:1764)[23]

[22] "A great many people, men and women both, studied singing with me," writes Goshirakawa, "but all abandoned their study with their art yet imperfected. Now there is no one to succeed me. What a pity that I have no students to whom I might securely transmit my art, despite years of dedication to imayō!" (*Ryōjin Hishō*, "Kudenshū," 10:113). [The *Ryōjin Hishō* originally consisted of ten fascicles of songs and ten containing instructions (kuden) on training and performance technique. Approximately ten percent of the original corpus survives.—Trans.]

[23] [The Sinified Japanese phrase, "kyōgen kigo" (wild words and fancy language) passed into the language, and it was often evoked during the Middle Ages.—Ed.]

The passage also appears in song form in the *Wakan Rōeishū* (*Collection of Japanese and Chinese Songs*, 2:200). Goshirakawa may in fact allude to the song, famous in his day, rather than to Po's own text. The meaning of the former sovereign's statement was probably not affected by the context of Po's "Postscript." Consequently, Goshirakawa's words would have been interpreted as a defense of all linguistic compositions: he advocates preserving even the most frivolous, impious pieces, because all may someday help us to attain the supreme truth of the Dharma. Through rigorous study, Goshirakawa eventually mastered the once plebeian imayō; he was equally untiring in his efforts to communicate a correct performance method to future generations. He may have been motivated by the belief that the singing of imayō was as likely a way to enlightenment as the more conventional practice of reciting the *Lotus Sūtra*.

Practical logic cannot explain why plebeian songs are ultimately identical to the sutras as means of expounding the truth of the Dharma. The concept is explicable, however, in terms of the logic of Tendai Buddhism. Tendai, the preferred school of thought among twelfth-century intellectuals, is characterized by its doctrine of Ten Worlds Concurrent (Jikkai Gogu). "Ten Worlds" refers to the worlds of Hell, Hungry Spirits, Animals, Asuras, Humanity, Celestial Beings, Arhats, the Self-Enlightened, Bodhisattvas, and Buddhas. Each of the Ten Worlds exists independent of the others. An inhabitant of the world of Humanity, for example, might be reborn in the world of Hell or the world of Celestial Beings, depending on conduct during the human life. The human world is, therefore, separate from the other nine worlds. On the other hand, although Tendai acknowledges the mutual exclusivity of the Ten Worlds, it also conceives of each world as simultaneously comprising within itself all other nine worlds. For instance, the world of the Buddhas is not confined to buddhas: since it also comprises the other nine worlds, its buddha-inhabitants can occasionally appear in human form. Conversely, a dog or cat from the world of Animals can become a buddha. Thus a single world is the Ten Worlds, and the Ten Worlds are a hundred worlds. Such logic enables us to find a link between plebeian songs on one plane, and celestial music and the Buddha's teachings on another. Virtuosity in imayō can then be perceived as a path that might lead to birth in the Pure Land.

The doctrine of Ten Worlds Concurrent—that one world is the Ten Worlds, and the Ten Worlds are a hundred worlds—can be reduced to the more general statement that one is many and many are one. In practical application, this logic yields the characteristic Tendai doctrine of Endonkai, the Perfect and Immediate Precept. Hīnayāna Buddhism demands that its religious observe all the precepts determined for their sex: 250 precepts for monks, and 348 for nuns. This is called Gusokukai, the Observance of Multiple Precepts. While not quite so exacting, Mahāyāna Buddhism requires that all the important precepts be observed: these forbid murder, theft, fornication, falsehood, and consumption of alcohol.

The doctrine of the Perfect and the Immediate Precept, first advanced by the founder of Tendai Buddhism, Saichō (767-822), is unique to Japan. It stipulates that the perfect fulfillment of a single precept ensures the fulfillment of all the rest, because they are all contained in the single precept. This reasoning can also be applied to secular arts: by comprehending the innermost meaning of an art, a specialist will also grasp the innermost meaning of all other arts, because they are encompassed within the one. This concept, linking specialization to universality, represents the stage at which the vocation of michi becomes an established ideal.

The twelfth century seems to have possessed the elements necessary to form this medieval ideal of artistic vocation, but it may not have developed the connection between specialization and universality. By the thirteenth century, however, michi was a distinct ideal. The following passages appear in *Shōbō Genzō Zuimonki* (ca. 1235), a record of the teachings of Dōgen, the founder of Sōtō Zen Buddhism.

> Someone born into a certain family and engaging in its profession [michi] should know the necessity to be diligent above all in the family's work. Learning an additional profession, one known to be outside the set scope, is to act in total error. (2:334)

> Rather than people—clerical or lay—pursuing several areas of study without mastering one, each should perfect a single pursuit, becoming so expert in it that it can be performed publicly. How much more does this apply to religious matters: Buddhism has been studied since time began, but never thoroughly. To this day, therefore, our scholarship remains inadequate. Then again, we students of Buddhism are not greatly gifted. One who approaches the vast, sublime subject of Buddhism by studying several aspects at once will fail to understand a single one. Even concentrating on one aspect cannot guarantee its thorough mastery in the space of this life, since one's natural gifts are inherently poor. All must definitely specialize in a single area of study. (2:344)

Dōgen advises that students of Buddhism should concentrate on a single specialty, since they do not have the mental powers to master all the specialized fields within Buddhism. His statement is based on a belief that the innermost meaning of Buddhism is attainable through command of a "single pursuit," a command equivalent to mastering "several aspects." The latter passage is alive with the logic of "one is many and many are one." This logic also applies to the former passage, which forbids someone engaged in "family work" to meddle in michi other than the family specialty. Dōgen's "One who . . . stud[ies] several aspects at once will fail to understand a single one" resembles Kenkō's dictum even in its mode of expression:

> If you are determined to carry out one particular thing, you must not be upset that other things fall through. Nor should you be embarrassed by other people's laughter. A great enterprise is unlikely to be achieved except at the sacrifice of everything else. (*Tsurezuregusa*, dan 188:226)[24]

Zeami also stresses that "one who wishes to excel in the michi of nō must not, above all, practice other arts" (*Kaden*, Preface, 14). Behind the injunction against involvement in other arts is the conviction that persistent pursual of one's own art will result in a revelation of its innermost meaning, one common to all arts. The formation of this belief marks the final phase in the creation of the michi ideal.

Dōgen perfected the ideal of artistic vocation. In the twelfth century, Tendai Buddhism had the potential to develop the concept of michi. A century later, Tendai was in decline, and new, Tendai-derived schools now took the lead. One of these was Zen: its prototype was evidently the Tendai concept of contemplation (shikan), and one of its central tenets was the logic of one as many and many as one. Zen therefore replaced Tendai as the driving force behind the formation of the michi ideal. Unlike the Rinzai branch of Zen, Sōtō has no tradition of kōan [catechetical questions to stimulate enlightenment]. Enlightenment is instead pursued through performing everyday actions—tidying the house and garden in the early morning, gathering firewood or drawing water, eating meals according to strict etiquette. The Sōtō approach is at one with the michi ideal, for michi maintains that the wisdom of sages can be found even in the act of climbing a tree.

The Relation of Michi to Literary Ideals

The ideal of michi, artistic vocation, is obviously important to high medieval literature, although the effect need not be the same in every genre. High medieval literature is characterized by its retrospectivity, subtlety, profundity, and fragmentation.[25] These characteristics are present in force in the ga genres of the High Middle Ages, but they are not easily discerned in the zoku ones. We may nevertheless limit the number of lit-

[24] [Keene, 1967, 161.—Trans. On Zen sects, see Miner-Odagiri-Morrell, 1985:375.—Ed.]

[25] In an earlier article (Konishi, 1953b, 24-25), I termed the second characteristic "microscopic" (bishiteki). Here I call it "subtle" (saishiteki). The opposite concept would be "obvious" or "accentuated" (soshiteki).

erary characteristics to the four given above, since any inquiry into the nature of the High Middle Ages demands that principal attention be given to ga genres (see vol. 1, General Introduction). Moreover, zoku is never incompatible with, or excluded from, literature dominated by the michi ideal, which regards even "wild words and fancy language" as potential manifestations of universal truth.

Retrospectivity—or, more precisely, a retrospective orientation—refers to a composer's constant awareness of the link between present work and preexisting expression. Retrospectivity is most notably present in diction. Fujiwara Teika (1162-1241), for example, writes that waka poets "should employ ancient diction" in their compositions. Teika also makes a more specific requirement, that "waka diction ought not deviate from usage found in the Collections of Three Eras.[26] Exceptions are diction used by great masters and poetry by the ancients that appears in the *Shinkokinshū*. Such usage is equally acceptable" (*Eika Taigai*, 114).[27] Poetic conception and design tended to emulate past forms. Any enterprising person who attempts to read through the last thirteen royal waka anthologies, beginning with the *Shinchokusenshū* (ca. 1235), must be very persevering. Even the freshest and most innovative of the thirteen, the *Gyokuyōshū* (1313) and the *Fūgashū* (1343-49), largely celebrate what was long since set in language and conception. This tends either to bore or enrage modern readers. Before rushing to condemn fourteenth-century tastes, however, we ought first to recall that the poets represented in the last thirteen royal waka anthologies composed verse in set ways because it was considered desirable. Literature conforming to earlier types was esteemed. The set and typical become even more pronounced in renga, linked poetry. It is difficult indeed to find any original concepts or diction in the several thousand surviving renga compositions.[28] The seventeenth-century *Renga Haja Kenshō (Falsehoods Dispelled and Truths Revealed in Linked Poetry)* defines renga as the linking of ordinary stanzas.[29] There is much in common here with the ideas of transmission associated with michi.

Renga demands a typical, set treatment of subject matter as well as the

[26] [The "Collections of Three Eras" (*Sandaishū*) refers to the first three royally commissioned waka anthologies: the *Kokinshū* (ca. 905-20), the *Gosenshū* (951), and the *Shūishū* (ca. 985).—Trans.]

[27] [The *Shinkokinshū* was compiled by Teika, among others, ca. 1201-1206. It includes works by such poets of the Ancient Age as Kakinomoto Hitomaro (fl. ca. 680-700), as well as waka by the compilers and their contemporaries. Teika recommends emulating only the diction used by the former group.—Trans.]

[28] We do not yet have a precise number, research into the subject being incomplete. Well over ten thousand renga compositions survive.

[29] *Renga Haja Kenshō* was written by a linked poetry master named Saijun, of whom nothing is known. The text survives only in a woodblock edition dated 1693. There is no revised edition in movable type.

perpetuation of past concepts and diction. The subject "spring rain" (harusame) is one example. Spring can be a time of heavy rainfall; but in linked poetry, spring rain must always be portrayed as sprinkling silently, gently obscuring the speaker's view. As Yamada Yoshio has shown, this typifying is called the hon'i (essential nature) of spring rain (*Renga Gaisetsu*, 1937, 129-36). Every frequently used renga subject has its own specified hon'i, a practice made possible by limiting renga subjects to those appearing most often in preexisting waka. If there had been no limits set on the number of renga subjects, linked poetry would probably not have developed the idea of essential nature. Hon'i may be defined as a set form for treating an individual topic.

High medieval art is characterized by single compositions consisting of several such set forms. A nō libretto, for example, is made up of several units (shōdan, "small sections"), each with its own modality: the introductory song, the travel song, the entrance song, spoken dialogue, the first choral song, the exchange, the thematic song, the withdrawal of the protagonist (shite) at the end of the first part of the play, and so on, down to the concluding lines.[30] Each section follows a set form within a larger configuration. The music accompanying a nō play also comprises various specific forms, including the ageuta, sageuta, kuri, sashi, and waka.[31] The movements of performers are similarly structured: actors must sing and move according to predetermined forms. It would hardly be exaggerating to say that the nō actor has no formal scope in which to exercise his creativity. These impersonal forms are sustained by the conformist ethic—the idea that the most sublime art emerges only through rigidly observed form.

Twelfth-century writers and poets were clearly interested in following literary precedent. Judgments handed down at waka matches reflect this: the words "familiar usage" and "frequently encountered scenes" are always employed in a positive sense. An example of the retrospective atti-

[30] The brief introductory song (shidai) is performed by the protagonist (shite) and deuteragonist (waki) on entering the stage. After the waki announces his intended destination, he sings the travel song (michiyuki). The entrance song (issei) is performed by the shite as he stands on the bridge leading to the stage. His spoken dialogue (mondō) with the waki concerns the history of the place in which the play is set. The first song performed by the chorus is called "shodō." The exchange (kakeai) is a duet sung by the shite and the waki, in which each states impressions of the circumstances. The chorus sings the thematic song (kuse), during which the shite may dance in time or remain seated at stage center. The withdrawal of the shite from stage at the end of the first part of the play is called "nakairi." [Auth., Trans.]

[31] The ageuta is sung principally at a high pitch and in regular time (i.e., eight beats to twelve syllables). The sageuta is a shorter song, also in regular time, that begins at a medium pitch and ends on a low pitch. The kuri is a high-pitched melody sung to free tempo. The sashi, a kind of recitation, is also sung in free time. Waka (not to be confused with the thirty-one syllable verse form of the same name) is a short song in free tempo, performed by the shite at the end of his dance. [Auth., Trans.]

tude appears in *The Palace Minister's Waka Competition of 1118 (Gen'ei Gannen Naidaijin Ke Utaawase)*. Mototoshi, one of the judges, nominated the following poem by Fujiwara Tamezane (dates unknown) as the winner of round twelve. The topic is "Late Chrysanthemums."

Oku shimo no	If the frost
Nakaramashikaba	Had not settled on their blossoms
Kiku no hana	Would the chrysanthemums
Utsurou iro o	Have changed to lightly faded hues
Kyō mimashi ya wa.	That we wish to see today?

Mototoshi selected this poem because of its last two lines, which contain "fairly familiar usage" (*HCUT*, 6:1769). Another instance, this time connected with a negative judgment, appears in *The Waka Match of the Kamo High Priestess of Rokujō (Rokujō Saiin Ke Utaawase)*. The topic of the round is "Cormorant Fishing on the River" (*HCUT*, 4:994).

Kagaribi no	The fishing flares
Hima shi nakereba	Burn everywhere upon the water—
Yoru shi mo zo	Nighttime though it is,
Ukawa no soko wa	The river where cormorants fish
Kakurezarikeru.	Is illumined to its depths.[32]

The judgment: It is reasonable enough to have a poem in which the reflected light of flares makes the water seem aflame. But flares cannot illuminate the bottom of a river. The poet would be well advised to compose on more frequently encountered scenes.

These judgments follow the criterion that consonance with past literary precedent constitutes beautiful language. Retrospective orientation is not only a high medieval hallmark: it dominates all medieval literature that is based on the ga aesthetic.

Subtlety, another characteristic predating the High Middle Ages, often accompanies retrospective orientation. The single-minded pursuit of frequently used language is not likely to yield fresh impressions or evoke intense emotions, because it contains nothing new. Since freshness is the lifeblood of literature, an absence of freshness can only signify withering and decay. Frequently used expression, therefore, was desirable only if joined by an element of freshness. Freshness was most highly appreciated in nearly imperceptible amounts. The assumption, in other words, was

[32] [Cormorant fishing takes place at night. Flares, contained in iron baskets and suspended over the water from fishing boats, attract the fish, which are caught by tame cormorants. The birds are tethered to lines held by the fishermen. A ring round the cormorant's neck prevents it from swallowing any but the smallest fish.—Trans.]

that both composer and audience were thoroughly acquainted with the kind of language perceived as "frequently used," and were able to respond sensitively to subtle variations in that vocabulary (see vol. two, ch. 3). Just as one can clearly hear the rustle of falling leaves on a still morning, so could people accustomed to composing and receiving set, typical writing distinguish a minute quantity of freshness. Excessively accentuated variations would undoubtedly have annoyed, if not pained, the sensitive recipient. To the uninitiated eye, the most characteristic nō masks—those known as the "young woman," the "Zō," the "Ōmi woman," "Magojirō," and the "girl"—all look like roughly identical masks of young women's faces.[33] How much more difficult it is, then, to distinguish among an ordinary "Zō" mask, a "gnarled Zō," and a "somber Zō"![34] On the other hand, any sensitive person familiar with nō masks will easily perceive the grace of the "young woman" mask, the restraint and elegance of the "Zō," the allure of the "Ōmi woman," the melancholy beauty of "Magojirō," and the amiability of the "girl" mask. Such a person, moreover, would vigorously protest any move to make the grace and elegance of a mask more perceptible by accentuating its expression.

Renga is also grounded on the assumption that its audience will reap abundant significance from certain subtle features. Those who see renga as groups of repetitious, set stanzas must also be unbearably bored by the act of hearing or reading renga, or by watching a nō play, for that matter. In fact, renga audiences consist solely of people able to derive enormous pleasure from discovering the minute innovations in a given stanza. When it is their turn to compose, they refrain as best they can from presenting outstanding stanzas, instead offering ones of scant interest. This is evidence of the affective-expressive attitude: a composer or performer intentionally suppresses what he would ordinarily express because he assumes the audience will at least sense and comprehend what is being suppressed and may comprehend more than what was originally suppressed (see vol. one, General Introduction). Similarly, a nō audience tends to consist of

[33] The "young woman" (wakaonna) mask depicts the face of a woman in her early twenties; its nonspecific beauty makes it adaptable to various roles. The "Zō" mask (named for Zōami, an early fifteenth-century nō actor and mask maker) communicates noble, refined beauty. The "Ōmi woman" (Ōmi onna) mask expresses voluptuous beauty. The "Magojirō" mask is named for Kongō Magojirō, and it communicates a sense of sorrow. The familiar "girl" (ko omote) mask depicts a girl in her late teens, charming and radiant with health. [Auth., Trans.]

[34] The prototype of the "gnarled Zō" (fushiki Zō, in the collection of the Hōshō school of nō) was created by Zōami (see n. 33). It gives a greater sense of warmth and intimacy than that possessed by the more imposing Zō which is used to depict aristocratic ladies and supernatural women, as the "gnarled Zō" is not. The Hōshō school uses the gnarled Zō mask for roles that the Kanze school plays with the "young woman" mask. The "somber Zō" (naki Zō), true to its name, has a graver expression than is found on ordinary Zō masks, and its complexion is paler; it is rarely used. [Auth., Trans.]

people with at least some formal education in practical nō techniques. Anyone lacking such experience will not know when and where the actor displays subtle innovations. Questions of individual proficiency aside, members of a nō audience are, or seem, capable of joining the acting cast. This phenomenon is even clearer in linked poetry. Only those who can compose renga will participate in a renga gathering. We have already seen how the Early Middle Ages are characterized by the practice of audience members doubling as performer-composers (see vol. two, ch. 3; see also above in this chapter). This practice is closely connected to the retrospective view.

The characteristic here termed profundity does not appear until the High Middle Ages, and so its link to michi is stronger than those of retrospectivity and subtlety. "Profundity" derives from the resolve to grasp the essential presence of an object rather than its superficial aspects. This is literary activity performed at a level of deep thought understandable only by similarly deep thought by the reader. Consider the following waka by Teika, from his *Shūi Gusō* ([=*SG*], "Inka Hyakunijūhachishu"):

Haru	*Spring*
Naniwagata	The Bay of Naniwa:
Akeyuku tsuki no	Dawn approaches with the moon
Honobono to	Casting a faint glow
Kasumi zo ukabu	Upon the very haze that floats
Nami no irie no.	Above the waves within the cove.
	(2:1509)

Natsu	*Summer*
Yukinayamu	Straining as it goes,
Ushi no ayumi ni	The bullock's every footstep
Tatsu chiri no	Raises up the dust
Kaze sae atsuki	In the breeze that stirs up hot
Natsu no oguruma.	Summer in my little carriage.
	(2:1525)

Aki	*Autumn*
Tabibito no	The man in travel,
Sode fukikaesu	His sleeves are blown back and forth
Akikaze ni	By the autumn wind
Yūhi sabishiki	When the evening sun turns desolate
Yama no kakehashi.	The hanging bridge between the peaks.
	(2:1535)

Fuyu	*Winter*
Hashitaka no	The windhover's wings
Kaeru shirafu ni	Show, as it returns, white spots
Shimo okite	Where hoarfrost settled;
Onore sabishiki	How the desolation deepens
Ono no shinohara.	Ono and its stand of bamboo grass.[35]
	(2:1555)

A Meiji poet might have read these poems as examples of objective portrayal. But all four were composed on the same day: the eighteenth day of the Ninth Month, 1196. The spring, summer, and winter poems obviously do not describe contemporaneous natural scenes. Neither does the autumn poem—composed at the urban residence of the Palace Minister Gokyōgoku Yoshitsune (1168-1206)—depict a scene before the poet's eyes. And yet these waka exude reality. The meaning of their reality differs from that acquired through our senses and described accordingly. The reality within Teika's four waka leads the reader toward the essence inherent in the phenomenon that forms each poetic subject. Such reality pertains to an unusually deep stratum of awareness.

The approach shown in these poems apparently originated out of esteem for the hon'i of a subject. The practice of composing waka on set topics, which reached its height in the twelfth century, included experimenting in various styles. The poet was chiefly concerned with capturing the essential nature of the topic, its hon'i. The goal was reached by focusing one's mind on the elemental aspects of the topic (see ch. 8). This procedure is identical to Teika's concept of ushin. Teika's principle, which eliminated the distance between subject and poet, maintains that a subject cannot be grasped on a superficial level of thought. Instead, a poet must focus thoughts deep within the mind, where the reality of the subject lies.

Teika's stance differs completely from the witty *Kokinshū* style, in which the poet intentionally shapes the essential nature of a subject. The "profound" stance requires that a poet's own impressions be set aside in order to draw near to the very essence of the subject. Once that essence is obtained, the poet may once again grasp forms reflected in superficial thought. Poetry produced in this fashion communicates a sense of profound mystery to most readers, whereas poetic concepts grasped only on a superficial level are easily understood. The sense of mystery is termed "yūgen." Because Teika's four waka are so descriptive that they might be mistaken for realistic verse, they are perforce difficult to characterize as

[35] [The excellence of these poems (in the original at least) shows that "profundity" could imbue the familiar with fresh beauty and original meaning. Or, it might be said that the author now chooses exceptional poems after describing earlier the more typical thought of the Middle Ages.—Ed.]

yūgen. Nevertheless, contemplative expression generally tends toward yūgen. The process of recapturing the essence of a subject, therefore, has much in common with michi, for the latter ideal links us to formless, universal truth through concrete, specialized work.

Nō drama best characterizes profundity in artistic expression. *Izutsu (The Well-Curb)* is one of the most famous nō plays, but it may be indescribably tedious when viewed at a superficial level of consciousness. Its plot development is practically identical to that of other nō plays with young female protagonists, and it has no intensely dramatic scenes. To be deeply moved by *Izutsu*, a spectator must sense the presence of the moon in the play. The moon is more than a celestial phenomenon. It symbolizes the theme of the play: the purity of a first love. Although the play is based on a story in the *Ise Monogatari* (*Tales of Ise*, ca. 950; dan 23), *Izutsu* does not retain the original plot.[36] The only events acted out in the play are a monk's visit to the ruined temple of Ariwaradera, his encounter with an unearthly woman, and the beautiful dream he has afterwards. The audience first senses the presence of autumn in the plumegrass placed onstage. Then, as the word "moon" (tsuki) is repeated throughout the libretto, the audience begins to feel that moonlight is flooding the world of *Izutsu*. Moonlight is the focal point of the work, the expression of a pure love blossoming in childhood and cherished through adulthood.

We lose sight of *Izutsu* as a nō play, however, when we scrutinize the performance for moonlight as the symbol of purity. To understand that A is a symbol of B is to judge according to superficial levels of consciousness, so that the purity one grasps from "moonlight symbolism" in *Izutsu* evokes shallow emotion, feelings that can be fully expressed in words. But the emotions I experience during a master actor's performance of *Izutsu* baffle my powers to explain and describe. Such emotions are felt only when superficial judgment is stilled and one is absorbed into the performance of the play. Direct experience of the essence of a subject, made without recourse to the medium of intellect, may also spring from a source in common with the michi ideal. In michi, after all, the most familiar, ordinary actions embody universal truth.

The characteristic termed fragmentation, like that of profundity, does not appear until the High Middle Ages. Renga provides an excellent example of fragmentation in literature, but it is also conspicuous in waka beginning with the thirteenth century. Fragmentation—division of a poem into relatively distinct parts—is most clearly discerned in a waka form that reserves its first half for stating emotion, and the second half

[36] The entire *Ise Monogatari* may be characterized as "pristine passion." This is particularly true of the twenty-third episode (see vol. two, ch. 8), on which *Izutsu* is based.

for a description of nature. The poem is in effect broken by the division, as in Jakuren's famous waka:

Sabishisa wa	As for loneliness,
Sono iro to shi mo	To say that it is one color
Nakarikeri	Is impossible:
Maki tatsu yama no	Black pines rise upon the hills
Aki no yūgure.	In the autumn twilight.
	(*Shinkokinshū*, 4:361)

The break in the poem creates a blank, a gap. We might supplement it by explaining how Jakuren expresses loneliness with an autumnal scene: twilight deepens in an evergreen forest in the mountains. When the semantic blank is more pronounced, however, reasoned explanation on a superficial level of thought can do no more than make the poem intelligible. It cannot kindle emotions. Consider this poem by Teika:

Musubikeru	How cruel you are
Chigiri mo tsurashi	To pledge and then withdraw your love.
Aki no no no	In the autumn fields,
Sueba no shimo no	Hoarfrost on the tips of branches
Ariake no kage.	Tinged by moonlight in the dawn.
	(*SG* [supernum. fasc.], 3140)

The lover's reproach must be directly sensed as hoarfrost covering branch tips under a dawn moon. Intellectual comprehension must be suspended in order to achieve this end. The reader is obliged to take a deep contemplative stance toward the essential nature of the subject, just as does the nō spectator who senses the purity of first love in the plumegrass nodding in the moonlight. The connection between fragmentation in literature and the idea of grasping the essence of a subject through contemplation was probably effected at much the same time that universality was added to michi, as was discussed in the first part of this chapter.

CHAPTER 6

The Writing and Reception of Literature

The High Middle Ages may be characterized as a time of growing independence for writers and poets. This liberalizing process began in the twelfth century. Literature had previously belonged exclusively to the ga sphere, in which composers doubled as recipients (see vol. two, ch. 3). By the twelfth century, however, there appear a few writers who do not read others and, even more, literary audiences consisting of people who, lacking the necessary creative powers, wish to read or listen to literature composed by others. Several major factors account for this trend.

The first is the increasingly sophisticated nature of works composed. All medieval arts—calligraphy and music as well as waka, wabun, and prose and poetry in Chinese—required substantial practice before a satisfactory composition or performance could be produced. Anyone who created a highly sophisticated work within a given artistic sphere would have found it extremely difficult to perform equally well in other spheres. The only reasonable course of action for such a person would be to abandon any hope of excelling in more than one activity and, for other artistic activities, to take their place instead among the rest of an audience. As artistic spheres became dominated by virtuosi, the shared circle of composer-recipients began to contract. The twelfth-century reverence for specialization, which effected great accomplishments in every artistic sphere, also marks the beginning of the end for literary amateurs. Their withdrawal from the literary scene was unavoidable in some cases, since other writers intentionally restricted their access to the literary world.

One kind of withdrawal is exemplified in the literature of seclusion written by quasi-monastic recluses. There were various methods of withdrawing from the secular world during the Middle Ages. One was to search earnestly for the truth and concentrate on achieving salvation, an approach recorded in *Ichigon Hōdan*. Secluding oneself from the world could also serve as a means of creating one's ideal life: it has been termed "seclusion for accomplishment's sake," in which one leaves the secular world behind so as to perfect a given accomplishment (Mezaki, 1978, 100-106). Since "accomplishment" denotes a high level of achievement, a person beginning a life of seclusion was unlikely to be "accomplished" in more than a few areas. Kamo no Chōmei's accomplishments lay in waka, the zither, and the lute (*Hōjōki*, 89). Saigyō was an adept at kickball (Horibe, 1943, 445-56), but seems to have focused exclusively on waka after becoming a recluse. Chōmei's and Saigyō's decision to concentrate on their chosen accomplishments did not signal their rejection of all other arts, however. Both men probably had enough cultural background to understand and appreciate arts other than their specialities. The role of composer became separate from that of recipient when writers like Chōmei and Saigyō retained interest in arts they did not practice.

A second factor is the growing number of genres. The increasing esteem for fictional monogatari provides perhaps the most outstanding example. Although prose fiction did not originate as a ga genre, its composition and reception was taken fairly seriously after the appearance of *The Tale of Genji* in the early eleventh century. Several of the ladies attending the Kamo High Priestess of Rokujō were writers of prose narratives who participated in a monogatari match held at the High Priestess' residence (*Rokujō Saiin Monogatari Utaawase*). Since these ladies also formed part of the audience for fiction written by their fellows, a closed circle of fiction writers doubling as recipients was established among the High Priestess' entourage.

Prose fiction truly entered the sphere of ga once waka poets acknowledged the indispensability of the *Genji* to their art.[1] The new respect for fiction also accorded legitimacy to factual monogatari. Jien's (1155-1225) *Gukanshō*, not an especially ga composition, evidently received a serious reading in the thirteenth century. The *Jinnō Shōtōki (A Chronicle of Gods and Sovereigns)* of Kitabatake Chikafusa (1293-1354) is a similar instance. Yoshida Kenkō's *Tsurezuregusa (Essays in Idleness)* marks the appearance of a new genre, the zuihitsu or miscellany. The kikō (travel account) genre is yet another fourteenth-century development. Renga, a ga-zoku diversion during the twelfth century, was elevated in the fourteenth to the status of true ga literature. Several other ga or quasi-ga genres appear during the High Middle Ages. Cultivated people of this period could easily have joined the audience, appreciating any of these genres, but no one could perform as an outstanding composer in all. In this respect, too, the closed circle of composer-recipients becomes less and less dominant.

The participation of new social classes is a third factor. Ga literature had formerly been produced entirely by members of the upper and middle nobility. Lower-ranking nobility and quasi-monastic recluses were admitted to this sphere in the twelfth century. Quasi-monastic recluses differed from traditional monks: the latter group generally entered a great monastery in childhood, received religious training there, and was even-

[1] A statement made by Fujiwara Shunzei (see ch. 2).

tually received formally into the religious community. The recluses were motivated by certain circumstances to become monks in their middle years. They may be characterized as an illegitimate branch of the monastic family tree. The conventional monastic orders drew their members from the upper and middle aristocracy, while reclusive monks had various family backgrounds. Saigyō is an excellent example: before he went into monastic seclusion, he was a professional warrior. Yet these "illegitimate" monks were perceived as equalling the clergy of the great temples in their services to the Buddha. Like their "legitimate" brothers, therefore, reclusive monks had access to members of the upper aristocracy. Their entrée into high society has great significance for Japanese literature.

Another important development was the role played by the warrior class, from the thirteenth century on, in composing and appreciating literature. Even the shōgun Minamoto Sanetomo (1192-1219) could not excel in every literary genre. Imagawa Ryōshun (1326-1417) and Tō no Jōen (1401-94) were far more blessed than Sanetomo with opportunities to broaden their knowledge, but neither made a mark outside the sphere of waka. In every other literary genre, Ryōshun and Jōen were audience members. One of the hallmarks of the High Middle Ages is this gradual disappearance of the closed circle of composer-recipients.

As composer and recipient came to adopt mutually exclusive functions, changes occurred in the reception process itself. One such change was the growing practice of reading native Japanese prose in illustrated format. Another was the development of aural reception with musical accompaniment. Both methods of reception had existed since the tenth century. By the thirteenth, they had gained a firmer footing, and the way in which they did so is characteristic of the High Middle Ages.

Reading illustrated monogatari and setsuwa was not an unusual practice in the tenth and eleventh centuries.[2] An instance appears in a source heretofore unnoted, a forenote in a variant manuscript of the *Yoshinobu Shū*: "Illustrations had been made for *The Story of Sumiyoshi*, and some contained no waka. His Majesty's opinion [. . .] was that these too should have waka. My poems were written in response to the royal request."[3] Some of the waka in the *Yoshinobu Shū* correspond to scenes in *The Story of Sumiyoshi (Sumiyoshi Monogatari)*; Horibe, 1940, 50-57). During the late tenth century, then, *Sumiyoshi* was being read in an illustrated ver-

[2] *Sambōe* provides an early example of this practice; the intertextual "captions" in *Utsuho Monogatari* are another. Tamagami Takuya has made the important finding that visual and aural reception occurred at roughly the same time (Tamagami, 1943, 113-14).

[3] Two manuscripts survive, one in the Reizei family collection, and a copy of the Reizei manuscript in the Royal Household Library. The latter has been published in modern printed form in *Katsura no Miyabon Sōsho* (Yōtokusha, March 1960), 1:247-303. [Dots in brackets indicate a lacuna in the extant text.—Trans.]

sion. The nature of the reception process is not known, but it probably combined visual and aural reception: the principal recipient looked at illustrations of scenes in a work while an attendant read the text aloud (see vol. two, ch. 7). The growing popularity of illustrated scrolls (emakimono) in the mid-twelfth century changed this process. Illustrated scrolls enable a reader to see both text and illustration at once.[4] The earliest surviving example is the famous *Genji Monogatari Emaki (Illustrated Scrolls of The Tale of Genji)*.[5] Not long afterward, probably in the late twelfth century, two illustrated setsuwa scrolls appear: the *Shigisan Engi (Legends of Mt. Shigi)* and *Ban Dainagon Ekotoba (The Ōtomo Major Counselor, an Illustrated Story)*.[6] Scrolls are well suited for visual reception, since their gradual unrolling matches the chronological narrative development of a monogatari. On the other hand, it is not easy to look only at the illustrations in a scroll while someone else reads its text. We may conclude that a given textual passage was read and its illustrations were viewed at more or less the same time.

The popularity of illustrated scrolls led to another important development: the idea of illustrating stories that were presented in other than scroll form. The continuous unfolding of a scroll corresponds to the progression of narrative events. The bound booklet (sōshi), by contrast, contains illustrations on pages other than those of the text. The small break created in the reader's experience by separated text and illustrations obliterates the unity between the two elements. This notwithstanding, monogatari booklets were frequently illustrated from the thirteenth century on. The practice was a result of the vogue for reading illustrated texts initiated by the popular picture scrolls. An interesting phenomenon appears in this connection. Thirteenth- and fourteenth-century booklet illustrations are uncaptioned, whereas illustrations in fifteenth- and sixteenth-

[4] Because a scroll is read by unrolling, illustrations and text must be read together. If an illustration is to be viewed while listening to a read text, the illustration and text either have to be contained in separate books, or, like the pien-wen texts collected by Paul Pelliot, the illustration must be on one side of a page (to show to the audience) and the text on the other (for the use of the lector).

[5] A late twelfth-century work (1162-84). Surviving sections are divided among the Tokugawa Reimeikai, the Gotoh Museum, and the Tokyo National Museum. Minamoto Morotoki records that "*Genji* pictures" were going to be painted at the residence of the former sovereign Shirakawa (*Chōshūki* [27.XI.1119], 183). It is interesting to speculate whether the surviving *Genji* scrolls are the fragmentary survivors of Morotoki's "*Genji* pictures"; there is no definite proof, however (Meech-Pekarik, 1982, 173-76).

[6] The *Shigisan Engi* depicts the legends connected with a holy man, Mōren; these legends appear in the Umezawa manuscript of the *Kohon Setsuwa Shū* (231-46) and in the *Uji Shūi Monogatari* (8:238-44). The scroll is thought to date from between 1169 and 1180 (Suzuki K., 1960, 458-61). *Ban Dainagon Ekotoba* illustrates the arson committed on the Ōtemmon, one of the palace gates. The event is mentioned in *Uji Shūi Monogatari* (10:281-84). The scroll is dated ca. 1163-1177 (ibid., 504-507). [The meaning of "setsuwa" here is mythic, legendary, or folk tales; a narrower meaning for some examples involves lore about temples and shrines. For a yet more limitedly defined usage, see ch. 4.—Ed.]

century booklets contain explanations of the illustrated scene. There are, however, no captions in Naraehon, illustrated booklets of the sixteenth and seventeenth centuries (Kuwabara, 1967, 94-95).[7] The earliest illustrated booklets probably preserved the emphasis on illustrations originated by the picture scroll form. In later centuries, however, a desire to read text and illustration as a single unit led to including captions. As emphasis shifted toward colored illustrations with the Naraehon, captions were again omitted.

Despite such shifts in fashion, it gradually became fixed practice to illustrate fictional narratives and similar works. By the time otogimonogatari [popular stories of kinds preceding those next mentioned, the kanazōshi] appear in the sixteenth century, illustrations are the rule rather than the exception. Seventeenth-century woodblock editions followed the earlier example: illustrated texts were standard for such kinds as the kanazōshi, the ukiyozōshi, and the several eighteenth-century genres generally grouped together as kesaku. The major Japanese newspapers today observe a peculiar custom: each publishes novels—usually two at any given time—in serial form, despite the far fewer pages in major Japanese newspapers than in Western ones. An unwritten rule dating from Meiji times stipulates that each serial section be illustrated. The format is inherited directly from that of the late-Tokugawa kesaku, but the ultimate source of both is the twelfth-century illustrated scroll. An ancient form of reading thus remains active today.

The gulf between audience and composer/performer was further widened with aural reception. Heikyoku, the recitation of passages from *The Tale of the Heike*, presents an apt example. During the Middle Ages, the *Heike* was usually aurally received, being recited to lute accompaniment. The Kakuichi version, the standard one of the *Heike* text, now exists as a written document available to readers in modern printed and revised editions. Its text, however, evolved in the process of recitation (see ch. 11). Two other narratives dealing with war and military exploits, the *Hōgen Monogatari* and the *Heiji Monogatari*, were also recited by biwa hōshi, blind, itinerant monks who accompanied themselves on the lute.[8] There is evidence that the *Soga Monogatari (The Soga Brothers)* was recited,

[7] A collective name for booklets bearing colorful illustrations. Naraehon flourished during the sixteenth and seventeenth centuries; many survive in Western collections. An inventory has been compiled by Barbara Ruch and M. H. Charles (Naraehon Kokusai Kenkyū Kaigi, 1982).

[8] "On speaking of biwa hōshi: 'Indeed, when Master [name insertable] recites from the *Heiji*, the *Hōgen*, and the *Heike*, he has committed everything to memory, and never stumbles over his lines. His voice, facial expressions, and gestures are splendid and compelling' " (*Futsū Shōdō Shū* [*Handbook of Commonly Used Subjects for Sermons*, 1297], 1:68). See ch. 11.

too, although this may not have been standard practice.[9] The lute accompaniment was obviously intended to be heard by the general public, not only by those proficient in lute performance. The closed circle of performer-recipients thus ceased to exist once stories were recited to musical accompaniment. As nō drama has become more technically refined and standardized—a process beginning in the seventeenth century—its audience has tended to be limited to students of nō song, drum playing, or other arts connected with nō performance. Prior to the seventeenth century, however, this closed circle did not exist in nō. Knowledge of the libretto and the performance techniques was confined to the nō actors and musicians. The medieval separation between performer and audience was still more pronounced in the case of kōwaka ballad-drama songs and with sekkyōbushi, recited secular narratives. The custom of listening to a recited text accompanied by music (and sometimes gestures), like that of reading illustrated texts, evolved from a growing distinction between performer and recipient.

Not all literature was presented in company with illustrations, music, and/or gestures. Some kinds preserved traditional forms of reception. The transmission of waka reveals just such conservative tendencies. Moreover, two literary emphases coexisted in the High Middle Ages: one was oriented toward accurate transmission of existing texts, while the other felt free to add new elements to a text.

Fujiwara Teika's copying of classic texts is an example of the former. Prior to the twelfth century, manuscript-copying standards appear to have been rather inexact. The quality of the finished product varied with the nature of the work copied, of course, but even royal waka anthologies, the most likely candidates for faithful transmission, survive from this period in highly contaminated versions. The Gen'ei manuscript of the *Kokinshū* is one example of an early, contaminated text.[10] The establishing of the Rokujō and Mikohidari waka schools in the late twelfth century led to the consolidation of authoritative texts (shōhon) for each school. Such texts were considered vital to the very authority of each school. Teika was the foremost copyist of authoritative texts.

Consider, for instance, his copying of *The Tosa Diary*. Ki no Tsurayuki's holograph text still existed in Teika's time. Teika reproduced the holograph as conscientiously as possible; he even appends a sample of Tsu-

[9] The *Zakki* (1347; Daigoji coll.) mentions that the Soga Brothers story was recited by "a rural blind man" (see ch. 17). Prior to this time, therefore, the story of the Soga Brothers was a subject of recitation; we have no way of knowing how closely the recited version matches the extant text of *Soga Monogatari*, however.

[10] The manuscript has a postscript dated Gen'ei 3 (1120), hence its name. The Gen'ei manuscript is deduced to have been copied by Fujiwara Sadazane (1063-1131). This ancient manuscript contains many errors and omissions and includes waka not in the original anthology (Kyūsojin, 1961: 59-62).

rayuki's calligraphy, copied from his exemplar. In other cases, Teika delegated much of the copying to members of his household but had them leave blanks in the text where proper nouns occurred so that he could write them in himself at a later time. In the course of doing so, Teika also checked the copy against the exemplar, thus carrying out a kind of proofreading (Horibe, 1943, 1-21). Several wabun works copied by Teika remain the definitive versions. All commentaries and analyses of *The Tale of Genji*, for example, are based on the manuscript line descended from Teika's Aobyōshi ("Blue Covers") recension. The standard version of the *Genji* in the thirteenth and fourteenth centuries was the Kawachi recension, compiled by Minamoto Mitsuyuki (1163-1244) and his son Chikayuki (dates unknown). From the fifteenth century on, as Teika's reputation as poet and scholar grew (see ch. 14), his "Blue Covers" *Genji* became the dominant version. Any manuscript copied by Teika was considered authoritative.

The sense of authenticity communicated by Teika manuscripts and their descendants makes them the definitive texts for scholars and readers alike. In addition to the *Genji* and *The Tosa Diary*, other works survive that were copied by Teika.[11] All are easily interpreted. By contrast, works not copied by Teika—including the *Kagerō Nikki (The Gossamer Years)* and the *Utsuho Monogatari (The Hollow Tree)*—contain many vexed passages. Whether an easily understood text is necessarily faithful to the original is a question beyond our present scope. The "Blue Covers" recension, however, shows fewer signs than the Kawachi version of altering the text to facilitate comprehensibility (Gatten, 1982, 87-90).

The converse of this approach advocates liberal alteration of an original text. *The Story of Sagoromo* is an outstanding testament to this attitude (see ch. 3). Taken one step further, liberal alteration can develop into rewriting. An early example is the twelfth-century *Ima Torikaebaya (The New Torikaebaya)*, a rewritten version of an earlier, no-longer-extant monogatari. The practice of rewriting monogatari became increasingly popular from the thirteenth century on, as indicated by the surviving text of *The Story of Sumiyoshi* and by the Nakamura manuscript version of *Yowa no Nezame* (*The Tale of Nezame*: see ch. 3).

Rewriting also appears in setsuwa, and in far more striking fashion. The many setsuwa collections compiled during the High Middle Ages tend to have certain stories in common. Versions of a given story vary considerably among collections, however. The variants are often substantial, including changes in plot. "Setsuwa," a word suggesting oral transmission, may imply that story changes were made at will in the process of oral narration. This is contrary to fact. Analysis of setsuwa variants

[11] The *Kokinshū*, the *Gosenshū*, the *Shūishū*, and the *Ise Monogatari*, among others.

clearly demonstrates that they originated in the process of written transmission. The same attitude that obtained in orally transmitting "light" setsuwa was perpetuated in written transmission, sanctioning the creation of significant textual variants.[12] "Weighty" setsuwa, by contrast, were transmitted without a single variant; in such cases, oral transmission was more accurate than writing. But reciters were granted considerable license in altering light setsuwa. This attitude was apparently transferred to written transmission: copyists seem to have felt justified in altering what they perceived as unimportant details.

Written alterations tend to be more extreme than those made through oral transmission. Because oral compositions are often combinations of formulas, even minor elements can easily be presented in the same way (see vol. one, pp. 156-60). The simplest way to transmit a story orally is to tell it exactly as it was memorized. Motifs are particularly difficult to change in oral transmission. A copyist, by contrast, has no audience present and so is free to change minor motifs at will.[13]

Writing also makes alteration of expression easier. The bamboo-cutter [taketori] setsuwa, for example, is transmitted in several versions, each with the same motif.[14] Only written transmissions of the bamboo-cutter story have variant major motifs; oral transmissions seem to vary only minor motifs. Zuikei Shūhō (1392-1473) records an unusual version of the bamboo-cutter setsuwa in his *Gaun Nikkinroku Batsuyū (Extracts from Gaun's Diary)*.[15] The setsuwa, which was told to Zuikei by a blind man named Jōryo, is a rare instance of oral transmission. Jōryo's version differs considerably in its major motif from the existing text of *Taketori Monogatari (The Bamboo Cutter)*; but the major motif of Jōryo's transmission is identical to that found in other versions preserved in the *Kaidōki*, the *Kokinshū Chū*, the *Katsuragawa Jizō*, and the *Sangoku Denki*. Jōryo thus probably recited a story whose major motif was created through written transmission. *Heike* recitation provides other instances of written transmissions communicated orally by blind men.

Altered texts (idembon) resulted from the accepted practice of changing any part of a light setsuwa, including its motif, in the course of written transmission. "Altered text" signifies a text in which content has been intentionally changed. An altered text is to be distinguished from a variant version (ihon) of a given text, which is produced through miscopying, misbinding, or other unintentional factors. *The Tale of the Heike* and *The*

[12] "Light" setsuwa do not require accurate transmission (see vol. one, p. 170, and in this, pp. 101-2).

[13] Motifs may be divided into the basic motif (the framework for an entire story) and the partial motif; the latter is subdivided into major plot motifs (which concern plot progression) and minor plot motifs (which are limited to details).

[14] Mitani, 1956, 321-44.

[15] *Gaun* [entry for 20.II.1447], 11-12. [Gaun is another name for Zuikei.—Trans.]

Soga Brothers both survive in several altered texts, created by the same kind of copyists who produced altered setsuwa texts. In fact, these monogatari contain elements of setsuwa. The same setsuwa will appear, with altered content and expression, in various transmissions of a given setsuwa collection.

Some transmissions of the same collection, moreover, contain more setsuwa than do others. The text of the *Hōbutsu Shū*, for example, survives in several transmitted forms, ranging from a single-fascicle version to a nine-fascicle text.[16] The difference is not due to lengthened stories, but to accretion: setsuwa not originally included were added to each new transmission. In other words, the *Hōbutsu Shū* was perceived as the same work regardless of the dramatic fluctuation in the number of stories and fascicles.

This attitude resembles another medieval view, discussed earlier: any number of setsuwa were seen as essentially the same story so long as all retained the central motif. Differences in major and minor motifs were not considered significant. This attitude may explain why certain sections of the *Heike* appear in some transmissions but not in others. Efforts are made, from time to time, to construct a textual stemma for *The Tale of the Heike*. They invariably prove futile. Works with setsuwa characteristics cannot be analyzed according to a stemmatic system, since stemma are designed to deal with bibliographically linked textual variants. *The Tale of the Heike* and similar works must be subjected to textual criticism based on principles [e.g., motifs] other than those applied to royal waka anthologies and nikki in Japanese prose (wabun).

[16] The single-fascicle transmission most closely approximates the form of Taira Yasuyori's original collection, while the other texts represent various stages of story accretion (Koizumi, 1973, 223-32).

PART THREE

The Formation of the High Middle Ages

CHAPTER 7

Poetry and Prose in Chinese: Stagnation

The Two Parts of the High Middle Ages

The High Middle Ages may be divided into two parts, each of which has mutually distinguishing features. The first half comprises the century and a half from the early thirteenth century through the middle of the fourteenth; this period is noted for masterworks in the traditional genres of waka, monogatari, and nikki. The second half of the High Middle Ages—the hundred and fifty years from the mid-fourteenth century up to the close of the fifteenth—is a time of high achievement in the new fields of linked poetry and nō drama. Shih poetry, a traditional genre, also evolves during the latter period, albeit in a direction categorized as "mad" by preexisting criteria.

Japanese society was devastated by the decade-long Ōnin War (1467-77). Yet those turbulent times proved to be a period of refinement for the intensely practical arts governed by the ideal of michi, or artistic vocation. This ideal reached perfection in the seventeenth century with the writings of Matsuo Bashō. The year 1499 marked the establishment of another new genre, haikai: in that year the first haikai anthology, the *Chikuba Kyōginshū*, appeared. The sixteenth century, then, is a transitional period combining characteristics of both the High and the Late Middle Ages.

Poetry and Prose in Chinese

Thirteenth-century Japanese shih poets generally carried on the ways of their twelfth-century predecessors. To be sure, no large-scale shih anthologies or personal shih collections (besshū) were compiled in the thirteenth century. Such works do not reappear until the following century, in the heyday of Zen monastic literature. The thirteenth century produced no shih poets worthy of representation in a major anthology, and in brief it is a period of stagnation for shih. Courtiers' diaries from this time indicate that gentlemen still attended the shih gatherings that formed a staple of aristocratic social life. The output of shih did not decline, but the quality did, as no new shih style appeared during the thirteenth century. My earlier discussion of the influence of Sung culture on the Japanese High Middle Ages was intended in a general sense. Thirteenth-century Japanese shih seem to present no evidence of Sung influence. I am careful to say "seem" because few Japanese shih survive from this period. We may, however, assume that there was no Sung influence. An example may be drawn from Sugawara Arimasa's "The Shrine: Three Poems," from the *Kyūreishū* (*The Dove Hill Collection*).[1]

> Hills are green where mists part, just as in a painting;
> Gauze curtains half-drawn, white clouds gather.
> By the crags, autumn trees give us a cool reception;
> Deep in the vale, ancient unseen pines speak to me.
> Woodcutters at sundown walk into northern winds;
> The night is quiet at Kayō: moonlight on the garden.[2]
> In the desolation of this garden panorama,
> Cranes visit monks in prayer, deer hearken to sutras.
> (*Kyūreishū*, 97)

Arimasa celebrates nature in a fashion typical of Late T'ang poets, each line employing time-honored diction. Yet the poem lacks focus and intensity. Its design, to show the passage of time from morning to afternoon and from evening to night, is pointless, and the impression conveyed is vague. Arimasa's shih appears poorer still when measured against Sung criteria, since Sung poetry is known for its abundant—and occasionally excessive—expression of a poet's or speaker's emotions. Let us consider another thirteenth-century Japanese shih, this time by Fujiwara Teika. He composed it in the First Month of 1212, en route to the hot springs at Arima. The shih, recorded in the *Meigetsuki*, describes a scene by the Mukogawa River.[3]

> Spring rains finally clear: the lake waters are high;
> A breeze blows soft on kindly waves: we look for a rich harvest.
> Pines greet me from afar, just like old friends;
> Men are startled by birdflocks vying to take the lead.
> At dawn, tears come with the moon to a river lodge;
> The vernal view resembles the sky over Tung-ting.[4]

[1] The *Kyūreishū* (preface dated 1295) is a collection of outstanding shih and Buddhist petitions presented to the Iwashimizu Hachiman Shrine. It was compiled by Ryōsei, a monk affiliated with the shrine. [Doves were believed to be messengers of the god Hachiman; hence the name of the collection.—Trans.]

[2] The Kayōkan'in was a mansion on the grounds of the Iwashimizu Hachiman Shrine.

[3] Teika writes in connection with this shih, "We passed by Lake Koya and entered the Muko Mountains" (*MGK* [21.I.1212], 144).

[4] [Tung-ting, the largest freshwater lake in China, has long been famous for moon-viewing. It is located in Hunan province.—Trans.]

I turn my head to gaze back over distant green peaks;
Our royal city recedes from sight: mountains, and then rivers.

Teika's poem has the same deficiencies as Arimasa's [conventionality, lack of intensity, etc.]. For the sake of his reputation as a waka poet, such compositions are perhaps best kept under wraps. Two rather good Late T'ang–style quatrains on nature precede this shih in the *Meigetsuki*, however: Teika may have been more comfortable composing in the shorter form.

Most thirteenth-century Japanese shih were probably on this general literary level. Late T'ang nature poetry does more than describe a natural scene: the poet unifies the work by fusing natural descriptions with personal concepts or emotions. Arimasa's and Teika's shih do not share this characteristic. They are obviously flawed when considered as complete poems; but many couplets from these and other shih are arresting as individual units. Let us consider some examples from *The Dove Hill Collection*.

Spring
By the Taira Former Consultant (Lord Tsunechika)

A warm breeze enfolds the willow, but its boughs remain indifferent;
Before the cherry trees blossom, haze turns the hills to crimson.
(83)

Thoughts on the Last Day of Spring
By the Fujiwara Former Provisional Middle Counselor (Lord Tsunenaga)

Breezes sweep the blossoming grove: shifting colors dance;
Returning to their valley home, warblers find abundant shade.
(86)

Other interesting couplets appear in the *Wakan Kensakushū*.[5]

Spring
By His Cloistered Majesty Juntoku

Amidst the cries of crow and sparrow, dawn in spring reveals bamboo;
Emerging through tinted mist, mountains show faintly in the dusk.
(1:115)

[5] The *Wakan Kensakushū* includes waka and shih from the ninth through thirteenth centuries, composed by literati adept in both genres. The collection was probably compiled in the late thirteenth century. Half the original twenty fascicles survive.

Gazing in Spring at a Village on the Water
By the Gokyōgoku Regent and Former Chancellor[6]

A shoreside hamlet belongs to a far-off, misty world:
Mirror-waters half engulf hills of willow and blossoming cherry.
(1:121)

Improvisation While Moon-Viewing
By Fujiwara Mitsutoshi

Stars linger in distant woods: bell and clock tell daybreak;
Winds rise in palace pines: autumn concertizing. (7:167)

On Entering the Henjōji Temple in Autumn
By Fujiwara Ariie, Minister of the Treasury

Green winds have blown past; nighttime mountains are still.
A white moon shines full; autumn waters are pure.
(7:170-71)

Autumn Foliage at a Mountain Dwelling
By Major Counselor Minamoto Michitomo

Two pines form a gate north of the shady path;
Gaps in bamboo eaves reveal mountains of red foliage.
(8:180)

The Last Day of Autumn
By His Cloistered Majesty Tsuchimikado

Autumn leaves pour down on steps: heavy evening rain;
The setting sun hangs on the rim: blue autumn sky is scarce.
(8:186)

These couplets are interesting only if read from a Japanese perspective; fragments of nature poetry are unlikely to impress Chinese readers. The thirteenth-century Japanese were carrying on a tradition of appreciating partial shih that dates back to the *Wakan Rōeishū* (*Collection of Japanese and Chinese Songs*; see vol. two, ch. 6). This explains why *The Dove Hill Collection* contains few complete shih and the *Wakan Kensakushū* none at all.

Waka also appear of course in the *Wakan Kensakushū*. The practice of reading a shih couplet or quatrain extracted from a longer work reflects the contemporary perception that a shih fragment approximated a tanka in terms of literary volume. In other words, a thirty-one syllable tanka was seen to express roughly the same content as a five-character shih quatrain or a seven-character couplet (see vol. two, ch. 7). If we agree that a tanka is roughly equivalent to a seven-character couplet in terms

[6] Fujiwara (Gokyōgoku) Yoshitsune.

of content, the Japanese preference for shih couplets over entire poems may become clearer.

The Japanese made a deliberate effort to approach shih as they did waka. Consequently, shih expression was readily incorporated into waka. Fragmentation, it has been noted, is a conspicuous element in high medieval literature (see ch. 5). The increased number of poets able to compose in both Japanese and Chinese during the thirteenth and fourteenth centuries contributed to the trend toward fragmentation. The composition of shih, originally a foreign poetic form, came to be carried out according to Japanese linguistic perspectives. Such shih would certainly puzzle Chinese readers, and before judging them as poetry, a Chinese would have to decide whether the shih were indeed written in the Chinese language. The tendency to employ non-Chinese expression in Japanese shih changed drastically in the late fourteenth century, when many Zen monks went to study in China. There were now Japanese shih poets who were fluent in spoken Chinese. The late fourteenth century also marked the arrival in Japan of several Chinese Ch'an [Zen] monks skilled in shih composition.

A similar phenomenon occurred in Chinese prose written by Japanese. There is no evidence that plain prose (san-wen) by great Sung stylists like Ou-yang Hsiu and Su Shih (Tung-p'o) was read in thirteenth-century Japan. During the Early Middle Ages, it will be recalled, Japanese writers of Chinese prose were unaffected by Han Yü's and Liu Tsung-yüan's manifestos on plain prose (see above, pp. 11-12; vol. two, ch. 6). The plain prose style advocated by Han and Liu did not flourish in China either, for parallel prose (p'ien-wen) reemerged as the dominant prose style of the Late T'ang period. During the Sung, however, plain prose was reappraised by Ou-yang Hsiu and his circle, gaining a secure position as the major prose style. Although parallel prose continued to be composed through the Ch'ing dynasty, it never regained its ascendancy after the Sung.[7] Thirteenth-century Japanese prose in Chinese shows no evidence of experiencing these vicissitudes. Parallel prose prospered as always. One reason for this phenomenon was the unavailability of accurate, up-to-date information on recent Chinese literary trends, once the official embassies to China had been discontinued. A more influential factor, however, was the lack of contact with spoken Chinese. The beauty of parallel prose, a metric form, can only be appreciated by those familiar with the correct Chinese pronunciation of the characters. The metric beauty of parallel prose vanishes when it is read in Japanese syntactic

[7] Since the ability to compose parallel prose was a requisite in passing the Chinese civil service examination, however, parallel prose composition was a valued pursuit until relatively recent times and even underwent some refinement (Liu Ling-sheng, 1936, 95-110).

order; all that remains is the parallelism forming the stylistic core. Thirteenth-century Japanese parallel prose was centered entirely on form.

Parallel prose was abundantly produced in thirteenth-century Japan because it was the official court document style. A few examples appear in *Honchō Monjū (Collection of Japanese Documents)*.[8] By this time, real power rested with the Kamakura bakufu, and official court documents dealt only with administrative formalities. They state no political opinions or philosophy. Formal, ordered parallel prose was, perhaps, the most appropriate means of lending authority to these meaningless documents. Parallel prose also thrived in Buddhist documents, especially the statement made on sponsoring a Buddhist service (hyōbyaku), the formal Buddhist prayer (gammon), and the concluding statement and offering at a memorial service (fujumon).

These liturgical documents, already in frequent use by the twelfth century, proliferated during the thirteenth. Enormous quantities survive, both in the *Collection of Japanese Documents* and in anthologies of sponsors' statements and formal prayers, including the *Tempo Rinshō*, the *Kaisōshū*, and the *Sokusōshū*. All follow essentially the same format: the purpose of the service is stated, the virtues of the deceased are praised, and prayers are said for the repose of the soul of the departed. The prayers were adjusted for general application by substituting the appropriate proper nouns and altering a few other items. In his *Futsū Shōdō Shū (Handbook of Commonly Used Subjects for Sermons)*, the monk Ryōki classifies the most common categories of phrases substituted in a given prayer.[9] Japanese parallel prose was an empty shell, but its formal, parallelism-centered beauty nevertheless attracted writers and audiences alike. The thirteenth-century fondness for parallel prose formed the foundation for incorporating Sinified expression into native Japanese prose and so created some of the great works written in the mixed style.

The situation outlined above roughly parallels that for contemporaneous Koryŏ. Sung culture was adopted somewhat earlier in Koryŏ, however. The Korean literati began showing interest in Sung culture as early as Sŏngjon's reign (1084-94); Kim Pu-sik (1075-1151) was a leading figure in this movement (see ch. 1). Nevertheless, Pu-sik continued to write poetry in the Late T'ang style. He composed both parallel and plain prose, an indication that this was a transitional period for Korean prose

[8] *Honchō Monjū*, in eighty fascicles, was compiled in the Edo period by the Shōkōkan in Mito. The collection reproduces over three thousand documents, chiefly royal edicts and other official documents drafted prior to the early eighteenth century. Because *Honchō Monjū* preserves texts of several documents otherwise nonextant, it is a valuable research tool.

[9] The single surviving manuscript copy of *Futsū Shōdō Shū* is in the Tōdaiji Library collection. The preface concludes with this passage: "Dated the third day of the First Month, Einin 5 [1297]. The monk Ryōki has here recorded facts he collected."

in Chinese. Korean shih seem to have resisted the Sung style. Yi Kyu-bo (1168-1241), who lived about one hundred years after Pu-sik, kept to the Late T'ang style of poetry. One of his shih is "A Summer Day" (*Tong Munsŏn*, 20:235).

In a light singlet, on fresh bamboo mats, I lie by the lattices;
My dreams are disturbed by warblers' voices raised twice or thrice in song.
Dense leaves, shady blossoms: those occur after spring;
Through wisps of cloud, sunlight filters bright among the raindrops.

To judge from this poem, Korean shih styles did not change greatly after Kim Pu-sik. Other works from this period, however, demonstrate that the Sung style had been adopted to some degree: "A Satire on Fishing for Fame and Fortune" (*Tong Munsŏn*, 4:42) and "Poem for Chancellor Cho" (ibid., 11:130), for instance, share a common philosophical outlook.

Korean prose in Chinese was apparently more amenable to Sung innovations. Yi Kyu-bo's "An Account of Moderation House" (*Tong Munsŏn*, 66:308) and "Preface to a Poem Sent to Historian Yi on the Occasion of His Official Departure for Kŏche" (ibid., 83:527) would not look out of place in a Sung prose anthology. On the whole, of course, Sung culture came rather late to Korea. In Yi Kyu-bo's old age, the Yüan dynasty was established in China. The Koryŏ government maintained its friendly relations with the Yüan, and in return the new Chinese government introduced much Sung culture to Korea. The major Korean literary figures of this period are Yi Che-hyŏn (1287-1367), Yi Saek (1328-96), and Yi Sung-in (1347-92). Sung culture may be said to have truly permeated Korean literati society in the late Koryŏ period.

Sung culture was absorbed more easily by the Japanese, thanks largely to the presence in Japan of Ch'an monks emigrated from Yüan China. Lan-ch'i Tao-lung (Rankei Dōryū, 1213-78), Wu-an P'u-ning (Gottan Funei, 1197-1276), Ta-hsiu Cheng-nien (Daikyū Shōnen, 1215-89), Wu-hsüeh Tsu-yüan (Mugaku Sogen, 1226-86), and I-shan I-ning (Issan Ichinei, 1247-1317), all major Ch'an figures, came to Japan in rapid succession. Their arrival was enormously significant in shaping the High Middle Ages. In addition to Ch'an (Zen) Buddhism, they brought with them a knowledge of Neoconfucianism and Sung literature.

The results of the sporadic Japanese embassies to T'ang China cannot rival the role played by Ch'an monks in introducing Chinese culture to Japan. Language did present problems in effecting this introduction. Since the Ch'an monks continued to use Chinese in order to communicate with Japanese monks and laymen, their explanations of Zen, Neoconfucianism, and literature must have been quite incomprehensible to Japanese in general. Of course, there was no shortage of interpreters: Japanese Zen monks had been studying increasingly in Sung and Yüan China.

But there are limits to understanding through interpreters. Sung culture was in fact introduced into Japan by Japanese Zen monks, who explained (in Japanese) what had been taught them (in Chinese) by the immigrant Ch'an monks. The process of communicating their knowledge from master to disciple to the disciple's disciple took more than half a century. Sung culture, therefore, first entered Japanese life in the late fourteenth century. By contrast, Neoconfucianism was introduced to Koryŏ during King Ch'ungyŏl's reign (1275-1308); it reached its height in the early fourteenth century, ten years after Paek I-jŏng returned to Koryŏ from study in China.[10] One of his shih, entitled "Hideaway," is as follows.

My lonely little house is only twenty feet square;
Incense burns while I quietly read the sages' books.
Rather than material rewards, I seek the moral virtues;
Like a grove in autumn, worldly passions daily diminish.
(*Tong Munsŏn*, 20:243)

The poem is typically Confucian; one also perceives the prolix Sung style put into practice. Japan adopted Sung culture about fifty years later than did Koryŏ.

[10] Paek I-jŏng's dates are not known. He returned from China in 1298 and instructed Yi Che-hyŏn at some point thereafter; thus his active period would be ca. 1300.

CHAPTER 8

The Rise of Waka

TOWARD NEOCLASSICISM

True to its name, Japanese neoclassicism strives to outdo the classical past in its grasp of beauty. The goal was to be achieved by giving further polish (yū) to an ancient ideal, en (refinement), and, by combining the two elements, create a new aesthetic: yūen, or refined charm. The neoclassical drive to surpass the beauty created by past poetry signified more than active amplification. In waka, neoclassicism is justly noted for its understatement, a negating element that marks a departure from past aesthetics. Another neoclassical characteristic is a marked shift in poetic focus: where beauty had previously been depicted as an entity independent of the poet, the neoclassical aesthetic demanded profound emotional or spiritual involvement with external subjects. The concept of kokoro (the spirit or conception of a waka) thus came to present poets with a dilemma for literary creation that was inconceivable to their predecessors. Both the traditional, external focus and the contemplative approach were acknowledged practices in Shunzei's day. Although Shunzei never fully resolved the dichotomy, his son Teika achieved a synthesis in his own waka.

Yūgen and Ushin

Shunzei believed that ideally waka should leave much unsaid; he conceived of the best poems as understatements conjuring a vision in the mind of the recipient. Such poetry, he remarked, is "both en and yūgen" to the ear (ch. 2). Yūgen—a sense of profundity—emerges paradoxically from incomplete expression. Some scholars have interpreted Shunzei's statement to mean that he both acknowledged yūgen as the supreme literary tone and endorsed a yūgen style of waka. This is erroneous. Shunzei uses "yūgen" as a critical term a total of fourteen times (counting the above instance) in his extant waka-match judgments. At no time does he state that yūgen is a concept central to waka. The fourteen instances are rather dubious proof that Shunzei espoused yūgen as a leading poetic ideal, and they become still less convincing when compared to the 279 times that Shunzei employs "yū," or his ninety-six recorded uses of "en" (ch. 2). Shun'e (fl. 1160-80), a somewhat later figure than Shunzei, was the first to recognize the vital significance of yūgen (Konishi, 1975a, 59).

"Yūgen" (Ch. yu-hsüan) was originally used to describe Lao Tzu's and

Chuang Tzu's perception of the profundity of the Tao. Both components of the word, "yu" and "hsüan," signify "reddish-black." The association with concepts of darkness and obscurity led to the words acquiring a more abstract sense: they came to mean "uncertain," "unclear," "difficult to understand." Eventually "yu" and "hsüan" were used in reference to philosophical depth. During the Six Dynasties period, San-lun Buddhism [J. Sanron, the "Three Treatise" sect founded in Nara in 625] used Taoist terms to explain the doctrine of emptiness (Skt. śūnyatā); "yu-hsüan" was used as a compound from this point. In the Sui dynasty T'ien-t'ai [J. Tendai] Buddhism, also centered on the emptiness doctrine, frequently used "yu-hsüan." In later centuries, Ch'an [J. Zen] employed the term to express the profundity within non-being (Ch. wu, J. mu; Konishi, 1943b, 13-22).

Buddhism did not communicate "yu-hsüan" directly to waka critical vocabulary, however. "Yūgen" was first used as a general expression meaning "difficult to perceive," "not obvious." Later it became a technical term used in verse-topic shih (kudaishi). "Yūgen" was apparently incorporated into the waka vocabulary about this time. In verse-topic shih, the Chinese verse that serves as topic is usually divided in the composition: the first part of the topic thus appears in the first line of the shih, and its second part is found in the second line.[1] For example:

Vernal Colors Know No Bounds
By Minamoto Takamichi

Vernal colors in the distance: here and there they show;
Gazing at them, truly my emotions *know no bounds.*
The heavens range fathomless beyond wisps of haze;
Far-off lands are discerned, although not easily.[2]

This is the basic form. Sometimes, however, a shih expresses the verse-topic text in more indirect fashion. *Sakumon Daitai (Basics of Composition)* lists three techniques for incorporating verse-topics indirectly. These are the "fragmented topic form" (in which the topic is first broken down into individual characters, then characters corresponding in meaning or theme to the topic components are incorporated into the shih text); the "generally-expressed topic form" (in which the general sense of the verse-topic is communicated without use of or reference to its characters); and the "implied yūgen form" (which implies rather than states the verse-

[1] "In verse-topic shih, the first lines generally present all the words used in the topic" (*Sakumon Daitai*, 73).

[2] *Honchō Reisō* [= *HR*], 1:205. The forenote has been slightly shortened to give only the verse-topic.

topic). An example of the last form, given in *Basics of Composition*, is a couplet taken from a poem by Yoshishige Yasutane. The verse-topic is "Where Has the Cool Breeze Hidden?"

> People are wise to wait for it with bamboo mats outspread!
> Master Lieh has housed his carriage; he will make no rounds.[3]

In other words, people do well to wait on cool bamboo mats, because the wind may not rise for a while: Master Lieh, who rides the wind, has "housed his carriage" for the time being. Yasutane implies that cool breezes will eventually be on the way. His subtlety is praised by the author of *Basics of Composition* as "truly embodying the yūgen form."

Waka poets adopted the shih poets' concept of yūgen in the twelfth century. It was employed as a term of praise, signifying "indirect," "blurred," or "not explicit," and implying the presence of profundity (Nose, 1944a, 228-29). That Shunzei followed this usage is demonstrated in his judgment of a poem composed for the *Waka Match at the Hirota Shrine* (Round Two: "Gazing Far Across the Sea"):

The Left: The Former Major Counselor (Sanesada)

Muko no umi o	The sea at Muko
Nagitaru asa ni	Has grown calm with the morning,
Miwataseba	And gazing far beyond
Mayu mo midarenu	I see unruffled eyebrows—
Awa no shimayama.	The Awa island mountains.

Shunzei commented,

> The poet does not blindly adhere to time-honored diction.[4] The sense of desolation in the poem seems to be deliberate, moreover. "I see unruffled eyebrows— / The Awa island mountains" is reminiscent of such shih lines as "Painted-eyebrow colors gaze across the azure sea" and "Lung-men peaks face each other: indigo-paint eyebrows."[5] Here indeed we seem to have yūgen. (*HCUT*, 7:2262)

[3] Master Lieh, a Taoist philosopher, was known for riding the winds through the sky. "Master Lieh used to ride the wind nimbly and marvelously" (*Chuang Tzu*, 1:40). The couplet states that Lieh seems to have housed his wind-carriage for the indefinite future.

[4] Shunzei refers to the fourth line of the poem, "Mayu mo midarenu" (I see unruffled eyebrows), an unconventional use of diction. [Auth., Trans.]

[5] The first shih line is from "Pai-chang Mountain," by Ho-lan Hsien (*Wakan Rōeishū*, 2:491). The second is by Po Chü-i, from his "Evening View from Five Phoenixes Tower." Both compositions allude to a practice, common among T'ang noblewomen, of shaving the eyebrows and painting thick blue or indigo lines over them. T'ang poets often compared the blue-green of distant wooded mountains to a lady's eyebrows. [Auth., Trans.]

Sanesada's waka explicitly mentions the topic, "Gazing Far Across the Sea," in the words "umi o" ("the sea") and "miwataseba" ("gazing far beyond"). Shunzei therefore does not refer to "yūgen" in the sense of indirect allusion to a verse-topic. "Yūgen" may rather signify the indirect approach of the poem itself: by alluding to well-known Chinese shih, it conjures up a vision of beautiful women.

Shunzei regarded yūgen, like sabi (desolation), to be a poetic manner rather than a major literary ideal. Shun'e, not Shunzei, was the first to declare that understatement was the very core of waka. Shun'e cautioned poets against directly expressing their emotions: they should instead be sensed by recipients. For this reason, Shun'e dared to criticize what is generally thought one of Shunzei's masterworks, a waka prized by the poet himself (ch. 2):

Yū sareba	As evening falls,
Nobe no akikaze	From along the fields the autumn wind
Mi ni shimite	Pierces to my heart,
Uzura naku nari	And the quails can be heard to cry
Fukakusa no sato.	At Fukakusa lost in deep plants.[6]

Shun'e believed that the third line, "Mi ni shimite" ("Pierces to my heart") was too expressive. Instead of stating the speaker's emotions, Shunzei should have used some other phenomenon to suggest that the autumn winds indeed pierce the speaker's heart (*Mumyōshō*, 73). Shun'e was not the only critic who praised incomplete expression. A few of his contemporaries were also enthusiastic advocates. They termed the incomplete, understated tone "the yūgen manner." Here "yūgen," signifying understatement, is used in a more general, praiseworthy sense than that of Shunzei's "yūgen." Kamo no Chōmei was another strong supporter of yūgen in that larger sense of the word, as in the following [mostly paraphrased] from his *Mumyōshō* (*Untitled Writings*, 82-88):

1. Yūgen is a difficult concept. It evolved when poets realized that they had been writing in the same styles since the *Shūishū* period. Waka had consequently lost its freshness. The purpose of yūgen is to recapture an ancient poetic style.[7]

[6] [Adapted from Brower-Miner, 1961, 17. Shunzei alludes to an exchange of poems between Narihira and a lady (*Kokinshū*, 18:971-72; *Ise Monogatari*, dan 123). By Shunzei's time, the village of Fukakusa ("deep grass") was only a legend, its very location being unknown.—Ed.]

[7] Chōmei perhaps refers to Ariwara Narihira's style, characterized in the *Kokinshū* as having "too much kokoro and not enough words" (Kana Preface, 18). An excellent example of a famous but unclear waka by Narihira is this: Tsuki ya aranu / Haru ya mukashi no / Haru naranu / Waga mi hitotsu wa / Moto no mi ni shite. (This is not that moon! / Nor is this spring the spring that was / In those days by gone! / My being is the single thing /

2. The ideal mid-antique style (chūkofū, the waka style modeled on *Shūishū*-period poetry) "expresses matters completely and forthrightly, in a mild manner." It would seem reasonable that poets writing in this style would reject the difficult yūgen style. In fact, however, both the mid-antique and the yūgen styles are apparent in the *Kokinshū*. To reject the yūgen style is to ignore the bases of the mid-antique style.
3. Although Chōmei found nothing fresh produced by gatherings of poets working in the mid-antique style, Gotoba In's waka gatherings brimmed with vitality. Inexperienced poets are cautioned against imitating the style advocated by Gotoba and his circle, for the end result will be "Zen gibberish" (Darumashū) rather than yūgen poetry.
4. The yūgen style can be summed up as "possessing overtones not expressed in words, and presenting scenes whose form is not described." "When the motif is profound and the diction most refined," poetry is produced in the yūgen style. Only the most accomplished members of an audience can respond to it.

By invoking the *Kokinshū* in his plea for a fresh waka style, Chōmei clearly shows that he holds a neoclassical position.

Two important points emerge: the former sovereign Gotoba was a proponent of the new yūgen style; and inept imitations of the style would produce "Zen gibberish." Both points suggest that Teika was the principal composer in the yūgen style. Teika compiled and copied his own private waka collection, *Shūi Gusō*, in which he reminisces,

> During the Bunji and Kenkyū eras [1185-98] I was criticized by all levels of society for writing faddish, Zen-nonsense poetry. I seriously considered giving up waka composition. In the Shōji and Kennin eras [1199-1204] I was succored by the Deity of Temmangū, patron of literary pursuits, and benefited from the kindness of His Enlightened Majesty.[8] The traditions of my school thus came to be perpetuated, and I continued to follow the Way of Waka. (Supernum. fasc., 376)

Teika's reference to "Zen-nonsense poetry" is literally to "Darumauta." "Daruma," the Japanese pronunciation of "Bodhidharma" (d. 528?), is

Remaining as it ever was . . .) [As so often in Asia, literary innovation is proposed by Chōmei as a return to a pristine past.—Ed.]

[8] ["Temmangū" is a reference to Sugawara Michizane (845-903), literatus, statesman, and scholar. Michizane was deified and given the name Temman Tenjin ca. 950. He is worshipped principally at the Kitano Temmangū Shrine in Kyoto and at the Dazaifu Temmangū Shrine in Northern Kyushu. Dazaifu was the site of Michizane's exile and death.—Trans.]

used here as a synonym for Zen Buddhism.[9] This recently imported religion seems to have baffled many Japanese literati. Teika was condemned for composing "Zen-nonsense poetry" because he was one of the first to write in the yūgen style. "His Enlightened Majesty" refers to Teika's patron, the abdicated Gotoba. A great many poems typical of the new *Shinkokinshū* style were composed during the Shōji and Kennin eras, with Gotoba providing poets the necessary setting.

What specifically was it like, this new style of poetry dubbed both "yūgen" and "Zen nonsense"? The *Roppyakuban Utaawase (Waka Match in Six Hundred Rounds)*, convened in 1193, provides several instances of the yūgen style. The first round on Spring, on the topic, "The Palace Banquet on New Year's Day," begins with a poem by Fujiwara (or Gokyōgoku) Yoshitsune:

Aratama no	Bright as a new jewel
Toshi o kumoi ni	Is this year we turn to welcome
Mukau tote	At the Court of Clouds;
Kyō morobito ni	Today each and every one
Miki tamau nari.	Partakes of the finest sake.
	(Spring, 1:6)

Yoshitsune divides the topic into two parts: "New Year's Day" is expressed by "Aratama no / Toshi o" (Bright as a new jewel, / Is this year . . .) and by "Mukau" (welcome); "The Palace Banquet" appears as "Miki tamau" (Partakes of the finest sake). Kenjō, a member of the Rokujō school, is true to its traditions in directly paraphrasing the topic:

Mutsuki tatsu	The First Month begins
Kyō no matoi ya	With this gathering today;
Momoshiki no	Surely, this is the first
Toyonoakari no	Of the New Year's celebrations
Hajime naru ran.	Convened at the manifold Court.
	(ibid., 8)

The "New Year's Day" of the topic corresponds to Kenjō's "Mutsuki tatsu" (The First Month begins); "The Palace Banquet" is rendered as "Toyonoakari" (the New Year's celebrations). Jakuren, a member of Teika's Mikohidari school, makes this somewhat anomalous contribution:

[9] The Indian monk Bodhidharma brought the meditation techniques known as dhyāna (Ch. ch'an, J. zen) to China. He is regarded as the founder of Ch'an/Zen Buddhism. [Auth., Trans.]

Momoshiki ya	The manifold Court
Sode o tsuranuru	Where we join sleeve to sleeve
Sakazuki ni	To pass the winecup,
Ei o susumuru	Our intoxication speeded
Haru no hatsukaze.	By the first soft breeze of spring.
	(ibid., 9)

Jakuren hints at "New Year's Day" with his "Haru no" (of spring) and "hatsu-" (first). Unlike Yoshitsune and Kenjō, however, he does not refer directly to this part of the topic. Jakuren was criticized for improperly expressing "The Palace Banquet." It was felt that the significance of His Majesty's palace celebration was not well summed up by a line like "Our intoxication speeded."[10] [By conventional standards,] Teika's waka marks a complete departure from the topic:

Haru kureba	As spring arrives
Hoshi no kurai ni	The stars in their brilliant ranks
Kage miete	Show a finer light,
Kumoi no hashi ni	And on the stairs that lead to clouds
Izuru taoyame.	Celestial maidens come to view.
	(ibid., 8)

The Right criticized the poem: "The Left's waka is written in an incomprehensible style." The Right team included Takanobu, Ietaka, and Jakuren, all members of the Mikohidari school. Yet even these likely allies seem to have been unimpressed by Teika's poem. Shunzei, acting as judge, stated that he did not understand what the Right meant by "incomprehensible"; even he could not respond to the poem, however. It was ruled the loser.

Teika's loss was guaranteed by the criteria used at waka matches, criteria grounded in the tradition of composition on fixed topics. Teika accurately expressed the topic from his perspective, which happened to be dominated by the new yūgen style. His poem proclaims that spring seems to have made the many ranks of stars more luminous, as they watch lovely women climb the palace stairs of heaven.[11] This celestial event is a metaphor for the royal New Year's banquet. The Pole Star corresponds

[10] Shunzei expostulated, "The poem might just as well concern a private stream-banquet where men delight in peach blossoms seen against the sky!" (*RU*, "Spring, 1" 10).

[11] "Hoshi no kurai" (lit. ranks of stars) is an inversion of "kurai no hoshi" (stars of rank). Another inversion appears in Teika's "Beginner's Hundred-Poem Sequence," composed at the age of nineteen: what should be "Tsuki koso aki no / Hikari narikere" (But it is in fact the moon / Illuminating autumn) is given as "Aki koso tsuki no / Hikari narikere" (But it is in fact autumn / That illuminates the moon; *SG*, 1:37).

to the tennō (see vol. one, ch. 7), and the subordinate stars ranging round it represent his vassals. On a superficial level, the waka states that the wintry-cold starlight is made more brilliant by the arrival of spring; but the poem also hints at the enhanced splendor of the assembled vassals. The celestial maiden-stars who mount the steps are singers and dancers from the Female Dancers' and Musicians' Office, summoned to perform for the banqueters.[12] Teika's poem communicates a sense of brilliance and celebration. The singers and dancers are not mentioned in any of the other eleven waka composed on this topic. Teika may have done so because he thought the performers embodied the brilliance and celebratory atmosphere most characteristic of his topic, "The Palace Banquet on New Year's Day."

The "most characteristic" element of a waka is its hon'i or essential nature. Prior to Teika's time, waka poets composing on set topics were expected to evoke only the most stereotyped hon'i of a topic. Anyone hearing or reading such a poem would immediately realize that it depicted the "most characteristic" aspect of its topic. When, for example, the topic was Mount Fuji, a poet customarily mentioned the smoke emerging from its crater (see ch. 2), because that was the hon'i of Mount Fuji. By contrast, Teika's decision to capture his topic by conjuring up a vision of brilliance and celebration was an act wholly unmotivated by precedented, communal, formulaic factors. Teika acted out of independent inspiration.

If brilliance and celebration had indeed been an accepted hon'i for "The Palace Banquet on New Year's Day," Teika's depiction would not have been condemned by the Right as "incomprehensible." Teika's concept, though independently inspired, was hardly beyond the grasp of the other participants. It was, however, something not ordinarily conceived. Once expressed, the concept cannot help but elicit a response, even from modern readers. His poem shows us something that exists at no routine level of awareness, revealing something not usually perceived. Despite its generally elusive nature, that "something" is bound to be recognized as a true aspect of the topic. The Right side should have responded in such a fashion, and yet they protested that Teika's style was "incomprehensible." Their protest was probably motivated by his flouting of topic conventions. As he well knew, the most characteristic aspect of a topic was an entity agreed upon by everyone and pertained to a normal level of awareness. He defied convention by composing a poem on a nonformulaic aspect of the topic. For him, the hon'i occupied a different dimension and had thus to be sought in mental depths (see ch. 5). Yūgen underwent

[12] Women were instructed in dance and music by the Female Dancers' and Musicians' Office. The tennō customarily gave an annual banquet for his personal attendants around the twentieth of the First Month, at which women from the Office sang and danced (see vol. two, ch. 6).

a corresponding evolution. The yūgen defined by Chōmei and Teika belongs to a different dimension from "yūgen" as invoked by Shunzei and his predecessors. In his last years, Shunzei was not at all attracted by the yūgen style. We must therefore conclude that Teika, not Shunzei, established yūgen as a waka style.

The yūgen style may strike readers as a blurred poetic focus communicating a sense of diffuseness. Nor is this view peculiar to readers. A poet without a firm grasp of his subject will produce a work in which intended understatement becomes merely diffuse language. It is absolutely necessary that understated expression—which gravitates toward diffuseness—be accompanied by a cohesive grasp of the subject. What gave the poet this cohesive grasp? I believe it was kokoro [mind, spirit, conception]. Earlier, we considered a poem by Shunzei:

Omokage ni	I set the vision
Hana no sugata o	Of the flowers' configuration
Sakidatete	Before me as I go;
Ikue koekinu	How many mountains have I crossed,
Mine no shirakumo.	Oh, white clouds that wreath the peaks?

The speaker does not declare that he longs to see cherry blossoms; he tells us instead how a vision of blossoms has lured him across countless peaks. Indirection strengthens the received impression of the speaker's longing. Shunzei's poem was praised as moving, impressive (ch. 2). The poem focuses on "shirakumo," white clouds. Cherry blossoms are not described in the poem. When the white cloud imagery enters the mind, however, an image of the clouds will drift through the imagination, transforming into a vision of cherry-blossom. A reader who probes more deeply into the cloud imagery will find the imagination invaded by the image of cherry blossoms looking like white clouds clinging to distant peaks. At this point the reader understands the speaker's claim to have crossed countless peaks, and what had previously seemed exaggerated now makes perfect sense. Such poetry remains incomplete without a committed imaginative approach from the reader. In Shunzei's poem, the recipient is caught up in the poet's cherry-blossom-obsessed imagination. He and poets contemporary with him called this quality "kokoro fukashi" (moving, impressive; deep in conception).

The "kokoro" of "kokoro fukashi" refers directly to the speaker's kokoro or heart and indirectly to the poet's. Kokoro is the functioning of the human heart, with its wide range of emotions. Tsurayuki uses "kokoro" in this sense when he writes that "Yamato poetry takes the human spirit as seed" (*Kokinshū*, Preface, 9). In the twelfth century, another kind of kokoro developed in tandem with the practice of composing on set topics. The "kokoro of a topic" refers to the most characteristic aspect of a given topic—its hon'i, or essential nature (see ch. 2). As we know, hon'i was not produced through individual poetic responses. It was a convention created through consensus: everyone agreed that a given topic was to be treated in a given fashion. We have seen how the kokoro for the topic "Mount Fuji" was agreed to be "spouting smoke." When the kokoro of a topic was properly expressed in a waka, it was hailed as "possessing hon'i." Both kinds of kokoro, the emotive and the conventional, appear in waka. We would do well to distinguish between the emotive kokoro—the speaker's or poet's range of feeling—and the conventional kokoro, a product of mutual agreement that is unconnected to a poet's individual emotions. The emotive variety will be termed "subjective kokoro," and the convention will be called "objective kokoro." Because both kinds of kokoro can serve as the focal point of a poem, however, they may also be referred to jointly as the "expressed kokoro."

"Kokoro" is used in yet another sense, to designate the entity functioning in the design or technique of a poem. An example of this usage appears in a judgment of a poem on the topic "Wind," composed in the Eighth Month of 1116 in the *Waka Match at Ungoji, Held at a Banquet Following the Copying of Sūtras (Ungoji Kechienkyō no Kōen Utaawase).*

Ogi no ha no	The leaves of reeds
Soyo to mo sureba	Rustle and awaken me
Matsu hito ni	As I wait for him—
Odorokarenuru	But what has startled me from sleep
Aki no yūkaze.	Is the wind at autumn dusk.

Mototoshi, the judge, remarked: "The approach has kokoro, especially in the speaker awakening to the rustling of reeds and thinking it is her lover. This strikes me as a well-wrought poem" (*HCUT*, 6:1728). The approach "has kokoro" (kokoro aru sama) because it creates interest by having the speaker mistake one sound for another. The rustling of reeds in the wind awakens a woman who has fallen asleep waiting for a tardy lover; she thinks the rustling comes from his silk robes. Here "kokoro" does not signify the speaker's feelings, but the poet's witty conceit. This illustrates how "kokoro" can be used to designate the conception leading to composition instead of the hon'i or essence of a poem. Kokoro in this sense will be termed the "expressing kokoro," as contrasted to the "expressed kokoro." A poem that skillfully displays an expressing kokoro "has kokoro" (kokoro ari); when skill borders on mastery, the poem is praised as "kokoro okashi," "well devised" (pleasing in kokoro).

The earliest instances of "kokoro" pertain to the subjective category.

The "expressing kokoro" appears next, followed by objective kokoro. The Japanese language makes no distinction among these categories, which are all grouped together as "kokoro." This gives rise to considerable confusion. Almost all waka can be clearly assigned to one of the three categories.

For all his experience in judging at poetry matches, in his late years Shunzei occasionally found it difficult to categorize kokoro within certain waka. One such problematic work, on the topic "Fallen Leaves," was composed by Teika for the *Match in Six Hundred Rounds*.

Katsu oshimu	Some parts I regret:
Nagame no utsuru	The colors in the garden,
Niwa no iro yo	How they shift in view!
Nani o kozue no	What will be in those branches
Fuyu ni nokosan.	As something left for winter?

Shunzei comments, "It seems to have kokoro. But I have also taken note of the Right's statement that the poem is incomprehensible" ("Winter, 1" 180). Subjective kokoro is present in the speaker's lamenting the gradual disappearance of leaves at the onset of winter. The poem also has an objective kokoro: the hon'i of "fallen leaves" is the image of autumn foliage gradually vanishing from the trees.

The same match also contains a poem that taxed Shunzei's capacity to distinguish between an expressing and an expressed kokoro. The waka in question is by Jakuren, on the topic "Typhoon."

Omoiyaru	I am so concerned
Waga kokoro made	That I am drenched with despair
Shiorekinu	To my very heart,
Nowaki suru yo no	Another of the many flowers
Hana no iroiro.	On this night of the typhoon.

Shunzei remarks, "The line 'To my very heart' ['Waga kokoro made'] suggests that the poem has kokoro. The Right has indeed grasped the hon'i of the topic 'Typhoon' " ("Autumn, 1" 132). In Jakuren's poem, the speaker is so concerned about his various flowers, battered by the storm, that his heart also is drenched—with despair.[13] Subjective kokoro is manifested in the speaker's concern for the fate of his flowers. A ty-

[13] "Shi[h]oru" means "to be wet, drenched," and may also signify "to be dispirited, despondent." Its medieval pronunciation was very similar to that of "shi[w]oru," "to wilt"; hence the two words function as a pivot. [The two verbs are pronounced identically today, as "shioru." When the poem was composed, however, there would have been a slight distinction between them.—Trans.]

phoon, moreover, is conventionally perceived in waka as ruining flowers: this is its hon'i. Hence Shunzei says that Jakuren's poem "grasped the hon'i of the topic 'Typhoon.'" Not only the flowers but the speaker's heart are "drenched with despair." The pivot word "shiore-" (to be drenched, to despair) gives further interest to the poem by intertwining the physical damage to the flowers with the speaker's emotional response. This is an example of the "expressing kokoro" in action. Shunzei's difficulty in distinguishing a specific kind of kokoro in these poems is significant because it demonstrates that his age produced poems defying categorization. It is not for us to force such waka into categories (Konishi, 1951b, 128-32).

Waka styles became fixed in the late twelfth century, when composing on set topics grew widespread. Each topic had its own, predetermined hon'i, and a poem yielding any but the prescribed hon'i was invariably a failure at poetry matches. The most esteemed poetry was consequently composed according to accepted form. Of course, overemphasis on form tended to quash spontaneity and leave the mere shadow of hon'i. Shunzei's emotive style was intended as an alternative to fixed composition forms (see ch. 2). He believed in poets giving free rein to emotion; but he also wished to honor the ga aesthetic, and he does not therefore reject the accepted treatment of hon'i. What kind of style did Shunzei have in mind? I believe he envisioned the style eventually developed by Teika: yūgen. Like Shunzei, Teika respected the hon'i of a topic, its most characteristic aspect. Teika differed from his fellow poets, however, in the nature of the hon'i he pursued. His hon'i were not features likely to occur to anyone, not features reinforced by ordinary thought. For Teika, the essence of a topic could only be grasped at a deep mental level.

An example of Teika's approach occurs in round 75 of the *Waka Match of Fifteen Love Poems, Held at the Minase Mansion (Minasedono Koi Jūgoshu Utaawase)*, held in 1202. The topic is "Winds and Love"; the judge is Shunzei (391-92).

The Left: Lord Teika

Shirotae no	White as pure hemp,
Sode no wakare ni	The sleeves at morning parting
Tsuyu ochite	Brighten with dew drops,
Mi ni shimu iro no	While with its heart-piercing color
Akikaze zo fuku.	Chill autumn wind blows through.

The Right: [Fujiwara] Masatsune (Winner)

Ima wa tada	Now again it is
Konu yo amata no	A night you fail to visit me,

Sayo fukete	A night grown late,
Mataji to omou ni	And as I think to wait no longer,
Matsukaze no koe.	The waiting wind cries in the pines.

> The Left has not done badly with its "While with its heart-piercing color / Chill autumn wind blows through." The Right's "And as I think to wait no longer, / The waiting wind cries in the pines" is by far the better, and is thus declared the winner.

The topic "autumn winds" (akikaze) contains a pivot word, "aki-," that signifies both "autumn" and "cooling passion." In love poetry, therefore, cooling passion is the hon'i of "autumn winds." Both Teika and Masatsune respect the hon'i of their topic. In Masatsune's poem, the speaker, realizing her lover will not come, is just about to abandon her wait for him. Then she hears the sound of wind in the pines (matsukaze). "Matsu," like "aki-" in Teika's poem, is a pivot word: "matsukaze" can also mean "the waiting wind." The speaker, sensing that the wind in the pines is "waiting," decides to join it in waiting for her lover.

Masatsune clearly portrays a waning love. Teika's poem presents no such picture. The lovers in his poem have spent the night together, sleeve resting upon sleeve; dew falls on the sleeves when they (and their wearers) are parted at dawn. Dew, a metaphor for tears, is associated with lovers' parting at daybreak; it has no specific connection to waning passion. The poem concludes with autumn winds blowing. What color have winds that blow "with its heart-piercing color"? We are not told. Anyone familiar with the Five Elements [gogyō] system, however, will know that the autumn wind is represented by the color white.[14] The pillow word "Shirotae no" ("White as pure hemp") alerts those who remain unaware of this fact. Teika's use of "Shirotae no" is unconventional, because the pillow word is made to function as a color image. The focal point of the poem is whiteness. Concentration on the penetrating whiteness of the autumn winds in the waka will evoke a sense of waning love. Only then does the reader understand that the lovers' "parting of sleeves" is not a present event, but a memory of an earlier, happier time.

Teika's extremely understated poem might easily evoke random associations that in turn lead to a diffuse, disorganized response. Whiteness, the focus of the poem, performs an important function in this respect. Concentrating on whiteness will purify the phenomena in the poem, until all that is left is a sense of emptiness: the love affair is over. The white, empty perspective then becomes a vantage point from which to discover a broader, unexpressed meaning within the phenomena of the poem. Teika's unified expression yields a far richer and subtler work than is first

[14] [For such seasonal and directional symbolism, see Miner-Odagiri-Morrell, 1985, 404. An ensuing note in the original has been transferred, with some adjustment, to the main text.—Ed.]

apparent. Shunzei's comment, that Teika "has not done badly" with his poem, probably means that Teika's work, though intelligible up to a point, ultimately failed to summon a response from Shunzei. Masatsune's poem, the winner by default, has little else but its pivot between "wind in the pines" and "waiting wind."

Teika's poem met with little better favor from the same judge when it was entered again on the twenty-ninth day of the Ninth Month in the same year at the *Waka Match in Fifteen Rounds, Held at the Sakura Shrine in Minase (Minase Sakura no Miya no Jūgoban Utaawase).* Lady Kunaikyō (d. 1205?) wrote the opposed poem.

Kiku ya ika ni	Have you heard how
Uwa no sora naru	Even the heedless wind that moves
Kaze dani mo	Through the upper sky
Matsu ni otosuru	Habitually goes in visit,
Narai ari to wa.	They say, to the waiting pines?

Shunzei declared the match a draw: "Both the Left and the Right have good poems" (Round 14:394).

Even the perceptive Shunzei was incapable of responding fully to Teika's poetry; others inevitably condemned it as Zen nonsense. How was Teika able to create such individualistic poems? He was, I believe, inspired through the practice of Tendai contemplation (shikan [or, cessation and insight]). The process of contemplation or meditation is similar to Teika's practice of concentrating deeply on the essence of a subject. In Tendai contemplation, worldly thoughts are banished from the mind, which concentrates instead on a given object, and the goal of the process is for the meditating person to become one with the essence of the contemplated object.[15] The object is known as the "sphere" (Ch. ching), and the unifying mental function is termed "cognition" (chih). If, for example, Amitābha is the object or sphere, the meditator contemplates and seeks to become one with the compassion that Amitābha personifies. Since compassion is an abstract concept, the meditator facilitates assimilation by conjuring up a mental image of a familiar painting or sculpture of Amitābha. The form that is contemplated must be unmistakably Amitābha's; the more stereotyped the image, the more effective will be the contemplative process. When the meditator concentrates more deeply, the visual image diminishes and vanishes. Assimilated into Amitābha's

[15] "Shikan," or Tendai contemplation, is a composite word. "Shi" (concentration or cessation) signifies the stilling of external stimuli and inner turmoil in order to concentrate on a specified object. "Kan" (realization or insight) refers to the correct cognition of the object, a cognition achieved through concentration. The *Maka Shikan* gives practical directions for four kinds of meditation processes (sammai). [See notes 18-19 for further information on *Maka Shikan*.—Trans.]

pure compassion, the meditator also becomes filled with mercy. The process of assimilation is known as "fusion" (chü-jung).

Let us apply the process of contemplative fusion to waka. Our object, or sphere, shall be cherry blossoms. Yūen, refined charm, is the essence of cherry blossoms; we shall therefore focus our minds on refined charm. The facilitating image is a blossom; not any image of cherry or plum blossoms, but a specific blossom. If cherry blossoms are our focus, contemplation is facilitated by conjuring up a stereotyped image recognizable to anyone. This is the expressed kokoro of cherry blossoms. The cognition process—the deep contemplation of a specific cherry blossom—corresponds to the expressing kokoro. When the poet is assimilated into the refined charm that is the essence of cherry blossoms, refined charm becomes a living presence within, and all distinction vanishes between blossoms and poet. This is fusion, also known in Tendai contemplation as "object and cognition as one" (ching-chih pu-erh; J. kyōchi funi).

Earlier in this section we encountered examples of waka that clearly "had kokoro," but could not easily be categorized as possessing either "expressed" or "expressing" kokoro. When a skilled writer adopts the contemplative approach described, all distinctions vanish between the poet's kokoro and that of the blossom. (We cannot be sure that Shunzei made intentional use of the contemplative method. He may have composed in a semi-contemplative stance, which came to be reflected in his criticism.) When a "sphere" is contemplated as a mental process, it is termed a "thought-object" (ching-ssu; J. kyōshi); when it possesses concrete form, it is a "form-object" (ching-hsiang; J. kyōshō). The former entity corresponds to subjective kokoro, and the latter to objective kokoro. The relationships are diagrammed in Figure 8.1.

Waka created from grasping an object through deep contemplation are said to follow the "ushin style" (the style that has kokoro), according to the poetic treatise *Maigetsushō*. Ushin is described there as the most important of the ten basic waka styles, with the addition that ushin (a compound also read as "kokoro ari," "to have kokoro") is also a requisite for the other nine basic waka styles. Composing in the ushin style is described as follows (*Maigetsushō*, 128):

> It is difficult to have a complete understanding of this style. A poet who approaches it with wavering mind will never be able to compose in the ushin style. Only after meticulously purifying the heart and entering into a single sphere [kyō] can one compose ushin poetry—and then only rarely. That is why I limit good waka to those possessing profound kokoro.

The author certainly advocates a contemplative stance. A poet must purify the heart—quieting the mind and concentrating on a single object—

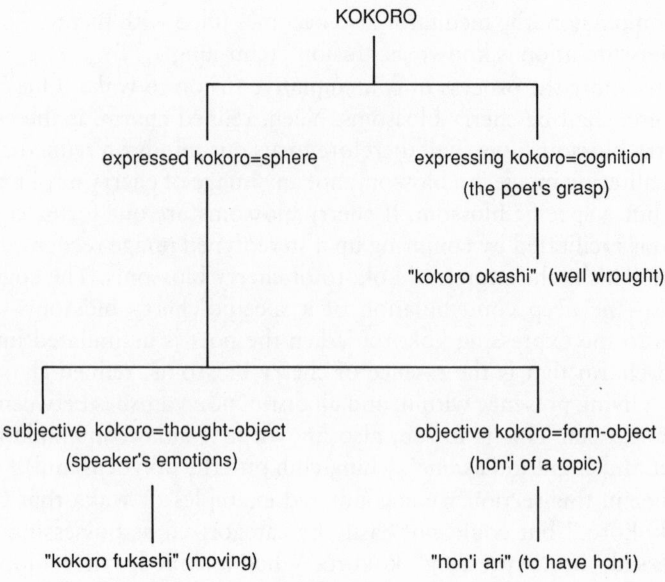

FIGURE 8.1 Varieties of Kokoro Distinguished

in order to compose in the ushin style. This act corresponds to "shi" (Skt. śamatha, cessation or concentration), the word forming the first half of "shikan," (cessation and insight). The second half, "kan" (Skt. vipaśyanā, insight or realization), corresponds to the poet's "entering into" (deeply concentrating on) a poetic subject. "Kan" signifies the correct cognition of the poetic subject at a profound conceptual depth. The author of the *Maigetsushō* also uses "sphere," a technical term employed in contemplative practice, to refer to the subject of a poem. Deep contemplation will produce fusion between the expressed and the expressing kokoro: this is the kokoro achieved by the ushin style. We have no way of knowing whether the *Maigetsushō* passage was directly inspired by contemplative practice. The *Shih-ke* of Wang Ch'ang-ling has a very similar discussion on grasping the poetic subject, which again is termed the "sphere."[16] Ch'ang-ling's exposition too may be based on contemplative practice. Regardless of its inspiration, the *Maigetsushō* passage aptly describes Teika's method while guiding us toward full appreciation of Teika's waka.

The *Maigetsushō* is attributed to Teika. Yashima Chōju has disputed

[16] "Literary composition demands that you formulate various plans, explore all possible avenues, and rack your brains for concepts. Then block from your mind your own worldly state, for you must not become caught up in such thoughts. If an idea is not quick in coming, let your mind move freely: this will facilitate the creation of a sphere [ching; J. kyō]. Elaborating on this sphere will yield an idea; as soon as it occurs, compose on it. If you can summon neither sphere nor idea, you cannot compose" (Konishi, 1953e, 164).

the attribution, giving rise to long-standing debate.[17] I do not join the majority of scholars in endorsing the traditional attribution. The *Maigetsushō* postdates Teika's time: it could not have been written before the late thirteenth century (see ch. 14). It is nevertheless quoted here because the above passage, at least, accurately transmits Teika's intentions. To call the *Maigetsushō* a forgery would be to brand it as totally unreliable, when in fact certain passages are well worth our notice. Various documents in the keeping of the Reizei family transmit Teika's poetic theories; some of these would have provided source material for the *Maigetsushō*. Its authenticity has remained largely unquestioned because it contains opinions attributable to Teika alone.

Teika (1162-1241) began formal study of Tendai contemplation in old age.[18] Shunzei mentions one of the Tendai canons, *Mo-ho Chih-kuan* (J. *Maka Shikan*), in his *Korai Fūteishō*.[19] Shunzei's interest in Tendai thought may be connected to his usage of the critical term "to have kokoro": in waka-match judgments, he generally uses the term to connote unity between object and cognition. If his critical attitudes were indeed shaped by Tendai thought, the still youthful Teika may have acquired his contemplative approach to waka from his father. Needless to say, hardly any of Shunzei's waka require contemplation in order to be understood. Although Shunzei framed the basic concepts of the ushin style, he did not put them into action. As was the case for yūgen, Teika, not Shunzei, transformed a crucial concept into actual composition.

Teika's move toward new expressive forms may be said to involve two energies, yūgen and ushin. Where yūgen is diffuse, intense feeling embodies the concentration of ushin. Not only are these seemingly mutual opposites mutually dependent, they also share certain aspects. The interest in yūgen stems from its way of capturing ushin; ushin is a requisite for creating yūgen. "Yūgen" and "ushin" are terms used respectively by Chōmei and the compiler of the *Maigetsushō* to refer to aspects of Teika's art. Yet Teika did not call these elements "yūgen" and "ushin." It is virtually meaningless, therefore, to investigate the number of times Teika used the word "yūgen" or to determine how old Teika was when his poetry was first judged "ushin" at a waka match.

[17] Yashima, 1953, 1-21. Mizukami Kashizō succinctly summarizes both sides of the debate (Mizukami, 1969, 106-20).

[18] Teika copied, punctuated, and collated the ten fascicles of the Tendai text *Mo-ho Chih-kuan (Maka Shikan)* between 18.III.1229 and 12.VIII.1230 (*MGK*, 3:85-232). Teika's name in religion, Myōjō ("Clarity and Tranquility"), is probably based on the passage, "The clarity and tranquility achieved by contemplation is not known to have existed in past ages" (*Maka Shikan*, 1:1; Konishi, 1952b, 19-20).

[19] *Kōrai Fūteishō*, 1:303-304. The *Mo-ho Chih-kuan* is a collection of teachings expounded by the Great T'ien-t'ai Teacher, Chih-i (538-97) in 594 and recorded by his disciple Kuan-ting, the Great Chang-an Teacher.

TEIKA'S ACHIEVEMENT

Teika and Other Shinkokinshū *Poets*

The Bunji and Kenkyū eras (1185-98) marked Teika's first attempt at writing in the yūgen style, and his results were generally criticized as "Zen-nonsense poetry." This period covers Teika's twenty-third through thirty-sixth years. The waka composed during the first half of this time are hardly so aberrant as to deserve being called "faddish and unfounded." They do make striking use of caesuras, however. Two examples date from the Bunji era.

Miwataseba	As I look afar
Hana mo momiji mo	The blossoms and bright autumn leaves
Nakarikeri	Are no longer needed;
Ura no tomaya no	Wretched thatched huts along the shore
Aki no yūgure.	In the thickening autumn dusk.[20]
	(*SG*, 1:135)

Kaerusa no	While he now returns
Mono to ya hito no	Is this something he gazes on
Nagamu ran	After our brief tryst?
Matsu yo nagara no	Through the night hours of my waiting,
Ariake no tsuki.	The moon now fading in the dawn.
	(*SG*, 1:379)

The distinct break after the third line of both poems makes the poems reminiscent of two stanzas of linked poetry. Naturally, a reader or hearer will have some difficulty supplementing the blank created by each caesura; but this is little labor indeed for those familiar with Teika's ambiguous later work. If, on the other hand, the poems are one's introduction to Teika's understated art, they might well seem as impenetrable as a Zen kōan [paradoxical questions for spiritual illumination]. Even connoisseurs of Teika's poetry discover ambiguities in his Kenkyū-era work; his

[20] [One of Teika's famous poems, this is the third of the "sanseki," or consecutive poems ending "Aki no yūgure" in the *Shinkokinshū* (4:361-63). There is still no agreement as to what the poem means. One, the "literal," interpretation holds that "Nakarikeri" means that cherry blossoms and colored leaves are absent from the scene; another holds that the line means they are not needed. It seems agreed that the poem is less interesting with the first interpretation. Varieties of the second exist, whether or not with relations to the allusions (to a poem and to the *Genji Monogatari*). One of the most interesting holds that the speaker had come to the scene with images in his mind of cherry blossoms and autumn-tinged leaves but that, with the very differently moving scene before him, the conventional beauties are unnecessary. For a discussion, see Ishida Ayao, *Uta no Fukasa* (Sōgensha, 1971), 114-17. It will be clear why Teika's contemporaries might be confused and why translating his work reduces multiple possibilities to fewer. The author has asked that our translations not overemphasize a single, unambiguous interpretation.—Ed.]

entries for *The Waka Match in Six Hundred Rounds (Roppyakuban Utaawase)* are particularly problematic. The difficulty of this poetry was discussed above. Other examples from the *Match* include:

Kōriiru	Frozen quite solid,
Mirume nagisa no	The seaweed I see along the shore,
Tagui kana	That is the kind of thing!
Ue seku sode no	A sleeve checks the outer flow,
Shita no sasanami.	Inside resistless waves of tears.
	(*RU*, "Love, 1" [Hidden Love] 230)
Toshi mo henu	The years have passed
Inoru chigiri wa	With prayers, for love, to the Kannon
Hatsuseyama	On Mount Hatsuse.
Onoe no kane no	From its hilltop the temple bell
Yoso no yūgure.	And evening just for others.
	(*RU*, "Love, 2" [Prayed-for Love] 245)
Omokage mo	You beside me,
Wakare ni kawaru	A vision changed to parting,
Kane no oto ni	At dawn's temple bell
Narai kanashiki	It is always sad to find
Shinonome no sora.	The sky streaked with first light.
	(*RU*, "Love, 4" [Love at Dawn] 281)

Putting these and many more of Teika's poems into modern Japanese, much less English translation, is an exercise in futility. These three poems were criticized at the *Match* as follows. The Right (the opposing side) found that the first poem, "Kōriiru" ("Frozen quite solid"), "does not state all that it should"; Shunzei, the judge, pronounced it "quite incomprehensible." The judgment for the second, "Toshi mo henu" ("The years have passed"), was "The speaker's emotions, though deeply portrayed, seem imprecisely expressed." The last poem, "Omokage mo" ("You beside me"), moved the Right to note that "the poem is incomprehensible unless one has read it ahead of time"; Shunzei remarked, "The style is like Kisen's—'incomprehensible from start to finish.' "[21]

Some of the participants in *The Waka Match in Six Hundred Rounds* were members of two rival schools of waka: Teika, Ietaka, Jakuren, and Takanobu represented the Mikohidari school, while Suetsune, Kenjō, Tsuneie, and Ariie made up the Rokujō contingent. If we assume that unaffiliated participants—Yoshitsune, Jien, Kanemasa, and Iefusa—re-

[21] "Kisen, a monk living in Uji, has vague diction. His poems are incomprehensible from start to finish" (*KKS*, Japanese Preface, 19).

mained neutral throughout the match, we may conclude that the event essentially pitted the Mikohidari waka against those of the Rokujō school.[22] The Mikohidari began its ascendancy in 1171 with the death of its principal rival, Fujiwara Kiyosuke, leader of the Rokujō.

Taniyama Shigeru's calculations reflect this trend. In poetry matches held between 1160 and 1169, the Rokujō won an average of 55 percent of the rounds versus 40 percent for the Mikohidari. In the next decade, 1170-79, the Mikohidari moved ahead with a 47 percent winning average versus 43 percent for the Rokujō. A virtual tie existed from 1190 to 1199: the Mikohidari averaged 45 percent of the victories, while the Rokujō had 44 percent. (No records survive of matches held between 1180 and 1189 that were attended by both sides.) In the three years from 1200 through 1202, however, the Mikohidari gained a clear advantage, winning 51 percent versus 41 percent for its rival (Taniyama, 1943, 257-320). *The Waka Match in Six Hundred Rounds*, convened in 1193 in the midst of this power shift, was the scene of momentous battles between the Mikohidari and the weakening Rokujō. Yet the final score of the *Match* was hardly decisive: the Rokujō won 110 rounds and lost 165, while the Mikohidari had 114 wins and 164 losses. The relatively balanced outcome reflects Shunzei's extremely impartial judgments; it also indicates how obscure Teika's contemporaries found his yūgen style.

The Rokujō managed to recoup its losses six years later. It won 56 percent of the competitions at *The Waka Match at Omuro (Omuro Senkaawase)* versus 44 percent for the Mikohidari.[23] Teika himself won no rounds, lost five, and was given three draws. His 31 percent average placed him a pitiful sixteenth in a field of eighteen participants. Shunzei served as nominal judge. Victors were, however, determined by "written judgment," a summarized version of the open discussions conducted during the match.[24] The match was sponsored by the cloistered prince Shukaku (1150-1202), a close friend of Kenjō, and the discussions seem to have favored the Rokujō side. Shunzei, whose task it was to transcribe the proceedings, was unable to make substantial revisions (Ariyoshi, 1968, 36-38).

The Waka Match at Omuro was a rearrangement of earlier poetic se-

[22] Kenjō's later rebuttals to Shunzei's judgments (commonly known as *Kenjō's Refutation*) suggest that the opposing sides had heated arguments during the *Match*. A later source, *Seiashō*, records disputes between Kenjō and Jakuren (6:99). [The author's next note has been entered as a parenthesis in the text below.—Ed.]

[23] All manuscripts give 1200 as the year of the match; but the official titles of the participants, noted in the match records, indicate that the event actually took place between 23.III.1199 and 22.VI.1199 (Ariyoshi, 1968, 24).

[24] A "written judgment" was produced through on-the-spot discussions among participants at a match. The discussions were later summed up in writing by one of the participants, acting as secretary. The judgment is essentially a record of participants' opinions, but the secretary's bias is often discernible through his choice of words.

quences into the format of a poetry match. Its source, *The Fifty-Poem Sequences Composed at the Residence of the Cloistered Prince Shukaku* (*Shukaku Hō Shinnō Gojusshu*; also known as *Fifty Poems from Omuro, Omuro Gojusshu*, etc.), was compiled two years prior to the match.[25] The sequence composed by Teika for the occasion appears in his *Shūi Gusō*.[26] Some of its poems are acknowledged examples of his best work:

Ōzora wa	Across the heavens
Ume no nioi ni	In the fragrance of plum blossoms
Kasumitsutsu	The haze increases;
Kumori mo hatenu	The thin clouds do not exempt
Haru no yo no tsuki.	The moon on the brief spring night.
	(*SG*, 2:1632)

Shimo mayou	Lost in the frost
Sora ni shioreshi	In the sky that has dampened
Karigane no	The wild geese's wings,
Kaeru tsubasa ni	Returning to their northern home,
Harusame zo furu.	There the soft spring rain is falling.
	(*SG*, 2:1634)

Haru no yo no	On the brief spring night,
Yume no ukihashi	The floating bridge of dreams
Todaeshite	Breaks all apart,
Mine ni wakaruru	And from a mountain peak a cloud
Yokogumo no sora.	Takes leave into the empty sky.
	(*SG*, 2:1638)

Yūgure wa	In the twilight,
Izure no kumo no	Which cloud will be provider
Nagori tote	Of the memory,
Hanatachibana ni	As from the flowering orange trees
Kaze no fuku ran.	The fragrant breeze blows here?[27]
	(*SG*, 2:1644)

[25] The sequence was evidently composed between 9.XII.1198 and 23.III.1199, to judge from the official titles of participants (Ariyoshi, 1968, 23).

[26] Teika composed his sequence well in advance. A note in the *Shūi Gusō* (2:1629-78) states, "50 waka for the Ninnaji prince [Shukaku]; Summer, Kenkyū 9 [1198]."

[27] The scene of orange blossoms was thought to evoke memories of someone absent or dead. Teika's poem alludes to a *Kokinshū* poem (3:139): Satsuki matsu / Hanatachibana no / Ka o kageba / Mukashi no hito no / Sode no ka zo suru. (When I smell the fragrance / Of the blossoms of the oranges / That wait till June to come, / It is the fragrance of the sleeves / Of that person of my past.) The "cloud" of Teika's poem is a conventional allusion to the dead, whose spirit rises in the smoke of the funeral pyre and becomes a cloud. [Auth., Trans.]

None of these poems appears in *The Waka Match at Omuro*. The Rokujō group would have regarded them as utter nonsense. The Rokujō, in fact, was probably the first to characterize Teika's poetry as "Zen gibberish."

Soon, however, the Rokujō resistance was no longer a substantial hindrance for Teika. He recalls in his diary how, during the Shōji and Kennin eras (1199-1204), he gained the confidence necessary to devote himself to the Way of Waka. His confidence was bolstered by a patron, "His Enlightened Majesty," the abdicated sovereign Gotoba. Teika also remembers an earlier period, the Bunji and Kenkyū eras, when he was scorned by all levels of society. During this period, Teika served the regent, (Fujiwara) Gokyōgoku Yoshitsune, and presented new compositions at the regent's waka gatherings. Fujiwara Kiyosuke, the Rokujō leader and the most eminent waka poet of his day, had enjoyed entrée to Yoshitsune's household when the latter's father, (Fujiwara) Kujō Kanezane (1149-1207), was alive. The Rokujō continued to dominate the regental salon after Kanezane's death. The Mikohidari school was also represented at these early Kujō waka gatherings: Shunzei first appeared there in 1178, and Teika followed in 1186. The Mikohidari was clearly a minor presence, however. Its few members—Shunzei, Takanobu, Teika, and Jakuren—faced such major Rokujō poets as Suetsune, Tsuneie, Motosuke, Akiie, Ariie, Yasusue, and Kenjō. Teika was as yet an unprepossessing poet (Fujihira, 1969, 24-35).

The Mikohidari position was gradually strengthened as Teika began to gain the support of Yoshitsune and his uncle Jien, Kanezane's younger brother. These influential backers enabled the Mikohidari to achieve its 1193 draw with the Rokujō, in *The Waka Match in Six Hundred Rounds*. After this point, as we have seen, the Mikohidari became the dominant force in waka. The Rokujō nevertheless remained a power to be reckoned with: given the proper chance, they might well have engineered another Mikohidari debacle like *The Waka Match at Omuro*.

An ambitious waka gathering convened by Gotoba in 1200 aided Teika in consolidating his victory over the Rokujō school. In the Seventh Month of 1200, Gotoba envisioned that several prominent poets should each submit a hundred-poem sequence for a grand waka gathering. Teika was a likely participant; but his candidacy was opposed by the Palace Minister, Minamoto Michichika (1149-1202). The Minister had become a power in court politics after successfully engineering the downfall of his rival Kanezane in the Eleventh Month of 1196. Suetsune, a Rokujō poet, promptly placed himself under Michichika's patronage. Michichika's intervention was perceived as a Rokujō plot by the furious Teika.[28] Shunzei

[28] "At first His Majesty [Gotoba] was most favorably inclined toward my participating in

submitted a written opinion on the matter to Gotoba. The document, which has come to be called *The Memorial in Japanese, Dated Shōji 2*, requested that His Majesty include three gifted poets in the gathering: Teika, Takafusa, and Ietaka.[29] Moved by Shunzei's reasonable petition, Gotoba agreed to add Teika and the others to the designated group of poets. One waka in Teika's hundred-poem sequence won Gotoba's especial admiration.

Birds

Kimi ga yo ni	Our lord once decreed
Kasumi o wakeshi	That a crane among the reeds
Ashitazu no	Emerge from the mists;
Sara ni sawabe no	Now once again its voice
Ne o ya naku beki.	Will be heard along the marsh![30]
	(*SG*, 1:993)

Teika's fine sequence won him entrée to the Courtiers' Hall in the tennō's royal residence (Ariyoshi, 1968, 52-60). Thus began the connection between Teika and Gotoba, an acquaintance that was to have enormous bearing on the creation of the *Shinkokinshū*. Teika's grateful reference in his memoirs to "the kindness of His Enlightened Majesty" in the Shōji and Kennin eras is to the events just related.

Though already an abdicated sovereign, Gotoba was only twenty years old when this controversy took place. One wonders how well he understood Teika's yūgen style. Conjecture is impossible, given the paucity of data on Gotoba's early waka. His style resembled Shunzei's during the Shōji and Kennin eras. Apparently Gotoba did not wholly endorse Teika's new style. The former sovereign admired Teika's poem on the crane among the reeds for its skillful metaphorical treatment of a specific situation.[31] Despite Gotoba's lukewarm response to his poetry, Teika worked

the gathering. Then the Palace Minister [Michichika] intervened, and matters quickly worsened. . . . Dazzled by Suetsune's bribes, the Minister has become involved in an intrigue to drive me out of the affair. Both Suetsune and Tsuneie are under the Minister's patronage. I do not write this out of enmity for them; but the situation appears hopeless" (*MGK* [18.VII.1200], 161).

[29] *Waji Sōjō*, 275. Shunzei was eighty-six at the time.

[30] The poem is metaphorical. Teika is the crane that is now permitted to "sing again" in the marshes—that is, Gotoba is allowing him to present his poetry at the royal palace. The first half of the poem alludes to an earlier waka by Shunzei that extricated Teika from an unpleasant situation; see n. 31. [Auth. Trans.]

[31] Teika was apparently hot-tempered in his youth. He was once expelled from court for beating a fellow courtier with a candlestand (*Gyokuyō* [25.XI.1185], 118). Shunzei presented the following waka (*SZS*, 17:1155) to Gotoba, then the reigning tennō, as a plea for Teika's reinstatement: Ashitazu no / Kumoji mayoishi / Toshi kurete / Kasumi o sae ya /

hard at his hundred-poem sequence (generally known as *The First Hundred-Poem Sequence of the Shōji Era [Shōji Shodo Hyakushu]*). On the ninth day of the Eighth Month, he was unofficially notified that he was to participate in the gathering. He worked on his sequence continually from that point.[32] Shunzei and Yoshitsune were asked to comment on the results. On the evening of the twenty-fifth, Teika submitted his sequence to Gotoba (*MGK* [25.VIII.1200], 166-67). It contains some of Teika's finest poetry.

Ume no hana	Blossoms of the plum
Nioi o utsusu	Transfer their fragrance from the tree
Sode no ue ni	To the moistened sleeve
Noki moru tsuki no	Where moonbeams vie in shining
Kage zo arasou.	As they filter through the eaves!
	(*SG*, 1:906)

Koma tomete	There is no shelter
Sode uchiharau	Where I can rest my weary horse
Kage mo nashi	And brush my sleeves:
Sano no watari no	The Sano ford and nearby fields
Yuki no yūgure.	Spread with a twilight in the snow.[33]
	(*SG*, 1:967)

The gathering of 1200 was followed by a burst of poetic activity within Gotoba's salon. Teika and the other Mikohidari poets had joined Yoshitsune and Jien as members of the royal circle. The active period encompasses more than five years, beginning in 1200 with the first hundred-poem-sequence gathering and concluding on the sixteenth of the Second Month, 1205, when poems were composed at a banquet marking the completion of the *Shinkokinshū*. This period yielded thirty-nine surviving records of waka matches, hundred-poem-sequence gatherings, and waka gatherings sponsored by Gotoba (Fujihira, 1969, 85-86).

Gotoba's salon during this period was steeped in the *Shinkokinshū*

Hedatehatsu beki. (A crane left the reeds / To go astray through the clouds; / Now with the old year past, / Will the warm haze of springtime / Also hide him from the view?) The poem moved Gotoba to pardon Teika and restore him to his former rank (*Ienaga Ki*, 81-82). Teika's "Kimi ga yo ni" in the poem "Birds" alludes to this incident and to Shunzei's poem (see n. 30).

[32] "My writing costs me such painful effort that I never have time to go out" (*MGK*, 1200:166). [Seventy-nine of the hundred poems of the sequence—including three by Teika—were included in the *Shinkokinshū*. Brower, 1978, offers numerous pertinent comments.—Ed.]

[33] [The translation is adapted from Brower-Miner, 1961, 306.—Trans.]

style—so much so that the purpose behind his various waka gatherings might well have been to generate material for the anthology. The first of Gotoba's hundred-poem-sequence gatherings was immediately followed by another, convened in the Twelfth Month of 1200 and known as *The Second Hundred-Poem Sequence of the Shōji Era (Shōji Saido Hyakushu)*. A third such gathering *(The Third Hundred-Poem Sequence of Gotoba In; Gotoba In Sando Hyakushu)* was held in the Sixth Month of 1201. This last group of sequences was recast as a waka match; it took place between the Ninth Month of 1202 and the spring of 1203 and is known today as *The Waka Match in Fifteen Hundred Rounds (Sengohyakuban Utaawase)*. Ninety-one of its waka appear in the *Shinkokinshū*. By contrast, thirty-four waka were selected from *The Waka Match in Six Hundred Rounds* and seventy-nine from *The First Hundred-Poem Sequence of the Shōji Era* (Ariyoshi, 1968, 537-38). One year earlier, on the twenty-sixth of the Seventh Month, 1201, the Bureau of Waka (Wakadokoro) had been established. This strengthens our surmise that the third hundred-poem-sequence gathering and its reappearance in waka-match form were indeed intended to produce material for the *Shinkokinshū*.

Teika's new style emerged gradually over a fourteen-year period, from 1190 to 1203.[34] During this time his most appealing waka style, that called yōen or ethereal beauty, came into full flower. This was also an active time for waka poets in general, as they apparently worked on material for the *Shinkokinshū*. These fourteen years may thus be said to constitute the *Shinkokinshū* period in its strictest sense. Although the *Shinkokinshū* is true to its name—*The New Collection of Ancient and Modern Poetry*—in containing poems both from the past and from Teika's time, those in the latter group were almost all composed between 1190 and 1203. Teika's yōen style, evoking an ethereal beauty, first emerges in 1201; as early as 1186, however, the Rokujō school criticized his waka as "faddish and unfounded."

Teika's poetry sparked resistance because his method—deep contemplation—made no sense to recipients following traditional approaches. Or, to put matters another way, contemplative poetry first became an issue among waka poets when the Rokujō raised its objections. Teika's contemplative approach could still function after he abandoned the ethereal style, and it is that approach, therefore, that aids in defining other,

[34] The period has been divided into two sub-periods: that of the Gokyōgoku waka circle and that of Gotoba's salon. Such subdivisions are unnecessary: Teika's waka style does not change from one sub-period to the other. Yoshitsune and Jien were the focal members of Gotoba's salon.

broader boundaries for the *Shinkokinshū* period. This period, in the broad sense of the term, encompasses approximately thirty years. The boundaries are established by extending the fourteen years of the "narrow" period in both directions.[35]

We work from a modern perspective in determining the boundaries of the *Shinkokinshū* period. In other words, we must take into account facts that were very likely unknown to the thirteenth-century poets themselves. The result is that our methods may not match thirteenth-century standards. This is perhaps best illustrated by considering which poets are best represented in the *Shinkokinshū*. Saigyō ranks highest with ninety-four poems. He is followed by Jien with ninety-one poems, Yoshitsune with seventy-nine, Shunzei with seventy-two, Princess Shokushi with forty-nine, and Teika with forty-six. In all cases, the choice was probably influenced by contemporary tastes. Other major waka poets of the period are represented in the *Shinkokinshū* as follows: Jakuren, thirty-five poems; Gotoba, thirty-three; Shunzei's Daughter, twenty-nine; Fujiwara Masatsune, twenty-two.[36] During his lifetime, then, Teika was not considered the foremost poet of the age. But periodizing is at least partially accomplished by considering facts unknown to the people of the period under examination; hence Teika's—and his group's—position among contemporary waka poets need not be a powerful determinant. The *Shinkokinshū* period, in the narrow sense, begins two years before the compilation of the collection itself, because the style of ethereal beauty (yōen) begins to fade from that time. This development will be discussed below. We shall now investigate the nature of ethereal beauty, one of our periodizing criteria.

Teika and Ethereal Beauty

Scholars of Japanese literature almost universally consider ethereal beauty (yōen) the typical poetic mode of the *Shinkokinshū* period (in the narrow sense). Ethereal beauty is also generally regarded as exemplifying Teika's waka style. Neither view is erroneous. We ought, however, to ask ourselves whether the ethereal beauty we sense in Teika's waka actually matches Teika's own concept of yōen. His *Kindai Shūka* (= *KDSK*; *Superior Poems of Our Time*, 1209) contains a famous statement:

[35] Various studies have attempted to define the *Shinkokinshū* period, beginning with Kazamaki Keijirō's monumental work (Kazamaki, 1932, 84-130). The specific content of this thirty-year period is discussed later in this chapter.

[36] "Shunzei's Daughter" refers to Shunzei's adopted daughter (d. 1254), also known as the Zen Nun of Koshibe. She is not to be confused with Kenju Gozen (see ch. 10).

> The clever, witty waka composed by Tsurayuki in times past have a loftiness that is not easily equalled. His preferred style was clear in its diction and pleasing in form. He did not compose in a nuanced, ethereal mode. (*KDSK*, 100)

What does Teika mean by "a nuanced, ethereal mode"? He continues:

> A good many poems have recently been written that modify this straightforward form and favor antique diction. One occasionally finds poets writing in styles neglected since the days of the Bishop of Kazan [Henjō], the Ariwara Captain [Narihira], Sosei, and Ono no Komachi.[37] People unaware of the nature of things have declared such poetry an innovation that is altering the Way of Waka. (*KDSK*, 101)

The "innovation" mentioned in the passage refers to the waka style developed by Teika and his group. According to Teika, their "innovative" poetry continues the tradition established by such waka immortals (kasen) as Henjō, the Bishop from Kazan.[38] Somewhat later in *Superior Poems*, Teika writes, "You favor antique diction, seek new kokoro, and wish to achieve an effect of unparalleled loftiness. You will surely be benefited by studying waka from the Kambyō [889-98] and earlier eras" (*KDSK*, 102). Teika's poetic models clearly predate the witty waka produced by Tsurayuki and his followers. Although Teika refers only to a general era, he has a specific poet in mind. The nuanced, ethereal mode Teika invokes is epitomized by the waka of Ariwara Narihira (Tanaka, 1965, 107-21).

Teika's statements should not mislead us into believing that ethereal beauty was his supreme ideal. He faults Tsurayuki's waka for lacking nuance (yosei): they are unsatisfactory because (to borrow a phrase from Kamo no Chōmei) they "state everything in exhaustive detail."[39] Teika maintained that yūgen (profound) expression creates rich nuance. Narihira's waka, famed for their unstated content, are excellent early models of the yūgen style. Waka written during the Kambyō and earlier eras struck Teika and Chōmei as ideal primarily because they were understated. Yōen, ethereal beauty, is the nuanced tone produced by such un-

[37] Teika refers to four of the "six waka immortals" (rokkasen) mentioned in the Kana Preface to the *Kokinshū*. He understates the case: he and his followers were revolutionizing waka, not merely "modifying" it, and they composed on a frequent basis, not "occasionally." [Auth., Trans.]

[38] One of the six waka immortals who composed in a period thought "recent" (chikaki yo) by the *Kokinshū* compilers. Their "recent" times immediately precede the "modern" (kin) compilation period. See volume two, ch. 7.

[39] *Mumyōshō*, 83. See the first section of this chapter.

derstatement; its value is thus secondary to that of understatement itself. Let us inquire further into the meaning of ethereal beauty.

"Yōen" is a word frequently used in judgments handed down at waka matches. Their records therefore provide data useful in determining the contemporary meaning of "ethereal beauty" as an aesthetic term in waka. "Yōen" is used in a twelfth-century judgment made during *The Waka Match at the Residence of Akisuke, Assistant Master of Her Majesty's Household* (*Chūgū no Suke Akisuke no Ke no Utaawase*; "Love," Round 4), an event that took place in the Ninth Month of 1134. The judge was Fujiwara Mototoshi.

The Left: The Minister of the Treasury[40] (Winner)

Mi ni tsutsumi	It lies within my heart,
Ii dani idenu	And cannot be declared in words:
Ikemizu no	A pond of waters,
Nagare mo yaranu	Prevented from free flowing—
Koi o suru kana.	That is the nature of my love!

The Left has produced a waka with rich, elegant diction tending toward the ethereal [yōen]. One particularly appreciates its zest. A very good poem indeed! (*HCUT*, 7:1981)

How does this poem display ethereal beauty? Love waka ought to have en, a sense of refined, gentle amorousness, and yet this poem does not strike us as particularly en. Mototoshi, however, probably found one element of the poem quintessentially en (or, in other words, yōen): the image of pent-up water to describe the speaker's repressed love. Note that Mototoshi uses "yōen," ethereal beauty, to designate en that is understated.

Shunzei comments as follows in *The Waka Match in Fifteen Hundred Rounds*.

The Left: A Court Lady[41] (Winner)

Kaeru kari	Geese returning north
Mine no kasumi no	Flying by the peak where haze
Harezu nomi	Never clears up;
Uramitsukisenu	Unexhausted their resentment
Haru no yo no tsuki.	In moonlight on a night in spring.

"Kaeru kari" [Geese returning north] evokes ethereal beauty throughout the Left's poem, in both configuration and conception. (Round 166 ["Spring, 3"]:78)

[40] Fujiwara Tsunetada, 1075-1138.
[41] The pseudonym used by Gotoba.

The Left: Lord Takanobu (Loser)

Tazunekoshi	I came to visit
Yamaji wa hana o	A mountain path guiding me
Shirube ni te	To cherry blossoms:
Chiru konomoto ya	It would be fine indeed to dwell
Sumika naru beki.	Beneath the falling petals!

The Left's poem is ethereal in concept: the speaker wishes to live beneath the cherry blossoms. (Round 220 ["Spring, 3"]:107-108)

In the first poem, wild geese regret that haze veils the moon from sight. Gotoba's birds respond to the moon as human beings conventionally do: this may be what Shunzei perceived as ethereal beauty. The speaker of the second poem wishes to lodge beneath a cherry tree. It is not a tree in full bloom, but one whose blossoms are falling. The poem is faintly reminiscent of a verse by Po Chü-i: "Beneath cherry blossoms, I forget to return: the cause is lovely scenery."[42] These elements evidently produce ethereal beauty in Takanobu's poem.

Teika uses "yōen" in a written judgment at *The Waka Match in One Hundred Rounds* (*Hyakuban Utaawase*, 1216).[43]

The Right: Tsunemichi (Winner)

Kore zo kono	This it is, this,
Waga mi ni itou	That I find so very hateful:
Aki no shimo	An autumn frost
Tsumoreba hito no	Settling on another's sleeve
Sode no tsukikage.	Glistening like moonlight.

The poem evokes the rhapsody on autumn written by P'an Yüeh of the Chin dynasty.[44] It also calls to mind our own Narihira's conception of hating to grow old.[45] Both allusions produce a sense of ethereal beauty in the waka, and so I found it the winner. (Round 54 ["Autumn"]:211–12)

At first glance, Tsunemichi's waka shows no signs of en. Teika, however, seems to have sensed a latent en in the concept of "autumn frost," a frost

[42] "Beneath cherry blossoms, I forget to return: the cause is lovely scenery. / Before the winecask, I am urged to drink—by the breezes of spring" (*Wakan Rōeishū*, 1:18; *HKS*, 13:1929).

[43] [For "written judgments," see n. 24.—Trans.]

[44] "In the fourteenth year of the Chin dynasty [265], when I was thirty-two years old, I discovered my first white hairs" (P'an Yüeh [247-300], "Autumnal Rhapsody," *WH*, 13:267).

[45] A reference to Narihira's poem (*KKS*, 17:879): Ōkata wa / Tsuki o mo medeji / Kore zo kono / Tsumoreba hito no / Oi to naru mono. (Generally speaking, / I do not admire the moon, / And this is it, this: / As the moons accumulate, / One's discovery is old age.)

occurring so early that the speaker still retains vivid memories of beautiful autumn foliage. And for him as well as Shunzei, subtle allusion to the literature of the past seems to have involved part of ethereal beauty.

Teika uses "ethereal beauty" again in a written judgment in *The Waka Match Held on the Fourth Day of the Eleventh Month, Kempō 5* (*Kempō Gonen Jūichigatsu Yokka Utaawase*; 1217). The topic is "Snow on a Wintry Sea."

The Left: His Majesty[46] (Loser)

Kaze samumi	With the wind so cold
Hikazu mo itaku	The many days pass heavily
Furu yuki ni	In falling snow:
Hito ya wa oran	Is he indeed gathering
Ise no hamaogi.	The shoreside reeds of Ise?

The windswept snow scene is portrayed through diction of truly ethereal beauty. This is both welcome and rare. (Round 33:258)

Again, the waka does not immediately strike us as en. Teika probably found a certain en in the concept of the man gathering reeds: the speaker, a woman, tenderly imagines her journeying husband or lover preparing a shelter for the night.[47] The en of the waka is enhanced by snow imagery; the result is yōen.

Teika's independent judgments—as distinguished from his written ones, the product of consensus—survive only from his later years. Teika served as judge of *The Waka Match at the Wakamiya, Iwashimizu Shrine (Iwashimizu Wakamiya Utaawase)*, held in the Third Month of 1232. He comments as follows on a waka from the match; the topic is "Haze by the River."

The Right: Lord Shunzei's Daughter (Winner)

Hashihime no	The Lady of the Bridge—
Sode no asashimo	The morning frost upon her sleeves
Nao saete	Makes them yet colder,
Kasumi fukikosu	And the spring haze is swept along
Uji no kawakaze.	By the Uji river wind.

[46] Juntoku Tennō (r. 1210-21).

[47] The honka to Juntoku's poem is by the Wife of Go no Dan'ochi (*MYS*, 4:500): Kamikaze no / Ise no hamaogi / Orifusete / Tabine ya su ran / Araki hamabe ni. (The divine winds blow / On the shoreside reeds of Ise— / Do you gather them / As bedding for sleep in travel / There on that jagged coast?) Go no Dan'ochi may be a nickname. "Go" is written with the same character as that used for the board game Go; this suggests that the man was a master of the game. "Dan'ochi," a Buddhist term signifying "donor" or "benefactor," may indicate that the man was known for his generosity to Buddhist clergy and establishments. [Auth., Trans.]

> The Right wins because "Hashihime no/ Sode no asashimo" [The Lady of the Bridge— / The morning frost upon her sleeves] truly reveals the yōen mode. (Round 1:272)

En is discerned fairly easily in the poem, owing to the well-known subject: the Lady of the Bridge (the guardian goddess of the Uji Bridge) is a profoundly romantic subject in waka.[48] But Shunzei's Daughter presents a gloomy scene: the goddess is hidden in the haze blown by river winds, and the morning frost covering her sleeves pierces the speaker with cold. Rather than being present within the poem itself, en seems just beyond the speaker's visual field.

Teika uses "yōen" again in a later judgment from the same match. The topic is "Cherry Blossoms in Darkening Mountains."

> The Right: Lord Shunzei's Daughter (Winner)

Tsukikage mo	The moonlight, too,
Utsurou hana ni	Like fading cherry blossoms
Kawaru iro no	Makes all seem white
Yūbe o haru mo	Even as evening is seen in spring
Miyoshino no yama.	On the fine peaks of Yoshino.

> The Right's poem may be said to produce a yōen effect. It fully merits our appreciation, and therefore wins the round. (Round 18:275)

The cherry blossoms of the poem, now past their prime, can be fully appreciated only in the imagination. The image of moonlight further enhances the poem by lending a quiet beauty to the scene.

Other examples of Teika's use of "ethereal beauty" in waka judgments appear in his remarks on the poems in several rounds of *The Waka Match at the Residence of the Kōmyōbuji Regent* (*Kōmyōbuji Sesshō Ke Utaawase*), held in the Seventh Month of 1232.[49]

> The Right: Tadatoshi (Draw)

Omoishire	Know that my underrobes
Mune ni taku mo no	Are scorched by a breast as hot
Shitagoromo	As burning seagrass:
Ue wa tsurenaki	On the surface, coolness reigns,
Keburi naritomo.	Although inside I smolder.

[48] The waka that comes first to mind is from the *Kokinshū* (14:689): Samushiro ni / Koromo katashiki / Koyoi mo ya / Ware o matsu ran / Uji no hashihime. (For her bedmat / She spreads out a single robe: / And again tonight / does she do so waiting for me, / The Woman of the Uji Bridge?) The alluring Lady of the Bridge might be seen as a Japanese version of the Goddess of Mount Wu [and although a goddess, by legend seems to be a woman of pleasure in this poem, according to the author.—Ed.]

[49] The Kōmyōbuji Regent is Kujō Michiie (1192-1252). [Auth., Trans.]

The ethereal beauty in the last four lines of the poem is of especially high quality. (Round 4 ["Clothing and Love"]:282)

The Right: Tadatoshi (Loser)

Nagekiwabi	In grief and sorrow,
Sate furu hodo no	I lapse into remembrance
Omoide ni	Of times now gone,
Musubi mo hatenu	But I cannot recapture
Yume no tamakura.	The dream of that pillowing arm.

Several participants remark that "Yume no tamakura" ["The dream of that pillowing arm"] has ethereal beauty. (Round 48 ["Pillows and Love"]:289)

The Right: Tadatoshi (Loser)

Hakanashi ya	How ephemeral!
Sono yo no yume o	That of that night's now vanished dream
Katami nite	Only this for memory:
Utsutsu ni tsuraki	A reality so cruel,
Toko no samushiro.	Bedclothes in a lonely chamber.

Although several of the participants maintain that the Right's poem has ethereal beauty, the Left wins the round at the Regent's request.[50] (Round 81 ["Bedclothes and Love"]:293)

Tadatoshi's three poems, which all concern love, manage to communicate a sense of en while presenting a lover's conventional complaints: the speaker of the first poem must appear "cool" (tsurenaki) on the surface; in the second poem, the speaker experiences "grief and sorrow" (nagekiwabi); and in the third, reality is "cruel" (tsuraki). We can only conclude that "ephemeral beauty," "yōen," is used in late twelfth- and thirteenth-century waka criticism to designate a style that—allowing for differences of degree—conceals en within a superficially gloomy, subdued, negative setting. Teika uses "ethereal" in this sense when he criticizes Tsurayuki for "not compos[ing] in a nuanced, ethereal mode" (*KDSK*, 100).

Scholars have tended, however, to describe Teika's "ethereal" style as a bright, positive beauty in which en is explicitly expressed. They support their interpretation by quoting waka such as these, which appeared earlier in this chapter:

Ōzora wa	Across the heavens
Ume no nioi ni	In the fragrance of plum blossoms

[50] Michiie, the host, is careful to ensure that no one poet (such as Tadatoshi) wins too many rounds; hence his concern that the Left win this round. [Auth., Trans.]

Kasumitsutsu	The haze increases;
Kumori mo hatenu	The thin clouds do not exempt
Haru no yo no tsuki.	The moon on the brief spring night.

Haru no yo no	On the brief spring night,
Yume no ukihashi	The floating bridge of dreams
Todaeshite	Breaks all apart,
Mine ni wakaruru	And from a mountain peak a cloud
Yokogumo no sora.	Takes leave into the empty sky.

Ume no hana	Blossoms of the plum
Nioi o utsusu	Transfer their fragrance from the tree
Sode no ue ni	To the moistened sleeve
Noki moru tsuki no	Where moonbeams vie in shining
Kage zo arasou.	As they filter through the eaves!

A similar case can be made for Teika's followers.

Composed for The Waka Match in Fifteen Hundred Rounds.
By Shunzei's Daughter

Kaze kayou	A breeze comes calling,
Nezame no sode no	Bringing to my sleepless sleeves
Hana no ka ni	The blossoms' fragrance,
Kaoru makura no	Perfuming my lonely pillow
Haru no yo no yume.	For a dream on a brief spring night.

(*SKKS*, 2:112)

On the topic "Love in Spring," composed for
The Waka Match at Minase on Fifteen Love Poems.
By Shunzei's Daughter

Omokage no	Memories of you
Kasumeru tsuki zo	Emerge from a misty moon
Yadorikeru	Whose light is lodged
Haru ya mukashi no	In the teardrops of a sleeve
Sode no namida ni.	Thinking of those springtimes past.

(*SKKS*, 12:1136)

Composed upon submitting a hundred-poem sequence.
By Lord Fujiwara Ietaka

Ume ga ka ni	As plum blossom fragrance
Mukashi o toeba	Leads me to seek out the past,
Haru no tsuki	The moon in spring

Kotaenu kage zo	Sends an enigmatic light
Sode ni utsureru.	That is reflected on my sleeves.

(*SKKS*, 1:45)

These poems exemplify the style usually thought to embody "ethereal beauty." If so, "ethereal beauty" may no longer mean what Mototoshi, Shunzei, and Teika thought it meant. The general modern scholarly view is not incorrect, however: "ethereal" (yao-yen) is the term used in Chinese shih to describe a similarly bright, positive beauty. The first instances of "ethereal beauty" in Chinese poetry appear in the early third century. The concept, which became linked with Taoist magical practice during the Six Dynasties period, came into frequent use during the T'ang (Ōta S., 1958, 148-49). Several Six Dynasties passages connect "ethereal beauty" to descriptions of beautiful women:

> Mao Ch'iang, Hsi Shih, Ching Chi, and Ch'in Ying all had fine figures and ethereal beauty. A single amorous glance from any one of them could reduce a capital to ruins.[51] (Chung Hui [225–64], "Rhapsody on Chrysanthemums," *I-wen*, 81:2083)

A similar linkage appears in T'ang literature, which concentrates on the famous beauty Hsi Shih. One example will suffice: "An ethereal beauty obsessed the king, whose harem was in turmoil; / Vassals, true as blue hills and seas, labored for the state" (Kuan-hsiu [832-912], "Passing by the Ruins of the Royal Palace of Wu," *CTS*, 837:9434). The title of the poem suggests the identity of the "ethereal beauty": Hsi Shih was the favorite of the King of Wu. "Ethereal beauty" was not used exclusively to describe women of outstanding loveliness, however. The term is often used in connection with anonymous beauties.

In the days of armored steeds and war chariots,
Singing boys and dancing girls had ethereal beauty.

(Tu Wei [fl. ca. 750], "Miss Coral,"
CTS, 145:1465)

Ch'ang-an reveres the great houses;
Countless are its ethereal beauties.

(Wei Ying-mu [736-90?],
"Five Miscellaneous Poems,"
CTS, 186:1896)

[51] Extraordinarily beautiful women are conventionally portrayed in Chinese literature as potentially dangerous forces. An amorous glance from such a woman might captivate the Emperor; his dalliance with her would lead him to neglect government duties. The country would grow weak under poor leadership, fall prey to enemy forces, and see its capital city sacked—all because of one devastatingly beautiful woman. [Auth., Trans.]

Flowers, especially peonies, are also described in T'ang literature in terms of ethereal beauty.

> Azaleas in full bloom have ethereal beauty;
> People of the capital, alas, know little of them!
> (Shih Chien-wu [b. 791], "A Song of Azaleas," *CTS*, 494:5592)

> Their ethereal beauty agitates men's hearts;
> The country, mad for peonies, will pay any price.
> (Wang Jui, "Peonies," *CTS*, 505:5743)

> Heaven grants that flowers in full bloom shall not be shabby;
> Spring teaches them the ethereal surpassing splendor.
> (Hsü Yin [b. 865], "Two Poems on Peonies," *CTS*, 708:8150)

Peonies are often associated with female immortals in Chinese poetry.

> Could they be the Goddess of the River Lo transformed?
> Their voluptuous figures are glimpsed through morning mists.
> (Hsü Ning [d. 840?], "Peonies," *CTS*, 474:5382)

> Clusters of immortal splendor emerge from the flames;
> For an instant, rare fragrance wafts from the heavens.
> (Li Shan-fu, "Peonies," *CTS*, 643:7377)

If peonies symbolize the female immortals, ethereal beauty characterizes their appearance. Because female immortals possess an idealized version of mortal women's beauty, "ethereal beauty" has highly positive connotations (see vol. 2, ch. 5). Plum blossoms were not thought ethereal: "They do not open when ethereal flowers blossom; / They prefer the season when days are darkest" (Wei Chuang [836-910], "On Plum Blossoms," *CTS*, 700:8055). Ethereal beauty, in this sense, was known to early medieval Japanese. An example is provided by Kose no Shikihito (fl. ca. 823) in his "Matching his Majesty's Poem on 'A Solitary Wife's Grief in Spring' " (*BSS*, 2:244): "I was once an ethereal beauty, aged sixteen years: / My appearance was as dazzling as peach and damson blossoms." "Ethereal beauty" is used here to suggest a showy beauty, like that of the peonies in the T'ang verses quoted above. Yoshimine Yasuyo compares lotuses to women of ethereal beauty in one of his shih, "On the Topic, 'Autumn Lotus,' Composed at His Majesty's Command at a Banquet in the Shinzen Gardens on the Ninth Day of the Ninth Month" (*RUSS*, 119). One of its couplets runs: "Ladies of ethereal beauty no longer bloom for us; / That is why I join our ruler at the lakeside arbor."[52] Yasuyo celebrates the lotus, a less flamboyant flower than the peony, as an example of ethereal beauty. This may well mark the origin of the more muted yōen that emerges in the High Middle Ages.

These examples illustrate why scholars are not mistaken in using "ethereal beauty" to describe that bright, attractive element characterizing the major works of Teika and his group. The scholars' usage conforms to the traditional Chinese view of "ethereal beauty." Their approach has its problems, however, when applied to Teika, who does not use the term "ethereal beauty" in this sense. Of course, Teika's approach might well be explained by means of terms he never used. Earlier in this chapter, for example, Teika's poetic mentality was analyzed in terms of "yūgen" and "ushin," as defined respectively by Kamo no Chōmei and the author of the *Maigetsushō*. Teika's use of these terms was not considered in the analysis.

Difficulties arise, however, when he is presumed to have thought things that could never have entered his head. It is wrong, in other words, to conclude that his "nuanced, ethereal mode" signifies a bright, attractive beauty and that this bright beauty was his ideal poetic mode. He was deeply dissatisfied with his waka style in 1209, when he compiled *Superior Poems of Our Time*.[53] Having emerged from this inactive period, he began to write waka in which en was generally concealed or understated (see the next section of this chapter). One is hard pressed to find bright, attractive elements in Teika's waka during this crucial period. The confusion arises because one fact is disregarded: "ethereal beauty" changes its meaning. "Ethereal beauty" in T'ang shih means something different from "yōen" as defined and developed by Mototoshi, Shunzei, and Teika. In the discussion that follows, I shall try to avoid confusion by assigning a different name, "loveliness" ["kambi," the author's coinage, literally means "sweet beauty"; cf. Greek "kalos"], to the bright, attractive waka written by Teika and his group.

The young Teika and his followers did indeed create a lovely style, one so distinctive that it became a criterion defining the *Shinkokinshū* period (in the strict sense). Equally indisputable, however, is that waka produced during the more broadly-defined *Shinkokinshū* period are characterized by concealed en. They consequently possess a muted, understated beauty. Both aspects—loveliness and concealed en—must be taken into account

[52] The speaker hopes to feast his eyes on human "lotuses" (court ladies), since real lotuses are no longer in season. The shih was composed in mid-October by the solar calendar. [Auth., Trans.]

[53] "Having encountered old age, I now find myself afflicted by grave illness and plunged into deep grief. I have forgotten the varied colors of words in flower, my fount of inspiration has dried up, and I am unable to conceive waka of any sort. I think increasingly of abandoning poetry altogether" (*KDSK*, 102).

if the *Shinkokinshū* style is to be understood. We should take note that Late T'ang poetry is similarly duofaceted. Late T'ang shih are generally regarded as individualistic poetry centered on the concept of ornate beauty (ch'i-li), as contrasted with the more sober approaches of High and Middle T'ang poetry. Ornate beauty in Late T'ang shih differs from Six Dynasties poetic ornateness: where the richly decorated language of Six Dynasties shih tends to have little connection to the speaker's or poet's sentiments, Late T'ang poetry maintains a balance between ornate diction and content. Late T'ang shih also have a more delicate, subtle texture than that found in Six Dynasties poetry.

All this applies, of course, to the principal Late T'ang poets, including Li Shang-yin (812-58), Wen T'ing-yün (812-72?), and Han Wo (844-923). It has less to do with poetry by notable but peripheral figures like Lu Kuei-mao (d. 881) and P'i Jih-hsiu (833?-88). There are two sides to the central concept of ornate, subtle beauty: in some shih it is clearly expressed, while in other works it is concealed under a muted, negative facade. An extreme example of the former tendency occurs in the poetry of Han Wo, who was apparently an anomalous figure in the Late T'ang shih circle. His poem on "Napping" illustrates his approach (*CTS*, 683:7837).

Blue paulownia deeply shades the screened window between us:
Her fan drives off golden geese; the pretty mat is hot.[54]
She paints her face: a fragrant form becomes sleeker still;
She sheds her clothes: the only garment visible, a crimson singlet.
Stifled, she reaches for a chilled ice-jar;
Tired of pillows, she lifts her head and loosens a fine chignon.
Why exhaust your spirits, why dream of love, my dear?
Wang Ch'ang himself lives right next door![55]

Han wrote other poems in much the same vein, including "Bathing" (*CTS*, 683:7834), "Giggles" (ibid., 7837), "On Disliking Falling Blossoms" (ibid., 7840), "Boudoir Sentiments" (ibid., 7845), and "Boudoir in Spring" (ibid., 7847). Their charm is overwhelming. The *Shinkokinshū* poets never attempted to adapt this style of waka, although Teika and his

[54] The woman's fan is decorated with figures of geese embroidered in gold thread. The speaker, looking up at the woman as she waves her fan, seems to see the geese chased by the fan.

[55] Wang Ch'ang, like Casanova in the West or Narihira in Japan, is the prototypical amorous man. (Wang Ch'ang is a fictional figure, however.) The speaker of the shih invokes the name to make clear his romantic intentions. "Next door" (lit. "the house east of the hedge") refers to the aspiring suitor's house, located to the east of the woman's house. A suitor conventionally climbs the hedge to reach his ladylove's house. "If he climbs the hedge of the house to the east and abducts the young lady, he may have her as his wife. If he does not abduct her, she shall not be his wife" ("Kao Tzu, Pt. 2," *Meng Tzu*, 274).

group hint at similar scenes in their work. This is the point at which "loveliness" develops as part of the new style.

Charming subjects notwithstanding, Han Wo's poetry is typical of the Late T'ang in focusing on visual beauty. The following examples are all couplets taken from longer poems, since couplets are more easily compared to waka.

Beneath broad skies, every hill is white with distant trees:
I cannot tell if they are plums in bloom or willow catkins.
(Chiao Yü, "Spring Snow," *CTS*, 505:5744)

A red-bedewed corolla and its white, honeyed pistil
Are visited by yellow bees and purple butterflies.
(Li Shang-yin, "Boudoir Sentiments," *CTS*, 539:6178)

Late at night, blue skies outline a rugged mountain range;
Light shatters on jewelled waves: moonbeams fill the boat.
(Wen T'ing-yün, "The Narcissus Song," *CTS*, 576:6704)

Upon the lake, scarlet lotuses are white with dew;
Within the garden, green grass is joined by yellow twilight.
(Han Wo, "A Bending Stream at Night," *CTS*, 682:7818)

This style recurs in Late T'ang poetry. The rich sense of color permeating the Late T'ang shih corpus is also a hallmark of the *Shinkokinshū* style. Compare Chiao Yü's couplet, "Beneath broad skies," for example, with a waka by Gotoba:

Uguisu no	The warbler sings,
Nakedomo imada	But there is no interruption
Furu yuki ni	Of the falling snow,
Sugi no ha shiroki	For cryptomeria needles are white
Ōsaka no yama.	In the forest on Mount Ōsaka.
	(*SKKS*, 1:18)

Teika's early waka are even more vivid. One such poem is this:

Kurenai no	Crimson is the dew
Tsuyu ni asahi o	That catches and reflects
Utsushimote	The rising sun:
Atari made teru	A glow spreads all around
Nadeshiko no hana.	Wild carnation flowers.
	(*SG*, 1:223)

The beauty of this scene corresponds to that described by Ch'en Piao: "Emerald grounds bloom with scarlet beauty; / Azure skies at dawn drift with rosy haze" ("Peonies at a Monastery," *CTS*, 508:5771). Their conceptual foci are also similar.

We have seen that Late T'ang poetry is characterized by a fine, subtle texture. The result of such verse is not simply beauty, but delicate beauty. A couplet by Wen T'ing-yün provides an apt example: "Lush shade makes a curtain for red roses at evening; / Misty rain, fine as smoke, turns the grass spring-green" ("Written at the Secluded Abode of Recluse Mr. Li," *CTS*, 578:6717). Wen's logic is apparent in his conceptual focus: colors appear dark because of the shade, and misty rain enhances the fresh greenness of new grass. The logic is subtler than the Six Dynasties obliqueness, however: one senses very little that is expository. Because logic in Late T'ang poetry is dependent on beauty, the reasoning process is itself camouflaged by the beauty of the poetry. The *Shinkokinshū* shares this delicacy, as exemplified by another poem by Teika.

Sumire tsumu	I gather violets
Hanazomegoromo	In a robe of flowery colors,
Tsuyu o omomi	And with heavy dew,
Kaerite utsuru	My sleeve is dyed yet again,
Tsukigusa no iro.	Rubbed with dayflower blue.
	(*SG*, 1:516)

Reaching out a hand to gather violets, the speaker finds her sleeve heavy with dew. When brushed against a dayflower, the gaily dyed sleeve takes on the blue color of the flower.[56] This unlikely situation has been engineered by fabricated logic. But Teika's logic, wrapped in layers of color imagery, bears little resemblance to the explanatory reasoning characteristic of the *Kokinshū* style. The poet's subtle response renders his reasoning processes equally subtle. The poem has so delicate a beauty that the casual reader will not even realize that logic is present. Teika's poem is very much in the Late T'ang style.

One aspect of Late T'ang poetry, then, is its easily perceptible ornateness. But much poetry from this period conceals its ornate beauty under a surface of muted scenes and emotions. Two examples of this latter category follow.

[56] [The dayflower (tsukigusa, Commelina communis), known today as tsuyukusa (dewflower) or bōshibana (hatflower), is a low-growing perennial with fleshy leaves and small blue flowers. A member of the Tradescantia family, it is related to the spiderwort and the wandering jew. Dayflowers stain clothing easily and were used to produce a blue dye.—Trans.]

Before the shrine, evening colors reach a wintry river;
The sunken sun dyes distant sails with its last rays.
(Wen T'ing-yün, "The Shrine to Lao Tzu," *CTS*, 578:6726)

Evening mists drape the dark lanes of a lonely village;
Setting sunrays fade along neglected garden beds.
(T'ang Yen-ch'ien [dates unknown], "Chrysanthemums," *CTS*, 885:10004)

The chrysanthemums blooming in the scene set by the latter couplet are of course beautiful, but they also communicate a sense of immeasurable loneliness. On the other hand, the scene is not wholly negative. The flowers are bathed in the light of the setting sun: the scene fuses desolation with splendor. The visual effects produced by sunsets were apparently a favorite subject of Late T'ang poets. Consider this couplet:

Haze at sunset as wild geese return through clearing showers;
A traveler, facing the sandy plain, is bathed by evening light.
(Shen Pin, "By the Fortress," *CTS*, 743:8456)

The couplet is set in spring; if the season were changed to autumn, one of Teika's waka (*SKKS*, 10:953) would present a similar scene:

Tabibito no	The man in travel,
Sode fukikaesu	His sleeves are blown back and forth
Akikaze ni	By the autumn wind,
Yūhi sabishiki	When the evening sun turns desolate
Yama no kakehashi.	The hanging bridge between the peaks.

I do not mean to suggest that specific waka were influenced by specific Late T'ang poems. Teika's autumn poem is quoted here because it has a tonal similarity to Shen's couplet: in both poems, the subdued splendor of the setting sun illumines the lonely form of a traveler.

A subdued, negative tone first appears in Japanese shih during the twelfth century. Minamoto Tsunenobu's "View from a Farmhouse on an Autumn Day," quoted earlier, is one such example (see ch. 1). The scene is deeply autumnal: bare trees and shrivelled grasses are illumined by the moon. But its cold, pure light also provides a faint vision of these plants at the height of their beauty and vigor. Like T'ang Yen-ch'ien's "Chrysanthemums," Tsunenobu's shih is not entirely negative.

Subdued, desolate scenes are even more common in thirteenth-century Japanese shih (ch. 7). In some cases, these works emphasize negative elements excessively and so forfeit any sense of implied brilliance. Teika is guilty of this in his shih. In 1212 the poet, aged fifty, made a journey to the hot springs at Arima. Having arrived at Kanzaki, a stop en route, in the rain, he composed a shih and a waka (*MGK* [21.I.1212], 144).

> These sandy riverbanks see few travelers when it rains;
> At length I find a fishing boat and go in search of lodging.
> The moon is dark, clouds lower: soon it will be night;
> Still I gaze upon the river, wandering quite alone.

Harusame no	If the spring rains
Asu sae furaba	Should fall again tomorrow,
Ikaga sen	What can be done?
Sode hoshiwaburu	Our clothes still suffer wetness,
Kyō no funabito.	We boat passengers today.

These travel jottings are not proper examples of Teika's poetic style. They do demonstrate, however, that some of Teika's compositions are thoroughly lackluster.

A shih composed on the following day of his journey displays a certain brilliance, however.[57]

> The setting moon lies deep in haze: spring is still young;
> Mountain clouds are first to show the growing colors of dawn.
> A village among fields; rain having lifted, what will block my
> view?
> One thing only—the fragrant breeze from early plum blossoms.

Questions of workmanship aside, Teika's poem is definitely in the Late T'ang style.

Teika's style thus corresponds to both facets of Late T'ang poetry: it has a bright loveliness as well as splendor and refinement (en) hidden beneath a subdued surface. What is more, both Teika's waka and Late T'ang shih are known for their delicacy. We may thus conclude that Japanese shih were the medium through which Teika incorporated the Late T'ang poetic style into waka. Further impetus was probably provided by Teika's patron, Gokyōgoku Yoshitsune, who was learned in shih (Fujihira, 1969, 54-56). That aspect of Late T'ang poetry used to extreme effect by Han Wo produced exquisite results in waka by Teika and his coterie. But to borrow a phrase from Zeami, the style was a "temporary

[57] "The 22nd. The rain stopped during the night, and a cold wind blew at dawn. We left before daybreak, by the light of a late moon" (*MGK* [22.I.1212], 144). The shih was written under these circumstances. See ch. 7.

flower" (jibun no hana); Bashō would have found it "mutable" (ryūkō). Teika realized this when he was about forty-three, during his confrontations with Gotoba.

Teika and Nonrefined Beauty

A banquet was held at the palace in 1205, Teika's forty-third year, to celebrate the formal completion of the *Shinkokinshū*. This event marks the pinnacle of the *Shinkokinshū* period (in the stricter sense of the term). Teika, on the other hand, was suffering through an extremely inactive creative period. In 1201, when he was thirty-nine, he wrote 314 waka. His output dropped to fifty-one in 1202, twenty-eight in 1203, and sixteen in 1204. Some sign of recovery appears in 1206, when Teika, then forty-four, wrote forty-three poems; sixty-two appeared the following year. But he composed only two in 1209. Teika returned to writing significant quantities in 1214, at the age of fifty-two, when he produced forty-five. His inactive period thus encompasses a decade. He seems to have fully recovered his powers by 1215, when he was fifty-three; that year he composed 211 waka, and 109 the following year.[58] These figures are based on extant compositions; more waka were actually composed. The decade from 1204 through 1213—Teika's forty-second through fifty-first years—nevertheless remains a period of stagnation. The poet himself frequently lamented his inability to compose as he would wish.[59] Why did he become so inactive?

We ought to note that Teika's inactive period exists only in terms of the quantity of waka composed. What was the quality of the poems written during this period? The loveliness that had characterized Teika's earlier

[58] Teika's stylistic preferences apparently changed after his forty-ninth year (Kazamaki, 1932, 473). Quantitative data follow, with the first number the year, the second Teika's age that year, and the third the number of waka composed. [The year (in italics), Teika's age (in parentheses), and the number of poems are given.]

1178 (16), 3; *1181* (19), 100; *1182* (20), 100; *1184* (22), 4; *1186* (24), 5; *1187* (25), 211; *1189* (27), 254; *1190* (28), 311; *1191* (29), 232; *1192* (30), 33; *1193* (31), 113; *1194* (32), 15; *1195* (33), 37; *1196* (34), 187; *1197* (35), 2; *1198* (36), 50; *1199* (37), 12; *1200* (38), 139; *1201* (39), 314; *1202* (40), 51; *1203* (41), 28; *1204* (42), 16; *1205* (43), 23; *1206* (44), 43; *1207* (45), 62; *1208* (46), 12; *1209* (47), 2; *1210* (48), 11; *1211* (49), 2; *1212* (50), 24; *1213* (51), 14; *1214* (52), 45; *1215* (53), 211; *1216* (54), 109; *1217* (55), 97; *1218* (56), 162; *1219* (57), 25; *1220* (58), 124; *1221* (59), 22; *1224* (62), 3; *1225* (63), 30; *1226* (64), 1; *1227* (65), 16; *1229* (67), 44; *1230* (68), 1; *1231* (69), 3; *1232* (70), 116; *1233* (71), 78.

[59] "I have been asked to present ten waka at the palace. Waka composition is unbearably difficult in my old age" (*MGK* [25.IX.1212], 183). "Lord Kiyonori was asked to draw up a document indicating three waka topics. I am to present twenty waka on each topic. Not having received such a request in recent years, I have quite forgotten how to compose. My expression is worn and poor indeed, but I do not know how to improve it" (ibid. [22.XI.1212], 213).

waka disappears from works composed between 1204 and 1213. The following poems exemplify his new style:

Composed in the Seventh Month of 1204, during a royal progress to Uji, on the topic "The Storm."

Kaerimiru	Looking back, I see
Susono no kusaba	That field plants on the foothills
Katayori ni	Are bent all one way—
Kagiri naki aki no	No place in autumn fails to feel
Yamaoroshi no kaze.	Winds of the mountain tempest.
	(*SG*, 3:2142)

Composed in the Seventh Month of 1206, at a match held at the Waka Bureau: "Moon by the Seashore."

Moshio kumu	Ladling the seabrine,
Sode no tsukikage	The sleeves reflect the moonlight,
Onozukara	Which of itself
Yoso ni akasanu	Would not shine in other places—
Suma no urabito.	Denizens of the Suma shore.
	(Ibid., 2149)

One of three love poems presented at the palace in the Third Month of 1213.

Kage o dani	Our reflections—
Au se ni musube	Where the two Streams of Longing meet,
Omoikawa	May they join at least—
Ukabu minawa no	What matter if, like drifting foam,
Kenaba kenu tomo.	We soon vanish on the waters!
	(Ibid., 2444)

A substantial change has taken place. Careful perusal of these poems reveals that en, refined beauty, is concealed beneath their somber scenes and emotions. The second poem, for example, appears at first glance to be a simple nature poem. "Sleeves," however, suggests love, which in turn evokes memories of such amorous Suma exiles as Ariwara Yukihira and the radiant Genji.[60] This abstruse refinement is precisely what Teika

[60] Teika equates sleeves with unhappy love in several poems, including the following (*SG*, 3:2436). Sleeves wet from tears conventionally reflect moonlight; the moon is said to "lodge" in the sleeve [Auth., Trans.]: Yadorikoshi / Tamoto wa yume ka / Tobakari ni / Araba au yo no / Yoso no tsukikage. (It lodged here— / Or was my sleeve only dreaming? / If only briefly / You should visit me when some night / The moon will brighten other sleeves.)

meant by "nuanced, ethereal beauty" (see the previous section). It can be sensed only through very careful reading indeed. The difficulty characterizing his poems adds an important subtlety. These difficult, subtle aspects are at the heart of the poet's estrangement from Gotoba.

During the decade in question, Teika dealt severely with waka—his own included—that did not display profundity, subtlety, and concentration. Gotoba, on the other hand, praised poetry that clearly stated the composer's emotions and the circumstances of composition. Conflict between the two men was inevitable. On the twenty-fifth day of the Second Month, 1203, the palace sponsored an informal gathering to view cherry blossoms. Teika's poem for the occasion expresses his chagrin at being repeatedly passed over for promotion.[61]

Haru o hete	These many springs
Miyuki ni naruru	Royal outings have grown familiar
Hana no kage	To this tree in bloom;
Furiyuku mi o mo	I wonder if my aging self
Aware to ya omou.	Arouses pity in it?
	(*SG*, 3:2068)

Gotoba praised the waka for its "gentle, retrospective kokoro." He was impressed by the able contrast drawn between the splendor of the blossoms and the poet's personal woes. Gotoba believed that Teika should be justly proud of such a masterpiece. The poem appears in the *Shinkokinshū* (16:1454), no doubt because of the royal opinion. Teika, however, was bored by what he considered an obvious poem; he repeatedly emphasized its mediocrity at *Shinkokinshū* editorial meetings. Gotoba was apparently much displeased by his behavior (*Gotoba In*, 148-49). In the Eighth Month of 1204, Saionji Kintsune told Teika that Minamoto Ienaga had spoken ill of Teika before Gotoba; the former sovereign had then formed the opinion that Teika was insolent (*MGK* [22.VIII.1204], 380). Teika would certainly not have lost favor with Gotoba because of Ienaga's story alone. We can only conclude that the ultimate source of Gotoba's displeasure was the unpleasantness over Teika's cherry-blossom poem, "Haru o hete" (Fujihira, 1969, 73-74).

A further clash occurred over screen waka composed for Gotoba's Saishō Shitennōin chapel. In the Fourth Month of 1207, Gotoba commissioned forty-six screen paintings of utamakura [or nadokoro; land- and seascapes long associated with waka]. Each was to be accompanied by an

[61] Teika was a provisional captain in the Left Division of Bodyguards, an undistinguished post for a man of his years. His official duties included accompanying the tennō on outings and gatherings like the present cherry-viewing party. He alludes to this duty in his poem. [Auth., Trans.]

appropriate poem composed for the occasion. The task was divided among ten poets, including Teika and Gotoba himself. Teika placed high hopes on one of his poems, written to accompany a painting of the Ikuta Forest.

Aki to dani	Autumn though it is,
Fukiaenu kaze ni	The winds do not fit the season;
Iro kawaru	Yet colors change
Ikuta no mori no	In the forest of Ikuta
Tsuyu no shitakusa.	With its dewy undergrowth.
	(*SG*, 2:1827)

The poem was selected, then rejected in favor of one by Jien. Gotoba's negative opinion was the opposite of his response four years earlier, when he praised Teika's cherry-blossom poem. But again Teika disputed the royal decision. He apparently made disparaging remarks about Gotoba's critical sense. The former sovereign, hearing of this, was understandably annoyed. His criticism of Teika's "Ikuta Forest" poem, while revealing a certain amount of vexation with the poet, is nevertheless entirely fair.

> In the way this poem begins with "Aki to dani" [Autumn though it is], continues the rhythm through "Fukiaenu kaze ni / Iro kawaru" ["The winds do not fit the season; / Yet colors change"] in the second and third lines, and concludes with the placement of "Tsuyu no shitakusa" ["With its dewy undergrowth"], there is perfect correlation between the upper and lower verses—truly, it seems the epitome of the polished style. And after all, it does appear superior to Jien's poem on "The Forest of Ikuta" that was chosen for the painting. At the same time, such lapses of taste and judgment are likely to occur over and over again, not only on my part but with others as well. One mistake surely should not be held against a person forever.
>
> It is instructive to consider the foregoing poem in detail. Apart from the gentle, refined beauty [en] of the diction, there is nothing particularly striking about either the conception [kokoro] or the nuances. "Beneath the trees of the forest are some slightly withered plants"—apart from this, the poem presents no special visual attraction, no element of wit or ingenuity, and yet how splendid it is in the lovely cadences of its flowing diction! People who know little about waka of this nature would utterly fail to appreciate such a poem. As a consequence, relatively few of Lord Teika's poems are universal favorites, although their superiority is acknowledged by all. And if this does occasionally happen, it is not because people have been truly moved. The finest poems of Shunzei and Saigyō are not only

polished and gentle in diction; they are also unusually moving, and are associated with stories about the poets themselves. As a result, it would be impossible to count the poems of theirs that are always on people's lips. (*Gotoba In*, 149-50)[62]

Gotoba admits that Teika's poem is better than Jien's and proceeds to ponder the reason why he chose the lesser contribution. He prefers Jien's poem, according to the passage, because Teika's offering has two serious faults: the poem is not sufficiently moving, and refined beauty (en) is evident only in its diction. Gotoba adds that the "Ikuta Forest" poem is symptomatic of a general, serious stylistic deficiency: it lacks conviction. What is more, Teika's immoderate diction ensures that his poems will be difficult to understand; that is why contemporaries acknowledge few of his works as masterpieces.[63] Gotoba's opinion must have been a severe blow for Teika; but he was not one to submit meekly.

Gotoba and Teika must have had fundamentally different views of the "kokoro" of a poem. By pondering the most characteristic aspect of his object, Teika grasps an essence: that essence, he believes, is the kokoro of a poem. Concrete phenomena and personal emotions are of secondary importance. Gotoba, on the other hand, believes that following the true Way of Waka means composing on those very phenomena and emotions that Teika dismisses as secondary. That is doubtless why Gotoba mentions the lack of "visual attraction" (keshiki) and "ingenuity" (kotowari) in Teika's poetry and contrasts it unfavorably with Shunzei's and Saigyō's verse. Gotoba's opinion—that true waka are composed on actual phenomena and ordinary emotions—would be strongly supported today. Teika's method, to seek out the essence of an object, bears some resemblance to the approach used by modern poets in the West.

Gotoba's and Teika's mutual estrangement resulted because neither bothered to understand the other's approach. Both men esteemed a profound, moving "kokoro." Gotoba's "kokoro" corresponds to what has earlier been termed the "subjective kokoro." Teika's perception is more complex: he objectivizes the subjective kokoro and enters the objective kokoro to grasp it again at a deep level of awareness (see the first section of this chapter and Figure 8.1). Since Teika's concept of "kokoro" cannot be explicitly expressed, he embeds his poetry with clues that will aid a reader in gaining a deeper understanding of the poetic object. Understanding Teika's poetry was no easy matter for those unsympathetic to contemplative reception. All the same, Teika must have been mortified by Gotoba's criticism of the difficulty of his poetry. To characterize its ko-

[62] [Adapted from Brower, 1972, 40-41.—Trans.]

[63] *Gotoba In Gokuden* was written long after the event, but we may safely assume that Gotoba's opinions remained the same as those he expressed in 1207.

koro as having "nothing particularly striking" about it would have wounded Teika, who believed his poetry embodied profound kokoro.

Teika emerged from his inactive decade in 1215, at the age of fifty-three. His waka output, comparable to that of his prolific earlier years, may signal regained self-confidence. He nevertheless continued to use his contemplative approach to produce understated, difficult poetry. We might better understand his renewed poetic output, therefore, more as a new confidence in his style than in himself. One such poem, submitted by Teika in his *Hundred-Poem Sequence on Famous Places in Poetry, Sponsored by the Palace* (1215), also appears in *Teika's Solitaire Waka Match in One Hundred Rounds.*[64]

Ikomayama	On Mount Ikoma,
Arashi mo aki no	The color of autumn blows
Iro ni fuku	Even in the storms,
Tesome no ito no	For spinning my hand-dyed threads
Yoru zo kanashiki.	Makes the night so desolate!
	(*SG*, 1:1241)

The poem, which is also found in *The Match of Selected Waka by Lords Teika and Ietaka (Teika Ietaka Ryōkyō Senkaawase)* and the *Gyokuyōshū*, was prized throughout later centuries. The stated content of the waka appears in the last line, "Yoru zo kanashiki" ("Makes the night so desolate!"). The preceding four lines are a preface (jo) culminating in a pivot word, "yoru," meaning both "to spin" and "night." The purpose of the preface is to evoke "night." The theme of the poem, "night so desolate," is a boudoir lament (to use a term from Chinese poetry). The speaker, envisioned as a refined, charming woman, reproaches the husband or lover who fails to visit her. Nothing is said in the poem about the nature of the reproach. The preface provides several hints, although it has no semantic connection to the meaning of the last line. Mount Ikoma, a famous site for viewing scarlet leaves, suggests deep red; this in turn is associated with the woman's longings. The image of bright leaves scattering in the storm signals her uneasiness. "The color of autumn" (aki no iro) is, in this case, the color of the leaves. The wind blows so hard that it becomes red itself as it scatters hosts of scarlet leaves throughout the mountain; here the wind suggests the violence of the woman's emotions.

[64] The widely circulated version of the *Solitaire Waka Match (Teika Hyakuban Jikaawase)* has a short preface stating that the first draft, dated II.1216, was revised in VI.1217. The text, however, includes one waka from 1229 and eight from 1232, suggesting a second revision. The first revised version survives in a manuscript copy attributed to Sanjōnishi Kin'yasu (1398-1460) and in another manuscript formerly in the Sanjōnishi collection (Higuchi, 1953, 29-39). "Ikomayama" is the winner of Round 33 of the *Solitaire Match*.

"Aki," "autumn," is also a homonym for "satiation" or "tiring"; hence the man's cooling attachment is superimposed on the seasonal imagery. Teika's use of the pivot-word "yoru" seems a bit radical; yet it is based on a similar device in a *Man'yōshū* poem:

Kōchime no	A Kōchi woman,
Tesome no ito o	I spin the thread I dyed by hand,
Kurikaeshi	Then spin it once again;
Kataito ni aredo	Though it be a single strand,
Taen to omoe ya.	Shall I fear that it will break?
	(*MYS*, 7:1316)

The reader is aware that the speaker constantly worries that her thread "will break" (taen) during spinning. Her reluctance to entrust the dyeing to anyone but herself reveals devotion to the lover for whom she spins; the twisted thread suggests the complexity of her thoughts.

Teika's preface in his "Mount Ikoma" poem has no bearing on the meaning of the thematic final line. The details of his poem just discussed do not amount to elucidation of the speaker's feelings, but rather assistance to the reader for imagining any number of things. It would not be incorrect to say that the preface contains symbols, in the broadest sense of the term. But we might do well not to call them symbols, since that might imply Western senses of the term. In the West "symbol" generally signifies an image, serving as vehicle or signifier, that is necessarily linked to the tenor or signified meaning: the image vehicle more or less clearly conveys the meaning. Such an assumption may lead to the conclusion that a vehicle may have only one tenor. Teika's technique is to leave clues for his reader or hearer, whose responsibility is to capture a tenor or tenors from those clues. There is no single correct tenor. Any tenor is correct, providing the reader does not violate the terms of the poem. Teika never changed his basic poetic assumptions: they remain the same from his youth through his inactive period and on through his return to prolific composition. This being the case, why did he experience a decade of inactivity? His clashes with Gotoba were unquestionably the cause.

Gotoba sought excellence in poems that required response on a normal level of consciousness. For Teika, an outstanding poem grasped the essence of a poetic object on a deep level. Gotoba's and Teika's perceptions of poetry occupied two different, irreconcilable dimensions. We have seen how fairly Gotoba dealt with Teika's poetry. He continued to do so even after the compilation process of the *Shinkokinshū* led to further clashes. Forty-six of Teika's waka appear in the anthology, reflecting Gotoba's impartiality. One of these was the much-disputed cherry-blossom poem.

The choice is indicative of Gotoba's nature: he was not one to retreat from an earlier position. Teika, who had so gratefully acknowledged the "kindness of His Enlightened Majesty," was all the more deeply pained by this confrontation.

The dispute was not likely to force him to change his beliefs, however; the opinionated Teika could not always muster respect for his father Shunzei's waka. As Gotoba remarked, "Teika . . . found his own father's poetry shallow" (*Gotoba In*, 148).

His ten bad years behind him, Teika resolved to push on with his contemplative style. The confidence with which he carried out his goal seems to have further strained relations with Gotoba. On the thirteenth of the Second Month, 1220, Juntoku Tennō gave a waka gathering. Enraged by a poem Teika presented at this event, Gotoba declared him persona non grata at all future palace waka gatherings (Fujihira, 1969, 76-77). The Jōkyū Civil War broke out in the Fifth Month of the following year, and with Gotoba exiled to Oki, Teika's punishment was no longer enforced.

Teika believed that kokoro lay in the essence of an object. This essence could be grasped only at mental depths by penetrating that object. Since "kokoro," according to his definition, does not reflect individual thought processes, the resulting poem could be fully appreciated without knowing anything of the poet or the circumstances of composition. This position might be taken one step further (although he did not do so): a poet's identity has no connection to the reception of a poem. Here are two, by different poets, that measure up to Teika's criteria.

Hana no ka no	The cherry blossoms,
Kasumeru tsuki ni	Their fragrance casts in haze the moon
Akugarete	That I so long for,
Yume mo sadaka ni	And recently my dreams as well
Mienu koro kana.	Seem to have grown indistinct.
Ume no hana	The plum blossoms—
Akanu iro ka mo	Their scent and color always fresh,
Mukashi nite	And from times bygone
Onaji katami no	They are alike the keepsake
Haru no yo no tsuki.	Of the moon on brief spring nights.

One need not know which poem is by Teika and which by Shunzei's Daughter to appreciate them.[65]

On the other hand, Gotoba's virtuosity can only be recognized if we know two things: that *he* composed the following poem and that it con-

[65] [The author's point will not be spoiled by identifying the former as Teika's, in *Shūi Gusō*, and the latter by Shunzei's Daughter in *Shunzei Kyō no Musume no Shū*.—Ed.]

tains the circumstances of composition ("a story about the poet himself," to use Gotoba's expression):

Ware koso wa	It is I myself
Niishimamori yo	The new guardian of the island!
Oki no umi no	Here by the Oki sea,
Araki namikaze	You winds that roughen waves,
Kokoroshite fuke.	Blow with consideration!
	(*Masukagami*, 2:279)

We cannot properly appreciate the poem without considering the sad circumstances of Gotoba's exile to the island of Oki. The poem becomes a still more vivid statement when we take into account the former sovereign's personality. Gotoba's poem has been interpreted heretofore as a request: the new, melancholy guardian of Oki—the former sovereign—asks the ocean winds not to blow too violently. But Gotoba, a lavish host at his Minase villa and a man ambitious enough to attack the shogunate, was unlikely to have become a whining weakling as soon as he landed on Oki.

His poem is better interpreted as a stately declaration: now that he is lord of the island, the rough sea winds would do well to blow respectfully![66] This reading yields a poem far more characteristic of Gotoba. A poem may well be taken as an entity judged solely on its own terms, rather than by its connection to its author. But this idea cannot entirely negate the opposing position, that understanding is enriched by a knowledge of the poet and the circumstances in which a work was created. These two views are still being debated. The conflict between Teika and Gotoba, representing the two extremes, is an early example of an ongoing controversy among critics.

I noted earlier that 1204, the beginning of Teika's inactive period, also marks the gradual withdrawal of "loveliness" from his poetry. This event is unrelated to his differences with Gotoba. Several "lovely" waka by Teika and his followers were selected for the *Shinkokinshū* by Gotoba himself. Their inclusion is one reason why that tone has come to exemplify the *Shinkokinshū* style. Loveliness must therefore have disappeared from Teika's poetry for a personal reason: he had exhausted its potential. Realization of this ideal by him and his followers seems to have achieved "maximum value," and no amount of effort could yield a higher beauty.[67]

[66] This is Katō Shūson's reading. He told me (though he has probably forgotten having done so) that he conceived this interpretation on a visit to Oki in 1943.

[67] "Maximum value" is a mathematical term used in graphs. It is not synonymous with "greatest value." [That is, Teika and his circle had fully realized what they could create by "loveliness."—Ed.]

Let us suppose that Teika and his group had continued to compose in the lovely style. What would have been the result? A waka may be beautiful, but if its loveliness resembles that of its predecessors, the outcome will be surfeited readers. For their part, the poets would have had to compose yet lovelier poems if they were to be successful. But there can be no further amplifying a loveliness that has attained its maximum value. In lamenting that his "expression is worn and poor indeed, but I do not know how to improve it," Teika reflects his struggle against the limitations of his style of loveliness (see n. 59).

Teika endured a decade of public opposition to Gotoba's literary views and struggle in private with the style he himself had created. By the time he was fifty-three, Teika had determined new poetic boundaries for himself. They represented a new style: Teika's waka, like Late T'ang shih, now concealed their refined beauty within muted, negative scenes or emotions. At this point he realized that his earlier, lovely style was only a "temporary flower."

Teika's new orientation began to reveal itself in the way in which he selected waka for anthologies. *Teika Hachidaishō (Teika's Extracts from the Collections of Eight Eras)*, probably compiled in 1215, includes 567 poems from the *Shinkokinshū*. None of the selected poems by his contemporaries (including Shunzei and Saigyō) displays overt loveliness. These, for example, were excluded from the *Extracts*:

Kaerikonu Mukashi o ima to Omoine no Yume no makura ni Niou tachibana.	The past returns And I think of it as now In longing sleep Whose dreams came to a pillow Fragrant with orange blossoms. By Princess Shokushi (*SKKS*, 3:240)
Omokage no Kasumeru tsuki zo Yadorikeru Haru ya mukashi no Sode no namida ni.	Memories of you Emerge from a misty moon Whose light is lodged In the teardrops of a sleeve: Thinking of those springtimes past. By the Daughter of Shunzei (*SKKS*, 12:1136)

Teika included sixteen of his own poems in the *Extracts*. None, however, exemplifies the lovely style as do these excluded [and previously cited] poems:

Haru no yo no	On the brief spring night,
Yume no ukihashi	The floating bridge of dreams
Todaeshite	Breaks all apart,
Mine ni wakaruru	And from a mountain peak a cloud
Yokogumo no sora.	Takes leave into the empty sky.

Ume no hana	Blossoms of the plum
Nioi o utsusu	Transfer their fragrance from the tree
Sode no ue ni	To the moistened sleeve
Noki moru tsuki no	Where moonbeams view in shining
Kage zo arasou.	As they filter through the eaves.

Some of the poems by Teika in the *Extracts* possess a concealed beauty:

Tabibito no	The man in travel,
Sode fukikaesu	His sleeves are blown back and forth
Akikaze ni	By the autumn wind,
Yūhi sabishiki	When the evening sun turns desolate
Yama no kakehashi.	The hanging bridge between the peaks.

Toshi mo henu	The years have passed
Inoru chigiri wa	With prayers, for love, to the Kannon
Hatsuseyama	On Mount Hatsuse.
Onoe no kane no	From its hilltop the temple bell
Yoso no yūgure.	And evening just for others.

Shirotae no	White as pure hemp,
Sode no wakare ni	The sleeves at morning parting
Tsuyu ochite	Brighten with dew drops,
Mi ni shimu iro no	While with its heart-piercing color
Akikaze zo fuku.	Chill autumn wind blows through.

Teika did not entirely reject the lovely style, however. Some poems using it appear two years after the compilation of *Teika's Extracts*, in his *Solitaire Waka Match in One Hundred Rounds* (first revision):

Kasumi tatsu	The haze rises
Mine no sakura no	On peaks of cherry blossoms
Asaborake	In dim morning light:
Kurenai kukuru	The river waves of Heaven
Ama no kawanami.	Are tie-dyed in crimson.

(*SG*, 604; *Teika Hyakuban Jikaawase* [= *THJA*], Round 7)

Hana no ka no Kasumeru tsuki ni Akugarete Yume mo sadaka ni Mienu koro kana.	The cherry blossoms, The fragrance casts in haze the moon That I so long for, And recently my dreams as well Seem to have grown indistinct. (*SG*, 907; *THJA*, Round 4)
Ōzora wa Ume no nioi ni Kasumitsutsu Kumori mo hatenu Haru no yo no tsuki.	Across the heavens In the fragrance of plum blossoms The haze increases; The thin clouds do not exempt The moon on the brief spring night. (*SG*, 1632; *THJA*, Round 2)
Na mo shirushi Mine no arashi mo Yuki to furu Yamazakurado no Akebono no sora.	True to its name, Storm Mountain's blustering winds Fall like the snow; From the door mountain cherries Under the sky lit by the dawn. (*SG*, 2075; *THJA*, Round 12)
Konu hito o Matsuho no Ura no Yūnagi no Yaku ya moshio no Mi mo kogaretsutsu.	He who does not come I await at Matsuho Bay In the evening calm As seagrasses burn for salt And my body chars with longing. (*SG*, 2447; *THJA*, Round 62)

Although loveliness was no longer typical of Teika's style, he continued to see it as an appropriate mode for certain circumstances. Some believe that the poems just given were selected for the *Solitaire Waka Match* because Teika wished to include poems representing each stage of his career. He composed "Na mo shirushi" ("True to its name") at the age of fifty-two, however, and "Konu hito o" ("He who does not come") at fifty-four. What is more, Teika selected both waka for the *Shinchokusenshū* (1235). This strongly suggests that Teika did not disparage or reject the lovely tone in the later years of his life. On the other hand, the *Solitaire Waka Match* is clearly not dominated by loveliness. *Teika's Extracts* displays similar inclinations: they grew more pronounced as Teika aged.

An important aspect of the *Solitaire Waka Match* is the presence of a few poems that were both composed and intended to be appreciated on an ordinary level of awareness. Two examples:

Inochi dani	So long as I live,
Araba au se o	I will await the chance to meet
Matsuragawa	At Matsura River:
Kaeranu nami mo	For the wave that does not return
Yodome to zo omou.	Shall be trapped in stagnant waters.
	(*SG*, 1173; *THJA*, Round 76)

Yomosugara	Throughout the night
Tsuki ni ureete	I shall tell the moon my anguish
Ne o zo naku	And not cease to cry;
Inochi ni mukau	"My life hangs in the balance,
Monoomou to te.	I love so much," will be my words.
	(*SG*, 1375; *THJA*, Round 44)

The former was written by Teika at fifty-three, the latter at fifty-four; both can be appreciated without recourse to contemplation. He did not write exclusively in the contemplative stance. In fact, the majority of his poems involve less intense, less deep mental processes. He had once perceived these less intense works to be merely second- or third-rate poetry; hence his pique in 1203 when one such work, his cherry-blossom poem, was praised by Gotoba. Fourteen years later, when he made his first revision of the *Solitaire Waka Match*, he realized that a few of these poems were masterworks. Perhaps a similarly accommodating attitude would have softened his confrontation with Gotoba, and yet we must remember that Gotoba forbade him to compose at the palace in 1220, three years after the *Solitaire Waka Match* was first revised. The differences between him and the former sovereign had evidently become irreconcilable by 1217.

As he aged, Teika grew increasingly tolerant of those poems he had composed with less profound mental exertion. He compiled the *Shinchokusenshū* at the age of seventy-three, completing in 1235 a clean copy of this, the ninth royal waka anthology. This collection is well known for its paucity of "lovely" poems. The anthology might also be characterized by the larger number of his poems composed without contemplative depth. A corresponding event took place at much the same time: his second revised version of the *Solitaire Waka Match*, carried out after 1232, was augmented by these and similar poems.

Ima no ma no	Only just now
Wagami ni kagiru	Are my actions dictated
Tori no ne o	By the crowing cock—

Tare ukimono to Kaerisomeken.	Who was it feared exposure And suddenly hurried home?
	(*SG*, 1461; *THJA*, Round 61)
Haruka naru Hito no kokoro no Morokoshi wa Sawagu minato ni Kotozute mo nashi.	Far, far distant Is my faithless lover's heart— A true Cathay— And to my agitated harbor No communication comes.
	(*SG*, 1467; *THJA*, Round 76)
Miyako idete Asa tatsu yama no Tamuke yori Tsuyu okitomenu Akikaze zo fuku.	I leave the capital As morning rises on the mountains, And upon its crest, The dew of parting scatters In the gusts of autumn wind.
	(*SG*, 1476; *THJA*, Round 88)

His movement toward such poetry in his old age has given rise to simplistic explanations. It has been interpreted, for example, as indicating a transition from respect for ethereal beauty in the *Shinkokinshū* period to a preference for plain, simple beauty in the *Shinchokusenshū* era. Anyone who reads the above three waka will realize the error of that approach. All three poems employ fairly elaborate, difficult techniques; they are definitely not plain, simple poetry.

The conventional hon'i (essential nature) of the cock's crow in the first poem is that it is a nuisance for lovers. Because the cock's crow signals the arrival of dawn, the lover, though reluctant to leave his lady, must make haste to depart.[68] Teika's speaker, however, criticizes men who passively return at the first cock's crow. The sound he hears exists only in the present: the speaker must decide whether to follow its urgings and return, or to dare to stay by his lady's side. His cock's crow is a separate matter from the cock's crows heard by lovers of old. Problems may occur; but the speaker decides to stay all the same.

His treatment of the subject violates the hon'i of the cock's crow, which inevitably signifies parting; a reader familiar with this hon'i would thus be surprised by the poem. Aware that the speaker has resolved to stay, the reader, surprised by his unconventional decision, also comes to realize

[68] A classic example is this (*KKS*, 13:640): Shinonome no / Wakare o oshimi / Ware zo mazu / Tori yori saki ni / Nakihajimetsuru. (In the early light, / I so regret our parting / That I first of all— / Well before the cock himself— / Have begun to utter cries.)

that the speaker's resolve applies restrictedly to "Only just now" ("Ima no ma"). He will leave his beloved that morning, just as men have always left their ladies. Teika invites the recipient's surprise by seemingly violating the hon'i; in fact, he respects it. It is unexpected that a poet aged seventy would use so risky a technique.

He composed the other two poems in the same year as the poem on the cock's crow. The former is on the topic, "Lovers Meet but Do Not Share a Bed." Cathay ("Morokoshi") is a metaphor for the man's distant emotions, while the restless harbor represents the woman's unsettled heart. Each image is accompanied by complex overtones. The last poem associates the image of dew with the traveler's tears. "Tsuyu" (dew) is also used adverbially as a pivot (signifying "entirely" or "[not] at all") to suggest that the speaker, reluctantly leaving the capital, is hurried on his way by a manifestation of the travelers' guardian deity—in the form of the autumn wind. This delicate, intricate design can only be appreciated with considerable concentration.

It is of course erroneous to call Teika's late tone plain or simple. For lack of a better term, let us call it "non-en" or "nonrefined." The *Shinkokinshū* period, in the stricter sense of the term, may be defined as a time (1190-1203) dominated by "loveliness." His orientation toward nonrefined beauty becomes apparent after 1203. Thus the period from 1204 onward, although still part of the *Shinkokinshū* period, had best be considered in the broader sense of the term. The *Shinkokinshū* was presented to the tennō and a final celebratory banquet held in 1205. But that marks only the nominal completion of the anthology. Frequent additions and deletions continued to be made after this time. The final compilation process was probably completed between 1210 and 1216.[69]

Around the year 1217, when Teika made his first revision of the *Solitaire Waka Match*, he realized that superb waka could be written and appreciated at a normal mental level. His realization occurred at roughly the same time as the completion of the *Shinkokinshū*. The years after 1217 thus mark a transitional period between the *Shinkokinshū* and the *Shinchokusenshū* eras. If the close of the *Shinkokinshū* period is seen to coincide with Teika's turn toward a less than contemplative intensity, the *Shinkokinshū* period (in the broad sense) must be defined as a time in which poetry was dominated by the contemplative emphasis. This period begins around 1186, when Teika began to frequent Yoshitsune's salon and produce difficult, contemplative poems that were soon criticized as

[69] Changes continued to be made to the text of the *Shinkokinshū* after Gotoba's exile to Oki. One result was the "Oki Manuscript" of the *Shinkokinshū*. This manuscript need not be taken into account in delineating time periods, however, since it had no bearing on the principal waka poets.

"faddish and unfounded." The *Shinkokinshū* period, in its broad sense, thus encompasses roughly three decades (see the first part of this section).

Teika's contemporaries would not have been pleased that his poetry had become the standard defining the *Shinkokinshū* period. We would arrive at a different periodization if we employed Gotoba's perspective. By the fourteenth century, however, Teika's ideas and principles had become supreme literary touchstones, influencing linked verse and nō drama as well as waka. He is unquestionably the outstanding figure of the *Shinkokinshū* period. His changing styles thus provide the best criteria for defining it.

Connected Breaks and Polyresonant Unity

The *Shinkokinshū* period, in the broader sense, is known for a characteristic tone and handling of subjects. Another of its hallmarks concerns the form and content of a waka: the use of caesuras. A caesura most typically occurs after the third line in a poem that ends with a noun:

Sabishisa wa	Desolation grows
Shimo koso yuki ni	Increasing more with the frost
Masarikeri	Than when snow falls;
Mine no kozue no	Tips of branches on a peak
Akebono no sora.	Against the sky at daybreak.
	(*SG*, 1:362)

Of course waka often have other kinds of caesuras. Pronounced syntactic breaks appear occasionally in the Ancient Age and the Early Middle Ages, but they become a conspicuous feature of waka only in the broadly-defined *Shinkokinshū* period. Multiple caesuras are particularly characteristic of the period.

Two poems by Gokyōgoku Yoshitsune, for example, are quite unprecedented:

Aki zo kashi	It must be autumn!
Koyoi bakari no	Will I spend only tonight
Nezame ka wa	Without sleep?
Kokoro tsukusu na	Do not exhaust my heart,
Ariake no tsuki.	O moon at break of day.
	(*Akishino*, 1:834)

Kyō kurenu	Today is at an end.
Asu mo karikon	Let us come hunt tomorrow too.

Katanohara	In the Katano fields,
Kareno no shita ni	From beneath the withered plants,
Kigisu naku nari.	Other pheasants seem to be heard.
	(Ibid., 4:2117)

Such fragmentation is anomalous in waka, a genre generally distinguished by its continuous flow of language (see vol. one, General Introduction).

Special factors, such as Yoshitsune's wide knowledge of shih, may account for multiple caesuras in his poems. Influenced perhaps by his older brother Yoshimichi's (1167-88) accomplishments in Chinese prose and poetry composition, Yoshitsune was already producing "torch shih" at the tender age of fourteen.[70] He dabbled in waka prior to 1185, but only as a means of relaxing after shih gatherings (Kubota, 1973, 497-502). Yoshitsune's acquaintance with Teika commenced in the mid-1180s, when he first developed a serious interest in waka. Teika began to frequent Yoshitsune's salon in 1186, and his patron's influence may account for the marked increase in caesuras in Teika's waka from this time. With its several caesuras, the following poem, composed by Teika in 1189, is strongly reminiscent of Yoshitsune's style.

Chiraba chire	Scatter if you must!
Tsuyu wakeyukan	O dew, I shall be passing by.
Hagihara ya	Fields of bush clover—
Nurete no nochi wa	The wetting will prepare me
Hana no katami ni.	To recall the cherry blossoms.
	(*SG*, 1:538)

Syntactic breaks, rather than formal caesuras, are more typical of the *Shinkokinshū* style. One of Teika's waka, quoted earlier, was pronounced untranslatable:

Toshi mo henu	The years have passed
Inoru chigiri wa	With prayers, for love, to the Kannon
Hatsuseyama	On Mount Hatsuse.
Onoe no kane no	From its hilltop the temple bell
Yoso no yūgure.	And evening just for others.
	(*RU*, "Love, 2" 245)

[70] The slender torch (shisoku) used for "torch shih" was intended for interior use. Made of pine, it was approximately 18 inches long. One end was soaked in tallow; elapsed time was calculated by measuring the length of the unburned portion. A "torch shih" was composed in the time it took to burn a given length of the torch.

Two breaks occur in this poem, after the first and the third lines; neither break functions semantically in the poem. Such breaks are usually explained as signalling unstated feelings. But nothing has been left unsaid in these breaks: they are, quite simply, blanks. Motoori Norinaga (1730-1801) praises this poem from the second line on, but criticizes the blank after line 1: " 'The years have passed' [Toshi mo henu] is not an effective statement. Its insignificance is due to its lack of semantic connection to the rest of the poem" (*Mino*, 4:404). It was perhaps inevitable that Norinaga, a student of Nijō waka theory (on which see below, pp. 261, 390), would find this blank a defect. Viewed from the opposed Kyōgoku standpoint, however, Teika's poetic blank spot is praiseworthy, because it allows the reader to imagine numerous motives and emotions. Compared to the break after line 1, those after lines 3 and 4 are minor. There is no break in meaning between these lines, which state that the Hatsuse temple bell is tolling. On the other hand, if the "Hatsu-" of "Hatsuse" is seen as a pivot with the verb "hatsu," "to complete, be over," the reader is left with yet another inexplicable blank. The place name Hatsuse in love poetry is conventionally linked with romantic successes.[71] In Teika's poem, however, the affair is over, and the tolling of the bell is now meaningless to the speaker. The evening bell, signaling the time that lovers meet, rings in a world "other" (yoso) than the speaker's. The break between lines 3 and 4 is situational, therefore.

Waka follows the natural properties of the Japanese language in its continuous linguistic flow. Conspicuous breaks in waka result from the influence of shih expression. Yoshitsune is a highly significant figure in this respect. He was seven years Teika's senior, and in his time the most powerful patron of waka. Teika joined Yoshitsune's salon during the regent's most intense involvement with waka. Yoshitsune was on the verge of making astonishing strides in composition. Teika may well have encouraged Yoshitsune's tendencies toward fragmented waka. The younger man would certainly have been eager to harmonize with Yoshitsune's tastes. Although caesuras are a normal feature of an isolating language like Chinese, they are somehow dissonant in waka, as Norinaga was perceptive enough to see. He criticizes one of Teika's best known poems as follows.

Tabibito no	The man in travel,
Sode fukikaesu	His sleeves are blown back and forth
Akikaze ni	By the autumn wind,

[71] As in the *Kokin Rokujō* poem (3:293): Hatsusegawa / Ikuse ka wataru / Wagimoko ga / Okite shi kureba / Yase koso watare. (Hatsuse River—/How many shallows will you cross,/ My beloved wife? / My leaving you to come here / Makes eight shallows to be forded!)

Yūhi sabishiki	When the evening sun turns desolate
Yama no kakehashi.	The hanging bridge between the peaks.
	(*SKKS*, 10:953)

"The autumn wind" [akikaze], "the evening sun" [yūhi], and "the hanging bridge between the peaks" [yama no kakehashi] each form independent, unconnected units. The last three lines, moreover, have no connection with "The man in travel" [tabibito] of line 1. Things are collected and scenes presented quite at random. The style resembles that of the *Gyokuyōshū* and the *Fūgashū*. (*Mino*, 3:385)

Norinaga's Nijō approach to poetics naturally limits his critical perspective. There are no caesuras in this poem, but Norinaga still calls attention to the fragmented content. He finds the poem anomalous, a response evidently based less on Nijō doctrine than on the essential continuous nature of waka.

The most profound breaks occur in waka when the first half states emotion and the second half depicts nature. The break is particularly dramatic when the halves are semantically unconnected. A good example of such a break appears in a poem composed by Teika on the thirteenth of the Ninth Month, 1192.

Musubikeru	How cruel you are
Chigiri mo tsurashi	To pledge and then withdraw your love.
Aki no no no	In the autumn fields,
Sueba no shimo no	Hoarfrost on the tips of branches
Ariake no tsuki.	Tinged by moonlight in the dawn.
	(*SG*, supernum. fasc., 3140)

If the blank spots are filled in by intellectual means, the poem will become more easily understood, but that will be the only benefit. No emotional response will ensue unless the speaker's reproach to his lady is directly sensed as frost-coated branch tips under a dawn moon. If this is to be achieved, the reader must suppress intellectual processes. Expression of this kind appears often in Chinese poetry from the High T'ang period on; and it probably inspired similar approaches in waka.

I miss our days of laboring at verses;
Skies are cold, and waters flow on swiftly.
(Chia Tao [779-843], "Longing for a
Friend in Po-ling," *CTS*, 572:6647-48)

The emotions expressed in the first line of the couplet are next symbolized by the image of a river coursing under the winter sky. But the emotions evoked by the shih diminish in direct proportion to the effort exerted to explain it. The first two lines of Teika's "lover's reproach" might be seen as a forenote, and the last three lines as the poem itself. Their relationship would then correspond to that between the following poem and forenote.

Discrimination of Merits

Tobu tori no	Where birds fly best,
Asukagawa kaze	Asuka whose river winds,
Sore mo ga to	Desiring blossoms,
Sode fukikaeshi	Excite one's sleeves to blow about
Hana zo furishiku.	As the petals fall in showers.
	(*SG*, 3:2750)

Teika may be alluding to a passage in "Discrimination of Merits," the seventeenth chapter of the *Lotus Sūtra*, in which the Buddha's preaching produces auspicious signs:

There rain down heavenly flowers,
  Great clusters of heavenly flowers;
And Indras and Brahmas, like Ganges' sands
  In their numberlessness, come from the Buddha-lands.
Powdered sandalwood and aloes rain down,
  Mingling together as they fall;
Indras and Brahmas, like birds falling from the sky,
  Scatter the incense as offerings over the Buddhas.
    (*Hokkekyō*, 17:46; adapted from Hurvitz, 1976, 248)

The splendid merits of eternal Truth are symbolized by the explicit description of beautiful blossoms scattering. From his poem, we may think Teika an early practitioner of a technique perfected by the abdicated sovereign Hanazono in the fourteenth century—that of using pure description to symbolize a conceptual tenor (see ch. 14).

Expression that is both fragmented and somehow connected appears not only in individual poems but also within collections. In the latter, the poems were originally freestanding works, and the principal concern was with how the poems were linked one to another. In royal anthologies, poems are ordered according to certain designs that follow the principles of progression and association (see vol. two, ch. 7). Progression, the first principle to appear, is joined by the principle of association around the time the *Kin'yōshū* was compiled. The following sequence appears in that collection, which is arranged more or less according to the principle of progression.

Composed on the topic "The First Day of Autumn," from a hundred-poem sequence.
By Kinzane, Master of the Crown Prince's Household

<table>
<tr><td>Toko to wa ni
Fuku yūgure no
Kaze naredo
Aki tatsu hi koso
Suzushikarikere.</td><td>Always, one might say,
The wind can be expected
To blow at dusk,
Yet on the first day of autumn
Its coolness is so refreshing.
(3:165)</td></tr>
</table>

On the topic "Meadow Grasses Are Touched with Dew."
By Nagazane, Assistant Governor-General of Dazaifu

<table>
<tr><td>Makuzu hau
Ada no ōno no
Shiratsuyu o
Fuki na midari so
Aki no hatsukaze.</td><td>Kudzu vines extend
On the grand plain of Ada,
The pearl-like dew
Is not to be blown about,
O first breeze of autumn!
(3:166)</td></tr>
</table>

On the topic "Waiting for Flowers to Bloom."
By Lady Mino of Her Majesty's Residence

<table>
<tr><td>Fujibakama
Haya hokorobite
Niowanan
Aki no hatsukaze
Fukitatazu to mo.</td><td>Purple trousers plant,
Make haste to undo your buds
And come into bloom—
Although the first autumn wind
Has not yet begun to blow.
(3:167)</td></tr>
</table>

On the topic "The Seventh Night," composed during the reign of Goreizei Tennō at Her Majesty's Waka Match on Spring and Autumn Topics.
By Lady Tosa, Court Handmaid

<table>
<tr><td>Yorozuyo ni
Kimi zo miru beki
Tanabata no
Yukiai no sora no
Kumo no ue nite.</td><td>For age upon age
Your Majesty will behold
The celestial lovers
Making their heavenly rendezvous—
From your Palace of the Clouds.
(3:168)</td></tr>
</table>

Poems 165 through 167 follow a seasonal progression. Kinzane's poem concerns the first day of autumn, while the next two poems, by Nagazane and Lady Mino, are composed on the first autumnal winds. The choice of the next poem, by Lady Tosa, is less obvious. There seems little sense in moving from the first winds of autumn to the Seventh Night. Here Lady Mino's "purple trousers" poem becomes crucial to the configuration. "Purple trousers"—a literal translation of "fujibakama," a purple-blossoming wild aster [Eupatorium Fortunei]—is used as a pivot for "[a lady's] undertrousers" in the poem. The speaker urges the "purple trousers" to "undo your buds" (hokorobite). The clothing imagery calls to mind a poetic convention in which the Weaver Maid, awaiting the arrival of her Herdboy lover on the Seventh Night, undoes the waistband of her trousers.

There may be some connection between the twelfth-century development of this linking technique and the practice of arranging setsuwa by thematic links between contiguous stories. The successive setsuwa in the *Konjaku Monogatari Shū (Tales of Times Now Past)* roughly follow the principle of progression. Some contiguous stories appear at first sight to have no thematic link, yet closer investigation reveals an element shared by both stories (see ch. 4). *Tales of Times Now Past* is unique among setsuwa collections in possessing this feature. The configurational principles used in waka collections probably inspired the compiler of the *Tales* to arrange his setsuwa collection similarly.

During the *Shinkokinshū* period, waka arranged by association become a noticeable feature of hundred-poem sequences as well as royal anthologies. An apt illustration of association from this period is found in the first ten poems from Book 12 of the *Shinkokinshū*.[72]

On the topic "Love and Clouds," composed on presenting a fifty-poem sequence to His Majesty. By Shunzei's Daughter

Shitamoe ni	Burning secretly
Omoikienan	Love will consume me in its flames;
Keburi dani	Smoke from my pyre
Ato naki kumo no	Will vanish among the clouds
Hate zo kanashiki.	Making my unhappy end!
	(12:1081)

[72] Other instances appear in *SKKS*, 1:1-15 and 10:896-904; they are discussed in Konishi, 1958a, 69-82 and 92-99. Progression and association in seven winter poems from the *SKKS* (6:667-73) are discussed in Brower-Miner, 1961, 324-28.

Composed for a waka match in one hundred rounds, held at the residence of the Regent-Chancellor. By Lord Fujiwara Teika

Nabikaji na	You do not yield,
Ama no moshiobi	Though I begin to burn with love
Takisomete	(A fisher's seagrass fire),
Keburi wa sora ni	And my smoke rises skyward
Kuyuriwabu to mo.	Curling about in misery.
	(12:1082)

A poem on love, presented to His Majesty with a hundred-poem sequence. By the Regent-Chancellor [Yoshitsune]

Koi o nomi	It takes only love:
Suma no urabito	This denizen of Suma Bay
Moshio tare	Dripping seagrass brine;
Hoshiaenu sode no	The wet sleeves will never dry—
Hate o shiraba ya.	Whatever will become of them?
	(12:1083)

A Love Poem
By Lady Sanuki, Attendant to the Nijō Consort

Mirume koso	The branching miru
Irinuru iso no	Is a plant that flourishes
Kusa narame	In waters of the shore,
Sode sae nami no	But flooded under waves of tears
Shita ni kuchinuru.	My sleeves will surely rot away.
	(12:1084)

Composed on the topic "Long-Lasting Love." By Lord Shunrai

Kimi kou to	Born to love you,
Narumi no ura no	I remain like the oaks that stand
Hamahisaki	At Narumi Bay,
Shiorete nomi mo	Feeling only being drenched
Toshi o furu kana.	As one year follows that before!
	(12:1085)

On the topic "Secret Love."
By the Former Chancellor [Fujiwara Yorizane (1155-1225)]

Shiru rame ya
Ko no ha furishiku
Tanikawa no
Iwama ni morasu
Shita no kokoro o.

How could you know?
My love remains unspoken,
A valley stream
When the leaves have thickly fallen
And yet seeps through between the rocks.

(12:1086)

On the topic "Secret Love," composed when I was General of the Left and held a match of hundred-poem sequences at my residence.
By the Regent-Chancellor

Morasu na yo
Kumo iru mine no
Hatsushigure
Ko no ha wa shita ni
Iro kawaru to mo.

Do not let it out—
O beclouded mountain peak—
Though the first drizzle
May subtly affect the colors
Of even the lowest hanging leaves.

(12:1087)

Composed after having written several love poems.
By the Gotokudaiji Minister of the Left
[Fujiwara Sanesada (1139-91)]

Kaku to dani
Omou kokoro o
Iwaseyama
Shita yuku mizu no
Kusagakuretsutsu.

You see how I love you,
Yet I cannot speak my heart;
It is a stream whose flow
By the base of Mount Iwase
Is concealed by undergrowth.

(12:1088)

On the same topic.
By Lady Taifu, Attendant to Princess Imbu Mon'in

Morasaba ya
Omou kokoro o
Sate nomi wa
E zo Yamashiro no
Ide no shigarami.

Oh, to tell it all!
To suppress a longing heart—
What a vain attempt—
It seeps even through the weirs
Of Ide in Yamashiro.

(12:1089)

On the topic "Secret Love."
By Konoe Tennō (1139-55; r. 1141-55)

Koishi to mo	To say "I love you":
Iwaba kokoro no	Those words could be expected
Yuku beki ni	To bring me peace,
Kurushi ya hitome	Yet what an agony to hide
Tsutsumu omoi wa.	My feelings from the eyes of others!
	(12:1090)

Love poetry in the *Kokinshū* is arranged according to the principle of progression. The poems depict the progress of a love affair: a man's love evolves into intense passion which, having been satisfied, begins to cool. Eventually his love is gone, and his lover is left alone with her grief and resentment.[73] The sequence just given does not always follow the *Kokinshū* precedent. Love poetry in the *Shinkokinshū* often displays no logical, comprehensible arrangement yielding the *Kokinshū* style of progression. That the sequential configurations of the *Shinkokinshū* are nevertheless thoroughly interesting is due in large part to the technique of association, which gives a fine texture to the sequence.

If our sample sequence is to be appreciated fully, we must concentrate on the poems alone. Individual circumstances of composition—the facts stated in the respective forenotes—should be disregarded. The first poem in the sequence, number 1081 (by Shunzei's Daughter), shares one word with poem 1082 (by Teika): "keburi," "smoke." "Clouds" (kumo) in 1081 evokes "skyward" (sora) in 1082, moreover. The fairly conceptual "Burning secretly" (shitamoe) of poem 1081 may be seen to correspond to the concrete "burn" (taki-) of 1082. Similarly, in poem 1081 the base ending "-hi" (modern "-i") of the inflected verb "omohi-" (modern "omoi"; love) is a homophone for "fire"; this draws our attention to the "seagrass fire" (moshiobi) of poem 1082.[74] The "love"/"fire" homophone in 1081 also associates "hi" with "kiyu" ["-kienan"], "to consume," later in the poem. We do not know the speaker's location in poem 1081. When 1081 is linked to 1082, however, we take it that the former poem takes place near the sea. Poem 1081 thus acquires a meaning not implied by its original status. All the poems through Shunrai's (1085) are situated by the sea. Yoshitsune's poem (1083) shares the word "moshio" ("seagrass brine") with 1082, and the two poems are also associated by

[73] In royal collections, seasonal and love waka are typically arranged largely according to the principle of progression alone (see vol. two, ch. 7).

[74] The love/fire homophone "omi[h]i" occurs earlier, for example, in *KKS*, 11:470: Oto ni nomi / Kiku no shiratsuyu / Yoru wa okite / Hiru wa omoi ni / Aezu kenu beshi. (Nothing but rumors: / As dew settles on chrysanthemums / I lie awake at night, / While by day, the fires of love / Threaten to consume me.)

the "dry" (hoshi-) of 1083 and "fire" (-bi) in 1082. Lady Sanuki's poem (1084) is joined to 1083 by the word "sode" (sleeves); her "shore" (iso) also corresponds to Yoshitsune's "bay" (ura), just as her "branching miru" (mirume, a delicate seaweed) is linked to his "seagrass" (mo). Shunrai's poem (1085) also has "bay" (ura) to join it to the preceding "shore" of 1084.

Yorizane's poem (1086) moves the scene from the sea to the mountains, but its setting remains concerned with water: "valley stream" (tanikawa) corresponds to "bay" in 1085. The association is thus effected through a "waterplace" (or suihen; a term from linked poetry). Poem 1087, by Yoshitsune, has three words in common with 1086: "morasu" (to seep or leak; to let it be known), "ko no ha" (foliage, leaves), and "shita" (beneath; subtly, unspoken). Yoshitsune's "drizzle" (-shigure) is homologous with "stream" (tanikawa) in 1086, since both deal with water; and his "mountain peak" (mine) corresponds to "valley" in the preceding poem, since both are features of mountain topography. Poem 1088, by Sanesada, is also linked by the word "shita" (beneath; base). Its "Mount" (-yama), like "mountain peak" in 1087, belongs to the renga category of Peaks (sanrui). Similarly, "undergrowth" (kusa) in 1088 corresponds to "lowest hanging leaves" in 1087: both are members of the Plants (uemono) category in linked poetry. "Stream" (mizu) in 1088 corresponds to "drizzle" in the preceding waka. Lady Taifu's poem, 1089, has "omou kokoro" (a longing heart) in common with 1088, and its mention of the place name Ide evokes associations with the "stream" of the preceding poem.[75] Poem 1090, by Konoe Tennō, has only the word "kokoro" (heart, thoughts) in common with 1089; there may, however, be an indirect connection effected by a homophone of "tsutsumu" (to hide; also, to envelop) and "moru" (to let out; to speak my heart) in the preceding poem, since any attempt to suppress water will result in its seeping out.

Qualitative considerations are also at work in arranging a sequence. Thirteenth-century waka poets arranged sequences in patterns of what they called "ji" (background) and "mon" (design). Background poems are plain, inconspicuous works; they are also called mumon, or nondecorative. Design poems contain strikingly superior expression; an alternate term is "umon," possessing decoration. All waka ideally belong to the design category when read as individual works, for no one will be impressed by a background poem on its own. But if a sequence consisted entirely of design poems, each superlative work would cancel out the others, and the good qualities of individual poems might be diminished. Background poems are useful in sequences because their inconspicuous

[75] As, for example, in *Senzaishū*, 2:111: Haru fukami / Ide no kawamizu / Kage sowaba / Ikue ka mien / Yamabuki no hana. (Spring so advanced, / The river waters of Ide bear / Bright reflections— / Layer upon layer can be seen / Of the golden kerria blossoms.)

presence draws the reader's attention to the fine points of neighboring design poems. When properly set off by background poems, design poems appear to even greater advantage than in their original settings.[76]

The design poems in our ten-poem sequence are numbers 1081 through 1085, and poems 1086 through 1090 are background poems. The *degree* of "design" or "background" also varies poem by poem. The first two poems of the sequence, those by Shunzei's Daughter (1081) and Teika (1082), use extremely difficult techniques; when finally understood, these poems produce a strong impression. Although technically outstanding, poems 1083 through 1085 are ultimately less effective than the preceding pair. The latter group may be termed "semi-design" (yaya mon) waka. Similarly, the background poems 1086 through 1088, though not especially striking, employ more interesting techniques than poems 1089 and 1090. The somewhat more outstanding members of this category, then, may be termed "semi-background" (yaya ji). [These fine discriminations do not always survive translation or interpretation by reader without ample training and knowledge.]

The motif of poem 1081 is the mingling of love and death. The speaker, a victim of excessive longing for her beloved, is on the verge of death. When she dies, she will be cremated, and the smoke from her pyre will vanish into the clouds. Her love now burns within her, like a pyre that continues to smolder. Shunzei's Daughter uses two very complex concepts in her poem: she mixes present and future, and she uses "fire" not only as a conventional metaphor for romantic yearnings but as the flame actually consuming the speaker's corpse. Although it also likens the violence of love to fire, Teika's poem (1082) uses the imagery of burning seagrasses. The deep-sea plants were harvested and burned to produce salt. The salt image suggests the pains of love, as its cares are represented by the smoke. "Nabiku" (yield, lit. to bend), an associative word, describes how the smoke "lingers" above the burning seaweed; but it also signifies that the speaker's lover may be "yielding" after all.

Poem 1083, by Yoshitsune, is by contrast relatively straightforward: his speaker's sleeves, always wet with tears, will rot some day. "Su-" (to perform an action; in this case, to love) in the second line pivots with the place name Suma, which in turn calls to mind the waka on which Yoshitsune's is based. It is by Ariwara Yukihira.

Wakuraba ni	If, by some chance,
Tou hito araba	Someone inquires after me,
Suma no ura ni	"There at Suma Bay

[76] This is easily understood when considered in connection with "figure" and "ground" in gestalt psychology.

Moshio taretsutsu	Dripping with seagrass brine,"
Wabu to kotaeyo.	Answer that "he suffers so!"

(*KKS*, 18:962)

Yoshitsune's poem would gain greater romantic import, on the other hand, if Genji's exile at Suma were evoked (*GM*, "Suma," 30). Lady Sanuki's waka (1084) is based on a *Man'yōshū* poem about love between fisherfolk.[77] Her poem may thus be interpreted as a similar statement: lovers who are busy gathering "miru grass" (mirume, a kind of seaweed) have little time for a rendezvous (mirume, chance to meet). That is why the speaker's sleeves, constantly wet with tears, are nearly rotted through. The base poem provides the concept of the lovers having "little time." In Shunrai's poem (1085), oaks growing by the shore are coated by salt spray borne on strong sea winds. A pivot word is at work here: "shiore-" signifies both "being salty" and "being damp or wetted" (usually by tears). Shunrai's technique is rather impressive; unlike poems 1081 and 1082, however, with its simple conception his poem does not possess a strikingly poignant theme. That is why it is a "semi-design" poem.

The gradual shift from design to background ensures that the next design poems to appear will be properly set off. Although background waka are commonplace in themselves, they perform a vital function in sequences. The background-design pattern seems first to have been used in hundred-poem sequences. Gotoba remarks of Yoshitsune's waka:

> The late regent composed mainly in the lofty style, although he employed other styles as well. There was something extraordinary about his diction—which was impeccable—and his delicately devised waka. One might, however, criticize the paucity of background poems in his hundred-poem sequences. (*Gotoba In*, 146)

Gotoba firmly believed that a hundred-poem sequence should have background poems.[78] This rule was later to be observed in linked poetry (Yamada Y., 1937, 98-99), an indication of the close relationship between renga and the *Shinkokinshū* approach to arrangement in collections and hundred-poem (or other length) sequences.

During the *Shinkokinshū* period, individual waka were incorporated into a sequence by linking them through various kinds of association. The

[77] *MYS*, 7:1394: Shio miteba / Irinuru iso no / Kusa nare ya / Miraku sukunaku / Kouraku no ōki. (When the tide is full, / The seagrass by the shoreline / Sinks beneath the waves: / How infrequently we meet, / How often do I yearn for you!)

[78] Tameie has a detailed discussion of background poems (*Eiga no Ittei*, 354-55). Robert H. Brower has conducted a comprehensive investigation of background and design in Teika's *First Hundred-Poem Sequence of the Shōji Era* (Brower, 1978, 37-102).

resulting sequence unfolds as a single harmonious unit, although the degree of intensity varies poem by poem. The effect thus achieved is a polyresonant unity. Not all *Shinkokinshū*-period waka poets seem to have been equally devoted to achieving such unity. Gotoba displays the strongest tendencies. His first sequence, *The Hundred-Poem Sequence Composed in the Eighth Month of 1200*, has an intricate design determined by both progression and association, as well as by a proper distribution of background and design poems. The same is true for his hundred-poem sequences on topics concerning, respectively, the Inner and Outer Shrines of Ise (both composed in 1201), and for his *Five-Hundred-Poem Sequence* (date unknown).[79]

Teika is almost as strongly drawn toward polyresonant unity. The first signs appear in his *Hundred-Poem Sequence Composed in Haste* (1189) and his *Hundred-Poem Sequence for a Waka Match* (1193).[80] Teika's associative techniques matured in 1200 with his *Hundred-Poem Sequence at the Former Sovereign's Palace.*[81] His interest in polyresonant unity continued into old age, although Gotoba far outdid him in observing the principle of association.[82] Association is much less noticeable in hundred-poem sequences by the other editors of the *Shinkokinshū*, Michitomo, Ariie, Ietaka, and Masatsune. The *Shinkokinshū* is, in a sense, Gotoba's compilation and his leadership probably had much to do with the importance accorded association in the anthology. Prior to their estrangement, Gotoba and Teika probably worked together to achieve this goal.

Polyresonant unity is achieved through progression and association. The principle of progression, distinguished by tradition, retained an imposing presence in royal waka anthologies after the *Shinkokinshū*. Association, on the other hand, became an increasingly minor feature of anthologies and sequences. Association rarely appears in hundred-poem sequences after the middle of the thirteenth century. Gotoba's dedicated promotion of association may have triggered a reaction to the principle. More importantly, however, the principle of association declined because a new poetic age was dawning: the late thirteenth through the fourteenth centuries mark the evolution of linked poetry. Because renga practitioners took a lively interest in association, there was no longer an aesthetic need for intricate associative design in royal anthologies and hundred-poem sequences.

[79] *Gotoba In Gyoshū*: 1-100, 201-300, 301-400, 601-1099.

[80] *Sōsotsu Hyakushu* and *Utaawase Hyakushu*, respectively. The latter (in *SG*, 1) appears in the *Roppyakuban Utaawase*.

[81] *Sentō Hyakushu*, another title for the *First Hundred-Poem Sequence of the Shōji Era*. [See n. 78.—Ed.]

[82] A thorough discussion of this point, in connection with *Kindai Shūka*, appears in Brower-Miner, 1967, 48-131.

Toward Pseudoclassicism

The authority of Teika's waka school became unshakable after the Jōkyū Civil War of 1221. For the next two centuries, Teika's descendants were the sole leaders among waka poets. In 1209, at the age of forty-seven, Teika presented his *Kindai Shūka (Superior Poems of Our Time)* to the shogun Sanetomo.[83] The shogun had probably used Kujō Kanezane, Teika's close associate and a nobleman on intimate terms with the bakufu, as an intermediary in requesting Teika's instruction in waka composition. Teika's association with Sanetomo led to friendships with Utsunomiya Yoritsuna (1182-1259) and other warriors from the eastern provinces. The bakufu had great confidence in Teika. His position was further strengthened in the waka circle following Gotoba's failed coup d'état.

The lack of true poets in the Rokujō school accounts in part for the leadership exercised by Teika and his descendants from the thirteenth century on. One telling manifestation of this fact is the identity of the compilers of royal waka anthologies from this period. Becoming the compiler of a royal anthology resulted, apparently, from being publicly acknowledged as a supremely authoritative waka poet. Excepting the *Fūgashū* (1343-49), supervised by Hanazono In, and the *Shinshokukokinshū* (1433-39), compiled by Asukai Masayo, all the anthologies known collectively as "The Collections from Thirteen Reigns" had Teika or his descendants among their compilers.[84] One characteristic of the Middle Ages—perpetuating the Way of Waka through a "family" (ie) or school—was established by Teika and his descendants.

The Mikohidari did not, however, always encounter easy passage in consolidating its waka authority. Its efforts involved considerable opposition and resistance. The trouble probably originated when people began to have doubts about the poetic opinions of Tameie (1197-1275), Teika's heir to the Mikohidari legacy. Tameie revered the plain waka style, a position said to have been advocated by Teika in his old age. The plain style was perpetuated by the Nijō house and was to influence not only waka but linked poetry and nō as well. There is no factual evidence, however, to support the belief that Teika advocated the plain style in his later years. We have already seen how Teika moved markedly toward the "non-en" style in his old age, otherwise maintaining a style unchanged from that of

[83] In the *Azuma Kagami* (passage dated 13.VIII.1209), Teika is recorded to have presented Sanetomo with his "secret transmissions of waka composition, written in one fascicle" (19:646). This is believed to refer to *Kindai Shūka*, also probably composed in 1209. [On pseudoclassicism—gikotenshugi, which also might be translated imitative classicism—see ch. 6, n. 1.—Ed.]

[84] [Although the work was performed by Kōmyō Tennō, Hanazono closely supervised compilation of the *Fūgashū*. Not even Uda or Daigo had been so involved (for the *Kokinshū*). The "In" for Hanazono seems to be a courtesy title. See Miner-Odagiri-Morrell, 1985, 160 and 467-69.—Ed.]

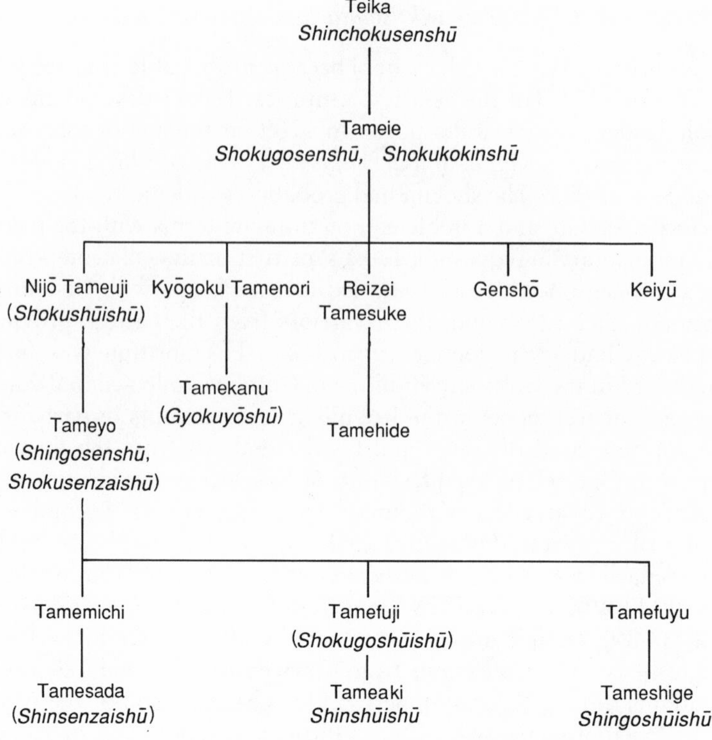

FIGURE 8.2 Descendants of Teika

his youth: he continued to enter deeply into a subject to obtain a contemplative grasp of it and maintained the same subtle design. He may not even have turned away from the yōen style of waka. On the other hand, almost all of Tameie's 5,730 surviving waka are in the plain style (*Fujiwara Tameie Zenkashū* ["Kaisetsu," 586]). He may well have consciously adopted this standard. Tameie describes his ideal poetic form in *Eiga no Ittei (The Single Style of Waka Composition).*

> Diction that flows clearly and smoothly produces good poetic form. The style may be acceptable, but disjointed diction will expose one to reproach: "Alas, here is good material gone to waste!" When considering a composition, therefore, closely observe the state of your diction. The second half of your poem might go first, and the first part last. A skillful poet hears the same things but makes his poem flow smoothly. If one or two syllables grate on the ear, all thirty-one are besmirched. How much more true it is, then, that one poorly-written line will negate the rest of a fine poem and render it quite hopeless. (356)

> If you wish to make a name for yourself as a poet, and as a skillful one at that, . . . you must dedicate the rest of your life to eliminating bad elements from your verse. It is said that waka should be fresh and innovative, compositions unique to oneself. There are few new subjects, however. You must strive instead to transform traditional subject matter by creating a style whose presentation and flow of diction makes everything sound fresh. (366)

Tameie follows his own advice in his compositions. It is quite another question, however, whether Tameie's opinions coincide with Teika's.

Fujiwara Mitsutoshi (1203-76) doubted that they did. A pupil of Teika's during the Kangi and Jōei eras (1229-33), Mitsutoshi was probably fairly familiar with his teacher's late style.[85] The poetic ideal, according to Mitsutoshi, is as follows:

> In general, . . . lofty, vivid waka exemplify the supreme poetic style. Another style, indescribably fine, is that of profound [yūgen] waka. Poets writing in this style rack their brains to produce verse whose suggested meaning stimulates deep thoughts. Such poetic composition seems centered on kokoro rather than diction, a marvelous thing indeed. This style cannot be imitated by ordinary poets. (*Hi no Kawakami*, 62)

Mitsutoshi's position contrasts markedly with Tameie's. The former assigns the highest value to waka possessing majestic import, as well as praising waka in the deep, contemplative style. Mitsutoshi's opinion is, I believe, closer to that held by Teika near the end of his life. The differing views held by Tameie and Mitsutoshi led to arguments among waka poets, culminating in open confrontation in 1246.[86] Mitsutoshi's allies included three from the Rokujō house—Tomoie, Akiuji, and Yukiie—as well as the influential poets Gosaga In (r. 1242-46), Kujō Motoie (1203-80), and Kinugasa Ieyoshi (1192-1264). The Mikohidari side boasted a principal lineup of Tameie, Tameuji, Genshō, Keiyū, Ankamon'in Emon no Suke (later known as the nun Abutsu), and in-laws like Saionji Saneuji (1194-1269) and Tsumori Kunisuke (1242-99; Fukuda, 1972, 67-73).

The confrontation lasted about thirty years. Although originating in a difference over poetics, it came increasingly to take on the nature of a power struggle among poets. This was particularly clear and intense when the decision was made as to who would—and who would not—

[85] "Lord Mitsutoshi (name in religion: Shinkan) joined the company of waka poets as a pupil of this house around the Kangi or Jōei era [ca. 1229-33]" (*Genshō*, 1). Mitsutoshi's relationship with Teika began several years earlier, around 1213 (*MGK* [1213], 278).

[86] Genshō writes that Mitsutoshi's disagreements with Tameie began in 1232 and quickly became serious (*Genshō*, 1-2). Mikohidari poets were kept from participating in *The Waka Match at the Wakamiya Shrine of Kasuga*, held in the Twelfth Month of that year. This indicates an open break between the two factions (Yasui, 1973, 184-85).

compile a royal waka anthology. Because Tameie had been the sole compiler of the *Shokugosenshū* (1251), it was assumed that he would occupy the same position with the next anthology. The Ninth Month of 1262, however, saw Tameie joined in his labors by Motoie, Ieyoshi, Yukiie, and Mitsutoshi. Since Mitsutoshi was the only one of the four who was likely to raise dissenting views, the upshot of the group appointment was that Mitsutoshi and Tameie served as co-compilers.

The product of their joint efforts, the *Shokukokinshū*, was submitted to the throne in the Twelfth Month of 1265. Tameie was said to have been too disgusted by the experience to have made more than a feeble effort in selecting poems. Mitsutoshi had succeeded in being made co-compiler because of a strong recommendation from the bakufu—he taught waka to the shogun, Prince Munetaka—and from the recommendation of his younger brother, Hamuro Sadatsugu, an official in attendance on Gosaga In (Yasui, 1973, 187-88). Discord within bakufu circles forced Prince Munetaka to resign in the Seventh Month of 1266, however, and Mitsutoshi quickly lost both his prominent poetic position and entrée to Gosaga's palace.[87] For nearly ten years after his fall, Mitsutoshi was barred from active poetic participation at court. The way again became open with Tameie's death in 1275, but Mitsutoshi died one year later. The Mikohidari house had established its leadership.

The dispute between the Mikohidari house, begun by Shunzei and now headed by Tameie, and its opponents, led by Mitsutoshi, was originally centered on a literary matter: whether or not Teika's waka style was being transmitted accurately. At some point, the confrontation evolved into a struggle for material power. This may account for the fact that there is no great difference between the compositions of the two factions. Tameie and Mitsutoshi clearly differ in their poetic philosophies; but these were evidently formulated solely to clarify the position of each side and so justify their respective roles in the conflict. Waka by the later Mikohidari poets are of course written entirely in the plain style. Nevertheless, although something akin to the contemplative style occasionally appears in anti-Mikohidari waka, most are written in a manner nearly indistinguishable from the plain style. If we were to put ourselves in the place of the rival faction members, we would naturally see considerable difference in their waka styles. To an outsider like myself, however, both sides seem to produce more or less the same kind of poetry. Once the Mikohidari had consolidated its poetic leadership, an internal struggle arose. Unlike the earlier, external confrontation, this one was accompanied by clear stylistic differences.

[87] "In the Seventh Month of the following year [1266], Prince Nakatsukasa [Munetaka] returned to the capital. Shinkan [Mitsutoshi] was also denied access to the retired sovereign's palace" (*Genshō*, 2).

During Tameie's lifetime, the Mikohidari house became subdivided into three independent families headed by three of his sons. The families were known as Nijō, Kyōgoku, and Reizei. The three houses eventually engaged in such battles that one might more properly speak of the disintegration of the Mikohidari rather than its subdivision. These battles were instigated not by differing views on waka composition but on the exceedingly worldly matter of rights of property inheritance. Following Tameie's death, his sons Nijō Tameuji and Reizei Tamesuke disputed which stood to inherit Tameie's estate at Hosokawa. The dispute led to a lawsuit that lasted thirty-nine years.[88]

Another point at issue in the lawsuit concerned which son was entitled to own the poetic treatises passed down from the time of Shunzei and Teika. Contemporary inheritance law decreed that the treatises be given to the eldest son, Tameuji. Tameie, however, seems to have favored a younger son, Tamesuke—or, perhaps, his favor was centered on Tamesuke's mother, Abutsu. In any case, Tameie bequeathed the documents to the younger son. The Nijō family's case seems to have been persuasive, because the court ruled as follows: the deed to the Hosokawa manor was to be given to the Reizei family, while the poetic treatises, accumulated over several generations, were to be restored to the Nijō house.

The Reizei did indeed inherit the Hosokawa manor, but a sizeable portion of the poetic treatises apparently was not returned to the Nijō family. Kitabatake Chikafusa (1293-1354) declares so in his *Kokinshū Jochū (Commentary on the Japanese Preface to the Kokinshū)*. According to Chikafusa's account, among the poetic materials bequeathed to the Reizei family by Tameie were two chests filled with Teika's secret waka transmissions, probably in holograph form.

> There are two chests with writings about waka composition by Lord Teika. One has a picture of a cormorant inlaid on the lid, the other a picture of a heron. The chests, called "Cormorant" and "Heron," did not leave Lord Tameie's side. When he died, her ladyship, the nun Abutsu, took the poetic treatises with her when she went to Kamakura. The heir, Lord Tameuji, later lodged a suit against her, and because of this Kameyama In issued a proclamation to the military government in Kamakura. When the time came for the disputed documents to be given to Tameuji, an old catalogue was used to ensure that all the documents were handed over. But the papers contained in the Cormorant and Heron must not have been well known to his

[88] The lawsuit was apparently lodged in 1275, the year of Tameie's death. The final ruling came in 1313. The laws governing courtiers differed from warrior law in the matter of the force carried by an oral testament. Moreover, the administration of manors tended to pass between court and bakufu. A final judgment was thus difficult to reach, and once attained, resulted in repeated appeals (Fukuda, 1972, 225-86).

> lordship, because they were kept back while other papers were substituted and passed over in their place.[89]

Chikafusa was twenty at the time of the judgment; it is not known how he acquired his information, nor is there any evidence to support his account. If, however, we assume his story is true, interesting conclusions emerge. At much the same time as the judgment, forged documents purporting to have been written by Teika began to surface in large quantities. Two of these spurious documents, *Guhishō* and *Sangoki*, had the alternate titles *Cormorant* and *Heron*, respectively. Other works from this group, including *Gukanshō, Miraiki, Uchūgin, Kiri Hioke*, and *Teika Jittei*, were believed original until the end of the nineteenth century.[90] The provenance of these forged treatises is easily explained by one of the following accounts: (1) the Reizei family forged works that were handed over to the Nijō and, eventually, went into general circulation; (2) the Nijō family, finding itself lacking certain necessary treatises, forged them rather than acknowledge that it did not have them; or (3) a combination of the first two explanations.

The forgeries have no significant value in themselves. We should, however, note the very fact that they were forged. The forgeries reflect the medieval view that waka composition and reception are ensured high value when they are based on knowledge handed down from the past. A house proved that its inherited knowledge was correct by displaying its ancient documents as evidence. We note that all the forged treatises are attributed to Teika. This tells us that fourteenth-century waka poets perceived the Mikohidari patriarch to be Teika, not Shunzei. In order to assert their respective claims of legitimacy, the three descendant families would each have preferred to show the world that it possessed all the works compiled by Teika. This proved to be impossible, at least for the Reizei family, and the Kyōgoku was probably far from possessing all Teika's poetic treatises.

Even the Nijō family probably soon discovered that the documents returned to it were not in fact written by Teika. Its claim to legitimacy, bolstered by possession of all the family documents on poetics, was therefore weakened. The point of dispute among the three families consequently shifted to the correct manner of passing on Teika's poetics. The next generation—Nijō Tameyo, Kyōgoku Tamekanu, and Reizei Tame-

[89] *Kokinshū Jochū*, 554. The general veracity of this account has been acknowledged for some time (Brower-Miner, 1961, 349-52). A recently discovered letter written by Tameyo between 1294 and 1299, in the Sonkeikaku Library collection, reveals that the Reizei family did indeed keep the poetic treatises transmitted from Teika's and earlier times. Tameyo also states that the Reizei were ordered by Gouda In to return the documents to the Nijō family, but that they never actually did so (Tsugita, 1964, 48-49). [A portion of the original note has been moved to the main text to replace a paraphrase there.—Ed.]

[90] *Guhishō* and the other forgeries ascribed to Teika all appear in *NKGT*, vol. 4.

hide—based their opposition on matters of propriety and quality in waka composition, not on material possession. The forgeries ascribed to Teika were most likely written during their lifetimes.

It was not always clear, of course, what kind of waka style was advocated by the earlier generation of Nijō Tameuji, Kyōgoku Tamenori, and Reizei Tamesuke. Tamenori's son Tamekanu delineated the Kyōgoku style. The Reizei poetic style, on the other hand, remained so undefined that it can only be deduced through the work of two later poets, Ryōshun and Shōtetsu. The Nijō style was fairly distinct. We can discern it by considering Tameuji's choice of waka for the *Shokushūishū*, through reading Genshō's *Waka Kuden*, and through statements in the anonymous treatise *Nomori no Kagami.* The Nijō style was, in a word, the plain style faithful to Tameie's practice—a practice that probably came naturally to the Nijō. The Nijō house and the plain style it espoused were the mainstream of waka for years to come. Modern readers, however, tend to assign little value to the Nijō achievements in waka, which have been essentially ignored. The Nijō waka style nevertheless had an enormous impact on the poetry of later generations. Tameie's discussion, quoted earlier in this section, can be summarized:

1. A waka should appear in toto as a harmonious flow. It is not good when an audience is struck by only part of a poem.
2. Instead of searching for fine phrasing, one would do better to concentrate on eliminating bad elements from one's poetry.
3. Nothing good is to be found in new subjects. Only subjects that have appeared in earlier poems should be treated. These subjects are to be presented in such a way that they exude a sense of freshness.

Tameie's position is a model of pseudoclassicism (gikotenshugi). The great waka masters of the past have already accumulated splendid expression, according to Tameie. Hence present-day waka poets will find that "there are few new subjects." They should instead focus on "traditional subject matter." The process of breathing fresh life into old subjects became the rule in linked poetry. The practice reached its apex with Sōgi and was further perfected by Jōha. Zeami's principle of the "flower," in his nō treatises, is also based on this idea. It was, moreover, a basic principle of such nonliterary arts as the tea ceremony and flower arrangement. We would do well to stress the immense significance the Nijō house possessed as a source for focal aesthetic ideals in the High Middle Ages.

Toward Anticlassicism

The internal and external conflicts of the Mikohidari house revolved around poetic leadership rights. In the provinces, by contrast, waka poets looked to the capital for their leadership. They made no attempt to assert their own styles. The shogun Minamoto Sanetomo (1192-1219) provides a good example. He asked his waka teacher, Teika, various questions on the subject; Teika answered them by writing *Superior Poems of Our Time* and presenting it to the shogun. Sanetomo always paid attention to the styles current at court, working to incorporate them into his own poetry. This tendency is clearly visible in his personal waka collection, *Kinkai Wakashū* (=*KKWS*). A few of his poems caught the attention of Masaoka Shiki, Saitō Mokichi, and other poets of the modern *Araragi* group (originated 1908). They praised Sanetomo as the greatest poet to emerge since *Man'yōshū* times. The waka admired by the *Araragi* poets include:

Hail

Mononofu no	The warrior straightens
Yanami tsukurou	The arrows in his quiver,
Kote no ue ni	While on his gauntlet
Arare tabashiru	The hail scatters as it falls
Nasu no shinohara.	On the bamboo fields of Nasu.
	(*KKWS*, 1:348)

I emerged from the Hakone mountains and saw an islet washed by waves. "Do you know the name of this bay?" I asked my attendant. He answered, "It is called the Sea of Izu." Thereupon I composed this verse.

Hakoneji o	Having come across
Waga koekureba	The Hakone mountain road,
Izu no umi ya	I now behold
Oki no kojima ni	The Sea of Izu where waves wash
Nami no yoru miyu.	An islet in the offing.
	(*KKWS*, 2:593)

Composed upon receiving a letter from the former sovereign.[91]

Yama wa sake	This may be a world
Umi wa asenan	Where the mountains crumble
Yo naritomo	And where seas dry up,
Kimi ni futagokoro	But could I ever be the one
Waga arame ya mo.	Who proved faithless to my lord?
	(*KKWS*, 2:680)

[91] Probably Gotoba.

Composed upon watching the waves strike a rocky beach.

Ōumi no	Along the vast sea
Iso mo todoro ni	When the shores are thundering,
Yosuru nami	The waves beating in—
Warete kudakete	They are broken and are splintered
Sakete chiru kamo.	And are rent and scattered.
	(*KKWS*, 2:696)

Composed when I saw a small child crying bitterly for its mother by the roadside. Both its parents, I was told, had died.

Itōshi ya	Ah, how pitiful!
Miru ni namida mo	As I look upon one child
Todomarazu	Tears will not cease:
Oya mo naki ko no	The child that lost both parents
Haha o tazunuru.	And wishes to find its mother.
	(*KKWS*, 2:717)

On the topic "Compassion."

Mono iwanu	They may lack speech
Yomo no kedamono	But the beasts throughout the world—
Dani sura mo	Verily I say,
Aware naru kana	How they do move my heart
Oya no ko o omou.	By the love they show their young.
	(*KKWS*, 2:718)

There was a great flood in the Seventh Month of Kenryaku 1 [1211]. Concerned with the people's suffering, I presented this poem as a prayer to a sacred image of the Buddha.

Toki ni yori	When it exceeds
Sugureba tami no	The limits, then your people
Nageki nari	Know only suffering.
Hachi Dai Ryūō	Oh, Eight Great Dragon Kings,
Ame yametamae.	Will ye not make the rain to stop!
	(*KKWS*, 2:719)

Shiki and Mokichi read these poems wearing *Araragi*-colored glasses. In the *Araragi* view, plain description constitutes ideal literary expression;

hence their lavish praise for Sanetomo's poetry. Let us take another look at Sanetomo's work without benefit of the *Araragi* lenses.

There are 719 poems in the *Kinkai Wakashū*, of which only seven—those given above—merit the praise of the *Araragi* faithful. Other of Sanetomo's waka are highly regarded, but one suspects that they are excessively praised so as to enhance Sanetomo's reputation still further. The poem numbered 348 in the seven above has a sense of freshness: its subject is arms, something never before treated in waka. It cannot be thought superior, however, to Tsunenobu's or Yoshitsune's waka in its techniques of nature description. Poem number 593 simply restates the forenote. Its rhythmic beauty aside, there is little that is good about it. Number 696 is notable for its violent tone, particularly in the last half of the poem: "Warete kudakete / Sakete chiru kamo." Numbers 680, 717, 718, and 719 are direct expressions of the "subjective kokoro." None contains expression that would be suitable to formal waka. All were probably composed in informal situations. There is a marked tendency in poets from the twelfth century on to give direct statements of the subjective kokoro in informal situations. The approach does not originate with Sanetomo. Poems 680 and 719, on the other hand, are valuable because the emotions expressed there are felt by a man burdened by great administrative responsibilities. The poems communicate a new sense of tension.

Sanetomo might well have created even greater masterpieces of informal waka had he not been assassinated at the age of twenty-seven. A few of his informal waka must be deemed inferior work:

On watching charcoal being produced in the mountains.

Sumi o yaku	I am moved
Hito no kokoro mo	By the feelings held by those
Aware nari	Who make charcoal.
Sate mo kono yo o	And yet, it is their way
Suguru narai wa.	To get on in this world.
	(*KKWS*, 1:389)

At Year's End

Chibusa sū	With the tiny child
Mada itokenaki	Still helpless as it suckles
Midorigo no	At its mother's breast,
Tomo ni nakinuru	I join in tears to bewail
Toshi no kure kana.	The year that now draws to its close.
	(*KKWS*, 1:406)

Had these poems been more polished, they might have given rise to a new kind of zoku.

Very few of Sanetomo's waka are oriented toward zoku. Some of his formal waka, however, contain expression in the style of the *Shinkokinshū*, while his informal waka experiment with free language and new techniques. The monk Kōben, also known as Myōe Shōnin (1173-1232), further pursued the path opened by Sanetomo. Kōben was unlike Sanetomo in that he had no interest in communicating with the central waka authorities; hence most of his poetry disregarded accepted techniques. This is not to say that he was ignorant of formal waka techniques. All twenty-seven of his waka selected for inclusion in royal anthologies contain some degree of conventional technique. And yet, although Kōben's ratio of familiar techniques is on the opposite end of the scale from Sanetomo's, Kōben himself did not think highly of technique. Consider the following poem, which appears in the *Shinchokusenshū*.

I spent one autumn night, after the meditation period, gazing at the moon. Although its light shines on all without discrimination, I felt that night that it was shining on me alone.

Kōben Shōnin

Tsukikage wa	Although the moonlight
Izure no yama to	Makes no choice of the mountains
Wakazu to mo	That it brightens,
Sumasu mine ni wa	Yet my illuminated peak
Sumimasaru ran.	Seems to shine more clearly still.
	(16:1083)

Kōben mentions this poem in his autograph letters: "I am vexed at being too caught up in conventional waka techniques. . . ."[92] The poem emphasizes that whereas the moon shines everywhere impartially, the speaker feels that the moonlight seems purer on the mountain peak where he purifies his heart during meditation. There is logic in the poem, though it is not especially insistent. Teika apparently included it in the *Shinchokusenshū* on the grounds that it "could be described as yūgen."[93]

Kōben thought little of such poetry, however. When a waka contained the logic characteristic of the *Kokinshū* and subsequent anthologies, he

[92] Property of the Ōhashi family, Kyoto. I draw on Akamatsu Toshihide's research (Akamatsu, 1944, 62-64).

[93] Teika writes: "The Holy Priest Chōsei . . . came to visit me with some waka Myōe [Kōben] had written him in reply. On close examination, I found they could be described as yūgen. I told Chōsei I would do what I could" (*MGK* [3.VII.1233], 371). The entry is also pointed out by Akamatsu, 1944 (see n. 92).

found it "too caught up in conventional waka techniques." A similar view of waka appears in Kōben's *Kyakuhaibōki (Memoranda)*.[94] His waka master's testamentary admonition is recorded there as follows: "It is a foolish thing to strive to produce fine waka. If a poem conforms to what is in the poet's heart, it may be a mere trifle carelessly tossed off, but it will nevertheless be perfectly acceptable" (1:542). What kind of poetry is produced when a poet follows such advice? One principal characteristic is the substantial use of vocabulary outside the realm of accepted waka diction. Consider two examples from Kōben's personal waka collection, *Myōe Shōnin Kashū* [= *MSK*].[95]

Shingechi no	The lunar mind
Sumu ni *mumyō* no	In its shining clears away
Kumo harete	Maculate clouds
Gedatsu no *mon* ni	And at deliverance portal
Matsukaze zo fuku.	The wind blows in the pines.
	(88)

Shohō muga no	Utter selflessness
Matsu no arashi no	In the pines of the tempest
Sabishisa ni	Leaves desolation,
Zehi tokushitsu mo	In which I have forgot entirely
Wasurarenikeri.	Being, nonbeing, gain, and loss.
	(102)

Both poems are full of Chinese loanwords [indicated by italics] that were not considered appropriate to waka. Sanetomo has similar poems, such as the following.

A Poem on Obtaining Merit

Dainichi no	From Vairocana's
Shuji yori idete	Mystic Sanskrit letter comes
Samayagyō	The Vow Pagoda,
Samayagyō mata	And thereupon the Vow Pagoda
Songyō to naru.	Becomes an august Personage.
	(*KKWS*, 2:650)

[94] The *Kyakuhaibōki* is a notebook of Kōben's conversations, assembled in 1235 by Jakuebō Chōen, a disciple. Chōen's holograph manuscript survives at the temple Kōzanji in Toganoo.

[95] *Myōe Shōnin Kashū* was compiled in III.1248 by another of Kōben's disciples, Junshōbō Kōshin. The only surviving manuscript, a fourteenth-century copy, is in the Tōyō Bunko collection.

Such language appears occasionally with Sanetomo [italics again indicating Sinified words], but it is commonplace in Kōben's waka.

The most characteristic aspect of Kōben's waka is not his diction, however. It is his habit of stating forthright, unrevised impressions received from the subject of his poem. He does *not* produce objective descriptions of nature. When Kōben sees wisteria, he does not write about it, nor does he write about bamboo when he sees bamboo. Instead he expresses the feelings given him by the wisteria or bamboo (Yamada S., 1973, 70-74). Kōben's waka have points in common with Impressionist painting. The difference between the two is the complete lack of design in Kōben's verse. If, for example, the following poem was turned into a well-designed painting, the result would be Impressionist:

Composed on noticing that the pines by my eaves are faintly visible through the mist.

Sora no iro no	It looks as if
Kami ni egakite	Someone has painted on paper
Miyuru kana	The color of the sky—
Kiri ni magiruru	This scenery of the pine trees
Matsu no keshiki wa.	Confused among the swirls of mist.
	(*MSK*, 48)

Kōben believed that expressing an impression precisely, rather than artistically, gave it religious significance. Surely he thought so because he felt that adding human design would distort the natural aspect that is the manifestation of basic principles of the universe. Kōben's principle applies not only to scenes of nature but to poems on the emotions.

Tsuru no ko no	If I were to speak
Sumu ki iite wa	Of the tree where baby cranes live,
Hito shiran	Someone would find them.
Sodatan made wa	Until they have been taught to fly
Kakushi okaba ya.	I shall have to keep it secret.
	(*MSK*, 51)

Kōben's reaction to the situation reflects the basic principle of the universe, and so his emotions must be expressed precisely as they are felt. His response occasionally tends toward idiosyncrasy, as in the following poem.

I mused that the Bamboo Grove Gardens of Kalandakaveṇuvana in India, favored by the Buddha, probably contained the same species of bamboo as those in our country. Deeply moved at the thought of bamboo as a remembrance of the Buddha, I planted a stalk of bamboo before my study and called it the Stalk of the Bamboo Grove.

Chikurin'on no	In my longing
Take no hayashi no	For the forests of bamboo
Koishisa ni	In the Bamboo Grove Gardens,
Chikurindake to	I give the name "Bamboo Grove"
Nazukete zo miru.	To the stalk on which I gaze.
	(*MSK*, 83)

The poem merely restates the content of the forenote and employs no techniques at all. The response is peculiar to Kōben, moreover; it cannot be called a general reaction. Seen from the perspective of kū (Emptiness), such an attachment to bamboo signals delusion. It is, however, human to love something to the point of delusion. Kōben's precise expression of delusion is thus a correct representation of humanity as one manifestation of the basic principle of the universe. It cannot be helped that his response is overly personal and idiosyncratic.

Siddham [Holy Sanskrit Syllables]

Karasugawa ni	Even the noises
Saru no kikimeku	Of what seems monkeys chattering
Oto kiku mo	By Raven River
Kokoro sumu ni wa	Are to the unclouded heart
Shittan no jibo.	The syllables of "siddham."
	(*MSK*, 94)

On once having passed through the fields of Uchino with another monk.

Hiroki no ni	Across broad fields
Sugagasa uchikite	Wearing our wide sedge hats
Yuku ware o	As we walk along—
Muma no kusotake to	I wonder if others take us
Hito ya miru ran.	For two horseapple mushrooms?
	(*MSK*, 147)

Kōben was interested in whether his poem captured his precise feelings at a given moment, not in whether others would understand his feelings and respond appropriately. This poet wished to express in language various matters concerning nature and mankind. The shapes reflected in his poetry hold what Kōben sensed as the basic principle of the universe. Such poetry may be called a verbal mandala.

Aka aka ya	Bright, oh bright!
Aka aka aka ya	Bright, bright, oh bright!
Aka aka ya	Bright, oh bright!
Aka aka aka ya	Bright, bright, oh bright!
Aka aka ya tsuki.	Bright, oh bright, the moon!
	(*MSK*, 152)

This cannot possibly be thought a waka by ordinary criteria.

Saigyō's poetry is another source of the view that waka reflect the basic principle of the universe (or, indeed, the Buddha) rather than merely describe nature and individual emotions. A biography of Kōben, *Toganoo Myōe Shōnin Denki*[96] (title hereafter abbreviated to *Myōe Den*), mentions that Saigyō often visited Kōben and discussed poetry with him.[97] The story is improbable, given their respective ages.[98] The incident was devised, more than likely, because Saigyō and Kōben both perceived waka as verbal mandalas. Their discussions on poetry and poetic theory are mentioned as a way of expressing this understanding. The concept of the waka as a verbal mandala was apparently well known during this period. Mujū's declaration that waka are dharani means much the same thing, though it is put somewhat differently.[99] If language is thought limited in its ability to communicate meaning and incapable of fully elucidating the basic principle of the universe, the logical conclusion is that true expression can be found only by transcending ordinary linguistic significance. Zen and the esoteric schools of Buddhism make this assertion, which was in fact given a logical basis by the Kegon school. Kōben, a Kegon monk with esoteric leanings, naturally agreed with Saigyō on the concept of waka as verbal mandala.[100]

If this view had been held only by Saigyō, Kōben, and Mujū, it might be perceived as restricted to Buddhist monks and therefore be of little concern for mainstream waka. Kōben's ideas on waka, however, are im-

[96] The biography was compiled by Kōben's disciple Girimbō Kikai. The two surviving texts (a manuscript dated 1599, in the collection of Kōzanji temple, and the printed edition of 1662) are probably not faithful transmissions; both seem to include later accretions.

[97] *Myōe Den*, a, 456-57.

[98] Saigyō died in 1190, when Kōben was seventeen years old. One year earlier, at the age of sixteen, Kōben had taken his monastic vows and had had his name added to the Register of Religious. He would probably not have had time by then for other matters than religious observance.

[99] "I understand the way of waka . . . it is in fact dharani" (*Shasekishū*, 5:222).

[100] Kōben regarded Kegon and esoteric Buddhism as doctrinal equals (Ishii, 1928, 20-41).

portant because they influenced Kyōgoku Tamekanu and, through him, fourteenth-century waka poets. The passage below appears in the biography of Kōben.

> Moved that so many years had passed before I [Kōben] had entered the mystic gate of profound Mahāyāna, I chanted, "May all the many forms of existence attain peace." I heard the evening bell tolling from high above the valley and recited,
>
> | | |
> |---|---|
> | Mine no arashi ni | When I proclaim |
> | Shoissaishu to | "May all creation find its peace" |
> | Agetareba | In the mountain storm, |
> | Tani yori tsuguru | From the valley slopes there comes |
> | Iriai no kane. | The sound of the evening bell. |
>
> Someone later told of Lord Tamekanu having praised this poem. His lordship said, "This is a fine poem indeed, one that should set a standard for other poets. I was taught that the wise men of old composed in this fashion. Nowadays," he lamented "poems are twisted, and no longer seem like real poetry." (*Myōe Den*, b: 282-83)

The final part of the passage, in which Tamekanu praises the poem, appears only in the printed edition of 1665 and must therefore be considered a later accretion.[101] It is nevertheless a well-informed accretion. Tamekanu writes in his *Tamekanu Kyō Wakashō*,

> Myōe Shōnin is quite right in his preface to *Kenshin Wakashū*: " 'To like' means 'what the heart likes.' This does not always conform to the demands of diction. 'Pleasing' means 'a pleasing spirit.' How can this take a specific shape?" Myōe wrote things down exactly as he felt them. He composed interesting poems about our everyday world; others of his poems have crude diction like works in the *Man'yōshū*. Yet the dictates of his heart never vary in the least. (*Tamekanu Shō*, 160)[102]

Here is Tamekanu's frank opinion of Kōben's waka. Had he had the opportunity, he would certainly have praised the poem just quoted from Kōben's biography.

[101] The accretion probably predates 1456. A late thirteenth-century copy of *Myōe Den* in the collection of the temple Kōfukuji has the waka "Mine no arashi ni" followed by the statement, "Lord Tamekanu was later said to have praised this poem highly" (*Myōe Shiryō*, 1:299). A postscript to the manuscript is dated 1456; thus Tamekanu's connection with the poem was known prior to that year.

[102] *Kenshin Wakashū* is a collection of Kōben's waka, compiled by the poet himself. It does not survive in its entirety. Kōshin's *Myōe Shōnin Kashū* is based on the first half of *Kenshin Wakashū*.

The influence of Kōben's waka on Tamekanu can also be ascertained from Tamekanu's own poetic corpus. The Nijō school produced two waka treatises attacking Tamekanu, *Nomori no Kagami* and *Kaen Rensho Kotogaki*. The former work quotes a waka as an example of Tamekanu's style.

Ogi no ha o	Closely, closely
Yokuyoku mireba	Looking at the leaves of reeds,
Ima zo shiru	I now realize
Tada ōkinaru	That in fact they are large grown
Susuki narikeri.	Plumes of the eulalia.

The poem is criticized as unworthy of the name of waka (*Nomori no Kagami*, 1:70). It is so crude that one is tempted to wonder if it was fabricated by an agent provocateur of the Nijō faction. Recently, 244 rough poetry drafts were discovered written on the back of a copy of the *Kammon Nikki* in the Royal Library collection. These poems verify that Tamekanu did indeed write waka along the lines of the one quoted in *Nomori no Kagami*. Many of them are faithful, unadorned expressions of the poet's emotions (*Kammon Shihai*, 164-77).

Kyō yori wa	As of today
Haru to wa shirinu	I know full well that it is spring.
Shikari tote	Nevertheless
Kinō ni kawaru	There is nothing that has made it
Koto wa shi mo nashi.	Different from yesterday.
Haru o mukaen	To greet the spring
Koto wa kokoro ni	Is a thought that makes my heart
Isogedomo	Beat on faster,
Toshi no nagori wa	And yet there is also sadness
Oshiku mo aru kana.	For the loss of the year now gone.
Haru no shirushi wa	What do we see
Nani to ka wa min	Of the usual signs of spring?
Yuki chirite	The snow still falls—
Kasumi mo tatazu	Not only does the haze not rise
Uguisu mo nakazu.	But also no warblers sing.
Kaku bakari	Have they blossomed
Tagui naki iro ni	In just this way whose color
Sakikeru mo	Has no precedent
Hito ni nagori o	To show that they have sympathy
Aiomoe to ka.	With my longing thoughts of her?

Fukaki michi wa	The profound Way—
Kamo no yashiro ni	It is at Kamo Shrine
Arikeri to	Where it can be found:
Koto ni furete zo	That is what is important
Omoiawasuru.	As I think again, again.
Kimi o inoru	I pray for our lord
Sore yori yomo no	And beyond that for the good
Yutaka naran	Of all his subjects;
Kokorogokoro o	I am overjoyed to think
Omou mo yorokobashi.	Of the joy in all those hearts.

These poems contain much everyday language, diction that was not supposed to be used in waka: "shikari tote," "aiomoe to ka," "koto ni furete," "yorokobashi." The difficulty with the poems does not lie in their diction, however. The conception of each waka is expressed precisely as it has been thought, and each appears with no poetic design whatsoever. The Nijō poets criticized Tamekanu justly.

Informal waka permit straightforward descriptions of nature and emotions, while formal waka require ga conception and language. Shunrai, Saigyō, Sanetomo, and even Kōben observe this rule. Tamekanu dared to use highly zoku expression in his formal waka. The poem drafts written on the back of *Kammon Nikki* form two sets of hundred-poem sequences. One is titled "One Hundred Waka on the End of the Year. Composed, by Royal Command, by Fujiwara Tame."[103] The other is called, "One Hundred Poems on the Beginning of Spring, by Fujiwara Tamekanu, Provisional Captain of the Left Bodyguards." The sequences were probably composed between 1275 and 1289, to judge from Tamekanu's official title. This period encompasses his twenty-first through thirty-fifth years. We should note that the former sequence was composed by royal command.[104] Whoever may have issued the command, it marks the work as formal. Tamekanu's poetic convictions, as set forth in *Tamekanu Kyō Wakashō*, induced him to attempt using expression such as we have seen in the series of poems just mentioned. The generally assumed compilation date of Tamekanu's *Wakashō*, between 1285 and 1287, matches the period in which the hundred-poem sequences were composed.[105] Tamekanu's mention of Kōben in his treatise is extremely important: Tamekanu's waka criteria are here imbued with a religious perspective.

The bald presentation of commonplace scenes and everyday emotions

[103] "-kanu" is omitted in the text.

[104] A sequence composed "by royal command" was prepared in response to a request from a member of the royal family [i.e., not necessarily the tennō.—Ed.].

[105] The compilation period has been deduced by Kyūsojin Hitaku (*Kagaku Taikei*, 4 ["Kaisetsu"]:18-19).

deserves condemnation from a literary standpoint. In this respect the Nijō critics were correct for criticizing Tamekanu out of concern for literary criteria. Religious criteria, on the other hand, require that a poet try to perceive the basic principle of the universe in the faint rustle of a leaf. A work may be inferior as literature and still move its audience when reception is based on religious rather than literary experience. We cannot, of course, determine the propriety of incorporating religious criteria into literary criticism. Rather, let us consider that, whatever his theology, Tamekanu could not be applauded by the literary world for writing works that were inferior by literary criteria. As will be seen in another chapter, however, he was gradually evolving styles whose poetic results would be acknowledged as superior literature.

CHAPTER 9

The Formation of Codified Renga

Renga was a ga-zoku form of literature in the twelfth century, a time of popularity for "chain renga" (kusari renga) and short sequences of linked stanzas. The people of the time probably perceived it as more of a zoku art. It was not entirely so, however, since the *Kin'yōshū* contains a section devoted to renga.[1] Linked poetry was not, of course, a pastime for formal occasions, but it was a challenging art all the same. Participating in a renga session was impossible without sharp wits and skill in waka composition. The tone of renga was then basically comic (mushin, non-standard, without kokoro), unrelated to the waka tones of yūen and desolation. From this standpoint, renga is not a ga form. Neither are the unconventional waka (hikaika, also haikaika) in the *Kokinshū* [book 19]. The comic, unconventional nature shared by renga and hikaika may be termed "haikai." The use of the term "haikai" could, however, lead to confusion with the later genre of haikai renga, a genre eventually known simply as "haikai." That is why I have substituted "ga-zoku" as a literary principle. Renga from the thirteenth century on underwent striking changes in both its external form and in its essential nature.

Let us begin with the essential nature of renga. One major change was the composition of renga in a non-humorous vein. Such renga are known as serious or standard (ushin) renga. The practice of composing linked poetry began in 1206, in circumstances meticulously detailed by Fujiwara Teika in his *Meigetsuki* (where ushin/mushin renga is mentioned a total of eleven times). A middle controller, Nobukata, invited Teika, Masatsune, and other friends from the Bureau of Waka to "stretch out with some crazy linked poetry." Nobukata's guests "countered this with proper waka diction." After their third session, news of the unconventional gathering reached Gotoba.

The former sovereign hosted a session in which each of two sides pitted its linked stanzas against the other's. One side, known as the mushin or nonserious group, intentionally composed only crazy verses. The serious

[1] [The tenth, the last, book of the *Kin'yōshū* contains a number of poems known as short renga (tanrenga) as opposed to the chain renga (kusari renga) or long renga (chōrenga) discussed in this chapter. Short renga are effectively capped poems, one person composing one part (usually the first three lines) of a tanka and another the other (usually the last two).—Ed.]

group cast their links in the diction acceptable to waka. Gotoba's gathering began in the evening of the eleventh day of the Eighth Month, 1206, and went on well into the night. Tentative rules were worked out beforehand: if one side composed before the other a total of six consecutive links, the other side would be driven from the floor. Gotoba's side, the serious one, eventually succeeded in making six consecutive links. The nonserious side was punished by having to leave the room and sit on the ground outside (*MGK* [1206], 469). Gotoba was apparently much taken with the event. Seven days later there was another renga session between the serious and nonserious groups; the thematic directive (fushimono) of the session was "Floating and Sinking" (ibid., 471).

These directives are a special convention of renga, varying in nature over the centuries. By the late fifteenth century they were either perfunctory or served to provide part of a title, as in the *Minase Sangin "Nanihito" Hyakuin (One Hundred Stanzas Devoted to "Person" by Three Poets at Minase)*. Early in the thirteenth century, however (the period under consideration here), the fushimono directives bore thematically on a major word or image in each stanza. For example, to compose according to the double directive, "Floating and Sinking," each stanza had to include, in alternation, something that would float (a leaf, a straw) and then something that would sink (a stone, a key). In the course of time, lists of directives were drawn up, each preceded in a designation by "nani" ("what"). "Hito" ("person") gradually became the most popular.[2]

The completion of the *Shinkokinshū* had been celebrated a year previously, in 1205, by a grand royal banquet. Waka had reached perhaps its ultimate refinement during this period. Those who had dedicated themselves to consolidating the *Shinkokinshū* style amused themselves by composing linked poetry, as their forebears had in the twelfth century (ch. 2). But waka was more refined in the early thirteenth century than it had been in Mototoshi's and Shunrai's day. Poets were consequently not satisfied to divert themselves with the old, comic renga. "Crazy renga" (kyōrenga) and "crazy stanzas" (kyōku) probably connote the new trend toward more incisive humor in linked poetry. The serious (ushin) group of poets tended to link an overly comic verse with a serious one framed in conventional language, since they could not possibly win with a run-of-the-mill comic verse. Because renga was still essentially a game, its keynote remained humorous. Serious links in a renga sequence generally acquired a humor of their own from the context in which they appeared. Consequently, renga in a serious tone were not then (1206 ff.) a standard

[2] [For a list of fushimono, see Yamada Yoshio and Hoshika Sōichi, eds., *Renga Hōshiki Kōyō* (Iwanami, 1936), 13-20, a list prepared by the poet Shōhaku.—Ed.]

feature of sessions. The experiments conducted in this period did, however, lead several years later to the popular practice of using waka diction in linked poetry. The *Tsukuba Shū* contains links of this kind.

Mimuro no yama wa iro masarikeri	On the slopes of Mimuro the colors take on deeper hue

The added stanza, by His Majesty Gotoba:

kurekakaru mine ni hikage no sasu mama ni	as it grows dark the peak is brightened as the rays of the sun fall on it
	(13:1302)

Again:

Kameyama no iwane o sashite fuku kaze ni	At Tortoise Hill rocky crags are chosen out by the strengthening wind[3]

The added stanza, by the former Middle Counselor Teika:

taki no kazu sou tama zo kudakuru	the waterfall rivals in number jewels as it cascades down
	(13:1317)

Such verses form a considerable presence in *Tsukuba Shū*. This is not the result of selecting only the "meaningful" stanzas from sessions between ushin and mushin poets. Such stanzas were then composed independently of larger sequences—hence their large number.

Renga, as we have said, originated as a game. Could interest in linked poetry remain high once the serious tones of waka gradually began to be used in renga? Interest was apparently sustained through the thematic directive (fushimono) signalling that certain subjects are to appear within the verses to be composed. Here are some examples from the *Tsukuba Shū*.

From a renga session held during Gotoba's reign [1183-98], in which the directive was "White and Black."

Toyo no akari no yuki no akebono	At the Harvest Festival daylight breaks upon the snow

[3] Kameyama (Tortoise Hill) is located in the Saga district of Kyoto; it faces Arashiyama across the Ōi River. The hill is also called Kamenooyama (Tortoise-tail Hill).

The added stanza, by Mitsuyori the Inspector:

ko wa ika ni	what have we here?
yareueginu no	a tattered formal court robe,
migurushi ya	a horrid sight!
	(19:1986)

Wata no kuzu nite	With leftover fluff from silk
hitai o zo yuu	I tie my forehead with a band

The added stanza, by the former Middle Counselor Teika:

ōhige no	what a large beard
mikurumazoi no	has that guardsman who attends
kita omote	the royal carriage
	(19:1987)

Mitsuyori's link counters "snow" in the preceding stanza with the image of an inspector's formal black court robe. Teika's verse mentions a beard—assumed to be black—in opposition to the white silk fluff in the preceding stanza.[4] The humorous tone of these verses was the norm for the time, as it was for the earlier renga period. Clearly Teika did not always compose serious renga. Interest would have been generated not only by humor, but by devising and appreciating words to fit the directive of "White and Black." When renga later developed a tone close to that of waka, people still seem to have enjoyed composing with theme words. The following links are also from *Tsukuba Shū*.

Taken from a session held during Gotoba's reign. His Majesty was presented with a hundred-verse sequence centering on chapter titles from The Tale of Genji *and on the names of the provinces.*

Itsumo midori no	Always at Izumo the dew
tsuyu zo midaruru	is strewn about like emeralds

The added stanza, by Lord Minamoto Ienaga:

yomogiu no	the wormwood patch
nokiba arasou	stretches toward the eaves
furusato ni	at my old home
	(13:1278)

[4] The first stanza, "Wata no kuzu nite," signifies that the speaker's forelocks are decorated not with the usual twisted cords tied around the head, but with bits of silk floss twisted together. The linking stanza, "ōhige no," responds to this unusual sight with another, that of a fully-bearded bodyguard attending the carriage of a former tennō.

Without knowing the circumstances described in the forenote, these stanzas might seem to imitate waka. In fact, however, they play on words: "itsumo" (always) can also be read "Izumo" (the name of a province), and "yomogiu" (the wormwood patch) is both a common noun and the name of a chapter from the *Genji.*

The linked poetry of this period was greatly concerned with thematic directives. When Teika mentions or describes a renga session, he generally includes its directive. One reason for his doing so is that directives were used as criteria to determine literary value. Their appropriate and skillful use was therefore an important consideration in judging a link. In the first two renga matches between the proponents of serious and nonserious stanzas, the losing side had been penalized by being made to sit on the ground. This, however, was the exception, not the rule. The more usual custom was to award prizes—objects or cash—commensurate with the participants' scores. The custom of giving prizes remained popular in centuries to come, indicating how much of an amusement renga originally was.[5] Its playful aspects gradually receded between the end of the thirteenth through the early fourteenth centuries. At that point renga moved to become a highly polished, ga genre.

The ga language characteristic of waka eventually dominated renga and altered its essence. A similar phenomenon occurred externally: from the thirteenth century on, renga was transformed when it took on a formal aspect of waka. There is no question but that from the hundred-poem or fifty-poem—at least the fixed-number—waka sequence renga derived its one-hundred- or fifty-stanza length. As opposed to "short renga" and "chain renga," what had been called "long renga" did not mean merely a large number of stanzas. Rather, in considering the standardizing of an ordered group of stanzas, I have chosen to speak of one-hundred-stanza and fifty-stanza sequences as "codified renga." The standard form of the two is the hundred-stanza variety; the fifty-stanza type was perceived as an abbreviated version.[6] This practice reflects two older perceptions: that

[5] "The renga session commenced. . . . There were goods intended as prizes for the participants. Each time a link was composed, a prize was given. The governor of Mimasaka (I forget his name) was charged with placing the prizes before our host so he could award them. Prizes consisted of fans and patterned crepe paper (a flowing stream formed the background of the paper; a design of red or white plum blossoms was added to this)" (*MGK* [16.IV.1225], 422). [Note that each link is judged and prizes allotted accordingly. A difficult link might merit a fan, while an easier one would be rewarded with five sheets of paper. Links were not composed by a set order of participants. All participants were free to contribute a verse for a given link; the judge would then determine the best of the lot and award the prize to the winner.—Auth., Trans.] Yoshida Kenkō also mentions returning from a renga session with prizes (*Tsurezuregusa*, dan 89:152-53).

[6] The hundred-stanza form is the unit for larger sequences. Multiplied by 10, it yields a 1,000-stanza sequence; multiplied by 100, it produces a 10,000-stanza work. Abbreviated forms include the yoyoshi (44-stanza sequence) and kasen (36-stanza sequence).

the hundred-poem sequence (hyakushu uta) is the standard in waka, and—as *The Hundred-Poem Sequence from Horikawa's Reign* demonstrates—the fixed sequence yields a variety of designs. A hundred-waka sequence might well touch [like a royal collection] on the four seasons, love, and miscellaneous topics, arranged according to the principles of progression and association. This configuration was incorporated into renga.

Renga is, of course, a group creation. One of its basic rules is that a stanza links with its preceding stanza but that there must be no connection between the stanza just composed and that preceding it by two or more. [See the "Appendix."] Renga thus evolves by accident, which is its essence. No one can predict how a sequence will develop. If, on the other hand, a sequence is *nothing more* than an accidental development, chaos ensues. Renga is contradictory in demanding both incidental linkage and orderly development. The renga poets of the early thirteenth century rose to the challenge by making partial use of the hundred-waka sequence structure. A certain number of stanzas were determined to pertain to the seasons, love, and miscellaneous topics; these were not to be confusedly ordered. When, for example, the stanzas are progressing through the topic "Spring," one cannot include verses on autumn and winter.

Limits were placed on the number of stanzas dedicated to a given topic, since too many stanzas on one subject would increase the sense of predictability. If a sequence has from three to five stanzas on spring or autumn, or one or two on summer and winter, development remains spontaneous. The renga becomes yet more spontaneous if there is another rule: no stanza on a given season is allowed unless the last one on that season appeared at least seven stanzas earlier. The renga practice of allotting a larger number of stanzas to spring and autumn over summer and winter is probably directly influenced by the hundred-waka sequence, although royal waka anthologies also distribute their seasonal waka in such proportions.

Various kinds of poetic material appear in a sequence of one hundred waka. Such material is not confined to hundred-waka sequences; it is general information that happens to be applicable to all waka composition. Knowledge of such general material was thought necessary as far back as the late tenth century (see vol. two, ch. 7). The hundred-waka sequence will lose its sense of harmony as a whole if the same kind of material appears at random within this limited number of poems. Regulation thus becomes desirable. Because the hundred waka in such a sequence are a static configurational unit, overlapping can be avoided by arranging the poems according to the same principle, namely, progression, employed in the royal anthologies. In renga, however, sequential development is left up to chance, so ruling out extensive use of progression. A rule was devised to act in place of progression: the same type of poetic matter—kuzai, "stanza material," in renga terminology—cannot appear within a specified interval. Young herbs and pine trees both belong to the category of plants, for example; they must therefore be separated by at least three stanzas. Consider young herbs and dianthus, or pine and cryptomeria: both cases concern plants, but closely related plants. Because the first pair are perennial herbacious plants and the second pair are trees, the necessary interval in both cases must be five or more stanzas.

We have been considering relatively physical matters up to now. The hundred-waka sequence also influenced the spirit of renga, particularly in the use of association to link one stanza with another. Renga, linked poetry, is a genre that by its very name stresses continuity. Despite its obvious sequentiality, however, renga consists of single, separately composed stanzas. Without a design to link individual stanzas, there is no such thing as a work of linked poetry. Order is created in a sequence of one hundred waka by arranging poems so that they progress in time. Thus the section on "Spring" moves gradually from early through late spring with topics like "Lingering Snow," "The Warbler," "Plum Bossoms," "Cherry Blossoms in Full Bloom," and "Falling Cherry Blossoms." Such inexorable development is not permitted in renga, a basic element of which is that two stanzas separated by another are unconnected in meaning. Renga thus relies chiefly on association rather than on the principle of progression as it is used in hundred-waka sequences. If a renga stanza is concerned with plum blossoms, for example, its link may deal with the warbler; a stanza on kerria blossoms can be linked by one on the singing frogs of Ide, a famous place for viewing kerria.

Subjects that are fixed in waka are combined in renga, so that individual stanzas are linked associatively while appearing semantically distinct. We have seen how progression came to be superseded by association in royal waka anthologies and hundred-poem sequences from the *Shinkokinshū* period on. A similar phenomenon occurs during the formative period of codified renga. The popularity of renga undeniably accelerated associative configurations in waka sequences as well. Association as a configurational principle nevertheless originated with waka and is best regarded as having been incorporated into renga under waka influence.

These configurational principles represent a later fixed form; renga were not composed according to such principles in the early thirteenth century. Fifteen renga points are discussed by the former sovereign Juntoku (1197-1242) in his *Yakumo Mishō* (1:203-206). Five of them deal with thematic directives; the remaining points are not so organized as to represent a code. The *Yakumo Mishō* thus can only suggest what renga were like at the time. Rules for composing renga were also apparently written by Teika and Tameie, among others, but these were probably outlines rather than treatises, judging from the evidence we have. For example, the *Reizeike Zō Sōshi Mokuroku* (*The Inventory of Codices in the Possession of the Reizei Family*), containing a postscript dating it as a copy from the Bumpo era (1317-19), lists the following under the heading "Renga" (Katagiri, 1962, 2-7):

Rules: same as above. By Takasuke.
Hananomoto Style [of renga]. Compiled by the same.
Rules: same as above. By Nobuzane.
Rules: same as above. By Yukiie, compiled of other rules in his *Rules of Renku and Renga.*
Rules: same as above. By his lordship the Kyōgoku Middle Counselor [Teika].
Rules: same as above. By his lordship the Novice Monk, formerly Minister of Popular Affairs [Tameie].
Rules: same as above. By Dōshō, Hananomoto style.
Rules: same as above. Compiler unknown.
Rules: same as above. [Compiler unknown.]
A Guide for Beginners in Renga. [Compiler unknown.]
Limits to Mentioning Similar Subjects in Renga.
New Rules of the Hananomoto Style.[7]

According to Nijō Yoshimoto (1320-88), two kinds of renga codes, the "original" and the "new" codes, were in use from about 1264 to 1287, while Tamesuke's Fujigayatsu code was used in Kamakura (*Tsukuba Mondō*, 101). The codes of this time were evidently observed more or less by renga poets. Although nothing is known of their content, quite a lot can be deduced from data supplied by renku, linked shih verses. Ryōki discusses renku composition in "Kōshi no Koto" ("Explications of Shih"), part of his *Ōtaku Fuketsu Shō.*[8] The Chinese thought of a linked shih simply as a poem composed by more than one person. The genre developed independently in Japan from the thirteenth century on, however, coming to take on a form akin to renga. Renku thus enable us to surmise the state of renga codes during this period. A summary of Ryōki's renku rules follows.

1. A poet cannot compose a line on a subject that has appeared in a recent line of verse. Lines treating the same subject are not separated by a specific number of lines, however. To paraphrase this state of affairs in the diction used by later renga poets, "kirai"

[7] [A note here has been entirely taken to the main text.—Ed.]

[8] *Ōtaku Fuketsu Shō* survives in a fourteenth-century manuscript in the collection of the Hōshōin Shimpukuji Temple, as well as in woodblock print editions dated 1624 and 1634. There is no modern printed edition. [As should be clear, "renku" here refers to linking Chinese verse, not to haikai, called renku in modern times.—Ed.]

(topical variance) had evolved but "sari" (suspensions of topics and diction) had not yet been determined.

2. Repeating the same kind of import—an occurrence later termed "rinne" in renga—is forbidden.
3. The opening stanza, or hokku, must deal either with the season at the time of composition (later called "tōki" in renga), or describe the location (the later "tōza").
4. Lines on blossoms or the moon are to appear a total of three times in each quarter of the sequence.[9]
5. There are rules about theme words, but their content is not known.

Ryōki's *Ōtaku Fuketsu Shō* was compiled between 1275 and 1278. We can therefore conclude that similar rules had been drafted for renga at a somewhat earlier point (Konishi, 1951a, 123-30). Renga rules gradually grew more detailed and codified in nature. They became recognized in Yoshimoto's time as *The New Code of the Ōan Era* (*Ōan Shinshiki*).

We would also do well to note the influence of Chinese shih treatises on the evolution of renga codes. Six Dynasties and T'ang poets isolated and forbade various practices, which were called "poetic diseases." Treatises on these "diseases" made their way to Japan soon after. The "grouping disease" provides one example of a poetic affliction: if, say, "clouds" appears in the first line of a shih couplet, "mist" may permissibly appear in the second. If, however, more words are mentioned that signify celestial phenomena—such as "wind" or "moon"—the couplet suffers from "grouping disease." Waka afflicted with this phenomenon are said to suffer from the "same-conception disease," since a subject is not supposed to appear twice in a 31-syllable poem. The same stricture was adopted by renga, as we see in Juntoku's discussion of rules for linked verse:

> The disease must be eschewed within a three-stanza run. Be careful in using the same subject even within a four- or five-stanza run. One need not insist on this, however. It is generally bad form to have too many instances of the same subject in a renga session. (*Yakumo Mishō*, 1:204)

It would be impossible entirely to prohibit recurrence of the same topic in a renga sequence; it is quite acceptable, on the other hand, to require that the same subject be suspended by a specific number of stanzas. The concept of suspension is probably directly derived from the Chinese treatises on poetry diseases. Shih poetics prohibit diseases called "the same

[9] A later standardized form for renga specified one mention of blossoms and two of the moon in each quarter of the sequence. [That is, one hana or flower stanza per sheet and one tsuki or moon stanza per side, thereby two per sheet.—Ed.]

sound," "the same consonant," "the major vowel," and "the minor vowel." The "same sound" disease refers to a case in which a shih in five-character lines contains the same sound within the space of ten characters (the tones of the two homophonic characters may differ).[10] In the "same consonant" disease, the same consonant appears within the space of ten characters within a shih in five-character lines. The "major vowel" disease involves the reappearance within a nine-character interval of a vowel used for rhyme in a shih in five-character lines. In the same poetic form, the "minor vowel" disease signifies the reappearance of a vowel within a nine-character interval, whether or not it has been used in rhyming.

Although these prohibitions are concerned with tone, they resemble the restrictions known as sarikirai (variations and suspensions) in renga. Both shih and renga critics held, moreover, that a sense of overlapping can be avoided by maintaining a certain distance between poetic units of similar nature. The basic renga concepts are therefore practical applications of the Chinese "poetry diseases" (Konishi, 1951a, 116-18).

[10] In standard Medieval Chinese, there were four tones, including three long (level, rising, falling) and one short. Standard Modern Chinese has lost the short tone but has four because of a second kind of level tone. The number of tones varies from regional dialect to dialect, with some southern ones having eight or more.

CHAPTER 10

Retrospection in Japanese Prose Literature

IMITATIVE FICTIONAL MONOGATARI

Thirteenth-century Japanese prose followed the same course toward ga and zoku as did contemporary prose and poetry written in Chinese. People of considerable talent wrote the three principal stories (monogatari) of the late eleventh century: *Sagoromo Monogatari (The Story of Sagoromo), Yowa no Nezame (The Tale of Nezame)*, and *Hamamatsu Chūnagon Monogatari (The Nostalgic Counselor)*. From that point on, both writers of fiction and their audiences realized that no one would ever write a better narrative than that found in the superlative *Genji Monogatari (The Tale of Genji)*. Authors reacted in two ways. One method, the next best thing to rivalling the *Genji*, was to create a similar monogatari through the use of related subject matter and narrative style. The second kind of response was to experiment with unusual subjects and so create something fresh, something different from the *Genji*. *Ariake no Wakare (Parting at Dawn)* is a twelfth-century work belonging to the former category. The latter category comprises three twelfth-century narratives, *Torikaebaya Monogatari (The Changelings), Matsura no Miya Monogatari (The Tale of the Matsura Shrine)*, and "Mushi Mezuru Himegimi" ("The Lady Who Loved Insects").

The former approach set the standard for fictional monogatari from the thirteenth century on. This trend resembles the evolution of Nijō pseudoclassicism as the mainstream waka style from Tameie's time onward. Fictional monogatari composed in the style of the *Genji* are generally termed imitative monogatari (giko monogatari). They were apparently composed in vast quantities. Nearly two hundred existed when the *Fūyōshū* was compiled in 1271.[1] If we include imitative classical monogatari written after the *Fūyōshū*, the number probably exceeds three hundred. Most of this corpus has been lost. The thirteenth century certainly marked the zenith of fictional monogatari in quantitative terms. Compare their number with that estimated for earlier monogatari. Thirty-one works, including ones now lost, were written before the eleventh century

[1] The *Fūyōshū* is a waka collection of poems selected from fictional monogatari and compiled according to the arrangement of royal waka anthologies. The compiler is unknown. The text that survives is an augmented version of the original. The final two of the original twenty books do not survive.

(vol. two, ch. 8), and seventy-four monogatari, including those no longer extant, are thought to have been written in the eleventh and twelfth centuries.[2] The marked increase in monogatari during the thirteenth century probably mirrors an equivalent increase in readership. In one presumably thirteenth-century work, *Waga Mi ni Tadoru Himegimi*, one of the characters, the sovereign Saga, comments on a certain Minister of Popular Affairs:

> "He need only see something once to remember it—really, who can rival him? When he first came to attend us at the palace, he had a reputation for knowing the three great waka anthologies and all the monogatari that were ever written. . . . That gentleman is indeed a marvel." (6:366-67)

Saga's statement, that the minister's superhuman powers of memory enable him to be conversant with "all the monogatari that were ever written," makes no sense unless we assume that fictional monogatari existed in vast quantities at this time. Even if we allow for fictional license, the Minister of Popular Affairs likely mirrors similarly well read members of thirteenth-century society.

Authors frame a narrative to accord with their anticipated audience. If the audience is well read, the narrative must take this into account. Consequently, an author may place greater reliance on earlier works of fiction. The fact that the Minister of Popular Affairs has memorized the "three great waka anthologies" (the *Kokinshū,* the *Gosenshū,* and the *Shūishū*) as well as a monogatari corpus signifies that waka and monogatari were held to share the same status. Waka achieve truly poetic expression when they draw on earlier waka. Similarly, monogatari acquire a status worthy of the genre when they draw on already extant monogatari. That is why authors mined earlier monogatari for subject matter and stylistic ideas.

A common theme of thirteenth-century imitative monogatari is a protagonist's rise, setbacks, and downfall [or success] placed against a background of intrigue over the royal succession. The narrative is interwoven with subplots of love affairs at court and embellished with various complex relationships. The characters' thoughts, responses, and actions in the

[2] Fifty-eight now nonextant fictional monogatari postdating the composition of the *Genji Monogatari* are mentioned in such early thirteenth-century documents as the *Shūi Hyakuban Utaawase* and the *Mumyō Sōshi.* The number is not definitive, since some nonextant works may have been listed in these documents under more than one title and so counted more than once. [Monogatari often had variant titles.—Trans.] The number seventy-four has tentatively been arrived at by adding the sixteen surviving works composed after the *Genji* to the fifty-eight nonextant monogatari. Only three extant fictional monogatari predate the *Genji: Taketori Monogatari, Utsuho Monogatari,* and *Ochikubo Monogatari* [discussed in vol. 2—Ed.]. Twenty-eight others are nonextant, known only by their titles. If these two figures are added, the total number of monogatari predating the *Genji* comes to thirty-one.

face of events are described exactly as in tenth- and eleventh-century monogatari. It follows that not even principal characters are given much family or career background when they are introduced to the story. Consider, for example, the opening passage of *Sayogoromo*.[3]

> Summer rains come every year, but this time they persisted for days on end. With all his usual finely-scented visitors kept away by the bad weather, the prince was seized with ennui. Fortunately his daughter, the royal consort, was home for a visit. Several of her ladies-in-waiting amused themselves in her presence by playing go and backgammon. (1:5)

Later in the text, the prince and consort are described somewhat more fully.

> The prince I recently mentioned was the elder brother of the Reizei sovereign. He had few sons and one daughter, the present royal consort. The consort's younger brother, Prince Hyōbukyō, was perhaps two years short of twenty. His person, nature, and abilities were so superior that they were unmatched even in Korea or China. People wondered if he might not be a buddha in disguise. (1:7)

The passage gives only the ranks and blood relationships of the principal characters. The character of the hero, Prince Hyōbukyō, is not described. This is not an isolated instance: no such passage appears in *Sayogoromo*. The absence was not a matter for concern among thirteenth-century authors and their audiences. Fictional monogatari contain very few types of protagonists. An audience familiar with earlier works would simply match an undescribed character like Prince Hyōbukyō with similar heroes from earlier stories. The same method applied to plot development. *Sayogoromo* consists of a love story intertwined with a wicked-stepmother motif. Because the *Sumiyoshi Monogatari (The Story of Sumiyoshi)* and the *Ochikubo Monogatari (The Story of Ochikubo)* had already described similar events, the audience of *Sayogoromo* accommodated itself to unnarrated aspects of the plot by supplementing it with available information. The author thus relied passively on earlier works. The author also anticipated a more active response from readers. An example is provided by this passage from *Sayogoromo*, in which Prince Hyōbukyō goes to visit a lady living in the mountains.

> As he moved deeper into the mountains, his loneliness grew. He imagined how these surroundings must affect a lady beset by gloom. The prince encountered chill autumn winds that were as yet strang-

[3] The composition date of *Sayogoromo* is not known. One manuscript copy of the work (in the Royal Library Collection) has a postscript attesting that the manuscript was copied in 1364. Thus the original work may predate the mid-fourteenth century.

ers to the city; the mountain forests were already tinged with fall colors. No matter where we may be, autumn touches our hearts. How grieved must his lady be, then, whenever she seated herself near a veranda and heard the moan of mountain winds and the sad chirp of crickets in the garden hedges! A few faint strains from a zither blended with the breeze rustling through the pines. (1:74-75)

The passage becomes more moving when superimposed on a scene from *The Tale of Genji*. In the "Sakaki" ("Sacred Tree") chapter, Genji visits the Rokujō lady at Sagano under similar circumstances.[4]

Sayogoromo often draws on the *Genji*, as the following excerpts show.

Needless to say, the nun did not again rise from her bed. She had no sorceror at her command to seek out her beloved, whose destination and condition must perforce remain unknown. The nun reproached the fates for letting her live to see this day. (2:143)

"You could court an out-and-out goddess and she wouldn't refuse you! You have made too many conquests—they all think you heartless, which means you are bound to suffer as well." (2:150)

Day dawned, but still Prince Hyōbukyō did not arise. The women complained among themselves. "How late he is this morning! His breakfast is getting cold." When the sun had climbed high in the skies, the prince summoned Lady Saishō. Saishō bustled over and was told to come inside the prince's bed-curtains. "I have brought someone unexpected with me. Come and greet her," he said, drawing away the covers from a recumbent person. Saishō smiled happily when she saw it was the girl. (3:215-16)

A reader who knows that these three passages are based, respectively, on passages from "Kiritsubo" ("The Paulownia Court"),[5] "Hahakigi" ("The Broom Tree"),[6] and "Aoi" ("Heartvine")[7] gains greater apprecia-

[4] *GM*, "Sakaki," 368. A translation of the relevant passage is given in vol. two, ch. 8.

[5] "She [the Kiritsubo lady's mother] lay overcome by the darkest grief" (*GM*, "Kiritsubo," 34). " 'If only a sorcerer would seek her out' " (ibid., 40). [This is part of a poem composed by the tennō after the death of his favorite concubine, the Kiritsubo lady.—Trans.] " 'Because I see how cruel it is to live long . . .' " (ibid., 36). [The speaker is the late concubine's grieving mother.—Trans.]

[6] " 'If you fell in love with an out-and-out goddess . . .' " (*GM*, "Hahakigi," 81). " 'A wholeheartedly amorous woman is interesting when considered solely from that standpoint' " (ibid., 77). [Both quotations are from the famous "Rainy Night's Discussion of Women" ("Amayo no Shinasadame") conducted by Genji and his friends. The first quotation is from Tō no Chūjō's story of a woman he loves and loses; the second is from Sama no Kami's tale of a fickle, amorous woman.—Trans.]

[7] "What could have happened between them? Although their new relationship attracted little notice from the attendants, Murasaki often stayed in bed while Genji rose early" (*GM*, "Aoi," 357). "Genji went to the south side of the house and summoned Koremitsu" (ibid., 358). "Genji parted the curtains and saw Murasaki lying in bed with the covers pulled over

tion by supplementing the narration in *Sayogoromo* with the relevant *Genji* passages. The technique resembles allusive variation (honkadori) in waka. In the thirteenth century the existence of an audience sufficiently sophisticated to recognize allusions to an earlier work must signify that fictional monogatari already constituted a ga sphere.

Authors also anticipated that an audience thoroughly familiar with monogatari would demand various subplots and interesting minor events. Although twelfth-century fictional monogatari already show a trend toward limited subjects, they clearly strive for innovations in plot. Critical standards shifted a century later: the highest praise became reserved for plots similar to those of past monogatari. An important factor in this shift was the rapid increase in the number of fictional monogatari, which made it difficult to devise new plots. Another factor was the authorial surmise that audiences familiar with monogatari would delight in the understated freshness of subtly varied subplots or minor events. Seen from this perspective, the more similar a plot was to its predecessors the more its new approach to a subplot or minor occurrence would stand out to the discerning reader. The principal plot, moreover, ought not to be complex, according to this view. A convoluted, eventful plot obliterated the impression generated by subplots.

Rewritten monogatari clearly demonstrate this attitude. *The Tale of Nezame* provides a particularly good example, because a part of the original text survives along with a rewritten version. The rewritten version tends to condense any passage that, in the original text, has a hint of longueur or convoluted plot twists. The result is not altogether satisfying, although there is a certain miniaturist attraction. This veneration of the small scale generally means that psychological description is sacrificed, because complex psychological description has a negative effect on the appeal generated by subplots and minor events. Psychological description is reduced to the following level in *Matsukage Chūnagon* (Sonkeikaku manuscript), for example.[8]

> She brooded over yesterday's poem. How she regretted writing it! He was sure to find something ludicrous in it if he read it over carefully enough. Her worries made sleep increasingly difficult. (1:9)

---

her head" (ibid., 357). [All three passages describe the difficult first day of Genji's marriage to a very young Murasaki.—Trans.]

[8] Because *Matsukage Chūnagon* is not represented in the *Fūyōshū*, it was probably written after the late thirteenth century. A manuscript copy of *Matsukage Chūnagon* in the Tōhoku University Library bears a postscript dating the copying as 1371. Thus the monogatari was probably written before the mid-fourteenth century. [Chūnagon, Middle Counselor, is the rank of the central male figure of most of these stories, and in the *Hamamatsu Chūnagon Monogatari*, the figure never changes in rank, something as strange as Sagoromo's ascending the throne in the *Sagoromo Monogatari*.—Ed.]

> He stood on the veranda and looked out. The capital city, always in his thoughts, lay far across the sea. It was sad indeed to think that the mists rose to hide it from his view. (3:78)

Natural description is similarly scant and poor in quality. Again, the precedence allotted to subplots and minor events may account for this phenomenon.

A similar tendency appears in other surviving imitative monogatari, including *Koke no Koromo, Ama no Karumo, Yaemugura, Iwade Shinobu, Shinobine Monogatari, Iwashimizu Monogatari*, and *Kaze ni Tsurenaki Monogatari.*[9] It is also present in rewritten works like *Sumiyoshi Monogatari.* This was the result of a positive response from a homogeneous audience. Behind this trend was a heightened interest in and knowledge of the classics, as exemplified by manuscript collating and copying carried out by the aged Teika and by Minamoto Mitsuyuki and his son Chikayuki (see p. 172). A more important factor still was the imitative pseudoclassical spirit, the conviction that good resides in the past. Thirteenth-century fictional monogatari, works whose familiar plots depend on fresh details to generate interest, are not at all different from the waka of the Nijō school.

Imitative Factual Nikki

In the twelfth century, the fictional nikki genre vanished, leaving only factual accounts. This phenomenon was accompanied by a tendency among authors to give direct expression to their emotions, in what may be seen as a return to the style originally present in Japanese prose nikki of the tenth and eleventh centuries. The thirteenth century, by contrast, marks the appearance of several nikki that provide objective descriptions of public events at court. The style of these "public" nikki resembles that used by eleventh-century court ladies in their nikki; one example is the first part of the *Murasaki Shikibu Nikki.*[10] To say the same thing differently, the style employed in thirteenth-century nikki thus corresponds to the move toward the imitative in fictional monogatari. Examples of public nikki include *Kenshun Mon'in Chūnagon Nikki*, by Kenzu Omae; *Ben no Naishi Nikki*, by the daughter of Nobuzane; and *Nakatsukasa Naishi Nikki*, by the daughter of Nagatsune. We might also note that some of the public nikki that appear at this time were written by men. Two such works are the *Tsuchimikado Naidaijin Nikki*, by Minamoto Michichika (1149-1202), and *Minamoto Ienaga Nikki*, by a principal organizer

[9] Although *Iwade Shinobu* and *Kaze ni Tsurenaki Monogatari* survive only in fragments, we may assume that the lost portions differed little in nature from what remains.

[10] Corresponding to Richard Bowring's "Part A" (Bowring, 1982, 43-119).

of the *Shinkokinshū*, Minamoto Ienaga (1170?-1234). Private nikki, first-person accounts that record personal events, also survive. Three principal examples are *Kenrei Mon'in Ukyō no Daibu Shū*, by Ukyō no Daibu (the daughter of Sesonji Koreyuki), and Abutsu's *Utatane no Ki* and *Isayoi Nikki*. Private nikki by men include three by Asukai Masaari (1241-1301): *Haru no Miyamaji, Miyakoji no Wakare*, and *Saga no Kayoi*.

The *Tsuchimikado Naidaijin Nikki* was the first of the surviving thirteenth-century nikki to be written. Why did men begin writing nikki in Japanese prose? One factor, though not necessarily a direct one, was the rise in status of Japanese prose. Fictional monogatari, originally invented to amuse bored noblewomen, had acquired commentaries by the twelfth century.[11] This demonstrated beyond doubt that Japanese prose was perceived as capable of producing classic literature. Another reason was an increasing awareness of the literary aspects of utilitarian prose written in Chinese. Public documents were regarded as a compositional form: the *Chōya Gunsai* includes not only shih, fu, prefaces, and inscriptions, but a massive amount of utilitarian documents written in Chinese.

The work now known as the *Tsuchimikado Naidaijin Nikki* is a travel account of the visit of the former sovereign Takakura to the Itsukushima Shrine in 1180, together with a record of Takakura's death in the following year. The latter section, entitled "The Death of Takakura In," was written in 1181. Its marked use of parallel prose techniques sets it apart from pure Japanese prose. The style may well presage that used by Kamo no Chōmei in his *Hōjōki* (*An Account of My Hut*). The former section, titled "The Royal Progress of Takakura In to Itsukushima," also shows signs of the influence of Chinese prose, but it is written in the style of a true Japanese prose nikki. An example from "The Royal Progress" follows.

> An extraordinary fragrance drifts from the sanctuary, filling many with awe and amazement. The experience reminds me of the immortal woman from Yang-t'ai on Mount Wu. She descended to Kao-t'ang, appeared to the emperor in a dream, became his lover, and promised him that he would see her again as morning clouds and evening rain.[12] It is daybreak. The cocks of the shrine raise their varied voices in chorus to announce the dawn. Waves crash against the

[11] Sesonji Koreyuki's (d. 1175) *Genji Shaku*, a commentary on the *Genji Monogatari*, is the normative example (see vol. two, ch. 8).

[12] The following passage appears in "Kao-t'ang Fu," by Sung Yü: " 'I am a woman of Mount Wu. I have journeyed to Kao-t'ang. Hearing that you too were travelling to Kao-t'ang, I am here in the hope that you will share my bed.' The king thereupon made love to her. As she was leaving, the woman said, 'I live on a craggy precipice on the southern side of Mount Wu. Clouds rise there in the morning and rain falls in the evening. When you see the clouds and rain, remember me' " (*WH*, 19:393).

> fences of the shrine. Has the tide risen? I remember Po Chü-i's verse, "I can hear the sounds of high tide."[13] The poet was able to give a skillful description of a scene on hearsay alone. These events and scenes, though right before my eyes, are difficult to describe satisfactorily. (*Michichika Ki*, 353)

The style of the nikki reveals its author's deliberate use of beautiful prose to describe a public event. "The Royal Progress" was probably written between 1198 and 1202, long after the journey to Itsukushima.[14]

Michichika apparently required much time for experimentation before producing a nikki in true Japanese prose. The *Minamoto Ienaga Nikki* was written somewhat later than Michichika's work. The nikki begins with Ienaga's first days at court in 1196 and ends with the dedication of the Saishō Shitennōin. The work is, of course, valuable as data on the composition process of the *Shinkokinshū*, as it contains several interesting passages about editing and revising the anthology. That this public nikki also contains moving descriptions of nature suggests that it, too, was consciously intended as literature.

Those public nikki written by women have a strikingly imitative style. Kenzu Omae, an elder sister of Teika, was sixty-two years old in 1219 when she wrote *Kenshun Mon'in Chūnagon Nikki* as a memoir of her days at court. She thus had ample time to shape her subject and structure her narrative. The result is highly unoriginal. The nikki concludes with an appendix consisting of Kenzu's rough drafts, together with a postscript:

> These were copied down by a later person who came upon trifles lacking beginnings and ends, little pieces that had been casually dashed off. Bit by bit and scrap by scrap, the papers were collected and copied. (*Kenshun*, 205)

If the appendix, an amalgam of "bits" and "scraps," is compared to the main text, compiled by Kenzu herself, one discovers that the structural

[13] The quotation is from Po Chü-i, "Composed in the Seventh Month of [822] at Lan-ch'i, en route to assume the governorship of Hangchow, having left the Secretariat" (*HKS*, 8:1848): Yü-hang is a town widely famous; / The city walls rise above river embankments. / Imagining twin mountains at the river's mouth, / I can hear the sounds of high tide. By "hearsay," Michichika means that he thinks it splendid that Po, who had yet to see Yü-hang, based these lines solely on what he had already heard and imagined.

[14] There are nine errors of fact in the text. "The Royal Progress" also records that "the dawn moon sets behind the island of Awaji," an event impossible to witness while en route to Itsukushima. The statement probably originated when Michichika accompanied the former sovereign Gotoba to Kumano in VIII.1198 and X.1199; the author later confused his recollections (*Michichika Ki*, "Kaisetsu," 124-26). Michichika, it will be recalled, played the principal villain's role in the circumstances surrounding Teika's *Hundred-Poem Sequence of the Shōji Era* (p. 206).

deficiencies of the appendix are not markedly greater than those in the text. The main text is followed by a postscript written by Teika:

> I did not know of this book while she lived. It was only after her death that I discovered it. She wrote it for amusement at her residence south of the Takahashi mansion, while recovering from one of those illnesses that afflict the elderly. I was told that she asked her adopted daughter, the Zen nun, to copy it for her. Both its style and its diction are worse than what one usually sees. Although reluctant to bring it before the public, I have no intention of destroying it. (*Kenshun*, 204-205)

Teika presents his sister's nikki as written "for amusement"; he notes that he does not want to show the world a style "worse than what one usually sees" and so has tentatively decided to keep it under wraps. Modesty plays some role in Teika's response, but his literary criteria are also at work in this negative evaluation. Kenzu herself was apparently rather proud of her nikki. The main text, compiled by the author, has this postscript: "Finished on the third day of the Third Month, [1219]. I am in the west room of my house. It is daytime, a slight breeze is blowing, and I have asked someone to read it to Lady Shōnagon" (*Kenshun*, 204).[15] Kenzu may have wanted to ask Shōnagon's opinion of her work before she asked her daughter, the Zen nun, to make a clean copy.

Kenzu's action demonstrates that nikki, like fictional monogatari, were occasionally read aloud and listened to rather than read silently. It also shows that Kenzu thought of her nikki as literature on a par with fictional monogatari. The same can be said for *Ben no Naishi Nikki* and *Nakatsukasa Naishi Nikki.* Contemporary readers would have delighted in reading about who wore what kind of clothes at a court function, what an individual carried, how the rooms were decorated, and what actions were performed. Texts that gave pleasure became de facto literary works.

Several thirteenth-century private nikki are also concerned with personal experiences. The *Kenrei Mon'in Ukyō no Daibu Shū* and *Isayoi Nikki* are outstanding examples.[16] We would do well, however, to reassess the reasons why they are thought to be outstanding. The *Kenrei Mon'in Ukyō no Daibu Shū* begins in 1174, the year after the daughter of Sesonji Koreyuki entered the retinue of the consort Kenrei Mon'in, and concludes around the year 1232. The work begins with a kind of preface;

[15] It was apparently customary to ask the opinion of someone reliable before having a clean copy made.

[16] For a discussion of shū, see vol. two, ch. 8. Much the same description applies to "shū" composed in the thirteenth century. An alternate title for the *Ben no Naishi Nikki* is *Gofukakusa In Ben no Naishi Kashū (The Personal Waka Collection of Ben no Naishi, Lady-in-Waiting to Gofukakusa)*; this suggests that the border between "nikki" and "shū" remained vague for some centuries.

events are arranged chronologically; and the nikki concludes with a postscript-like passage that clearly displays an awareness of the overall structure of the work.

Ukyō no Daibu probably compiled her nikki toward the end of her life. Its continued high reputation is due to its interesting subject, the author's love affair with Taira Sukemori (1158-85). The lovers frequently exchange waka in the nikki. When the Heike flee the capital in the Seventh Month of 1183, during the Gempei War, Sukemori and the author meet for the last time. Sukemori died in battle in 1185, at the age of twenty-seven. The severed heads of the most important Heike clan members killed in battle were brought to the capital and paraded down the main thoroughfares. Koremori drowned at Kumano and Kiyotsune at Dazaifu, while Shigehira was captured and sent under guard to the capital. These events and more like them, though nearly unbearable for the speaker-author to relate, appear one after the other in the nikki.

> When I hear that Captain Shigehira has been taken prisoner and has been brought back to the capital for a while, I think dejectedly of how among all those I have known he has been especially close to me. He says such amusing things, and even in the most trivial matters he is so considerate towards other people. He is indeed an exceptional person: what can he have done in a previous life to bring this upon himself? Those who have seen him say that his countenance is unchanged, and they cannot bear to look at him. I cannot describe how painful, how grievous it is to hear this:

Asa yū ni	By day, by night,
Minaresugushishi	How often we would meet
Sono mukashi	In those days not long ago:
Kakaru beshi to wa	Never did I imagine
Omoite mo mizu.	That it would come to this.[17]
	(*Ukyō*, 63-64)

Despite the tragic event, Ukyō no Daibu's waka is a trifling response. It is a crude, flat statement of predictable sentiments. The prose passage is equally undecorated and bereft of design. Yet one surmises that the author had a point in conceiving this style. The Japanese believe that extremely keen emotions are best expressed with restraint.[18] If Ukyō no

[17] [Trans. adopted from Harries, 1980, 199.—Trans. Following the author's definitions and discussion in volume two, we have altered Harries' past to present tense for nikki usage.—Ed.]

[18] An educated Japanese knows to respond to small or ordinary favors with courteous thanks but to utter only a few simple words in thanks for a great favor rendered in connec-

Daibu had added decorative language to her passage, it would have lost its sincerity. Circumstances like those described above are better expressed in commonplace fashion than through finely wrought, technically superior language. The *Ukyō no Daibu Shū* would be less moving if its author had intended it as an elegantly shaped outlet for her pathos and regrets.

On the other hand, this is wholly unadorned expression. The audience must be fully familiar with the circumstances in which the *Ukyō no Daibu Shū* was written in order to find the work moving (Harries, 1980, 65-66). The author wrote under the assumption that her audience would be as informed as herself about the members of the Heike clan. The anticipated audience would therefore find excessive information detrimental to an appreciation of the work. Even the best read modern readers, however, cannot match the thirteenth-century court literati in knowledge of the Heike, and so the modern response cannot be the same.

The nikki is nevertheless esteemed today thanks to the *Heike Monogatari (The Tale of the Heike)*, which has familiarized modern readers with the characters and events described in *Ukyō no Daibu Shū*. Readers supplement the plain expression of the nikki with their remembered response in reading of the tragic fate of the Heike clan in *The Tale of the Heike*. This approach kindles emotions similar or superior to those evoked by minute description. Because the *Heike* did not exist during the lifetime of Ukyō no Daibu [the Enkei manuscript of the *Heike* was copied some eighty years after the *Ukyō*], she could not have imagined that the emotional impact of her nikki would be augmented by a literary work like *The Tale of the Heike*. We may, however, conclude that the author fully expected her audience to use personal knowledge to supplement or augment her simple expression.

Abutsu's *Isayoi Nikki* owes its fame to similar circumstances. The *Isayoi Nikki* is a record of Abutsu's journey to the shogunal seat in Kamakura to respond to a series of lawsuits challenging her son Tamesuke's inheritance (see ch. 8). The author does not, however, write of legal matters or of her anxieties over Tamesuke's prospects. If one were to read the text of the nikki without knowing the identity of the author, one would probably conclude only that the work is a travel record made up of waka and prose.

The Nijō-Reizei lawsuits, however, had become a cause célèbre by the time Abutsu wrote the *Isayoi Nikki*. Fourteenth-century and later readers thus tended to project onto this work the sentimental image of an elderly mother risking a journey to Kamakura out of love for her son. Conse-

tion with one of life's major passages. Gratitude for a great favor is supposed to be expressed in actions, not words.

quently, this ordinary travel account is generally recognized as an outstanding example of Japanese literature written by women. This opinion was established around the eighteenth century and remains undisputed to this day. The *Isayoi Nikki* lacks a stirring setting—something equivalent to the sad scenes of lovers parting during the Gempei War found in *Ukyō no Daibu Shū*—and so demands considerable knowledge of the author and her situation if a reader is to be moved by the work. One useful source is *Utatane no Ki*, written by Abutsu in her youth and focusing on her romantic concerns. Other useful data are provided by Masaari in his *Saga no Kayoi* (31-32):

> The seventeenth. I go there during the day. A lector is about to begin the *Genji*; the mistress is summoned. The lector recites from behind the blinds. Her performance is outstanding. She does not recite as people ordinarily do—she must have received special instruction. She reads as far as "Wakamurasaki" ["Lavender," the fifth chapter]. That evening we drink sake. The master has two women serve it. The mistress of the house calls to me from near the blinds.
>
> "The master of this house is the grandson of a compiler of the *Senzaishū*, the son of a compiler of the *Shinkokinshū* and the *Shinchokusenshū*, and himself a compiler of the *Shokugosenshū*," she tells me. "He inherited a famous villa on Mount Ogura from a poet who carried on the ancient family waka traditions. . . ."
>
> I am moved that she solaces herself by speaking of such elegant matters. She continues, and so adds charm to the occasion.
>
> "People today are not the same. At the villa, one has the feeling of being at one with the great poets of the past."
>
> The master of the house, an elderly gentleman of sentiment, has drunk enough to shed tears of joy.

The "master of the house" is Tameie, and the talented and learned mistress will later be known as the nun Abutsu. She was about thirty years old at the time this passage was written. The lady gives Masaari a detailed account of something he would already have known well, the family waka lineage dating back to Shunzei and Teika. Her staunch loyalty to the family traditions later precipitated the great lawsuit.

Enough related material survives to make conjectures about Abutsu's personality. Such material supplements the *Isayoi Nikki* to create an interest not present in the text itself. Masaari's is rather a different case: his career was relatively calm, and little material on his life survives. As a result, the several nikki written by Masaari over his lifetime are not likely to be so highly appreciated as the *Isayoi Nikki*, a work of equal or lesser quality. Is it perhaps improper to look for the principal element of reception in external, related events rather than in the work itself?

The *Isayoi Nikki* emerges as third-rate literature at best if it is evaluated solely on its own merits as an object of reception and evaluation, free from external circumstances. There is nothing wrong, on the other hand, with appreciating literature in various ways. If we agree that the *Isayoi Nikki* can be evaluated on the basis of more than one criterion, the esteem enjoyed by Abutsu's work from high medieval times onward becomes closed to question. Had Teika's best waka, composed during the *Shinkokinshū* period (in the strict sense), appeared as anonymous, untitled works, they would retain the same virtuoso qualities. Yet we approve of the process of determining the aged Teika's masterworks by linking a poem itself with its circumstances of composition (pp. 235-241). The *Kenrei Mon'in Ukyō no Daibu Shū* and *Isayoi Nikki* can be masterpieces or ordinary nikki, depending on the relationship each establishes with its audience. They may best be thought at once great and commonplace.

CHAPTER 11

The Advance of Prose in the Mixed Style

Literary Accounts and Travel Records

Although prose in the mixed style existed in the twelfth century, the thirteenth century marks its consolidation as a genre ranking with prose written in Chinese and in pure Japanese. The new genre emerged not simply when conventional language was used to paraphrase the Chinese classics into Japanese prose, but after works of potential value as literature had been written in the mixed style. The *Hōjōki (An Account of My Hut)* was the first such work.

There is little doubt that the author of *An Account of My Hut*, Kamo no Chōmei (1153-1216), intentionally cast his "account" (ki)—an established literary genre—in a new style. Both the title and content of Prince Kaneakira's "Chiteiki" ("An Account of My Lakeside Arbor")[1] and Yoshishige Yasutane's work of the same name[2] show that they are tenth-century antecedents for Chōmei's *Account of My Hut* (Kaneko H., 1942, 34-60). Both "Lakeside Arbor" essays are usually assumed to have been based on Po Chü-i's "Around My Lake: A Poem and Preface."[3] Their content and their use of "ki" in their titles suggest, however, that Po's "An Account of My Thatch-roofed Arbor" ("Ts'ao-t'ang Chi") is a closer parallel.[4] It may not matter which of Po's essays was the inspiration for the two "Lakeside Arbor" essays. We ought rather note that both Japanese accounts describe the joys of living in a cottage with gardens and a nearby lake, and both include implicit censure of the worldly pursuit of power and profit. In China, the account (chi) was originally an objective exposition of facts, but during the zenith of the genre in the T'ang period, Chinese accounts incorporated the author's opinions or contentions.[5] Po Chü-i's accounts have philosophical themes, as do Kaneakira's and Yasutane's "Lakeside Arbor" essays and Chōmei's *Account of My Hut.*

At the time in which Chōmei wrote, nikki in pure Japanese prose described phenomena close to the author's own circumstances. They did not

[1] *Honchō Monzui*, 12:297-98.

[2] Ibid., 298-300.

[3] "Chih-shang P'ien," *Po-shih Ch'ang-ch'ing Chi*, 68:1699-1700.

[4] Ibid., 43:1063-65.

[5] "The principal aim of an account [chi] . . . is to have a factual style. Later writers, ignorant of the original style, have introduced personal opinions into their accounts" (*Wen-t'i Ming-pien*, 145).

contain speculative or philosophical themes. *An Account of My Hut* attempted to break the precedent set by nikki by employing prose in the mixed style. Rather than settle for narrating miscellaneous matters bearing on himself, Chōmei centers his account on the theme of evanescence (mujō), a basic Buddhist concept. This weighty theme is communicated through an artificial parallel prose style. If we analyze the famous opening passage of *An Account of My Hut* in the terminology of parallel prose, the result is as follows (see ch. 1).

Indeterminate alternating parallelism:

The flow of the river is ceaseless
And its water is never the same.
The bubbles that float in the pools, now vanishing, now forming,
Are not of long duration:

Free-form phrase:

So in the world are man and his dwellings.

Interjection:

In the glittering capital,

Short parallel couplets:

Ridgepole rises by ridgepole,
Tiled roofs vie for splendor
In the great
And in the humble

Interjection:

Dwellings of man.

Free-form phrase:

It might be imagined that they remain unchanged from one generation to the next, but when we examine whether this is true, how few are the houses that were there of old.

Heavy alternating parallelism:

Some were burnt last year
And rebuilt this year;
Great houses have crumbled
And become hovels.

Interjection:

Those who dwell in them have fallen no less.

Short parallel couplet:

The city is the same as ever,
The people are as numerous,

Free-form phrase:

But of those I used to know, a bare one or two in twenty remain.

Heavy alternating parallelism:

I do not know: those who are born and die,
Where do they come from, where do they go?
Nor do I know: in building houses that last but a moment,
For whose benefit does man torment himself, for what reason is his eye delighted by them?

Interjection:

Which, the master or his dwelling,

Free-form phrase:

Will be first to go? Neither differs from the dew on the morning glory.

Equal alternating parallel couplets:

The dew may fall and the flower remain—
Remain, only to be withered by the morning sun.
The flower may fade before the dew evaporates,
But though it does not evaporate, it waits not the evening.[6]

(*Hōjōki*, 75-76)

There can be no complete correspondence between this Japanese "artificial parallel prose" and true parallel prose written in Chinese, because the natures of the languages differ. Chinese parallel prose consists chiefly of lines of four and six characters, with anomalous lines introduced occasionally to vary the rhythm. The Chinese version is also characterized by tonal patterns at the ends of lines and of course by frequent use of parallelism. The vocal symmetry disappears in "parallel prose" written in Japanese, leaving only the parallelism. Alternating parallelism (an a/b/a′/b′ configuration) in true parallel prose can be subdivided into the "light" form (in which lines a and a′ contain four characters each, and lines b and b′ each contain six characters) and the "heavy" form (lines a and a′ = six characters; lines b and b′ = four characters).

It is impossible to discriminate between the two forms in Japanese prose. The next best thing, in translating from Chinese to Japanese, is to use phrases roughly corresponding to light or heavy alternating parallelism. For example, the lines beginning "Some were burnt last year" are designated as heavy alternating parallelism because they have more words in their first half than in the second. Contemporary readers would

[6] [The translation is adapted from Donald Keene, trans., "An Account of My Hut," in *Anthology of Japanese Literature* (New York: Grove Press, 1955, reprinted 1960), 197-98.—Trans.]

have perceived even so slight a stylistic element as characteristic of parallel prose, because formal Buddhist prayers (gammon) and the statements made by sponsors of Buddhist services (hyōbyaku) were written in parallel prose. These documents, read aloud in Japanese syntactical form at Buddhist services, accustomed the contemporary audience to the parallelism, if not the euphonic beauty of Chinese parallel prose.

Ki no Tsurayuki and his collaborators attempted to incorporate a parallel prose style into the Japanese Preface to the *Kokinshū*, because they wished to add a certain gravity to the preface to a royal anthology. Not obliged to use a solemn style, Chōmei chose nevertheless to experiment with a parallel prose-type style because it was used in Buddhist prayers and sponsors' statements and was thus appropriate for prose written with a Buddhist theme. Although Chōmei's theme, the impermanence of all things, is stated explicitly in the section on the five great disasters that afflict the capital and the country, there are few instances of parallelism there.[7]

The accounts of these calamitous events are strongly realistic, probably because Chōmei is describing things he actually witnessed. Such raw description cannot be expressed in a Japanese approximation of parallel prose. The section on the five disasters corresponds to two essential elements in a medieval Buddhist sermon, the illustrative anecdote (hiyu) and stories of the buddhas' and bodhisattvas' previous existences (innen). These stories, which clarify the message propounded in a sermon, were related in colloquial Japanese, not in parallel prose (see ch. 4). Their objective was to give the congregation a strong sense of the unsettled, undependable nature of life. They pose a problem, and a method for solving it must then be found. The solution, according to Buddhist sermons, was faith in the Three Treasures (the Buddha, the dharma, and the priesthood). Chōmei's answer is somewhat different.

Living in seclusion is Chōmei's response to the ephemerality of life. His method—to live in a simple grass house in the hills of Hino, cut off from worldly fame and fortune—may seem to recommend total abandonment of the world. An audience familiar with the two "Lakeside Arbor" accounts would, however, have clearly perceived the aristocratic aesthetic that underlay this description of the simple life. For Chōmei, the Hino hermitage was the "lakeside arbor" reduced to its simplest form. A lakeside arbor is a small retreat in an artistically designed garden of water, rocks, and trees. Although simplicity is its essence, the simplicity is relative. Only when compared to the grand residences of the powerful nobility did such a retreat seem simple. A garden landscaped with water, rocks,

[7] The five disasters described by Chōmei are the great fire of 1177, the windstorm of 1180, the transfer of the capital to Fukuhara, also in 1180, the famine of 1181-82, and the earthquake of 1185 (*Hōjōki*, 76-85).

and trees was certainly not cheap to build. It was beyond the reach of the lower aristocracy.

The Chinese began to be interested in close contact with nature from about the time of Hsieh Ling-yün (385-433). Communion with nature, an activity connected to Taoism, became more marked in the T'ang period. The ideal life for a T'ang literatus included both public observance of Confucian austerities and private enjoyment of Taoist pleasures. Po Chü-i exemplified this life. Those high officials who were too busy to commune with nature by journeying to famous mountains and magnificent lakes instead built gardens—with water, rocks, and trees—at their city residences or country villas. They concentrated their minds on the model scenes of nature there, delighting in the view from the garden arbor. Chinese landscaping skills were probably not transmitted to early medieval Japan, but the Japanese nevertheless gained a sense of Chinese gardens through such works as Po's accounts of his garden retreats. They used Chinese literary material to construct gardens patterned after nature's own designs. Prince Kaneakira's and Yasutane's lake arbors provide two examples of the success of such endeavors. Each wrote his "Account" as evidence of a spiritual lineage, reaching back to China, that perpetuated a continental love for nature in Japanese gardens.

Hino had scenery untouched by human artifice. Chōmei nevertheless considered his landscape as an extension of the gardens carefully crafted by Prince Kaneakira and Yasutane. Chōmei's seclusion in Hino was not a move to attain absolute freedom by rejecting aristocratic culture and returning to nature; nor did he wish to imitate T'ao Ch'ien's productive country life of farming and sericulture.[8] Negative conditions drove Chōmei into seclusion. The five major calamities described in his *Account of My Hut* represent the dangers threatening society in his day. The elegant (fūryū) life of past centuries could no longer be maintained. Chōmei, a member of the lowest stratum of nobility, resigned himself to lowering his standard of living so that he could escape the concern of keeping up appearances. He wished to keep alive only one part of the old fūryū life, its loftiness of spirit. That is why Hino, as depicted in *An Account of My Hut*, is nature seen through the eyes of a country recluse whose heart remains in the capital.

Pastoral poetry in the West advocates recapturing harmony with nature. This view holds that humanity, which originally lived in total harmony with nature, has become estranged from it through human failings. Pastoral poetry is not the product of shepherds minding their flocks, but the creation of intellectuals who imagine an ideal, unsullied world situ-

[8] T'ao Ch'ien's "Six Poems on Going Back to Live in the Country" (*Tōshi*, 2:414-15) describe how the poet, a small landowner, earned his living by farming.

ated in the distant past. By evoking this world, symbolized by pastures and fields, in their poetry, these intellectuals attempt to transcend the real, polluted world. Pastoral poetry is thus oriented toward simplicity. The hallmark of the genre, however, is its inner store of sophisticated ideas. Pastoral poetry is, moreover, technically complex. The form is a fusion of narrative and dialogue framed in hexameter or pentameter. Despite its countrified exterior, then, pastoral poetry is rooted in urban perceptions. In this sense, *An Account of My Hut* is pastoral. There are differences: whereas pastoral poetry looks to the remote past for its ideal world, Chōmei's recollections go back only to the tenth century, the composition period of the two "Lakeside Arbor" accounts. The difference corresponds to the differing perceptions of a golden age held by the West and Japan. By the High Middle Ages, the Japanese had located their golden age in the relatively recent past, designated "nakagoro."

The Buddhist principle of evanescence is a complete denial of all existence. This perspective does not accord at all with Chōmei's approach—to seek an ideal world in the elegant life of the tenth century and maintain a spiritual bond with it, while also lowering his living standards in order to avoid the torments of worldly disappointment. Chōmei has no answer to the great question: how does man respond to the evanescence of all things? This life at Hino is tasteful seclusion: he has fled from worldly problems so that he might discover taste and elegance within himself.[9] Buddhism regards such goals as attachment and delusion, and their pursuit as contrary to the true meaning of seclusion. The later *Ichigon Hōdan*, composed of anonymous declarations, describes the true hermit as one willing to abandon even the necessities of life.[10] Chōmei's half-hearted seclusion (only his *favorite* musical instruments go with him to Hino) is shocking by comparison.[11] This is not meant as criticism. The literary essence of the last half of the High Middle Ages appears in this very approach: to aim at a spiritually lofty realm while living far from worldly fame and fortune. Chōmei's stance is also an essential source of the literary ideal of artistic vocation (michi).

The *Kaidōki*, written by an unknown author about a decade after *An Account of My Hut*, describes a way of life similar to Chōmei's. In the opening passage, the narrator uses the third person to introduce himself (*Kaidōki*, 5):

[9] "Suku" (to act with taste) signifies an attitude centering on perceived high values rather than simple liking. In his *Mumyōshō* (48-51), Chōmei remarks that one Tōren "is a man of formidable taste" because he goes off in a rainstorm to question a man who knows much about the rare "masuho plumegrass." People like Tōren are hard to find these days, Chōmei laments: "People with taste and feeling become fewer with each passing year."

[10] "Know that those concerned with salvation are not to own so much as a pickling pot" (*Ichigon*, 2:201). See n. 30 below.

[11] "I construct a hanging bamboo shelf on the southwest wall. . . . By its side I place a zither and a lute" (*Hōjōki*, 89).

Short parallel couplet:

In the region of Shirakawa,
In the foothills of Nakayama,

Free-form phrase:

A solitary gentleman dwells in a lonely, simple house.

Light alternating parallelism:

Because his nature and potential cannot be controlled,
He must do more than master accomplishments and study the arts;
Because his fate has always been precarious,
He cannot take refuge in shame when retribution comes, nor curse the destiny meted out by Heaven.

Indeterminate alternating parallelism:

He has become as insignificant as the toad of Pauper's Spring;
Weeping helplessly, he compares himself to a floating waterplant.
He is a useless, fallen tree in Straitened Valley,
Whose heart no longer sends out shoots and blossoms.

Light alternating parallelism:

Finding his worthless life all too precious,
He is not profound enough to drown himself in a deep chasm.
Because his feeble mind maintains its rash existence,
Thorns of agony flourish in his grieving heart.

Dense alternating parallelism:

In spring he breaks off fern shoots, staving off imminent starvation;
As he is not the sage Po-i, no one will condemn him.[12]
In autumn he gathers nuts to cure the ills of poverty;
Dr. Hua's medicine will not work, for he is already starving.[13]

Nakayama is the name of a hill in Kurodani. The reclusive narrator of *Kaidōki* who lives there, taking part in literary activities and placing his faith in the Buddha, resembles Chōmei in his attitude toward life and in his credo.[14] The two works differ in that *Kaidōki* is principally an account

[12] ["Po-i hated the Chou dynasty and chose to starve on Shou-yang Mountain rather than serve under it" (Burton Watson, trans., *Records of the Grand Historian of China* [New York: Columbia University Press, 1961], 2:453.)—Trans.]

[13] Hua Ch'a was a famous physician who lived in the latter part of the second century A.D. He is mentioned in the *History of the Later Han*. [Auth., Trans.]

[14] The concluding passage of *Kaidōki* is wholly Buddhist in content, beginning with the sentence, "One shows true gratitude by relying completely upon nature" and concluding with the waka that ends the work (82-93): Kawaraji na / Nigoru mo sumu mo / Nori no mizu / Hitotsu nagare to / Kumite shirinaba. (There is no difference! / It may be sullied, may be clear, / The Dharma stream / Flows on as a single thing / As I know in drinking it.)

of a journey. Because its approach is the same as that used by Chōmei, the exchange of the word "kaidō"—signifying travel—for "hōjō"—a kind of dwelling—may alert the reader that this is a work of similar nature. Travel literature existed in the past. The *Tosa Nikki (Tosa Diary)* is one of the oldest. The *Sarashina Nikki* is partially a travel account, as is the *Isayoi Nikki*. Travel literature written in Chinese prose includes Ennin's *Nittō Guhō Junrei Kōki (The Record of a Pilgrimage to China in Search of the Dharma)* and Jōjin's *San Tendai Godaisanki*. These are generally gathered under the rubric of "travel accounts" (kikō). I believe that these works need not be set apart because they deal with travel; they should all be considered as nikki.

The *Kaidōki* does not belong in the nikki genre, however; the works mentioned earlier record an individual's journey, but they contain no explicit statements of how the journey leads the traveler to discover new significance in his life. The *Kaidōki*, on the other hand, is a travel record prefaced and concluded by serious explications of human existence. We must conclude that the journey is recorded to serve as a theme relating to human existence. I shall therefore designate a new genre, the travel account (kikō), defined as records of journeys that have human existence as their theme. Chōmei also wrote an account of a journey, *Ise Ki*. As it survives only in fragments, it cannot suggest how Chōmei's philosophical views would have been reflected in it.[15] The travel account, as here defined, must begin with the *Kaidōki*.

Saigyō and Nōin were two eminent earlier travelers. Nōin visited utamakura, locales associated with specific events mentioned in waka. He did not record his journeys. Even had he done so, they would probably not have dealt with the theme of human existence. The protagonist of the *Kaidōki* visits places where specific events have occurred, instead of happening across places at random in the course of a journey. Some of the events that attract the narrator-protagonist are connected with waka. Utamakura are not necessarily linked to a specific event. In many cases, a locale becomes an utamakura simply because someone composed a poem that had some connection to the place.

That the waka composed was memorable enough to remain in people's memory may be an event in its own right, of course. Because certain facts were assumed to form basic elements of a famous waka, anyone coming into direct contact with those facts was believed to receive the elemental power that created the famous poem. This was undoubtedly what was anticipated by visitors to utamakura sites. A similar process applied to those visiting sites where something special had taken place. One went

[15] Twelve fragmentary quotations from *Ise Ki* survive in *Fuboku Wakashō*. They appear with the following beginnings: "Chōmei's *Ise Ki* has, '. . . .' " (Yanase, 1937, 552-56).

there to be addressed directly by the spirits of those involved in the event. If the visitor was a Buddhist ascetic, his contact with these spirits would enable him to know evanescence as a living reality as well as a concept. The author of *Kaidōki* envisioned travel in this sense.

Saigyō seems to have found it more important to visit places associated with past events than to travel to utamakura sites. Sometimes the events attracting him had occurred just as he heard them, but others would inevitably have become setsuwa (traditional stories) in the course of repeated tellings within the local area. In the latter case, the story itself would be far from factual, but the spirits related to the event would speak with greater vigor. To gain contact with their speechless voices one had to visit the site of the event. Saigyō's travels were probably linked to setsuwa for this reason and eventually led to Saigyō himself becoming the subject of setsuwa. Saigyō's image as a traveller was probably largely shaped by the early fourteenth century. His "acts of austerity" are mentioned by the daughter of Masatada in the *Towazugatari* (5:330), although these austerities are not specified. They probably do not reflect the strongly fictionalized image of Saigyō found in *Senjūshō* and *Saigyō Monogatari*. If Saigyō's "acts of austerity" are instead invested with the kind of travel description found in the *Kaidōki*, we may well obtain a fair sense of his early fourteenth-century reputation.

Assumed to be by the unknown author of the *Kaidōki*, the *Tōkan Kikō* is set in 1242, a year probably not far distant from the actual time of composition. Like the *Kaidōki*, it is written in the mixed style and makes frequent use of parallelism in the style of parallel prose. On the other hand, it says little about the significance of the protagonist's journey with regard to human existence. The author nevertheless knew the connection between the journey and life, as is seen in the opening passage.

> My age nears half a century, and my sidelocks grow ever more frosted. Yet I live an idle existence, with no place for a permanent dwelling. I agree with Po Lo-t'ien's [Po Chü-i's] moving verse, "You drift like a floating cloud, your sidelocks are like frost." (*Tōkan*, 1)[16]

Because the connection between life and travel was apparently fairly well known, the author seems to have felt no need to stress the metaphysical significance of facts in his journey. *Tōkan Kikō* represents the first instance in which "kikō" appears in the title of a work. The title, however, was probably given the work in the eighteenth century.[17] It was originally

[16] "A literary man who loves his wines is elderly Mr. Hsiao; / You drift like a floating cloud, your sidelocks are like frost" (*HKS*, 18:2025-26, "Sent to Mr. Hsiao"). ["Lo-t'ien" (J. Rakuten) was the literary sobriquet of Po Chü-i (J. Haku Kyoi).—Trans., Ed.]

[17] The title *Tōkan Kikō* appears only with the texts in *Gunsho Ruijū* and *Fusō Shūyōshū* (both eighteenth-century compendia). Many woodblock editions, beginning with the print-

titled *Chōmei Michi no Ki (Chōmei's Account of the Road)* out of an erroneous attribution to Chōmei. Despite the error, the original title is significant in being called *Michi no Ki*, an "account of the road" or "account of a journey."

The title demonstrates an early recognition that works describing a journey belong to an independent genre and not to a subcategory of nikki. The pure Japanese expression "michi no ki" can be rendered as "kikō" in Sino-Japanese; the terms themselves present little problem. The difficulty is with what underlies the term "travel account." The observations and descriptions that make up a travel account reflect the view that factual accounts of a journey have a special nature. This nature stems from the truths of life one encounters on a journey, truths of which one is ordinarily unaware. This is the conceptual backdrop for the many travel accounts that commence in the fourteenth century and culminate in the seventeenth with a grand series by Bashō.

Historical Treatises and Buddhist Essays

The advance of prose in the mixed style produced a genre that presented an author's thoughts in treatise form. Because the indigenous Yamato language was deficient in conceptual vocabulary, treatises could not exist without a massive infusion of Chinese loanwords. Not that imported vocabulary alone made a treatise. What was also needed was a logical treatment whereby an author structured thoughts into a clear line of reasoning. I define "logical" as characterizing a mental approach in which the matter at hand is aptly analyzed and various elements are interpreted according to a single principle. This was a weak point for the Yamato people. Only those rare Japanese whose mental processes had been refined by foreign culture were able to master the logical approach. The monks Jien and Dōgen are early, eminent examples.

Jien (1155-1225) exerted a considerable influence on waka poets during the *Shinkokinshū* period. A younger brother of Kujō Kanezane, Jien was the abbot of Enryakuji and superior of the Tendai sect of Buddhism. His and his nephew Yoshitsune's support for the Mikohidari was a motivating force behind the great poetic output of Teika and his group. Jien has ninety-two waka in the *Shinkokinshū*, second only to Saigyō in numerical representation. The *Shūgyokushū*, his personal waka collection, has 6,117 poems. Despite Jien's eminence among his contemporaries,

---

ings of 1648 and 1789, have *Chōmei Michi no Ki*. Other variant titles are *Chōmei Hōshi Michi no Ki, Kamosha Ujibito Kikutaifu Chōmei Michi no Ki, Azumaji no Ki*, and *Chikayuki Nikki*. One undated woodblock copy is titled *Kamo no Chōmei Kamakura Kikō*. Another example from the same edition is titled *Chōmei Michi no Ki*, however. The former book probably had its title page changed.

however, his poetry is undeniably inferior not only to Teika's but also to Yoshitsune's and Princess Shokushi's. The reason is Jien's attachment to logic. Although his approach differs from the oblique logic used by *Kokinshū* poets, the intellectual judgments made in his poetry are unconnected to direct emotion. Jien's approach was a natural one for a man trained since youth as a scholarly Tendai monk.[18] Tendai is known for logical erudition. The orderly systemic structure of its doctrine, its strict conceptual provisions, and clear doctrinal statements are reminiscent of nineteenth-century Western philosophy. While such erudition occasionally backfires in waka composition, it provides an unclouded, penetrating view of history.

Jien's *Gukanshō (The Future and the Past)* is usually regarded as a work of history. This is not a mistake. Jien begins by discussing Jimmu Tennō and continues with a chronologically ordered summary of political events up to the reign of Juntoku Tennō. The *Gukanshō* is based on reliable documents; oral statements from participants in events are chosen with a full awareness of their relative reliability. Jien's objectivity is certainly that of a historian. For all that, the *Gukanshō* is more than a history. It not only sets forth events from the past; it also asserts that the events discussed in the text can aid in determining the future of Japan. The future is, of course, unknown to human beings. Realizing that knowledge of the future was beyond his grasp, Jien sought to capture the "causation" (dōri) that would govern the future as it did the past and present. To quote Jien:

> All dharma (hō) is maintained in a single word, "causation." Aside from causation, there is nothing. It is vital that one discern whether a falsehood originates from causation. The path of causation is trodden from the beginning of time until its end, and from the end of time back to the beginning. Causation is the sole doctrine to be followed by states large and small, new and old. (*Gukanshō*, 7:324)

The idea that all dharma (phenomena and concrete existence) owes its identity to causation is based on the premise that identity was originally part of Emptiness (kū).[19] Water, fire, trees, and people have all become what they are through combinations of various main and supplementary causes. When their respective karma is exhausted, the identity of each will dissolve. All phenomena and existence are, in other words, Emptiness. Causation provides the sole reason why water, fire, trees, and people each possess a being, ephemeral though it is. Both good and evil exist in the

[18] Jien took monastic vows in 1167, at the age of twelve (Manaka, 1974, 28).

[19] The Sanskrit root for "dharma" is "dhṛ," "to hold." The various identities of existence are "held"; these identities are basic components of dharma. Jien's use of the words "motsu nari" (translated as "is maintained") is based on this derivation.

world. Evil, however, owes its very existence to causation. The world governed by causation seems infinite to humans, because it spans a period from the beginning of time through the path of decline that leads to the end of time. Just before mankind is extinguished, the Buddha will direct that the world revert to its primeval form. Since the time period spanned by human nations, both great and small, is insignificant compared to this grand, seemingly infinite period, their historical progress tends toward decline. This is causation. The *Gukanshō* attempts to capture the significance of causation-based historical events. We might thus more accurately call the *Gukanshō* a historical treatise than a history.

To conclude that the world is in headlong decline is to assume no escape. That attitude produces only pessimism and lamentation. Jien adds a very original idea to this position. He sees the universe as repeating the process of decline and zenith in units of time so long as to seem infinite. The repetitive process occurring in the universe is mapped to display a length of time recognizable to human beings. Although the inverse image has a vast, seemingly infinite domain of definition, the mapped image of the domain corresponds accurately to the prototype. In a mere millennium on earth, therefore, one can expect alternations of decline and zenith. On the other hand, since the overall trend is toward decline, only strong willpower and wise governance can move a state or society toward its zenith. Jien envisions changes taking place on earth as follows:

> One hō represents sixty years.[20] That is the length of time required for a complete zodiacal cycle. A statesman takes the cycle into consideration. A gradual decline will eventually reverse and bring prosperity. When the cycle points to prosperity, statesmen of the past, as today, have guided their countries from decline to gradual improvement. (*Gukanshō*, 3:147)

When a statesman "guides" his country to improvement, the result in absolute values is a momentary rise in the midst of a downward curve. It is nevertheless an improvement over the period prior to the upward trend. The willpower and governance that produce a gradual improvement stem from correct judgments based on a knowledge of causation. In the finite, material human world, causation is the mapping of the infinitely great, basic principle that pervades the universe. History therefore moves in accordance with causation.

Causation is most concretely manifested in sovereign law (ōbō). The purpose of this human norm is to bring the proper kind of prosperity to nations and society. Sovereign law is based, in turn, on causation. Since

[20] A hō (Ch. pu) is a unit used in Chinese historical metaphysics. One hō is usually equated with a seventy-six-year period. We do not know what source Jien used to arrive at his sixty-year figure.

humanity is naturally disposed toward making the wrong judgments, however, sovereign law tends to be breached, bringing confusion and decline upon state and society. Human norms are thus an insufficient motivating power in effecting a gradual improvement in the fortunes of a state. Another essential ingredient is the causation of the Buddhist dharma, which transcends human intelligence. When the dharma declines, so too does sovereign law. Jien attempts to use his knowledge of causation to determine whether a given situation indicates rise or fall.

The judgments given in the *Gukanshō* are consequently not Jien's individual opinion. His judgments are linked by extension to general causation and by further extension to the basic governing principle of the universe. The extent to which the *Gukanshō* puts these principles into effect is problematic. Nevertheless, their application gives a new meaning to various facts. The method is certainly impressive. The *Ōkagami (The Great Mirror)* also contains judgments based on a principle called "dōri." In its case, however, dōri signifies commonsense or conventional criteria, not a unified principle (vol. two, ch. 8). Critical judgments in the *Gukanshō* are far more advanced than those in the *Ōkagami*. Another work that uses historical facts for its raw material, *Rokudai Shōshiki*, also has critical assumptions.[21] Its criteria, however, pertain solely to sovereign law and remain in the realm of common sense. Its critical views do not bear comparison to the *Gukanshō*, which creates fresh insights by breaking the mold of common sense.

Shōbō Genzō, by the monk Dōgen (1200-53), is quintessentially logical.[22] This scholarly, conceptual record (1231-53) of one man's search for the basic governing principle of the universe is written from the Zen perspective and has no literary pretensions whatsoever. I have nevertheless chosen to discuss it because it has highly noteworthy stylistic hallmarks that strongly influence later literature. These traits of *Shōbō Genzō* originate from knowledge acquired while Dōgen was studying Ch'an (Zen) in China. He stayed in China for four years and four months, from 1223 through 1227.[23] During his stay, he had many consultations with Zen masters throughout the country. He had an almost constant dialogue with his master, T'ien-t'ung Ching-tsu (1163-1225), during his period of

[21] The *Rokudai Shōshiki* is an anonymous work in eloquent mixed-style prose. It relates important events that occurred during six reigns, beginning with Takakura's (r. 1168-80) and ending with Gohorikawa's (r. 1221-32).

[22] Dōgen wrote two works titled *Shōbō Genzō*. One is in Chinese prose (arranged in three hundred soku, or items); the other, in ninety-two fascicles, is written in the mixed style of Japanese prose. I am concerned here with the latter work, a compendium of sermons given between 1231 and 1253.

[23] Dōgen probably returned to Japan in the Eighth Month of 1227 (Ōkubo, 1953, 174-79). He left for China in the Third Month of 1223.

study at the Ching-fu Temple in Ming-chou. He must obviously have been fluent in Chinese.

This fluency is reflected in *Shōbō Genzō* when Dōgen creatively adapts Chinese loanwords to fit his own contextual requirements. Ideally speaking, the Chinese loanwords employed by Japanese in their Chinese or in the mixed Sino-Japanese style follow or closely approximate Chinese usage, since they were originally words of foreign provenance. Chōmei is one of many who observe this stricture: loanwords are not forced to follow Chōmei's own style. Dōgen, on the other hand, experimented with the commonly accepted forms of usage in order to express most appositely the essence of what he wished to say. His usage is not wrong in the lexical sense. Dōgen's Chinese vocabulary is semantically correct but used in unprecedented ways. In a way, Dōgen creates neologisms by giving established loanwords new meaning. "Existence and Time" ("Yūji"), the twentieth chapter of *Shōbō Genzō*, provides one example. The chapter presents the thesis that "the expression 'existence and time' signifies that time is existence, and existence is time" (20:189). Dōgen's discussion begins by quoting an eight-line psalm attributed to "a great Zen master."[24] The psalm opens with the couplet:

> There is a time [yūji] when I stand high atop mountain peaks;
> There is a time [yūji] when I dive deep to the sea floor.

"Yūji," as it is used in the psalm, corresponds to our modern "sometimes." Dōgen, however, interprets "yū" as meaning "existence." According to his reading of the psalm, the existence of mountain peaks and sea depths is in fact time, and the time-oriented action of climbing or sinking is also existence. Dōgen's individualistic usages are probably open to criticism from hair-splitting linguists. Dōgen nevertheless dared to devise a new usage for the word "yū" in order to assert an Einsteinian opinion that being and time are indissoluble and identical.

Originality in word usage results in a speedily-developed thesis. Although the speed may astonish denizens of the commonsensical world, it can be arrested by Dōgen's logic.

> Therefore both a pine tree is time and a bamboo is time. One should not grasp only that time passes, or study passage as the sole function of time. If passage is perceived as the unique property of time, there will be gaps. Failing to grasp the Way of Existence and Time comes from studying only how time passes. In essence, all be-

[24] Dōgen uses "great Zen master" (J. kobutsu, little Buddha) as a term of respect for Yao-shan Wei-yen (751-834). The *Ching-te Ch'uan-teng Lu* (*Keitoku Roku*, 28:440) informs us that the psalm is by Yao-shan.

ings in all worlds are interconnected, and each is time. Since they exist as time, we too exist as time. (20:191)

Dōgen presents a paradox in his idea that time both passes and does not pass. What keeps his argument from ending as paradox is his logic: if we accept that time does nothing but pass, we must conclude that, after all time has passed, something that is not time will remain. Dōgen acknowledges a four-dimensional world of time and space.

> Mountains are time; seas are time. Without time, neither mountains nor seas can exist. One must not conclude that time does not exist in mountains and seas at the present moment. If time were to vanish, so too would the mountains and seas. Within this logical framework, the Morning Star appears, the Buddha comes into the world, eyeballs emerge [i.e., spiritual eyes are opened], and a plucked flower is flung out [i.e., the dharma is correctly transmitted to a disciple]. All these are time. If they were not time, nothing whatsoever could exist. (20:193)

Dōgen intends the phrase "the present moment" (shikin) to mean a fusion of "now-itself" and "presentness." Thanks to his unusual neologism, Dōgen can present us with amazingly advanced concepts. Such content could not possibly be expressed in the indigenous Yamato language. Mountains and seas exist because they exist *now*. If there were no "now," there would be no room for existence. Time encompasses past, present, and future. The present, however, is truly here, while the past and future exist only in relation to the present. Past and future could not exist without the present; and the absence of past, present, and future would mean the absence of room for existence. It thus follows that mountains and seas can both be perceived as time.

When Dōgen expresses his logic through the new concept embodied by his phrase, "the present moment," the received impression is of moving from the root to the equation. Simple calculation is fruitless, but careful thought given to the meaning of "the present moment" will yield the result that time and existence are equivalent. On a superficial level, this may seem a rapidly-reached announcement. Yet in fact it has an inexorably logical structure. We usually think of Zen as a sphere where people instantly grasp highly illogical language. The view is not mistaken so long as it concerns Rinzai Zen.[25] On the other hand, Sōtō Zen, which Dōgen

[25] The Rinzai (Ch. Lin-chi) school of Zen was founded by Lin-chi I-hsüan (d. 867). Rinzai discipline centers on grasping supralogical, instantaneous solutions to kōan (catechetic questions to contemplate during meditation). The Sōtō (Ch. Ts'ao-tung) school was founded by Tung-shan Liang-chieh (807-69) and Ts'ao-shan Pen-chi (840-901). Sōtō focuses on gradual attainment of enlightenment through the performance of everyday duties.

transmitted to Japan, has a logical framework resembling mathematics. Sōtō requires the kind of accumulated thought processes that go into patiently solving a set of simultaneous equations in two or more unknowns. Because the process is dispassionate, literary beauty is hard to find in *Shōbō Genzō*.

Beauty nevertheless exists there—the beauty appreciated by mathematicians when they call a solution or the left side of an equation "elegant." Dōgen's thought is unlike mathematical theory in one respect: he expresses a thought process through universally understood symbols and methods. Consider Dōgen's way of expressing great enlightenment: "The Morning Star appears, the Buddha comes into the world, eyeballs emerge, and a plucked flower is flung out." Shakyamuni, as is well known, attained Buddhahood while the Morning Star (Venus) glimmered in the east.[26] "The Buddha comes into the world" is also easily understood. The first two clauses thus present little difficulty. But the last two are extraordinary expressions. Attaining enlightenment means that the eyes of the mind have opened; to have "the eyeballs emerge," however, is odd. Similarly, "a plucked flower is flung out" seems a most unreasonable way to refer to the story of the disciple who smiled when the Buddha plucked a flower—a story that signifies the complete transmission of enlightenment.[27]

Dōgen's practice of creating new expressions that press toward the immoderate reflects his view that truth does not live unless it is framed in one's very own language. If, on receiving a problem from his master, Dōgen had solved it in meditation and then told his master the answer in already existing language, he would certainly have been met with a negative reaction. His master would have remained silent and driven Dōgen from the room, scolded him sharply, or struck him with a staff. Enlightenment is experienced when it is expressed in one's own unique way. That is why Dōgen always uses his own language in important passages of his writings. The practice was characteristic not only of Zen. It was also common among the new schools of Buddhism that appeared in the thirteenth century. Shinran (1173-1262) gives the following answer to a believer who has traveled from eastern Japan to the capital to ask the great master what he must do to attain salvation and enter paradise.

There are no kōan. The "Zen Buddhism" known in the West is Rinzai Zen as introduced by Suzuki Daisetsu (D. T. Suzuki).

[26] "The night was quiet as Venus rose. All—those with business and those with none—were still asleep. It was at this time that the Bhagavat attained enlightenment" (*Hongyōkyō [The Sūtra of Buddha's Life on Earth]*, 30:795). "Bhagavat" (virtuous man) is an honorific name for Shakyamuni.

[27] Once, while giving a sermon, Shakyamuni plucked a flower and showed it to his listeners. Everyone fell silent; only Mahā-Kāśyapa smiled. Shakyamuni told him, "I have transmitted the true dharma to you" (*Wu-men Kuan*, item 6:293).

"I shall answer from my own experience. I was blessed by the teachings of a great man.[28] He told me, 'All you need to do is chant the Buddha's Holy Name and pray for Amida's succor.' If you accept this, nothing else is necessary. I do not know whether chanting the Buddha's Name is indeed the pathway to rebirth in the Pure Land, or whether it is the deed that dooms one to Hell. But even if the saintly Hōnen has given me false advice and I am cast into Hell for chanting the Holy Name, I shall not regret the consequences." (*Tannishō*, 193)

Shinran stresses that chanting the Buddha's Name is the requisite for salvation. This is the supreme dogma for believers of Pure Land (Jōdo) Buddhism. Had anyone but the great Shinran therefore uttered the above paradox—that he does not know if chanting the Buddha's Name will ensure salvation—it would surely be seen as falsehood. Shinran's radical paradox matches his famous dictum, "Even the virtuous will reach paradise; how much more is this true for the wicked!"[29] Scholars of Jōdo Shinshū have variously interpreted and explained these declarations in order to justify the implied defiance of the basic Buddhist principle that good acts yield good results and bad acts, evil results. The more successful these scholarly efforts, the more lifeless Shinran's vast religious experience becomes. We can strongly perceive Shinran's unique way of expressing himself only when we confront his writings without commentary.

The names of Dōgen and Shinran are clearly linked to their declarations. But attribution was not necessary: anonymous recluses joined Dōgen and Shinran in declaring that the living truth must be expressed in one's own words. *Ichigon Hōdan*, the collection of anonymous declarations, attributes each statement to "a certain man."[30] These declarations also are framed in language peculiar to each recluse.

In contemplating salvation, make your thoughts like a spear that pierces the heart of a beast. (1:186)

Working for salvation is like working in the world. When the day nears its end, time slips by quickly although one is no longer working. Suddenly the year has been frittered away; your life will pass just as easily. When you lie down at night, lament how you have let things go by. At dawn, awake and vow to worship the Buddha all day long. (2:202)

[28] Shinran refers to his religious master, Hōnen (1133-1212).

[29] *Tannishō*, 193.

[30] *Ichigon Hōdan* was compiled anonymously around the year 1300. It is principally a collection of statements made by recluses who have severed all bonds with the secular world and who perceive that salvation consists of a peaceful death.

> The essence of turning away from the world is—smoke trailing off into faint wisps. (2:204)
>
> Do not be covetous. Although it is easy to accumulate things, it is far more important to leave them behind. (2:206)
>
> Those who set their minds on salvation stop doing as they please, because the human heart desires only evil things. (2:214)

The narrative style of the second passage is reminiscent of the *Tsurezuregusa* (*Essays in Idleness*) of Yoshida Kenkō.[31] Nevertheless, the speaker in *Ichigon Hōdan* is striving for individual expression. Another characteristic the anonymous recluses share with Dōgen is the basing of their assertions on a reasoning process. Theirs naturally differ from Dōgen's. Where his structure will yield a solution when pushed to its logical limits, the anonymous recluses' assertions often omit logic. They never distance themselves from reasoning, however. Shinran's paradoxes seem to transcend logic. They are like equations using complex numbers that appear anomalous only if Dōgen's real-number logic is our criterion. Yet both are equations.

Setsuwa and Recited Narratives

The Evolution of Public Buddhist Services

The public Buddhist services celebrated in twelfth-century Japan probably followed the same basic form as the T'ang popular services (su-chiang) brought from the continent by Ennin and later Japanese monks. Thus tenth-century Japanese services may also have resembled the Chinese form (see ch. 4). Although the service had some entertainment value for its audience, it was perceived as a solemn ceremony by those who performed it.[32] We know from Ennin's record of his experiences in China that the T'ang popular services were strongly bound by etiquette, despite their "popular" nature. A change in attitude occurred in Japan around the end of the twelfth century. As Kokan Shiren states in his *Genkō Shakusho*,

> Public Buddhist services: . . . In the Chishō and Yōwa eras [1177-82], the monk Chōken preached. His sermons were based on scholarship transmitted by his father, the minor counselor, and on the teaching methods used by his erudite Buddhist master.[33] His wide learning, which illumined Confucian scholarly circles, was splendid

[31] An example is in *Tsurezuregusa*, dan 189:227. [Note abbreviated—Ed.]

[32] See ch. 4, n. 18.

[33] "The minor counselor" refers to Fujiwara Michinori (1106-59).

as a flower in full bloom. Knowledge came from his lips like water from a bubbling spring. No sooner did he mount the pulpit stairs than all hearkened carefully. As Chōken did not keep the commandments in his later years, he fathered children. His eldest son, Shōgaku, was as talented as Chōken; he undertook to direct public Buddhist services. The family had able successors from Shōgaku through several later generations. Shōgaku was succeeded by his son Ryūshō, Ryūshō was succeeded by his son Kenjitsu, and Kenjitsu was succeeded by his son Kenki. The court, grateful for the family's many contributions to the enlightenment of the people, chose to overlook their relations with women. That is why there were so many descendants. A man called Jōen lived during the Kangen era [1243-47]. He was a monk attached to the temple of Onjōji. Jōen was a brilliant speaker who, like Chōken, founded a line of preachers. Anyone today who is known for his sermons has received instructions from either Chōken's or Jōen's school.

Because good preaching presents difficult philosophical systems in easily understood terms, enlightens and instructs us on several levels, moves countless people, and clears paths on which we would otherwise stumble, its effects are wide-ranging and its influence splendid. Nothing is more beneficent than preaching. Unfortunately, as soon as a monk begins to reap financial gain from his sermons, he is likely to forsake the pursuit of truth. When a fortuneteller's livelihood depends on predicting the time of a man's death, his accuracy will falter, because thoughts of gain interfere with his inspiration. So it is with preachers. Those today speak only of what interests their audience. They put on odd performances, shaking their heads and bodies and making their voices sound seductive. Although their sermons are replete with parallelism, the content is either maudlin or laudatory. The sponsor of the service is always mentioned, together with a guarantee that he or she will be enriched by the Buddha. Preachers make such strong appeals to the emotions that they are often quicker than the audience to weep at their own anecdotes. How shameful it is that the transmission of pure Truth has become degraded to an art practiced by deceitful actors! (29:433-34)

The passage, itself a slice of medieval literary history, needs little restating. The severe criticism of latter-day preachers' histrionics is a valuable indication of the changes undergone by public Buddhist services over the centuries.

Kokan Shiren (1278-1346) was born too late to witness Chōken's and Shōgaku's sermons. When he writes of "shaking their heads and bodies and making their voices sound seductive," Kokan is describing services as they existed in the late thirteenth century. The art of histrionic sermonizing, however, very likely began in Chōken's and Shōgaku's day. A descendant of the medieval public Buddhist service, the fushidan sekkyō, barely survives today. Up to the first part of this century, it was a flourishing form preached by its many adepts in a highly emotional style.[34] Although Chōken and Kokan are separated by about a century, we may assume that the narrative style employed in the sermons of both periods was essentially the same. When the public Buddhist service, originally celebrated by Buddhist monks for the general good, evolved into a professional activity, sermons began to be preached in a histrionic manner. In his *Essays in Idleness*, Yoshida Kenkō describes how a man hoping to set himself up as a preacher takes lessons in singing popular songs so that, when invited to a sponsor's house, he will have some talent to contribute to the drinking party that follows the service (*Tsurezuregusa*, dan 188:224). Preaching, then, was well on its way to becoming professional entertainment by the early fourteenth century. Kokan and his fellow Zen monks found this cause for great lamentation. In terms of the history of entertainment, on the other hand, this trend means nothing more than that a new kind of diversion had appeared: the public Buddhist service.

The transformation that occurred in public Buddhist services around the turn of the thirteenth century set them apart from services of the past. The earlier services should therefore be treated separately from those middle-period services that commence with Chōken's time. Yet another turning point occurred in public Buddhist services at the end of the fourteenth century. This resulted in what may be called the late period of Buddhist services, characterized by the lower social class and provincial origin of their preachers and officiants. There is, however, no distinct dividing line between middle- and late-period services. Thirteenth-century services were performed by men who were thoroughly trained in kangaku, the curriculum of Chinese studies. Kokan takes considerable pains to point out that Chōken followed in the footsteps of his father, the eminent scholar Fujiwara Michinori. The erudition of thirteenth-century preachers led to the compilation of a great many compendia of sponsors' statements and formal Buddhist prayers. These works contained much prose that could be written only by the erudite. Contemporary public Buddhist services were thus probably performed with the same solemn ceremony as those in the early period.

The histrionics condemned by Kokan may have appeared chiefly in the anecdotal parts of the sermon. Collections of sponsors' statements and

[34] Fushidan sekkyō were narrated in a style that strongly appealed to the audience's emotions (Sekiyama, 1978, 25-31).

formal prayers had largely ceased to appear by the late fourteenth century. The statements and prayers themselves continued to be composed, of course, but their quantity declined radically. Engi, legends explaining the origin of a ceremony or religious institution, developed rapidly in place of the more formal compositions.[35] This phenomenon reflects the evolution undergone by public Buddhist services: the old, formal variety sponsored in the capital by aristocrats and royalty was giving way to services commissioned on an ad hoc basis by provincial shrines or temples. The former situation demanded polished, individualized sponsors' statements and formal prayers to declare to the public the requests and eminence of the sponsor. Such elements were only a matter of form in the latter case. What was important in a provincial service was to tell everyone about the august provenance of the shrine or temple and the marvelous miracles that had occurred there. The legends were very likely told in those parts of the sermon that originally contained illustrative anecdotes (hiyu) and stories of the buddhas' and bodhisattvas' previous existences (innen).

The nature of the sponsor distinguishes middle-period services from late ones: the former were sponsored predominantly by individuals, while provincial shrines and temples were the chief sponsors of the latter. The boundary between the two periods is not easily determined. Public Buddhist services are believed to have occurred at provincial shrines and temples as early as the thirteenth century; a few collections of legends describing origins of shrines, temples, and ceremonies also survive from this period. Sermons apparently retained their traditional form into and beyond the fourteenth century, moreover. The nō play *Jinen Koji* depicts its protagonist, the preacher Jinen Koji, offering a public Buddhist service to raise funds for the reconstruction of his temple, Ungoji.[36] The play probably reflects an actual contemporary situation. The service itself seems to correspond roughly to the format described in the thirteenth-century *Hossokushū* (see ch. 4).

The middle and late periods thus cannot be distinguished solely by whether a service occurs in the provinces or the capital. Yet, the two periods clearly differ in the social standing and educational level of their preachers. Chōken's and Shōgaku's relations with women were tolerated by the court, an indication that these preachers enjoyed a special status freeing them from the strictures of celibacy. Preachers in the late period

[35] Two examples are *Kogawadera Engi* and *Hachimangūji Jumpaiki*. I use the term "engi" (stories about the history of shrines, temples, or ceremonies) to refer to works on the subject that are written in the mixed style. I do not include works on the subject that are written in Chinese prose.

[36] Jinen Koji, a historical figure, was a disciple of Mukan Fumon (1212-91) and lived at the temple Ungoji (*Nihon Meisōden*, 437).

did not obtain similar status, nor were they erudite. We shall see below that middle-period services are linked to the composition process of *The Tale of the Heike*, just as late-period services are connected to the composition of the *Soga Monogatari* and the *Gikeiki*. The different levels of learning displayed in services from the middle and late periods had a considerable influence on the quality of these three works.

Although public Buddhist services in their earliest period had little that was entertaining, setsuwa (traditional stories) evolved from the anecdotes and pious stories told during sermons and eventually found their way into setsuwa collections. The collections probably originated as source books for preachers seeking likely anecdotes for their sermons. Setsuwa collections also gave a more general audience the opportunity to read stories that usually appeared only in recited form. There is a similar connection between public Buddhist services and setsuwa in both the middle and late periods.

Another phenomenon not found in the early period is the creation of a new genre, the katarimono (recited narrative). A katarimono contains two kinds of narrative, one recited to musical accompaniment and another which is not. The musical accompaniment is tuned but has no time measure. The texts of the *Heike*, the *Hōgen Monogatari*, and the *Heiji Monogatari* are all recited narratives performed to biwa accompaniment. The *Soga Monogatari* was once a recited narrative as well, although we know little of how it was performed. We can only conjecture that the *Gikeiki* was recited; there is no evidence that in fact it was.

Recited narrative stands in opposition to utaimono, or sung texts. The text of the latter, sung to measured musical accompaniment, is not chiefly narrative. Recited narrative and sung texts also differ in their respective styles of musical accompaniment. The emotional content present in the text of a recited narrative is expressed through the voice of the reciter, but in sung texts there is no direct translation of emotion from libretto to melody or voice. The stylistic difference can be better understood when we recall that the evolution of the recited narrative is linked to public Buddhist services. It will be recalled that the monk Kokan found the popular services of his day to be overly emotional. The histrionic influence of public Buddhist services on recited narrative extends even to the style of its musical accompaniment.

The recited narratives that emerged from the latest period of public Buddhist services may be subdivided into hikigatari and sugatari. Hikigatari designates genres like jōruri (various popular entertainments) that are sung to tuned accompaniment on biwa and (later) shamisen. Sugatari refers to genres like kōwaka bukyoku (accompanied warrior mime) in which a decorative rhythmic accompaniment (by hand drum or fan) is unrelated to the actual time measure.[37] Nō performances present a skillful synthesis of recited narrative and sung texts. The nō presentation is accompanied by a musical accompaniment consisting of flute, small hand drum, large hand drum, and occasionally floor drum. The flute carries the melody. The drums perform two functions: they beat time in sections with a time measure and provide a decorative beat in unmeasured parts of the play. The corresponding text consists of songlike sections performed in meter of syllabic sevens and fives and chanted lines following an indeterminate syllabic meter. Nō is, however, more than a mixture of recited narrative and song. It is, essentially, a synthesis tending more strongly toward the sung text. Like the sung text, nō never directly translates the emotion in the text into musical or vocal treatment. We are speaking only of nō performed today, of course. We cannot know how it was performed in its earliest period.

Recited narrative, as we have seen, is divided into parts performed to musical accompaniment and parts that are not. This is important. From heikyoku (recitations drawn from the text of the *Heike*) and nō libretti through the many kinds of jōruri down to the naniwabushi (various kinds of recitations accompanied by shamisen) of the late nineteenth century, all recited narrative contains sections with musical accompaniment as well as others that are unaccompanied. This is certainly due to the influence—whether direct or indirect—of anecdotes told during public Buddhist services (Konishi, 1960c, 103-108). Its influence is particularly marked in *Heike* recitation. That its musical accompaniment is derived from shōmyō (Buddhist chant) is most naturally explained by concluding that the libretto was composed by an officiant of public Buddhist services.

Nō presents a somewhat different case. Nō as it is known today was incorporated into its parent, sarugaku, around the end of the thirteenth century (see ch. 18). Prior to this point, sarugaku seems to have been much like conventional spoken drama. Preachers who were associated with provincial shrines and temples probably created the nō prototype, a fixed form consisting of accompanied and unaccompanied parts. The public Buddhist service in its most basic form is, in any case, the ultimate source of two-form recited narratives. The genesis of recited narrative cannot be considered apart from the public Buddhist service.

The T'ang version of the public Buddhist service, imported by Ennin and other Japanese monks studying in China, is the basic form as it was known in Japan. In China as in Japan, public Buddhist services gave rise to literary phenomena. Pien-wen (prosimetric, semicolloquial tales) are, in effect, scripts for public Buddhist sermons. With few exceptions, the

[37] My use of "sugatari" is for convenience. [Usually it refers to the combination of shamisen and other jōruri elements.—Ed.]

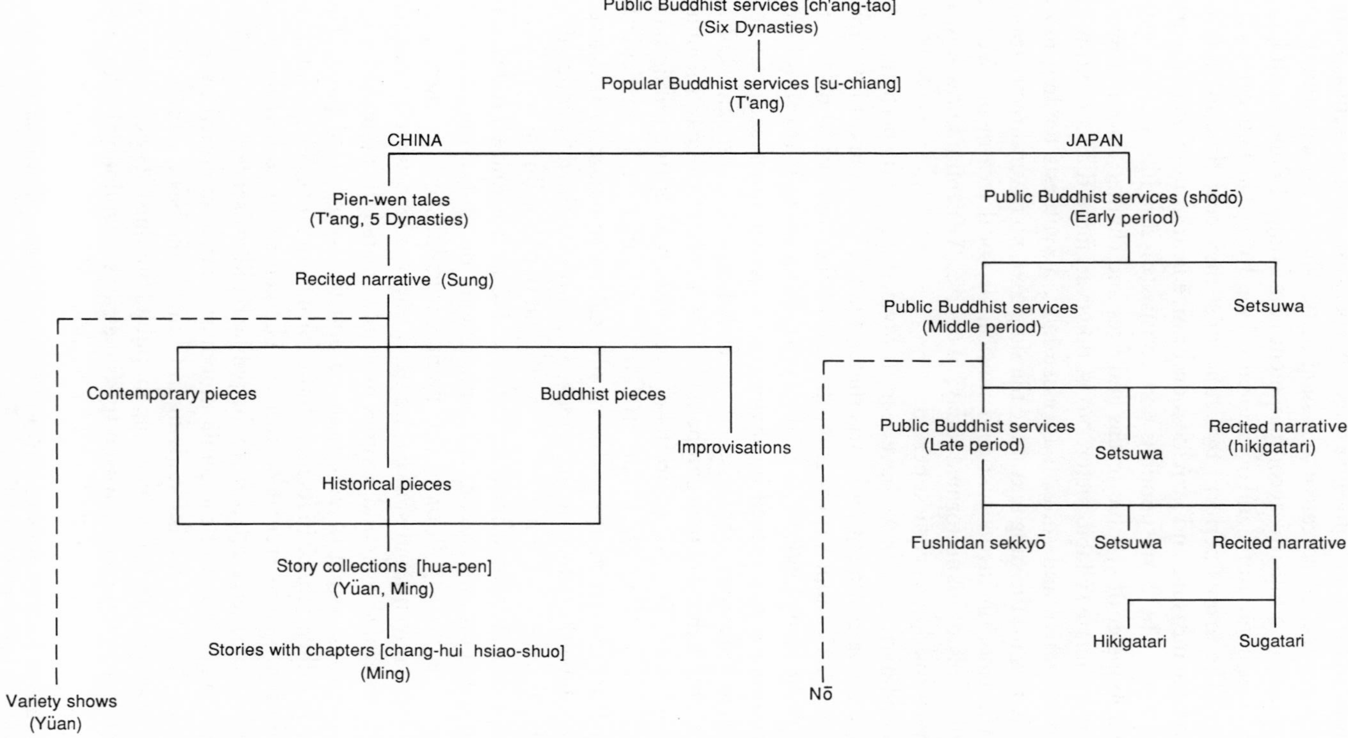

FIGURE 11.1 Public Buddhist Services and Their Descendants

basic form of a pien-wen tale is twofold: parts recited to musical accompaniment are called "yin," and unaccompanied parts are called "pai."[38] A later genre, the recited narrative (shuo-hua) of the Sung period, has a similar form. In the capital cities of the Northern and Southern Sung dynasties, Pien-ching and Lin-an respectively, entertainment districts contained variety halls (wa-she) in which recited narrative was performed.[39]

Roughly speaking, there are four kinds of Chinese recited narrative: historical pieces (chiang-shih), contemporary pieces (hsiao-shuo), Buddhist pieces (hun-ching), and improvisations (ho-sheng). Each kind was performed in its own makeshift theatre. Nothing is known of their performance methods. Orally recited narratives were set down in writing in the Yüan and Ming periods. These story collections (hua-pen, meaning "prompt books") enable us to make limited deductions about recited narratives of the Sung period. Historical pieces (also called chiang-shih-shu and yen-shih) were the most popular variety during the Northern Sung. Two such narratives were so popular that they became independent subgenres: one dealt with the Three Kingdoms period, and the other with the Five Dynasties. They survive in the early Yüan compendia *Ch'üan-hsiang P'ing-hua* (in five versions), the *Hsin-pien Wu-tai-shih P'ing-hua*, and the *Ta-Sung Hsüan-hua I-shih*. These works suggest that the historical narratives involved prose passages interspersed with singing. The Ming-period *San-Sui P'ing-yao Chuan* includes the story of a woman named Hu Mei-erh who calls in a storyteller to relieve her boredom.[40] The man begins to recite (*P'ing-yao Chuan*, 15:101):

> The blind man Ch'ü thereupon cleared his throat, struck the table one smart blow with his baton, chanted a quatrain for his preface, and then moved into the main story. He told the tale of King Chou and Ta, his consort. . . . When the story was over, he chanted another quatrain.
>
> Everyone says His Majesty dearly loves Consort Ta,
> But no one knows she is in fact a fox-spirit in disguise.
> Crafty and wise a fox may be, but is she any match
> For those resourceful mortals, the empresses Lü and Wu?[41]

[38] A few pien-wen tales are written entirely in verse, such as "Shun-tzu Chih-hsiao Pien-wen." There are also a very few pien-wen written entirely in prose, like "Liu-chia T'ai-tzu Pien." The essence of pien-wen is their composite form (Hu S., 1980, 33).

[39] "Wa-she" (variety halls) were also called "wa-tzu," "wa-shih," and "wa-ssu." The meaning evolved from the idea of designating a special place in a district where people gathered for entertainment.

[40] *San-Sui P'ing-yao Chuan* was originally attributed to Lo Kuan-chung. The title may apply to a book in twenty rounds in the Tenri Library collection. The widely circulated text, in forty rounds, is said to have been expanded by Shih Nai-an. I quote from the latter work.

[41] Empress Lü lived in the Han dynasty, Empress Wu Tse-t'ien in the T'ang. Both women attained supreme political power. The last two lines state that Consort Ta may be a fox-

The story in *San-Sui P'ing-yao Chuan* is set in the Sung period. Although we cannot be certain that such a historical tale was told as described above, the account is nevertheless useful as a description of Ming or even earlier conditions. Recited narrative flourished during the Southern Sung. Only Ming examples survive, among them *Ching-pen T'ung-su Hsiao-shuo*, a collection displaying characteristics of the genre as it existed in the Southern Sung; it follows a form in which prose recitative is interspersed with song.[42]

The Buddhist pieces (hun-ching) have great significance when we consider why the song-and-prose format, original to pien-wen tales, was incorporated into recited narrative. The Buddhist pieces are humorous tales (Hu S., 1980, 114-18). These works appear in the *Ta-T'ang San-tsang Ch'ü-ching Shih-hua*.[43] It may seem strange to have Buddhist narratives performed in variety halls. The presence of Buddhist pieces on the bill of entertainment must have been due to the long-standing connection between recited narrative and popular Buddhist services. During the Sung period, variety halls were located in entertainment districts and produced all kinds of acts—collectively called tsa-chi, or variety shows—in addition to recited narratives. Similar variety shows were performed in temple precincts during the T'ang period.

The move to urban entertainment districts took place during the Sung. Recited narratives certainly evolved when the illustrative anecdotes used in sermons were made somewhat more worldly and so turned into temple entertainment. It follows that recited narratives would draw often on Buddhist subjects as well as perpetuating the song-and-prose format of public Buddhist services. The humorous Buddhist pieces continued to be performed as before, even after historical and contemporary narratives became popular. The continuing popularity of Buddhist pieces was due to factors similar to those motivating Japanese setsuwa to retain large elements of Buddhist subject matter.

Chinese recited narrative was originally short. Subject matter was broadened and the texts lengthened during the Ming period. The expanded stories are still punctuated at a certain stage by units called "rounds" (hui), perhaps to evoke the original, orally-recited stories found in the older story collections. Long, punctuated stories were called "sto-

---

spirit, but she still cannot compete with mortal power-holders like the above two empresses. The story is probably a version of "Wu-wang Fa Chou P'ing-hua" ("The Story of How King Wu Subjugated King Chou"—one of five kinds of illustrated story).

[42] The *Ching-pen T'ung-su Hsiao-shuo* is said to be a compendium of Southern Sung tale collections. Books 10-16 were reissued by Miao Ch'üan-sun (1844-1919). The original number of books in the collection is unknown.

[43] According to the colophon to *Ta-T'ang San-tsang Ch'ü-ching Shih-hua*, "Published by the House of Chang in Middle Wa-tzu," the work is a Sung composition. This is the accepted opinion. It is more likely of Yüan date, however, since the House of Chang (a bookstore in Lin-an) was also in business during the Yüan period (Kuo C., 1939, 159-60).

ries with chapters" (chang-hui hsiao-shuo). We know that these stories originated from the collections called hua-pen because both groups share certain raw material. There are, for example, material correspondences between *San-kuo Chih P'ing-hua*[44] and *San-kuo Chih Yen-i*, between *Ta-Sung Hsüan-hua I-shih*[45] and *Chung-i Shui-hu Chuan*, and between *Ta-T'ang San-tsang Ch'ü-ching Shih-hua* and *Hsi-yu Chi*. Japanese setsuwa did not undergo expansion, probably because of the native preference for brevity of form (see vol. 1, General Introduction). Japanese began expanding stories in the eighteenth century, when Chinese "stories with chapters" were first imported.

Another noteworthy aspect of the Chinese recited narrative is that its song-and-prose form was incorporated into tsa-chi, variety shows. True to its name, the variety show is a melange of singing, spoken lines, and acting. Although it differs from Western opera, it corresponds closely to nō. A theory in circulation since the eighteenth century postulates that nō evolved when Japanese monks studying in Yüan China saw variety shows and, on returning to Japan, had actors imitate what the monks had seen. A few scholars still seriously support this view (Shionoya, 1938, 7-10). Nō, however, had already consolidated itself by the later fourteenth century, when large numbers of Japanese monks went to China for study. There is thus a chronological contradiction in the theory. All the same, the variety show and nō are curiously alike. Like nō, the variety show did not evolve from the public Buddhist service, but apparently was developed from theatrical forms that had existed well before, gradually assuming the form of conventional drama. One could trace this development to the foreign source of the public Buddhist service form that Ennin and other monks imported from T'ang China. Both did combine chanting and speaking. But it really was without any relation of influence that there later followed in both countries the kind of analogous results just described (Konishi, 1948, 482-83). Although in the genres of both countries we find the same fundamental features, the specific analogous phenomena were spread out over a number of centuries. Popular Buddhist services and their developments in the two countries offer rich material for comparative literary study.

Setsuwa and Public Buddhist Services of the Middle Period

We have seen the role played by public Buddhist services in the evolution of setsuwa. It may be a natural consequence that performing elements

[44] One of the five kinds of illustrated story.

[45] Said to be a Sung work. It seems to have Yüan accretions and revisions (Yüeh, 1969, 159-63).

survive in some quantity in the narrative style of setsuwa. A noteworthy development was the growing tendency away from listening to recited setsuwa and toward reading them in one of the many collections that appeared in the thirteenth and fourteenth centuries. The preference for reading over listening to a narrated setsuwa has a bearing on the gradual process by which setsuwa, originally a zoku genre, became characterized by ga. Eighty-four of the 197 setsuwa in *Uji Shūi Monogatari (A Collection of Tales from Uji)* also appear in similar form in the earlier *Konjaku Monogatari Shū (Tales of Times Now Past)*.[46] The eighty-four stories thus make excellent subjects for comparison. Let us consider one such setsuwa, the story of Toshihito and the attendant of the Fifth Rank who would like to eat his fill of yam gruel. The setsuwa is well known because Akutagawa Ryūnosuke drew on it for his story "Imogayu" ("Yam Gruel").[47] The two setsuwa versions begin as follows.

From *Tales of Times Now Past*:

> In a time now past there was a man known as General Toshihito. In his youth, he was called [lacuna in text]. He faithfully served the most eminent man of the day. Because Toshihito was the son-in-law of [lacuna in text] Arihito, a powerful man in Echizen province, he spent all his time there. At New Year's, his lord the Chancellor gave a great banquet—in those days, after the New Year's banquet was over, his lordship would have the beggars driven out, not admitting them onto the premises, so that food left over from the feast was given instead to the lord's attendants—where one of the guests at the banquet was an attendant holding the fifth court rank and who, after long years of faithful service, had been favored by his lord. (*KMS*, 26:458)

From *A Collection of Tales from Uji*:

> Long ago, when General Toshihito was a youth, he faithfully served the most eminent man of the day, the Lord Chancellor, who gave a New Year's banquet—in those days, when the New Year's banquet was over the chancellor forbade beggars admission to the premises to eat up the leavings, which were eaten by the retainers who had been doing the serving—and among the retainers in the house was an attendant holding the fifth court rank whose long record of service earned him the favor of his lord. (*Uji*, 1:78)[48]

Where the version from *Tales of Times Now Past* proceeds by ascertaining one fact after another, the story in *Tales from Uji* is told as a coherent

[46] The compiler and the date of *Uji Shūi Monogatari* are unknown. The work was completed between the late twelfth and mid-thirteenth centuries.

[47] *Akutagawa Ryūnosuke Zenshū*, 1 (Iwanami Shoten, 1977):203-26.

[48] [Adapted from Mills, 1970, 155.—Trans.]

whole. This is evident from the fact that the former version consists of five sentences in the original text while the latter consists of only one sentence. Of course a work intended to be read is defined by more than the length of its sentences. Nevertheless, stories that are orally performed and aurally received tend to avoid long sentences, since narration must communicate who is doing what in easily understood fashion.

Tales from Uji also reveals, in the design of its subplots, a strong tendency toward visual reception. In the example given above, the *Uji* version leaves out the explanation in *Tales of Times Now Past* that Toshihito "spent all his time" in the province of Echizen. The *Uji* version omits this detail not because it is superfluous, but because it is more effective if, later in the story, the attendant of the fifth rank suddenly learns that he is being taken to Echizen to eat his fill of yam gruel. Early in the story, Toshihito overhears the attendant grumble that for once he'd like to eat as much yam gruel as he wants. Toshihito promises that he will grant the man's desire. One day, he invites the attendant to go with him to a bathhouse. The attendant, assuming that the bathhouse is nearby, agrees. When they have passed through Yamashina and crossed Mt. Ōsaka, the attendant asks Toshihito where they are going. Toshihito replies that he is taking him to Tsuruga in far Echizen. The mention of Tsuruga at this point in the story surprises the reader as much as the attendant of the fifth rank. The intended surprise effect is the reason why nothing is said at the beginning of the story about Toshihito spending all his time in Echizen. The technique is effective when the story is read, because a reader has time to take in the structure of the entire story.

Another technique concerns the psychology of the characters in the story. The *Uji* version does not discuss it explicitly, preferring instead to suggest it to the reader. Again, the effect may not come off unless the story is read. When the attendant of the fifth rank learns he is on his way to Tsuruga, he remarks that, had he known he was going so far, he would have brought servants with him. Toshihito derides his companion, claiming that he, Toshihito, is as strong as a thousand men. The version in *Tales of Times Now Past* begins this part of the story with the attendant of the fifth rank grumbling and fussing at Toshihito:

> "What a madman you are! If you had told me this back in the city, I would have known to bring along some manservants. How can I make such a long journey without a single servant?" So he spoke in his fear. (*KMS*, 26:459)

This explains why Toshihito mocks the attendant. The latter is frightened because provincial roads were poorly patrolled and extremely dangerous during this period. The compiler of *Tales from Uji*, on the other hand, probably did not anticipate a readership so unsophisticated as to need to be told that the attendant's cowardice is the object of Toshihito's derision. In this respect, *Tales of Times Now Past* reflects a larger degree of influence from public Buddhist services. Preachers who habitually addressed large audiences made up of all kinds of people would have known that many would not be able to understand a story without detailed explanation, while others would understand certain matters without being told explicitly.

Ga literature is not only predicated on purely visual reception but also on interest in sensing things left unstated in a text. Setsuwa collections display a tendency toward the ga aesthetic in structure as well as in narration. *Kokon Chomonjū (Collection of Early and Recent Famous Tales)* is one example.[49] The title is probably modeled after the *Kokin Wakashū (Collection of Early and Recent Japanese Poetry)*, the full title of the first royally commissioned waka anthology. Both works are divided into twenty parts, begin with a Chinese preface and end with a preface written in Japanese,[50] and are arranged according to unified principles.[51] Setsuwa concerning poetry, music, dancing, and singing can easily be narrated in a ga manner, but stories dealing with earthier or seamier sides of urban life—gambling, robbery, satisfying old grudges, fighting, eating, and drinking—cannot and tend toward the zoku. The lower setsuwa were probably regarded in the same fashion that hikaika and renga [i.e., tanrenga, not long, codified renga] were in royal waka anthologies.

These resemblances illustrate how setsuwa became an acknowledged literary genre. Not a few setsuwa collections existed prior to the thirteenth century. They, however, were never regarded as a genre on a par with royal waka anthologies, nor did they employ the kind of narrative devices used in Japanese prose nikki and monogatari. Needless to say, setsuwa could never attain a level of ga commensurate with that of waka; at best they attained the status of a ga-zoku genre. Its emergence as a literary genre nevertheless demonstrates that the ideal of michi had finally reached maturity. The concept that even lowly acts contain lofty philosophy is embodied in the literary setsuwa collection (see ch. 5).

The evolution of setsuwa toward ga is a noteworthy event in thirteenth-century Japanese literary history. Despite this trend, however, setsuwa—

[49] *Kokon Chomonjū* was compiled by Tachibana Narisue (d. 1272). According to the Preface, the work was completed in 1254.

[50] The surviving version of *Kokon Chomonjū* situates the Japanese Preface somewhat before the end of the last fascicle. At some point after the work was completed, five additional stories were appended to the end of *Kokon Chomonjū*. This accretion moved the preface from its original location (the end of the work) to its present one. [Of the five characters used for the title of the work, the first two and the last can also be read "Kokinshū," and like the *Kokon Chomonjū*, *Kokin Wakashū* has two characters between the first two and the fifth—hence the author's comments on the title.—Ed.]

[51] The twenty parts of the *Kokon Chomonjū* are classified—Shinto Deities, Buddhism, Plants and Trees, Fish and Insects, etc.—and each part is arranged in chronological order, so giving the work an integration like that of the *Kokinshū*.

which first emerged from illustrative anecdotes told during a zoku event, the public Buddhist service—retained much of their original nature. One such characteristic is arbitrariness. A setsuwa does not have unified narration: different parts of it are told in differing ways. Over the centuries, moreover, a setsuwa collection often acquires stories that were not present in the original collection. Stories of similar content exist among setsuwa collections from the thirteenth and even earlier centuries. Such stories generally share a central motif and plot but differ substantially in details. The story of Toshihito and the yam gruel is an exceptional case: the compiler of *Tales from Uji* probably drew directly on *Tales of Times Now Past* for the story. It is more usual for substantial variants to appear among setsuwa that tell essentially the same story. There is, moreover, considerable fluctuation in the number of setsuwa in a collection and in their configuration within a collection. Taira Yasuyori's *Hōbutsushū*, for example, exists in versions of one, two, three, seven, and nine fascicles.

The different texts cannot be explained by concluding that the collection grew from an original single-fascicle text to one consisting of nine.[52] Kamo no Chōmei's *Hosshinshū* survives in versions of five and eight fascicles, but neither matches the form taken originally by the collection.[53] Because changes in structure are principally matters of quantitative fluctuation of, and changes in, story units, the number of variant texts is enormous. Variants in narratives and fluctuations in the number of setsuwa are probably phenomena influenced by public Buddhist services, which reached the height of their popularity during the period in which setsuwa collections were compiled. The illustrative anecdotes used by preachers were essentially auxiliary means of clarifying the point of a sermon and could thus be varied at pleasure. Regular members of the audience probably welcomed an occasional variation. The anecdotal origin of setsuwa cannot be considered apart from an accompanying assumption that it was permissible to alter anecdotes. This is the apparent reason why thirteenth-century setsuwa collections contain so many radically emended versions.[54]

A second major link between setsuwa and public Buddhist services is an emphasis on edification. Since sermons were preached to edify the laity, the anecdotes used in sermons had to be didactic as well as interesting.

[52] Although the seven- and nine-fascicle versions of *Hōbutsushū* are organized differently, the texts belong to the same family. Their common ancestor was probably compiled before the Jōō era (1222-24; Koizumi, 1973, 269-85).

[53] The *Honchō Shojaku Mokuroku* lists *Hosshinshū* as having three fascicles. This may have been its original form (Yanase, 1938, 35-41).

[54] A variant manuscript (ihon) is a manuscript copy differing from the standard text because of variants unconsciously created during the copying process. An emended manuscript (idembon) displays conspicuous variants created by deliberate revision or emendation.

That is why stories in *Tales of Times Now Past* usually end with an appended moral (ch. 4). The practice was also observed in thirteenth-century setsuwa collections. Of course, collections like Mujū's (1226-1312) *Shasekishū (Sand and Pebbles)*[55] and *Zōtanshū* (*Casual Digressions*, 1305),[56] containing many stories of people edified by Buddhism, do not always have a moral appended to the conclusion. Such stories tend instead to contain morals imbedded within the main text.[57] The following opinion is stated in *Shasekishū* in the course of a five-part story about wives who successfully resist jealousy.

> Many women are serious victims of jealousy. A woman so afflicted will become enraged and suspicious, beat her husband's mistress to death, develop an ugly countenance, a flushed face, and glaring eyes, and will indulge in violent language. Such behavior only drives a husband farther away, for how can he feel affection for one who seems to have become a demon? She will end up either as a vengeful spirit or a serpent. Really, this is foolishness indeed! If, therefore, you study the example of thoughtful women of the past and learn to dispense the virtue of reverent love in this life, you will surely escape a future life of suffering in the World of Serpents. (*Shasekishū*, 7:294)

This passage could be an extract from a Buddhist essay if it were read free of its setsuwa context. Yet again, the text would seem quite at home in *Essays in Idleness*, were somewhat more profound thoughts stated in a more polished style. A similar phenomenon appears in an entire setsuwa collection, the *Jikkinshō*.[58] It has ten chapter titles, two examples of which are "Maintain a Stable Mental Outlook and Behavior" and "Avoid Haughtiness." Each title has a short preface explaining its import, followed by setsuwa chosen to match the didactic point of the chapter. What is worth noting here is that the edificatory nature of each setsuwa is not always confined to Buddhism, despite the Buddhist perspective emphasized by the general preface to the collection: "The book describes how to shun extravagance and promote a proper way of living. How can these goals not accord with the intent of Buddhism?" (*Jikkinshō*, Preface, 10). Some of its setsuwa contain Confucian morals, while others are simply based on common sense current in the society of the time. One especially good example is the chapter, "Strive to Excel in

[55] The *Shasekishū* was begun in the summer of 1279 and completed in the autumn of 1283. There are many emended versions of the *Shasekishū*, which does not survive in its original form.

[56] *Zōtanshū*, in ten fascicles, was completed in 1305.

[57] Jūshin's *Shishu Hyaku Innenshū* (completed in 1257) is an exception. It does not touch on edifying subjects.

[58] The compiler of *Jikkinshō* is unknown. According to the preface, the work was completed in 1252.

Scholarship or Art" (10:95-186). "Scholarship" refers to the Chinese curriculum, waka, and calligraphy, and "art" to the playing of string and wind instruments, the singing of such song kinds as imayō, rōei, kagura, and saibara, and the sport of kickball. The preface to the chapter summarizes the edificatory nature of the forthcoming setsuwa:

> Those born into a specialized house, as well as those who are not, have a certain amount of ability in accordance with natural gifts. Among such people are those disqualified by lack of accomplishment from assuming leadership of a house. Others not born into a specialized house have the good fortune and talent to reach the pinnacle of their profession. Thus those who would inherit the leadership of a house or rise to master an art must work hard. (10:95)

In other words, an artistic vocation—be it knowledge valued by society or an art ensuring no public recognition—is resolved into the Buddhist dharma, the universal cosmic principle. The artistic sphere widens in *Kokon Chomonjū* to include martial arts, horsemanship, sumō wrestling, and painting. Thirteenth-century sermons probably included frequent edifying remarks about these arts.

A third connection between setsuwa and public Buddhist services is the increased factualness of subject matter. The illustrative anecdotes used in sermons could touch on anything, so long as they held the interest of the audience. Unrealistic or fantastic stories were highly effective in certain cases and with certain audiences. As the average level of education rose in an audience, the preacher found it easier to drive home his moral and move his audience if he spoke of actual events known to them. It is a very natural process to treat such subject matter as if it were a real event. This explains why the secular setsuwa in *Tales of Times Now Past* are often made to give with care the time and place in which a story took place, as well as the means whereby it was transmitted. The practice reflects the trend toward realism in sermons. Factuality is an outstanding characteristic of thirteenth-century setsuwa collections in general, and Keisei's (1189-1268) *Kankyo no Tomo* in particular.[59] It is common practice in setsuwa to give the provenance of a story. Keisei sometimes serves as the witness of a story's origin:

> The story of the Reverend Seikai is supposed to be contained in *Shūi Ōjōden*,[60] but since I did not find it there, I wrote it down here. (*Kankyo*, 1:80-81)

> While in China I heard someone tell this story. (Ibid., 2:140)

[59] *Kankyo no Tomo* survives in its original form. It was written between 1216 and 1222 (Hirabayashi M., 1970, 35-46).

[60] Compiled by Miyoshi Tameyasu. See ch. 4, n. 14.

Real events form the subject matter for these setsuwa. A story was told essentially as it happened, allowing of course for some dramatization on the teller's part. Contemporary society abounded in such information. If it was shaped into a factual monogatari, the result was a work like the *Imakagami (The New Mirror)*; whereas *Fukegatari (Lord Fuke's Stories)* and *Chūgaishō (Notes on Matters Inside and Outside the Capital)* were the result of information presented in the form of a factual nikki. The incorporation of such information into setsuwa—producing what might be called factual setsuwa—was apparently achieved through the medium of public Buddhist services. One good example of a factual setsuwa is the story of a quiet journey to Ōhara made by the cloistered former sovereign Goshirakawa to visit the former royal consort Kenrei Mon'in, now a nun:

> Upon his arrival, His Majesty saw an old, shabby nun. He asked her, "Where might I find Her Majesty the cloistered consort?"
>
> The nun answered, "She has gone up into the hills to pick flowers." His Majesty was deeply moved by her words.
>
> "How can this be?" he asked. "She has indeed turned away from the world, but to perform such acts herself!" The nun replied. . . . (*Kankyo*, 2:146-49)

Despite the factual nature of Goshirakawa's visit to Ōhara, no one was likely to have been present to record this conversation between the former sovereign and the old nun. This is surely a dramatic embellishment added by a storyteller. The passage thus becomes a kind of setsuwa. During the thirty-six-year period between Goshirakawa's visit to Ōhara in 1186 and the completion of *Kankyo no Tomo* in 1222, the story underwent considerable changes as it evolved into setsuwa. Keisei himself writes of the story, "This account appears in documents that record matters pertaining to His Majesty [Goshirakawa]. It would seem that people were attracted to these matters and so wrote accounts of them" (*Kankyo*, 2:149). The story of Goshirakawa's journey quickly reached the level of written transmission. Specialists are well acquainted with linguistic similarities between the *Kankyo no Tomo* passage and the chapter entitled "Ōhara Gokō" ("The Royal Journey to Ōhara") in *The Tale of the Heike*. The relevant passage in one *Heike* manuscript line, the Enkei (6a:973-92), is known to have a particularly close relationship to Keisei's version (Asahara, 1970, 23-31). Although we do not know if both works are based on "documents that record matters pertaining to His Majesty," we can be sure that, by the early thirteenth century, written material existed that had made a setsuwa of the account of Goshirakawa's journey. This material was incorporated in written form by both *Kankyo no Tomo* and the *Heike*. If we consider this fact together with another, that preachers of public sermons contributed to the formative process of the *Heike*, we may conclude that such written material was very likely also available to preachers. It follows that a preacher could have been the author of the Ōhara setsuwa and the man who turned Goshirakawa's visit into setsuwa.

Recited Narratives and Public Buddhist Services of the Middle Period

One commonly identified genre in Japanese literature is the monogatari dealing with accounts of war or battles (gunki/senki monogatari). *The Tale of the Heike*, the *Taiheiki*, and the *Soga Monogatari* are thought the most prominent members of this genre. In spite of usual designations, however, none of these works can be said to contain a large proportion of battle scenes. Not a single battle in the *Soga Monogatari* provides a solution for the political problems depicted there. The *Gikeiki* culminates with the scene of Minamoto Yoshitsune's (1159-89) death in battle but completely ignores the most important event in Yoshitsune's life—the battle that destroyed the Heike. These works differ considerably, then, in nature from the meaning usually suggested by "war account" or "battle record." The *Heike*, of course, has many battle scenes; yet most of the text describes subjects quite distant from the warrior's life—political infighting, tragic love affairs, and stories centered on certain waka. The hallmark of these works is their historical content rather than an emphasis on battles. By "historical" I do not necessarily mean that they relate historical facts, but that such facts provide the raw material for fictionalized stories.

The stories thus resemble the historical narratives (chiang-shih) recited in Sung China. In both cases, the narratives were orally performed and aurally received. There is a great difference in subject matter between works like the *Heike Monogatari* and the *Taiheiki*—in which civil war becomes the only means of solving national political disputes—and other narratives like the *Soga Monogatari*, which are solely occupied with private vendettas. I shall term the former group "monogatari of war and peace" to differentiate it from the latter, "monogatari of private vengeance." The *Gikeiki* may be assigned to the latter category, since the battles depicted therein are not based on political claims.

MONOGATARI OF WAR AND PEACE: THE ISSUE OF MARTIAL HEROISM

A major characteristic of monogatari dealing with war and peace is that they depict war, the basic feature of military behavior, as nonetheless essentially oriented toward peace. There is no irony in the fact that the *Taiheiki (An Account of the Great Peace)* has the largest number of battle scenes of any work in the genre. The title reflects the theme of the narrative: peace on earth. The idea did not originate with the *Taiheiki*: it appears as early as the tenth century with *Shōmon Ki* (also titled *Masakado no Ki*; either way, *An Account of Masakado*). The author of the latter work regards the rebellious Masakado's destruction as "divine punishment" but also takes pains to point out that Masakado's insurrection was touched off by faulty provincial administration. *An Account of Masakado* is written from a historical viewpoint in which war and peace are presented as inextricably bound together. The *Mutsu Waki (An Account of the Mutsu Rebellion)*, written about 120 years later, also depicts war from the perspective of peace. The *Hōgen Monogatari* and *Heiji Monogatari* duplicated this treatment in the thirteenth century.

Because a historical point of view implies that facts are narrated from a rational perspective, monogatari so narrated are not likely to develop a style reminiscent of martial heroic poetry.[61] If there indeed exists a genre of monogatari concerned with warfare and battles, then its raw material should come from miscellaneous battle stories, just as waka narratives (utamonogatari) draw on oral waka stories. The author of the *Account of the Mutsu Rebellion*, for example, used several oral sources as well as documentary material.[62] Oral sources can easily veer from the original facts, even if they describe a very recent event. The desire to add interest to a story, moreover, often leads to the incorporation of fictional elements. Consequently, embellishing oral battle stories in Japan could potentially lead to the creation of a kind of battle story resembling Western heroic poetry. When the raw subject matter of a story is an actual, well-known event or series of events, the story cannot contradict central historical features without risking opposition from its audience. On the other hand, when an audience could not know details about historical characters, a storyteller would have a fairly free rein in filling out personalities. Idealized heroes, however, do not appear in *An Account of Masakado* or *An Account of the Mutsu Rebellion*.

The characters in the *Hōgen Monogatari (The Tale of the Hōgen War)* and the *Heiji Monogatari (The Tale of the Heiji War)* seem to be somewhat idealized. Characterization in these works, however, is extremely meager when compared with that in the *Chanson de Roland* and the *Niebelungenleid*. The protagonists of the *Hōgen* and *Heiji Monogatari* cer-

[61] Heroic poetry has not developed in highly intellectual societies. Individualism, unfettered by communal thoughts and emotions, flourishes in an intellectual society and hinders the heroic spirit. China and Israel are examples of countries that did not develop heroic poetry (Bowra, 1952, 12-15). Heroic poetry declines when it comes into contact with an advanced foreign culture (ibid., 537-39).

[62] *Mutsu Waki* concludes with the words, "This book, in one volume, is based on provincial government documents and information communicated orally by the people of the area" (*Mutsu*, 56).

tainly cannot be called heroes. In his *Gukanshō*, Jien records a passage in which the warrior Minamoto Tameyoshi explains to the former sovereign Sutoku why their forces are inferior to those of Toba, another former sovereign:

> "Our men have all gone with Yoshitomo to serve at the royal palace. I have only a couple of inconsequential fellows still with me. What good are they? If we were to wait for the enemy to attack your majesty's residence, things would surely not go well for us." (*Gukanshō*, 4:220)

Jien no doubt used reliable oral sources in writing this passage. The "couple of inconsequential fellows" mentioned by Tameyoshi are his own sons, Yorikata and Tametomo. Even if we allow for the customary practice of referring disparagingly to one's own children, there is still something artificial about calling Tametomo, famed for his valor, an "inconsequential fellow." Tametomo is famous for having led an insurrection in Kyushu.[63] That signifies only that he was an unmanageable ruffian, a man occupying a dimension other than that of the fully superior being. Tametomo becomes a superior being, however, in the *Hōgen Monogatari*:

> As for Tametomo, . . . not even the foulest demon or wickedest deity would wish to make him its enemy. His demeanor was of course imposing; . . . no man, past or present, could rival him in bravery or in martial arts. (*Hōgen*, Kotohira manuscript, 81-83)

Although the passage appears in several variant versions, Tametomo is presented in all cases as a superior being. Clearly the author was strongly motivated to idealize this character. Tametomo never develops into a true martial hero in the *Hōgen Monogatari*, however. He is only one of many commanders active in the battles described in the narrative, not the central character around whom the theme is built. If Tametomo bears no comparison to Roland and Siegfried, the villain Yoshihira in the *Heiji Monogatari* falls even shorter of the heroic prototype.

Tametomo and Yoshihira are not heroic martial figures because the battle scenes that are their center stage serve only as subplots. Both the *Hōgen* and *Heiji Monogatari* are focused on power struggles over royal succession. The civil war that erupts from this dispute is not the central issue of either work. That is, both give substantial, exhaustive explanations of the circumstances leading to and aggravating political strife. Clearly the envisioned audience was highly intelligent, and audience so-

[63] "Minamoto Tametomo, while in Bungo province, disrupted the Southern Headquarters [Dazaifu] and menaced the district under jurisdiction. Thereupon His Majesty commanded the Southern Headquarters to suppress those who had joined forces with Tametomo" (*Hyakurenshō*, 7 [3.IV.1155]: 71).

phistication is incompatible with the spirit of heroism. Both works, moreover, devote considerable space to sympathetic accounts of the fate suffered by Tameyoshi and Yoshitomo, both members of the losing side. This stance is based on the realization that war always demands tragic sacrifices. The narration of the *Hōgen* and *Heiji Monogatari* is lyrical and at times sentimental. Since lyricism and sentimentality are incompatible with martial heroism, the two stances are mutually contradictory.

The same applies to *The Tale of the Heike*. Kobayashi Hideo sees military episodes like "Ujigawa no Senjin" ("The First to Cross the Uji River"; *HM*, 9:164-71) as the essence of the narrative, which he describes as "the gleam of the sun and the sweat of men and horses."[64] Such episodes are, however, relatively few, and the characters acting as the protagonists of such episodes are not especially heroic. Only Yoshinaka and Yoshitsune come close to being martial heroes. Yoshinaka is depicted as a hero at the battle of Kurikara Valley,[65] but his comic behavior during a stay in the capital quite cancels out his earlier heroism.[66] His last appearance in *The Tale of the Heike* strikes a melancholy note: with only one retainer, Kanehira, by his side, Yoshinaka finds that his usually comfortable lightweight armor weighs heavily on him. In the end, unable to kill himself in a heroic manner, Yoshinaka meets a pitiful end when his horse becomes mired in a paddy field.[67] Although Yoshitsune is depicted as a brave general at the battles of Ichinotani and Yashima, his gallantry is only that appropriate to a field commander; it has nothing to do with decisions made or actions taken by a man on whom depends the rise of the Genji and the fall of the Heike.[68] On the other hand, heroism is found often among minor characters. Examples of such characters who die heroic deaths are Sanemori, who dyes his white hair black so that he might fight and die in battle;[69] Kanehira, who dies fighting like the strongest man in Japan;[70] and Noritsune, whose heroic fight ends when he drowns himself, taking two Genji warriors with him to the bottom.[71] Only their deaths are heroic, however: their other acts are not so described. Decidedly unheroic characters are presented in a highly sympathetic manner: Kiyotsune kills himself when he grows weary of war,[72] and Koremori leaves the scene of battle and eventually drowns himself out of love for

[64] Kobayashi H., 1942, 21. See vol. one, General Introduction.
[65] *HM*, 7:72-75.
[66] *HM*, 8:139-41.
[67] *HM*, 9:179-81.
[68] *HM*, 9:209-12; 11:304-10.
[69] *HM*, 7:79-81.
[70] *HM*, 9:181.
[71] *HM*, 11:340-41.
[72] *HM*, 8:134-35.

his wife and children.[73] Neither character resembles a medieval Western hero.

Warfare is not a central subject dictating the treatment of characters in *The Tale of the Heike.* Rather, war is a secondary phenomenon within the framework of government. The Genji and the Heike fight because the political situation demands it. Yet government is (or ought to be) essentially motivated toward achieving peace. Shigemori most clearly displays this understanding. He wears civilian dress when he visits Kiyomori's residence, which is swarming with soldiers uniformed for battle. Shamed by Shigemori's behavior, Kiyomori puts his monk's habit over his armor to receive his guest.[74] Shigemori admonishes Kiyomori with splendid Confucian ethical declarations that the latter, despite his authority as leader and father, cannot refute. Confucianism, present in Japan from the seventh century, makes its debut as literary expression in this passage. Confucianism is, of course, a product of accumulated, refined knowledge gained from experience and applied with a sense of moral responsibility. The Confucian spirit consequently thrives in a highly intellectual context; it cannot easily coexist with the more primitive heroic, martial spirit.

Confucianism is concerned with sovereign law. There is another philosophical basis running through *The Tale of the Heike*, that of the Buddhist dharma. The principle of sovereign law assures order in this world. The dharma, especially as it was interpreted by Jōdo (Pure Land) Buddhism in the late twelfth through thirteenth centuries, is focused on the eternal peace of the world to come rather than peace in this life. The deserters Kiyotsune and Koremori are depicted sympathetically despite their shameful deeds, because the story is written with the view that it is of ultimate value to find salvation in the world to come. Kumagae Naozane shows timidity unbefitting a soldier when he suffers anguish at having to kill Atsumori, a boy the age of his own son. The event is nevertheless narrated approvingly because it motivates Naozane to become a monk.[75] The ideals of sovereign law appear in fairly restricted areas of the work, whereas the concept of dharma permeates the entire work. The heroic martial spirit requires subjugating problems in this world through human ability and bravery, unaided by superhuman powers. Religious ideas are thus not only incompatible with the heroic spirit but often weaken or even destroy it. The old Viking ways, for example, were annihilated by the growing influence of Christianity. It makes sense, then, that heroic characters are not likely to emerge in *The Tale of the Heike.*

Those who regard Prince Yamato Takeru as the first Japanese hero (see vol. 1, ch. 2) have also tried to discover a heroic age in *The Tale of the*

[73] *HM*, 10:267-84.
[74] *HM*, 2:170-75.
[75] *HM*, 9:220-21.

Heike. Other, unrelated scholarship has tried to make analogical connections between *The Tale of the Heike* and the *Chanson de Roland*.[76] In thirteenth-century Japan, there was no literary foundation upon which to shape a heroic image. The conditions necessary to bring the heroic spirit to fruition were not present in a world governed by sovereign law and the Buddha's dharma.

MONOGATARI OF WAR AND PEACE: STYLE AND THEME

Of all the monogatari of war and peace, *The Tale of the Heike* is particularly steeped in Buddhism. This is apparently due to the participatory role played by celebrants of public Buddhist services in the formation of the narrative. The style of the work testifies to this. The famous opening passage can be broken down into the phrase and couplet types of parallel prose. The following structure emerges when the passage is fitted into parallel prose categories.

Equal alternating parallel couplets:

The sound of the bell of Jetavana
Echoes the impermanence of all things.
The hue of the flowers of the teak-tree
Declares that they who flourish must be brought low.

Light alternating parallel couplets:

Yea, the proud ones are but for a moment,
Like an evening dream in springtime.
The mighty are destroyed at the last,
They are but as the dust before the wind.

Free-form phrase:

If thou askest concerning the rulers of other countries far off;

Short parallel couplets:

Chao Kao of Ch'in,
Wang Mang of Han,
Chu I of Liang,
Lu-shan of T'ang,

Interjection:

All these,

Loosely alternating parallel couplets:

Not following the paths of the Kings and the Emperors who went before them,

[76] There are many valiant characters in the *Heike* but only one heroic figure, Yoshitsune, whose character has been contrasted with that of Roland (Satō Teruo, 1973, 2:402-409).

Sought pleasure only; not heeding remonstrance
Nor considering the disorders of their country,
Having no knowledge of the affliction of their people,

Free-form phrase:

They did not endure, but perished utterly. (*HM*, 1:83)[77]

The passage conforms to a style often employed in public Buddhist services when a sponsor's statement or formal prayers are read according to Japanese syntax. The resemblance may indicate that the celebrants of public Buddhist services contributed to the composition of *The Tale of the Heike*.[78] Of course, a decorative style patterned after parallel prose could appear wherever one desired beautiful phrasing; it was not limited to public Buddhist services. The point is less that the style of the passage is reminiscent of parallel prose than that such a style appears in the opening passage. Japanese approximations of parallel prose appear infrequently in the work, which is principally one of plain prose.[79] A similar dichotomy existed in public Buddhist sermons. The illustrative or edifying anecdotes used in sermons were apparently narrated in colloquial Japanese, the linguistic keynote of the service. Japanese prose modeled after parallel prose was reserved for the formal commencement of the service and for other parts demanding an emotional climax. The *Heike* follows this format. By contrast, the Kotohira manuscript of the *Hōgen Monogatari* uses an approximation of the parallel prose style throughout. The constant use of this style proves that celebrants of public Buddhist services did not contribute to its composition. The opening passage of the *Heike Monogatari* is influenced by public Buddhist services not only stylistically but in its emphasis on the theme of evanescence.

There is further evidence that the officiants of public Buddhist services participated in the formation of the *Heike Monogatari*: the narrative is interspersed with setsuwa that implicitly praise the temples to which participating monks belonged. In its most basic form, a public Buddhist service began with solemn statements and prayers. The next major event was

[77] [Trans. by A. L. Sadler, *The Ten Foot Square Hut and Tales of the Heike* (Sydney: Angus and Robertson Ltd., 1928; reprint Tokyo: Charles E. Tuttle Co., 1972), 22—Trans.] The conclusion of the original passage can be translated literally as, "They are the people who perished in a brief space of time" (hisashikarazu shite bōjinishi monodomo nari). Because the predicate follows the subject in Japanese, the word corresponding to "they are" (nari) comes at the end of the sentence in the original text. "Monodomo nari" (They are the people) corresponds to the concluding phrase (sōku) in parallel prose terminology. The concluding phrase has been omitted here and "monodomo nari" incorporated into the preceding free-form phrase because the concluding phrase cannot be properly rendered in English. [Auth., Trans.]

[78] This was first pointed out by Yamagishi Tokuhei (Yamagishi, 1942, 297-98).

[79] Another example of a decorative "parallel prose" style is "Seinan no Rikyū" ("The Royal Villa Southwest of the Capital," *HM*, 3:267-68).

a sermon that interpreted a text or preached on general Buddhist principles. The sermon was interspersed with illustrative anecdotes and stories of the buddhas' and bodhisattvas' previous existences, which is to say, a sermon was enlivened by setsuwa. Setsuwa, which helped to keep an audience interested, might vary according to time and the nature of the audience. A good preacher was valued for his ability to tell stories appropriate to the situation at hand. The interposed setsuwa in the *Heike Monogatari*, corresponding to the illustrative anecdotes and stories in a public Buddhist service, were originally regarded as tales to be varied at the storyteller's discretion. Depending on the manuscript consulted, a given story will be present or absent; if present, it will be told in markedly different ways.

Such extreme variants reflect the medieval perception of subsidiary stories in the text of *The Tale of the Heike*. Since several officiants in a service would have been attached to a given temple, they would alter a given *Heike Monogatari* episode so that it told of their temple or, indeed, told a new story entirely. The story of Ogata Koreyoshi, for example, contains the Mount Miwa motif, found throughout Japan.[80] The connection to Koreyoshi was probably made by a preacher associated with the Usa Hachiman Shrine, which also figures in the story. Similarly, the story of Ariō's visit to Shunkan on Devil's Island was probably produced by a monk from Mount Kōya (Yanagida, 1940, 66-79).[81] Shunkan's fellow prisoners, Yasuyori and Naritsune, build a branch shrine of Kumano on the island and pray there for a safe return to the capital. They are eventually pardoned and leave the island; only Shunkan, who did not join in their prayers, is left behind. This part of the story was probably added by preachers associated with Kumano. The story of Rokudai may be the product of a preacher connected to the temple of Hasedera: on the verge of execution, Rokudai is saved by the Kannon of Hase and allowed to live another twenty years.[82]

Anecdotes used in sermons were not drawn solely from Buddhist setsuwa. Stories might be purely secular, so long as they ended with Buddhist-related comments. The new style of public Buddhist services inaugurated by Chōken and his line moved their audiences through various theatrical techniques. Similar artifices were probably applied to the text of the service. Thanks to the large, general audiences of public Buddhist

[80] *HM*, 8:130-31. The legend of Mount Miwa is as follows. A handsome young nobleman begins courting a woman who lives near Mount Miwa. He will not tell her his name or his dwelling. The woman, curious to know his identity, attaches a threaded needle to the man's clothing as he prepares to return home. Following the trail of thread, the woman reaches a small cave on Mount Miwa. The man is in fact a snake that inhabits the cave. The legend survives in many variants. [Auth., Trans.]

[81] *HM*, 3:232-39.

[82] *HM*, 12:422.

services, the storytelling art that evolved there acquired a fresh narrative style and skillful colloquialisms. These features first appear in monogatari during the thirteenth century. Without the addition of such elements, derived from public Buddhist sermons, the present *Tale of the Heike* might be less vivid in content and language.

When I refer to the "present" aspect of the work, I have in mind the textual line descended from the Kakuichi manuscript, the principal version. The *Heike Monogatari* was apparently performed to biwa accompaniment from its inception. As the musical art of its recitation became more polished, the text required further refinement. A musical text naturally becomes more elaborate as the art of music becomes more technically advanced. Unless subtle accompaniment has a polished text, the combination will be unsuccessful. Music and text evolve together and mutually affect each other. Jōichi, a master of *Heike* performance, lived at the beginning of the fourteenth century. Two of his pupils were Kakuichi and Jōgen. The Ichikata school, founded by Jōichi, was systematized by Kakuichi, who added new melodies to the repertoire and reordered the text.[83] The Ichikata school thus became more influential than the Yasaka school founded by Jōgen. The Kakuichi manuscript line eventually acquired the status of a widely circulated text. It combines a textual authority reminiscent of Teika's Aobyōshi recension of *The Tale of Genji* with a highly polished text appropriate for skilled biwa accompaniment.

In addition to its polished text, the Kakuichi manuscript is known for its splendid structure. In other manuscript lines, for example, the story of Kenrei Mon'in's last years is scattered throughout the narrative. The Kakuichi line, on the other hand, gathers all parts of the story into its final section, "Kanjō" ("The Initiates' Chapter"). This section corresponds to the opening words of *The Tale of the Heike*: "The sound of the bell at Jetavana." Transience is clearly announced as the theme of the work. Informed by this theme, the stories of valiant battle become descriptions of brave men destroying one another. This interpretation alerts us to the motif of death that runs throughout: *The Tale of the Heike* is the story of various people dying in various ways. Some die in the agony of fever, others on the field of battle; some kill themselves, while others are captured and executed. The *Heike* is, in other words, the story of the annihilation of the Heike clan. The Yasaka manuscript line places the story of Rokudai's death at the end of the work in order to signal the extinction of the Heike: "The execution of the Sammi Priest [Rokudai] marked the

[83] Kakuichi died in the Sixth Month of 1371; his year of birth is unknown. The earliest record of a performance by Kakuichi is 1340; thus he was evidently active during the early fourteenth century (Atsumi, 1962, 71-73). [As opposed to the Yasaka School of reciters, the Ichikata wrote "ichi" at the end of their names.—Ed.]

end of the Heike line" (*HM*, Yasaka manuscript, 593).[84] This would seem a far more effective way to end the work. Yet salvation is not attained through the extinction of the Heike clan. According to the preachers of public Buddhist services, there was a more convincing way to bring home the reality that evanescence is inescapable and all are fated to perish: evanescence should be linked to the hope that Amida's mercy will lead one to rebirth in the Western Paradise. In this sense, "The Initiates' Chapter" makes splendid use of the theme of evanescence and follows a design more worthy of a sermon. The section is structured so that Kenrei Mon'in, whose tragic fate exposes her to what seems the ultimate in human suffering, quietly attains salvation.

The Kakuichi manuscript line has one striking characteristic with regard to the various ways in which characters die in the story. Besides those who die from disease and drowning, many are executed or die in battle. One would therefore expect to encounter gory descriptions of the latter categories of death. The Kakuichi line, however, contains no descriptions that include bloodshed. In rare instances, the Kakuichi line may show a character's feet bleeding from walking on a steep mountain path,[85] but it does not contain a single description of bloodshed connected with death. This phenomenon is limited to the Kakuichi line. Both the Enkei[86] and Nagato[87] manuscripts contain descriptions of gory deaths; so does the *Gempei Jōsuiki* (or *Seisuki*; *An Account of the Gempei War*).

> Holding Sammi's head in his right hand, he leaned on his bowstaff, took paper from his breast, and wiped the blood from the head. The paper seemed a cinnabar color. (*HM*, Enkei manuscript, 772)

> They broke down the wall when they saw blood coursing out. Inside, they found a man's head. It was the governor of Izu. To this day the entrance is called "Suicide Gate." (*HM*, Nagato manuscript, 287)

> Gen Taifu Hōgan was wounded under his helmet by an arrow. The arrowhead pierced straight through the nape of his neck; blood ran into his eyes. The Hōgan, near death, saw the world grow dark. He

[84] The Sammi Priest, also known as Rokudai, was the son of Taira Koremori. The designation "sammi"—"the third rank"—comes from the rank Koremori held at court. [Auth., Trans.]

[85] *HM*, 8:134.

[86] The original manuscript was dated Enkei 2-3 (1309-1310) in a postscript. It no longer survives. A copy dated 1419-1420 is in the collection of the Daitōkyū Bunko.

[87] Part of the Nagato manuscript, in twenty fascicles, is in the collection of Akama Shrine; other parts are in other collections. The Nagato manuscript may originally have been structured in six fascicles (Atsumi, 1962, 106). It has many points of resemblance with the Enkei manuscript.

> could neither hold his bow nor draw his sword. (*Gempei Jōsuiki*, 15:462)

These are a few of many examples. Gory scenes also appear frequently in the *Hōgen Monogatari* and *Heiji Monogatari*, as in this description of Yorinaga's death:

> The minister of the left, growing weaker, finally fell from his horse. Blood gushed from his body like coursing water. His riding clothes, lined in white silk, were dyed crimson by his blood. (*Hōgen*, Bumpo manuscript, 117)

The decapitation of Nobuyori is told as follows:

> And, finally, his head was cut off. Nobuyori was a big, stocky man. When his head was severed, the body fell forward. They threw sand over it. Just then it began to rain, so that the fluid from his spinal column, mixed with blood, ran crimson. (*Heiji*, Kujō manuscript, 51)

In addition to descriptions of bloodshed, these narratives contain passages linking death to decomposition. Consider the scene from the *Hōgen Monogatari* in which Yorinaga's body is disinterred and his body identified:

> The decaying corpse was bloated and festering. Pus and blood oozed from the burst body. A dreadful stench filled the air; everywhere was foulness. No one could gaze at so dreadful a sight. Unable to look again at the corpse, they had it reinterred. (*Hōgen*, Yasutoyo manuscript, 68)

Virtually the same passage appears in the Enkei manuscript version of the *Heike Monogatari* (167-68). Whichever version is the original, a description of a decomposing corpse is unusual to find in thirteenth-century Japanese literature. Death may have been fairly routinely envisioned in terms of physical decay in the West from the fifteenth century on.[88] In Japanese literature, however, such an approach is highly exceptional. Ji sermons often included mention of corpses, skeletons, and ghosts (Tsukudo, 1938, 60).[89] The Jishū stands out among Jōdo subsects as being particularly drawn to darkness and gloom. Sermons delivered by Jishū preachers may have had a partial influence on certain versions of the *Hōgen*, the *Heiji*, and the *Heike Monogatari*.

[88] This is discussed in detail by Huizinga (Huizinga, 1919, 124-35). Although the West has beautified death (Ariès, 1977, 409-74), death is generally thought loathsome and ugly.

[89] The Jishū was a Jōdo order founded by Chishin Ippen (1239-89). One of its leaders, Yugyō Shōnin, travelled through Japan urging the people to recite the nembutsu. Jishū members were exclusively ascetics preaching no specific doctrine.

By comparison, the Kakuichi manuscript line eliminates bloodshed from its death scenes and presents death as one of several processes leading to rebirth in the Pure Land paradise. Death is considered from a contemplative point of view. The contemplative approach to death is linked to the Jōdo school founded by Hōnen (1133-1212). The Kakuichi version does not see physical death as a literary object, but rather as the imagistic equivalent of a majestically beautiful setting sun coloring the sea at Naniwa. The Kakuichi manuscript line is more interested in the aesthetics of death than in recording it. Like Hōnen, the compiler of the Kakuichi manuscript had a contemplative approach: both depict and meditate on the Buddha and his Pure Land in their innermost heart. The words and deeds of characters in the story reflect this contemplative stance. Taira Tadanori's valiant death, for example, is described in this way in the Kakuichi manuscript line (9:216):

> Tadanori, seeing that all was over, said, "Leave me a while. I wish to recite ten invocations to Amida." He flung Rokutaya from him so that he fell about a bow's length away. Then turning toward the west, he chanted, "Hail to Amida Buddha" ten times in a loud voice, and prayed, "O Amida, who sheddest the light of thy presence through the ten quarters of the world, gather into thy radiant heaven all who call upon thy name!"[90]

Doctrine in Jōdo Buddhism developed along two positions. One, advocated by Hōnen and his Jōdo school, maintains that birth in paradise is achieved by repeated recitation of the nembutsu: "Namu Amida Butsu" ("Hail to Amida Buddha"). This practice is called "many-calling" (tanen). Shinran (1173-1262) and his Jōdo Shinshū school proposed instead that salvation could be achieved with a single recitation of the nembutsu—the "once-calling" (ichinen) approach. Despite the spread of Jōdo Shinshū in the late thirteenth century, the doctrine of many-calling is retained by the Kakuichi version. This indicates that the text was written by Jōdo monks involved with public Buddhist services.

The varied, colorful text of *The Tale of the Heike* came to be considered in terms of the Kakuichi manuscript line, a version oriented toward Hōnen's vision of Jōdo Buddhism. A somber tone, symbolized by the opening lines—"The sound of the bell of Jetavana"—becomes the dominant key underscoring all the events in the work. Kobayashi Hideo's arbitrary—or wishful—statement that the essence of the work lies in the "gleam of the sun and the sweat of men and horses" is something sensed only when specific passages are read in isolation. Kobayashi's interpretation is wholly inapplicable to a reading of the entire Kakuichi manuscript

[90] [Adapted from Sadler, trans., 1972, 153.—Trans.]

version. Nor need we discuss further the inadvisability of using the Kakuichi version, with its finely-developed religious (or sectarian) perceptions, as base data for comparison with the martial heroism of the *Chanson de Roland.*

MONOGATARI OF WAR AND PEACE: TEXTUAL LINES AND VERSIONS

There can be no doubt that the celebrants of public Buddhist services participated in the composition and transmission of *The Tale of the Heike.* That does not mean, however, that they composed the entire work. Several accounts of the war between the Genji and the Heike, extant by the early thirteenth century, seem to have provided important material. *Gyokuzui,* the diary of Kujō Michiie (1193-1252), contains the following entry:

> I sent Arinaga to ask Lord Mitsumori for some of his accounts of the Heike [Heike ki]. That gentleman has a great store of writings on the Heike clan. He responded favorably to my request. (Entry for 20.IV.1220)

Some thirty years after the destruction of the Heike forces at Dannoura, then, several accounts of the war existed. Taira Mitsumori (d. 1229), a nephew of Kiyomori, may have possessed his exceptionally large collection of "Heike accounts" in memory of his ill-fated clan. Michiie's reference to "accounts of the Heike" is to a group of documents, not to the title of a work. Their contents are of course unknown. They may have recorded oral eyewitness accounts.

Eyewitness accounts generally suggest highly reliable sources. In this case, however, there seem to have been a great many dubious witnesses. Jien's *Gukanshō* mentions various reports about the death of the minister of the left, Yorinaga, followed by this passage:

> People spoke of such matters among themselves. When one made inquiries into the veracity of individual accounts, however, the stories changed. We would know exactly what happened if we had listened carefully, putting together this story and that. (*Gukanshō,* 4:223)

Jien asserts that correct deduction and evaluation of a report's reliability will eventually yield accurate facts. His opinion also tells us indirectly of the opposite situation: that even eyewitness or participants' reports are not fully reliable unless subjected to full investigation. This strikes us as reasonable. Even today, newspaper accounts of an event one happens to have witnessed usually have slight (and occasionally unpardonable) errors. We can hardly expect complete accuracy from twelfth- and thirteenth-century purveyors of information wholly untrained in the art of data gathering. Jien's account of Yorinaga's death and that given in *Hōgen Monogatari* differ rather significantly.[91] There are few differences, on the other hand, in accounts of Yorinaga's death as it appears in the various manuscripts of the *Hōgen Monogatari*. This is an important fact.

"War accounts" were narrated to biwa accompaniment by itinerant, usually blind performers in monastic dress [known as biwa hōshi, "biwa monks"].[92] A view widely supported in the scholarly community maintains that the enormous number of emended texts originates from their varied narrative versions (*Hōgen*, "Kaisetsu," 9-10). The view is based on misinterpretation, however, since it does not take into account contemporary performance conditions. Blind performers recited a memorized text. Given the strong memorizing powers of the blind, textual changes probably did not evolve from errors of memorization in the course of narrating. All the same, it was difficult to narrate a text over the years without committing errors. Blind performers thus apparently corrected their memorized version by having a written text read to them. This practice required the existence of many manuscript copies of a given "war account." Textual variants emerged in the process of transmitting written texts, not because of inaccurate oral transmission. There are substantial differences between Jien's oral sources and those in the *Hōgen Monogatari*, but barely any differences are apparent among any but the Kotohira manuscript of the *Hōgen Monogatari*. This indicates that the variants emerged from written transmission. If the textual change had originated from oral transmission, some of the variants would occupy a middle ground between the accounts in the *Hōgen Monogatari* and the *Gukanshō*. Such variant versions do not exist, however, and as we shall see below, copyists are obviously responsible for the Kotohira manuscript variants.

Textual variants are more easily created by written than by oral transmission. Why, then, do the extant versions of *The Tale of the Heike* and other recited narratives possess so large a number of emended texts? The question might be considered in light of the fact that manuscript variants often concern chapter units. Manuscript A, for example, might have the chapters "Giō" and "The Burning of the Zenkōji Temple" while manuscript B has neither. A compiler obviously decided to add or to eliminate chapters in such cases. The process differs entirely from that in which faulty oral narration creates textual variants. Setsuwa collections also

[91] *Hōgen*, 2:120-31.

[92] One account appears in *Futsū Shōdō Shū* (see ch. 6). Another is: "We summoned the blind musician Yuishin and had him play the biwa for us. At the touch of his fingers, the instrument produced a tonic range so broad that he seemed to be playing a thirteen-stringed koto. The music was so marvelous that it cannot be described accurately. Yuishin accompanied his playing with recited stories of the Heiji era [1159-60] and the Heike clan. Several ladies-in-waiting also heard his performance" (*Hanazono Ki* [16.IV.1321], 238).

survive in emended texts created by adding or subtracting certain stories from the corpus. This shared characteristic probably arises because both setsuwa and recited narrative evolved from public Buddhist services. Twelfth-century and later setsuwa collections are made up of tales based on illustrative anecdotes and pious stories told in sermons. Sermon anecdotes were not stable compositions: they could be varied to suit the circumstances of a given sermon.

The basic form taken by a public Buddhist service begins with the recitation of the sponsor's statement and prayers and is followed by the highlight of the service, the sermon. The body of the sermon, an interpretation of scripture or a pronouncement on general Buddhist principles, was interspersed with interesting setsuwa. If this structure is applied to *The Tale of the Heike*, the result is as follows. The opening passage corresponds to the opening statement and prayers, written in parallel prose; the history of the rise and fall of the Heike is the expository meat of the sermon; and the setsuwa of Ssu Wu, Kūkai (Kōbō Daishi), and the like that are scattered throughout the narrative correspond to the diverting anecdotes told during a sermon. Like the preachers who varied anecdotes to suit their audience, performers and copyists of the *Heike Monogatari* freely altered and shifted the location of the setsuwa interspersed through the narrative.

The Tale of the Heike undoubtedly possesses a nucleus accompanied by subsidiary parts. The latter group was perceived as open to narrative variation, while alteration of the former was forbidden on the grounds that the narrative would lose its identity. Variants among manuscripts are so substantial both in quantity and quality that some of the more extreme variant versions of the Heike story, particularly the *Gempei Jōsuiki*, have often been treated as separate works. All emended versions nevertheless contain passages in common that point to their identity as variants of *The Tale of the Heike*. All *Heike* manuscripts, even the *Gempei Jōsuiki* version, contain the opening passage. Passages common to all texts, with the exclusion of minor variants, may be deduced as having existed in an ancestor text from which all surviving versions descend. The ancestor will be called the original text. Its nature is of course unknown. We can, however, conclude that sections not present in all existing manuscripts—especially subsidiary setsuwa—represent later changes or additions made to the narrative and that the original text would have been shorter than those extant today. There has long been discussion of a text in six parts that predated the twelve-part version preserved in the widely circulated text (Yamada Y., 1911, 516-45). The theory has recently gained validity by the discovery of a letter written on the back of a manuscript copy of *Hyōhanki* (Higashiyama Library manuscript), the diary of Taira Nobunori, that mentions a *Chishō Monogatari* in six parts.[93]

[93] [The title *Chishō* is significant because the Gempei War took place in the Chishō era

We cannot of course conclude that the *Chishō Monogatari* mentioned in the letter is in fact the original text of the *Heike*, since we cannot ascertain if it had the same opening passage present in all extant manuscript versions of the *Heike Monogatari.* The existence of a *Chishō Monogatari* in six books nevertheless supports the deduction that surviving *Heike* manuscripts evolved from a shorter original text that was later augmented to produce emended texts. To take a different perspective, the fewer additional sections a *Heike* manuscript has, the more ancient its form. "Ancient form" refers to proximity to the original, and there has been much discussion in scholarly circles about that Ur-form. The absence of a clear definition of "ancient form" has rendered these discussions fruitless. If we define "ancient form" as "proximity to the original text," we will avoid the tendency of previous theories to duplicate themselves or miss the point altogether.

Proximity to the original text does not necessarily mean that the form of a manuscript is chronologically ancient. The postscript to the Enkei manuscript, for example, attests that the manuscript was copied in the late thirteenth century, an early date for manuscripts of the *Heike Monogatari.* Yet the Enkei manuscript has a great many narrative passages not present in other versions. In this respect, the Enkei manuscript is distant from the original text. On the other hand, its six-part structure, including main and subordinate sections, is patterned after an ancestor reminiscent of the nonextant, six-part *Chishō Monogatari.* The Enkei manuscript retains an ancient form in this sense. These facts suggest another trait of the ancient form: it need not survive whole in a manuscript. That is, we cannot determine a single text unit that defines the ancient form. For instance, we cannot conclude that the Enkei manuscript line displays a more ancient form than the Shibu Kassenjō manuscript, because the former is a combination of relatively recent accretions coexisting with ancient forms.[94]

The case is similar for the *Hōgen Monogatari* manuscripts. The Nakarai and other related manuscripts have a section not present in the Kotohira manuscript version, a chapter called "Tametomo's Voyage to Devil's

(1177-81).—Trans.] When Fujiwara Teika copied *Hyōhanki* between 1240 and 1243, he supplemented his paper supply by using the backs of old letters and other documents. One such letter, from an unknown writer, is dated the eleventh day of the Seventh Month, 1240. It includes the statement, "*Chishō Monogatari*, in six parts (also called *Heike*). I have been copying it recently. I am not yet through, but when it is done I would like you to see it" (Akamatsu, 1970, 183-86).

[94] The Shibu Kassenjō manuscript is written in a style imitative of Chinese prose. According to its postscript, the exemplar for the Shibu Kassenjō manuscript was copied between 1446 and 1447. The work is thought to have been compiled in 1323 or 1324 (Takahashi, 1978), 421-29).

Island and His Death" (*Hōgen*, Nakarai manuscript, 103-108).[95] Because the Tametomo of this chapter has been so changed by setsuwa that he differs from the character appearing earlier in the work, the chapter must be a later accretion. With regard to this chapter, therefore, the Kotohira manuscript preserves a more ancient form than the Nakarai manuscript. That does not, however, mean that the Kotohira manuscript has on the whole a more ancient form than the Nakarai. The Bumpo manuscript of the *Hōgen Monogatari*, for instance, describes the half-dead Yorinaga's return to Nara in this fashion:[96]

> Placing Yorinaga in a carriage, they went as far as Saga, where they were stopped by many monks emerging in front of the Shaka Hall. They entreated the monks, with successful results. The group proceeded to Umezu, traded hempen clothing for the use of two small boats, lashed them together, threw in some bundles of brushwood, and rode downriver disguised as woodcutters. (*Hōgen*, Bumpo manuscript, 127)

The Kotohira manuscript has the following passage in place of "They entreated the monks, with successful results."

> Shigenori, the senior assistant minister of ceremonial, entreated the monks, ". . . ." Thus he entreated them, devising various means of persuasion. The monks listened closely, with heads bowed and tears flowing. "Quickly, go quickly!" they said, letting the party pass. (*Hōgen*, Kotohira manuscript, 129-30)

The speech omitted from the above passage occupies twenty-two lines in the *Nihon Koten Bungaku Taikei* edition of the *Hōgen Monogatari*. The Kotohira version suffers by comparison to Jien's eyewitness-based accounts of the same event in the *Gukanshō* (4:222-23). To have the monks bar the way is pure fabrication. What is more, Shigenori's speech, a splendid prose passage drawing heavily on Confucian and Buddhist literature, is so long in the Kotohira version that it throws the episode off balance. The speech is a secondary fabrication appended to what is already a fictional event. As a whole, the Kotohira manuscript cannot be said to possess an ancient form.

The approach outlined above attempts to grasp ancient form in quantitative aspects alone, with no consideration of quality. This is unavoid-

[95] The Nakarai manuscript is in the collection of the Cabinet Library and the Shōkōkan Bunko. Only Part 2 of its ancestor, the Bumpo manuscript, survives; thus our only means of deducing the first and third parts of the Bumpo manuscript is through the Nakarai.

[96] The Bumpo manuscript is in the Shōkōkan Bunko collection. The completed copy was made on the third day of the Eighth Month, Bumpo 2 (1318), hence its name. The Bumpo manuscript is the oldest surviving copy of the extant *Hōgen Monogatari*.

able. The quantitative approach is predicated on the likelihood that the original text did not have accretions. Since we do not know the *nature* of the original text, however, we have no criteria by which to determine qualitative proximity. Factual correspondence to historical reality has been seen as one criterion of the ancient form. This approach, used to compare *Heike* versions to Jien's *Gukanshō*, concludes that those *Heike* manuscripts closest to the *Gukanshō* in content preserve the ancient form.[97]

The method confuses raw material and its expression as literature, however. It also assumes that the original text of the *Heike Monogatari* allotted equal importance to historical fact and to the records that served as its subject matter. The extent of dependence on source materials, a matter left up to the individual author, is not necessarily connected to the antiquity of manuscript form. If preachers in public Buddhist services were indeed associated with the composition of the original text, they would have altered the original story to accord with the tastes of differing audiences. Although the "accounts of the Heike" that served as source material for the original text may well have been historically accurate, the preachers who drew on them were not likely to have incorporated the accounts verbatim into their narrative. Conformance with historical fact is unrelated to ancient manuscript form.

The same holds true for the *Jōkyūki (An Account of the Jōkyū War)*. This work is not a recited narrative, because its composition process has no connection to the celebrants of public Buddhist services. The subject of the *Jōkyūki* is Gotoba's unsuccessful coup d'état against the Kamakura bakufu. The work survives in four principal manuscript groups, each of which differs from the others in substantial textual variants: (1) the Jikōji manuscript line; (2) the Maeda manuscript line; (3) the widely circulated text line; and (4) the *Jōkyū Ikusa Monogatari (The Tale of the Jōkyū War)*. All except the first group have areas that were rewritten or enlarged along the lines of the *Azuma Kagami* (*Mirror of the East*; Sugita, 1974, 63-74). Passages that incorporate excerpts from the *Azuma Kagami*, a history of sorts, are closer to historical fact than corresponding passages in manuscripts that do not draw on the *Azuma Kagami*. This does not enable us to conclude, however, that the Jikōji manuscript line is less likely than the others to approximate the ancient textual form. It is equally difficult to discover the ancient form in a narrative style modeled on historical works. The Shibu Kassenjō manuscript of *The Tale of the Heike*, ordered chronologically, undoubtedly shares features of the annalistic "accounts of the Heike." But that in itself does not mean that the Shibu Kassenjō manuscript transmits the original form of the *Heike*: the

[97] This approach was proposed by Akamatsu Toshihide (Akamatsu, 1967, 3-25).

original text could have been recast in the style of the "Heike accounts"; nor does this mean that the Shibu Kassenjō shows a late form. The annals that served as the immediate ancestor of the Shibu Kassenjō manuscript may well have existed in the thirteenth century. The ancestor probably did not resemble the original text, however, because it possessed accretions of the same nature as those found in the Enkei manuscript.[98] The date of a manuscript must be clearly distinguished from its proximity to the ancient form and its consequent proximity to the original text of the *Heike*.

[98] Even if we assume that the Shibu Kassenjō manuscript postdates the Enkei manuscript, the two are closely related (Mizuhara, 1979, 141).

CHAPTER 12

Song and Lyrics in Seven-Five Meter

In the history of Japanese song, the Middle Ages commence with the inception of 7-5 syllable meter (vol. two, ch. 9). [The 7-5 rhythm for certain songs, nō, etc., is taken by Japanese to contrast with a dominant 5-7 rhythm for poetry.] This holds true for both lyrics and melody. The 7-5 meter, not a characteristic of ancient song lyrics, became a major element of medieval song. This distinction between the Ancient Age and the Middle Ages concerns an upper stratum of song in which individual creativity shapes or alters culture. Obvious changes rarely occur in song from a lower stratum, which is composed and received communally. Periodization of song from a lower stratum is thus rendered difficult. Even when differentiation between periods is possible, the periods discerned will not always correspond to those created by the upper stratum. Because individuals who composed these songs tended to be anonymous communal entities, song never emerged from the zoku sphere to associate itself with the medieval ga aesthetic. Or, to rephrase the statement, song entered the Middle Ages later than waka and prose written in Japanese and prolonged its Ancient Age for a much longer time. On the other hand, imayō, a song form popular from the early eleventh century, entered a ga period by the mid-twelfth century when it established a 7-5 metric text and quatrain form. Not only did aristocrats listen to imayō, they also performed them and composed lyrics. Imayō, once the exclusive province of prostitutes and itinerant female entertainers, developed ga expression as it moved into aristocratic society.

Aristocratic imayō were of such a conventionally literary quality that tennō might sing them without causing a stir.[1] Their lyrics, however, lacked the liveliness of the imayō in *Ryōjin Hishō (The Secret Store of Marvelous Song)*. The aristocratic version would strike modern readers as tedious. Asobi, the waterfront prostitutes who first brought imayō proper into noble society, later circulated two new, different kinds of imayō: the shirabyōshi and the rambyōshi. Both appeared in the middle of the twelfth century. They cannot be discussed, since no lyrics survive

[1] *Towazugatari* contains a passage in which the former sovereign Gofukakusa sings an imayō beginning, "How sad it is to see an aged charcoal peddler" (1:83). In another, Gofukakusa and another abdicated tennō, Kameyama, sing an imayō written by the former, which begins, "I cannot forget it, it pierces my soul" (3:180).

from that time. Both kinds of songs were performed to hand-drum accompaniment; hence both were highly rhythmic songs. "Shira" and "ram" (or ran) in their names may refer to a certain rhythmic form. We know that shirabyōshi was accompanied by dancing; the same may have been true for rambyōshi.

Early shirabyōshi lyrics consisted of existing imayō songs and waka. By the thirteenth century, lyrics were composed exclusively for shirabyōshi performance. The new texts seem to have been longer than the old imayō quatrain, but that is all that can be said of their form.[2] Ennen, a kind of entertainment given by and for the monks of powerful temples, included performances of various arts including shirabyōshi and rambyōshi. No rambyōshi lyrics survive. Shirabyōshi texts composed for ennen entertainment are fairly long, follow a 7-5 metric beat, and make skillful allusions to Japanese and Chinese literature and culture.[3] These songs were special cases, composed by monks for personal diversion. The shirabyōshi sung at banquets by female entertainers were not necessarily similar. We would do well, however, to note the presence of long, polished song texts in 7-5 meter that make abundant allusion to the Japanese and Chinese cultural traditions, because that is the form also taken by banquet songs (enkyoku).[4]

Banquet songs (or "fast songs," songs in fast time, sōga), have medium-length or long texts in 7-5 meter. The shortest banquet songs are fourteen lines long ("Udonge," for example); the longest, like "Jūeki," are 168 lines. Several collections of banquet songs survive. Myōkū compiled the *Enkyokushū*, *Enkyokushō*, *Shinkyokushū*, *Kyūhyakushū*, and *Shūkashū* between 1296 and 1306. The *Shūkashō*, *Besshi Tsuikakyoku*, and *Gyokurin'en* were compiled anonymously between 1314 and 1319. Another collection, *Sotomono*, was compiled at some point after the middle of the fourteenth century. A total of 173 song lyrics are contained in these collections. There are two kinds of texts in the banquet-song collections: one is modeled after pure Japanese, while the other follows the diction of the

[2] *Ayanokōji Toshikazu Kyō Ki* includes a fourteen-line text entitled "Mizu no Shirabyōshi" ("Water: A Shirabyōshi"; *Toshikazu Ki*, 622). A work titled *Ryōjin Hishō Kudenshū* (not the imayō collection compiled by Goshirakawa) includes the same song title but no text (*Ryōjin Hishō*, 14:166). If the earlier title matched the "Mizu no Shirabyōshi" text, the song would date from the twelfth century. There is, however, no firm external evidence to support this. *Ayanokōji Toshikazu Kyō Ki* is a record of the annual public ceremonies and festivities that occurred in 1514.

[3] In 1362 the monk Jūkai of the temple Hōryūji composed seven surviving songs collectively titled "Hōryūji Engi Shirabyōshi" (*Enkyoku Zenshū*, Appendix, 1-15). Jūkai's holograph manuscript, in the collection of Hōryūji, has measured breaks to facilitate singing (Nose, 1932, 372).

[4] Enkyoku is a modern term. The genre was originally called sōga, songs in fast time. I use the modern "enkyoku" because "sōga" is easily confused with a variety of kagura having the same name, as well as the sōga variety of imayō (in the broad sense).

mixed style. "Autumn," an example of the banquet song in its pure Japanese style, appears below (*Enkyokushū*, 1:55):

Torishi sanae no itsu no ma ni
Inaba no naruko hikikaete[5]
Akikaze fukeba Tanabata no
Tsuma mukaebune ni chigirite ya
Toki shi mo koe o ho ni agete
Kumoi o wataru karigane[6]
Ochi no yamaji ya kirikomete
Tomo mayowaseru tabibito wa
Sugusanu aki ya tsurakaran.

Young rice-seedlings moved to the fields
Have grown to leafy plants guarded by bird-clappers.[5]
Autumn winds blow—is the Weaver Maid
Now rowing off to meet her lover's boat?
Just then, lifting their voices like sails,
Wild geese fly across the realm of clouds.[6]
Yonder mountain path is shrouded in mist;
The traveller whose companion went astray
Must find unending autumn hard to bear.

"The Full Moon" (ibid., 1:56) is an example of a banquet song in the mixed style.

Kōtakeyo shizuka ni shite
Seimeitaru tsuki no yo
Meigetsukō no akatsuki
Yū Kō ga rō ni noboreba
Chisato ni tsuki akiraka nari[7]

[5] Rice is sown in a small seedbed and grown there until seedlings are large enough to transplant into rice paddies. As the plants mature they become attractive food for birds, and so clappers are constructed in the fields to frighten away birds. "Naru" means both "to mature" (as with rice plants) and "to make a noise" (hence "naruko," bird-clapper). [Auth., Trans.]

[6] [This couplet alludes to an autumn poem in the *Kokinshū* (*KKS*, 4:212): Akikaze ni / Koe o ho ni agete / Kuru fune wa / Ama no to wataru / Kari ni zo arikeru. (The boat approaching / With voices raised high as sails / In the autumn wind / Proves to be a line of geese / Winging across the heavens.) Trans. by Helen Craig McCullough, *Kokin Wakashū: The First Imperial Anthology of Japanese Poetry* (Stanford: Stanford University Press, 1985), 55.—Trans.]

[7] Ming-yüeh (Full Moon) Ravine is a scenic spot in Szechuan province. Yü Liang (289-340) of the Chin dynasty is famous for having constructed a magnificent turreted mansion in Chianghsi province with a spectacular view of Mount Lu and the Yangtze River. Yü and his retainers would view the moon from the south wing of the mansion. "At night, mounting

Zangetsu mado ni katabukite
Kyūrō masa ni nagakereba
Utsu ya kinuta no yorozugoe
Chitabi nezame no toko no ue ni
Harai mo aenu tsuyushimo o
Katashiku sode ni ya okisoen.

The hour grows late, all is quiet
On a night when the moon glows bright.
Were I at Full Moon Ravine in China,
Or gazing with Yü Liang from his towered mansion,
I would see the moon clearly for a thousand miles.[7]
Before the dawn moonbeams strike my west windows,
There is yet time, for autumn nights go slowly.
The fuller's mallet sounds in myriad voices;
A thousand times, as she lies in bed,
She cannot brush away the frost and dew of tears,
But must increase their number on her lonely sleeves.

Both are noteworthy examples of the progress made by song texts in 7-5 meter [as opposed to songs in older rhythms]. The latter variety is especially significant, because prose in the mixed style entered the sphere of ga following the example of just such songs.

Banquet songs were considered a ga art. We can tell this from the *Enkyokushū*, which is structured along the lines of the royal waka anthologies. The song texts of the *Enkyokushū* are studded with allusions to Chinese and Japanese classics.[8] The allusions are so numerous that modern scholars have criticized them as pedantic. It is, however, natural for ga literature to be expressed in precedented language. All that is at issue here is the gulf between such precedents and the knowledge of modern readers. The interesting thing about banquet-song texts in the mixed style is instead that in them Chinese loanwords achieve ga status for the first time. For waka composition, Chinese loanwords are clearly outside the realm of ga. In fact, except for unusual kinds of waka, the use of Chinese loanwords in waka was forbidden along with colloquial language. The practice was picked up by renga, which relegated verses containing Chinese loanwords or colloquial language to the category of haikai renga. The overwhelming presence of Chinese loanwords in banquet songs, and the accompanying belief that allusions from the Chinese classics were per-

Yü Liang's mansion towers, / I see the moon clearly for a thousand miles" (*Wakan Rōeishū*, 1:374). [Auth., Trans.]

[8] Banquet songs have their own categories arranged around a basic thematic framework of: Spring, Summer, Autumn, Winter, Congratulations, Shinto, Love, Travel, Evanescence, and Buddhism.

missible in such songs, is highly significant for Japanese literary history. The lyrics themselves manage to follow the rules of Japanese grammar while incorporating elements of Chinese prose and poetry so skillfully that nothing anomalous is sensed. Banquet-song texts written in this style use a language perhaps better called a fused Sino-Japanese style rather than the mixed style.

The phenomenon of fusion was fostered by the environment in which banquet songs were created. Composed and appreciated chiefly by members of the warrior class, banquet songs were most popular in the shogunal seat at Kamakura. There are twenty-three known composers of banquet songs. Many were high-ranking warriors serving in the Kamakura bakufu, monks living in temples near Kamakura, or courtiers with close ties to the bakufu (Tonomura, 1965, 127-51). Reizei Tamesuke, significantly, is one of the twenty-three composers of banquet-song lyrics. Unable to confront the rival Nijō house successfully at court, the Reizei branch decided instead to instruct Kamakura warrior households in the art of waka. In addition to preserving a certain amount of prestige, the Reizei gained economic support from this arrangement. This was the context in which Tamesuke formulated his renga code in Kamakura (ch. 9). Consequently, the Reizei family and the courtly culture they embodied had a substantial impact on Kamakura warrior society in general and banquet songs in particular.

This held true, however, only for the early period of banquet songs. Kamakura itself gained the cultural edge during their mature period. We can conclude this because Myōkū, who systematized both banquet-song texts and melodies, was probably a monk of Gokurakuji in Kamakura with connections to Mimuraji in Hitachi province (Tonomura, 1965, 15-41).[9] Gekkō, another monk who distinguished himself in composing lyrics and music for banquet songs, was also a member of the Kamakura cultural sphere (ibid., 102-21). Myōkū did not elevate banquet songs by adding further polish and definition to an already developed art.[10] He took a rather radical, even revolutionary approach, at least to the music. Although the two songs quoted above, "Autumn" and "The Full Moon," generally follow 7-5 meter, they occasionally contain hypermetric and hypometric lines. These were made to conform to 7-5 meter by shortening or extending the final syllables. The twelve syllables that make up a line in 7-5 meter are sung to eight beats.[11] The five-syllable subgroup in a line,

[9] Myōkū's dates are unknown. He compiled the *Sen'yō Mokuroku* in 1306 and is known to have been active after that time. Despite lack of firm evidence, some maintain that Myōkū and Gekkō are the same person.

[10] Myōkū composed lyrics to eighty-one songs and the music for 111. In output alone, he is certainly the greatest name in enkyoku. Myōkū is followed by Gekkō, who composed the music to twenty-four songs and the lyrics to twenty-one.

[11] The 8-beat measure also applies to hiranori, the basic rhythm in nō. If the twelve syllables in a 7-5 meter line are sung to six beats, two of the eight are left over. These last two

however, has two kinds of rhythm. Almost all banquet songs follow a form we shall call A. Only eleven preserved songs belong to form B, and they are fairly short. Many songs in B have undistinguished melodies with hardly any lines cast in the measureless form called nobebushi. These form-B works apparently preserve an ancient song form. By contrast, the rhythmic style of form A is very lively. The ample presence of nobebushi in form A makes the rhythm far more impressive. Myōkū seems to have been the first to enliven banquet songs (Yokomichi, 1960, 302-31). The revolution in banquet songs kept them popular until the early sixteenth century. Of course, both the lyrics and the music of banquet songs had gradually become fixed by the early fourteenth century.

Both shirabyōshi and banquet songs are written in 7-5 meter and have clearly rhythmic melodies. Their relationship, however, is unclear. Kusemai, songs originating in the early fourteenth century and flourishing through the fifteenth, are on the other hand an offshoot of shirabyōshi. Like the shirabyōshi, kusemai singing is accompanied by dance. The two also have structural similarities. They can be compared as follows (Nose, 1932, 384-87).

1. Introduction.
   In shirabyōshi: rōei, waka, or short imayō are sung. These later come to be called shidai.
   In kusemai: shidai, kuri, and sashi are sung.[12]
2. Development.
   In shirabyōshi: songs specific to the genre (i.e., long imayō) are sung.
   In kusemai: songs specific to kusemai (the first part) are sung.
3. Ending.
   In shirabyōshi: a fast dance is concluded with the singing of waka.
   In kusemai: songs specific to kusemai (the second part) are sung in quick tempo. The performance ends with shidai.

Though few kusemai texts survive from the fourteenth century, many of their titles are extant. They suggest that kusemai lyrics were concerned with Buddhist concepts and the origins of shrines and temples. Kusemai is itself less significant than its two offshoots: kuse, a new kind of music incorporated into nō drama, and kōwaka bukyoku, a fifteenth-century

are taken up by drawing out the final syllables and adding drumbeats and cries to arrive at the total of eight sung beats (Malm, 1975, 108-18). Banquet songs follow a similar rhythmic pattern. This undoubtedly will appear strange to a Western musical perspective. The Sonkeikaku manuscript score of banquet songs is reproduced in *Enkyoku Shūsei* (Koten Bunko).

[12] Kuri is a short, unmeasured, high-pitched song. Sashi is a nonmelodic, unmeasured chant in which the last syllables of each line are drawn out. [Auth., Trans.]

kind that evolved plots similar to those in recited narratives (katarimono).

The lyrics of shirabyōshi, banquet songs, and kusemai are all sung in 7-5 meter. That metric development was natural, given the Japanese preferences in syllabic rhythm (see vol. one, General Introduction). The 7-5 meter is not limited to song; it is also occasionally incorporated into prose. The *Taiheiki* account of Toshimoto's journey to Kamakura is an excellent example. It begins:

> Rakka no yuki ni / fumi mayou // Katano no haru no / sakuragari // momiji no nishiki o / kite kaeru // Arashi no yama no / aki no kure // hitoyo o akasu / hodo dani mo // tabine to nareba / monouki ni // on'ai no chigiri / asakaranu // waga furusato no / saishi o ba // yukue mo shirazu / omoioki // toshi hisashiku mo / suminareshi // kokonoe no / teito o ba // ima o kagiri to / kaerimite // omowanu tabi ni / idetamau // kokoro no uchi zo / aware naru. // Uki o ba tomenu / Ōsaka no // seki no shimizu ni / sode nurete // sue wa yamaji o / Uchide no hama // oki o haruka ni / miwataseba //. . . //[13]

> Wandering among a snowfall of petals // viewing cherry blossoms at Katano in spring // returning home dressed in brocade made by colored leaves // as autumn evening deepens on Arashi Hill, // even a single night of wakefulness // is unbearable for a traveller // whose bonds of gratefulness and love are strong // for his wife and children left at home, // their future always to be unknown to him; // these many years he passed in // the ninefold-walled royal capital, // and looking back for the last time // he embarks on an unforeseen journey // and is moved to the depths of his heart. // His sadness is not arrested at the Ōsaka barrier // where his sleeves are wetted // by a mountain spring; // the hilly path leads them to // the beach of Uchide, // as he gazes afar at the offing //. . . //[14]

Why is this section alone in 7-5 meter? Certainly the popularity of banquet songs is not sufficient explanation. The passage describes Toshimoto's journey from one geographical location to another—a michiyuki. But why must a michiyuki be composed in 7-5 meter? I would like to consider this question in the light of another passage in 7-5 meter, this time from

[13] *Taiheiki*, 2:67-68 ("Lord Toshimoto Again Travels to the East").

[14] We have worked to make the English translation reproduce the peculiar syntax of the original text. The narration is not easily understood in Japanese. The passage consists of fragmentary impressions of Toshimoto's visits to and passages through various locales. There is no unified structure. Toshimoto's impressions are arranged in an order reminiscent of linked poetry. The passage differs from renga, however, in its implied context: Toshimoto is making his journey under duress, having been captured in Kyoto, and is now travelling under guard to Kamakura. [Auth., Trans.]

the Kotohira manuscript version of *Heiji Monogatari.* In the following passage, Tokiwa and her three small children are wandering alone, trying to avoid discovery and arrest by Heike forces.

> Teradera no / kane no oto // kyō mo kurenu to / uchishirase // hito o togamuru / sato no inu // koe sumu hodo ni / yo wa narinu. // Shibaori kuburu / tami no ie // keburi taesezarishi mo // tazura o hedatete / haruka nari. // Baika o // otte kōbe ni / hasamedomo // jigetsu no yuki / koromo ni otsu. // Kawara no ue no // matsu mo nakereba / shōkon ni // tachi yadoru beki / kokage mo naku // jinseki wa yuki ni / uzumorete // tou beki tozashi mo / nakarikeri. //[15]

> From temple to temple, bells toll: // "This day too is over," they tell her, // village dogs reproving mankind // bark with uncanny clarity on this quiet night. // Peasant cottages made of brushwood: // smoke rises always from them // but they lie across the rice fields far, far away. // Like a spray of scattering plum blossom // spring snow falls on her hair and dress. // In place of a tiled roof // she can find no pine branches, // no massive roots to give them shelter; // footprints are buried by the snow; // there is no dwelling where she might ask assistance. //

Both passages describe a scene in which people are travelling prior to dying. Two kusemai—"Saikoku Kudari" ("The Journey to the Western Provinces") and "Azumakuni Kudari" ("The Journey to the Eastern Provinces")—have a similar subject. The former relates the journey made by the Heike after evacuating the capital; the Heike warrior Morihisa makes the latter journey when he is captured and brought under guard to Kamakura. "The Journey to the Eastern Provinces" describes circumstances that closely resemble those in Toshimoto's journey, quoted above. The 7-5 meter in the two kusemai may seem natural to the genre. Both songs, however, have a higher incidence of the meter than is usually found in kusemai. "The Journey to the Western Provinces" maintains the 7-5 song meter even in its chanted sections (sashi):

> [Sashi] Juei ninen no / aki no koro // Heike saikai ni / omomukitamau. //
>
> Seinan no rikyū ni itari // miyako o hedatsuru / Yamazaki ya // Sekido no In ni // tama no mikoshi o / kakisuete // Yawata no kata o / fushiogami // namu ya Hachiman / Daibosatsu // ninnō hajimaritamaite // jūrokudai no / sonshu tari. // Mimosusogawa no / soko kiyoku // sue o uketsugu / onmegumi // nado ka sutesasetamau beki. // (*Rangyoku Kusemaishū*, 33)

[15] *Heiji*, 2:282 ("Tokiwa Leaves the Capital"). This episode does not appear in some *Heiji* versions, including woodblock editions.

> [Chant] In the second year of Juei [1183] during the autumn // the Heike journeyed to the western provinces. //
>
> They came to the detached palace south of the capital // and Yamazaki, marking countryside from city; // at the site of the old Barrier Palace // they lowered the royal palanquin, // prostrated themselves toward Yawata and said, // "All hail, Hachiman, great bodhisattva // who reigned as the sixteenth // ruler of our land! // You and our lord are of lineage pure as the sacred Mimosuso River of Ise, // and you who ruled mercifully // shall surely not forsake our lord!"[16]

An already existing tradition that the michiyuki should be in 7-5 meter thus extends even to the kusemai chant, normally presented in nonmetric prose. But why must the michiyuki be in 7-5 meter?

All three examples describe people in unusual circumstances. All concern journeys embarked upon unwillingly at the dictates of fate. Another kind of michiyuki occurs in the first section of a nō play when the waki [secondary character, described in ch. 18] describes his journey to the scene of what are to be the chief events in the play. This description, in 7-5 meter, is also called a michiyuki. Most nō plays begin with the waki's michiyuki, even though it has become an overly obvious plotting stratagem. It is indispensable because a waki must be specially qualified to meet a ghost, demon, or other supernatural entity during his journey. The waki recalls events that occurred at each of several famous places through which he has travelled. Each event is associated with active spirits of gods and people.

The waki's contact with these local spirits transmits special qualifications to encounter a demon or the ghost of a certain person later in the play. That is why the locales mentioned cannot be ordinary places. They must be locations that remind people of a specific event or association; an utamakura [in particular, a place famous in poetry] would be one such kind of location. Such places were believed to be inhabited by particularly active spirits. The kotodama must be operative, if one is to speak to the spirits of a place. This requires a specific form of speech; ordinary address is not effective (vol. one, ch. 1). In the Middle Ages, the specific form with which to address spirits was 7-5 meter.

At each location, the waki addresses the local spirits in 7-5 meter. Each time, he experiences increased powers of communication with the spiritual world. When he reaches his destination, therefore, the waki is able to converse with the shite, a ghost or demon. If the waki is to acquire the

[16] Ōjin Tennō, who probably ruled in the late third or early fourth century, is identified with Hachiman. Ōjin-Hachiman is worshipped at the Iwashimizu Shrine, close to Yamazaki. Hachiman, a Shinto deity, was also worshipped as a bodhisattva in medieval Japan, since gods were seen as manifestations of buddhas and bodhisattvas. [Auth., Trans.]

necessary qualifications, he must address the local spirits in the first person. That is why the michiyuki in nō is never sung by the chorus.[17] The nature of the nō michiyuki differs somewhat from the *Taiheiki* passage quoted earlier. The michiyuki made by Toshimoto, Morihisa, and Tokiwa are told from the narrator's point of view. In all three passages, the characters are about to die. They are looking forward to future happiness—probably birth in paradise—as they pass through each location. The narrator, speaking for the character, addresses the local spirits from a third-person perspective and links the road travelled by the character to the path to paradise. Although narrative michiyuki thus differ somewhat from the nō variety, both are concerned with communication with another world.

The source of these michiyuki appears in a category of imayō called "songs about miraculous places." Here is one such song, from *The Secret Store of Marvelous Song* (*Ryōjin Hishō*, 2:312):

Kompon Chūdō e mairu michi
Kamogawa wa kawa hiroshi
Kannon'in no sagarimatsu
Naranu Kakinoki Hitoyadori
Zenjizaka
Suberishi Mizunomi Shirōzaka
Kiraradani
Ōtake Za no Ike
Akoya no hijiri ga tatetarishi
Sembon no Sotoba.

The path trod by pilgrims to the Central Hall on Hiei,
The broad stretches of the Kamo River,
Drooping pine branches at the Kannon'in Temple,
Barren Persimmon Tree where Hitoyadori folk take shelter,
The Slope of the Azari Master,
Slippery Rock, Drinking Place, Shirō's Hill,
Mica Valley,
Great Peak, Serpent Lake,
Thousand Stupas where
The travelling monk Akoya once stood.

This is more than an enumeration of place names. The song was undoubtedly sung in the anticipation that uttering the names would motivate the latent spiritual nature within these places to perform some kind of action.

[17] The jiutai, often translated "chorus," consists of two rows of six or eight people each seated stage left. They narrate the action in sung chorus; they have no spoken lines. [Auth., Trans.] [See Miner-Odagiri-Morrell, 1985, 307-16 and especially 334-35.—Ed.]

Note that this song too is in 7-5 meter. The michiyuki in nō apparently evolved from such songs. Michiyuki narrated in the third person, by contrast, seem to have evolved somewhat later.

As the impact of Jōdo Buddhism grew greater on society, the latter variety of michiyuki developed into an important mode. In such michiyuki, the narrator addresses local spirits in 7-5 meter, beseeching them to make sure that the characters travelling the road to death find it connected to the path to paradise.[18] The third-person michiyuki reached its zenith in the seventeenth and eighteenth centuries. A superlative example is the michiyuki of Ohatsu and Tokubei in the jōruri (puppet theater) *Sonezaki Shinjū (The Love Suicides at Sonezaki)*, by Chikamatsu Monzaemon.[19]

The 7-5 meter, which brought the michiyuki mode to this high point, originated in the Japanese Buddhist hymn (wasan; vol. two, ch. 9). This metric form was originally a foreign syllabic rhythm, an important fact in Japanese literary history. Because the kotodama could only be activated by a special linguistic form unique to Yamato, the 7-5 meter was undoubtedly perceived as a native syllabic rhythm. Since the syllabic units most natural to Japanese are 5 and 7 (vol. one, ch. 5), it is hardly strange that the 7-5 meter was regarded as a Yamato form. Nevertheless, the precedent of Chinese poetry and prosimetric writing meant that foreign influence determined that the dominant song meter would be 7-5 rather than 5-7. If we consider this as a literary phenomenon rather than in the light of contemporary perceptions, we must conclude that a foreign element fused with native Yamato elements and thereby eliminated zoku in its pure Yamato form. This means that, in the genre of song, the level of ga was achieved very late, and for song the Middle Ages begin in the thirteenth century.

Modern readers perceive 7-5 meter only as decorative, elegant prose. A poem or prose piece written in 7-5 meter today would meet with scorn and derision. This is because the kotodama has been virtually extinguished in our world, and because we are unable to communicate with the other world through the special 7-5 metric form. In the past, people could sense a vision of the other world in 7-5 meter. Those people wept and were moved to the bottom of their hearts by the michiyuki of Ohatsu and Tokubei.

[18] [On the relation between michiyuki—from early to late classical times—with death, see Nakanishi Susumu, "The Spatial Structure of Japanese Myth: The Contact Point Between Life and Death," Miner, 1985, 106-29.—Ed.]

[19] *Chikamatsu Zenshū*, 6:616-17.

PART FOUR

The Achievement of the High Middle Ages

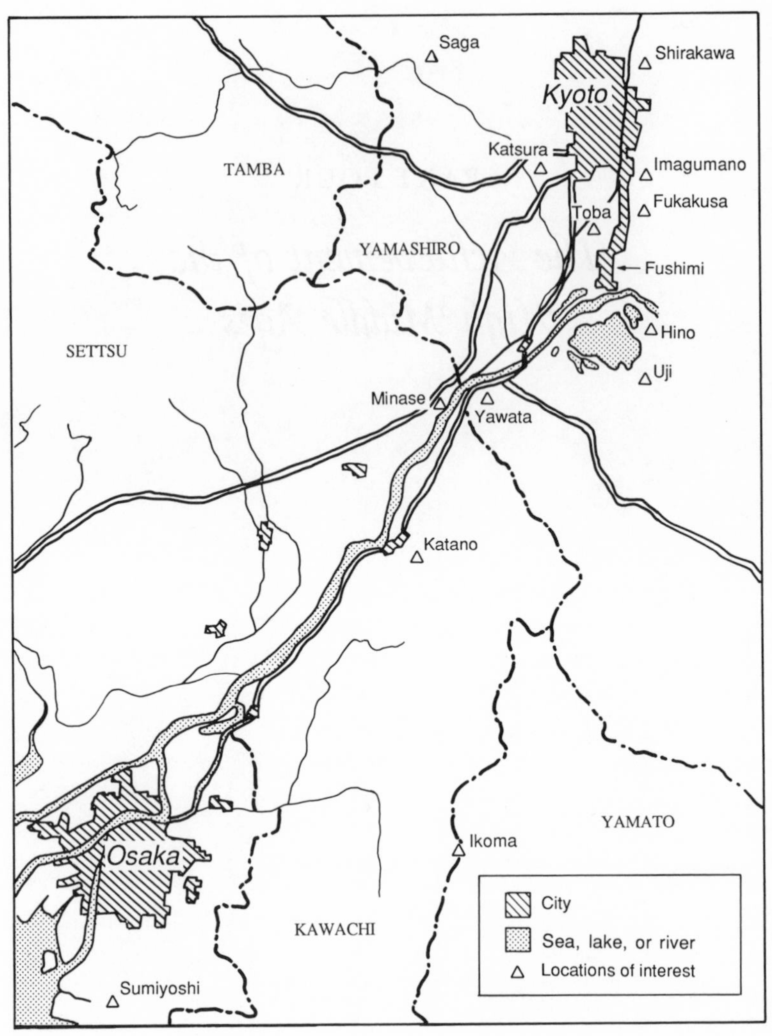

MAP 2: Detail of the Kyoto-Osaka Region

CHAPTER 13

The Revival of Poetry and Prose in Chinese

The first part of the High Middle Ages (from the beginning of the thirteenth century) was one in which existing genres flourished and the theoretical foundations for superior literature continued to be found in the teachings of the established Buddhist sects, particularly Tendai, Kegon, and Shingon. In contrast to this, the second part, encompassing the fourteenth and fifteenth centuries, witnessed the emergence and the ultimate perfection of new genres given their theoretical bases principally in Zen Buddhism.

The Zen sects were introduced from the continent at the beginning of the thirteenth century, but their unusual methods of thought did not win easy acceptance in Japan. Indeed Zen modes of thought did not begin to affect waka and nō materially until the second half of the fourteenth century. In the sixteenth century, the influence of Zen on these genres would bring about the ultimate culmination of ga in the aesthetics of wabi and sabi. On the other hand, the version of zoku that emerged around the time of the Ōnin War (Ōnin no Ran, 1467-77), was united with existing concepts of ga to form a new aesthetic of ga-zoku. This not only spurred the development of new ga-zoku genres but, after the beginning of the seventeenth century, would make the Late Middle Ages a period dominated by ga-zoku.

Reason (Ri)

Ocean transportation between Japan and the continent became somewhat easier after the beginning of the thirteenth century. As a result, Sung Dynasty culture, including Zen, exerted a strong influence on Japan during this period. After Myōan Eisai (1141-1215) introduced the Zen Buddhism of the Rinzai sect (Ch. Lin-chi) in 1191, interest in Zen grew steadily. Research on the *Honchō Kōsōden* ("Biographies of Outstanding Japanese Monks," "Jōzen," 3:1-23) has revealed that ninety-three monks travelled to Sung or Yüan China during the thirteenth and fourteenth centuries and that eighteen Chinese immigrated to Japan from China during the same period (Okada, 1929b, 300). That almost all belonged to Zen sects is an indication of the high level of interest in Zen during the period. Moreover, the Japanese Zen monks brought back with them not only the teachings of Zen but also knowledge of Sung Neoconfucianism and poetry.

From the Han through the T'ang, the chief object of Confucianism had been to derive guiding principles of life from an enormous accumulation of fact and experience. The work of Confucian scholars had been devoted principally to the exegesis and annotation of the classics. The Neoconfucianism of the Sung, however, sprang from a synthesis of Confucianism and Buddhism, particularly the teachings of the Hua-yen (Kegon) sect (Takeuchi, 1936, 267-69), and attempted to establish an order of all facts on the basis of a conception of unifying ri (Ch. li), or reason. In fact, Neoconfucianism was so closely involved with this attempt that it was alternatively termed rigaku (Ch. li-hsüeh), the study of ri, or shōrigaku (Ch. hsing-li-hsüeh), the study of fundamental nature and reason.

In all likelihood, the Japanese monks who travelled to China studied Neoconfucianism as well as Zen, precisely because they had points in common. While Kegon and Zen are very different in actual practice, they have strong philosophical affinities. For this reason Kuei-feng Tsung-mi (780-841), for example, could study Kegon and Zen at the same time. It is natural that Zen and Neoconfucianism should have become bound together, given their mutual affinities to Kegon.

The Zen monks also returned with Sung poetic texts. The central emphasis of Zen is fūryū monji (Ch. pu-li wen-tzu), or non-reliance on writings. Even emphatic interest in the sutras was discouraged. Given that, a monk's enthrallment with secular literature would be thought reprehensible.[1] Nonetheless Zen monks produced a great volume of secular literature in Japanese and Chinese during this period, and this literature is given the name of Gosan, that of Five Temples.[2] It was enormous. If one were to select only the so-called Gosan editions—works actually edited and published by modern scholars—and even if one devoted full time to their study, three years' work would allow little more than a passing glance.[3] This apparently contradictory phenomenon can be explained by the great fondness and respect for secular poetic writings among Sung Zen monks, and Japanese monks in China followed the Chinese example. Sung Zen monks were intimate with members of the highest levels of society. Not only did they receive great respect from high officials, but many of them came from families of high rank. These former members of the

[1] "Literature—prose, poetry in Chinese, poetry in Japanese—all these are of no use. There is no need to debate the propriety of abandoning them" (*Zuimonki*, 2:341).

[2] [On the Gosan temples, see ch. 1, n. 12.—Ed.]

[3] The two anthologies of Gosan literature are *Gosan Bungaku Zenshū* (4 parts) and *Gosan Bungaku Shinshū* (8 parts). Together they make up 12,562 pages. It should be noted that Gosan literature also includes works by Zen monks associated with temples and monasteries outside the "five" major temple complexes.

upper classes had mastered the art of exchanging poems as an essential medium of social intercourse, and they brought this secular poetry with them into the monasteries (Tamamura, 1955, 53-54). This Zen poetry has two opposing aspects. On the one hand, it displays a great respect for ri, as defined by Sung Neoconfucianism; but, on the other, it inclines sharply toward the beautiful.

Sung poets reacted against the excessive ornateness (kirei; Ch. ch'i-li) of Late T'ang poetry. They held increasingly that highest respect should be given to poetic ideals featuring the pristine (ku), simple (p'u), or crude (cho). These ideals were based on Taoist theories. They do not appear in the T'ang or earlier dynasties, and now make first appearance in the Sung (Aoki, 1929, 196-97). Of course, not all Sung poets acceded to the new taste. During the early Northern Sung, the Hsi-k'un style of Li Shang-yin, Wen T'ing-yün, and others, which imitated the tone of Late T'ang poetry, enjoyed great popularity, and, similarly, the *San-t'i Shih (Shih in Three Modes)*, which consists mainly of Late T'ang poetry, was widely read during the Southern Sung.[4] Nevertheless, when the Sung is viewed as a whole, the poets who advocated the so-called simple and crude were clearly preeminent, and their particular style gives the poetry of the Sung its distinctive character. Kokan Shiren (1278-1346) discussed this aspect of Sung poetry in the following:

> When the people of the Chao-Sung criticized poetry, they prized the simple, the pristine, and the plain, despising novelty, artfulness, and gorgeous beauty. This, I think, was because they did not understand the true intentions of the poets. In general, poetic expression is not limited either to pristine plainness or to novel artifice. Rather, it is of the first importance that it should be consistent with ri. (*Saihokushū* [=*SH*], 11:228)[5]

This respect for ri in poetry—and for giri (Ch. yi-li), the rationality that makes one aware of ri—provides the mainstream of Sung poetics from Ou-yang Hsiu (1007-72) and following. It was formulated on the same

[4] The Hsi-k'un style takes its name from the *Hsi-k'un Ch'ou-ch'ang Chi (Anthology of Poems Exchanged Among the Immortals)*, which is the representative collection of shih by this group of poets. Hsi-k'un (the western K'unlun) is a reference to Mount K'unlun, a mountain to the west of the Chinese mainland. Mount K'unlun actually exists, but for the Chinese of the Sung it was an imaginary mountain of pure jade, the abode of the Taoist immortals. The Hsi-k'un group of poets likened themselves to the immortals. *San-t'i Shih* is an abbreviation of *T'ang-hsien San-t'i Shih-fa*. Compiled during the Sung by Chou Pi, it classifies shih according to the manner of connecting lines and provides examples of each style. Perhaps because it is an excellent guidebook for composing shih, it was also widely circulated in Japan.

[5] There were two Sung dynasties: that (420-79) of the Six Dynasties period and the better-known one (960-1279) which follows the T'ang. The earlier is known as Liu-Sung, the latter (of interest here) as Chao-Sung.

basis as the Neoconfucian aspiration for ri (Aoki, 1935b, 67-68). Poetry that gives prominence to giri (rationality) is easy to understand, but it has a tendency to lapse into a quality called chiang, or excessive explanation. A shih by Gidō Shūshin (1325-88), "Camellia Blossoms" (*Kūgeshū*, 2:1389; Ury, 1977, 94, revised), provides a good example:

My ancient hut's a ruin, half hidden under moss—
Who'd have his carriage pause before my gate?
But my servant boy understands I have invited a guest of rare taste,
For he leaves unswept the camellia blossoms that strew the ground.

The import of the poem is quite plain: no one of a rank that would allow him to travel by carriage visits my old house, secluded as it is on a road half covered with moss. But my servant boy understands that I expect a visit from someone who loves true beauty, and so he has not swept up the fallen camellia blossoms that blanket the grounds.

The colorful device of contrasting the green of the moss with the light red of the camellia blossoms succeeds, and the mental state of the speaker of the poem who lives in this place is refreshing. The skeletal structure of the poem is formed by the following logic (giri): only a person who understands the beauty of quiet tranquility should visit this place; a guest of power and influence would not be appropriate. This logic is extremely easy to understand from the poem, and that is at once the poem's strongest point and its worst failing.

It is by no means true that only shih placing emphasis on giri (rational logic) were popular in the Zen temples that became the focal points of Gosan literature after the beginning of the fourteenth century. Even if it may have been only a result of imitation of the opinions of Sung poets, the Gosan monks did recognize the greatness of Tu Fu (712-70), who had been ignored in Japan before the fourteenth century. Moreover, the fact that there are three extant Gosan editions of *San-t'i Shih*, which is composed mainly of Late T'ang poetry, may be seen as evidence that their tastes were not limited to giri.[6] Zekkai Chūshin (1336-1405), for example, was able to harmonize these different styles, and his poetry won high praise from Chinese poets themselves. "Mist on the River" (*Shōkenkō*: 1933; Ury, 1977, revised) is a good example of Zekkai's style:

The single band of the river's flow steeps heaven in coolness,
Distant and nearby peaks have merged in the autumn mist;

[6] Books and scrolls published by Zen temples during the period from the mid-thirteenth century through the sixteenth century are called Gosan editions. Many of the providers employed in the temple complexes came from China. For research on the Gosan editions of *San-t'i Shih*, see Kawase, 1970, 1:275.

It seems she'd bar men's view with green gauze—
The goddess of the waters, too modest to show her lovely self.[7]

The scene of this poem is truly beautiful. The richness of color may be seen as a feature of Late T'ang styles. Moreover, while the poem takes as its subject the female immortal Mi-fei of Lo-ch'uan, that Taoist immortal of the river is not made to appear in the scene herself but, rather, is depicted as a fleeting vision. This is reminiscent of Shunzei's conception of yūgen (mystery and depth), as well as of Mototoshi's ideal of yōen (ethereal charm).[8] However, the flow of meaning that runs through the poem as a whole is extremely lucid, without the slightest suggestion of vagueness. In this aspect of precision in giri, or the thread of logic, the poem bears close affinities to Sung poetry.

Zekkai's poetry is also beautiful tonally. When the two poems above are read aloud, even in modern Chinese, Zekkai's poem is clearly superior to Gidō's. Compared to Gidō, who spent no time in China, Zekkai's nine years on the continent certainly worked to his advantage. Indeed, because he was a Japanese poet who composed shih that would be appreciated by Chinese poets, we cannot but consider Zekkai preeminent among Gosan shih poets. Having said that, however, I cannot rank him as a first-rate poet in Chinese, and I have serious doubts that he would have ranked even as a second-rate poet in China. His poetry has insufficient thematic weight.

Su Shih (1036-1101), the premier shih poet of the Sung, sought to reveal the very fountainhead of human existence in his poetry, an ideal others before him had pursued without success. Moreover, his poetry is always imbued with a warm, encompassing love for humanity (Yoshikawa, 1962, 104-26). Zekkai's shih lack this thematic seriousness. On the other hand, it would be unfair to criticize Zekkai too harshly for this failing. The Japanese Zen monks employed shih as a means of social intercourse, and it was thought that weighty themes belonged rather to the province of geju (Skt. gāthā).[9]

An emphasis on giri and an aspiration for beauty coexisted also in prose, and this corresponds to the coexistence of Chinese plain prose (san-wen) and parallel prose (p'ien-wen). In this case, plain prose refers

[7] Mi-fei ["The Princess of the River"] appears in Ts'ao Chih's (192-232) fu "The Goddess of the Lo" (*WH*, 19:401-405), in which she is depicted as an incomparable beauty. See Schafer, 1973, 53-55.

[8] [For various discussions, see the Index, *s.v.* yūgen and yōen.—Ed.]

[9] Geju (Skt. gāthā) is a general term for Buddhist axiomatic verse, which in China took the form of shih. In fact, there are some differences between ge and ju, with ge tending to be more explanatory and ju having a more axiomatic character. Japanese researchers use the term geju for both types of verse, but occasionally they distinguish between them as I have done in this study. [Auth., Trans.]

to the prose styles of Han Yü and Liu Tsung-yüan, which were written in classical Chinese. This is often called the antique prose style (ku-wen). Styles in the manner of Po Chü-i's plain prose were already being employed in Japan in the Early Middle Ages, but the plain prose styles of Han and Liu, which were characterized by rigorous argument achieved through a tightly knit structure, found little acceptance. However, under the influence of Ou-yang Hsiu and Su Shih, the styles of Han and Liu became the mainstream of plain prose in the Sung, and this probably also accounts for the popularity of these styles in Japan after the beginning of the fourteenth century. Since Su Shih, the leading literary figure of the Sung, had a profound understanding of Zen, the Japanese monks in China of course became attracted even more to the plain prose styles he advocated.[10] Since this style is used to move the reader by the tightly knit structure of its argument, the refinement of giri (logical structure) was absolutely essential to its success. In contrast to this, the fundamental nature of parallel prose is beauty of diction much more than what is actually said, and this did not change in the parallel prose written by Zen monks.

Kokan Shiren strongly advocated the importance of plain prose, rejecting parallel prose. His *Tōshō ni Kotau (Reply to the Fujiwara Minister)* is representative of this argument (*SH*, 9:208). Kokan's theory, which he says is based on the argument of his teacher, takes as its premise a respect for giri.[11] It is summarized in the following (*SH*, 12:247):

> When thought has self-consciously grasped its own mode of being, I call it "hō" (conception). When thought is given form through verbal sounds, I call it "shō" (linguistic expression). Today, the learned place much emphasis on conception before it has become linguistic expression, and refuse to give emphasis to expression itself, regarding this as secondary. However, in the fact that everything is "dust" [a temporary mode of existence], whether before or after it has been expressed linguistically, there is no difference between them. If the ri (reasoning) that is to be expressed is excellent, then its expressed content will also be superior. If the ri is of little import, the thought that becomes the content of expression will also be insignificant. It is precisely the manner of expression that is the problem.

Kokan believed in the equivalence of thought, which constitutes the content of expression, to expression itself, asserting that the content of

[10] Su Shih's connection with Hua-yen has been pointed out previously (Yoshikawa, 1961, 267-71). However, he also exchanged questions and answers (mondō) with Fu-yin Liao-yün (1032-98) (*Eyō* 28: 454), and a Ch'an poem survives that he sent to Chao-chiao Ch'ang-tsung (1025-91; *Tōba* 23:2739). These and other facts suggest that he was on intimate terms with priests in the Ch'an sects.

[11] Kokan was the disciple of Tōzan Tanshō. In his study of literature, however, he received much of his training from I-shan I-ning (1247-1317), and it is quite possible that the teacher he mentions is the latter.

thought achieves or fails to achieve a high level depending on structure of its linguistic expression. This assertion reminds one of R. S. Crane, but Kokan's use of the concept of reasoning (ri) has a much narrower sense than does Crane's, referring as it does to the logical structure of a composition.[12] In his own compositions, Kokan's logic is always extremely clear, and one understands precisely what he is trying to say. This kind of writing had not existed in Japan previously, and it now developed for the first time from contact with Sung culture. It is especially worth noting that this way of writing penetrated Japanese prose in the standard styles, for example, in the new prose seen in certain sections (dan) of *Tsurezuregusa* (see ch. 16).

Of course, the Gosan monks did produce an enormous body of literature in parallel prose, and this literature is also rich in examples from Sung China. From the Five Dynasties to the Northern Sung, temples and monasteries in China established administrative systems that were very much bureaucratic organizations, and, as was true in the government bureaucracy itself, the management of these organizations was carried on through documents. This development was by no means limited to the Zen sect. In many cases, the scribes who prepared these documents were former men of letters, who had mastered parallel prose in preparation for the national examinations (k'o-chü). It soon came to be standard practice for the official documents of Buddhist temples and monasteries to be written in parallel prose, and this practice was copied by the Zen Buddhist establishments in Japan (Tamamura, 1955, 51-53). Kokan himself, who criticized parallel prose as the literature of dynasties in decline, compiles in it the *Zengi Gemonshū (Examples of Official Composition for Zen Priests)*, which is ample evidence of the high demand for composition in parallel prose.[13] This appears to be a case of not practicing what one preaches, but Kokan must have made a distinction between plain prose for writings that had a direct connection with Zen itself and parallel prose for secular or ceremonial uses.

Paradox (Ha)

While the poetry and prose dealt with in the previous section were written by Zen monks, the intrinsic quality of this poetry and prose itself did not differ from that of secular poetry and prose. The kind of poetry called geju (Ch. chieh-sung) was, however, unique to Zen circles. Geju belong to poetry in its broad definition, but they take as their themes the ultimate

[12] See Crane's concept of structure in *The Languages of Criticism and the Structure of Poetry* (Crane, 1953, 128-39). Kokan himself uses ri for a concept better termed giri (Ch. yi-li).

[13] "Plain prose is popular in flourishing times, while parallel prose is used in waning times" (*SH*, 208).

truths to which Zen aspires. Unlike shih, which express personal thought and emotions, geju are characterized by impersonality. Moreover, they are not necessarily bound by the normal formal restrictions of shih, and they do not exclusively value precedented language. Therefore, when geju are judged by the same criteria applied to shih, they are almost invariably inferior or even outside the pale of discussion. But if they are read without reference to shih standards, geju have an amazing expressive power. Even I, with no experience of zazen, have been extremely moved by some geju.

For Zen monks, there must originally have been no other poetry besides geju. Chinese Zen monks such as Lan-ch'i Tao-lung (1213-78), Wu-an P'u-ning (1197-1276), and Ta-hsiu Cheng-nien (1215-89), who came to Japan in an early period of contact between the two countries, have left only geju. Among other Chinese monks who came to Japan, Wu-hsüeh Tsu-yüan (1226-86) and I-shan I-ning (1247-1317) seem to have been relatively interested in shih but, on the evidence of extant sources, neither wrote a great number. The advance of secular poetry and prose into the Zen temples did not occur until the early fourteenth century, when Japanese disciples of the Chinese monks who had returned to Japan began to write actively. It was in the period of Tettan Dōshō (1260-1331), Shūkan Dōsen (1263-1323), Musō Soseki (1275-1351), and Sesson Yūbai (1290-1346) that styles of shih besides geju began to gain ascendancy among Japanese Zen priests. Kokan Shiren did not study Zen as a disciple of a Chinese monk, but he did learn prose and poetry styles from I-shan I-ning.

Among these priests, Sesson wrote an unusually large number of shih, achieving a high degree of mastery. But even he produced his best work in geju. In 1313, the seventh year of his study in China, relations between Japan and China grew strained, and Sesson was arrested on suspicion of espionage, after a time being sentenced to death. Just as he was about to be executed, he recited the following ge with perfect composure:

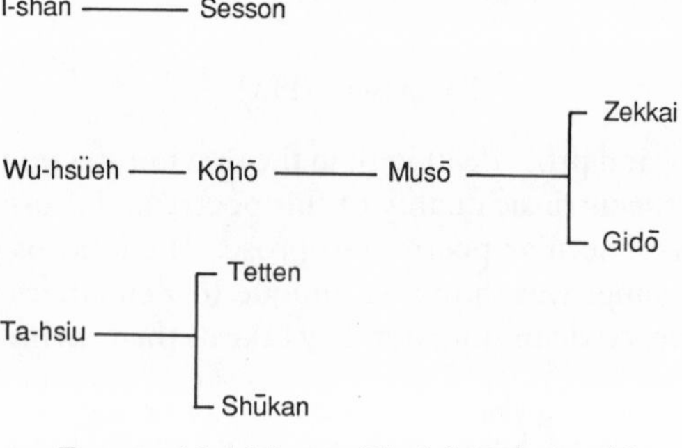

FIGURE 13.1 Master-Disciple Relationships Between Chinese and Japanese Zen Priests

In all heaven and earth there is no place to stand a staff.
It is wonderful that man is Emptiness, substantial existence is Emptiness.
The long sword of the great Yüan is wonderful.
In the moment of a flash of lightning, it cuts the spring breeze.

The Yüan officials were so impressed with this performance that they released Sesson.[14] The ge had been composed earlier by Wu-hsüeh when he was on the verge of being killed by Yüan soldiers, who spared him because of its mastery. Sesson used it to the same effect. Later, Sesson wrote the following ge, incorporating the earlier ge by Wu-hsüeh (*Bingashū*, 2:890):

In all heaven and earth there is no place to stand a staff.
Yet, though my body truly exists, I am in a place where it cannot be seen.
At midnight a wooden man mounts a stone horse,[15]
And crashes down the hundred walls of iron, the thousand walls of iron, that encircle him.[16]
It is wonderful that man is Emptiness, substantial existence is Emptiness.
The millions of worlds of the cosmos are confined in a bird cage.[17]
Sin disappears, my heart is void in the ultimate third pleasure of Zen,
And who would say that Deva or I am imprisoned?[18]
The three-foot sword of the Great Yüan is wonderful,
Its light glittering like cold frost over ten thousand leagues.
The weathered skull opens its eyes again;[19]
Its eyes like flawless jewels worth fifteen capitals.[20]
In the moment of a flash of lightning, the sword cuts the spring breeze,
And the god of Emptiness bleeds crimson.

[14] *Sesson Daioshō Gyōdōki* (568/40), compiled in 1432 by Daiyū Yūsho.

[15] There are many examples of similar lines, of which the most famous is: "The wooden man sings and the stone woman rises to dance" (*Tōsan Roku*, 515).

[16] Cakravāda-parvata, the outermost of the nine mountains surrounding the central world of the Buddhist universe, is said to be entirely composed of iron.

[17] The "millions of worlds" is an abbreviation or simplification of the quintillion worlds of the Buddhist universe. [Auth., Ed.]

[18] Āryadeva, the disciple of Nāgārjuna and the founder of Mahādhyamika philosophy. He defeated anti-Buddhist philosophers in a debate in Pātaliputra, the capital of Magadha, but was later killed because of his victory.

[19] Similar imagery may be seen in other geju. For example: "The eyes within the skull are beady" (*Hekigan Roku*, 1, item 2:14).

[20] This is the treasury of a jewel that King Chao of Ch'in proposed as the ransom for fifteen walled cities.

He surprises Mount Sumeru, making it stand on its head,[21]
And jumps into the hole of a lotus root to hide himself.

The fourteenth line of this ge, "The god of Emptiness bleeds crimson," is extraordinary and representative of the paradox of the poem. Emptiness is sūnyatā (J. shunnyata), the absence of substantial existence, and its god is of course its deification, without shape or color. But when the great sword of Yüan cuts through the spring breeze like a flash of lightning, Emptiness bleeds colorfully. This kind of expression is unique to geju and so would never be found in a normal shih.

The explanation for this bizarre mode of expression lies in the ultimate truth of Zen, Emptiness. The concept entails that all existence is without substantiality; but when this concept is expressed in that way, the expression itself has a substantiality. Thus, in order not to allow expressed content to have substantiality, a mode of expression was devised that deliberately had no meaning, that should convey no meaning. For example, the sixth line of the poem, "The millions of worlds of the cosmos are confined in a bird cage," defies reason, but the reader must not attempt to understand intellectually why the speaker of the poem has made this kind of statement. The concept of a huge existence confined within something tiny may also be found, for example, in "The Good Morrow" by John Donne (1572-1631):

And now good morrow to our waking soules,
Which watch not one another out of feare;
For love, all love of other sights controules,
And makes one little roome, an every where.

(8-11)[22]

Unlike the brutal image of prison and execution that hovers in the background of Sesson's ge, the scene of this poem is suffused with the ardent murmurs of two lovers. They delight in the consummation of their love, and their "one little roome" (a tiny space curtained off within the bedroom) in which it has taken place. The poet attempts to transcend his story of love in the specific space of this "one little roome" and the time depicted—in order to rise from a specific space to the universe and a specific time to eternity, so to be elevated from particular phenomena to uni-

[21] Sumeru is the name of the mountain that is said to rise at the center of the most central world of the Buddhist universe.

[22] W. H. Auden and Norman Holmes Pearson, *Poets of the English Language* (New York: The Viking Press, 1953), 2:374.

versality.[23] This "one little roome" becomes any place in the world, or in the universe.

The conception of Donne's poem is thus of the same character as Sesson's "the millions of worlds of the cosmos are confined in a bird cage." In the case of Metaphysical poetry, however, even if the poem is conceived on the basis of a radical image, the conceptual focus of the poem is the device of reaching a solution through a kind of intellectual tightrope walking. The irrationality of geju denies any such intellectual assistance. It should require no further argument to establish that in this sense, the expression found in Zen poetry is not the same as that of Metaphysical poets.

The last two lines of Sesson's ge, "He surprises Mount Sumeru, making it stand on its head, / And jumps into the hole of a lotus root to hide himself," are of the same character. Radical images to which it is impossible to respond with our usual consciousness of space are presented and powerfully affirmed. The first line of the ge, "In all heaven and earth there is no place to stand a staff," also presents a conception of space that, while opposite in intent from that of the other lines quoted, is equally radical. This kind of spatiality is also taken up in Donne's "The Sunne Rising."[24] It opens with the speaker of the poem exclaiming to the sun: "Busie old foole, unruly Sunne." It transpires that, because it is morning, the sun is peeping through the curtains, trying to arouse two lovers. About halfway through the poem, we find the following lines:

> Looke, and to-morrow late, tell mee,
> Whether both the Indias of spice and Myne
> Be where thou leftest them, or lie here with mee.
> Aske for those Kings whom thou saw'st yesterday,
> And thou shalt heare, All here in one bed lay. (16-20)

Both the kings and the Indias have taken the shape of the speaker and his lover lying in bed beside him: "She is all States, and all Princes, I, / Nothing else is" (21-22). The poem eliminates spatiality by transcending it. This is a denial of the spatiality of distance, and to the extent that it denies the substantiality of specific spaces the imagery of this poem has much in common with the Zen imagery of Sesson's ge: paradoxically, the apertures in a lotus root are not small, and the space in all heaven and earth

[23] "Donne's 'one little roome' is a chamber, a curtain-bed, in which the two lovers awake and find in their joy that all they desire is right there. It is, then, a specific, felt place at a specific, felt time, and the urge to transcend rather transforms the time and place than aspires for that which is beyond" [Miner, 1969a, 105].

[24] *Poets of the English Language*, 2:375.

is great. However, in the case of the Zen poem, the reader is not permitted to say, "Of course." *Not* comprehending is required.

The reader who thinks such writing intellectual, and the reader who thinks it is super-intellectual, will be both radically surprised. But because this surprise is not surprise in the dimension of heightened experience, specialists have given it the name "metaphysical surprise." The nature of this metaphysical surprise is exemplified by Sesson's "At midnight a wooden man mounts a stone horse, / And crashes down the hundred walls of iron, the thousand walls of iron, that encircle him."

When metaphysical surprise is accompanied by dread and loathing, it is called a "metaphysical shudder" (Williamson, 1930, 90-98). T. S. Eliot's "Whispers of Immortality" is a good example of a poem that evokes this response by employing metaphysical imagery:

> Webster was much possessed by death
> And saw the skull beneath the skin;
> And breastless creatures under ground
> Leaned backward with a lipless grin.
>
> Daffodil bulbs instead of balls
> Stared from the sockets of the eyes!
> He knew that thought clings round dead limbs
> Tightening its lusts and luxuries. (1-8)[25]

The imagery of bulbs staring from the sockets of a skull whose eyeballs have rotted and disappeared is very close to Sesson's concept: "The weathered skull opens its eyes again." However, Sesson's imagery is intended to affirm the absolute contradiction that "the fact of not being is precisely the fact of being," and the extraordinary nature of the contradiction must never be rationalized.

I RATE Sesson's ge as the finest of its kind. That judgment refers to its excellence as Zen writing, for if the standards of shih are applied to this poem, we can just as easily criticize it as awkward and crude. I have had occasion elsewhere to comment on Burton Watson's translation of the poem, stating that while his translation was extremely interesting as a poem in English, I was not impressed by the original (Konishi, 1970c, 24).[26] The criteria used were those of the traditional, refined techniques of Chinese shih poetry. Poetry in English is not restricted by such rules,

[25] *T. S. Eliot: The Complete Poems and Plays, 1909-1950* (New York: Harcourt, Brace & Co., 1952), 32-33.

[26] For Watson's translation, see Keene, 1955, 312-13.

and for that reason I found Watson's translation much more interesting than the original.

In general, the writers of geju assumed that recipients would be people who, like themselves, were actively engaged in Zen. Based on their own experience, such readers could be expected to understand modes of expression unique to such thought. In short, we amateurs are ignored completely as unqualified readers. Thus, if we want to apply the standards of secular literature to geju and evaluate them one way or the other, it has nothing to do with the devotee of Zen. At the same time, of course, if we want to respond to geju in the manner of a Zen adept, there is no reason for the Zen professional to deny our attempt. What I mean by responding as an adept is an attitude that does not attempt to understand its extremely paradoxical, irrational modes of expression intellectually, but to respond to the logic of its writing—that is, it is precisely the irrational that is rational. Reading again Sesson's geju with this attitude enables us to say that it is the finest of its kind.

There is the danger that ultimate truth will become no longer truth in the instant it is spoken, and yet truth is not communicated by simply remaining silent. To deal with this dilemma, imagery was devised that completely excludes intellectual understanding, and that imagery may be termed the greatest special feature of Zen. For example, there is the following Zen mondō (question and answer between monk and master; *Hekigan Roku*, 2, item 66):

> A certain priest questioned Tung-shan saying, "What kind of thing is the Buddha?" Tung-shan's answer: "Three pounds of hemp seed."[27]

Tung-shan Liang-chieh's (807-69) answer has become one of the most famous Zen kōan. However much the kōan is explained, such an explanation will never teach truth. Those trained in the nineteenth-century tradition of literary commentary will no doubt think that there must be some necessary connection between the signifying image of "three pounds of hemp seed" and the signified meaning, the Buddha, and they will endeavor to grasp it. This is because they believe that a single intention has been buried in the work and that the correct interpretation of the work is to excavate that intention and explain it in some one-to-one correspondence.[28] In fact, "three pounds of hemp seed" is posed as expression that

[27] I have suggested to the translator the word "pound" for Japanese "kin," a unit of weight that usually designated six hundred grams. In this class, neither the unit of measurement nor the number of kin has any significance—it could be one kin or seven hundred, one gram or a metric ton.

[28] The archaeological metaphor of digging for meaning as a means of literary understanding holds that meaning is a thing hidden in the text that can be excavated through interpretation. But it is no more than an artifact of the nineteenth century (Iser, 1976, 4-5).

does not mean anything at all, and one who would attempt to seek meaning in it runs the risk of being scolded or, worse, beaten soundly by a Zen master.

The essential nature of language is to communicate meaning and, therefore, if something has been said there must be meaning in it. In the dimension of everyday language, this way of thinking is absolutely correct. In Zen, however, one speaks precisely in order not to mean anything, and this we may call an infinite paradox. It is precisely this language of paradox that is the expressive medium of Zen; and because it destroys the mode of existence of ordinary language, I would like to call it ha or paradox.[29] And when this language of ha or paradox is brought to life in geju, we may call it paradoxical expression or ha expression. P'an-shan Pao-chi (744-825) left behind for his disciples the following problem: "In the entire universe there is no substantial existence. Where then exists the human heart?"[30] Many years later, Hsüeh-tou Chung-hsien (980-1052) composed this ju as an answer (*Hekigan Roku*, 4, item 37:188):

> In the entire universe there is no substantial existence.
> Where then to seek the human heart?
> Make of the white cloud a sunshade.
> Make of the water's flow a lute.
> Play one song, two songs—there is no one who understands.
> The rain has gone, and beyond the bank of night the water of autumn is deep.

In the whole universe, there is no existence that possesses self-identity. What makes all existence exist is a nonphysical existence that transcends individuals, but this existence itself does not exist as actual form. How will you deal with this? To this question, Hsüeh-tou replies: Make the white cloud into a sunshade, and listen to the flowing spring as if it were the sound of a lute. This imagery communicates no meaning whatsoever. Hsüeh-tou reasserts this fact in the line, "Play one song, two songs—there is no one who understands" (this imagery will not be understood by anyone), and then emphasizes it further with the allegorical line, "The rain has gone, and beyond the bank of night the water of autumn is deep" (the long autumn rain has stopped falling, and, as one stands on the embankment in the darkness of night, the depth of the water is unfathomable). Since the speaker of the poem himself assures us that the imagery "will

[29] ["Ha" means breaking, destroying, but by extension such other things as irrationality, absurdity, agitation, and development. We use "paradox" as translation, since the author has just shown that the ha principle is founded on using language in a radically paradoxical fashion.—Ed.]

[30] *Keitoku Roku*, 7:253.

not be understood by anyone," there is no need for us to endeavor to understand it.

This kind of imagery is the result of incorporating expression that is always used in mondō into the genre of geju.[31] Originally it was nothing other than a means of leading the recipient to awakening (satori). While I have no particular intention to achieve satori, however, I am able to respond to this Zen paradox from the point of view of literature. When one attempts to discover some tenor or signified meaning in the imagery of Emptiness bleeding crimson blood, nothing is there but an impenetrable strangeness. If one renounces this search for a significance and responds directly to the imagery itself, however, one is moved by a kind of powerful emotional impact not to be found in normal shih. There is no basis for saying that shih must mean something particular, for as long as shih contains language that arouses an emotional response, it can be recognized as literature. The imagery used by Sesson has this character. But one must not ignore the fact that the ge discussed above does, in fact, have a signified tenor that is present in the poem as a whole: since life and death are essentially the same, the fact of having been slashed by a sword is of no great consequence. Indeed, that this meaningfulness has been effectively linked with meaningless imagery is precisely the reason that I can say that this ge is an outstanding example of its genre.

BECAUSE ha or paradoxical writing is employed to break down routinized and fixed awareness, it must always be spoken in "one's own words." Even when one uses existing expression, it is essential that the way one uses it be "something that belongs to one alone." Sesson's ge includes diction that is similar to that of existing shih, but in the situations in which he uses this diction there is that which is unique to him. In the succeeding generation—the time of Gidō and Zekkai—this kind of individuality decreases to a certain extent, and there is a tendency toward writing that does not evoke such a powerfully vivid emotional response. One example of this tendency is Zekkai's "To Master Ch'u-shih" (*Zekkai Roku*, 2:749):

> Great masters are rare in the world of Buddhism today,
> And the great teaching can depend only on the vigor of your old age.
> The three-foot staff is made completely of iron,
> And on the back of Emptiness the red wound bleeds.

[31] There are many examples in the sayings of Zen masters. For example, see *Lin-chi Lu* (*Rinzai Roku*, 66-67). [Mondō means question and answer. As the author is showing, this may involve a kōan but is a much larger phenomenon in varieties of paradoxical (ha) expression.—Ed.]

The first half of the poem is fairly straightforward: today, when masters who have achieved satori are few, the teachings of Zen may rely only on your own robust health. In the latter half of the poem, however, the following imagery is used to express the depth of Ch'u-shih's mastery of Zen: he beats Emptiness with a staff of iron, and blood flows from the back of Emptiness, itself the ultimate truth.[32] If we were to read only this ge, we would be shocked by the strangeness of this expression. Because we have seen Sesson's "And the god of Emptiness bleeds crimson," however, the imagery of this poem is not so impressive. Moreover, in Sesson's case, the imagery is given power because we are reminded of the poet at the moment when it is uncertain whether or not he will be beheaded. Zekkai merely imagines that Emptiness is being beaten like an errant disciple in order to emphasize the greatness of his master, and his poem possesses less strength.

A similar tendency may be seen in the first of Gidō's "Two Ge on Seeing off Master Chin the Liaison Officer on His Way to the Funeral Service of His Great Teacher" (*Kūgeshū*, 3:1394-1395):

> His knowledge was like a boundless sea within his heart;
> The waves running high were never ending.

And this is the second:

> One night, a whale came and gulped up the waters,
> exposing the bottom;
> Two or three pieces of coral appeared exposed.

The second poem is a lament for the dead master, while the first speaks of his greatness.[33] Gidō attempts a paradox: a whale has drunk up the waters of the great sea, and a few pieces of coral have appeared on the bottom. This kind of absurd imagery is appropriate precisely for the expression of the ultimate truth to which Zen aspires, but when it is used to symbolize the greatness of an individual one has the feeling that a meat cleaver has been used to slice a chicken breast. Moreover, I do not think that this imagery is original with Gidō. Compare it with Zekkai's "Arousing the Spirit That Is Not in Thrall" (*Zekkai Roku*, 2:749):

[32] The "iron staff" is usually made by wrapping a bamboo rod with wisteria and applying lacquer. It is used to strike Zen practitioners who are dull in their response to Zen mondō or lose concentration in meditation. Either "sky" or "Emptiness" may be read from the Chinese character. In Zen Buddhism it designates the ultimate truth, the Emptiness as described earlier.

[33] The master is a liaison officer in the sense of being in charge of the temple's relations as an ambassador to, or a liaison with, the external world. [Auth., Ed.]

The true work of the mind is born when it is not in thrall.
The past, the present, and the future—
Splendid naming, but with whom in mind?
An enormous whale drains the waters of the sea,
And the moon is bright in the upper branches of the coral.[34]

I doubt that Gidō borrowed from Zekkai's ge, or vice versa. More likely, they both allude to a preexisting poem. Certainly the influence is not from Gidō to Zekkai. The theme of Zekkai's ge is Zen truth, and his use of paradox is not inappropriate. However, reliance on existing imagery cannot help but result in a weakening of the extraordinary quality inherent in paradoxical expression. Compared to the geju of Sesson and his predecessors, these examples reflect the technical improvements in normal poetry and prose that began to occur in the period of Gidō and Zekkai. But the evocative power of geju (as Zen poetry) seems to decline precisely to the extent that the genre approaches the technical mastery of shih. Quantitatively, Gosan literature enjoyed amazing prosperity after the beginning of the fifteenth century, but the geju of the Gosan monks of the time are remarkable only for the prevalence of hackneyed imagery. In short, the ha principle no longer produced adequately paradoxical writing, and geju fell into a condition that demanded the appearance of Ikkyū Sōjun's (1394-1481) "madness" (kyō). The use of the paradoxical or ha principle itself came to be assimilated into such other genres as waka and nō.

Madness (Kyō)

In the late fourteenth century, the period during which Gidō and Zekkai were active, there was already a tendency for geju to lose their quality of "one's own words." But in secular poetry and prose of the same period, writers continued strongly to grasp their own thoughts and emotions in the most appropriate diction. After the beginning of the fifteenth century, however, secular poetry and prose lapse into a monotonous sameness of expression, and only the *quantity* of literature written in Chinese during this period gives occasion for surprise. Similarly, the geju of this period are characterized by a constant repetition of stereotyped diction that is quite foreign to the rigorous intensity one expects of Zen writing. This is of course related to the systematizing of the Zen establishment proceeding at an increasingly rapid pace, with the support of the court and the bakufu. In the process of this regularizing, Zen monks themselves under-

[34] Zekkai's title is taken from a phrase in *The Diamond Sūtra (Vajraschedikā-prajnāpāramitā-sūtra)*, 763.

went a kind of bureaucratizing, in which conformity was the order of the day.

In literature, this resulted in a new Zen world of ga, in which the composition and reception of literature took place within a group that held common conventions of thinking and feeling. To the extent that this was in fact a world of ga, there is no particular reason to criticize this development. Poetry and prose in Chinese by Zen monks, however, are basically different in many respects from the world of ga discovered in waka and prose in Japanese. The fundamental approach of Zen is not to remain in the same state, an ideal refusal described as denial of attachment to a given state (which is a form of delusion). As expressed in Zekkai's ge, it is precisely the heart that has no place to reside that achieves satori. Thus the fundamental nature of Zen is uncongenial to the world of ga [with its rational, fixed categories]; and if Zen stagnates in such a world, it will itself be debilitated. An enervated Zen could not possibly produce superior ga expression.

Nankō Sōgen (1387-1463) was one of the Zen monks who became disillusioned with this fossilized and stagnant Zen establishment. Renouncing his status as a senior scholar at the temple Shōkokuji, Nankō spent the last half of his life in freedom, as a poet, following a life more suitable to a conscientious Zen devotee. Nankō's one-time student Ikkyū Sōjun (1394-1481), however, chose a way of life that, viewed simply, appears to have been the very antithesis of that of a conscientious Zen monk. In a word, he lived like an outlaw.

> A certain monk who had been a senior disciple of my teacher warned me against having relations with women and eating meat. My disciples became angry, so I composed this ge and read it to them.
>
> Preaching Buddhism for the sake of others, this is but seeking after worldly fame.
> This man, an ordinary person who yet assumes the guise of a monk, what's his name anyhow?
> If the old master's admonition makes your ears burn with anger,
> My humdrum character, evil yesterday, is quite good today.[35]
>
> (*Kyōunshū* [=*KUS*]: 154)

Unlike shih, ge require no regulated expression. All that is required is that the poem state a high principle of Buddhist thought. This ge, for example, gives the impression that Ikkyū has simply arranged everyday spoken language into seven-syllable lines. The phrase translated above as "what's his name anyhow?" is a Sung-period colloquialism that could

[35] [A note on Chinese usage is omitted.—Ed.]

never have been used in a normal shih. Nevertheless, the diction employed in this poem is weak in evocative power. Certainly it possesses nothing like the shocking imagery of Sesson's ge, and the impression of the language of the poem is rather weak in general.

Because of its extraordinary internal qualities we nevertheless receive a powerful impression from this ge. In the world of fifteenth-century Buddhism, enjoying oneself with women and eating meat were considered to be horribly immoral (drinking was perhaps considered to be a somewhat lesser sin). However, what Ikkyū calls his "humdrum character" desires all these things, and while they constituted immoral conduct for which, as a monk, he could only expect severe criticism, Ikkyū wrote about them constantly.

As I was about to leave Nyoian, I left this for Master Yōsō.[36]

> I have been ten days in this temple, and my spirit is restless.
> When I pull the scarlet thread near my feet, it reaches up long.
> If someday you come searching for me,
> I'll be in a fish shop, a sake shop, or a brothel.[37] (*KUS*, 79)

I have been at Nyoian (a detached temple of Daitokuji) for ten days, but somehow my spirit is not settled. I want a woman so badly I cannot endure it, and so I am going out. If you have need of me, look for me at a seafood restaurant, a bar, or a brothel. This is the tone of this lighthearted ge. Moreover, Ikkyū was by no means indulging in an idle jest: it seems that he actually did frequent brothels, for he wrote at least seven other ge on the subject. The following is a good example (*KUS*, 138):

Written in a Brothel[38]

> In the drenched affection of a beautiful woman, the river of my
> passion is deep.
> A prostitute and this old monk are singing on the second floor.
> I love to embrace her and kiss her,
> Having no desire to renounce the fire of worldly passions.[39]

[36] Yōsō Sōi (1376-1458), the twenty-sixth abbot of Daitokuji. Later, Ikkyū and Yōsō found themselves in bitter conflict and in his *Jikai Shū* Ikkyū denounces his former friend with horrible curses.

[37] The scarlet thread symbolizes lust for the opposite sex, and the "fish shop" is one serving fish as prepared food not to be cooked at home.

[38] This shih was probably actually written on the wall or a pillar in a brothel.

[39] The phrase translated here as "drenched affection" means "clouds and rains." In the legendary tradition of Mount Wu, however, it means sexual intercourse as in *Wen Hsüan*, 19:393, the "Kao-t'ang Fu." The phrase "fires of worldly passion" refers to the aggregate energy of worldly passion (desire, delusion).

Ikkyū declares that he loves embracing beautiful women but has no desire to discard his body—an accumulation of worldly passions—in order to seek buddhahood. Since the poet is the famous Zen monk Ikkyū, however, to the view of an ordinary person, the poem can only seem to be an expression of madness. But Ikkyū was no extoller of brothels. He also wrote two ju and a shih under the title "Deploring the Brothels in the Capital" (*KUS*, 333-35). He observes that brothels are prospering in the capital and exclaims that this is infinitely deplorable, an omen of the downfall of the country. He declares that those who spend their days enthralled in sexual intercourse are no different from cows, horses, dogs, and chickens. This seems blatantly contradictory, but for Ikkyū there was no contradiction at all. In Mahāyāna Buddhism, worldly passions and buddhahood are not different things, and this assertion is even more strongly emphasized in Zen. The idea of gradually reducing worldly passions until one finally reaches a state of buddhahood in which all worldly passions have disappeared is a Hīnayāna concept strongly rejected in Zen. The position of Zen is that the only method to attain buddhahood is to identify oneself with worldly passions and thereby deny them. Ikkyū pursued this method faithfully.

Ikkyū also had a concubine. They seem to have been together for some time but finally separated (*Kyōun Shishū* [=*KUSS*], 161-63). A woman who is called Oako also appears in Ikkyū's poems (ibid., 182). It is not clear whether or not she is the woman of the earlier poem, but Ikkyū has two poems that certainly deal with her.

Oako Estranged from My Bed

She who copulated with me has distanced her bedding more than
four feet,
My shore bird, who learned her tricks here beside me.
To sleep alone one night is like being three thousand leagues distant,
And does anyone's letter come from the skyways of the geese?
(*KUSS*, 209)

Oako Goes to Take a Bath

Her naked body appears somehow amid many others
As she washes the world's red dust from the verdant brows of her
flower-like face.
After this old priest has long soaked himself in the bath,
He could use a spring of divine treasure made in this hot spring!
(*KUSS*, 220)

The intimacy of the relation needs no comment.

Toward the end of his life, Ikkyū became passionately infatuated with a blind woman called Mori. Apparently, Mori had known Ikkyū and had been longing for him for some time before they finally formed a relationship in the spring of 1471, when Ikkyū was seventy-eight years old (*KUS*, "Supplement," 420). Ikkyū's love for Mori was intense, and in one sequence of shih he vividly describes sexual acts with her that can only be called perverted (ibid., 405-22). To what extent these poems describe fact or fiction is impossible to tell. But when this sequence is read as a kind of poetic novel, I find it much more powerful than Tanizaki Jun'ichirō's *Kagi* (*The Key*). Ikkyū, who publicly spoke of sexual acts that a normal person could not even voice, was truly a man of "madness" (J. kyō; Ch. k'ung), and well deserved the pen name he chose for himself, Kyōun (Mad Cloud).

There were also people of "madness" in China, such as the dissident and anti-moral "seven wise men of the bamboo grove." Yet the philosophical standpoint of the "seven wise men of the bamboo grove" was connected with Taoism. They are not in the same line as Ikkyū, who put into practice the Mahāyāna concept, "worldly passions are buddhahood." Apparently, Japanese intellectuals of this period approved of Ikkyū's madness. He was revered by three tennō: Gokomatsu (r. 1392-1412), Shōkō (r. 1412-28), and Gohanazono (r. 1428-64); and in 1474 the court appointed him abbot of Daitokuji. Owa Sōrin, a wealthy merchant and cultural figure of the new city of Sakai, and others were said to have been constantly concerned for Ikkyū's welfare, giving him large amounts of financial support.

As I have said, in terms of technique alone, Ikkyū's geju are not particularly impressive. I prefer to think, however, that this was not because Ikkyū was unskilled as a writer, but rather that he protested against how routine the absurd expression employed by Zen masters had become. To him, however much their mode of speech appeared to be of a kind that would startle people, in fact they were merely repeating hackneyed formulas again and yet again. Ikkyū was well versed in the traditional expressive techniques of shih, and his mastery of these techniques is remarkable in his descriptive landscape poetry.[40]

In spite of his ability, he did not use very impressive techniques of expression either in his geju or in most of his shih, which implies that he chose to give greater weight to originality of material and theme. Ikkyū's choice of subjects for his poetry was not limited to revelations of his bizarre behavior but also ranged over a wide variety of social phenomena that had never before been taken up in shih. He apparently had a strong interest in the performing arts, for he wrote shih on the nō performances of Komparu Sōin (1432-80) and Komparu Zempō (1454-1528?).[41] A

[40] See *KUSS*, 69, 72, 149-56, etc.
[41] *KUSS*, 216 and 266.

great number of references to nō plays appear in these shih. He also wrote shih on shakuhachi performances.[42] On the other hand, he wrote of the continual warfare during this period and of the poverty of the nobility. He wrote love letters for other people but also reviled the cupidity of women. Others of his shih depict beheadings at Rokujōgawara.[43] I have stated previously that the aspects of real life do not often become the subjects of Chinese poetry and prose written by Japanese (vol. two, ch. 6). Ikkyū brought all these aspects of secular life into the world of shih, and I view this introduction of zoku in a ga art as one indication that movement toward the Late Middle Ages had already begun by this time.

[42] *KUSS*, 76, 221, and 237.

[43] On warfare, see *KUS*, 155; *KUS*, "Supplement," 249; and *KUSS*, 148; on the nobility, see *KUSS*, 102; for a love poem for another person, see *KUSS*, 165; on women's cupidity, see *KUS*, "Supplement," 141-43, 192; and on beheadings, see *KUS*, 229-30.

CHAPTER 14

The Deepening of Waka

Confrontation in Poetic Circles

Conflict among the three branches of the Mikohidari house became even more intense from the end of the thirteenth century to the middle of the fourteenth. The already present antagonisms between the three branches developed into disputes connected with the lines of royal succession. On the occasion of his abdication, Gosaga (r. 1242-44) established the custom of having the descendants of Gofukakusa (r. 1246-59), the Jimyōin line, and the descendants of Kameyama (r. 1259-74), the Daikakuji line, alternate as tennō. The Nijō family was connected with the Daikakuji line, while the Kyōgoku family allied itself with the Jimyōin line. Thus, whenever a royal waka anthology was commissioned, the editors were chosen from the family—Nijō or Kyōgoku only—connected with the line of the reigning tennō. The Reizei family always united with the Kyōgoku family in opposition to the Nijō, but the result of the practice was that Reizei family members were never chosen as editors. In general, the Nijō prevailed. They or their allies compiled the final twelve of the twenty-one royal collections, with but three exceptions: (1) *Gyokuyōshū* (properly *Gyokuyō Wakashū* [= *GYS*]); (2) *Fūgashū* (*Fūga Wakashū* [= *FGS*]); and (3) *Shingoshūishū (Shingoshūi Wakashū)*.

The compilers of these collections were Kyōgoku Tamekanu (1254-1332) for the *Gyokuyōshū* in 1313 or 1314, abdicated Kōgon (1313-64) for the *Fūgashū* about 1346, and (Fujiwara) Nijō Tameshige (1325-85) for the *Shingoshūishū* in 1383.[1]

Even in the case of the *Gyokuyōshū*, the only royal anthology edited by a Kyōgoku poet, there were extraordinary wrangles before the commission was finally awarded to Tamekanu. The Nijō family, which was the direct line of descent from Teika, took the position that compilers of royal anthologies should come from their family as a matter of course and that royal anthologies were beyond the province of the illegitimate Kyōgoku and Reizei lines. Moreover, this position was generally acknowledged. From the very beginning, there was no general recognition that a tennō from the Jimyōin line could appoint from the Kyōgoku fam-

[1] Ōgimachi Kinkage (1297-1360), Fujiwara Tamemoto, Reizei Tamehide, and Ayanokōji Shigesuke (1305-89) assisted Kōgon in the compilation of the *Fūgashū*. [As did abdicated Hanazono (1297-1348), who was formerly thought the compiler. As for Tameshige, although not a Nijō poet, he was closely allied with that house.—Ed.]

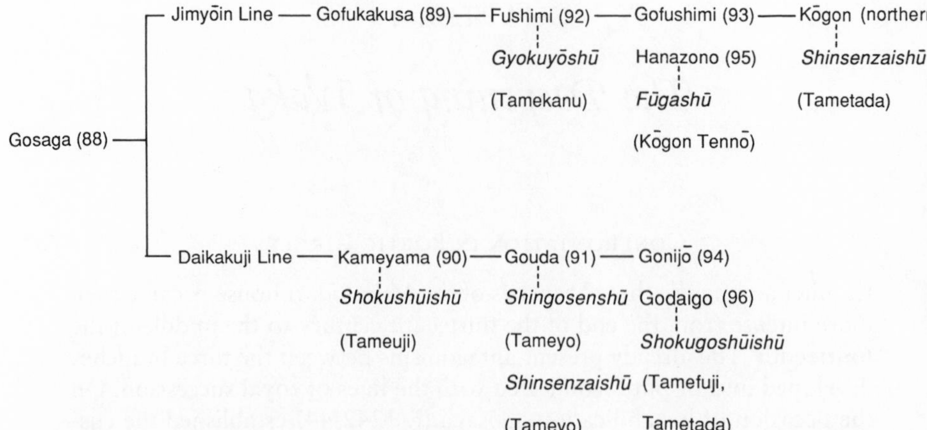

FIGURE 14.1 The Royal Lines After Gosaga, with Notice of Royal Collections and Their Compilers (Numbers in parentheses indicate a tennō's order in traditional numbering; names in parentheses indicate the compiler of the collection specified)

ily a compiler of a royal anthology. The first violation of the well-established Nijō family monopoly on royal anthologies occurred because Fushimi Tennō (1265-1317) wanted to appoint Tamekanu, who was one of his intimate circle.

In 1280, Tamekanu, who was in his twenty-seventh year, had become the personal retainer of the sixteen-year-old Crown Prince Hirohito (later to become Fushimi Tennō). Tamekanu was a talented and purposeful politician, and the young prince seems to have trusted him implicitly. As a poet, his daring experiments with new styles were extremely attractive to the prince and his retinue, and soon a new poetry circle had been formed in the palace of the prince. When Prince Hirohito ascended to the throne in 1287 at the age of twenty-three, he of course wanted to commission Tamekanu to compile a royal collection. This was the beginning of a bitter dispute that was to last nearly sixty years.

Given the conventions concerning royal anthologies [and the unprecedented appointment of a Kyōgoku], it would have been impossible for Fushimi to make Tamekanu the sole editor. Therefore, on the twenty-seventh day of the Eighth Month of 1293, Fushimi summoned Nijō Tameyo (1250-1338), Tamekanu, Asukai Masaari (1241-1301), and Kujō Takahiro (?-1298) to announce his plans for a royal anthology and to discuss editorial policies.[2] Reizei Tamesuke, who was in Kamakura at the time, later heard about the plan for an anthology and sent word to Fushimi that he would also like to be included among the compilers. This

[2] *Fushimi Ki* [27.VIII.1293], 326-27.

attempt was opposed by Tameyo, and Tamesuke did not receive his appointment.[3]

Selection of the anthology proceeded to a certain point, but in 1296 Tamekanu was dismissed because of slanderous accusations by his colleagues and, on the sixteenth day of the Third Month of 1298, he was exiled to Sado. On the fifth day of the Twelfth Month in the same year, Takahiro died, and on the eleventh day of the First Month of 1301 Masaari also died. At this point, work on the anthology was suspended. Tamekanu was pardoned in the Fourth Intercalary Month of 1302 and returned to the capital, where he apparently began working secretly on the anthology with the intention of completing it on his own. Gonijō Tennō of the Daikakuji line died on the fifteenth day of the Eighth Month of 1308, and Abdicated Tennō Fushimi's second son, Prince Tomihito, ascended the throne as Hanazono Tennō. Fushimi was once again firmly in control as Cloistered Sovereign, and Tamekanu's chances of becoming the sole compiler of the anthology were substantially increased.[4]

Tameyo was well aware of this situation, and sent appeals to the court and to the bakufu arguing that Tamekanu was unqualified to edit a royal anthology. Tamekanu responded with an angry rebuttal. Petitions flew back and forth in what came to be called "the warring petitions of two lords in the Enkei period." This great debate between Tamekanu and Tameyo began in the First Month of 1310 (Enkei 3) and raged until the third day of the Fifth Month of 1311, when Fushimi, with Kamakura's assent, issued an inden (command of the Cloistered Sovereign) commissioning Tamekanu to be the sole compiler of the anthology. He quickly submitted the *Gyokuyōshū* on the twenty-eighth day of the Third Month of 1312.

This was the first royal anthology from the Jimyōin line. Of course, as happened with other royal anthologies, the collection was only nominally complete at that time. It appears that the final version was submitted sometime between the sixth and the sixteenth days of the Tenth Month of 1313 [Tsugita, 1964, 65-66]. For a short period after its completion, the Kyōgoku family and the Jimyōin line were at the zenith of their power and influence. But Tamekanu's daring activities in politics earned him the

[3] Tamesuke's petition survives in the house collection of Prince Takamatsu. Official documents related to Tameyo's activities in thwarting Tamesuke's hopes are in the collection of the Sonkeikaku Library (Tsugita, 1964, 47; Fukuda, 1972, 317-18). [Some readers may wonder why "Tamekanu" and "Sanekanu" are given instead of "Tamekane" and "Sanekane." The author has observed that the forms used here are clearly and consistently used in a contemporary account, the *Towazugatari* by Gofukakusa In Nijō.—Ed.]

[4] [The system of cloistered sovereigns, insei, began with Shirakawa (cloistered 1086-1129). It was designed so that a sovereign could abdicate from the onerous formalities of being tennō and in effect rule from the cloister. To use the usual terms, at any given time there was only one regnant tennō, and there could be only one cloistered sovereign (in) as dominant individual. But there might be more than one abdicated tennō (jōkō) or abdicated sovereign in orders. For further details, see Miner-Odagiri-Morrell, 1985, 467-69.—Ed.]

displeasure of the powerful Saionji Sanekanu (1249-1322) and, on the twenty-eighth day of the Twelfth Month of 1315, Tamekanu was arrested on orders from Kamakura. On the twelfth day of the First Month of the following year, he was once again exiled, this time to Tosa. He was subsequently released in a general amnesty and travelled to the province of Kōchi (present Osaka prefecture), but he was never allowed to return to the capital before his death at the age of seventy-nine on the eleventh day of the Third Month of 1332. Moreover, he had no heir in the way of poetry, and with his death the Kyōgoku family ceased to play a major role as a poetic house.

However, the Kyōgoku style of waka was preserved by the Jimyōin royal line and its ladies: Hanazono, Kōgon, Yōfuku Mon'in (1271-1342), Princess Shinshi, Kian Mon'in (1318-58), Princess Gishi, Princess Shukushi, In no Ichijō, In no Hyōe no Kami, In no Reizei, Yōfuku Mon'in no Naishi, Yōfuku Mon'in no Emon no Kami, and others. In fact, rather than saying that these poets preserved the Kyōgoku style, it would be more appropriate to say that, in terms of quality, they refined the style even further, and that the central figures among the poets who wrote in Kyōgoku styles were Hanazono and Yōfuku Mon'in. The poems of this group were collected in the *Fūgashū*, which was completed in 1346. Its compilation has been attributed to both Hanazono and Kōgon, and it is likely that Hanazono first conceived the idea of an anthology compiled by the Jimyōin line and then entrusted the editing to Kōgon. In much the same way that Gotoba played an important role in the compilation of the *Shinkokinshū*, Hanazono's opinion must certainly have been important in determining the character of the anthology. But just as Teika and his collaborators are recognized as the compilers of the earlier anthology, Kōgon was the actual editor of the *Fūgashū*. Again, the date of 1346 is the nominal date of the completion of the anthology; it was actually finished in 1349, one year after Hanazono's death.

Armed hostility broke out in 1336 between the Northern (Jimyōin) and Southern (Daikakuji) courts, continuing off and on until 1392. The Kyōgoku style, which was associated with the Northern court, might well have been expected to flourish with it.[5] A dispute occurred, however, within the Ashikaga administration, which supported the Northern court and, as an indirect result of this dispute, the capital was temporarily occupied in 1351 by the Southern court. The abdicated Kōgon was taken to Yoshino; and the Kyōgoku faction, which amounted only to the small group composed of the Jimyōin royal line and its ladies, was suddenly annihilated. The political situation was finally brought under control in

[5] [This dispute between the Southern and Northern courts gave rise to the name for the period, Nambokuchō (Period of Northern and Southern Courts), after a similarly divided era in China.—Ed.]

1353, and with the accession of Gokōgon (1352-1371), the Northern court was restored to power. However, Kōgon did not return to the capital until 1357, and in the meantime, Nijō Tamesada (1285-1360) and Nijō Tameakira (1295-1364) launched a skillful campaign to ingratiate themselves with the Ashikaga bakufu and secured the bakufu's recommendation that a royal anthology should be compiled by a member of the Nijō family. In 1356, Tamesada received a royal commission to compile an anthology and submitted the *Shinsenzaishū (Shinsenzai Wakashū)* in 1359 (Inoue, 1961, 23-24). Subsequent royal collections were monopolized by the Nijō and their allies.

One reason the Nijō family was able to secure the leading role in waka circles was that it produced many outstanding poets. But an equally important factor was the fact that the Nijō style was influential among the lower nobility (jige), those who could not appear in the royal presence unless priests. These poets included Tonna, Kenkō, Jōben, Keiun, and Nōyo, who were all disciples of Tameyo, and they were the preeminent poets of the day. Tonna (1289?-1372) was the most talented poet of the Nijō faction and apparently was widely recognized. In fact, Tonna completed the *Shokushūishū (Shokushūi Wakashū)* after the untimely death of Tameakira, its Nijō compiler. Because he was of too low noble rank, Tonna worked as an "assistant," but in fact, he was the principal editor of the anthology. This reflects the spirit of the period, which held that adepts in an artistic vocation (michi) must be given respect, regardless of low social rank. It also reflects the fact that the respect for "men of letters" (Ch. wen-jen, J. bunjin), which had developed in Yüan China, had penetrated into Japan.

For a man of his low noble standing Tonna's activities were truly astounding. He had great confidence that he was the heir to orthodox Nijō waka ideals, and, in spite of his rank, he wrote the six-volume poetic treatise *Seiashō* and the *Gumon Kenchū*, in which he replied to questions on waka from Nijō Yoshimoto (1320-88), who was at various times regent (sesshō) or chancellor (kampaku) and the preeminent intellectual of the day.[6] Tonna's waka treatises were passed down from his son Kyōken to his grandson Gyōjin and finally to his great grandson Gyōkō (1391-1455). Then Tō no Tsuneyori (1401?-84?), Gyōkō's disciple, transmitted Tonna's teachings to Sōgi (1421-1502). The Nijō family itself ends as a waka house in 1391, when Tameshige's son Tamesuke was executed, for some unknown offense, by the shōgun, Yoshimitsu (Inoue, 1961, 31). As we have seen, however, the poetic teachings of the Nijō house survived among the lower-ranking noble poets. The Kyōgoku house had fallen al-

[6] [On regents, chancellors, and Yoshimoto's offices, see Miner-Odagiri-Morrell, 1985, 460-65.—Ed.]

ready, and with the end of the Nijō house, only the Reizei family remained, continuing as a waka house up to the present. At the end of the fourteenth century, the Reizei line was represented by Tamehide (?-1372) and Tamemasa (1361-1417), but sufficient documentary evidence does not survive to determine directly what their poetic views were. They can be discovered only indirectly through the waka treatises of their disciples, such as Imagawa Ryōshun (1326-1417?) and Seigan Shōtetsu (1381-1459). In general, the poetic ideals of the Reizei line were very similar to those of the Kyōgoku poets, and positions of the two houses can be compared with those of the Nijō poets:

Reizei-Kyōgoku

1. Various styles of composing should be recognized.
2. Excellent waka are born precisely from deep, silent contemplation.
3. Diction need not be precedented.
4. There is no need to be overly concerned about phrasing prohibited from use.[7]

Nijō

1. One should master thoroughly the style of elegant simplicity.
2. Excellent poetry is born when one composes with ease.
3. One must not use unprecedented expression.
4. One must not use prohibited phrasing.

To the first point, the Reizei school would add: "The style of refined charm (yūen) is particularly valued."

Shōtetsu emphasized this point in the following famous statement: "Anyone in the way of waka ignoring Teika will of course not receive the blessings of the deities and buddhas and, indeed, would receive their punishment" (*Shōtetsu*, 1:166). This statement does not reflect a vague respect for Teika, but rather a worship, and in making it Shōtetsu has in mind the magical tone of the style of ethereal charm (yōen) that is found in the poetry of the *Shinkokin* period (in its narrow definition). But Shōtetsu calls this style neither yōen or yūen (refined charm), but rather the yūgentei (yūgen style) which he explains in the following (*Shōtetsu*, 2:332-33):

> What kind of thing is it that can be called the yūgen style? . . . Should we call only a style that is obscure yūgen? Or should we call a style

[7] The prohibitions established during Tameie's period of activity set forth 48 famous lines or phrases by previous poets (*Eiga no Ittei*, 362-64). This list of interdicts was subsequently expanded by Genshō (*Genshō*, 29-34) and again by Keiyū (*Tsuika*, 402). These prohibitions were originally based on a sense of reverence for the creative powers of great poets of the past. Later, however, they became fossilized, and authority for the interdictions was founded simply on the fact of prohibition.

yūgen when it suggests a scene in which one is gazing upon four or five court ladies in all their finery beneath cherry blossoms in full bloom at the Southern Palace? It is difficult to say. When one is asked "What is there about this that is yūgen?" it is impossible to point to one thing and say, "This is yūgen."

When Shōtetsu presents as one characteristic of yūgen an undecidability of meaning which he compares to drifting clouds, he conveys the traditional usage. However, when he refers to the refined charm (yūgen) symbolized by beautiful women enjoying cherry blossoms, he is using yūgen in a sense that did not appear until the late thirteenth century. Yūgen was used in this sense by Ryōki, in his *Ōtaku Fuketsu Shō* (compiled between 1275 and 1278). In fact, Ryōki replaced the original Chinese character for yū in yūgen with the one for yū in yūen, emphasizing his concept of yūgen as a style of refined beauty (Nose, 1944a, 242-43). In his own waka, however, Shōtetsu does not always compose in a style consistent with this conception of yūgen:

Seeing Cherry Blossoms in a Spring Dream

Hana zo naki	There are no blossoms!
Sametaru matsu wa	The pines that have been awakened
Mine ni akete	Dawn upon the peaks,
Magaishi kumo mo	And the clouds I mistook for blossoms
Haru no yo no yume.	Also were a spring night's dream.

(*Sōkonshū*, 1467)

Summer Grasses on a Journey

Sode zo uki	My sleeves are wretched!
Mine no shita kusa	In the plants beneath the peaks
Wakeizuru	There filters through
Hikage wa nurenu	A sunshine that is not soaked
Nobe no asatsuyu.	By morning dew upon the plain.

(Ibid., 2045)

Plovers in Moonlight

Hamachidori	Plovers of the shore—
Ariake no shimo no	As dawn breaks the frost covers
Masagoyama	The high dunes of sands,
Tsuki ni koekuru	And across the moon there pass
Koe no samukeki.	The bird cries that are so cold.

(Ibid., 5561)

Evening Temple Bell

Yūgure no	As evening comes
Kokoro no iro o	The coloring of my heart
Some zo oku	Will be redyed—
Tsukihatsuru kane	From the bell no longer booming,
Koe no nioi ni.	The fragrance of its lingering sounds.

(Ibid., 8839)

The style of these poems is rooted in yūen. But their tone, which infuses them with a sense of lonely desolation, is especially characteristic of Shōtetsu's waka. More than with Teika, Shōtetsu has close affinities with Shinkei (1406-75), who advocated the style of chill (hie), and his poetry should be recognized as exemplary of a new Reizei style. Moreover, Shōtetsu does not compose on subjects just as he has seen them or just as he has been moved by them, but he attempts to grasp the scene and his emotions at a level of awareness deeper than usual: not the beauty of cherry blossoms, but the beauty of cherry blossoms that no longer exist now that the speaker of the poem has awakened from the dream; or the sunlight, reflected in dew, which should appear damp but is not.

This way of attempting to grasp poetic objects does not differ significantly from the Kyōgoku style as we have seen it. His attitude of attempting to grasp phenomena at a more profound level can also be seen in Shōtetsu's use of synaesthesia; for example, when he speaks of the coldness of the beach plovers' voices, he apprehends an aural sensation (voices) as a tactile one (cold). This feature of Shōtetsu's style is much closer to Kyōgoku and Reizei styles than to Teika, and it is also one of the artistic techniques characteristic of fourteenth-century waka.[8]

After the falls of the Kyōgoku and Nijō families, leadership of the waka world was assumed by the Reizei and Asukai families. Nijō Yoshimoto, the noble and premier intellectual of his day, received his training in waka from Tonna and became the principal supporter of the Nijō faction.[9] His recommendation of the Nijō style to Gokōgon was the direct occasion for the establishment of ties between the Nijō faction and the Jimyōin royal line.[10] Even though Yoshimoto spurned the "queer style" (ifū) of the Kyōgoku faction, he had a high regard for the Reizei style, was intimate

[8] It has been pointed out that poets of the Kyōgoku and Reizei families used synaesthesia in the *Gyokuyōshū* period (Brower-Miner, 1961, 383-85). It should be noted that this resulted both from an extension of *Shinkokinshū*-period poetics and from the assimilation by Shōtetsu (a Zen priest) of Gosan shih into waka (Inada, 1978, 718-32).

[9] The Nijō family to which Yoshimoto belonged was a different [and much more highly ranking] family from the Nijō branch of the Mikohidari house.

[10] "Abdicated Gokōgon composed in the style of Lord Tamesada and discarded the style of Fushimi Tennō. Indeed such queer styles are without merit" (*Kinrai Fūtei*, 144).

with Tamehide and Tamemasa, and was on good terms with Ryōshun.[11] Yoshimoto's regard for both the style of simple elegance (heitan) advocated by the Nijō school and the style of refined charm (yūen) of the Reizei poets exerted a strong influence on Zeami (see the last chapter). It was, however, an underlying cause of attenuation of the distinctive styles of the Nijō and Reizei poets.

The preservation of a characteristic Reizei style lasted until Reizei Mochitame (1401-54), but in the generation of his son Masatame (1445-1523), the Reizei style became increasingly difficult to distinguish from the Nijō style. Much the same may be said of the Nijō faction. The poetic ideals of Tonna remained influential among lower noble poets such as Tsuneyori, but the higher noble poets of the Nijō school lost anything distinctive that might be asserted as a style of their own, moving steadily closer to the style of the Reizei faction. This opened the way for a fusion of the two schools (Shimazu, 1953, 41-53). This does not necessarily mean a decline in creativity. Rather, it may be thought of as one step in the process that led to the formation of an established ga style in waka during the period from the middle of the sixteenth century to the beginning of the seventeenth.

Tamekanu and Hanazono Tennō

Originally, the conflict between the Nijō and Reizei families was a very worldly dispute over domains and the rights of possession to Mikohidari house documents, not a question of conflicting assertions concerning ideals of waka. As the two poetic houses attempted to make clear their respective reasons for being, however, sooner or later waka would inevitably become an issue. Kyōgoku Tamekanu seems to have been the first to realize this unhappy fact. He asserted that the proper realm of waka is the expression of "what one feels in one's heart" just as one has felt it, and he attempted ways of writing that were extremely unusual in his day.

At least one of the reasons he took this position was that he was trying to fashion a poetics for the Kyōgoku house in opposition to the ideas of the Nijō family. The theoretical basis of Tamekanu's new style was Kōben's concept of waka, and it is well worth noting that Tamekanu's theory had a religious focus from the very beginning. Kōben's view of waka was rooted, however, in his own practical experience as a poet and was therefore insufficient as the basis of a theoretical position that would enable Tamekanu to criticize the Nijō position. Tamekanu therefore turned to a theory of perception closely related to the Tendai concept of shikan

[11] Ryōshun himself states that he was familiar with Yoshimoto in waka and renga circles (*Rakusho*, 154-55).

(cessation and insight) contemplation. This theory seems to have been based on a treatise of Teika's that is no longer extant and on T'ang shih treatises that advocate very similar theories.

Tamekanu's theory of perception is clearly the position of shikan. He displays a deep mistrust of existing methods of composition, in which the poet is aware of the poetic object as something that exists apart from the poet, who grasps it according to logic (gi), and then expresses it with already mastered preexisting diction. Instead, he argues for an ideal of expression in which the poet's mind penetrates into the essential nature (kimi) of the object so deeply that the object and the workings of the mind that perceives it become one. In the theory of shikan contemplation, the object of contemplation is a world (kyō), and its essential nature (honsei, kimi) is penetrated by the working of intention or wisdom (chi). When this fusion of mind and object occurs, the language that the poet uses to express this state does not exist separately from the state that is to be expressed, and outside that language other language ceases to exist. Tamekanu argues strongly that this is the perfect ideal of waka composition (*Tamekanu Kyō Wakashō*, or *Tamekanu Shō*, 161):

> Certainly there is a difference between a poet's attempting to express a conception (kokoro) by putting it into words and by reacting precisely in accordance with conception that works at a deeper level. For the latter, whatever the situation is, when one composes on a certain thing the poet should become one with that thing and banish all other thoughts from the mind. The conception that composes and the object upon which it composes are fused into one, and the waka is completed. Indeed, there is a great difference between making a poem by comprehending intellectually the meaning of the object and composing a poem having become one with its essential nature.

This is precisely Teika's position, although there is no extant treatise in which Teika says it in so many words. Tamekanu expresses the concepts of "making oneself one with the object" with the words "narikaerite" and "nariirite," and we may interpret both words as having the same meaning as "irifushite," quoted above in the discussion of *Maigetsushō* (see ch. 8). Even if the extant text of the *Maigetsushō* is not itself the work of Teika, it is impossible to deny that it contains Teika's actual theories.[12]

[12] Until recently, I have taken the *Maigetsushō* to be one of Teika's own treatises (Konishi, 1975a, 61-63). I have come upon internal evidence, however, that forces me to conclude that it was written at the end of the thirteenth century: the fact that the theory of ten styles expounded in the treatise has much in common with the Zen concept of kyarai (the return). The theory holds that after one has achieved mastery and refinement of the style of mild gracefulness (sunao ni yasashiki sugata) it is also permissible to compose in the style of subjugating demons (rakkitei), which is otherwise not a desirable style (*Maigetsushō*, 127). This concept has roots in Sung shih treatises that held one should gradually move toward a style of plainness or elegant simplicity after first mastering an ornately elegant style. The

Of course, Tamekanu probably never saw the *Maigetsushō*. I say this because he makes no reference to kyarai (the return), which is the most important assertion in the *Maigetsushō*, and also because it appears that he was not yet interested in Zen in the period when he wrote *Tamekanu Kyō Wakashō* (1285-87).[13] Nevertheless, even though Tamekanu had not seen the *Maigetsushō*, his theory is consistent in terms of their mutual grounding in the Tendai concept of shikan contemplation. I have concluded that this is because there existed a treatise of Teika's at this time which is no longer extant, and that both Tamekanu and the compiler of the *Maigetsushō* relied heavily on this treatise.

Of course, there is no doubt that Tamekanu had reference to Wang Ch'ang-ling's *Shih-ke* when he restated the theory of shikan perception in his own words. The styles of argument in stating the theory in the two treatises are very close (Konishi, 1951a, 471-73). In the *Shih-ke*, Wang also bases his argument on the concept of shikan perception in Tendai Buddhism. Of course, as Hanazono pointed out in his own treatise, Tamekanu did not know that the *Shih-ke* was a T'ang dynasty shih treatise, and he thought of it as Kūkai's *Bumpitsu Ganshin (Essential Points of Literary Composition)*.[14] There is also a strong possibility that Tamekanu referred to other Chinese shih treatises from the Sung. For example, Tamekanu's "expressing the intention with diction" is very close to the following statement in Yeh Meng-te's (1077-1148) *Shih-lin Shih-hua (The Rock Grove Poetic Notes)*: "When the poet's intention fits his diction, and when diction is used precisely according to intention, the poem becomes perfect expression, and does not appear to have been created by a human being" (*Shih-lin Shih-hua*, 2760). It seems quite likely, therefore, that Tamekanu learned of this kind of theory from some Sung-dynasty poetic treatise (Konishi, 1951c, 39-41). Until 1270, the Yüan government promoted trade with Japan vigorously (Mori, 1948, 511-16), and Chinese poetic treatises and essays (shih-hua) must have been brought to Japan in great numbers.[15] The Sung was the golden age of critical writings on shih, and an enormous volume of shih-hua were written.

---

assumption closely resembles the Zen theory of kyarai, which held that one who has achieved true awakening should return to the state immediately preceding the awakening. This concept influenced both Sung shih treatises and the theory of ten styles in the *Maigetsushō*. Since, however, there is no evidence that Sung shih treatises entered Japan before the end of the thirteenth century, and since Zen itself did not become popular before that time, it is impossible to conclude that the *Maigetsushō* was written during Teika's lifetime [1162-1241]. A detailed study of the debate over authorship of the *Maigetsushō* may be found in Mizukami, 1969, 106-29. [Note curtailed.—Ed.]

[13] Internal evidence has been used to date approximately the completion of the *Tamekanu Kyō Wakashō*: Tamekanu refers to Chamberlain Sanetō; given the period during which the man held the rank and the year he changed his name to Sanetō, the date of completion has been set between 1285 and 1287 (*NKGT*, Introduction, 18-19).

[14] Based on an entry in *Hanazono Ki* dated 28.XII.1235, p. 160; Konishi, 1951a, 471-73.

[15] The *Shih-lin Shih-hua* is quoted frequently in Tōgen Zuisen's (1430-89) *Shiki Shō* (*A*

The *Tamekanu Kyō Wakashō* states Tamekanu's position during the period from his thirty-second to his thirty-fourth year, the period when his waka were being violently attacked by the Nijō faction in such treatises as *Nomori no Kagami (The Mirror of a Field Guard)*. Thus, the theory of waka in the *Tamekanu Kyō Wakashō* is an attempt to provide a theoretical foundation for a Kyōgoku style in the period when Kōben's influence was still dominant, and it does not correspond to the *Gyokuyō* style (or Kyōgoku style), which developed a few years later (ca. 1302). This becomes abundantly clear when one looks at the poetry produced by the Jimyōin group during this period: the *Kōan Hachinen Utaawase* (*Waka Match in the Eighth Year of Kōan* [1285]); the *Einin Gonen Jūgoya Utaawase* (*Waka Competition on a Night of the Full Moon in the Fifth Year of Einin* [1297]); and, the *Einin Gonen Tōza Utaawase* (*Impromptu Waka Match in the Fifth Year of Einin* [1297]). The waka composed at these competitions possess little of the flavor of the later *Gyokuyō* style.

Tamekanu was exiled to Sado in the Third Month of 1298 and did not return to the capital until the Fourth Intercalary Month of 1303. In some of the poetry of the *Shōan Gannen Goshu Utaawase* (*The Waka Match of Five Kinds in the First Year of Shōan* [1299]) and the *Shōan Ninen Sanjūban Utaawase* (*The Waka Match in Thirty Rounds in the Second Year of Shōan* [1300]), which were held during the period of his absence, one does see the germination of expression in the *Gyokuyō* style, but such waka were by no means numerous. The *Gyokuyō* style first shows itself clearly in the *Sentō Gojūban Utaawase (The Waka Match in Fifty Rounds at the Palace of His Abdicated Majesty)*, held in 1303, and the *Kengen Ninen Gogatsu Yokka Sanjūban Utaawase* (*The Waka Match in Thirty Rounds on the Fourth Day of the Fifth Month of the Second Year of Kengen* [1303]). For example, here are two poems from the former:

The Left: A Certain Court Lady (Winner):

Yamaarashi no	The mountain squall
Sugi no ha harau	Sweeps through the leaves of cedars,
Akebono ni	Leaving the dawn
Muramura nabiku	In which here and there soft piles
Yuki no shirakumo.	Of stark white clouds build up like snow.[16]

(Round 31: Winter Clouds)

Commentary on the Shih-chi), and it is therefore clear that it had already entered Japan by the mid-fifteenth century (Haga, 1956, 316). It is not known when it first entered Japan.

[16] The source for these two poems is the *Shinkō Gunsho Ruijū* edition, 9:467-75. "A Certain Court Lady" is a sobriquet for the cloistered Fushimi. [See ch. 2, n. 25, on this practice.—Ed.] This waka is paired with one by Tamekanu given just below.

The Left: Lady Chūjō [i.e., Yōfuku Mon'in] (Winner):

Kaze no oto no	The wind's strong sound
Hageshiku wataru	Violently passes over
Kozue yori	The tree tops where
Murakumo samuki	There comes between cold cloud banks
Mikazuki no kage.	The light of the crescent moon.
	(Round 40: Winter Clouds)

Tamekanu, who had just returned to the capital, participated in this match. But while he submitted five waka, none of them was awarded a victory, and his writing cannot be said to have achieved the *Gyokuyō* style:

The Right: Lord Tamekanu

Mine no yuki o	Blowing all together
Muramura kumo ni	The snow upon the mountain peaks
Fukimazete	And the clumps of clouds,
Wataru arashi wa	The passing gale can not decide
Kata mo sadamezu.	On the direction it would take.
	(Round 31: Winter Clouds)

This poem is in the descriptive mode, but nature poetry in that mode had been composed since the time of Tsunenobu, and that alone does not qualify it for recognition as a waka characteristic of the *Gyokuyō* period.

Although hers is also in the descriptive mode, the waka by Yōfuku Mon'in is remarkable for the attempt to grasp the object at a profounder level. Her poem is by no means simple description: while it is normal to infer the passing of the wind over treetops by seeing the branches swaying, she perceives it through the aural sensation of violent sound. Moreover, a cluster of clouds is not usually said to be cold—it is the wind that is cold—but the poet feels coldness in the color of the clouds. And that coldness is felt in the moonlight, which would normally be perceived visually. This is effective synaesthesia. But beyond synaesthesia, the special feature of the *Gyokuyō* style is the attempt to perceive poetic objects at a profounder conceptual level. In this attempt, *Gyokuyō* poets sometimes employ synaesthesia.

It is impossible to believe that Tamekanu continued to direct the poetic circle in the capital by correspondence during the more than five years of his exile. And given that waka in the *Gyokuyō* style were already being composed when he returned to the capital and that his own waka are still in his previous style, Fushimi and Yōfuku Mon'in, and not Tamekanu, must be the originators of the *Gyokuyō* style. Moreover, once this conclusion is reached, it is altogether natural that Nijō Yoshimoto should have referred to the style as "the style of the Cloistered Fushimi." Of course, this does not mean that Fushimi devised the *Gyokuyō* style independently. Undoubtedly the foundations for the new styles were formulated in the course of his conversations with Tamekanu before the latter's exile. Nevertheless, it would be difficult to think of any other candidates besides Fushimi and Yōfuku Mon'in (who never left the capital) as the poets who brought the *Gyokuyō* style to fruition. Why then did poetic styles shift from the wild freedom of Kōben's style to the rather formal *Gyokuyō* style? I find the reason in the assumption that Fushimi wanted to compile a royal anthology. A royal anthology must possess a level of ga appropriate to such a collection and, although waka in ga-zoku styles may be permitted occasionally in some sections, it is an absolute condition that the anthology as a whole preserve a tone of ga. Kōben's zoku alone could never provide a style appropriate for a royal anthology, and a new style of ga had to be created.

The creation of such a new ga style was by no means an easy undertaking. This becomes clear from an examination of the *Gyokuyōshū* [= *GYS*] itself. Up to now, only descriptive, seasonal waka have been quoted to represent the *Gyokuyō* style. However, nature poetry makes up less than half of the anthology, and it is a mistake to suggest that only they are characteristic. When one takes up the waka that depict subjective states—many examples of which are found in the love poems—it becomes clear that there is another remarkable feature of the *Gyokuyō* style. Psychological processes themselves become the subjects of poetry, and in many of these poems nothing that can readily be identified as technique has been employed.

Among some love poems
By the Former Major Counselor Tamekanu

Toki no ma mo	However brief the time
Ware ni kokoro no	It is of the heart within me
Ikaga naru to	That I wish to ask
Tada tsune ni koso	Always and just the same!—
Towamahoshikere.	"How go things with you just now?"
	(*GYS*, 11:1502)

Among ten love poems
By His Cloistered Majesty [Fushimi]

Hito wa shiraji	Others will not know.
Kokoro no soko no	At the bottom of my heart,

Aware nomi	There is only sorrow—
Nagasamegataku	I cannot alleviate it,
Narimasaru koro.	For it grows greater all the while.
	(*GYS*, 11:1558)

Among fifty poems I composed
By Jūsammi Tameko

Kokoro hiku	Only those people
Kata bakari nite	Who seek to entice my heart
Nabete yo no	Make up the world
Hito ni nasake no	Where absolutely no one
Aru hito zo naki.	Shows concern for one like me.
	(*GYS*, 18:2563)

One first notices that there is no imagery in these waka. Certainly, there are image-free poems in earlier royal anthologies, but not in the quantity found in the *Gyokuyōshū*. Moreover, these waka share a characteristic approach—they do not express subjective emotional states by saying "I am sad" or "I am happy," but instead observe the ways of feeling the emotions of happiness and sadness themselves as objects. One also discovers a search for reasons, an overt logical stance, concealed in the syntax of these waka. This technique of giving reasons for emotional states had not been unusual since the style of oblique expression in the *Kokinshū*, but before the *Gyokuyōshū* it is a technique for a refined intellectual interest in stating what the speaker of the poem wants to say in a roundabout fashion instead of expressing it directly. In the waka of the *Gyokuyōshū*, the reasoning process is presented in clear everyday logic (dōri). In the waka by Jūsammi Tameko, for example, the speaker of the poem says, in effect, "There are many people in the world who come around saying things to get you interested, but there is no one with real depth of feeling." One must judge this as a statement far removed from intellectuality or wit. Here is an even more excessive example:

On the spirit of "Yearning for the Past"
By His Cloistered Majesty [Fushimi]

Oshimu beku	What one must begrudge,
Kanashibu beki wa	What one must feel sadness for,
Yo no naka ni	In this world
Sugite mata konu	Are the passing days and months
Tsukihi narikeri.	That never come to us again.
	(*GYS*, 18:2616)

The poem is too obvious. One does not enough feel sufficiently moved to concur with its argument. This kind of direct statement of emotion was already being widely practiced by Tamekanu's group in the period when he displayed sympathy for the waka of Kōben—that is, the period when he composed the waka on the back of a page of a diary, the *Kammon Nikki.* The style was incorporated into the waka of the *Gyokuyōshū*, but the direct statement of emotion lacks the sama (the style or tone) expected in a royal anthology. Tamekanu sought a new sama in which a line of reasoning that would be persuasive to anyone is made the center of the poem and in which this reasoning is bound together with emotion.

How can the introduction of common sense into waka create a new tone (sama)? I have stated previously that I believe the introduction of this style was due to the infusion of Sung shih into waka (Konishi, 1960a, 171-81). As we have seen in the preceding chapter, Sung shih poets had a high regard for li (J. ri, reason) and yi-li (J. giri, the thread of reason), which is the logic by which li is perceived. Tamekanu's group knew that this style of composition was popular in Chinese shih circles, and they must have thought that it would also become a dominant style (sama) in waka. There are some historical problems, however. The Chinese poets who brought Sung shih to Japan were Zen monks, and if Tamekanu and his group had had contact with these monks, it stands to reason that they would have been influenced to some extent by Zen. But at least to the extent that we can judge from the *Tamekanu Kyō Wakashō*, the basis of Tamekanu's poetic theories in this period was the Tendai concept of shikan, and Tamekanu's contact with Zen must have occurred later. Ta-hsiu Cheng-nien came to Japan in 1269, Wu-hsüeh Tsu-yüan in 1280, and I-shan I-ning in 1299, but even if these Zen monks had been able to bring Chinese books to Japan, the study of Zen would still have been difficult for many Japanese, for none of these Zen masters could speak Japanese.

When psychological processes are made the objects of poetry, it is precisely a matter of the conception (kokoro) that becomes the subject, or of the "mind that is expressed" being observed by another "level" of intentionality—the "mind that expresses"—that composes the poem. However, when the conception that becomes the subject of expression is the poet's own, the relationship becomes complex and extremely subtle.

On the spirit of "Love Waiting"
By His Cloistered Majesty [Fushimi]

Chigirishi o	Because the heart
Wasurenu kokoro	That will not forget your vows
Soko ni are ya	Still is with you—

Tanomanu kara ni	Or because I doubt your coming—
Kyō no hisashiki.	What makes today seem without end?
	(*GYS*, 10:1379)

The mind that does not forget that the lover has promised "certainly I will come" is objectivized and observed, but the mind that observes it is the very same mind, that of the speaker of the poem. In this we may see a new poetic world that does not exist in previous waka. The doubtful tone of the first three lines intensifies the complexity. Since the speaker of the poem is a woman observing her own heart, there are features of the situation difficult to grasp precisely.

Composed on "Resentful Love" in a set of thirty poems commanded by His Majesty. By His Newly Cloistered Majesty[17]

Yoshi saraba	"If that is how it is
Uramihatenan to	I will hate that man completely!"
Omou kiwa ni	That moment's thought
Higoro oboenu	Brought with it a pity for him
Awaresa zo sou.	That had never crossed my mind.
	(*GYS*, 12:1703)

In contrast to the previous poem, which merely suggests the difficulty of perceiving one's own mind through its syntax, this poem takes up the mental state of the composer of the poem, who in the instant she resolves to hate her lover perceives a pity for him of which she had not been aware. This perceptual procedure, which makes the subject of composition the poet's mind at a profounder level, is one of the important characteristics of the *Gyokuyō* style.

The new style involved a shift from Kōben's style, in which one composes just as one has thought or felt, to what we have just been seeing by example, the advanced, double, or deeper awareness. The precursor of the new style was that using synaesthesia, already an object of practice by Fushimi and Yōfuku Mon'in before 1303. The movement toward a new style based on synaesthesia was accelerated by Tamekanu's return to the capital and to his fellow poets. During the ten years before the submission of the *Gyokuyōshū* in 1312, that peculiar poetic approach was established that can be termed the *Gyokuyō* style.

[17] [This newly cloistered majesty is Gofushimi (1288-1336), who was Gofushimi In during two periods, 1313-18 and 1331-33. It seems the former is involved here, which would make the "His Majesty" of the headnote Hanazono.—Ed.]

As has been proposed, the basis of this movement was no doubt a no-longer-extant waka treatise of Teika's and T'ang and Sung shih treatises; but to achieve the poet's end of mental states at a profounder level required a more direct theoretical grounding, which must have been the Tendai concept of shikan. When Tamekanu says, "penetrate and become one with it," the "it" to which he refers is the object of composition, with which the poet becomes one. As we have seen, in the terminology of shikan, this subject is called kyō (Ch. ching), sphere or world (i.e., both the object and state of recognition). There are ten types of kyō, and the basic and most elementary method of shikan is the contemplation of the kyō called onnyūkai (Ch. yin-ju-chieh).[18] Onnyūkai is a general name for all the various elements that make up our minds and bodies. Among these, shiki (Ch. shih; Skt. viñāna), or "the mind that distinguishes," first becomes the object of contemplation.[19] Not a particularly exalted dimension, the "mind that distinguishes" refers to nothing more than the workings of everyday awareness, in which the mind recognizes happy things as being happy and distinguishes what should be felt sad. That the working of this rather commonplace mind is made the first object of contemplation has important implications, for it suggests that even a poet who has only an elementary experience of shikan contemplation can make hate, pity, or sadness the subjects of poetry.

Shikan contemplation, however, is by no means merely the observation of the workings of one's everyday mind. The ultimate goal of shikan contemplation is a clear awareness that our minds, which experience the emotions of joy, anger, sadness, and pleasure due to illusion (bonnō), are actually manifestations of the ultimate truth that rules the whole universe. It follows that correct perception is impossible if the mind that observes the everyday mind is in the same dimension as the everyday mind. It is thus essential that the practitioner of shikan distinguish between the observed mind (shokan, Ch. su-kuan) and the mind that observes (nōkan, Ch. neng-kuan). Since both of these minds are the practitioner's own mind, this distinction is extremely difficult to make, but if the practitioner does not achieve a distance from personal everyday thought (from the

[18] Onnyūkai is a general term for the five elements (on) of human beings, the twelve elements (nyū) of recognition, and the eighteen elements (kai) of mental processes. These elements span physical and mental object and function; the term thus refers to the total physical and spiritual existence of human beings.

[19] "Even with a chang (3.11 meters), one pays attention to a ch'ih (1/10 chang). Even within that ch'ih, one pays attention to a ts'un (1/10 ch'ih). In the same way, of the five elements of the mind (physical existence, sensuous cognition, imagination, intention, and discrimination), one should not make an issue of the first four but should observe especially discrimination [shiki]" (*Maka Shikan*, 5 [I], 52). This theory separates human existence into the physical and the mental (or conceptual). The mind is further separated into four elements. In observing the essence of human existence, attention should be given especially to the function of discrimination.

observed mind), the functioning of the observing mind cannot exist. The poet's perception that the heart that does not forget the lover's promise "still suffers here" (*GYS*, 10:1379) corresponds to this elementary stage of shikan contemplation in which the observed mind (nōkan) is distinguished from the observing mind (shokan). While the kyō "world" as observed mind is still at a level where it can be observed intellectually—while it is an understandable object (shigi kyō, Ch. ssu-i ching)—it is not the ultimate object of shikan contemplation. Rather, the ultimate object of contemplation is a realm of the mind that the intellect cannot reach, and this realm is called the non-understandable object (fushigi kyō, Ch. pu-ssu-i ching). Thus, the onnyūkai kyō has two aspects: that of the understandable object and that of the non-understandable object. But the observing mind (nōkan) that is able to span both aspects and grasp the real truth of the kyō "world" as a whole may itself be thought of as an existence, and to the extent that it is an existence, it too can be observed and is thus an observed mind (shokan) in relation to the ultimate truth that rules the universe. In this dimension, therefore, an absolute distinction between the observed mind and the observing mind becomes impossible to make.

In the terminology of shikan, a poem corresponds only to the elementary stage of contemplation as long as the mind of the speaker of the poem focuses on the object of composition, observing it as a third person. An initiate, on the other hand, separates the observed mind and the observing mind. However, in waka just as in shikan contemplation, it is easy for the observing mind that has been distinguished from the observed mind to stop at the level of the understandable object (shigi kyō). There is a kind of aesthetic effect so profound that the reader or hearer is unaware of the reasons for being moved. That profound effect cannot arise from a poem in which the perceptual processes of nōkan as the observing mind are explained intellectually. Tamekanu was already aware of this fact in the period around 1286 (*Tamekanu Shō*, 160-61):

> Whether the object on which you compose is cherry blossoms, or the moon, or dawn, or sunset, if you would grasp that object, you should make yourself one with it, making clear its essential nature and engraving its state upon your own mind [conception, kokoro]. Direct the workings of your mind toward that object in the deepest recesses of your mind and leave the choice of diction to your mind. . . . Certainly, there is a difference between attempting to express the poet's conception by using diction and a diction reacting precisely in accordance with conception that works at a deeper level.[20]

[20] [Two notes on textual variants are omitted.—Ed.]

In writing about a natural scene as well, a poet is to project the perceiving mind into the scene that is to be the subject of the poem and, gaining a clear understanding of the most fundamental nature of the scene, engraving the understanding on the mind. Such a concept of mental processes applies to waka composition the shikan theories of kyōchi funi (Ch. ching-chih pu-erh), to be observed and to observe are not distinct; and guyū (Ch. chü-jung), the fusion of the observing and observed into one another. In such a mental process, various thoughts arise in the poet's mind concerning how to compose in order to achieve aesthetically moving language. But these thoughts belong to the observed mind at the level of everyday awareness, namely to the understandable object (shigi kyō).

To the extent that the poet goes no farther, it will be impossible to achieve thought capable of evoking a response so powerful that the reader is not aware of a reason for being so moved. When that state is reached, however, there is thought by the observing mind that corresponds to the non-understandable object. Therefore, the poet must "Direct the workings of [the] mind toward that object in the deepest recesses of [the] mind," and endeavor not to allow the "workings" control. When that is done, the mind of the poet that functions in the process of composition, on the one hand, and the mind that is in charge of seeing that this mind not be allowed to function, on the other, are equally the poet's mind (conception), but the kinds or levels of conception are different. One kind is the same as the conception that chooses diction, which is in Tamekanu's idea of "diction reacting precisely in accordance with conception that works at a deeper level." The other kind, the mind that functions in the process of composition, is the conception in Tamekanu's "attempting to express the poet's conception by using diction," the understandable object at the level of everyday awareness.

It may seem strange that Tamekanu was capable of expounding this theory of composition at this time, when he was still far from able to achieve such an ideal in his own waka.[21] But as I have argued earlier, this reflects the borrowing of theories set forth in the *Tamekanu Kyō Wakashō* from a no-longer-extant treatise of Teika's and Sung shih treatises and not opinions that sprang from his own experience of writing poetry. In the period of approximately ten years after 1303, Tamekanu and his group must have devoted immense efforts to eliminate this gap between their poetic ideals and their waka; the nature poetry, which is considered a special characteristic of the *Gyokuyō* style, was one of their experiments in that direction. Waka about nature, therefore, must not be thought of simply as pure nature poetry, for the same mental process of grasping

[21] That is, in the waka of the period in which Tamekanu was attacked in *Nomori no Kagami* [ca. 1285.—Ed.].

the object of composition at a profounder level is as prominent in waka on seasonal topics as in those on love and other subjective topics. For example:

On the night of the full moon in the Eighth Month,
when I commissioned people to compose a set of
fifteen waka on the topic "The Moon."
By His Cloistered Majesty [Fushimi]

Fukenu tomo	"Night soon will end"—
Nagamuru hodo wa	As long as I kept gazing out
Oboenu ni	That did not cross my mind,
Tsuki yori nishi no	But now westward of the moon
Sora zo sukunaki.	Its realm of sky has grown so small.
	(*GYS*, 5:712)

Gazing intently on the moon, the speaker of the poem does not notice that the night is growing late. But as the moon sinks in the west, the distance between it and the mountain's rim narrows and makes the poet conscious of time: "Night soon will end." Both the mind that has been made to become conscious (shokan) and the mind that observes that "ah, it (that other mind) has been made to become conscious" (nōkan) are present in the poem showing that this poem belongs to the same mode of thought we saw in Gofushimi's love poem, "If that is how it is" (*GYS*, 12:1703).

Here is another example, a poem on autumnal scenery.

An autumn poem composed by Her Majesty
at the Saionji mansion.[22]
By Yōfuku Mon'in

Obana nomi	Only pampas grasses
Niwa ni nabikite	Are swaying in the garden;
Akikaze no	I hear the autumn wind
Hibiki wa mine no	Reverberating in the limbs
Kozue ni zo kiku.	Of trees upon the mountain peaks.
	(*GYS*, 4:529)

This appears to be a pure nature poem. But it involves a consciousness (nōkan) that observes the speaker of the poem's own mind (shokan) on a deeper level. The autumn wind is blowing in the garden, and when the

[22] The mansion of Saionji Sanekanu, Yōfuku Mon'in's father.

poet observes the pampas grasses swaying, she is aware of the sound of the wind as if it were also coming from them. At the same time she understands that, in fact, she is hearing the sound of the wind (perhaps wind in the pines) in trees on the peaks. There is nothing in this poem like the expression "I had not noticed" in Gofushimi's, but there is another mind (nōkan) present that observes the mind (shokan) of the speaker of the poem. In this sense, the modes of perception are the same in both poems.

So, the nature poems in the *Gyokuyōshū* clearly cannot be dealt with by referring to a concept of direct, realistic poetic depiction like that held by the *Araragi* school of modern tanka poets. In the background of this *Gyokuyō* poetry, there is always a mode of thought, based on the theory of shikan contemplation, that grasps the poetic object at a profounder level than routine awareness. Let us consider a few of the outstanding poems in the *Gyokuyōshū*.

Composed on the topic "Spring Rain" for a poetry contest at my home.
By Former Major Counselor Tamekanu

Ume no hana	The plum in flower
Kurenai niou	Suffuses with a crimson glow
Yūgure ni	The evening scene
Yanagi nabikite	Where willow trees bend gently
Harusame zo furu.	And the spring rain softly falls.[23]

(*GYS*, 1:83)

Among poems on the topic "Summer."
By Former Major Counselor Tamekanu

Eda ni moru	The rays of sunlight
Asahi no kage no	That filter through the branches
Sukunasa ni	Are so very few
Suzushisa ni fukaki	That the coolness further deepens
Take no oku kana.	The back of the bamboo grove.[24]

(*GYS*, 3:419)

[23] [Translation adapted from Brower-Miner, 1961, 340.—Trans. In the second line of the poem "niou" ("Suffuses with a . . . glow") is a zeugma or yoking of both "Ume no hana" ("The plum in flower") and "Yūgure ni" ("The evening scene"). This technique differs from that of pivot words (kakekotoba), which involve distinguishing different meanings and usually parsing different words, syntax, and even grammar. The technique appears in poems quoted earlier: Fushimi In's "Yamaarashi no" (see "harau," p. 396) and Yōfuku Mon'in's "Kaze no oto no" (see "samuki," p. 397), and it will be found in the "fukaki" of the following poem. As will be seen in the next chapter, renga poets also employed this yoking.—Ed.]

[24] [Translation radically adapted from ibid., 366.—Ed.]

When I asked various people to write sets of thirty poems,
I composed this on "Dew on Flowering Plants."
By Former Major Counselor Tamekanu

Tsuyu omoru	The dew weighs heavy
Kohagi ga sue wa	And the tips of the bush clover
Nabikifushite	Bow toward the earth,
Fukikaesu kaze ni	And when the wind blows them back,
Hana zo iro sou.	The flowers take on another hue.
	(*GYS*, 4:501)

"On Lightning"
By His Cloistered Majesty [Fushimi]

Yoi no ma no	Early in the evening,
Murakumozutai	Skirting the gathering clouds,
Kage miete	A flash of light bursts forth:
Yama no ha meguru	It is the autumn lightning
Aki no inazuma.	Whirling about the mountain's rim.
	(*GYS*, 4:628)

On the topic "Pines in a Garden."
By His Cloistered Majesty [Fushimi]

Yūgure no	In the evening light
Matsu ni fukitatsu	The pines are shaken with the wind
Yamakaze ni .	Come from the mountains;
Nokiba kumoranu	It is cloudless only near my eaves;
Murasame no koe.	The sudden shower is all I hear.
	(*GYS*, 16:2195)

In the past, these poems have often been described in *Araragi*-school terms as "thoroughgoing realistic depiction," "purely objective and intuitive," or "depiction by a keen sensibility." Concerning only the surface levels of the poems, such descriptions are not mistaken. A reader who responds to them more profoundly, however, should experience an insight transcending ordinary understanding.

Consider the final waka, by Fushimi (*GYS*, 16:2195). Usually, a rainy sky is cloudy all over. But in this waka there are no clouds in the sky directly above the speaker's eaves, for the strong mountain wind breaks them up and scatters them. While the wind is strong near the peaks of the mountains, however, it does not reach the place from which the speaker of the poem observes it. Instead, the poet feels the violence of the distant wind in the sound of a gentler wind rustling in the pines in the garden. Moreover, while rain is falling all over the garden, the poet can see through the darkness of night a place in the sky where there are no clouds. Ordinary awareness is suddenly shattered and one feels that through the cracks one momentarily sees the colors of a deeper level of awareness. The speaker of the poem receives this feeling from the sudden shower, in which only the sky directly above the eaves of the house is not cloudy. For Tamekanu and his group, objective natural description, which is nothing more than mere depiction of the understandable object (shigi kyō), was a secondary ideal.

This shikan-style perception is not unlike Teika's way of composing waka, in which he attempts to penetrate deeply into the essential significance (hon'i) of the topic. Tamekanu must have believed that he, of all contemporary poets, had inherited and was correctly carrying on Teika's view of waka. The emphasis of Tamekanu's group on the non-understandable object among the concepts of shikan is somewhat different from Teika's view, but the fact remains that, like Teika, they based their waka styles on shikan.

A number of serious problems remain, however, in concluding that Tamekanu and his group perfected this style of shikan-style perception in the ten-year period before the compilation of the *Gyokuyōshū*. The five waka offered above as superior waka in the *Gyokuyō* style were, in fact, gleaned from the *Gyokuyōshū* only with considerable care, and, strangely enough, there are few poems in the collection that can be said to be in the *Gyokuyō* style. Unfortunately, even Yōfuku Mon'in, who became the central figure in the waka world after the deaths of Tamekanu and Fushimi, has no first-rate poems in the anthology. Moreover, there are not that many poems in the anthology that express nature directly with no admixture of subjectivity. Even in those that do, it is not clear to what extent they were composed with a full understanding of Tamekanu's theories. Many poets undoubtedly attempted to compose in this style simply because the descriptive mode was popular in the Jimyōin waka group, and many of the nature poems in the *Gyokuyōshū* were probably little more than imitations of Tamekanu's style. It would be mistaken to analyze all these waka by applying the concepts of shikan contemplation. In terms of both quantity and quality, it would be difficult to conclude that the *Gyokuyō* style had matured by the time of the compilation of the *Gyokuyōshū*.

The maturation of what I have been calling the *Gyokuyō* style occurred during the thirty-four years between the submission of the *Gyokuyōshū* in 1312 and the royal banquet that celebrated the official completion of the *Fūgashū* [=*FGS*], which was held in 1346. It may seem strange to refer to it as the *Gyokuyō* style, but there would also be problems with calling it the Kyōgoku style. In the Twelfth Month of 1315, Tamekanu was exiled once again and disappeared from the waka world. Moreover, Fushimi died in 1317. Even after they had lost its former leaders, however, the Jimyōin poets continued to mature steadily, with Yōfuku Mon'in as their arbiter of poetic taste and the abdicated Hanazono acting as their leader. What I mean here by maturation is that both the weak and strong points of the *Gyokuyō* style were amplified during this period to become clear, characteristic aspects of the style. This waka is exemplary of the weak points of the style:

"Topic Unknown"
By Junii Tameko

Ware mo iiki	I too said it:
Tsuraku wa inochi	"One who is so miserable
Araji to wa	Will soon lose life."
Uki hito nomi ya	Is it only heartless lovers
Itsuwari wa suru.	Who speak such falsehoods?
	(*FGS*, 12:1173)

With a few minor changes in syntax, this waka could easily become nothing more than a short sentence in a diary. Indeed, in translation, the 5-7-5-7-7 structure of the poem, which gives it what waka-like quality it has, will be lost, and it reads like prose. Direct expression of emotion in the style of Kōben was still valued by the compilers of the *Fūgashū*, but the recourse to prose diction is always a clearly negative quality in waka. On the other hand, however, the following outstanding poems from the *Fūgashū* are examples of the *Gyokuyō* style at a level of refinement achieved but rarely in the *Gyokuyōshū* itself:

On the topic "Cherry Blossoms in the Evening."
By Yōfuku Mon'in

Hana no ue ni	The evening sun
Shibashi utsurou	Flickers upon the cherry blossoms
Yūzuku hi	With a moment's light,
Iru to mo nashi ni	And though it does not seem to set,
Kage kienikeri.	Its light has disappeared.[25]
	(*FGS*, 2:199)

[25] [Translation adapted from Brower-Miner, 1961, 377.—Trans.]

From a set of thirty poems by Her Retired Majesty [Yōfuku Mon'in] on the topic "Summer Birds."

Kage shigeki	The shadows thicken
Ko no shita yami no	The blackness beneath the trees
Kuraki yo ni	In the evening darkness,
Mizu no oto shite	When I seem to hear the sound of water
Kuina naku nari.	As a rail taps out its cry.[26]
	(*FGS*, 4:376)

A poem on autumn by Her Retired Majesty [Yōfuku Mon'in]

Mahagi chiru	Bush clover falls
Niwa no akikaze	To the garden's autumn wind
Mi ni shimite	That pierces into me,
Yūhi no kage zo	And the light of the evening sun
Kabe ni kieyuku.	Disappears into the wall.
	(*FGS*, 5:478)

When I presented a hundred-poem sequence. By Yōfuku Mon'in Naishi

Someyaranu	The sun at dusk
Kozue no hikage	Does not give color to the boughs
Utsurisamete	As it fades below
Yaya karewataru	But seems to wither somewhat
Yama no shitakusa.	The plants beneath the mountain trees.[27]
	(*FGS*, 7:674)

When I presented a hundred-poem sequence. By Yōfuku Mon'in Naishi

Ame harete	Rain clears the air
Iro koki yama no	Of the mountains rich in color,
Susono yori	And from their hemline
Hanarete noboru	The clouds break loose and then climb up
Kumo zo majikaki.	Looking as though they were to hand!
	(*FGS*, 16:1688)

[26] The headnote refers to a thirty-poem sequence sponsored by Hanazono sometime in the period between 1338 and 1344.

[27] The headnote refers to a hundred-poem sequence sponsored by Kōgon in 1346.

From a sequence of a hundred poems by His Majesty.
By His Cloistered Majesty [Hanazono]

Yūdachi no	Sudden evening rain:
Kumo tobiwakuru	Its clouds are parted with the flight
Shirasagi no	Of the snowy heron,
Tsubasa ni kakete	And where its winds touch the sky
Haruru hi no kage.	The sunshine streams through the clear air.[28]
	(*FGS*, 4:413)

From a hundred-poem sequence by His Majesty.
By His Abdicated Majesty

Kusamura no	In clumps of plants,
Mushi no koe yori	From the crying of the insects
Kuresomete	Darkness begins,
Masago no ue zo	And upon the stretch of sand
Tsuki zo narinuru.	All is the radiance of the moon![29]
	(*FGS*, 6:579)

On the topic "A Rice Nursery."
By Princess Noriko [or Gishi]

Sakura chiru	They have diverted
Yamashitamizu o	The water below the mountain where
Sekiwakete	Cherry blossoms scatter,
Hana ni nagaruru	And the rice nursery in the field
Oda no nawashiro.	Has become a flow of blossoms.
	(*FGS*, 3:264)

Among some miscellaneous poems
By Kian Mon'in

Yūhi sasu	Where evening sun falls
Mine wa midori no	The greenness of the mountain peaks
Usuku miete	Shows to be pale,

[28] This sequence was also composed for Kōgon in 1346. [As often happens, here and with the preceding poem Hanazono is credited with being cloistered. He was never officially Hanazono In, but the "In" title appears with some regularity, and his diary has a very unusual combination of In and Tennō in its title.—Ed.]

[29] This is from Kōgon's own hand, one of the sequences he commissioned in 1346. Although he was then cloistered (Kōgon In), he is referred to as an abdicated or former sovereign here.

Kage naru yama zo	But the mountains cast in shadow
Wakite iro koki.	Are especially deep in hue.
	(*FGS*, 16:1649)

There are other fine poems in the *Gyokuyō* style, but let us compare Tamekanu's "The plum in flower . . ." (*GYS*, 1:83) with Yōfuku Mon'in's "The evening sun . . ." (*FGS*, 2:199). The former presents a beautiful scene in the Late T'ang style. It is dusk, and in the pale moonlight, made hazy by the light spring rain, the colors of the scene are washed out to a considerable degree. The speaker of the poem is seeing a scene much different from the crimson glow of plum blossoms and the vivid green of willow trees that one would see in the bright sunlight of spring. But it is precisely these images that float into the speaker's mind. The reader understands this from the strong impression made by the poet's use of language. "The plum . . . suffuses with a crimson glow" and "Where willow trees bend gently." Thus, the bright, colorful scene of afternoon and the same scene dimly perceived at dusk are superimposed in the mind of the speaker of the poem. The reflected image is rather close to the understandable object, however, and the response evoked by this rather light disruption of routine awareness is not very powerful.

In the case of Yōfuku Mon'in's poem, however, the sunlight that the speaker of the poem had felt was flickering upon the blossoms suddenly disappears. The response evoked by this sudden disappearance of sunlight is quite powerful, for everyday awareness leads one to believe that sunlight disappears gradually with the setting of the sun. In the physical world, of course, sunlight disappears gradually, but the speaker of the poem suddenly perceives that subtle moment in which it actually disappears completely. This perception is at once extremely subtle and delightfully keen. This keenness is not to be found in the poems I quoted from the *Gyokuyōshū*.

A change in the *Gyokuyō* style seems to occur after the departures of Tamekanu and Fushimi. Since this change was, in fact, an extension of the *Gyokuyō* style, it should not be seen as a shift to a different style. The following poem by Hanazono is a good example (*FGS*, 18:2056):

Tsubame naku	Swallows twitter
Nokiba no yūhi	At the eaves where evening sunlight
Kage kiete	Fades into dark,
Yanagi ni aoki	And with its willows the garden
Niwa no harukaze.	Stirs in the green breeze of the spring.

The vision of this poem combines those of Tamekanu's "The plum in flower" (*GYS*, 1:83) and Yōfuku Mon'in's "The evening sun" (*FGS*, 2:199). We seem to have a pure landscape poem. But the poem bears the following headnote:

> Composed on the topic "This is the real heroism; this the real worship of the Tathāgata with the true law," in the chapter on the Bodhisattva Bhaiṣajya-rāja [in the "Medicine King" chapter of the *Lotus Sūtra*].[30]

The imagery of "Swallows twitter" is a symbolic expression of the philosophical principle contained in the topic from the *Lotus Sūtra*, and so it becomes clear that this is not merely a landscape poem. The problem is in the way this imagery has been used. In modern criticism, this technique is usually called symbolism, and since it is to be expected that the vehicle or signifier and the tenor or signified meaning of the symbol will have a correspondence of meaning, one may very well make the mistake of thinking that the swallows, the setting sun, and the willows correspond as signifying images to create a consistent, signified other meaning.

But this would be a misunderstanding of the poem. The passage from the *Lotus Sūtra* and the waka have no explicable correspondence whatsoever at the level of meaning. Quite the contrary. The poet abandons the meaning presented by "This is the real heroism" as language and penetrates deeply into the phenomenal object (kyōshō) of the poem, and by doing so anticipates that the non-understandable object (fushigi kyō), grasped at a profounder level, will become one with the passage from the *Lotus Sūtra*. This is not different from the perceptual stance of shikan contemplation, but as Okami Masao has pointed out (1947, 11-12), it partakes even more directly of the Zen method of contemplation.

The Tendai concept of shikan and Zen meditation are not fundamentally different in essential matters. Yet, as a distinct sect, Zen has one characteristic aspect that makes it very different from the Tendai sect. That is its use of "language that means absolutely nothing." For example, the Zen master Hung-chih, or T'ien-t'ung Chen-chüeh (?-1157), addressed his disciples in the following manner (*Wanshi*, 1:5):

[30] *Hokkekyō*, 7 (Chapter on the Previous Existence of the Medicine King), 53. When the Buddha expounded the infinite quantity of the past, there was a certain bodhisattva in the audience. Since he had achieved awakening he was capable of taking any form. As a sign of gratitude to the Buddha, he poured various fragrant oils over his body and immolated himself. After burning for twelve hundred years, he was reborn. The other buddhas in the audience praised his act with their ge.

That real existence exists in itself is exquisitely evident.[31] That innate enlightenment exists in itself is evidently exquisite.[32] They are equal in size to the great sky, and they are governed by the same principles that rule the world. They correspond to both color and voice, and are just as one hears them and just as one views them. As past, present, and future exist everywhere, so do they exist, but they do not come and go. They enter into every relationship, but are not turned straight upside down. Do you understand?

When the clouds are low and the sun sinks,
Wild geese are strung out like a row of characters.
When the moon slips beneath the horizon,
A solitary monkey cries out in the loneliness.

There is deliberately no relationship that can be explained between the closing lines of poetry and the preceding prose, from "That real existence exists in itself is exquisitely evident" to "They enter into every relationship, but are not turned straight upside down." The relationship between the statement and the poem is precisely the same as that between the Buddha and "three pounds of hemp seed." It is also the same as the relationship between "This is the real heroism" and "Swallows twitter." It may also be seen in this waka by Hanazono (*FGS*, 18:2067)

On the topic "The three stages are one; they are not three but not one."

Mado no hoka ni	As I listen
Shitataru ame o	To the rain outside my window
Kiku nabe ni	Fall in gentle drops,
Kabe ni somukeru	I have turned my lamp around
Yowa no tomoshibi.	Dimming its light against the wall.[33]

[31] That is, true existence does not rely on anything outside itself, but exists in itself.

[32] That is, by birth a human being is endowed with the possibility of enlightenment. There is no difference between "evidently exquisite" and "exquisitely evident." [Auth., Ed.]

[33] The topic needs explanation. The three stages are kū (Emptiness: in all existence there is no substantiality); ke (the Transient: the concept that in all existence self being itself has no reality of its own); and chū (the Absolute: therefore, absolute affirmation that there is nothing that should be denied; in Chinese, k'ung, chin, and chung). However, all three stages are expressions of the same thing, and from that point of view it may be said that they are one stage. Thus, "the three stages are one; they are not three, but not one." [Translation is adapted from Brower-Miner, 1961, 388.—Trans.]

That this poem originates in Zen Buddhism is confirmed by another of Hanazono's poems (*FGS*, 18:2073):

> When I led an excursion to the Daibaizan Betsuden'in,[34] I recited the following account: "A monk asked Yün-men, 'What happens when the tree withers and the leaves fall?' Yün-men answered, 'It means my whole body will be exposed to the autumn wind,' " and I composed this poem.

Tatsutagawa	The Tatsuta River
Momijiba nagaru	Takes its course with colored leaves
Miyoshino no	To Yoshino,
Yoshino no yama ni	To lovely Mount Yoshino where blossoms
Sakurabana saku.	Of the cherries are in full bloom.

Hanazono had begun his study of shikan contemplation around 1318, when he abdicated at the age of twenty-two. From 1320 his interest turned to Zen, and Zen thereafter became his lifelong religious belief (Iwahashi, 1962, 133-56). His diary records, however, that he continued to practice shikan contemplation even after his conversion to Zen, probably because Tendai shikan is not very different in its essentials from Zen meditation. Yen Yü, a Zen poet of the Southern Sung, in his famous shih treatise, the *Ts'ang-lang Shih-hua*, propounded the theory that "poetry and Zen are in essence one" (Kuo S., 1947, 64-76).[35] This treatise was quoted in almost its original form in Wei Ch'ing-chih's *Shih-jen Yü-hsieh* (completed in 1244) and was published in a Gosan edition in 1324. Hanazono himself refers to his reading of this treatise in an entry in his diary dated the twenty-eighth day of the Twelfth Month of 1325 (*Hanazono Ki*, 160). We may therefore conclude that the assimilation of Zen imagery into the *Gyokuyō* style was the direct result of Hanazono's adoption of Zen and that this tendency was pushed forward further by the indirect influence of the theory that "poetry and Zen are in essence one" in Chinese shih treatises.

Hanazono was one of the leaders of the *Gyokuyō* poets in the later period of the *Gyokuyō* style, and his adoption of Zen, as well as his exploitation of Zen ways of expression in his poetry, led to a style in the later *Gyokuyō* period that displays somewhat different features from that

[34] The Betsuden'in is a detached temple of Chōfukuji. It was built for Gatsurin Dōkō (1293-1351). The quotation from Yün-men is found in *Pi-yen*, 145-47 (paragraph 27).

[35] Yen Yü was born during the reign of Kao-tsung (1145-48) and was alive until the reign of Li-tsung (1225-65; Tu, 1976, 424).

of the early period, which was based theoretically on shikan.[36] Zen expression gave this later style a more acute tone. As we have seen, even in the poems of a single poet like Yōfuku Mon'in, the approach taken in grasping the object in her later work, and therefore the tone of the poetry, is much keener than in her earlier work.

This keenness is the contribution of Zen. In Zen, and particularly in Rinzai Zen, dullness of expression is abhorred. Even if something is repeated, the statement that breaks down routine awareness and expresses something incisively is highly evaluated. This incisiveness of expression may be seen in records of mondō (dialogues) between famous Zen masters, which are infused with a tension suggestive of a life-and-death confrontation on a battlefield. When everyday awareness is radically broken down in this incisive fashion, conception of the non-understandable object (fushigi kyō) naturally should become stronger, and it is precisely this quality that appears in the *Gyokuyō* style of the late period. In the past, critics have analyzed the *Gyokuyō* style in terms of aspects of the understandable object (shigi kyō): the handling of light, the fluidity of time, and the abundance of color. Clearly one cannot approach the true value of the *Gyokuyō* style through that kind of analysis alone.

The Subtle Writing of the Nijō School

While there are now many critics who have come to esteem the waka of the *Gyokuyō* poets, it is still usual to describe the waka of the Nijō faction as insipid and dull. I acknowledge that, in a certain sense, such an evaluation is correct. The poems in the *Rika Wakashū* (abbreviation, *Rikashū*) for example, certainly deserve such a judgment:

In a one-thousand-poem sequence, on the topic "Haze."

Tachiwataru	Beneath the haze
Kasumi no shita no	That spreads wide across the scene,

[36] A recent interpretation argues that the *Gyokuyō* style had its theoretical basis in the theory of yuishiki (vijnāpti-mātratā) of the Hossō sect of Buddhism (Iwasa, 1983, 47-67). There is no doubt that this interpretation is a strong criticism of previous interpretations, which have always considered the style in connection with shigi kyō (the observing mind). However, the theory that true perception is impossible at the level of routine awareness and that one must go deep to the level of ariyashiki (ālayavijnāna) is propounded in the *Ta-ch'eng Ch'i-hsin Lun*; and after Ching-ch'ih Chan-jan (711-82), the theory of chen-ju sui-yüan—that all things and phenomena in the universe are manifestations of bhūtathatā (external truth)—had been assimilated into Tendai doctrine (Andō, 1968, 312-19). I believe that what appears to be based on the theory of yuishiki in the *Gyokuyō* style is rooted in the yuishin theory of Tendai doctrine.

Shirayuki wa	The white snow—
Yama no ha nagara	Along with the mountain rim—
Sora ni kietsutsu.	Is disappearing into sky.[37]
	(37)

Rice Seedling Beds

Shizu no o ga	The peasant men
Nawashiromizu o	Guide water for the seedling beds
Makaseirete	Into the land,
Kyō wa kadota ni	And in the field before my gate,
Kawazu naku nari.	Today the frogs are croaking.
	(148)

On the topic "The Moon among Bamboo"

Mado chikaki	The moon leaks through,
Take no ha wake ni	Dividing the bamboo leaves
Moru tsuki no	Near my window,
Kage sadamaranu	But its light has no direction
Yowa no akikaze.	In the autumn wind at midnight.
	(321)

Composed on the topic "Sea Ways"

Kureyukeba	With the setting sun
Ura kogu fune no	The boats plying across the bay
Minatoiri ni	Stir up the harbor;
Yūnami tatete	And what strokes up the evening waves
Shiokaze zo fuku.	Is the tidal breeze that blows.
	(713)

These poems are exemplary of the entire collection, and they seem to have not even one impressive point. But if one examines them more closely, each conceals a minute reasoning (ri). In the first poem, it is in the observation that although one should be able to see the snow remaining on the rim of the mountain, it disappears into the whiteness of the trailing haze, and the poet can no longer tell where the snow ends and the hazy sky begins. In the second poem, the poet observes that the exuberant rush

[37] The *Rikashū* is the personal collection of Prince Munenaga (1312-89). Its date of compilation is unknown.

of fresh water into the field has enlivened the frogs. In the third, the moonlight shining on the window through the bamboo leaves seems to move as the wind ruffles the leaves. In the final poem, the boats entering the harbor leave wakes behind them, creating waves higher than the gentle ones raised by the evening sea breeze. Since, however, the amount of reasoning in these waka is so much smaller than in the oblique expression of the *Kokinshū* style, it is impossible to respond to it without an extremely close reading. The very discovery of these minute threads of reasoning gives these waka a new interest, and for this reason, their expression must be clear and light, in the style of elegant simplicity. If the tone were vehement, the minute threads of reasoning would be blown away completely. A reader not also in a tranquil frame of mind will fail to amplify the minute reasoning of this kind of poetry.

This attention to minute details is essential not only in responding to individual waka in the Nijō style, but also in reading poems in sequences. The arrangement of sequences of waka according to the principles of progression and association is similar to that observed in the *Shinkokinshū* period, but it is particularly in the use of association that we find interspersed some extremely subtle techniques. The following is a sequence from Book Fifteen of the *Shin'yōshū*.[38]

Among some of His Majesty's love poems.
By Godaigo Tennō

Waga koi wa	As for my love,
Kumeji no hashi no	Like that bridge built in Kume
Nakataete	It has broken up—
Chigiri munashiki	Your promises are as hollow
Kazuraki no kami.	As the god of Kazuraki's.[39]
	(948)

[38] The *Shin'yōshū* was compiled by Prince Munenaga in 1381. Modeled on a royal collection, it is in twenty books. But breaking with the precedent of those collections, it includes only contemporary poets. Moreover, the poets are only those of the Southern Court (Daikakuji line). [Of the collection's 1,420 poems ninety-nine are labeled as by Munenaga, and another ninety-six are his but labeled "Anonymous," making him much the most heavily represented poet.—Ed.]

[39] According to the *Konjaku Monogatari*, 11:62-63 (see Ury, 1979, 82-83), there were powerful deities or demons who were great builders, making a bridge through the sky to join Mount Kazuraki and Mount Mitake. Because they feared to have their ugliness seen, they worked at night. This lore became associated with the deity of Kazuraki, who once agreed to do some building and then refused, so gaining a reputation for unreliability. The woman speaker of the poem draws on this lore for her accusation. [Auth., Ed.]

On love associated with the plant of forgetting.
By Shin Sen'yō Mon'in

Kayoikoshi — He who once came here
Hito wa nokiba no — Has left the forgetting plant
Wasuregusa — Beneath my eaves.
Tsuyu kakare to wa — Did he ever leave his promise
Chigiri ya wa seshi. — That I should dew it with my tears?[40]

(949)

Attached to a leaf of plant of forgetting
I wrapped up and sent to a certain person.
Anonymous

Wasuraruru — If I did not think
Mi o onaji na to — That I whom you have now forgot
Omowazu wa — Share this plant's name,
Nani ka nokiba no — Why also should this wretchedness
Kusa mo ukaran. — Affect the plants beneath my eaves?

(950)

Topic Unknown
By the Daughter of the Former Major Counselor Mitsutō

Karehateshi — He never comes now—
Hito ni wa tare ka — Who is to blame for teaching him
Sumiyoshi no — That plant's name,
Kishi naru kusa no — The one that grows so heavily
Na o oshieken. — On the Sumiyoshi coast?

(951)

On the topic "Love Associated with Longing Grass."
By Minister of Ceremonial Prince Koreshige

Karene tada — Wilt all away!
Obana ga moto no — You plant of the hateful name
Kusa no na yo — Beneath the pampas grass!
Tsuyu no yosuga mo — It is I myself whose misplaced trust
Arazu naru mi ni. — Leaves less to hope for than the dew.

(952)

[40] The plant of forgetting is the day lily, given the name because it was once believed that by adorning oneself with it, one would forget the sufferings one worried over. The "noki" of "nokiba" refers not only to eaves but, by a pun, to the man's going away.

On the same topic.
By Commander of the Right Military Guards Shigenao

Adanaran	Just as I thought!
Mono to wa kanete	The love grass has revealed to me
Omoigusa	What I cannot trust—
Hazue no tsuyu no	Like your promises, the dew
Kakaru chigiri wa.	Quickly forgets the tips of leaves.
	(953)

From a set of one thousand waka composed at the Palace in 1353, on "Love Associated with Moon Grass."
By Former Middle Counselor Tametada

Utsuriyuku	All your promises
Hito no chigiri wa	Come from one who changes quickly—
Tsukigusa no	Like a narrow sash
Hanada no obi no	Dyed light blue with moongrass flowers
Musubi taetsutsu.	Its knot comes constantly undone.[41]
	(954)

On the topic "Love Associated with Mugwort."
By Former Major Counselor Sanetame

Yomogiu no	The way to your house,
Moto koshi michi wa	Rampant now with untended mugwort,
Kawaranu ni	Is just the same—
Ika ni kareyuku	If my visits grow somewhat rare,
Chigiri naru ran.	Why should your vows wholly wither?[42]
	(955)

Among some love poems.
By Former Minister of the Center Taka

Kayoikoshi	All those promises
Hito no chigiri no	Made by him who used to come here:
Sue tsui ni	Nothing, after all—

[41] The speaker is a woman. Because it changes color so quickly, moon grass (tsukigusa) became an emblem of a man's unreliability.

[42] There is a wordplay on "kareyuku" as "wither away" and "go rarely." In the former sense it is an associated expression (engo) for mugwort, which Japanese think of as quickly growing rampant about a deserted or untended house. [Auth., Ed.]

Karureba shigeru	Like plants withered in my garden
Niwa no yomogiu.	Under the rampant mugwort.
	(956)

From a waka match in five hundred rounds.
By Major Captain of the Bodyguards
of the Right, Nagachika

Ukarikeru	It always happens
Mi no narawashi no	To one who is miserably sad
Yūbe kana	As the darkness falls.
Iriai no kane ni	The sound of the evening bell
Mono wasuresede.	Brings back to mind unhappy things.[43]
	(957)

We may describe the pattern of association and progression as follows: 948 and 949 are linked by "promise" (chigiri); 949 and 950 are linked by "forget" (wasure), "plant" (kusa-gusa), and "eaves" (nokiba); 950 and 951 are linked by "plant" (kusa—i.e., omoigusa); 951 and 952 are linked by "wither" (kare), "plant" or "grass" (kusa), and "name" (na); and 952 and 953 are linked by "grass" (kusa) and "dew" (tsuyu). This linking of adjacent waka that have common words or phrases is the same as that practiced in the *Shinkokinshū* period. The use of associated words (engo) in addition, however, is more subtle as a poetic technique. For example, while the "ji" of Kumeji in 948 had already come to mean "area" by this period, its original meaning was "road." This is linked to "made his way here" (kayoi) in 949. The "eaves" (noki) of 950 are part of a house, while the root meaning of the place name Sumiyoshi in 951 is "good for dwelling." Similarly the "way" (michi) of 955 is associated with the "used to come here" (kayoikoshi) of 956.

Another extremely subtle technique is the arrangement of the poems in such a way that the meanings of individual waka are changed completely by their association with the other poems of the sequence. For example, by itself and as originally composed, 950 would be understood as a waka with a female speaker and should be paraphrased as follows: if the "forgetting" ("wasure" in the name of the plant of forgetting, wasuregusa) did not make me so strongly conscious of my lot now that you have forgotten me, I would not grieve so much for the condition of the grass, also

[43] [As this sequence, and in it this poem best of all, show, when darkness fell a husband or lover was given to visiting the beloved woman to spend the night. The concept arose from earlier uxorilocal marriage and lover's trysts when most property descended matrilineally. By this time, inheritance was different, but poetic canons of love sustained earlier ideas.—Ed.]

forgotten, growing beneath my eaves. Once the compilers have placed 950 after 949, however, its point of view shifts, and it is understood as the answer of the male lover to the complaint of the female speaker of 949.

Thus, the paraphrase of the poem would have to be changed to something like this: You lament that you have been forgotten like the wasuregusa beneath your eaves, but that is only because you think of yourself as being in the same condition as the name of the grass. If you would only stop thinking that way, there would be nothing to be so unhappy about.[44] This kind of witty poetic exchange was extremely popular in the period of the *Gosenshū*, but then the poems were actually exchanged between lovers. Here the witty effect is achieved by the compilers' arrangement of two poems that were originally unrelated.

The use of this technique does not stop with the connection of these two waka. When it is read together with 951, 950 once again has a female speaker lamenting that she has been forgotten. In response to this lament, the speaker of 951 (probably another woman), says something like this: I wonder who it was that taught him—that man who has grown so distant—the meaning of "forgetting" in "plant of forgetting" (didn't you say something that would make him forget you?). This intent of 951, however, is present only when it is read as a response to 950. By itself, 951 should be read as a poem in which a female speaker berates herself: the person who taught him the name of that grass on the bluffs of Sumiyoshi (who is responsible for his forgetting me) was none other than I myself.[45]

This transformation of the meaning of waka by the way they are arranged has one other important feature. While the meaning of 951 is changed by its association with poem 950, it has no direct relationship with 949. Poem 949 does not give rise to a change in the meaning of 951, and there is a semantic break between non-contiguous poems.[46] This kind of settled, radical break had not existed previously among the principles of progression. Since the period of the *Kokinshū*, the principle of progression had yielded a progressive linking, in which one phenomenon gave rise to a succeeding phenomenon. A principle of progression that conceals those breaks somewhere in a sequence even while the sequence progresses

[44] On this revised reading of 950, its male speaker is replying to the female speaker of 949: you have thought all that in your self-centered way, but in fact it is I who suffer the problem of *your* forgetting me.

[45] [Unlike Japanese, English suffers from the tyranny of pronouns; so our translation of each poem has had to imply a specific sex for each speaker.—Ed.]

[46] [That is, as the author soon suggests, under the influence of renga Munenaga's waka sequentiality is semantically continuous only from one poem (or renga stanza) to the next: 950 and 951 are related in meaning, as are 951 and 952. But 952 has no semantic connection with 950. (See Appendix on renga.) Such breaks had occurred in earlier collections, but the influence of renga had made it a rule for Prince Munenaga's design.—Ed.]

continuously—a linked breaking—may be observed in the *Shinkokinshū*. But the techniques of arrangement we have seen in the present waka sequence were perfected in the *Shin'yōshū*.

The perfection of these new techniques was a result of the influence of renga. Yoshimoto had compiled the *Tsukuba Shū* (*The Tsukuba Collection* [= *TBS*]) twenty-five years before the compilation of the *Shin'yōshū*. Given the influence of renga, the kind of waka sequence analyzed above may be read as a renga with waka as its units rather than stanzas of 5-7-5 or 7-7 syllables. The principle of progression in which a waka is made to produce a new meaning by its connection with the waka immediately preceding it in the sequence is identical to the principle of stanzaic connection (tsukeai) in renga. The clearest example of this is the connection between poems 954 and 955. Since they have no common words or phrases, and since there is no link between the phenomena depicted in the poems, the progression of the sequence should have stopped here, according to the earlier rules of progression. In fact, however, in response to 954, which depicts the dilapidated dwelling of a woman who has been forgotten, 955 makes her the speaker of the poem, becoming a direct, first-person expression of her grief. By the canons of renga, they are superbly connected.

When we read the poems in this sequence individually, we find them stereotyped or even commonplace. But in their renga-like sequential connection, we discover an unexpected novelty, and our interest is aroused. The arrangement of poems inspires a feeling of novelty even while the poems themselves are written in the Nijō clear, light style of elegant simplicity. Novelty holds great importance as a basic principle of renga, but it was originally a stylistic ideal strongly advocated in Nijō waka treatises.[47] In fact, as we have seen, it can be traced back to Tameie, who argued for this standard in his own theory of waka. Tameie's approach became the mainstream in renga composition and also greatly influenced the principles of arranging waka sequences.

Those who are impressed by the poetry of the Kyōgoku poets will no doubt find the *Shin'yōshū* to be a collection of insipid, mediocre poems. From the Nijō standpoint, however, the techniques of arrangement displayed in the *Gyokuyōshū* and the *Fūgashū* could only be criticized as hopelessly heavy-handed and crude. Since individually the waka of the Nijō faction are written in the clear, light style of elegant simplicity, it is

[47] "There must be an enriching of technique. Not only did the great poets of the past insist on this, but so did my teachers (including my father, Tameuji). New techniques are, however, very hard to come by. Over many generations of royal collections and in the work of great poets, fresh techniques have been used up, and now there can be little that is original. The human face has always had eyes set side by side and a nose projecting between, but human faces are not what they were. The same is true of poetry." So Nijō Tameyo (1250-1338) in *Waka Teikin*, 115, giving a characteristic Nijō view.

difficult to judge between them. Therefore, the compiler's main task was not to choose outstanding poems and discard poor ones, but to take a collection of mediocre poems and arrange them appropriately in order to create a splendid whole, making an anthology that would become a wonderful aesthetic object in itself. Indeed, in a very real sense, it is less appropriate to call Prince Munenaga the selector for the *Shin'yōshū* than its maker.

To respond with great interest to the subtle devices contained in light, clear poetry and to discover the unexpected interest that arises from the arrangement of the poems—these are things impossible unless the reader possesses a truly refined sensibility. And of course a delicate sensitivity must be present to compose such poetry. It may appear, therefore, that Prince Munenaga must have composed or read poems in very tranquil surroundings. The truth, however, is quite the opposite. The period from the fourteenth to the fifteenth centuries was one of uninterrupted disorder. Besides such massive conflicts as the civil war between the Northern and Southern Courts, which lasted from 1331 to 1392, and the Ōnin War from 1467 to 1477, a glance at the chronology of this period will reveal that there is hardly a single year in which some sort of military struggle was not being waged. Prince Munenaga himself made his military headquarters in Shinano (present Nagano prefecture) and participated in battles in farflung Tōtōmi (present Shizuoka prefecture), Etchū (present Toyama prefecture), and Echigo (present Niigata prefecture), returning only occasionally to his mansion at Yoshino. One must wonder at the toughness of spirit of this poet who, not knowing what the morrow would bring, could respond to the novelty of extreme subtle expression in the setting of battle camps.

Compared to Chōmei, who did nothing but write pessimistic depictions of all the disasters that were taking place, Munenaga and the other nobles of the Southern Court appear to have been far more refined as human beings. The waka of the Nijō school is certainly attenuated. Yet it must also be said that the Nijō poets established the conviction that waka poetry is something of such high value that it should be composed and enjoyed even in the briefest interval between life and death.

CHAPTER 15

The Maturation of Renga

YOSHIMOTO AND KYŪSEI

Codified renga (hereafter simply renga) flourished from the middle of the thirteenth century. The creation of numerous canons and rules for composition must have been a major impetus to its development. According to Nijō Yoshimoto, during the reign of Gosaga (1242-1246), there were many skillful renga poets among the high nobility, and renga masters called Hananomoto ("Under the Cherry Blossoms") among commoners, but there were no really outstanding poets (*Tsukuba Mondō*, 78). Yoshimoto's reference to the Hananomoto poets provides evidence concerning two important aspects of the period: first, professional writers had appeared among the common people; and second, renga was linked to something incantatory. Yoshimoto goes on to describe the Hananomoto renga masters in the following:

> Dōshō, Jakunin, Mushō[1] and others used to gather great numbers of people of various classes under the cherry blossoms at Bishamondō[2] and Hosshōji[3] every spring to compose renga. Thereafter, famous renga masters from the lower nobility became numerous. (ibid.)

Dōshō and the other Hananomoto poets were monks, but it is difficult to believe that they were actually attached to temples or practiced Buddhist rites. In all likelihood, they were monks only in form, actually making their livings as judges (tenja) and leaders of renga groups.[4] These renga masters apparently had their own shikimoku (books of renga rules and canons). According to the *Reizeike Zō Sōshi Mokuroku (Catalogue of Books and Manuscripts in the Collection of the Reizei Family)*, there were shikimoku called *Hananomoto Yō (The Hananomoto Style)* or *Hanano-*

[1] The only thing known of the dates of three poets named is that they flourished in the middle of the thirteenth century.

[2] Bishamondō was the popular name for the temple Izumoji (Tendai sect) located in Izumoji in northern Kyoto. [The two words "Izumoji" have different third characters; "Izumo Temple" and "Izumo Street."—Ed.]

[3] Hosshōji was a temple built by Shirakawa (r. 1072-86) in Okazaki, Sakyōku of present Kyoto.

[4] Like performers of dengaku and sarugaku (predecessors of nō), performers of many other arts formally took orders. It seems likely that renga masters followed the precedent. There were certain advantages to being a monk: exemption from taxes and conscript labor; and possible freedom, if one was from the lower classes, to associate with people of high station.

moto Dōshō (Compilation by Dōshō of the Hananomoto) before 1317. Practical rules must have been necessary when the renga masters instructed others.

In any event, the Hananomoto poets advanced rapidly after the beginning of the fourteenth century. For example, in 1333 the shogunal army attacked Chihaya Castle, but could not at once seize it and was forced to wait out a long siege. To ease the boredom, they invited the Hananomoto renga masters from the capital and composed a renga in ten thousand stanzas (*Taiheiki* [=*THK*], 7:220). Whether or not this episode actually occurred is not important. Its very depiction in the *Taiheiki* demonstrates that professional renga masters were known to be active on a wide scale in the early fourteenth century.

Before they were conducted by professional renga masters, Hananomoto renga sittings had simply involved gathering groups beneath cherry blossoms in full bloom to enjoy composing and listening to renga. The custom of enjoying the grand displays of cherry blossoms has existed in Japan since the Heian period and continues to exist today (Yamada Y., 1938, 377-88). This custom implies more than aesthetic admiration of the cherry blossoms. It originated in the religious belief that anyone under the cherry blossoms in full bloom would be infused by the spirit of the flowers with some beneficial result. This partakes of the belief of the Chinkasai (Festival for the Deity of Cherry Blossoms), which celebrates the apotropaic powers of cherry blossoms. During this period, the association of Hananomoto renga with the cherry blossoms led to the belief that renga also had magical incantatory powers. For example, renga were composed as prayers for recovery from illnesses or for victory in battle.[5] These customs had their origins not in the renga composed at court but in Hananomoto renga.

Hananomoto renga composition led by professional renga masters began between 1356 and 1361.[6] As Yoshimoto wrote, renga masters not of high noble birth continued to flourish, producing many outstanding poets (*Renri Hishō* [=*RRHS*], 46): "There are also a few outstanding poets at the royal palace this time, but the real experts are among those of lesser station." Yoshimoto refers to the early fourteenth century, and during this period there were certainly a number of outstanding renga poets from

[5] The hokku (opening stanza) of the first hundred stanzas (hyakuin) of Sōgi's solo sequence, A *Thousand Stanzas at Mishima (Mishima Senku)*, was composed as an offering to the deity of the Mishima Shrine when Tō no Tsuneyori's son, Takeichimaro, was suffering during an influenza epidemic, and the thousand stanzas were presented to effect recovery. Sōchō also composed a solo senku, *A Thousand Stanzas on Call to Battle (Shutsujin Senku)*, as Imagawa Ujichika was about to go to camp (Yamada Y., 1937, 150-51).

[6] In the *Shinsatsu Ōrai (New Correspondence)* of 1367, it is observed that "Attendance at renga held under cherry blossoms at Jinshu and Washio Shrines has declined in recent years. Truly a regrettable thing" (*Shinsatsu*, 1:467).

the lower nobility. They include Zenna, Jungaku, Shinshō, Ryōa, and others, but Kyūsei (1284-1378) is the one who opens eyes. Kyūsei studied waka with Reizei Tamesuke and renga with Zenna.[7] Unlike Zenna, he infused his renga with the ga of waka. Yoshimoto describes Kyūsei's style in the following (*Jūmon*, 112):

> Kyūsei's use of diction was always remarkable. It possessed lovely depth (yūgen) and was impressive. He never composed renga with an eye to artifice. Rather, he connected stanzas well. Although few of his stanzas stand out by themselves, he made the most of poetic atmosphere (kakari), and his diction gave the feeling of fragrant blossoms.

The kind of writing this actually referred to can be seen from the following added stanza (tsukeku).

Inochi wa shirazu hi koso nagakere	No one knows how long life lasts but the spring day lasts on
shiratsuyu no tama no oyanagi ame furite	the bright dew drops bejewel the lovely willow as the light rain falls[8] (*TBS*, 1:70)

The stanza preceding Kyūsei's is a difficult one to connect with. Its speaker, perhaps an old man whose remaining time is short, is saying: "The span of my remaining life is uncertain, but the spring day is long." There is a certain uneasiness in the contrast between the long spring day and the shortness of life, but the speaker attempts to comfort himself with the balmy beauty of the spring landscape. With so complete a conception, an addition to the stanza is very difficult.

Kyūsei, however, changes the meaning of "span of life," making it refer not to a person but to the dew: "After the rainfall, how long will the raindrops remain on the leaves of the willow? I do not know, but it is the season when the days are long, so let us enjoy them while we can." Kyūsei also links the two stanzas by his use of pivot words (kakekotoba) and

[7] "Kyūsei is the disciple of Lord [Reizei] Tamesuke at Fujigayatsu and is able to compose waka to some extent" (*Rakusho*, 196). "Kyūsei studied with Zenna but has since left him" (*Jūmon*, 109). [Kyūsei (d. 1376 or 1378) is a name also pronounced Kyūzai, Kasei, and Gusai.—Ed.]

[8] [The author of the first two lines or stanza is not named, and that stanza is presented to show Kyūsei's skill in connection (tsukeai), as also because after the opening stanza (hokku), every stanza is complete only as an additional stanza is added, whether in the two- or the three-line stanza forms that alternate. Collections of renga stanzas give the previous stanza (maeku) so that understanding and appreciation of the added stanza (tsukeku) is possible.—Ed.]

word association (engo). The "o" (small or pretty) of "oyanagi" pivots a second meaning as "string," and this "string of jewels" associates with "nagakere" (long) in the previous stanza. Moreover, "tsuyu" (dew) associates with "inochi" (life) in the previous stanza.[9]

This subtle use of verbal association is what Yoshimoto refers to when he says, "Kyūsei's use of diction was always remarkable," or when he says that "he connected stanzas well." Yet if we consider Kyūsei's stanza by itself, it appears to be nothing more than a description of a beautiful spring landscape, devoid of the complex mental state of the preceding stanza. This is what led Yoshimoto to say that "he never composed renga with an eye to artifice"—that is, complex mental states or mental images. That his poems place primary emphasis on "poetic atmosphere"[10] and that his diction is sensually beautiful may also be seen in this stanza, in which the beauty of white drops of dew set against the green of willow leaves is further emphasized by the rhetorical flourish of referring to them as jewels. This is nothing other than the style of yūgen, which in this period was used in a sense almost precisely identical to that of yūen (elegant charm).[11] Yoshimoto's own statement that Kyūsei's "diction gave the feeling of fragrant blossoms" refers precisely to this quality of yūgen in Kyūsei's stanzas.

Here is another example of his skill in stanzaic connection (*TBS*, 4:332):

Tada hitomeguri	Come and gone in just one turn
aki zo shigururu	autumn drizzle goes its way
kusa ni saku	the plants in bloom
hanamiguruma no	the flower-viewing carriage
no ni idete	sets out over fields

In a beautiful meadow resplendent with blooming autumn plants, Kyūsei poses a carriage, which apparently belongs to someone of rank, making this truly a stanza of elegant charm. His poising of "kuruma" (a carriage or even a wheel) against the "hitomeguri" (in just one turn) of the rain is richly deserving of Yoshimoto's high praise for his language and connections. Moreover, as in the previous example, the poem has no particular

[9] See the anonymous love poem, *Gosenshū*, 13:895: "If I live on, / Perhaps I shall understand / His real heart, / But like the *dew* my *life* is fragile / And meanwhile I suffer so."

[10] "Kakari" may be rendered "poetic atmosphere" and is a word often found in Yoshimoto's late writings. More particularly, it resembles "sugata" (total effect, configuration). In opposition to a fixed, separate sugata, that with kakari is fluid, rhythmical, connected (Nose, 1946-47a, 155-57).

[11] Yoshimoto's usage of "yūgen" involves the beauty of elegant refinement (as if written with the "yū" of "yūen" rather than that of "yūgen"); there are implications of the sensitive and sensuous, along with youthfulness and splendor (Nose, 1944a, 303-307).

point of its own but places the focus of reading on its connection with the previous stanza, which is crucial in renga. Kyūsei's disciple, Shūa, who was the principal figure in the renga world from 1352 to 1379, wrote in a style that focuses interest on the stanza itself.[12] The view of Yoshimoto and Kyūsei that the interest of renga should always be in the connection between stanzas was revived by Bontōan, and after the appearance of Sōgi this became the dominant view.[13]

Kyūsei was the ideal collaborator for Yoshimoto in compiling the *Tsukuba Shū (A Collection of Renga)* and a new renga shikimoku *(The New Shikimoku of the Ōan Era; Ōan Shinshiki)*. The *Tsukuba Shū* was completed in 1357, and in the same year it was accorded a status just below a royal anthology. This was an epochal event in the history of renga, for the acceptance of the *Tsukuba Shū* as second only to a royal collection meant that renga, which had always been viewed as a literary form below waka, had finally been accepted as a premier art. Moreover, in 1372, the *Renga Shinshiki* was given royal sanction. Until then, a number of rule books (shikimoku) were in existence. It was not only that Yoshimoto unified this diversity, but that his achievement was given the authority of royal sanction.

In fact, Yoshimoto entrusted both of these important projects almost entirely to Kyūsei. This is an indication of Yoshimoto's trust in him, and that trust must have arisen from his stylistic consistency with Yoshimoto's own poetic ideals. Yoshimoto wrote many treatises on renga: *Hekirenshō (A Biased Treatise on Renga), Renri Hishō (A Secret Treatise on Renga Principles), Gekimoshō (The Gekimo Treatise), Tsukuba Mondō (The Tsukuba Dialogues), Jūmon Saihishō (A Top Secret Treatise on Ten Questions), Kyūshū Mondō (The Kyushu Dialogues)*, and *Renga Jūyō (The Ten Styles of Renga)*. From these and the opinions stated in his waka treatises, *Kinrai Fūteishō* and *Gumon Kenchū*, it is clear that his poetic ideals were a synthesis of the theories of the Nijō and Reizei poets. And it was Kyūsei who realized Yoshimoto's stylistic ideals in his renga practice.

Yoshimoto had both theoretical and practical reasons for taking a position that combined the principles of the Nijō and Reizei factions. On the theoretical side, his views represent an assimilation of Sung shih theories into waka and renga. We saw earlier that Sung shih treatises place emphasis on styles that are simple (p'u) or crude (cho), and that in special or extreme cases they advocated a style of elegant simplicity (heitan). However, Sung poetic ideals did not aspire merely to elegant simplicity.

[12] Shūa's dates are not certainly known. It seems he died in 1376 or 1377, and his stanzas begin to appear after 1355 (Kidō, 1971, 273-76).

[13] Bontōan's secular name was Asayama Morotsuna. He was born in 1349 and died sometime after V.1417 (Mizukami, 1950, 12-17).

As an ideal, it held that poets who had mastered ornate expression should gradually arrive at a style of elegant simplicity as they grew older. This ideal was propounded, for example, by Su Shih, who was greatly respected in Japan after the beginning of the fourteenth century, and his views are quoted in the *Shih-jen Yü-hsieh*. Yoshimoto refers frequently to this work in his own treatises. Considering that he borrowed many critical terms from Sung poetics (Konishi, 1955a, 1-9), it seems likely that he learned of the theory of advancing from ornate styles to a style of elegant simplicity from the *Shih-jen Yü-hsieh*.

For example, Yoshimoto writes as follows concerning the diction of renga (*RRHS*, 40): "One should choose diction with the intention of searching among flowers for the most beautiful flower, or searching among jewels for the most beautiful jewel." Here, flowers and jewels are metaphors for yūen, which in Yoshimoto's usage is equivalent to the beauty of yūgen. Although Yoshimoto basically affirms yūgen, however, he goes one step further to advocate the beauty of shiore (moisture) (*RRHS*, 41): "The stanzas of a person who uses diction effectively are easily linked and impressive, as if the flower or the jewel had been moistened by the morning mist." This passage follows the one above and suggests that when diction is used skillfully, the beauty of yūen is not sensed directly but in the way that one admires a beautiful flower when its luster is disguised by the dampness of morning mist. This kind of stanza is easy to link; but if yūen is too explicit in a stanza, it will be difficult for the following poet to compose a suitable linking stanza.

Yoshimoto comments further on the manner of forming the conception (kokoro) of a stanza (*RRHS*, 48):

> In all respects, the best approach is to avoid the artificial, to write of what is natural to oneself. To favor the unorthodox and seek the unusual is for the time when one has not yet achieved the deepest perfection. Renga is also like this. The essence of poetic ability lies in the genuineness of ordinary stanzas attractively and freshly connected with conceptual depth.

The advocacy of stanzaic connection at once attractive and fresh certainly does not deny originality. Although essentially affirming that the interest of poetry emerges from originality, however, Yoshimoto argues that ultimately clear and light writing constitutes the highest art.

The Nijō poets were the advocates of the style of elegant simplicity (heitan), while yūgen (defined as yūen) was associated with the Reizei faction. One reason that Yoshimoto incorporated both ideals into his own theory is that he had relations with the waka poets of both factions. His original adherence to the Nijō faction was a natural outcome of his close relationship with Tonna, but in waka circles he was also on intimate terms with Reizei Tamehide and Reizei Tamemasa. Yoshimoto himself made clear his reasons for assuming his position (*Jūmon*, 114-15):

> In all the arts, once the world decides upon a given track, one must go along, even if one's opinions differ. To persist in one's own opinion has no effect at all. Thus, when Dōyo favored a certain fashion, everyone began to use the same devices.[14] In our time, the atmosphere of his highness's [Yoshimitsu's] renga is lovely and, while he employs rather ordinary devices for his stanzas, his style makes them fresh. This wins my consent. In all the world there seems no effort likely to alter this dominant style.

One must go along with the styles that everyone prefers, and the present fashion is based on the style favored by Ashikaga Yoshimitsu (1358–1408). Yoshimoto himself preferred this style and saw no reason why the form of expression should change. This passage suggests the importance of Yoshimitsu's influence in the practical aspects of Yoshimoto's theory of renga.

Yoshimoto summarizes the principal features of Yoshimitsu's style in two points: (1) the feeling the reader receives from his writing is beautiful (yūgen/yūen), and (2) although he employs an ordinary style of composition, his stanzas have originality. Clearly, the first aspect of Yoshimitsu's style corresponds to Reizei principles while the second is characteristic of the Nijō school. Yoshimoto had no choice but to maintain relations with waka poets of both factions, a point that cannot be understood without reference to the influence of Yoshimitsu, for his patronage of both the Nijō and Reizei factions was one of the most important social realities of renga composition. The renga poet that best gave concrete expression to these ideals was Kyūsei. But it was Zeami, in the world of nō, who perfected Yoshimoto's ideals both in theory and in literary creation.

From Bontōan to Shinkei

Yoshimoto considered Bontōan to be the finest renga poet after Kyūsei and Shūa.[15] Bontōan was only forty when Yoshimoto died in 1388, and

[14] Dōyo, whose priestly name is Sasaki Takauji (1306-73), is a complex figure. Famous as a warrior, he also flouted authority by quarreling with the chief priest of Myōhōin, who was a prince, razing the main temple building (*THK*, 21, 337-39). On the other hand, he was a connoisseur of the tea ceremony, incense, formal flower arrangement, nō, and especially renga. Eighty-one of his stanzas were selected for the *Tsukuba Shū* (Yoshimoto has eighty-seven stanzas in the collection [Hasegawa, 1961, 204-12]).

[15] "It is reported that the Lord Regent [Nijō Yoshimoto] said, Morotsune [Bontōan] is the best renga poet since Kyūsei and Shūa" (*Kyūei*, 208).

yet Yoshimoto could describe his style in the following terms (*Kyūei*, 208):

> As the moon melts into the sky at dawn over the Seiryōden, the plum blossoms grow yet more fragrant, some young lord steps forth, and the young courtiers watching him wonder, "Is that a certain Middle Captain, or perhaps a certain Lesser Captain?" This vision represents Morotsuna's [Bontōan's] style.[16]

When Yoshimoto gives yūgen concrete expression in imagery, the result is writing of this kind. While yet in his thirties, Bontōan received this kind of recognition from Yoshimoto, but for some reason he left the capital not long after the Eighth Month of 1392. For the next fifteen years, until he returned to the capital some time before the Fifth Month of 1408, he wandered around the country as a nameless poet-priest (Mizukami, 1950, 14-16). In Ryōshun's *Ben'yōshō* (compiled in 1409; 186), we find this on Bontōan: "Apparently some people are saying that Asayama Bontōan's renga have declined recently, while others even say that he has become a poor poet."

Ryōshun himself disagreed with this general evaluation of Bontōan's later renga, and he follows the passage above with this: "Who in recent times surpasses Bontōan that such things should be said?" (*Ben'yōshō*, 186). Shinkei, who was in the same Reizei school, gave contradictory critiques of Bontōan. On the one hand (*Hitorigoto [Solitary Mutterings]*, 475), he wrote: "Since the Ōei years (1394-1428), the famous renga poets have been Imagawa Ryōshun, Jōa, the master of the hut called Bontōan . . . and Shōa, and they all had outstanding talent. Among them, it was Bontōan who remained famous even until later days and gained the reputation of having been the supreme master." In *Oi no Kurigoto (Ramblings of an Old Man)*, however, he writes (414):

> After the Master Bontōan . . . returned to the capital in his sixties, his poetry lost even its beautiful diction, as if the color and the fragrance of his flower had faded and the wellhead of his conception had become muddied. His style grew tottering, and it was said that he had forgotten to link his stanzas to those before them. Indeed, after living so long away from the literary world of the capital, it is only natural that he became so poor a poet.

It is very likely, in fact, that after Bontōan's return to the capital, Sōzei (1386?-1455) and Chiun (d. 1448) rather than the old poet himself developed his earlier style.

[16] [The Seiryōden was the tennō's residential quarters and was also employed for everyday ceremonies and other functions. See Miner-Odagiri-Morrell, 1985, 482-83 and 489.—Trans., Ed.]

At the same time that he was Bontōan's disciple in renga, Takayama Sōzei received instruction in waka from Shōtetsu.[17] Since he studied with both Bontōan, who revered the yūgen style of Yoshimoto, and Shōtetsu, who advocated the yūen style of the Reizei school, it is natural that his renga should have aspired to combine these two styles. Here is Sōzei adding a stanza as recorded in Sōgi's collection, *Chikurinshō* (*Bamboo Forest Miscellany* [=*CRS*]: 50).[18]

Hikage honomeku ame no asakaze	The sunlight streams but faintly in the rain blown by morning wind
yama wa kyō kumoi ni kasumu yuki kiete	today the mountain at the cloud bank hazes over the melting snow

In the stanza before Sōzei's, the light rain of a passing shower stills at dawn, and some raindrops are blown by a morning wind while the sun shines dimly through. Sōzei's stanza shifts the vision to a distant scene, one of haze filling the sky and of snow somehow melting on the mountain. The conception of both stanzas is light and clear, and the spring scene depicted by the linkage is truly beautiful. Of course, the scene is not directly observed. For one thing, the faint morning light is occluded by a passing shower and, for another, although the snow does seem to have melted, one cannot see all that well through a sky filled with haze. The beauty of the snow capping the mountain is present only as a vision, and it is therefore more beautiful than real snow, and the haze seems all the more peaceful. I think Yoshimoto's ideal of shiore (moisture) refers to just this kind of writing in which a charmed beauty is shrouded.

While it is not clear with whom Ninakawa Chiun studied renga, in waka he clearly belongs to the line of Shōtetsu.[19] Perhaps that explains why his renga stanzas display a yūen loveliness but at the same time are indirect. Here is an example from the *Chikurinshō* of Chiun's stanzaic connection (394).

[17] "While he was the disciple of Bontōan, Sōzei was also acquainted with the great master Shōgetsu. From him, he learned *The Tale of Genji* and studied the profound import of the vocation of waka" (*Azuma Mondō*, 208). "Shōgetsu" was Shōtetsu's pen name; it means "the one who would invite the moonlight into his house."

[18] The *Chikurinshō* is a privately compiled anthology (shisenshū) in ten books (completed in 1476) in which Sōgi collected and classified the stanzas of the seven poets he considered to be his teachers or senior masters: Sōzei, Shinkei, Senjun, Katamori (Sōi), Chikamasa (Chiun), Nōa, and Gyōjo.

[19] "Priest Chiun . . . was the disciple of the Devout Master Seigan, and received lectures from him in the vocation of waka, *The Tale of Genji, Tales of Ise*, and other texts" (*Tokorodokoro Hentō*, 308). "Seigan" is another name for Shōtetsu.

Furuki kado sasu	The old gate fastened up
haru no kuregata	twilight on a spring day
yomogiu ni	in the rampant plants
matsukaze fukite	the breeze blows through the pine trees
hana mo nashi	and no cherry tree blooms

The cherry trees are not blooming in reality but fill the speaker's mind as a lovely vision. Moreover, it is well worth noting that what hovers faintly over the cherry blossoms in this vision is sabishisa (loneliness). Kensai (1452-1510) gives this critique of the linked stanzas (*Keikandō*, 141).

> When he was prosperous, many people came to visit. But now even the cherry blossoms have scattered, the wind in the pines sounds even more lonely than usual, and he is sunk in misery, so that he closes his gate, thinking that no one will visit now. The point of the poem is in the phrase "and no cherry blossoms." The stanza has a dried up (karabitaru) tone.

Kensai was the first to use the concept of the dried up or dessicated—karabi (karabitaru)—to describe the tone of this kind of renga. Although karabi became established as a critical concept during the period of Kensai's activity and was used frequently after him, it was certainly not part of Chiun's critical vocabulary. There is no doubt, however, that Chiun would have approved of this critique of his stanza. At the temples of Saihōji and Daisen'in there are gardens called "dry landscapes" (karasenzui), in which there are no ponds or flowing streams, or in fact any kind of water at all.[20] They consist entirely of rocks and sand. The viewer of these gardens must draw a mental vision of water and, precisely because there is no actual water, the vision is more beautiful than water in reality. The assumption underlying appreciation of these "dry landscapes" is identical to Kensai's when he praises Chiun's stanza as "dried up." The cherry blossoms do not exist in reality.

Sōzei's and Chiun's use of this kind of expression represents a further deepening of the beauty of shiore (moisture) proposed by Yoshimoto and Kyūsei. As we have seen in the previous example of Kyūsei's renga, his stanzas are tightly linked to previous stanzas, in terms of both the phenomena depicted and the diction, especially through his use of engo (as-

[20] "The master of the hut Jōsuian came calling with some Chinese cakes that were named karasenzui. It seems that they are called this because they have almost no moisture. They were very tasty" (*Gaun*, [12.X.1446], 4). The concept of creating gardens entirely from rocks originated in China and was brought into Japan by Zen monks. It is quite likely that the "kara" of karasenzui was originally written with the character for China: thus, "Chinese landscapes." As in the case of the rice cakes, however, the pun on "kara," which is also the pronunciation of the character for "dry," and the fact that these gardens are in reality dry must have given rise to a later change in transcription and meaning (Haga, 1945, 682-86). By the time of Kensai, these gardens were already thought of as "*dry* landscapes."

sociated words). This close connection with previous stanzas, however, is not present in the renga of Sōzei and Chiun. The concept of linking stanzas not closely connected to preceding stanzas (maeku) had existed since Yoshimoto's day. Yoshimoto calls such a stanza a "buried stanza" (uzumiku), and his definition of the term suggests that uzumiku may be understood as a "hidden device" (*RRHS*, 50): "Uzumiku: In its surface meaning, it appears to be unconnected with the previous stanza, but at its bottom there is a profound significance." There are, however, almost no uzumiku among Yoshimoto's own stanzas; linking stanzas of this kind increase in number from the period of Sōzei and Chiun. Of course, Sōzei and Chiun also wrote many stanzas that were closely linked to their predecessors, whether by meaning or engo or both. In renga, the poet must have a variety of ways of stanza connection. Uzumiku—distant relation—alone will not do. In their total canons, Sōzei and Chiun use witty connections most frequently. But they could not assume that all the poets at a renga session would share their ideals. Even if the number of uzumiku is comparatively small, it is very significant that kinds of distant connection begin to increase from this time.

A SHORT while after Sōzei and Chiun, there appeared such famous masters as Nōa (1397-1468), Gyōjo (1405-69), Senjun (1411-76), and Sōi (1418-85). Renga enjoyed an unprecedented rise during this period, in terms of both the quantity and the quality of the poetry.[21] By far the most important poet of this period was Shinkei (1406-75). Shinkei is another poet whose master in renga is unknown, but for thirty years he studied waka of the then still vital Reizei school with Shōtetsu. Sōzei and Chiun were also Shōtetsu's disciples, but neither of them compares to him. It was he who assimilated and deepened Shōtetsu's waka style in renga.

The beauty of yūgen (redefined as the elegant charm of yūen), which had suffused renga since the time of Yoshimoto, was associated with the Reizei faction, but among the renga poets who studied with Shōtetsu there gradually emerged techniques that suppress explicit yūen, concealing it in the depths of a negative or introverted tone that is suggestive of the beauty of sabi (loneliness) or wabi (desolate solitude). Shinkei developed this tendency even further, bringing it to perfection. For him, whether in renga or in waka, the finest expression was that of "coldness" (hie) or "slenderness" (yase). Shinkei explains these terms in *Sasamegoto (Whisperings)*:

> It is of the greatest importance to distinguish between stanzas that have the air of gentleness and those that are truly elegant, and also between stanzas that are merely violent in tone and those that truly

[21] The stanza collections of this group of poets are contained in the *Shichiken Jidai Renga Kushū (An Anthology of Renga Stanzas of the Seven Masters Period)*.

> abound in strength. It is said that the outstanding stanzas are found among those that are concentrated in conception and detail among stanzas that are cold and slender. (1:128-29)
>
> Someone once asked a great poet of the past, "How should one compose a waka?" The master replied, "Pampas grass in a withered field, the melting moon at dawn." The lesson here is to pay attention to what is not expressed, and to be enlightened by knowing the chill and the solitary. (2:175)

The tones that Shinkei described with words such as "cold," "slender," "chilled," and "solitary" are all realized precisely because they are not being openly expressive. He makes this clear by emphasizing that poets should concentrate conception and diction and "pay attention to what is not expressed."

When this standard is applied not to the tone of individual stanzas but to the linkage between stanzas, it is an argument for stanzaic linking of distant relation (soku) as opposed to those of close relation (shinku). The concept of closely and distantly related stanzas derives from waka. That is, shinku referred originally to the link between the two parts or lines of a waka: its 5-7-5 syllable upper portion or lines (kami no ku) and its 7-7 syllable lower (shimo no ku). When there was an intimate link in meaning between the upper three lines and the lower two, the whole poem was thought closely related (shin). If the relationship was slight, the whole poem was thought distantly related (so).[22] When the concept of soku (distantly related stanza) is applied to stanza relation in renga, it refers to a stanza (tsukeku) that has little apparent relationship to the stanza preceding it.

Shinkei was quite explicit in preferring distant (soku) stanzaic linking (*Sasamegoto*, 2:186-87): "Lord Teika said, 'Excellent waka may be found only among soku; they are rare among shinku.'[23] There are many fine distinctions: shinku of conception, shinku of structure, soku of conception, soku of structure. I will omit these. Shinku is the existential aspect; soku is the nonexistential aspect." Thus, both in regard to the tone of the stanza itself and to the degree of relation between stanzas, that which is explicitly expressed is inferior to that which is not expressed.

As is clear from these statements alone, Shinkei believed that a nonexplanatory approach was the highest ideal for renga. This was by no means a simple-minded rejection of expressiveness, but an assertion of the aesthetic ideals of hie (chill) and yase (slenderness), in which are concealed a

[22] The earliest extant use of these terms is in the *Chikuenshō*. While the date of compilation of this treatise is not certain, it is thought to have been completed by the late thirteenth century (*NKGT*, 3:414-15).

[23] Shinkei quotes the *Sangoki*, wrongly believing it to be Teika's own work (*NKGT*, 4:351).

beauty (en) that cannot be sensed directly. Both hie and yase involve images that accompany a vision of plum blossoms. Consider Koken Myōkai's "On My Plum Blossom Retreat" (*Ryōgenshū*, 2099): "Profuse plum blossoms on the banks suit me well in my seclusion; / Their clear cold pierces my bones like ice or frost in my mouth."[24] The feeling received from the plum blossoms (perhaps the white plum) is grasped as a "clear cold" like that of ice or frost. This clear cold is what Shinkei means by the beauty represented as samu (cold) and hie (chill). There are also many examples of the use of slenderness (yase) in composing poetry on plum blossoms. Here is one from Gidō Shūshin's "Poems Written on Forty-two Fans" (*Kūgeshū*, 4:1431):

> After snow, plum blossoms finer on slender branches
> Whose shadows mingle as the moon rises at dusk.

Shinkei considered the delicate slenderness (yase) suggested by the plum blossoms to have much in common with their coldness (samu) and chill (hie), using all three as critical terms. Examples of their use abound in Sung shih, which had been brought to Japan by Zen monks. Here is Lu Yu's (1125-1210) "Sitting Before a Potted Plum Beneath a Lamp on the Eighth Day of the Eleventh Month" (*Chien-nan Shih-kao*, 4:95):

> Moving the lamp changes the shadow pattern
> of the slender plum branches I enjoy,
> I close the shutters to retain the fragrance,
> smiling at the self-indulgence.
> My cup reflects the chill charm of the blossoms,
> which exceeds that of the finest wine.
> One branch stretches toward my inkstone,
> where water freezes into icy blossoms.

It is of utmost importance to note here that Lu Yu not only uses slenderness to describe the branches, and ice as a metaphor for the blossoms, but he also describes their reflection in his wine cup as a "chill charm" (ling-yen, J. reien). It is even more important that the Sung poets used the terms "chill" and "slenderness" not only to express the beauty of plum blossoms but also as terms of praise in criticizing shih. The following couplet appears in a shih by Yang Wan-li (1124-1206):

> I sent a messenger on horseback to pay my respects to Councilor Fan. In his reply, Mr. Fan wrote two quatrains. I expressed my apprecia-

[24] Myōkai's dates of birth and death unclear. He was the disciple of Musō Soseki (1275-1351) and senior to Gidō Shūshin.

tion by sending another letter with a shih written in the same rhymes as his:

> Taking a spray of plums I compare its beauty with that of your new poem.
> The slenderness of the plum does not rival that of your poetry.[25]

This is a good example of how "slenderness," which was originally used to describe the branches of the plum tree, came to be used to express the feeling aroused by the blossoms. In this case, by saying that the slenderness of the blossoms does not measure up to the slenderness of Fan's poem, the speaker of the poem expresses his high evaluation of the shih. Here is a couplet from a shih by Gidō (*Kūgeshū*, 6:1500):

> [One of] two shih written in the same rhyme as that of a shih I received with pink and white plum blossoms in a vase.
>
> Your shih describes the view of a mountain;
> Its slenderness excels lingering snow.

Since shih and slenderness are counterposed in the parallelism of this couplet, slenderness is clearly being used to praise the shih. But at the same time it also partakes of the beauty of chill, which is symbolized by the lingering snow. There are a great many examples of these usages of "chill" and "slenderness" in Sung and Japanese shih, and we may conclude that Shinkei's use of these terms derives from them (Konishi, 1958b, 12-29).

From Shōtetsu, Shinkei received the Reizei concept of yūgen (as yūen). He went on to perfect the beauty of chill by making the beauty of yūen in his poetry more introverted. For Shinkei, "chill" and "en" were not essentially different concepts. Consider his famous statement on the subject (*Hitorigoto*, 469):

> Nothing else has the refined charm of ice. What elegant fashioning there is in the morning to thin ice on a harvested rice field, to icicles hanging from eaves covered with much aged cypress bark, or to the sight of dew frozen on plants and trees in a withered field! Are they not attractive? Are they not charming (en)?[26]

The examples Shinkei gives convey a sense of en (elegant charm) opposed to our ordinary ideas. There is an immediacy of experience to the charm we find in golden stands of rice cast in waves by a breeze, to the fresh smell of cypress in a new house, to autumn plants sparkling with autumn

[25] *Ch'eng-chai Shih-hua*, 16:146.

[26] The phrase "elegant fashioning" in the translation is meant to stress that "en" (elegant charm) was thought to be the product of human effort. It took a Shinkei to apply the term to the beauties of the natural world. [Auth., Ed.]

colors in the sunlight. And yet when the charm cannot be directly apprehended and the beauty is born from visionary apprehension the charm excels that of reality. The actual opportunity for direct sensory apprehension is denied by the cold or chill of winter, which can only weaken or kill all activity, and yet the ice image gives concrete expression to the symbolic force of rei (chill). It is thought that all colors are included in the colorless translucency of ice, a way of thinking shared by Shinkei's remark above that "soku is the non-existential as poet." The Emptiness (J. kū) of Tendai Buddhism and the Non-being (J. mu) of Zen do not constitute a simple existence. These concepts signify instead that the reality of existence attributed to all phenomena cannot be directly experienced or discussed and that all existence is contained in non-existence.

With these premises, we can understand that Shinkei's statement that "nothing has the refined charm of ice" carries Yoshimoto's ideal of shiore (moisture) one step further. Shinkei could do this because the en to which he aspired was much more profound than Yoshimoto's. Yoshimoto understood and sympathized with Reizei ideals of beauty, but because his origins lay in the Nijō school, he had his limits. By contrast, after thirty years of instruction by Shōtetsu, Shinkei naturally conceived of elegant charm (en) in his teacher's terms—as what probably should be termed the real charm (yūen). The profundity of Shinkei's ethereal charm depended on the intensity of effort to extinguish any immediacy in it. More than any gently moistening (shiore), the chill (hie) of dew formed into frost is essential to a profundity of charm. When this demand for internalizing is conceptualized, we get Shinkei's chill, an image that arose from the familiar appearance of the blossoming plum celebrated in the poetry of Sung Chinese and the shih of Japanese Zen priests. This is clear from the use of "chill charm" Lu Yu writes of in the poem quoted earlier.

It must be understood that the background of this ideal is just that highness and clarity (heitan) rooted in splendor that was designated the truly light and clear again and again in Sung poetic criticism. Here, for example, is Wu K'o in his *Ts'ang-hai Shih-hua* (5, verso):

> In general, one's literary works should first be ornate and later plain. This is precisely the same as the passing of the seasons. In spring things are resplendent. In the summer the ears of grain grow full. From fall to winter the fields are harvested. The saying then, "The outside seems to wither and die, but the inside is young and fresh," applies here. Splendor and abundance are enclosed within the plain.[27]

In 1488, Inawashiro Kensai recorded many of Shinkei's oral teachings in his *Shinkei Teikin*. Among them is the following (1123):

[27] Wu K'o lived ca. 1126-ca. 1173.

> The finest renga are like drinking water. They have no special flavor, but one never tires of them, however often one hears them. Unusual things are interesting when one happens to hear them, but gradually they lose their interest. However, if a novice were to attempt to compose in this mature way from the very beginning, the verse would be flat and soon the poet would no longer attract attention.[28]

This appears to be an assertion in the vein of Nijō poetics, but it is important here that Shinkei insists that beginners should not strive for this kind of expression. Elsewhere in the same treatise, Shinkei explains this argument further (ibid., 1121):

> When one is a beginner, one must not prefer the dry in writing. Strive for the orthodox and the beautiful.
>
> After one has accumulated many years and much experience, one's writing should grow dry. The beginner, and even those half way in their art, should compose in orthodox styles.

If read with the Sung shih treatise by Wu K'o quoted above, it is clear that Shinkei was stating the same idea. What raised this concept to the level of a conviction was the Mahāyāna Buddhist doctrine that the ultimate truth is found precisely in the absolute Emptiness (kū) or the Non-being (mu), each of which completely denies the substantiality of all existence.

Shinkei's position is also reflected in his own linking of stanzas. In renga one is given a stanza (maeku) to which another joins, and it is not always possible to compose in a tone consistent with one's own ideal. Certainly not all Shinkei's stanzas are composed in the style of chill or slenderness. This is true of his stanzas included in the *Chikurinshō* and the *Shinsen Tsukuba Shū*, and also in the one-hundred-stanza and one-thousand-stanza renga sessions in which he participated.[29] When compared to other poets, however, the number of Shinkei's stanzas in the style of reien (chilly charm) is remarkably large. Here is an outstanding example (*CRS*, 1:356):

Omou to mo	Will all your yearning
wakareshi hito wa	for the man who has betrayed you
kaerame ya	ever bring him back

[28] This may be regarded as faithfully representing Shinkei's opinions. However, it was Kensai who first employed the concept of karabi. In his *Entokushō*, for example, he criticizes those who fail to recognize the resplendent ornateness (karei) and refined charm (yūen) concealed in the depth of the chill, the slender, and the dry [*Rengaron Shū*, A.2:125]. "There are many people who hold that what is meant by saying that the way of waka is the chill (hie), the slender (yase), or the dried (karabi) is a dead willow tree, or a dead plum tree, or frost covering a bridge, or snow, or ice. If that were it, things would certainly be quite easy."

[29] There are nineteen one-hundred-stanza sequences and three one-thousand-stanza sequences collected in *Shinkei Sakuhinshū*.

yūgure fukashi	the hue of the evening deepens
sakura chiru yama	hills fallen with cherry blossoms

Considered by itself, Shinkei's stanza appears to be quite ordinary. It must be read as giving meaning to the preceding stanza, however. In that (once Shinkei's stanza is added), the speaker of the previous stanza wishes that the people who have gone home from a flower-viewing party would return to this place once again, but he realizes the irony of the wish. Sunset in the mountain village where the cherry blossoms have scattered completely is unspeakably lonely, and since the speaker is so melancholy it is hardly surprising that the people who have left will not return.[30] What appears on the surface of the poem is a limitless desolation, and as the shadows of evening thicken, the loneliness becomes more and more profound. Mountain villages are always lonely, and the speaker of the poem has become lonelier still because the cherry blossoms have scattered. But in the background of this loneliness is hidden the splendor of the blossoms in full bloom. Because the blossoms cannot be seen now, the vision of them is even more beautiful than they had been in reality. Yet, their lovely colors have become the colors of loneliness.

Here is another example (*CRS*, 3:728):

Shigure no ato no	After the autumn drizzle
tsuyu zo mi ni shimu	the dew has soaked my body
mushi no naku	the insects cry on
nobe no tōyama	in fields before far mountains
irozukite	turning yellow and red

Shinkei's added stanza (tsukeku) also appears to be nothing more than a seasonal stanza in the light-and-plain style. In his *Oi no Susami (Gibberish of an Old Man)*, however, Sōgi gave this stanza his highest praise: "The connection is effected in a fresh way, and the linking stanza itself is one that no ordinary poet could have conceived. Moreover, it presents the very view before the speaker's eyes. This kind of originality is truly wonderful" (151-52). Gazing at the dew that remains on the plants and the leaves after a brief passing shower, the speaker of the first stanza feels a transience soaking into the body. The feeling of loneliness in this stanza has some depth. In Shinkei's added stanza, however, the speaker shifts the gaze from the insects crying in the wet grass to the autumn scene of the fields, and then beyond to the mountains in the distance, where there seem to be faint autumn colors in the leaves. Because the mountains are in the distance, dazzling reds and yellows cannot be seen, but the speak-

[30] This interpretation follows Sōgi's critique in *Oi no Susami*, 150.

er's mind fills with beautifully colored leaves sparkling in sunlight with limitless charm (en).

This beauty is not immediately sensed, and in connection with the drizzle and the dew of the previous stanza, Shinkei's stanza evokes a response of chilly loneliness. The dew in the previous stanza soaks into one's body, hinting at the transience of life. In Shinkei's stanza it is transformed into the dew that dyes the leaves with autumn colors and becomes part of the scene before the poet's eyes—an element of natural description.[31] This way of dealing with dew was entirely novel in this period. Sōgi praised this stanza not for any extraordinary or surprising device, but for Shinkei's novel conception of linking it to the previous stanza by shifting the focus from the speaker's emotion to the natural scene, which gives the stanza a freshness despite its otherwise ordinary subject and meaning. This is a deepening of Yoshimoto's ideal.

Here is another renga connection by Shinkei (*CRS*, 6:1636):

Wakareji ni	When you went away
nagusamenishi mo	you took care to comfort me
utsuroite	but you are wholly changed
kaeru kuzuha mo	and in rich arrowroot leaves too
aki ni au iro	there are colors that suit autumn

The preceding stanza is a love stanza. Setting out on a journey, the speaker's lover had comforted her: "Don't forget me, for I will soon return." But he has broken his promise, and there is no word from him at all. In his added stanza, Shinkei introduces a third person who comments (by allusion to a waka) on the first speaker's condition: "just as the leaves of arrowroot that wave ["kaeru," also "return"] in the wind change color in the autumn ["aki," also, "grow tired of"] there is nothing to be done about it." The two stanzas are, then, linked by allusions:

Wasuru na yo	Do not forget!
Wakareji ni ouru	Thick are the leaves of arrowroot
Kuzu no ha no	Here where I take leave,
Akikaze fukeba	But when the autumn wind blows on them,
Ima kaerikon.	I shall return to you at once.[32]

[31] [The novelty lies in taking the imaginary or symbolic as the actual. The idea that moisture changes the color of leaves to yellow or red is, on the other hand, persistently Japanese, as in the close of a waka: "Unable to stand the drizzle / The leaves have turned in color" (Shigure ni aezu / Momijitarikeri).—Ed.]

[32] *SIS*, 6:306. This follows the interpretation in *Chikurinshō no Chū* (*Commentary on the Chikurinshō*, 51).

The same "utsurou" (change) that in the first stanza refers to the male lover's change of heart is altered with the allusion by Shinkei's linking stanza to mean the changing color of the autumn leaves, and "aki" becomes a pivot word (kakekotoba) meaning both "to become tired of" and "autumn." This amount of word play is ordinary in renga, however, and it does not particularly stand out in this linking stanza. But the tone of the stanza is crucial. On the one hand, it is negative, since it is composed on the arrowroot when it has lost its color in the autumn. Yet it is not completely so, for one responds to an unseen charm (en). Until late summer, the white underside of the leaves can be seen when the arrowroot is ruffled by the wind, making the vivid green of the upper surface even more impressive. This beautiful aspect of the arrowroot is present in the stanza as a vision. This is precisely the beauty of chill (hie), and it is so like Shinkei to employ this kind of expression in a linking stanza on love, in which an upswelling of emotion is expected.

No other renga poet equals Shinkei in the brilliance of his stanzas (tsukeku); and in terms of the quality of their beauty, I think it is undebatable that the beauty of chill (hie) and slenderness (yase) are the ultimate literary achievement of the Japanese Middle Ages. However, when we turn our attention from the greatness of Shinkei's stanzas to the hundred-stanza and the thousand-stanza renga in which he is recognized to have been the leader, it is clear that Shinkei did not always achieve perfect beauty. In renga, one should enjoy a kind of variation and transformation that is nevertheless integrated by a subtle harmony of the hundred-stanza or thousand-stanza sequence as a whole. If a certain stanza is particularly brilliant, it stands out—isolated—from the whole, and the harmony of the whole is destroyed. As we have seen, nineteen one-hundred-stanza renga and three one-thousand-stanza renga in which Shinkei participated have survived. In those in which it can be deduced that Shinkei directed the progression of stanza linking, he displays a marked tendency to strive for an interest in which the part dominates the whole.

The *Kawagoe Senku (Thousand Stanzas at Kawagoe)*, composed in 1469, provides a good example. Only Shinkei and Sōgi participated as professional renga poets, the other participants being wealthy provincial figures, warriors, and priests of the Kantō region. In renga such as this, one expects the general quality of the work to drift toward the humdrum or drab, but all the stanzas in this sequence are extremely refined, elegant. While the level of renga composition in areas outside the capital at this time is not entirely clear, it is hard to believe that stanzas of such uniformly high quality could have been produced by the provincial amateurs that took part in this sequence. Moreover, all the stanzas are infused with precisely the tone of sad loneliness that Shinkei preferred. Here are the first eight stanzas (*Shinkei Sakuhinshū*, 392).

	Opening Stanza (Hokku)	
1	Mumezono ni	It is a fragrance
	kusaki o naseru	that makes of the plants and trees
	nioi kana	a plum arbor[33]
	Shinkei	
	Mumezono ni	It is a fragrance
	kusaki o naseru	that makes of the plants and trees
	nioi kana	a plum arbor
2	niwa shirotae no	the garden spread with cloth of white
	yuki no harukaze	snow touched by a soft spring breeze[34]
	Dōshin	
	Niwa shirotae no	The garden spread with cloth of white
	yuki no harukaze	snow touched by a soft spring breeze
3	uguisu no	the warbler sings
	koe wa toyama no	its voice in the far mountains'
	kage saete	shadows grown cold[35]
	Sōgi	
	Uguisu no	The warbler sings
	koe wa toyama no	the voice in the far mountains'
	kage saete	shadows grown cold
4	nobe ni utsureru	as it meanders through the fields,
	michi no harukesa	the path grows ever fainter[36]
	Chūga	
	Nobe ni utsureru	As it meandered through the fields,
	michi no harukesa	the path grew ever fainter

[33] Shinkei skillfully compliments the assembled poets: the image of fragrance suggests their skill. [The hokku or opening stanza was the only one that should relate the seasonal circumstances about the assembled poets, although general comment on the times might subsequently be possible, as the author shows later. In its quotidian informality, comment in a hokku on the poets gathered, rather than on a season, seems more like haikai than renga; Dōshin's second stanza (waki) presents the scene as Shinkei might have done, and coming in the second stanza, it also has a haikai air.—Ed.].

[34] Dōshin's speaker comments that ordinary trees and plants appear to be (white) plums, because snow is on their branches. The fragrance is borne on the gentle breeze poetically essential to spring. ["Shirotae no" is an ancient pillow word (makurakotoba) meaning something like "white as paper mulberry," or "white as hemp," and it is used to modify "clothes," "sleeves," etc. The usage here is fresh in that the expression precedes "snow" ("yuki"), and so is an engo (associated expression: white-snow) as much as a pillow word.—Ed.]

[35] This stanza moves the scene of the previous one to a house situated in the shadow or loom of the mountain. The wind, associated with mountains, takes on cold in blowing over the snow. [The stanza completes the minimum run of three stanzas on a spring topic.—Ed.]

[36] The scene is rendered yet more distant.

5	narawazu yo	unused to travel,
	izuku no tsuki zo	where am I with this lovely moon
	tabimakura	and a traveler's pillow[37]
	Inkō	
	Narawazu yo	Unused to travel,
	izuku no tsuki zo	where am I with this lovely moon
	tabimakura	and a traveler's pillow
6	miyako izureba	having left the capital
	mishi aki mo nashi	the autumn is one I never saw[38]
	Nagatoshi	
	Miyako izureba	Since I left the capital
	mishi aki mo nashi	the autumn is one I never saw,
7	susamashiku	the chill comes on
	shigururu sora no	a shower drizzles from the sky
	kuresomete	that begins to darken[39]
	Eishō	
	Susamashiku	The chill comes on
	shigururu sora no	a shower drizzles from the sky
	kuresomete	that begins to darken
8	kumo yori ochi no	more distant than the clouds
	iriai no kane	sounds a temple's evening bell[40]
	Yoshifuji	

In terms of quality of writing, it is impossible to distinguish the stanzas by the professional poets from the capital. Obviously Shinkei revised the stanzas by the provincial poets. While Sōgi also participated in this renga, it is impossible to suppose that he would have been the leader when Shinkei, one of his teachers, was present. Moreover, the stanzaic linking and progression of the sequence is also characteristic of Shinkei's style.

Here are the first eight stanzas of *Yama Nani Dokugin Hyakuin (Hundred Stanzas on Mountains by Shinkei Alone)* which, like the previous

[37] The length of the road [in the previous stanza] has suggested travel, and there is a shift to more subjective description. [After one miscellaneous (zō) stanza, we get this autumn stanza and the first moon stanza, one of which belongs to each side except the last—see the appendix.—Ed.]

[38] The speaker becomes someone from the capital who has never experienced travel, so making skillful use of the preceding stanza's "narawazu yo" ("unused to travel").

[39] The speaker is someone of high rank who, for some reason, is now forced to wander in the provinces ["Drizzle" ("shigure") is an autumn or winter concept, and here brings to a close the usual, and minimum, run of three autumn stanzas.—Ed.].

[40] The drizzle (shigure) of the previous stanza seems to have suggested clouds (kumo), as "begins to darken" ("kuresomete") leads to the temple bell at evening.

example, make up the front of the first sheet (shoomote) of the written text of the sequence.[41]

1	Hototogisu	The hototogisu
	kikishi wa mono ka	what difference can its song make
	Fuji no yuki	Fuji crowned with snow[42]
	Hototogisu	The hototogisu
	kikishi wa mono ka	what difference can its song make
	Fuji no yuki	Fuji crowned with snow
2	kumo mo tomaranu	the clouds pass without stopping
	sora no suzushisa	such being the coolness of the sky
	Kumo mo tomaranu	The clouds passed without stopping
	sora no suzushisa	such being the coolness of the sky
3	tsuki kiyoki	the moon so clear
	hikari ni yoru wa	radiance lets me see at night
	kaze miete	movements of the wind[43]
	Tsuki kiyoki	The moon so clear
	hikari ni yoru wa	radiance lets me see at night
	kaze miete	movements of the wind
4	yume o odorokasu	I am awakened from my dream
	aki no karifushi	in brief autumn sleep at the front[44]
	Yume o odorokasu	I have been wakened from my dream
	aki no karifushi	in brief autumn sleep at the front
5	okimasaru	does not the dew
	tsuyu ya yadori ni	grow heavier on my shelter
	fukenu ran	as night goes on[45]

[41] *Shinkei Sakuhinshū*, 392. A commentary and discussion of the entire sequence may be found in Kaneko K., 1982, 257-321. See also Konishi, 1975b, 38-39.

[42] [The hototogisu (cuculus canorus) is taken from waka to be the quintessentially summer bird. It is quite unlike the Western cuckoo in song and legend and differs somewhat in nesting habits. Usual poetic treatment involves longing to hear it sing. This speaker is unorthodoxly indifferent to its song, such being the beauty of the mountain.—Ed.]

[43] [The first moon stanza, and therefore an autumn stanza immediately after two summer stanzas. As often in renga, the attributive form of the adjective ("kiyoki," "clear") is here used so as to apply both to the moon before and the radiance after. So also in stanza 6, "weaken" ("yowaki," an adjective) applies to both cries and plants. Other examples have been passed by unnoted. On this zeugma or yoking by adjectives and verbs, see ch. 14, n. 23.—Ed.]

[44] The moonlight is so bright that its streaming into the speaker's battle tent awakens him.

[45] Unable to fall asleep again, the speaker speculates on the scene outside.

	Okimasaru	Does not the wet
	tsuyu ya yadori ni	grow heavier on my shelter
	fukenu ran	as night goes on
6	mushi no ne yowaki	the cries of insects weaken
	kusa no murasame	plants caught in a gust of rain[46]
	Mushi no ne yowaki	The cries of insects weaken
	kusa no murasame	plants caught in a gust of rain
7	hagi ga e no	on bush clover stems
	shitaba nokorazu	none of the lower leaves remain
	kururu no ni	in the darkening fields[47]
	Hagi ga e no	On bush clover stems
	shitaba nokorazu	none of the lower leaves remain
	kururu no ni	in the darkening fields
8	iku hito mare no	very few are those who pass
	okagoe no michi	on the road across the hill[48]

If one compares this sequence with *Kawagoe Senku*, it is difficult to deny that the two sequences are very like in their stanzaic linking and progression. The striking individual stanzas act to impede a beautifully integrated flow with subtle shifts of scene and emotional effect. Of course, such a criticism is based on the standards of renga set by Sōgi. And since renga styles that place emphasis on subtlety in the variation and integration of the entire work were not established before Sōgi, it may be more appropriate to praise Sōgi than to criticize Shinkei.

Sōgi's Achievement

The origins of Iio Sōgi (1421-1502) are unknown, and as a result there has been a great deal of conjecture. It has been suggested that he came from extremely humble origins (Ijichi, 1943, 27-31), but a recent study argues that there are no grounds for such a conclusion (Kaneko K., 1983, 33-34). Both arguments lack conclusive evidence, and this point remains unclear. Evidently, however, Sōgi was not from the upper levels of society. Despite his lowly origins, he appeared in the presence of the shogun, various daimyo, and the nobility to teach renga and to lecture on classics of poetry and prose. He earned respect as the most important literary

[46] The rain weakens the insects, and in the wind their sound also seems to grow fainter.

[47] The scene widens, shifting from rural to visual imagery.

[48] The speaker's vision moves yet further in the distance. Now that it grows dark, passersby become fewer—much like the leaves on the bush clover.

figure of the time.[49] He was of course accorded such warm respect because of his extraordinary poetic talents and erudition, and we ought not ignore the social conditions of the period that made it possible for a mere professional renga poet with no official status whatsoever to participate in the exalted circles of the military aristocracy and the court. The masters of an art were respected regardless of the background and social status, for this is the period in which the authority of michi (artistic vocation) was widely recognized by people at all levels of society. The impetus for this recognition was surely the emergence of wen-jen (literati, J. bunjin) in China.

Yoshikawa Kōjirō has provided the clearest explanation of the concept of wen-jen as it developed in China, and what follows summarizes his main points. Literature or letters (wen) had been esteemed in China since ancient times, but the Chinese had almost never advocated an independent raison d'être for it. Its value was recognized only when it was combined with politics and philosophy. This tradition continued into the Sung dynasty. The outstanding poets of the Northern Sung, Ou-yang Hsiu, Wang An-shih, and Su Shih, were all politicians and philosophers. In the Southern Sung, the poets of the Chiang-hu school (Citizens' School)[50] were addicted to poetry and took a position unrelated to politics, but there was still neither composition nor appreciation of poetry based on a conception that art is supreme.

However, the situation changed rapidly after the beginning of the Yüan dynasty (c. 1280-1368). The Mongol government placed severe restrictions on participation in politics by Han Chinese, and as a result people who had skills in literature became socially alienated. They reacted to their disenfranchisement by deliberately turning their backs on politics, and in doing so escaped from a philosophy that buttressed the governing principles of society. Increasingly, the intellectuals of this period felt that only poetry offered a reason for living. To emphasize their values, they behaved in ways defying, to a greater or lesser extent, contemporary norms. Instead of criticizing them for their defiance, ordinary people were more inclined to treat them with respect and admiration. Another impor-

[49] "Sōgi is the greatest master of renga. Even Sōzei, the great master of the past, falls far below him. When he lectured on the *Kokinshū*, *The Tales of Ise*, and other classical works, high-ranking courtiers and many other people vowed to serve him as disciples" (*Rokuon* [26.VIII.1487], 9).

[50] Literally, the River and Lake School, but chiang-hu (rivers and lakes) came to have the meaning of citizens, of nonofficials. Ch'en Ch'i, a publisher in the Southern Sung capital of Hangchow, published the shih of one hundred and nine of his contemporaries as a series in the *Chiang-hu Shih-chi (The Citizens' Shih Collection)*. The Chiang-hu school took its name from this collection. Because the members of the school were minor poets, most of their biographies are unknown, but it appears that almost all of them were citizens without official rank (Yoshikawa, 1962, 177-79).

tant characteristic of the ideal wen-jen figure is refusal to specialize solely in literature, also working frequently in other arts, especially calligraphy and painting. While the word "wen-jen" had existed in China for some time, these poet-artists represented a kind not seen before. Hence it was near the end of the Yüan dynasty when the term was first applied to them (Yoshikawa, 1963, 441-42).

Ashikaga Yoshimitsu (1358-1408) made great efforts to expand trade with the Ming dynasty, which was established in 1368, and trade grew even further during the shogunate of Yoshinori (1394-1441; Akiyama, 1939, 507-26). The increase of trade naturally promoted cultural intercourse as well, and by the second half of the fifteenth century, when Shinkei and Sōgi were active, much information concerning Chinese society and culture must have entered Japan. Although it is not clear whether they knew the term "wen-jen," the well educated in Japan must have known that there were people among those out of power in China who were allowed special behavior and treated with respect because of their fame in the arts. I believe that in Japan this knowledge became linked to the existing authority of michi (artistic vocation) and that it must have been part of the reason that someone like Sōgi was treated by princes and shoguns with the respect due a teacher. In this sense, Sōgi could be called a Japanese-style wen-jen (J. bunjin), with Kyūsei and Nōa his forerunners. Not until the eighteenth century, however, did a great number of artists and writers begin to imitate consciously the Chinese wen-jen, with a thorough knowledge of their lives and ideals. Sōgi and his contemporaries were not aware of the Chinese wen-jen in this way, and the appearance of Japanese-style wen-jen during this period was not the result of direct imitation. Therefore, we must distinguish between later bunjin such as Buson (1716-83), who deliberately imitated the wen-jen, and early-period counterparts such as Sōgi (Konishi, 1967b, 39).

Sōgi clearly required a special authority in order to eliminate the handicap of his lowly origins. One indication of this is his devotion to classical literature. In his case this meant the study of waka and classical prose, principally the *Kokinshū* and *The Tale of Genji*. As Keijo Shūrin (1440-1518) states in "A Eulogy on the Portrait of Iio, Master of the Hut of Shugyokuan," Sōgi was taught for waka the precepts of the Nijō school (*Koro*, 11:560): "When he received the Nijō tradition it was as if the capital of flowers was in cultural full bloom. His elevation of the vocation of waka was as splendid as the rising of eight-layered clouds, or as the moon radiant over the mountain rim." Of course, the Nijō family had ended as a waka house with Tamesuke, but the Asukai family, which was related to the Nijō by marriage, had taken over their poetic styles. Sōgi studied waka composition with Asukai Masachika (1416-90) and re-

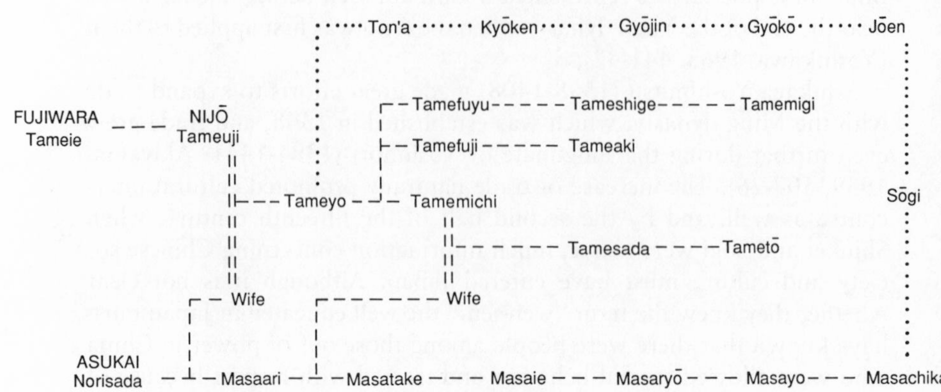

FIGURE 15.1 Sōgi and the Nijō-Asukai Descent

ceived instruction in the *Kokinshū* from Tō no Tsuneyori, a poet of the lower nobility who was also connected with the Nijō school.[51]

The line of one's teachers was fussed over in this period, and to the extent that one had not received instruction from an authoritative master, full social participation was difficult, no matter how outstanding one's compositions or criticism. Of course, social prestige did not come solely because of the lineage of one's teachers, and the superiority of Sōgi's scholarship was far more important to Sōgi's success than that negative factor. He seems to have received his instruction in *The Tale of Genji* from Ichijō Kaneyoshi (1402-81).[52] Commentaries on the *Genji*, such as the *Shimyōshō* and the *Kakaishō*, already existed at this time, and modern scholars have conjectured that Sōgi studied works like these on his own. There is no doubt, however, that it was also socially essential for

[51] Sōgi visited Tsuneyori's encampment at Mishima in the province of Izu to receive instruction on the *Kokinshū* from the twenty-eighth day of the First Month of 1471 to the eighth day of the Fourth Month. He received further instruction from Tsuneyori from the twelfth day of the Sixth Month to the twenty-fifth day of the Seventh Month of the same year. After reorganizing and revising his notes from both of these lecture sessions, he asked Tsuneyori for comments and corrections, and the manuscript was completed on the third day of the Fifth Month of 1472. This is the *Kokin Wakashū Ryōdo Kikigaki* (*Notes on Two Lectures on the Kokinshū*; Katagiri, 1981, 253-54).

[52] Sōgi's study with Kaneyoshi probably did not extend to detailed discussion of all *The Tale of Genji*, seeming to have been limited to questions on the details of court ritual and practices (Araki, 1941a, 157-58). [In the upheavals of the time, only the knowledge of a few people like Kaneyoshi enabled the court to maintain—or regain—its established practices.—Ed.]

him to receive instruction, if only on a few occasions, from Kaneyoshi, the greatest contemporary authority on ancient court practices and author of the *Kachō Yosei* (a thirty-part commentary on the *Genji Monogatari*).

Sōgi acquired fame as a classical scholar. His *Kokin Wakashū Ryōdo Kikigaki* and the *Gengo Henjishō* (*Shugyoku Henjishō*), on *The Tale of Genji*, remain important commentaries today. In his time, he was often invited to lecture on the classics by the high nobility.[53] Despite his low origins, he received such attention, even reverence, because he achieved a status corresponding to that of the Chinese wen-jen; such a status was widely recognized during this period, even at court. Had Sōgi concentrated only on renga, he would never have been able to enhance the social status of renga poets to the degree that he did. Sōgi's appointment by the court as the chief editor of the *Shinsen Tsukuba Shū (The New Tsukuba Collection* [= *STBS*]) is both an indication of the personal prestige he enjoyed and evidence of a general rise in the status of renga masters.

All this can only be understood from the fame that many renga masters achieved as classical scholars during this period. Kensai, who collaborated with Sōgi in compiling the *Shinsen Tsukuba Shū*, wrote the *Kokin Shihimon*, the *Gengo Hiketsu*, and other commentaries (Kaneko K., 1969, 217-24), and Botanka Shōhaku (1443-1527), who participated in the compilation of the *Shinsen Tsukuba Shū* as Sōgi's assistant, wrote many commentaries as well, including the *Ise Monogatari Shōmonshō* and the *Genji Monogatari Rōkashō*.[54] From the fifteenth century, this kind of knowledge of the classics came to be considered an indispensable qualification for a renga poet who aspired to fame. The result of this requirement that a renga master also be scholar of waka and classical prose was the development of a cultural milieu in which "total authority in literature entered the hands of renga poets" (Yamada Y., 1937, 193).

The *Shinsen Tsukuba Shū* was compiled under these conditions. The compilation was commissioned by Gotsuchimikado (r. 1464-1500) in the winter of 1494. The first draft was completed on the second day of the Sixth Month of the following year, and the second draft was submitted on the twenty-first day of the Sixth Month of the same year. In that revised form, the collection was accepted as a quasi-royal collection. The

[53] Sōgi lectured on the classics to such high-ranking noblemen as Sanjōnishi Sanetaka (1455-1537); Anegakōji Mototsuna (1441-1504); and Konoe Masaie (1444-1505; Araki, 1941a, 151-55). [Masaie was chancellor (kampaku) 1479-83, as Kaneyoshi had been 1467-70. This was the highest office a nobleman could hold, and members of only five families were eligible.—Ed.]

[54] [The author's point can be fully appreciated only if we bear in mind that Shōhaku, who studied under Sōgi and assisted him, was from a highborn noble family. See n. 60, below.—Ed.]

official copy of the anthology was presented to Gotsuchimikado on the twenty-sixth day of the Ninth Month of 1495 (Ijichi, 1943, 270-90).

The *Shinsen Tsukuba Shū* corresponds to the *Shinkokinshū* in waka, and no one would disagree that it occupies the highest position as a renga anthology. In its compiler's effort to achieve status as a classic for it, it shows characteristics of the *Shinkokinshū*. The diction employed in both linking stanzas (tsukeku) and opening stanzas (hokku) is purely ga in orientation. In this it is quite different from the *Tsukuba Shū*, which—perhaps for their historical significance—included not a few early renga with stanzaic linkings that are not yet highly refined. This may be seen clearly in the organization of the anthology itself. The new anthology does not follow the precedent of the earlier one, which includes an entire book of haikai renga (comic or otherwise nonstandard renga).[55] Sōgi and his collaborators eliminated haikai completely from the *Shinsen Tsukuba Shū*. Moreover, this was not done because haikai had declined; on the contrary, it was done in reaction to the spectacular vogue that the nonstandard version was enjoying during this period.[56]

The degree to which haikai renga flourished during the late fifteenth century can be seen in the *Chikuba Kyōginshū*, which had a preface dated the Second Month of 1499. Although the poets' names are not indicated in this anthology, external sources indicate that some at least of the stanzas were written by such famous masters as Sōgi, Shōhaku, Sōchō, and Kensai.[57] The majority of the other stanzas were likely written by these renga poets as well. The elimination of haikai renga from the *Shinsen Tsukuba Shū* should be thought, therefore, the result of the strengthening of the ga principles among its compilers. In this regard, we must accord high esteem to Yamada Yoshio's farsighted assertion that "it is here that the first chapter of the history of haikai truly begins" (Yamada Y., 1932a, 102).[58]

The enhanced social status of renga poets was also one of the important factors underlying this aspiration toward pure ga. This new status is manifested by the remarkable increase in the number of renga sessions held at the court in this period. In 1494 Gotsuchimikado commissioned the *Shinsen Tsukuba Shū*. During that year, fifty-nine renga sessions are recorded to have been held at court or the mansions of princes—if we include wakan renga.[59] One was a thousand-stanza sequence (Kaneko K., 1969,

[55] [Of course, by "haikai no renga" or "haikai" here, the author does not mean the basically serious kind by Matsuo Bashō and Yosa Buson, but nonserious, nonstandard (mushin) renga, out of which haikai of Bashō and Buson's kind later developed.—Ed.]

[56] *TBS*, 19, 1865-1993. This renga collection is arranged on the model of the *Kokinshū*.

[57] Notes on textual variants in the *Chikuba Kyōginshū*, 85, 90, 94.

[58] Since the *Chikuba Kyōginshū* was not discovered until 1963, Yamada's statement thirty-one years earlier is all the more impressive.

[59] Wakan renga are sequences in which stanzas in Chinese alternate with stanzas in Jap-

318-23). This is more than one session a week, and it means that renga, which had previously been a side event in occasions centering on waka, had been recognized as a premier art tantamount to waka. Given this recognition, the compilers of the *Shinsen Tsukuba Shū* should naturally have aspired to claim a ga status for their art.

The compilers' awareness of their new social status amplified this aspiration even further. Shōhaku was from the high nobility.[60] But both Sōgi and Kensai were from humble origins.[61] At the beginning of their careers, renga masters had not been respected by members of the high nobility. Sōgi had once been called "the beggar monk."[62] There is no question but that their awareness of their then dubious social position strengthened even more their desire to raise renga expression to the level of ga, to compile an anthology that would make renga appropriate as an art for the court. The respect accorded renga poets such as Sōgi and Kensai was always, however, recognition of their art. Their official status always remained that of non-noble, non-aristocratic (or military) renga poets.

For Sōgi to be recognized as an authority on waka and renga it was essential not only that he study with teachers from established lines but also that his own work be outstanding. Had he not composed superior waka and renga himself, he would not have been trusted by other poets as an arbiter of waka and renga. In terms of its content, Sōgi's critical theory is altogether simple. Indeed, its essential points are stated entirely in the following short passage from his *Chōrokubumi* (*Six Long Writings*, 117): "For renga, this: devote yourself to thinking its essential nature is yūgen [refined charm] with taketakaku [loftiness] and ushin [propriety of feeling]."[63] Yūgen and taketakaku relate to tone, while ushin refers to realization. But Sōgi's use of these terms differs in some respects from their usage in the thirteenth century.

---

anese. More properly, when the hokku is a stanza in Japanese (wa), the sequence is called a wakan renga (Japanese-Chinese renga). If the hokku is in Chinese (kan), it is called a kanna renga (Chinese-Japanese renga). [These were also important kinds in Gosan literature—Ed.]

[60] Shōhaku's father was Nakanoin Michiatsu (1379-1451), who held the position of minister at the Junior First Rank, there being only the senior rank above him. [See n. 54.—Ed.]

[61] Kensai's father is thought to have been Inawashiro Morizane, but Morizane's name does not appear in the genealogical table of the Ashina family, the head family of the Inawashiro clan (Kaneko K., 1962, 6-11). He was probably a warrior of such low rank that he was not included in the clan's genealogical record.

[62] Sōgi once donated one thousand hiki in cash (based on rice prices in 1984, some five thousand dollars) to the court for repairs to the Library of Official Documents (Kammu Bunko). Otsuki Masahisa commented: "That this beggar has done such a thing is truly rare and wonderful" (*Masahisa Kyō Ki*, 4.XI.1490).

[63] Sōgi seems to be expounding on the opinion of Sōzei: "Master Sōzei said, . . . 'In renga it is most important that the style be so lofty, so yūgen, and so ushin that one cannot identify what produces these effects' " (*Azuma Mondō* [*Dialogues from the East*], 226).

His yūgen (earlier, mystery and depth) partakes of Yoshimoto's usage, and so it has basically the same meaning as yūen (ethereal charm or refinement). However, Sōgi's yūen does not appear on the outer surface, which gives rather the feeling of elegant simplicity (heitan) or of the desolate (sabi). Similarly, his use of taketakaku (loftiness) differs somewhat from that of the thirteenth century, in which it meant sublime or impressive. He uses the term to mean that the conception of the scene expressed in the poem should be large in scale. Here are two of the stanzas that he gives in *Chōrokubumi* (18) as examples that are lofty and refined in appeal. The authors of the preceding stanzas are, as usual, not named. The authors of the added stanzas are Sōzei and then Senjun.

Aki samuge naru	Autumn has taken on a chill
kogarashi zo fuku	it is a wintry wind that blows
oshine moru	guarding the late rice
tōyama moto no	at the foot of distant mountains
kusa no io	a grass-thatched hut
	(*STBS*, 5:904)
Masaki chirikuru	Spindletree leaves flutter down
mine no akikaze	the autumn wind from the peaks
oshika naku	a deer is crying
toyama no oku ya	beyond these adjacent hills
shiguru ran	does cold drizzle fall[64]
	(*STBS*, 5:1015)

Although the arrangement of golden ears of rice and the red leaves of the spindletree within a scene depicting a desolate mountain village is certainly characteristic of Sōgi's yūgen, what gives these stanzas the quality of loftiness (taketakaku) is somewhat more difficult to discover. Here is another stanza, however, of which Sōgi said, "Is this not a lofty (taketakaku) style, indeed?" (*Asaji*, 327; the added stanza is Shōhaku's).

Ame uchisosogi	As the rain begins to fall
higurashi zo naku	clear voiced cicadas cry

[64] [The masaki (Trachelospermum asiaticum Nakai; spindletree) is a perennial vine. It blooms with white, perfumed flowers in the early summer, and its leaves turn red in the late fall.—Trans.] Sōgi writes of Senjun's stanza: "Priest Sōzei spoke fervently of this stanza, saying that it was indeed a superior stanza. Indeed, it affects one on each reading, no matter how many times it is read" (*Asaji*, 326).

Ikomayama	at Mount Ikoma
kumo fuku kaze ni	brought on a wind that bears the clouds
aki tachite	autumn has come
	(*STBS*, 4:580)

Judging from this poem, Sōgi's ideal of the "taketakaku style" is achieved by Shōhaku's shifting, enlarging the speaker's gaze from the foreground scene of the cicadas crying in the rain to the distance, where the clouds from which the rain is falling spread around the mountain. By its autumnal implications, the scene is conceptually enlarged in its temporal terms.

Sōgi's ushin (propriety of feeling) is not fundamentally at odds with that of the thirteenth century (conviction of feeling), but it does have some different elements. In his usage, propriety of feeling has its foundation in a universal reason (dōri), that is, shōri (correct reason). Sōgi gives eight stanzas as examples of the ushin style in *Chōrokubumi* (118-19), of which the following added stanza by Sōzei is typical:

Kanashi ya koishi	I am so sad and miss it so
yume ni dani mizu	not seeing it even in my dreams
tabi wa aki	the journey is autumn
furusato ika ni	and what about the house I left
arenu ran	how ruined is it[65]
	(*STBS*, 12:2305)

The added stanza enters into the yearning of the female speaker in the previous stanza, who laments that in the long days and months since parting she has stopped seeing her former lover, even in her dreams. But the added stanza transforms this into the sad yearning for home by a farflung traveler. For the modern reader, the stanza may seem to have a rather ordinary intent, yet by Sōgi's critical standards it is linked to the previous stanza in a new way. Unlike previous methods of stanzaic linking, which depended on witty transformation of the meanings of linked stanzas or on interesting uses of association (engo) and pivot-words (kakekotoba), the added stanza is dealt with in the same way topics (dai) are handled in waka. The poet enters deeply into the mental world of the preceding stanza just in the terms derived from that world.

[65] By itself, the preceding stanza is a love stanza, and for "it" we should translate "him." But the meaning of a stanza shifts in renga when what was the added stanza is itself added to. [Auth., Ed.] Sōgi had high praise indeed for this stanza: "The preceding stanza (maeku) is too complicated and deals with too many things. It would be difficult to link in the usual manner. Sōzei links it in this [excellent] fashion" (*Oi no Susami*, 160-61).

This creation by deep penetration into the world of the preceding stanza is not unlike the ushin style in waka (see ch. 8). For example, here is an example of Sōgi's commentary on a *Kokinshū* poem in his *Kokin Wakashū Ryōdo Kikigaki* (737):

Composed when women looked at me and laughed.
By priest Kengei

Katachi koso	Yes, I may appear
Miyamagakure no	Like an old tree that rots away
Kuchiki nare	Somewhere in far hills!
Kokoro wa hana ni	But if I make my heart a flower,
Nasaba nari nan.	It will blossom in your world.
	(*KKS*, 17:875)

Commentary by the master: "The reader should enter deeply into the composer's mind (kokoro)."[66] (Sōgi): This is a waka of true conception (kokoro aru).[67]

Sōgi's comment refers to the attitude the recipient should take in responding to the poem. Since the waka is in the ushin (conviction of proper feeling) style "of true conception," the reader or hearer must also enter into the mind of the composer (or, in more modern parlance, the speaker of the poem) in order to achieve a correct response. If we change this "enter deeply into the composer's kokoro" to "enter deeply into the intent of the previous stanza," Sōgi's conception of the ushin style in renga becomes clear.

Although Sōgi's ushin style does not differ from that of thirteenth-century waka treatises on this point, his concept is not exactly the same. When Sōgi uses "kokoro" as a critical term, he refers to individual psychological processes, but he believed these must also be supported by a universal principle (dōri). His added stanza on a traveler shows that in his age solitary wandering was widely held a true vocation (michi), and he himself wandered around the country for much of his life. This does not mean that he and his contemporaries denied the emotion of longing for one's home. Rather, for a person to lament that "I am so sad and miss it so" as he pursued his farflung wanderings was a natural expression of

[66] "Commentary by the master" no doubt refers to a written text of Tsuneyori's commentary on the *Kokinshū*. He had probably shown it to Sōgi before giving him personal instruction (Kaneko K., 1983, 151-53).

[67] ["Kokoro aru" and "ushin" use the two same Chinese characters in reversed order. See vol. two, index, on "fūryū."—Ed.] The "flower" ("hana") Kengei refers to represents not only the appeal he would exert in love but also in other bright (hanayakana) activities: poetry, music, and drinking.

human emotions, and the correct principle (shōri) was to compose poetry precisely as one was moved by that emotion. Here is another example of Sōgi's commentary in *Kokin Wakashū Ryōdo Kikigaki* (552):

Kimi ga tame	For your good sake
Haru no no ni idete	I venture into the spring fields
Wakana tsumu	To pick young greens,
Wagakoromode ni	And from the sleeves that did the work
Yuki wa furitsutsu.	The melting snow is dripping.
	(*KKS*, 1:21)

> This was paraphrased for me by my teacher [Tsuneyori], "This is work I do for you, but the drops collecting on my sleeves that keep out the snowflakes and water are tears of gratitude." In this, there is both the righteous way of the sovereign and nature, and this may certainly be said to be the ushin style.[68]

The hardship as I labor soaked in the drizzling snow is for your sake. This expression of faithfulness is grounded in the principle (dōri) that one should be devoted to those one loves, and Sōgi asserts that this principle is also applicable to the way of sovereigns, that it is the highest principle of politics.

To be loyal to this principle is precisely to be righteous (shō + jiki, i.e. shōjiki); and righteousness is also the most important ideal for poets.

> Shō (righteousness) is the heart that completely becomes itself.[69] The meaning of being itself cannot be explained with language. Thus, in the commentaries on the two characters of "shōjiki" [Ch. cheng-chih] we are told, "That which is the mean [chū, Ch. chung] even while it is not the mean is shō [cheng]. That which is crooked [wang] even while it is not crooked is called jiki [chih]. Chung is wu-chi [J. mukyoku, without extremity]." Thus we are told. It is a world that cannot be fathomed. In short, shō is the heart of the deity Amaterasu, and jiki is the principle that exactly reflects

[68] The author of the poem is Kōkō (fl. 884-87), son of Nimmyō (r. 833-50); Kōkō wrote the poem while yet a prince. The implied speaker and addressee may be variously interpreted. The person addressed as "Kimi" may be a parent, spouse or, in the traditional reading, the sovereign (Nimmyō?). The speaker implies that the work performed is for his own good as well as his addressee's, expressing satisfaction in doing service. Similarly, the waterdrops suggest tears of sensibility. It was then believed that if one ate young greens, their spiritual vitality would infuse one, preserving health. [Auth., Ed.]

[69] Jisei (the heart that completely becomes itself) refers to a person who exists without influence from outside. Tamekanu employs the same concept: "The waka of the *Man'yō* period are skillful in grasping the intention (kokoro) and the heart that completely becomes itself (jisei), in expressing to the outside the intention that moves within" (*Tamekanu Shō*, 158). Apparently, there are no examples of the concept in Sung Confucian treatises.

> her heart. The world is governed by the two characters of "shōjiki." Therefore, this collection makes shōjiki its basic form. When the three elements of heaven are grasped by the principle of shōjiki, heaven and earth are shō, and man is jiki. Because it is an art of this country, waka must preserve shōjiki. This is the most important point that waka poets must consider (*Ryōdo Kikigaki*, 545-47).

For modern readers who are inclined to support the theory of the autonomy of art, this frankly political position must seem ridiculous and completely unsupportable. To the extent that literature expresses the world of humanity, society, and nature, however, literature clearly cannot be separated from the fundamental logical principle (ri) that exists in all of them. Sōgi convincingly states that fidelity to that principle is the fundamental basis of literature. If we change the statement, "Shō is the heart of the deity Amaterasu, the jiki is the principle that reflects her heart" to something like, "Shō is the ultimate principle (ri) that governs the universe, and jiki is the reason that makes concrete this ultimate in the actual world," Sōgi can be said to have stated an opinion that has something new to say even in the modern world.

Chung (J. chū) is recognized as a technical term of Sung divination, in which it is often employed in compounds with the cheng (shō) and the chih (jiki) of cheng-chih (shōjiki), chung-cheng (chūshō, mean-just) and chung-chih (chūjiki, mean-straight; Imai, 1958, 50-51). According to Chu Hsi, ri is the fact of not being biased, and chung is the fact of ri having no particular character (ibid., 137). Clearly, the idea that shōjiki (cheng-chih) is "that which is the mean even while it is not the mean" came from Sung divination treatises, although the original source of this idea has not yet been determined. Since non-bias is a concept collateral with bias, the absolute non-bias presumed here must include bias even while remaining non-bias. The concept of shōjiki asserts that absolute non-bias (defined as chung) is shō. Wu-chi (mukyoku) is also a technical term from Sung divination and originally meant without limits (ibid., 133). Again, because mere limitless is simply a concept collateral with limits, an absolute limitlessness must also be inclusive of limits. Chu Hsi synthesized the tradition of Sung dynasty divination in the concept of the absolute character of "not having but not not having" (non-existent/non-empty), but I have never seen an example in which he expressed this absolute character as shō. Sōgi's formulation of the concept may have been based on a no-longer-extant treatise or on commentaries in Japanese. In any case, there is no room for doubt that it was inspired by Sung divination theory.

Sōgi was not the first to consider the political nature of poetry as an extension of the ushin style. In the *Guhishō* and the *Sangoki*, both falsely attributed to Teika, the styles of riseitei (the style of state management) and bumintei (style of caring for the people) are proposed as lesser styles within the style of ushin.[70] These styles were passed down in Nijō poetic treatises and, inspired by Sung divination, developed into the kind of theory stated above. The theory was transmitted to Sōgi by Tsuneyori. Unlike waka, however, in which each poem is complete in itself and can make political or ethical ideas its subject, a main characteristic of renga is precisely that the sequence does not have a single subject throughout the work. It is therefore impossible to develop a logical argument that will be convincing to readers.

The expression of political ideas may seem, consequently, quite impossible in renga. Renga poets of this period believed, however, that such expression was possible. Consider, for example, the following stanzas from the *Yunoyama Sangin Hyakuin (A Hundred Stanzas by Three Poets at Yunoyama)*. The preceding stanza is by Sōchō, and the added stanza by Sōgi.

Furusato mo nokorazu kiyuru yuki o mite	Even at my home I watch the snow disappear without a trace
yo ni koso michi wa aramahoshikere	if only there existed a correct way through our world[71]

Sōgi's added stanza makes the joint poem mean: I wish that a correct path (righteousness) would appear in contemporary society, just as the once covered path appears again when the snow melts in the spring. Here is a short sequence of stanzas with a political theme from *Sōgi Dokugin Nanihito Hyakuin (A Hundred Stanzas Related to Person by Sōgi Alone)*:

54	Kokorogokoro ni sawagu namikaze	Feelings upon feelings rise with the blustering wind and waves
55	yamakawa mo kimi no yoru yo o itsu ka min	shall we ever see the time your reign brings lasting peace even to hills and streams
	Yamakawa no kimi ni yoru yo o itsu ka min	Shall we ever see the time your reign brings lasting peace even to hills and streams

[70] *Guhishō*, 292, *Sangoki*, 318-20.

[71] *Yunoyama*, 153-54. [The "way" of the translation is of course a translation of "michi" and also represents the moral way (dōtoku), the Buddha's way (butsudō), and the way of the deities (shintō).—Ed.]

56	ayafuki kuni ya tami mo kurushiki	and will the land not fall to ruin with its commoners in distress
	Ayafuki kuni ya tami mo kurushiki	Will the land not fall to ruin with its commoners in distress
57	ueshi yori tanomi o tsuyu ni aki kakete	since the rice was planted the harvest that raised great hopes is chilled with autumn dew[72]

Stanza 55 in this sequence turns the images of stanza 54—a natural scene in which both the wind in the sky and the waves are in tumult—into metaphors for the disorder of society in the aftermath of the Ōnin War (1467-77). Stanza 56 comments specifically on the distress of the commoners, and the sequence is concluded with the following speculation: We have hoped ("tanomi") for the ripening of the rice ("ta no mi," the fruit of the fields) in autumn since we planted the paddies, but will we ever be able to harvest it safely? (The cold that blights hopes suggests the cold-heartedness of those carrying out rule of the country.) This sequence is a prayer for peace, based on the political ideal of mutual trust between rulers and the people. The *Sōgi Dokugin Nanihito Hyakuin* was composed in the period from 1491 to 1499. The lengthy Ōnin War had ended, but local conflicts and peasant riots occurred constantly, both in the capital and in the provinces. The desire for peace must have been deeply felt.

Of course, only one or two verses with political themes can be found in the entire hundred-stanza sequence, and by no means does the whole work develop a political theme. The modern reader may well ask if these few stanzas have any effect at all. But Sōgi expected a great deal of these stanzas mixed in with the others in the long sequence. In renga, whether the subject is a landscape or human affairs, almost all the stanzas are composed according to preexisting formulas. The composer never expresses raw emotions. Precisely for this reason, when stanzas like those above appear in a renga sequence—even if there be only one or two of them—they stand out remarkably. Moreover, Sōgi actually lived in an age of tumult and disorder, and his fervent prayer for peace is infused with the feeling of reality. One of the rules of renga composition is that with the exception of the opening stanza (hokku), all stanzas should depict scenes separate from the place (ba) of the composition and the actual situation of the composers. Even if a stanza expressing this kind of fervent emotion were attempted, the emotion would amount to nothing more than feelings spoken by the speaker of the stanza. They would have no relation to Sōgi himself or to Sōchō himself. Nevertheless, stanzas such as

[72] *Sōgi Nanihito*, 205-206. [Translations slightly adapted from Miner, 1979, 254-55.—For information on stanza impressiveness and relation, see ibid., 72-76.—Trans., Ed.]

the ones above that express the hopes of all the people of that period could not have failed to invoke a strong feeling of reality.

The first reception of renga occurs when the stanzas are recited as they are composed at the renga session (za) itself. When the composers' voices expanded into space, they expected that their kotodama would reach the deities and buddhas and that eventually moral politics would result. Since renga composed outside the circles of the court and the nobility had been believed to possess incantatory powers since the period of Hananomoto renga, stanzas infused with a strong feeling of reality were expected to move the deities and buddhas to intervene in the affairs of man. Himself a non-courtier poet, Sōgi of course lived in this tradition. But he discovered a theoretical basis for this belief in Sung divination theory, and it may be said that it was he who gave renga a metaphysics. This metaphysics established renga as a premier art form.

Sōgi's synthesis of a metaphysics for renga, ultimately linking it to universal principle (dōri), must have served to strengthen the confidence of renga poets. This does not mean that renga composition itself was refined by the metaphysics. The most important reason that Sōgi was lionized as the preeminent master of renga must be sought in his extraordinary powers of writing. In fact, almost all the techniques Sōgi employed had been developed before him, and there is none that might be called his own innovation. It is difficult, however, to discover either before or after Sōgi another poet that rivals him in his masterful varying and harmonizing of tone in a long sequence. Since renga were usually written and heard at za (renga sittings or gatherings) in which a number of composer/recipients participated, attention normally became focused on the interest of the individual stanzaic links immediately at hand, with little awareness of controlling the development of the entire sequence. Renga masters and senior poets were responsible for providing leadership and direction so that the sequence as a whole did not become disjointed. But if the master concentrated only on controlling the sequence, then variation—the very life of renga—would have been sacrificed. Its accidental quality, that one can never predict what kind of stanza will come next, is the fundamental character of renga; and if that quality is done away with, the interest of renga is lost. The role of the renga master was in fact much more difficult than that of a symphony conductor. The renga master guided the development of the sequence in such a way that the work as a whole achieved a harmonious integration while enjoyable and sufficient accidental variations also emerged as the sequence developed.

Moreover, no matter how much of his own effort the renga master devoted to the sequence, he could not expect a fine renga sequence if the participants in the session were not first rate. In this he must have felt a frustration similar to that of the symphony conductor confronted with an orchestra composed of second-rate and third-rate musicians. I consider Sōgi to be the greatest of renga masters, and this opinion is based on the *Minase Sangin Hyakuin (A Hundred Stanzas by Three Poets at Minase)* of 1488 and the *Yunoyama Sangin Hyakuin.* Botanka Shōhaku (1443-1527) and Saiokuken Sōchō (1448-1532), the two poets who participated with Sōgi in these wonderful sequences, are not much inferior to Sōgi in their mastery of the techniques of composing renga sequences. Sōchō does not measure up to Shōhaku at some points in the *Minase Sangin Hyakuin* (Konishi, 1971c, 159), but in the *Yunoyama Sangin Hyakuin* three years later, he displays an almost flawless mastery. With these two poets as collaborators, Sōgi could manifest full command of renga sequencing. Even in sequences that he led himself, Sōgi could not always guarantee that the result would be so outstanding unless the other poets participating were all as excellent as Shōhaku and Sōchō. Nevertheless, when compared to other renga masters, Sōgi stands out even in compositions that include stanzas by second- and third-rate poets. Certainly, in his later years Sōgi achieved a command of variation and harmony in renga as a single flow.

In renga, the shape of the entire sequence is understood only when the final stanza has been linked. It is extremely difficult to imagine the renga completely while stanzas are still being composed. Therefore, if the renga is to be integrated into a single splendid whole, the participants must already have a superior paradigm. Sōgi wrote his *Yodo no Watari* in order to provide such a model. Unlike previous renga treatises, which deal only with individual linking stanzas, *Yodo no Watari* discusses how a renga sequence should progress from the opening stanza (hokku) to the final linking stanza (ageku), and it includes a hundred-stanza sequence illustrating Sōgi's principles of progression. *Yodo no Watari* clearly reveals that, in his late years, Sōgi came to place great weight on the entire flow of a sequence. Although the treatise contains a wealth of knowledge about renga, one of its most important teachings is the following from Sōgi's exposition of his general theory: "The occurrence of fresh writing is rare. In recent times it has been thought best to alter only slightly what already exists. For this very reason, the variation of the existing is of high importance" (83). Sōgi seems to be saying that in renga the reader will only rarely get the impression of novelty. As he might have put it to those of his time, great renga composition results from the feeling of slight difference that gives an impression of the new. Given this reasoning, of unusual importance to renga composition is that it emphasize stanzaic connection with exceedingly subtle points of difference. Sōgi is asserting that Nijō position in forming the basis of his practice on the light, clear tone of classical elegance and on the interest of minute variations. Of course this does not entail full rejection of the new:

> Even people who claim to be first rate in the capital say of renga, "Use the practice today you used yesterday." You should compose renga so that even people who are not renga poets will read it and say, "That's it!" because of its inevitability. The most attractive writing is an unruffled kind that conveys subtleties. As I said earlier, it is best for beginners to make use of that which has been used already. (*Yodo no Watari*, 83)

Even in the case of "subtleties" however, Sōgi argues that in principle one should avoid that which is so striking as not to harmonize with an effect of light clarity (heitan).

When used in an individual stanza, this light clarity was called or judged ground (ji), and ground stanzas are contrasted to design (mon) stanzas, which stand out in their features. Sōgi considered it essential that ground and design stanzas be properly mixed, and however much Sōgi and his disciples valued the tone of light clarity, a sequence composed entirely of stanzas with the same tone would be monotonous.[73] For renga, the fundamental principle is variance, and monotony is the enemy to be avoided. For this reason, although Sōgi's renga sequences are composed with numerous ground stanzas, design stanzas do appear here and there in the sequence. Because the ground stanzas provide the basis of a renga sequence, too obtrusive design stanzas that would disrupt the harmony are to be avoided. If the participants in a renga session were poets who were able to respond sensitively to even the most subtle shifts of emotion in a stanza linking, a stanza that was more impressive than necessary was not considered outstanding but discordant. Moreover, if only stanzas that were clearly ground in nature and stanzas that were clearly design in nature were juxtaposed in a sequence, the contrast between them would stand out too much and give an unsettled feeling. To deal with this problem, renga masters developed techniques of interspersing stanzas that are between ground and design in impressiveness. Stanzas that are closer to ground were called jiyori (I shall call them jimon, or ground-design), while those closer to design in impressiveness were called mon'yori (monji, or design-ground). By interspersing ground-design and design-ground stanzas, the impression received from the renga as a whole is one of fluid variation that nevertheless preserves a beautiful harmony.

Ground (ji), ground-design (jimon), design-ground (monji), and design

[73] [In this and the preceding, the author implicitly contrasts Sōgi's genius for integral sequences with Shinkei's brilliant individual stanzas.—Ed.]

(mon) all refer to the features of *individual* stanzas. The same gradations are essential in the very different matter of *stanzaic connection*. There are added stanzas (tsukeku) that are intimately and clearly related to the previous stanza in terms of meaning and association and other stanzas that have no intimate relation. The intimate relation is termed shin (close) and the remote so (distant).[74] As in the case of ground and design stanzas, if all the stanzaic links in a renga were either clearly close or clearly distant, the flow of the renga would become monotonous. On the other hand, if the shifts between distant and close links were too violent, the sequential progression of the renga would lack integrity. Thus renga masters had to develop techniques in which connections closer to shin (shinyori) and those closer to so (soyori) were woven into the fabric of the renga in appropriate measures. Following the system of classification outlined above for the impressiveness of individual linking stanzas, I will call shinyori links close-distant (shinso) and soyori connections distant-close (soshin; Miner, 1979, 72-77). Naturally, the role of the leader of a renga session was to give direction concerning the mix of closely and distantly related stanzas to the other poets participating in the renga, who were inclined to be more conscious of the interest of individual stanzaic links than the fluid harmony of the whole.

In considering the variation and harmony of an entire sequence, careful attention must be given not only to tone, but also to features of subject and impressiveness in the sequence. If stanzas with the same kinds of subject and design have been linked over and over again, the flow of the sequence bogs down, and the feeling of the renga as a whole becomes heavily oppressive. Sōgi describes this phenomenon with the term "tsumaru" (choked) which, in renga composition, is considered unskillful. If it seems that the renga may become "choked," the leader should introduce a light shift. Sōgi describes this as "sending forward" (yaru), and a stanza that serves this function was called a "sending stanza" (yariku). Even if the writing of the sending stanza itself is ordinary, it would receive high praise if it worked well to carry the sequence forward in a renga that seemed likely to become choked. Here is a sequence from the hundred-stanza renga Sōgi composed as a paradigm (*Yodo no Watari*):

13	Tsuyu wa kie shimo mata oku no kusa karete	The dew has dried and now the frost replaces it withering the plants
14	hitome o shinobu sode ya hosu ran	afraid to be seen by others do you dry your wetted sleeves

74 [See the author's discussion of shinku and soku practice in waka (ch. 14), from which the renga conceptions and terms were taken.—Ed.]

	Hitome o shinobu	Afraid to be seen by others
	sode ya hosu ran	I try to dry tear-wetted sleeves
15	towaredomo	though he does not come
	nao taenu koso	my longing is unabated
	urami nare	how I detest it
	Towaredomo	Though he does not come
	nao taenu koso	my longing is unabated
	urami nare	how I detest it
16	sumu zo to omou	you must admit we live in
	onaji yo no uchi	the very same society
	Sumu zo to omou	One must admit it flows clearly
	onaji yo no uchi	in the same small village
17	take hosoki	slender the bamboo
	kakei wa mizu mo	whose pipes furnish them with water
	sukunaki ni	in only a trickle
	Take hosoki	Slender the bamboo
	kakei wa mizu mo	whose pipes furnish us with water
	sukunaki ni	in only a trickle
18	narete no nochi mo	although it seems familiar now
	sugoki yamazato	the mountain village is so sad

The thirteenth stanza follows several continuous seasonal stanzas. The fourteenth exploits the associative potential of dew to yoke it to sleeves wet with tears. Sōgi explains: "In a renga in which seasonal stanzas have been dominating, it is best to send it forward (yaru) by shifting to love stanzas." When the love subtopic has continued over three stanzas (from the fourteenth through the sixteenth)—even though this is the renga minimum—the progress of the renga begins to slow.[75] The stanzas on love do not have a very progressive nature. Since "it is difficult to send the renga forward after it has become choked," it is better to take the "sumu" (live) of the sixteenth stanza and switch its meaning to the "sumu" (flows clearly) of water, returning the renga to a seasonal theme (*Yodo no Watari*, 78). Given his mastery of this kind of sending "stanza," it is surely no exaggeration to say that Sōgi is unparalleled in renga mastery.

As he aged, Sōgi came to pay closest attention to the development of a renga sequence as an integer, and this was an epochal phenomenon in the

[75] In renga, up to five stanzas on love might be composed, but only three were required. In fact, from the seventeenth century on there are examples of runs of but two. [In haikai the number may drop to only one, even in sequences of the Bashō school. The author interprets stanza 16 as the male lover's reply to the woman's complaint in 15, and stanza 17 as a deliberate shift to another set of circumstances, so altering the meaning of 16.—Ed.]

history of renga. This may best be seen in *Sōgi Dokugin Nanihito Hyakuin*, which Sōgi composed at the age of seventy-nine. I do not know of a more beautiful renga. A renga sequence composed by a single poet, however, is not representative of renga in the strictest sense of the word. The *Minase Sangin Hyakuin*, in which Shōhaku and Sōchō also brilliantly participated, is more appropriate as an example of a renga in which Sōgi directed the overall progress of composition. On the front of the third sheet (san no ori, omote; see Konishi, 1975b, 38) is the following sequence, which provides an outstanding example of Sōgi's approach and which we may consider a sequence exemplary for conveying the interest of renga.[76]

	Itadakikeri na	Night after night the many frosts
	yonayona no shimo	have brought their whiteness to one's head
51	fuyugare no	Bleached by winter
	ashitazu wabite	the reed-crane suffers in the bay
	tateru e ni	where it takes its flight

Sōgi. Design-Ground. Close-Distant.

	Fuyugare no	Bleached by winter
	ashitazu wabite	the reed-crane suffers in the bay
	tateru e ni	where it takes its flight
52	yūshiokaze no	in the wind swelling with evening tide
	okitsu funabito	the boatman labors out at sea

Shōhaku. Ground-Design. Close-Distant.

	Yūshiokaze no	In the wind swelling with evening tide
	okitsu funabito	the boatman labors out at sea
53	yukue naki	the haze drifts on
	kasumi ya izuku	uncertain in its scope and place
	hate naran	unknown in its end

Sōchō. Design-Ground. Distant-Close.

[76] *Minase Sangin*, 239-40. [Translations from Miner, 1979, 204-09.] As we have seen, each stanza of a renga has a double presence: once as an added stanza (tsukeku) in relation to its predecessor (maeku), and once as a preceding stanza in relation to the next added stanza. Thus a given stanza may differ more or less in meaning when it is added to from when it itself is added to. [See n. 65.] Miner's presentation of each stanza twice illustrates this double presence. [And it follows the author's teaching as well as his example in Konishi, 1971c. The author's quotations from the *Tsukuba Shū* and *Shinsen Tsukuba Shū* will have implied already the double presence by his following the practice of the renga anthologies in giving the preceding stanza along with the added one that is chosen as exemplary, as is natural and inevitable for linked poetry, renga.—Ed.]

Yukue naki
kasumi ya izuku
hate naran
54 kuru kata mienu
yamazato no haru

The haze drifts on
uncertain in its scope and place
unknown in its end
in this mountain village spring
gives no sign of whence it comes

Sōgi. Ground-Design. Close-Distant.

Kuru kata mienu
yamazato no haru
55 shigemi yori
taedae nokoru
hana ochite

In this mountain village spring
gives no sign of whence it came
from luxuriant boughs
the fall of blossoms leaves behind
greater riches still

Shōhaku. Design. Close-Distant.

Shigemi yori
taedae nokoru
hana ochite
56 ko no moto wakuru
michi no tsuyukesa

From luxuriant boughs
the fall of blossoms leaves behind
greater riches still
beneath the trees I pick my way
on a path bright with the dew

Sōchō. Ground-Design. Close-Distant.

Ko no moto wakuru
michi no tsuyukesa
57 aki wa nado
moranu iwaya mo
shiguru ran

Beneath the trees I pick my way
on a path bright with the dew
even my rock-bound place
somehow is entered by autumn
drizzling with tears

Sōgi. Ground-Design. Close-Distant.

Aki wa nado
moranu iwaya mo
shiguru ran
58 koke no tamoto ni
tsuki wa narekeri

Even my rock-bound place
somehow is entered by autumn
drizzling with tears
on my mossy priestly sleeves
the moon has found familiar place

Shōhaku. Ground-Design. Close-Distant.

Koke no tamoto ni
tsuki wa narekeri
59 kokoro aru
kagiri zo shiruki
yosutebito

On his mossy priestly sleeves
the moon has found familiar place
the elegant taste
of the renouncer of this world
clearly is supreme

Sōchō. Ground. Close-Distant.

Kokoro aru
kagiri zo shiruki
yosutebito

The elegant taste
of the renouncer of the world
clearly is supreme

60	osamaru nami ni	it seems a boat launches forth
	fune izuru miyu	on a sea whose waves are stilled

Sōgi. Ground-Design. Distant-Close.

	Osamaru nami ni	It seems a boat launches forth
	fune izuru miyu	on a sea whose waves are stilled
61	asanagi no	in the morning calm
	sora ni ato naki	no trace remains across the sky
	yoru no kumo	of last night's clouds

Shōhaku. Design-Ground. Close-Distant.

	Asanagi no	In the morning calm
	sora ni ato naki	no trace remains across the sky
	yoru no kumo	of last night's clouds
62	yuki ni sayakeki	peaks ring the distance on all sides
	yomo no tōyama	pure with the snow that covers all

Sōchō. Design. Close-Distant.

	Yuki ni sayakeki	Peaks ring the distance on all sides
	yomo no tōyama	pure with the snow that covers all
63	mine no io	the leaves are fallen
	ko no ha no nochi mo	but at the hut upon the peak
	sumiakade	there is more to live for

Sōgi. Design-Ground. Close-Distant.

	Mine no io	The leaves are fallen
	ko no ha no nochi mo	but at the hut upon the peak
	sumiakade	there is more to live for
64	sabishisa narau	the voice of the wind in pines
	matsukaze no koe	makes the solitude familiar

Shōhaku. Ground-Design. Close.

The desolate winter scene (51) and the seashore at evening (52), which is an extension of it, both present rather negative images, and if they were followed by another stanza with the same tone, the renga would begin to have a "choked" feeling. Stanza 53 is not a pure landscape verse, however. It contains a hint of human psychological processes in "unknown in its end" (hate naran). Moreover, the image of "haze" (kasumi) is evocative for its association with the refreshing atmosphere of spring. Fifty-three thus sends the sequence forward. It does not do so sufficiently to qualify it as a usual sending stanza, but it gives rise to the spring scene of the mountain village in 54, and after 54 almost any kind of stanza could be linked. Stanza 54 broadens the range of possible linking verses and is an exemplary sending verse (yariku).

Stanza 54 has no particular interest of its own, and may therefore be called a ground stanza, but since it includes a slight hint of brightness (in "spring") I have given it the status of a ground-design. From this "spring" the brilliant scene of 55 emerges. This scene, in which blossoms fall from time to time against a background of luxuriant green, is suffused with a quiet beauty, and this must certainly be the kind of beauty that Sōgi considered to be yūgen. Because the previous stanza (54) is nearly a ground stanza, the beauty of stanza 55 stands out, and this makes 55 a design stanza. But if, for instance, the previous stanza (54) had been on the order of a design-ground stanza, 55 would not be so impressive.

The succeeding stanza (56) merely adds an element of human interest and is in fact a ground stanza. When one considers the vivacity of the shift from spring to autumn occasioned by "on a path bright with dew" (dew is classified as an autumn signifier), however, it is, after all, a ground-design stanza. The next two stanzas (57, 58) mingle human elements with seasonal elements, bringing the sequence back from its rather positive tone to the negative tone of desolate solitude. Sōchō's stanza (59), with its contemplation of renouncing the world is, however, wholly concerned with human concerns, and this third consecutive stanza in the sad vein of loneliness gives the strongest feeling that the sequence has been "choked up." Instead of scolding Sōchō and having him rewrite the stanza, Sōgi lightly shifts the tone with a poem glorifying the peaceful age (60). Here the negative imagery of Sōchō's stanza becomes appealingly positive, and this stanza is wonderful as a sending stanza. Moreover, this sending stanza kills two birds with one stone, for it could be expected that the kotodama of this prayer for peace on earth would be effective. Clearly, it is composed in Sōgi's ushin style. Sōchō must have been extremely impressed. But Shōhaku next responds to Sōgi's stanza with a beautifully refreshing seasonal stanza (61), enabling Sōchō to develop the grand conception of his following stanza (62). The scene of dawn breaking on the distant mountains capped with pure white snow of course makes this a design stanza, and there is no question but that its tone is representative of what Sōgi calls loftiness (taketakaku). Sōchō thus recovers his dignity. From the loftiness of this stanza, Sōgi once again returns the renga to the negative image of a lonely dwelling in the mountains (63), and Shōhaku links a very similar stanza to this (64). Stanzas dealing with eremitism appeared previously (57, 58, 59), but while those focused on the deprivations and loneliness of Buddhist austerities, in contrast Sōgi and Shōhaku take up the pleasure of solitude. Just as a sonata varies thematic motifs, renga supplies counterpart sequential interests.

Earlier I stressed the problem of progression in the subjects and tones of stanzas in a renga sequence. In comparison with the variety there emphasized in theory, this sequence may give an impression of monotony in the degree of closeness of stanzaic connection. In fact, in the estimations

I have offered, the great majority of the connections are close-distant. However, this phenomenon occurs only on the front of the third page (san no omote). Immediately before it, on the back of the second sheet (ni no ura), there are three close, six close-distant, one distant-close, and four distant connections. On the back of the third sheet (san no ura), there are four close, seven close-distant, three distant-close, and no distant connections.[77] If the proportions of degrees of relation were the same throughout the renga as a whole, the sequence would lack variation, and the large percentage of close-distant linkings on one sheet gives the entire renga an integrated rhythm and tempo that nevertheless encompasses shifts from fast to slow in progression and from high to low in tone.

Speaking again in terms of variation within an integrated sequence, Sōgi's paradigmatic renga already displays those techniques of progression that would not be established formally until later. This is the jo-ha-kyū rhythm, which was systematically formulated for the first time in Sōboku's (1488?-1545) *Tōfū Renga Hiji* (completed in 1542; 164). The introduction (jo), which is unified in a poised way, runs through the front (omote) of the first sheet of four (shoori) and often a stanza or two more into the back (ura) of the first sheet. The development (ha), the section of variety, is longest, running from the back of the first sheet to the front of the fourth and last (nagori no omote). The fast close (kyū), which brings a seemingly rapid but smooth conclusion, is represented as the back of the last sheet (nagori no ura), although it often begins a stanza or two earlier on the front. [See the Appendix.] In his later years, then, Sōgi established techniques of exploiting the accidental character of renga, which occurs because the composers themselves cannot predict how the renga will progress, within a structure that is full of variation but nevertheless has harmony in its entirety. When only his linking stanzas are considered, it cannot be said that Sōgi is a greater master than Shinkei. However, in the integrated beauty of the hundred-stanza sequences he led, no one equals Sōgi, and his style would become what was meant by renga.

[77] The basic renga sequence is that in one-hundred stanzas. [See Appendix; the present note is abbreviated.—Ed.] I have discussed elsewhere the distribution of close-distant and design-ground stanzas for each side of each sheet of the *Minase Sangin Hyakuin* as well as for the sequence as a whole (Konishi, 1971c, 178-234).

CHAPTER 16

From Classical to Quasi-Classical Japanese Prose

The Decline of Nikki and the Rise of Travel Accounts

"Classical Japanese prose" refers of course to literary works written in the same style as the nikki and monogatari of the tenth and eleventh centuries. In the fourteenth and fifteenth centuries this style had become a thing of the distant past, and only people with ample specialized training were able to write literary works in it. This is reflected in the marked decline in the number of classical Japanese prose works after the fourteenth century begins. Moreover, even in the few texts that were written in the classical style, there is a gradual influx of Chinese words as well as Chinese readings adapted from the Japanese method of reading classical Chinese by transliterating each character into its Japanese reading (kambun yomikudashi).[1] Ultimately, prose styles degenerate into a kind of quasi-classical Japanese prose that is an intermediate form between pure classical prose and Japanese prose in the later standard mixed style.

Lady Nijō's (b. 1257) *Towazugatari (The Confessions of Lady Nijō)* and Hino Meishi's (d. 1358) *Takemuki ga Ki (The Memoirs of Lady Takemuki)* are the only extant nikki written in classical Japanese prose from the fourteenth century, and there are no extant examples from the fifteenth century.[2] Moreover, the two fourteenth-century diaries have aspects that make it impossible to recognize them as works in pure classical Japanese prose. For example, in *Towazugatari*, Lady Nijō describes her grief at the death of her father in the following manner (42-43):

[1] [Kambun yomikudashi, a method of reading Chinese, was employed by scholars of Chinese and by priests.—Trans.]

[2] "Lady Nijō" is the name given the author by Karen Brazell (see n. 6). She was the daughter of the Great Counselor Koga Masatada (1228-72). "Nijō" (Second Avenue) was the name she used while in the service of Gofukakusa, and from that service she derives the appellation by which she is known to Japanese, Gofukakusa In Nijō. "Hino Meishi" also presents a problem. The "Meishi" is written with the "Na" of "Nagoya" and the "shi" of the character for child. There appears to be no such name as "Nako," but there must have been some Japanese pronunciation. Since it is unknown, the Sinified "Meishi" is given. Writers in Japanese are spared this problem, since all they need do is silently print the two characters. [Auth., Ed.]

> So black is my own mood that when I look up at the heavens I think the sun and moon must have fallen from the sky, and as I lie on the ground sobbing, my tears seem to be a river flowing from me. When I was two years old I lost my mother, but at that time I was too young to realize what had happened. However, my father and I had spent fourteen years together—ever since the forty-first day of my life, when I was first placed upon his knee. Mornings, looking in my mirror, I was happy to realize whose image I reflected; evenings, changing my gowns, I thought of my indebtedness to him. The debt I owe him for my life and my position is greater than the towering peak of Mount Sumeru, and the gratitude I feel toward him for taking my mother's place in rearing me is deeper than the waters of the four great seas.

Even in translation, this prose style is clearly not colloquial, but its formal effects are even more striking in the original.[3] Given the situation described, it is possible that Nijō attempted a mode of expression in the vein of Buddhist petitions (gammon hyōbyaku). If this were a work of the twelfth century, the stiff formality of this passage would make one wonder if it had indeed been written by a woman.[4] This impression is reinforced by the appearance of large amounts of Chinese words and syntax throughout the text and the use of the polite auxiliary verb "sōrō" in dialogue and letters.[5] These features are not found in Japanese prose works of the tenth and eleventh centuries. There are differences of degree, but *Takemuki ga Ki* displays the same elements.

That the prose styles of these two nikki are somewhat impure as classical Japanese prose seems to me to be a reflection of the stances of their authors: both Nijō and Meishi, but especially Nijō, attempted to write in an up-to-date style. *Towazugatari* is a nikki, and so it is natural that the author should have made her subjects the events of her own times. One may feel that this "modern" style is something of a superfluity. But this work contains many elements that are suggestive of the style of a monogatari [narrative in the past tense]. More than anything else, the happenings described in *Towazugatari* are too unusual for a factual nikki.

The heroine, who is of course also the first-person narrator, is initiated into love by His [cloistered] Majesty, Gofukakusa ("In"; r. 1246-59) at

[3] [Diction and patterned syntax are the grounds.—Ed.]

[4] In the depiction of one formal scene (the scene in which Masatada attempts to withdraw from official life), there is an example of male characters speaking in a manner suggestive of Chinese parallel prose (1:18-19), but in this scene the heroine is speaking to herself. The extent to which this diction is Sinified is not apparent in translation, but it is quite striking in the original. [For the author's discussions of nikki—not as diaries or memoirs but as narratives in "the present tense"—see vol. two, ch. 8.—Ed.]

[5] [We omit twelve examples of Sinified compounds given by the author—kukon, keisei, etc.—Ed.]

the age of thirteen. She also has passionate affairs with a courtier of high rank, whom she terms Snow Dawn (Yuki no Akebono) and with a high-ranking priest she calls Dawn Moon (Ariake no Tsuki). There is also an episode in which His Majesty requires the heroine to sleep with "the Konoe Minister," while he listens from the next room. Later, the young Dawn Moon, completely consumed by his uncontrollable passion for the heroine, falls ill and dies young. His Majesty, who had connived in her affair with Dawn Moon, cannot, however, forgive her when rumors arise that she has also had relations with Kameyama In, his younger brother and political rival. She is banished from the court. She renounces the world and from the Second Month of 1289 to the end of the nikki in the Seventh Month of 1306 (books four and five of the text) she wanders around the country. During this period, Gofukakusa dies. No longer of the rank to be allowed to participate in his funeral, the heroine must watch from the roadside as the procession passes. She follows after it barefoot. On the third anniversary of the death, she closes her nikki with the lament that her true desire has been the resolution to emulate "the manner of Saigyō's pilgrimages." Leaving aside for the moment the last two books, the heroine's tangled love affairs with His Majesty, high-ranking courtiers, and even a priest, which comprise the subject matter of the first three books, fall into the category of fantastic events (ayashigoto), and the happenings in the nikki have a fictional character that is impossible in a factual nikki.

In short, *Towazugatari* is a fictional nikki. As material, Nijō must have used her own factual nikki and perhaps also factual diaries written by others. For example, it is impossible to believe that she could have written the account of the ninetieth birthday celebration for the Quasi-Consort Kitayama (3:163-79) without some other written record to base it upon.[6] In fact, in all likelihood she used the *Kitayama Jugō Kujūga no*

[6] Sadako, the wife of Counselor Saionji Saneuji (1194-1269). The maternal grandmother of Gofukakusa and Kameyama, she was called the Quasi-Consort Kitayama and afforded the same treatment given the Consort. She was Nijō's great-aunt. The author presents some of her main characters in two distinct guises, as fictional and as historical persons.

Fictional (Japanese and English)	*Historical*
In—His Majesty	Gofukakusa
Shin'in—New In	Kameyama
Konoe Ōidono—the Konoe Minister	Takatsukasa Kanehira
Yuki no Akebono—Snow Dawn	Saionji Sanekanu
Ariake no Tsuki—Dawn Moon	No name given

The importance of fictionalizing can be judged from two of the specifications. The Konoe and Takatsukasa families were two of the five regent families, and to depict a Takatsukasa as a Konoe was to depart from history. Also, the absence of a historical counterpart for Dawn Moon suggests the degree of fictionalizing. Actually, two men have been identified as

Ki (*An Account of the Celebration of Quasi-Consort Kitayama's Ninetieth Birthday*; Matsumoto, 1971, 374-85). But this is not a matter of passages in the style of a factual nikki occasionally finding their way into the fictional narrative. The appearance of a detailed, factual account of the Quasi-Consort's birthday celebration at this point in the narrative is the result of scrupulous care on the part of the author. The heroine, who has had her own chambers in the palace and grown up accustomed to the golden life of a favorite of His Majesty, has been slandered, and it has been decided that she will have to leave. She probably has resolved already to renounce the world and begin her life of wandering. The Consort Dowager Ōmiya is aware of the heroine's circumstances and, thinking at least to give her one last cherished memory, arranges for her to attend this once-in-a-lifetime affair secretly.[7] Thus, the detailed description of the celebration from the point of view of the heroine, now merely a bystander with no important role to play, does not deal with the gorgeous banquet as straightforward splendor but rather as magnificence painted on a ground of sorrow. This is a dispassionately calculated strategy that makes this grandeur more gorgeous than the actuality on which it was founded. As the finale of the first three books of the nikki, it is brilliantly effective.

There are many other examples of meticulous planning in the conception of this work. The heroine recalls that at the age of eight she had seen an illustrated scroll called *Saigyō ga Shugyō no Ki (An Account of Saigyō's Pilgrimages)* and says, "I have envied Saigyō's life ever since,

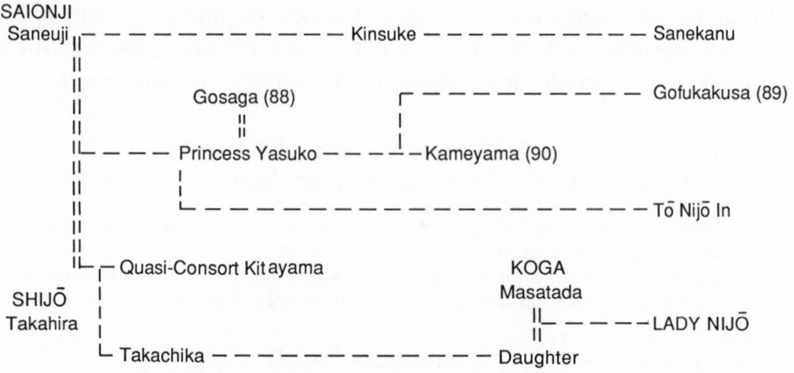

FIGURE 16.1 The Saionji Line and Lady Nijō's Descent (Numbers indicate the traditional succession of sovereigns; single lines indicate parent-child descent and double lines indicate marriage)

Dawn Moon: only the fictional version is clear. For a version of all this without these complexities, see Brazell, 1973. [Auth., Ed.]

[7] Ōmiya is Kitsushi, the middle consort (chūgū) of Gosaga (r. 1242-46). She was the mother of Gofukakusa and Kameyama.

and although I could never endure a life of ascetic hardship, I wish that I could at least renounce this life and wander wherever my feet might lead me . . . and make out of this a record of my travels that might live on after my death" (1:52). A child of eight could hardly have entertained such thoughts. Rather, this is a carefully planned foreshadowing of the last two books, which describe the heroine's wanderings. It is a fiction posited early on to foreshadow the heroine's realizing her desire to emulate "the manner of Saigyō's pilgrimages" in the last two parts (5:330).

The two examples given so far are easily understood, but correspondences that are much more complex and obscure have been devised in developing the major incidents of the story. The course of events that result in the heroine's banishment from court provide the best example. I wrote earlier that the cause of the heroine's banishment was slander, but the scandal arising from this slander is a mere pretext. Behind it is concealed the twisted psychology of His Majesty and a complex web of intrigue. While its existence cannot be discovered in a single reading of the work, in the course of several perusals one becomes aware of an elaborately structured design. One incident gives rise to another, compounding the complexities of the action, and from this complexity is born a degradation that inexorably leads the heroine toward catastrophe.

When the heroine is fourteen, her father dies (1:27), and this is an underlying cause of her downfall. As the daughter of a major counselor, she is well qualified to become a junior consort or a principal handmaid, but without an influential supporter (her father) she cannot expect to maintain a position of official marriage. She is forced to resign herself to the insecure status of one of His Majesty's concubines. While it is publicly acknowledged that she is a royal concubine, she is never given official status (Brazell, 1973, ix). The uncertainty of the heroine's position is one of the underlying reasons that she suffers the indignity of receiving the order for her withdrawal from the palace in a single private letter. The order is sent in a private letter to Shijō Takachika, minister of military affairs and the heroine's maternal grandfather, from the Middle Consort Tō Nijō In, who criticizes the heroine directly for lese majesty in respect to herself.[8] The heroine learns of it indirectly from her grandfather (3:160). Clearly, however, Tō Nijō In has acted with the implicit consent of His Majesty. Uneasy after receiving a message from Takachika that she should prepare to leave the palace permanently, the heroine presumes that this cannot be the intention of His Majesty and goes to his quarters. He merely glances at her coldly and asks, "Are you leaving this evening?"

[8] Tō Nijō In is Kimiko, the Middle Consort of Gofukakusa and the younger sister of Kitsushi.

Then he stands up to leave, "probably to go to Consort Higashi Nijō's apartments" (3:159).

Had he not abandoned the heroine, the Middle Consort could never have carried out her plan to force the heroine's withdrawal, no matter how bitter her rancor, for this is not the first time the Middle Consort had protested against the heroine's presence. Much earlier, when the heroine was His Majesty's favorite, the Middle Consort, whom she served as an attendant, had forbidden her to enter her apartments (1:54), and somewhat later the Middle Consort had sent a letter to His Majesty criticizing her arrogance. On the earlier occasion, he had been steadfast in his love and had replied to Tō Nijō In's complaints with a long letter defending the heroine's position (1:61-64). Had his love for the heroine been as strong as before, her downfall would not have come about. But the heroine is coldly abandoned. Given the contrast between these two episodes, one may well ask why His Majesty's feelings changed so drastically.

Not only because of her own character does the heroine become entangled in so many love affairs despite her uncertain position. She has unspoken royal consent in conducting her liaisons, and often His Majesty himself may be accused of initiating them. This is revealed most clearly in the two episodes in which he accedes to a drunken request of the Konoe Minister and presents the heroine to him as a bed companion (2:117-20). While it was not normal even in this period to send one's own lover to the bedchamber of another, even if he were a powerful courtier, the custom of taking a tolerant view of the sexual liaisons of court ladies seems not to have changed very much since the *Makura no Sōshi (The Pillow Book of Sei Shōnagon)* in the late tenth century. In brief, as long as the heroine's affairs were merely sexual dalliances, he would not consider them to be a major problem.

When the heroine actually falls in love with another man, however, it is an unforgivable act of betrayal. The heroine's lover is "Snow Dawn." The proof of this betrayal is that she describes her first encounter with him as "this unexpected bridal bed" (1:34), for she is already a royal concubine, and this use of "bridal bed" is strange unless it is interpreted as an expression of the heroine's true feelings rather than the facts of her sexual relations. Later, she says, about "Snow Dawn," "We had once enjoyed such a deep relationship that I might term him my first bridegroom" (3:128). For the heroine, "Snow Dawn" is her true love. His Majesty, however, mistakenly believes that Dawn Moon is the secret love who has stolen the heroine's heart, and this misunderstanding is the direct cause of her downfall.[9]

[9] The heroine begins to fall in love with Dawn Moon nearly five months after (3:134) their liaison is known to His Majesty (3:122-24).

At first disinclined to like Dawn Moon, she is caught up in an affair with him.[10] His Majesty falls ill and Dawn Moon is summoned to perform devotions for his recovery. He accosts the heroine in a small room beside the sanctuary where the devotions are to be performed, and unable to resist his burning passion, she yields to him virtually under the eyes of the other priests. As a Buddhist priest, Dawn Moon's sexual passion will condemn him to hell, and this affair has much more the character of an ugly swamp of lust than of sweet rapture. On another occasion when Dawn Moon is called to the palace, the heroine is summoned to attend him and His Majesty. When the latter is called away from the room, Dawn Moon breaks into tears, pouring out his love for the heroine. His Majesty returns unnoticed and overhears this conversation. Alone with His Majesty, the heroine confesses everything, but to her surprise he responds by saying that if Dawn Moon is so overwhelmed by passion, it must be the working out of some karma from a previous existence, and he promises to arrange for her to continue the affair in such a way that it will not be found out by others (3:122-24).

On the surface, this appears to be an extremely generous gesture, but it is at this moment that he ceases to love the heroine. We know this from his comparison of the heroine's situation to the tale of Consort Somedono, who was said to be seduced by a Blue Devil (the ghost of Archbishop Shinzei).[11] The Blue Devil who possesses Somedono corresponds to Dawn Moon, and His Majesty says of the consort that "it was beyond the power of the buddhas and bodhisattvas to prevent her from ruining herself with this incarnate fiend" (3:123). However indirectly, he is predicting that, like Somedono, the heroine will lose her position. Perhaps in order to emphasize this prediction, he brings up the story of Somedono again in the presence of Dawn Moon, deeply shocking the heroine by this repetition of the comparison (3:130-31).

Sometime after the heroine's confession, under the pretext that he has had a strange dream, His Majesty hints that she may be pregnant. She is not fully able to understand him. During a period when he does not send for her, however, she indeed feels the first signs of pregnancy. When he does summon her, he announces, "I've purposely avoided sending for you since my dream. I wanted to leave an interval of one month, but it has

[10] "And it is my usual foolish nature to feel unhappy, disagreeable, and even frightened" (2:88).

[11] Kakinomoto no Ki no Sōjō (Shinzei) was a senior disciple of Kūkai's and was revered by Montoku Tennō. He fell passionately in love with Somedono, but with no hope of consummating his passion, he died of a broken heart. His spirit was incarnated as a "Blue Devil" that seduced the empress, who yielded to him because he appeared to her as the tennō (*Hōbutsushū*, 2:99-103). Gofukakusa must be referring to a setsuwa in the same line in which the consort loses her position because of the incident. As an actual historical figure, Shinzei (800-60) was the compiler of the *Seireishū*.

been lonesome without you" (3:128). She is astonished to learn that he had a motive for his actions: to ascertain that the child to be born is indeed Dawn Moon's. This conduct clearly reveals that His Majesty's love for the heroine is already a thing of the past. But he cannot order her away from the palace without reason, and if he were to announce the true reason (her affair with Dawn Moon), his own reputation would be seriously affected.[12] In order to avoid this, he conducts the "ceremony of presenting the maternity sash" himself in his own chambers (3:135). This amounts to public announcement that he acknowledges the child as his own. The heroine, however, still cannot refuse the passionate entreaties of Dawn Moon, and as they continue to meet, they finally become the subjects of public gossip (3:144). Now confronted by the situation he had most hoped to avoid, His Majesty contrives an emergency solution. It happens that a lady under his protection has suffered a stillbirth. The heroine's child will be given to this lady, and it will be announced that her baby has died. This plan succeeds admirably, and the ugly rumors stop. The heroine is overcome with gratitude toward her protector, whose scrupulous concern has spared her embarrassment (3:146).

In fact, however, this plan was devised to save not the reputations of the heroine and Dawn Moon, but the face of His Majesty himself. He says, "Your affair with Dawn Moon is no longer a secret, and I hear that even rumors about my own conduct have been set afloat, falsely and with extreme exaggeration. It is all most deplorable" (3:144). Having given out that the heroine's child is his own, he dreads that if it were to resemble Dawn Moon the truth of the rumors would be established.[13] His true intention is to avoid a scandal involving himself. On the twenty-fifth day of the Eleventh Month, however, only a short time after the birth of the child on the sixteenth day of the same month, Dawn Moon suddenly succumbs to an epidemic disease (3:149-50). Had His Majesty ordered the heroine's banishment while he was alive, there would have been the danger that Dawn Moon would do something rash and that rumors would again flare up. But with Dawn Moon out of the way, there is no longer any danger that gossip about the heroine will affect him. Her future is sealed. At this point, however, there is still no reason that can be given for sending her away, and he does not want her banishment to appear to be his own doing.

[12] "Of course I realize that if word of this affair were to spread, your position would be difficult indeed" (3:132).

[13] The crown prince that was born between Hikaru Genji and Lady Fujitsubo bears a close resemblance to Genji (*GM*, "Momiji no Ga," 282), although the Kiritsubo Tennō does not recognize the resemblance (ibid., 284). In this later case, however, someone may notice. [His Majesty alludes to the *Genji* earlier when he relates his dream about Nijō's pregnancy by Dawn Moon (3:127): Genji hints to his wife, the Third Princess, that he knows Kaoru is not really his child but that he is willing to accept him as such.—Trans.]

In the middle of the Fourth Month of the following year, he sends her a poem saying, in effect, "Do you have the intention of having nothing to do with me?" At first, the heroine takes it as a complaint that she is still mourning the death of Dawn Moon. But it soon becomes clear to her that he is referring to rumors about herself and the "New In" (3:154-55).[14] These rumors concern an incident that had occurred six months earlier. His Majesty and the New In had taken an excursion to the Saga palace,[15] and the two brothers had slept in the same chamber. The New In had persuaded his brother to have the heroine sleep with them. Having drunk heavily at the evening's banquet, His Majesty quickly falls into a deep slumber. Near dawn, he realizes that the heroine is not beside him and murmurs, "I have been such a sleepy-head that even my chamber mate has deserted me." To this, the New In replies, "She was here until this very moment." The heroine, who seems to have been hiding behind a screen, thinks to herself, "It isn't my fault" (3:141-42).

Only three people are present in this scene, and the New In surely would not have spread rumors about it. Therefore, His Majesty himself must have been the source of the gossip. The heroine says of it, "At the time I knew nothing of this rumor" (3:155). She had known of the gossip about herself and Dawn Moon, but she knows nothing at all of the rumors that are circulating now. In fact, there are no rumors. They are a fiction manufactured by His Majesty. The circulation of this rumor would have been limited to a few of his trusted confidants. Since it could only prove embarrassing to himself and Kameyama, he would have wanted to avoid having it circulated more widely than necessary to make the heroine think that the rumor indeed existed.

At the beginning of the following year, the heroine senses that he has grown cold toward her. She writes in her nikki, "I sense a growing estrangement" (3:157). In the Seventh Month, after his waka, the order is given for her to withdraw from the palace (3:158-60). The heroine receives the order not from him himself but indirectly, as we have seen, in a private message from Tō Nijō In to her maternal grandfather. It is well known that Tō Nijō In harbors ill feelings toward the heroine, and it is for this reason that she is used. In this way, and over a period of time, His Majesty snuffs out one by one the rumors that threaten to involve the royal family in scandal.

It must be understood that we cannot take literally this portrayal of him as a realistic portrait of Gofukakusa (1243-1304). Not a few attempts have been made to explain his conduct in *Towazugatari* by refer-

[14] The "New In" (Shin'in) corresponds to Kameyama (1299-1305), but in *Towazugatari* designates a fictional character, as do other names in the story.

[15] A separate palace constructed and much loved by Gosaga (r. 1220-27). It stood in the vicinity of modern Tenryūji.

ence to the various historical documents that give glimpses of the character of Gofukakusa. This approach is wrong-headed, since to accept the happenings that occur in this work as historical fact is to ignore its character as a fictional nikki.

People tend to treat *Towazugatari* as a factual nikki, because most of the characters appear under real designations, and most of the incidents depicted accord with historical fact. But the fictitious names given to two of the work's most central characters, Snow Dawn and Dawn Moon, are an indication of the author's intention of eliminating the factual nature of the work. Previous scholars have argued, for example, that Snow Dawn is Saionji Sanekanu (1249-1322). But Sanekanu is cited by name and appears in various places as Major Counselor Saionji (1:29, for example) and Sanekanu (1:82). Why would the author use both real names and elegant sobriquets for this character? The answer to this question is that Snow Dawn is used only in love scenes between the heroine and this character; when a character appears with a name that could not have existed in reality, it indicates the fictional nature of the episodes. Even if Sanekanu actually saw this nikki, he would have enjoyed immensely the depiction of himself as an elegant playboy, fully aware that it was a fiction.

Dawn Moon never appears under a real name in *Towazugatari*, and so there has been a great deal of speculation as to his identity. Some have suggested that he is the priestly Prince Shōjo (1247-82), who was Gofukakusa's stepbrother. Others argue that he is Hōjo (1227-84), the son of Kujō Michiie, and the predecessor of Shōjo. It makes better sense to consider Dawn Moon's failure to appear with an actual name further testimony to his fictional nature, along with what transpires in the episodes where he appears.

The terms, "His Majesty" ("In") and "the New In" ("Shin'in") are also elegant sobriquets. In order to set the time frame of the work, the author does write, "When Kameyama In was the reigning tennō and upon that sovereign's abdication" (3:155). But in the scene in which the heroine and the two royal brothers share a bed chamber (3:179-83), only the sobriquet "the New In" is used. Therefore, the scenes in which "His Majesty" or "the New In" appear are fictional.

THE HABIT of calling the first three books of this work the "court section" and the last two books the "travel account section" has become established among critics. That is all very well, but it is important to bear in mind both that the last two books merely deal with subject matter that is suggestive of a travel account and that the travel account section has the same intrinsic character as the preceding books, that of a fictional nikki. On his death bed, the heroine's father says: "If you should incur the ill will of your Lord and of the world and find you are unable to manage, you are immediately to enter holy orders where you can work toward your own salvation, repay your debts to your parents, and pray that we might all be together in paradise" (1:25). The heroine takes these dying words to heart. She has seen the picture scroll, *An Account of Saigyō's Pilgrimages*, and has wished that she too might leave the world and write a record of her travels (1:52). The last two books are this "record of my pilgrimages" (shugyō no ki) and without it *Towazugatari* would be an unfinished work. The last two books do not give us a travel account (kikō no ki) at all, but an account of pilgrimages (shugyō no ki). How, then, does the addition of these two books make *Towazugatari* a finished work? The following famous verses appear in the parable of the burning house in the *Lotus Sūtra*:

> Already away from the burning house of the Three Worlds
> The Buddha resides in serene solitude in the forests and fields.
> (3:53)[16]

The Three Worlds, the space in which all living things exist, is a place of confusion and agony, like a burning house. In order to become a buddha, one must cleanse one's heart in the forests and fields. In both Tendai and Zen, the meditative practice of jōza sammai (spiritual concentration through sitting) is an important technique for achieving awakening. There is also, however, the less widely known meditative technique jōgyō sammai (spiritual concentration through walking). Originally, this referred to the technique of achieving spiritual concentration by walking around an image of the Amida Buddha within a temple's devotional hall, but it could also be extended to the act of walking in forests and fields. If one held an image of the Amida Buddha firmly in mind while walking, the act was no different from practicing jōgyō sammai in a temple. The idea that wandering around from province to province was a form of Buddhist devotion sprang originally from this kind of logic. We may, therefore, call the first three books of *Towazugatari* the "burning house section," and the last two books the "forests and fields section."

Of course, the idea that wandering around the country could become a form of Buddhist devotion did not originate with the author of *Towazugatari*. It had existed for some time, and in Nijō's period, *Saigyō no Shugyō no Ki (An Account of Saigyō's Pilgrimages)* was probably a typical statement of it. Unfortunately, there is no extant text of this work, and its nature is not known. From the allusion to it in *Towazugatari* (1:52),

[16] [On the parables and other features of the *Lotus Sūtra*, see Miner–Odagiri–Morrell, 1985, 385-88.—Ed.]

it does not appear to have been the same work as the *Saigyō Monogatari* or *Saigyō Monogatari Emaki*, but it must have been similar.[17]

In considering travel accounts after the mid-thirteenth century, it is also essential to bear in mind that a new presentation of Saigyō was created. For example, there are accounts of the *Senjūshō* that are written in such a way as to suggest that they are Saigyō's own work, and the figure drawn is the perfect image of a wandering poet-priest.[18] Here is a typical example (7:220): "Thinking that I would like to fulfill my long-held wish to renounce the world and make pilgrimages to hallowed sites while seeing interesting places. . . ."[19] This image is not necessarily consistent with the version of Saigyō available from his poems or their topic-prefaces (daikotoba). This is also true of the portrait of Saigyō that emerges from *Saigyō Monogatari*, and it may be concluded that the transformation of Saigyō's image occurred in the period in which these works were written.

The belief that traveling was a kind of religious devotion worked in the background of this transformation of Saigyō, in which he came to be thought of in terms of the vision of a wandering poet-priest, a vision that reinforced the identification of travel and devotion. Many travel accounts, both in classical Japanese prose and in quasi-classical Japanese prose, appear in the period from the fourteenth century to the seventeenth, and almost all are characterized by an underlying religious outlook. They are quite different from Chinese travel accounts, which are just that, travel accounts.

The religious outlook that informs Japanese travel accounts is not necessarily limited to Buddhism. It grows as well from beliefs about communing with place spirits that had existed since Yamato times long past. Everywhere a poet-priest went, he had to seek out the places that had adorned verse (utamakura). As a person dedicated to the vocation (michi) of poetry, it was natural for a poet-traveler to recall the famous waka that had given the famous place its renown and take pleasure in responding to it sensitively in the setting that had inspired it. But it was also extremely important for the traveler to commune with the soul of the poets who had written the poems and to come into contact with the vital atmosphere of this place that had inspired earlier poets to compose what was still treasured in a later age. These poet-priests believed that the local deities who

[17] There are many variant texts (idembon) of both *Saigyō Monogatari* and *Saigyō Monogatari Emaki*, and the dates of completion of the texts are difficult to deduce. It is likely, however, that they were compiled after the middle of the thirteenth century.

[18] There are two kinds of texts of the *Senjūshō*, of which the larger contains one hundred and twenty-one chapters. Four of these are written in a style very much like Saigyō's, eight more are close to this style, and nineteen may possibly be by him; *Senjūshō*, Introduction, 340-41.

[19] ["Interesting places" ("omoshiroki tokoro") refers here to the famous places (meisho), one kind of poetic adornment (utamakura).—Trans., Ed.]

had given the earlier poet inspiration lived on in each tree and blade of grass, as also in the mountains and rivers of the locality. It was essential to visit these places personally to engage in silent communion with these deities (Plutschow, 1983, 20-51).

This belief was not restricted to places celebrated in poetry, but also pertained to places where some famous incident of the past had occurred. The spirits of the main characters of these incidents, whose actions and circumstances had been recounted and passed down through generations and still lived in people's memories, remained in these places. Likewise, the deities who had influenced their actions continued to exert their subtle dominion. Communion with these spirits and deities would give people who visited the place something that they had not had before. This is a religion without doctrine or metaphysics, something that should be viewed as a pre-religious primitive mentality. Nevertheless, the Japanese of this period did not distinguish it from religion. It became linked with the Buddhist concept of travel as a religious act, and it was widely believed that visiting places of name (nadokoro), including shrines and temples, places famous in poems (utamakura), and the sites of historical incidents had the significance of a religious pilgrimage.

Travel accounts of this type based on religious mentality were written in great numbers after the beginning of the fourteenth century.[20] For the modern reader, however, they amount to nothing more than a huge collection of extremely boring texts. It is natural that people with no particular sympathy for Buddhist austerities and little knowledge of waka should discover nothing of interest in them, but their large numbers make clear that they were extremely appealing to contemporary audiences.

Among these travel accounts, the most outstanding is Sōgi's *Tsukushi Michi no Ki.* It depicts Sōgi's travels in Tsukushi [Chikuzen and Chikugo provinces in north central Kyushu] between the sixth day of the Ninth Month and the twentieth day of the Tenth Month of 1480. The account is taken up almost completely with pilgrimages to shrines and temples and visits to famous places. These correspond to the "hallowed sites" and "interesting places" in the *Senjūshō*, and Sōgi's assessments of these locations are especially revealing. For example, he describes his visit to Utsurahama in the following (*Tsukushi Michi no Ki*, 92):

[20] Fifty-one kinds of texts of travel accounts have been identified from the period between the beginning of the fourteenth century to the end of the fifteenth (Fukuda-Plutschow, 1975, 76-235). This list, however, is limited to texts for which there exist edited texts with colophons. If travel accounts that have been transmitted only in woodblock-printed texts or manuscripts were added, the number would be much greater. Until recently, Japanese scholars have had little interest in this literature, and with a few exceptions (Shirai, 1976) very little research has been done on them. However, Donald Keene (1984) has taken up the much neglected field and has brought to these works a detailed and sympathetic treatment.

> The pine forest near this beach stretches far into the distance, offering a view that is in no way inferior to the famous pines of Hakozaki. Indeed, it is without comparison. However, since this is not a place of name [nadokoro], I gave it no attention—just as in the vocation of waka, one would ignore a waka not composed by a poet of a recognized house or a person of high social standing.

Even though Sōgi recognizes that Utsurahama is at least equal to Hakozaki, he sees no need to accord it attention because it is not recorded as a famous place. He bases this judgment on the same logic that would lead him to disqualify a waka from inclusion in a royal anthology if it were not written by someone poetically or socially important. A place was acknowledged by society to be a place of name because it had a historic background and that historic background had been formed and maintained by a great number of people over a long period of time. The authority of this pedigree took precedence over the personal judgment of the talented individual. This logic was not unique to Sōgi but was shared by all the people of the period.

An interest in famous places grew after the beginning of the fourteenth century and so did the number of travel accounts. The *Meisho Hōgakushō*, which is said to have been compiled by Sōgi, is one of the works that satisfied the demand created by this swell of interest.[21] Whether or not a place should be acknowledged as a nadokoro was commonly decided by determining whether a famous waka had been written about it. For these reasons, a comprehensive guide to utamakura was called for, and Chōgetsu's *Utamakura Nayose* was compiled to meet the need.[22] The people who visited nadokoro were well versed in the classics, and it must have been a simple matter for them to write down their experiences. This accounts for the great volume of travel accounts written during the period.

Of course, there seem to have been many people who never felt the need to record every iota of a visit to a famous place. One indication of this is the character who commonly appears as the waki in nō, the monk wandering around the provinces. At the beginning of the performance, this character more or less simply enumerates the names of places he has passed before coming to the place where the incidents of the drama occur. This part of the performance of a nō play, the michiyuki, arouses little enthusiasm in all but a few in audiences today. But when these plays were

[21] Sōgi is usually considered the compiler, without firm evidence. From the wide circulation of the work, we may deduce at least that it was completed before the sixteenth century. Only manuscripts and woodblock editions are extant. [On poetic place names and for examples, see Miner-Odagiri-Morrell, 1985, 435-41.—Ed.]

[22] It has been inferred that the text was completed immediately before the compilation of the *Shingosenshū* in 1303 (Shibuya, 1979, 107). A hokku by Chōgetsu is included in the *Tsukuba Shū*, 20:2045.

written, people knew that each of the places the waki mentions held significance. The wandering priest has communed with the deities and spirits of all of these famous places, and having been infused with their charisma, he is already in no ordinary state. Moreover, the special place in which the incidents of the drama are about to take place is also a place of name (nadokoro). Here, the waki will encounter the incarnation of a dead spirit, the spirit of a living person, a buddha, or a deity, and fall into conversation. This is possible precisely because the monk is in the special state of having received the vitality of the deities of all the various famous places he has visited on his travels, and it is this that made the michiyuki an absolute necessity. Modern viewers who find the michiyuki scenes in nō performances a bore, will no doubt find Sōgi's travel account equally monotonous.

The End of Factual Monogatari

The appearance of the *Towazugatari* so long after the *Izumi Shikibu Nikki* marked the end of the genre of fictional nikki. As if in concert, the *Masukagami* (*The Larger Mirror*) brought to its conclusion the genre of the factual monogatari. Just as with the fictional nikki, the factual monogatari ended because it had become increasingly difficult by the fourteenth century for people to write literary works in pure classical Japanese prose. In such a period, the author of the *Masukagami* must have had special training in the classics. This has led to the theory, influential up to now, that the author was Nijō Yoshimoto. This theory lacks external evidence and does not rise above the level of conjecture. It is not conjecture but a positive fact, however, that the author must have been someone at Yoshimoto's level of erudition and talent.

Previous appraisals of *Masukagami* have been by no means uniformly favorable. The established view is that the author expended too much effort in depicting the eclipse of life at court and that serious political criticism is lacking. In terms of social criticism, the *Masukagami* may of course be compared to the *Ōkagami*, and it is certainly true that the earlier work contains more overt criticism of contemporary politics, based on the standard of justice (dōri) (see vol. two, ch. 8). However, the vigor of a work's social or political criticism should not be the only criterion on which to judge its worth.

In fact, there is overt political criticism in the *Masukagami*. In one passage the author comments on the fact that three cloistered sovereigns had been exiled during the Jōkyū War (1221). Again, rulers have often become embroiled in internal conflicts in both Japan and China, but, "There seems to be almost no precedent in this country for events such as occur today, when emperors war with subjects beneath notice and are ruined"

(2:277). This is frank enough criticism of the state of contemporary politics. After all, "subjects beneath notice" (muge no tami) refers directly to the de facto rulers of the Kamakura shogunate, the Hōjō family. In general, however, social and political criticism in the *Masukagami* is covert, and it is often difficult to comprehend how society and politics are being criticized. This is because the critical approach of the *Masukagami* involves simple relation of what has occurred, leaving it to the reader to draw negative judgments. The key to evaluation is hidden in the work, something I wish to show by one example from the *Masukagami.*

Ōmiya no In, the Middle Consort of Gosaga Tennō, invites Princess Yasuko, the former Ise Shrine Priestess and half-sister of Gofukakusa In, to Kameyama Palace in Saga.[23] It happens that Gofukakusa is also visiting Ōmiya no In. He is overcome by the princess's beauty and, although she is his half-sister, resolves to have an affair with her. He enlists the aid of a certain grand counselor's daughter and succeeds in seducing the princess. Once he has accomplished this seduction, however, he immediately loses interest in her and makes no further attempt to approach her. The broken-hearted princess is now approached by Saionji Sanekanu. His sincerity moves even the lady who had adopted the princess, and an informal marriage is publicly acknowledged.[24] Because of an unfortunate mistake, however, the princess spends a single night with Nijō Morotada (1254-1341). Sanekanu learns of that night and ceases his visits. In due course, she is known to be pregnant, and though his heart aches with jealousy, Sanekanu makes careful arrangements for the delivery, also taking measures to ensure that the child will be thought to be his own. When the princess dies fifteen years later, Sanekanu grieves deeply (*Masukagami*, 9:350-56). While this may appear to be a straightforward retelling of events, it must not be overlooked that there is incisive social criticism of royalty in the very fact that this incident is related in the *Masukagami.*

Like the *Ōkagami* and the *Imakagami*, the *Masukagami* is a factual monogatari, and as such it is natural that its principal subject matter should be political events. Contemporary readers, who were familiar with the public events of their time, must have felt it highly inappropriate that personal love affairs such as the ones related above were interspersed in the account. But this feeling of dissonance is precisely the key to the work's social criticism. Matters that do not normally appear in factual, historical monogatari are related in the *Masukagami* for no other reason than that the author thought they should be told.

The narrator of the *Masukagami* does not particularly criticize Gofu-

[23] Ōmiya no In was the mother of Gofukakusa and Kameyama (see n. 7). [The Former Ise Priestess Yasuko was the daughter of Gosaga and another lady.—Trans.]

[24] Among the daughters of Palace Minister Konoe Michitsune (1184-1238), there is a woman recorded as "The adoptive mother of Princess Yasuko."

kakusa's actions. In the passage in which Gofukakusa is first attracted to the princess, the narrator does insert the reflection that "his character is reprehensible" (3:351). This is a conventional expression, however, that appears often in the *Genji* and other monogatari and, in fact, it has something of a bantering tone. It should not be interpreted as serious criticism. Rather, the criticism implicit in this passage is precisely that intimate human actions that should not, given genre expectations, have been related in a factual monogatari are deliberately brought out.

This indirect means had been the orthodox method for criticizing the actions of historical personages in Chinese histories for centuries since the *Ch'un-ch'iu* (*The Spring and Autumn Annals*, 722-481 B.C.). By simply recording the facts of an action, without comment on its good or evil nature, this method forces readers to judge for themselves whether the actions depicted are good or evil—because of the fact itself that they have been recorded. Indeed, we must recognize that in attempting this kind of criticism that does not rely on direct statement of opinions, the author of the *Masukagami* shows a deeper understanding of the critical nature of Chinese histories than the author of the *Ōkagami*.

Criticisms of this nature may also be seen in the passage in which the speaker relates how Gofukakusa used as his go-between to the princess "the daughter of a certain major counselor, a person he employed near his person."[25] This lady was Nijō, the heroine of *Towazugatari*, and it was a widely known fact among the nobility of the late fourteenth century that she was Gofukakusa's favorite at this time. However permissive the period may have been in affairs of the heart, it must have been extraordinary to have one lover act as the go-between for another. It did not particularly matter that Nijō had written about this incident in a work belonging to the genre of the fictional nikki, but that it should be related in a work whose generic principle is the recording of historical fact—that was clearly a criticism of Gofukakusa.

In *Towazugatari*, Gofukakusa lost interest in the princess because she, unversed in the arts of love that would have enabled her to lead him on, yielded to him too easily (*Towazugatari*, 1:59). But while the heroine-speaker criticizes the princess and "has to agree" with His Majesty when he says "The cherry blossom is beautiful to behold, but its branches are fragile and too easily broken" (1:59), his selfish behavior in the affair is also not to be forgiven. The *Masukagami* states no opinion whatsoever on this incident, but instead places the emphasis on Sanekanu's sincerity. The corresponding passage in *Masukagami* concludes with the notation: "It is said that the major counselor was deeply saddened by the death of the princess on the fifteenth day of the Second Month of 1284" (3:356).

[25] The major counselor referred to here is of course Koga Masatada.

This has the effect of creating an impression of Sanekanu that stands in sharp contrast to Gofukakusa's "reprehensible character." However indirect, this is incisive criticism.

There are many other examples in the *Masukagami* of this kind of implicit criticism. It has often been pointed out that a characteristic aspect of the work is its minute description of a great number of court ceremonies and functions, and many scholars support the explanation that this is a manifestation of a spirit of longing for the elegant life (miyabi) of the court in its golden days. Such an explanation is not wrong. But was it only a longing for the past that inspired the author to record such an enormous number of ceremonies and functions in such minute detail? However much the author may have been addicted to things traditional, if the readers of the work had had no interest in descriptions of ceremonies and functions, such descriptions would have had no effect. There would have been no reason to repeat again and yet again such details as how the ceremonial halls were decorated, who was in attendance, what kinds of music and dance were performed, who wore what, and what waka were composed. There must have been no small number of people who found these descriptions "beautiful," and they would have belonged to the nobility. Now the reproduction of the elegant ceremonies and functions of the courtly past was nothing other than criticism directed at the warrior class, which suffered from backwardness in cultural matters.

It is important to note, however, that in the case of the *Masukagami*, this criticism is not a hostile view of the behavior of the warriors, criticizing their faults from nobles' point of view. Although the Kamakura bakufu [warrior government] had a certain respect for the culture of the court nobility, it was working to establish a tradition for the military houses. It was essential for them to have a system of norms for living and behavior that would be appropriate to a class whose mission was military affairs. Without such a system, the bakufu's administrative system would be unworkable. The birth of the so-called ancient conventions of the samurai was based on this requirement. Accordingly, this system of mores and norms was deeply rooted in the relatively simple customs of the local areas from which the warrior class sprang, and its rationale differed from the conventions of the court nobility, which were a collection of precedents accumulated over centuries (Fuji, 1949, 69-73).

In order to reorganize the conventions of the samurai into a systematic code of behavior, however, it was impossible for the bakufu to avoid incorporating many norms and customs of the nobility, which had reached a high degree of elaboration. As a consequence, the public, formal life of the warrior class gradually assumed more and more features of the court nobility. This tendency accelerated with the advent of the Muromachi bakufu. Indeed, Yoshimitsu (shogun, 1368-94), the third Ashikaga shogun, simultaneously held the court position of great minister of state (dajōdaijin), and from his time onward, the ceremonies and functions of the bakufu adopted the conventions of the court nobility on an increasingly large scale.

The aspiration of the warrior elite for mastery of the stately court traditions provided the nobles a clear reason for being—to provide an outstanding paradigm of the way of life of an advanced cultural elite. Therefore, while ceremonies and observances such as those depicted in the *Masukagami* were actually being performed in real life, the act of describing them repeatedly and in great detail in a literary work had the added benefits of pointing out the cultural differences between the warrior elite and the court nobility and of helping the warrior to approach more closely the level of the nobility. The didactic quality of guidance may be viewed as a form of social and political criticism. The *Masukagami*, which dates from the mid-fourteenth century, must have provided important information for the warriors of Yoshimitsu's period, during which the beauty of yūen was perfected.

The critical and pedagogical qualities of the *Masukagami* are not the only criterion upon which it deserves high esteem. Yet more important is the beauty of its classical prose style. There are few works of pure classical Japanese prose that equal the *Masukagami* in the High Middle Ages.[26] This may be easily appreciated by comparing it to other works that it used as source material. It is well known, for example, that one source of material for the *Masukagami* is *Towazugatari*, and this suggests the interest of comparing corresponding passages.[27] Here are the passages in which Gofukakusa succeeds in seducing the former Ise Shrine Priestess with the help of Lady Nijō.

> *Masukagami*
> His Majesty, . . . on calling to his side the daughter of a certain great counselor, a lady closely connected to and intimate with the Shrine Priestess, says to her with great earnestness, "It is not my intention that she should yield her favors, only that I should like just enough intimacy so that I could acquaint her with my affection, since once lost, this unexpected chance would be lost forever," and it may be wondered what thoughts may be going through the lady's mind, as the Shrine Princess in her case finds herself listening to him; it seems neither dream nor reality, so distressed are her spirits; and yet to him

[26] Book 16 of the *Masukagami*, "Kume no Sarayama," is translated almost in its entirety in Keene, 1955, 242-57 under the title "The Exile of Godaigo." The lucid, well-wrought, and elegant style of the text may be appreciated also in this English translation.

[27] Yamagishi, 1940, 351-56.

she seems neither about to expire nor faint but to have a beauty delicate and touching in its bearing. (351-52)

Towazugatari

No sooner was he in his own quarters than he turned to me and asked, "What should I do? What should I do?" I had foreseen this turn of events, but I was nevertheless amazed when he said, "You have been with me since you were a child. Now you can prove your love by conveying my feelings to her." Immediately I was sent with a message . . . and gave her the message. She blushed deeply and put the letter aside without replying, without even looking at it. "What shall I tell His Majesty," I asked. "I have no idea how to reply to such an unexpected message," she said, and went back to sleep. (1:57-58)

Given the differences in these passages between first- and third-person narrative and the approaches taken to characterization, it is difficult to make a simple judgment about the literary merits of the two works. Yet there is in *Towazugatari* His Majesty's importunate commission to Nijō, which can be paraphrased to show just how crass it is: "You have served me since you were a girl, and I have made much of you. If you can handle this business well, you will give me proof that you really love me." In contrast to this rude coercion, Gofukakusa's reasonable tone in the *Masukagami* is striking. It gives him a dignity befitting a cloistered sovereign (in) and a delicate sensibility of one used to dealing with women. With few exceptions, contemporary readers would have given high praise to the handling in *Masukagami.*

Moreover, following the passage in *Towazugatari* there is a detailed description of the heroine's leading His Majesty to the princess' bed chamber where, feigning sleep, she keeps track of their lovemaking from behind a screen. In *Masukagami,* this is dealt with by a simple but significant remark, "it may be wondered what thoughts may be going through the lady's mind. . . ." Scenes of seduction such as this appear in any number of previous fictional monogatari, and with details of these scenes readily available to contemporary readers, the terser version of the scene in *Masukagami* could have been easily appreciated by simply substituting details from earlier works.

Even from these few examples, it should be clear that the style of *Masukagami* possesses a wonderful lucidity, in which features of a scene that can be abbreviated are merely suggested, with a classical elegance that makes full use of diction precedented in the corpus of literature in pure Japanese prose.[28] It may be easier for modern readers to appreciate *To-*

[28] [Some readers at least may wish to gain a sense of the clear style of the *Masukagami*

wazugatari, with its persistent determination to tell all about fantastic happenings in a treatment that cannot be seen elsewhere, but for then-contemporary readers it must have been rather the language of *Masukagami* that was attractive. As pure classical Japanese prose, it combines the elements of lucidity, elaborate craft, and courtly elegance, and it deserves high marks even from our modern point of view.

It is well worth noting that the narration of *Masukagami* is in the present tense. According to my definition, the basic mood of monogatari is the past tense (vol. two, ch. 8). The use of the present tense in the *Masukagami* is related to the condition of Japanese prose in the fourteenth century as it became increasingly difficult, in terms of phraseology and diction, to write pure Japanese prose, and prose degenerated into something that may be called quasi-Japanese prose.

The Advent of Zuihitsu

As was just suggested, after the beginning of the fourteenth century, Japanese prose degenerated, transforming into a kind of quasi-Japanese characterized by an increasing number of Chinese elements. This phenomenon may be considered a reflection of the gradual transformation that had taken place in the Japanese language itself since the twelfth century, in which a considerable gap developed between the language actually spoken and the now classical language that had been employed by the court nobility of the tenth and eleventh centuries. Among the many causes of this transformation, the most important was the rise of intellectual thought in literature, which made writing impossible without the Sinified words and styles of diction borrowed from kambun [Chinese prose by Japanese]. Pure Japanese, the language of Yamato, is rich in vocabulary for expressing emotions and can distinguish subtle differences that are quite impossible to depict in English. On the other hand, it is limited in the kind of vocabulary necessary for expressing intellectual thought with precision. It was thus inevitable that writers were compelled to use increasingly numerous textures of Chinese prose and kambun. The advance of quasi-Japanese prose, and the rise of Japanese prose in the mixed style to become the standard in intellectual prose (bunshō) after the beginning of the fourteenth century, should be understood, therefore, to reflect the serious attention given to intellectual matters by literary writers

---

extolled by the author. Perhaps it will seem to them as to me an easier version of the *Genji Monogatari*, resembling the Uji chapters in shifts of point of view. Here, then, is the latter half of the quotation, beginning with (first two words) the thoughts of the Lady (Nijō): ". . . ikaga tabakariken, yume utsutsu to mo naku kikoetamaeba, ito kokoro ushi to obosedo, aeka ni kiemadoi nado wa shitamawazu, rōtaku, nayonayo to shite, aware naru onkewai nari."—Ed.]

of the time. This is consistent with the intellectual history of the period, during which the intellectual culture of the Sung was zealously imported.

Among these cultural imports was the literary genre of sui-pi (J. zuihitsu). The word sui-pi, which means "following the writing brush," was first employed by Hung Mai (1123-1203), who defined it as a literary work with neither systematic structure nor order, in which one writes things down just as they come to mind (see vol. two, ch. 8). If this is made the only criterion for defining the genre, all nonfiction prose works that have no particular order may be considered to be zuihitsu, and, in the late eighteenth century, the opinion appeared that even the *Makura no Sōshi (The Pillow Book)* is a zuihitsu, a view that is established even now. Besides the criterion defined by Hung Mai, another characteristic of Chinese sui-pi is interest in intellectual matters. This is clear from the actual works in the genre. Hung Mai did not touch on this point, but it would have been awkward for him to describe his own work as one "for the enrichment of the intellect." Moreover, he must have expected his readers to understand this point immediately when they read his work, the *Yung-chai Sui-pi*. The *Makura no Sōshi*, with its sensitivity of observation, should be classified generically as a Japanese prose nikki loosely ordered. It should not be entered into the genre of zuihitsu. Japan's first zuihitsu was Kenkō's *Tsurezuregusa (Essays in Idleness)* which was also the first fruit of direct reception of the new culture of the Sung.[29]

The route by which Kenkō (1283-1352?) came into contact with Sung intellectual writing is not clear, but his references to the *Lun-yü* (J. *Rongo*; *The Analects of Confucius*) in *Tsurezuregusa* are indicative of the connection of that work with Sung Neoconfucianism.[30] Before the thirteenth century, Japanese Confucian scholarship was mainly concerned with the study of the Five Classics.[31] The Four Books were transmitted to Japan in the twelfth century, but it was impossible in that period for the traditional houses of Confucian scholarship, such as the Ōe or Kiyohara families, to conduct study of them based on the new Sung commentaries.[32] This kind of study was first conducted and later developed

[29] Keene, 1967, 242-57. [Quotations and citations are taken from Keene with slight revisions.—Trans.]

[30] Kenkō was the son of Urabe Kaneaki, a low-ranking courtier. [His other surname, Yoshida, is from the place in Kyoto where he lived.—Ed.] Before renouncing the world, he held the fifth court rank and served in the royal guards of the right as Urabe Kaneyoshi (the Japanese reading of Kenkō, his priestly name). Kenkō refers to the *Analects* in dan (parts, sections) 122, 104-105; 129, 108; and 211, 174.

[31] The Five Classics (Su-ching; J. Gokyō) are the *I-ching* (J. *Ekikyō*; *The Classic of Changes*); the *Shih-ching* (J. *Shikyō*; *The Classic of Poetry*); the *Shang-shu* or *Shu Ching* (J. *Shōsho, Shokyō*; *The Documents of Old*); the *Li-chi* (J. *Raiki*; *The Rites*); and, the *Ch'un-ch'iu (Shunjū*; *The Spring and Autumn Annals)*. These books made up the required curriculum of the universities of the T'ang, and this tradition was continued in Japan.

[32] [The Four Books (Ssu-shu; J. Shisho) are the *Lun-yü* (J. *Rongo*; *Analects of Confucius*); the *Meng-tsu* (J. *Mōshi*; *Mencius*); the *Ta-hsüeh* (J. *Daigaku*; *The Great Learning*); and the

further by the Zen monks, who were in close contact with Sung scholarship and fully aware of its importance. Beginning with Enni Ben'en (1202-80), study had been advanced gradually by Rankei Dōryū (1213-78), Nampo Shōmei (1235-1308), and Kōhō Kennichi (1241-1316). The most striking developments occurred in the period of Kokan Shiren (1278-1346), Chūgen Engetsu (1300-75), and Gidō Shūshin (1325-88; Haga, 1956, 57-64). It is demonstrable that Kenkō wrote *Tsurezuregusa* sometime in the first part of the fourteenth century, a period in which secular literati were still highly conscious of the newness of Sung intellectual thought.[33] He came into contact with this new culture, making sui-pi, or zuihitsu, his own.

Even without presenting external evidence demonstrating how Kenkō obtained a text of the *Lun-yü* with commentaries by Sung Confucian scholars, or that the *Yung-chai Sui-pi* had entered Japan by the first half of the fourteenth century, it can be shown that it was his contact with Sung scholarship that induced Kenkō to write his *Tsurezuregusa*. The evidence involves his use of the concept of ri [Ch. li; reason, principle, etc.] characteristic of Sung Neoconfucianism and the resemblance of the *Tsurezuregusa* to Sung sui-pi.

One of the reasons that the *Tsurezuregusa* continues to offer much of interest today is that it presents completely unexpected opinions concerning the routine happenings of everyday life. Moreover, despite their apparent strangeness and even paradox, once fully pondered, they are eminently reasonable. Here are some examples:

> A house should be built with the summer in mind. In winter it is possible to live anywhere. (55, 50)[34]

> In everything, no matter what it may be, uniformity is undesirable. (82, 70)

> Three kinds of people make desirable friends. First is the friend who gives you things; second, a doctor; and third, the friend with wisdom. (117, 99)

Chung-yung (J. *Chūyō*; *The Doctrine of the Mean*). The Four Books were esteemed in China after the great synthesis of Neoconfucian thought by Chu Hsi (1130-1200). In Japan this esteem was not gained until after the beginning of the fourteenth century. For further information, see Miner-Odagiri-Morrell, 1985, 394-96.—Trans., Ed.] The *Chu-tzu Yü-lei (The Record of the Sayings of Chu Hsi)* and other Confucian commentaries of the time contain a large number of Sung colloquialisms beyond the comprehension of Japanese scholars of the Confucian families, who knew only written prose.

[33] There are a number of theories concerning the precise date of completion of the *Tsurezuregusa*, but each involves a premise based on some assumption, and in fact we do not know.

[34] [The first number in the citation is that of the dan or part in the original and the second the page number in Keene, 1967. The quotations given are not of complete dan but rather are famous "sayings" from the work.—Ed.]

> Are we to look at cherry blossoms only in full bloom, the moon only when it is cloudless? (137, 115)
>
> All people should be ignorant and without talent. (232, 190) [That is, the clever will outwit us, and the gifted will tyrannize us.]

If one reflects clearly on everyday life, all these observations are supported by a ri (rational principle) of which anyone would approve. Kenkō explains this logic in terms very easy to understand (143, 129):

> When I hear people say that someone's last hours were splendid, I always think how impressive it would be if they meant merely that the end was peaceful and free of agony; but foolish people embellish the story with strange and unusual details, singling out for praise words said or things done that suit their own preferences, but that hardly accord with the person's usual behavior.
>
> This great occasion is not to be evaluated even by an incarnation of the Buddha, nor can learned doctors judge it. As long as someone does nothing unseemly at the hour of death, nothing people may have seen or heard is of significance.

From this it is clear that Kenkō's ri is not unlike refined common sense, a characteristic his *Tsurezuregusa* shares with the prose works of the Sung.

Kenkō's ri is manifested not only in what he says, but also in the way he develops his arguments. In a number of dan, one discovers a logical structure appropriate to the character of the subject. An analysis of the thirty-eighth dan will provide an excellent example of this. Its theme is the vanity of wealth and fame. The theme is clearly sounded at the very beginning (38, 34).

> What a foolish thing it is to be governed by a desire for fame and profit and to fret away one's whole life without a moment of peace.

This topic sentence serves not only to introduce the argument but to state the conclusion. What follows is the development of the argument. Kenkō deals first with profit and then with fame, demonstrating that the pursuit of either is meaningless. His argument about profit leads to an intermediary conclusion: since riches are not the source of true happiness, "it is an exceedingly stupid man who will torment himself for the sake of worldly gain" (38, 34-35). This is followed by the discussion of fame, which is further divided into rank and position. Kenkō considers both to be nothing more than temporary existences and concludes that "a feverish craving for high rank and position is second in foolishness only to seeking wealth" (38, 35). In order to demonstrate why the pursuit both of profit and of fame is foolish, Kenkō argues that there is no absolute value intrinsic to the things usually sought, and in fact they are much the same as things agreed to be worthless. Those who pursue those things are deluded and mistaken. In his closing synthesis, Kenkō concludes: "All is unreality. Nothing is worth discussing, worth desiring" (38-36). The intellectual organization of the dan will emerge in the course of quoting the whole, with appropriate divisions and headings added.[35]

1. Introduction (and conclusion):

   What a foolish thing it is to be governed by a desire for fame and profit and to fret away one's whole life without a moment of peace. (34)

2. Development (profit and fame)

   (i) The denial of profit:

   Great wealth is no guarantee of security. Wealth, in fact, tends to attract *calamities* and *disaster*. Even if, after you die, you leave enough gold to prop up the North Star, it will only prove a nuisance for your heirs. The pleasures that delight the foolish man are likewise meaningless to the man of discrimination who considers a big carriage, sleek horses, gold, and jeweled ornaments all equally undesirable and senseless. You had best *throw away your gold in the mountains* and *drop your jewels into a ravine*. It is an exceedingly stupid man who will torment himself for the sake of worldly gain. (34-35)

   (ii) The denial of fame (rank and position)

   (a) Short introduction (the general character of fame):

   To leave behind a reputation that will not perish through long ages to come is certainly to be desired. (35)

   (b) Denial of the correlation between high position and a person's wisdom or folly:

   But can one say that men of high rank and position are necessarily superior? There are *foolish* and *incompetent* men who, *having been born into an illustrious family* and, *being favored by the times, rise to exalted position* and *indulge themselves in the extremes of luxury*. There are also many *learned* and *good* men who by their own choice *remain in humble position* and end their days without ever *having encountered good fortune*. A feverish craving for high rank and position is second in foolishness only to seeking wealth. (35)

[35] [The following passages constitute the entirety of the thirty-eighth dan. Italicized words and phrases are examples of parallelism in Kenkō's prose style, which will be discussed below.—Trans.]

(c) Denial of the permanence of fame:

One would like to leave behind a glorious reputation for surpassing wisdom and character, but careful reflection will show that what we mean by love of a glorious reputation is delight in the approbation of others. Neither those who praise nor those who abuse last for long, and the people who have heard their reports are likely to depart the world as quickly. *Before whom then should we feel ashamed? By whom should we wish to be appreciated?* Fame also inspires backbiting. A craving after fame is next most foolish. (35)

(iii) Denial of a fixed view of value:

If I were to address myself to those who nevertheless seek desperately to attain knowledge and wisdom, I would say that knowledge leads to deceit, and artistic talent is the product of much suffering. True knowledge is not what one hears from others or acquires through study. What, then, are we to call knowledge? Proper and improper come to one and the same thing—can we call anything good? The truly enlightened man has *no learning, no virtue, no accomplishments, no fame. Who knows of him, who will report his glory*? It is not that he *conceals his virtue or pretends to be stupid*; it is because from the outset he is above distinctions between wise and foolish, between profit and loss.

If, in your delusion, you seek fame and profit, the results will be as I have described. (35)

3. Conclusion (and emphasis through repetition):

All is unreality. *Nothing is worth discussing, nothing worth desiring.* (36)

Surely this is a truly well ordered, systematic structure. Kenkō's handling is very subtle, minutely calculated. His use of "foolishness" provides a good example. In (1) he introduces a generalized "foolishness," and then in (2, i) an "exceedingly stupid man," that is, a great fool. Finally, in (b) and (c) of (2, ii), Kenkō takes up the "next most foolish," a fool of a lower order. There is consummate skill in this repetition qualified by suitable variation.

Kenkō's mastery extends to his prose rhythms. Readers accustomed to the pure Japanese of earlier monogatari and nikki may well find the prose of *Tsurezuregusa* rather abrupt and choppy. In fact, however, there are many long sentences in this text. The feeling that sentences are generally short and choppy comes from the prose rhythm, not from the actual number of words in sentences. It may be traced further to Kenkō's use of parallelism, as in the italicized words and phrases in the passages above.

When words, phrases, and sentences of about equal length and with analogous meanings are juxtaposed, the balance so gained arrests the reader's attention. This parallelism slows the pace in just those passages where it is employed. It is extremely effective when used in places essential to the argument, where the author wishes the reader to pause and consider carefully. And even in sentences slightly long, this parallelism aids by introducing cuts (kire), saving the sentence from monotony.

Japanese literature had not seen before such logical construction to make prose impressive and persuasive, delighting a reader with the beauty of its reasoning. Nor was it known in China until the creation of new san-wen styles by Han Yü and Liu Tsung-yüan in the Middle T'ang. In their rhythm, the san-wen styles of Han and Liu possess a beauty of a different kind from p'ien-wen (elaborate, parallel prose) up to that time (vol. two, ch. 1). While these styles quickly degenerated in the Late T'ang, they were revived by Ou-yang Hsiu in the Northern Sung and reached an unprecedented level of perfection with the appearance of the great san-wen masters Su Shih and Wang An-shih. When Japanese Zen monks brought them from the mainland as one element of Sung culture, the san-wen styles of Han and Liu, which in fact dated from the eighth century, were still new for the Japanese of the fourteenth century. In *Tsurezuregusa*, Kenkō attempted to assimilate the "new" san-wen style into Japanese prose.

The style of the passage just discussed is not characteristic of the entire text. It is limited to dan that deal with intellectual themes; certain other dan are written in what can be called a pure Japanese prose style. Nevertheless, both qualitatively and quantitatively, Kenkō's philosophical reasoning style gives his writing its special quality, and this new prose style is the characteristic aspect of the *Tsurezuregusa* (Konishi, 1966c, 16-19). For Kenkō's contemporaries, it was a very new type of literary work.

Its novelty is to be found not only in its prose style, but also in the subjects with which it deals. If zuihitsu are considered to be "aggregates of unordered essays of no particular length," *Tsurezuregusa* is by no means new. It was preceded by *Makura no Sōshi*. However, in terms of the other salient feature of the genre—the aim to arouse or satisfy an interest in various intellectual concerns—*Tsurezuregusa* was the first true zuihitsu in Japan, and certainly the first to correspond to sui-pi in China. Here are some examples:

> Court caps in recent years have become much taller than formerly. (65, 58)

> The Toba New Road did not acquire its name after the Toba Palace was built. The name is an old one. (132, 111)

> There are honorary officials not only of the second rank but also of the fourth rank. It is so recorded in *Essentials of Statesmenship [Seiji Yōryaku]*. (198, 168)

Dan such as these are not very well regarded by modern scholars, who find in them little more than a bookish taste for antiquarian pedantry. In the fourteenth century, however, this kind of knowledge was essential even in warrior society. With the exception of a few learned scholars of the class of Ichijō Kaneyoshi, the knowledge was by no means available. The information was new for ordinary people, and the genre of the zuihitsu—which provided it in an intimate, accessible fashion—must have been extremely fresh and attractive.

The essential excellence of the *Tsurezuregusa* is found in those passages where a taste for learning leads to inquiry into intellectual issues of how to lead one's life or what it means to be human. Scholars widely share the belief that the reason this work remains so highly esteemed today is the profound, abundant understanding of life on the part of this "poetic philosopher of human life" (Nose, 1945, 12-13). Kenkō renounced the world to become a reclusive monk, but it is by no means true that he observes life only from the standpoint of Buddhism. Confucianism, the Taoist philosophy of Lao Tzu and Chuang Tzu, devotion to waka, and previous experience as a low-ranking courtier all become elements in the formation of his insights into our lives. Had he merely recorded all this knowledge at random, his zuihitsu would not be the compelling collection of insights that it is. His knowledge and experiences had to be refined until they achieved a rational principle (ri) that integrates them and gives them a synthetic structure. And it is in Kenkō's work that this kind of ri became michi (vocation).

We have seen that the michi ideal can be expressed by "many is one, one is many," and that is most explicitly defined in *Tsurezuregusa*. Of course, this clarity originates in Kenkō's humane depths. But we must not overlook that the characteristic feature of Sung Neoconfucian scholarship was the attempt to discover a unified ri in a synthesis of Confucianism with Buddhism and Taoism. *Tsurezuregusa*, which also has this character, was certainly new. Indeed, it seems to have been too new at this time, for there are no indications that it was read by many of Kenkō's contemporaries. Not until the seventeenth century, when Sung culture had spread so thoroughly, was the work widely read.

It is clear that with the *Tsurezuregusa* there was born a new Japanese literary kind of the same character as that of Chinese sui-pi. Yet we should not overlook special features that do not exist in sui-pi or in subsequent Japanese zuihitsu. While each dan of Kenkō's work is independent, study of the whole reveals subtle connections between them, achieved through techniques of association. This fact was discovered by Katō Bansai (1625-74), who called this technique raii, or linkage.[36] This immediately suggests the principle of association in royal waka anthologies, but it is even closer to the principles of tsukeai (stanzaic connection) in renga. Kenkō's period coincides with that during which the focus in renga had begun to shift from individual stanzas to the progress of entire one-hundred-stanza sequences. It is perfectly natural that he should have hit upon the happy idea of exploiting similar techniques in arranging the dan of *Tsurezuregusa*. The linkages between dan have various characters, and it appears impossible to explain them by a single principle.[37] But it is undeniable that *Tsurezuregusa* becomes even more interesting when one reads it with an appreciation of these subtle linkings (raii).

[36] The principles of raii are discussed in Bansai's *Tsurezuregusa Shō (A Commentary on Essays in Idleness)*, a work in thirteen books published in 1661. There is no extant copy of this text bearing a publisher's seal or a colophon. It is important to note here that Bansai approaches *Tsurezuregusa* from the standpoint of Tendai shikan: "Kenkō wrote of T'ien-t'ai's *Mo-ho Chih-kuan* in a gentle style, easily understood by the people."

[37] One of these interpretations follows Bansai, attempting to explain raii in terms of the ten stages of meditation in shikan contemplation outlined in the *Mo-ho Chih-kuan* (Suzuki Hisashi, 1975, 1-2). While it would be difficult to explain all of the instances of raii in *Tsurezuregusa* in such terms, the interpretation has great explanatory power in no few instances.

CHAPTER 17

The Dissemination of Prose in the Mixed Style

Historical Treatises and Embellished Histories

Sung culture was centered on conceptions of ri (Ch. li; reason, principle), and in the fourteenth century the concept became important to various aspects of Japanese culture. The transformation of historical writing during the period provides one example. Jien had already established the genre of historical treatises with his *Gukanshō* (*The Future and the Past*; 1219-20), but the concept of ri in his treatise shares many points in common with the metaphysics of Tendai Buddhism; it does not offer a criticism of contemporary society in the vein of political science. Kitabatake Chikafusa's (1293-1354) fourteenth-century treatise *Jinnō Shōtōki (A Chronicle of the Correct Succession of Deities and Sovereigns)* discusses the proper course of contemporary politics on the basis of his own political ideals. Although this work too is a historical treatise, Chikafusa's standpoint differs from Jien's. I believe that this new approach came from Sung historiography.

All Chinese histories were written for the purpose of political commentary. Even when they record only historical facts, there is always a silent but rigorous critical attitude hidden beneath the objective surface. In the Sung, this critical emphasis was further reinforced by a deliberate attempt to criticize the course of political events by the concept of ri. In particular, the attempt to formulate a theory of orthodoxy concerning the imperial succession was taken up as a powerful new theme of historical scholarship. The *Tzu-chih T'ung-chien (A Chronicle of Instructive Precedents for Contemporary Politics)*, compiled by Ssu-ma Kuang (1019-86), is one of the outstanding works that emerged from this attempt.[1] Chikafusa's historical treatise was written from the same standpoint as this important Sung record. Moreover, a direct influence may be recognized in this case, for it is known that Chikafusa studied the *Tzu-chih T'ung-chien*.[2]

[1] The *Chronicle* offers a chronological history covering the period from Chou Wei-lieh Wang (King Wei-lieh of the Chou dynasty, r. 424-401 B.C.) to Hou-Chou Shih-tsung of the later Chou (r. A.D. 954-60). The chronicle proper comprises one hundred and ninety-four books, the catalogues thirty books, and the variant traditions thirty books. It was compiled in 1084, during the Northern Sung.

[2] "People are receiving lectures on such works as *Tzu-chih T'ung-chien* and *Sung-chao T'ung-chien*. Among them Priest Kitabatake, of the rank of quasi-empress, is conducting

The *Jinnō Shōtōki* offers political criticism that takes as its standard a synthetic ideological system, and in this it truly succeeds to the spirit of Sung histories. This is clear from Chikafusa's explanation of the title of his treatise, in which he emphasizes the ideology of shōri (Ch. cheng-li, correct principle).

> Matters concerning the Shintō deities [shintō] are not readily revealed. Yet if the divine basis of things is not understood, such ignorance will surely give rise to disorder. To rectify this evil influence, I shall take up my brush. Since my chief aim is to discuss as correct principle (shōri) direct succession to the throne from the age of the gods, I will not write of things one hears all the time. Therefore, I shall name this *A Chronicle of Correct Succession of Deities and Sovereigns.*[3]

Although Chikafusa's propounding of ri clearly follows Sung scholarship, the shō (correct) to which his concept of ri aspires is not the same as the shō (i.e., Ch. cheng) of Sung China. Moreover, the *Jinnō Shōtōki* differs from the *Gukanshō*, as it does from factual monogatari such as the *Ōkagami*, in beginning with the age of the Shintō deities. Had he intended to write a dynastic history, it would have been natural to begin with the reign of the first tennō, Jimmu.[4] Instead, Chikafusa takes it upon himself to expand on the deity setsuwa (see vol. 1, ch. 2), from the very creation of heaven and earth as if it were historical fact, asserting that all the tennō are truly descendants of the deities. *Jinnō Shōtōki* accordingly begins:

> Great Japan is the divine land. The Heavenly Progenitors founded it, and the Sun Goddess bequeathed it to her descendants to rule eternally. This is true only of our country; there are no similar examples in other countries. This is why our country is called the divine land. (1: 41)

There is the central theme of the treatise. In brief, there are three points: (1) Japan is superior to all other countries; (2) this is because it is a divine land; (3) Japan is a divine land because the line of the tennō has succeeded unbroken since it was bequeathed to her descendants by the Sun Goddess Amaterasu (Varley, 1980, 7). The principle of the unbroken line of tennō is, in fact, Chikafusa's shō, and this differs from the Sung concept of cheng. In China, when an emperor was unvirtuous, a person with no blood relationship to him whatever would overthrow him and begin a

especially deep research" (*Sekiso Ōrai*, 607). The *Sekiso Ōrai (Anthology of Short Letters)* was compiled by Ichijō Kaneyoshi (1402-81). The rank of quasi-empress was given to court ministers of particularly high merit, even if they were male.

[3] [With minor revisions, translations of *Jinnō Shōtōki* are from Varley, 1980.—Trans.]

[4] [In the traditional order of sovereigns, Jimmu is first and Heisei Tennō (r. 1989-) is 125th. Before Jimmu was the Age of the Gods.—Ed.]

new dynasty. According to Chikafusa, this was the reason that China was inferior to Japan.

Even while it takes as its paradigm Sung scholarship, Chikafusa's view of history leads him to the very un-Chinese assertion that Japan is superior to China. This bears a close resemblance to the process in which Sung Neoconfucianists made use of Kegon and Zen Buddhist paradigms, but created their own intellectual system, in which Buddhism was not esteemed.[5] Chinese emperors received "the mandate of heaven," and it was on the basis of this mandate that they conducted politics. Also, if the emperor himself were guilty of misconduct, heaven would send its mandate to another, who would then become emperor. Who this new emperor would be made no difference to the governed as long as the person who received the mandate of heaven had a measure of virtue befitting an emperor. Chikafusa's shō differs radically from this concept of cheng. He made no issue of virtue or lack of virtue, crediting only the unbreakability of the line of tennō. Moreover, in fact, he was not overly concerned with legitimacy in the sense of actual blood relationships; rather, what was important for him was precisely the principle of continuous succession (Yamada Y., 1932b, 753-55).

While this way of thinking about the Japanese royal line was established by Chikafusa, it was not original with him. It had its foundations in the Watarai Shintō of the Ise Shrine. The offices of the Inner Shrine (naikū) of Ise were manned primarily by members of the Arakida family, while those of the Outer Shrine (gekū) were occupied by the Watarai family. Watarai Shintō was a theoretical synthesis formulated by the shrine officers of the Watarai family in perhaps the thirteenth century. Religious beliefs connected with the Ise Shrine were born from the native mentality of the Yamato race and had neither a body of doctrine nor an ecclesiastical authority appropriate to what one would call a religion. Something approaching a body of doctrine was developed when the theoretical system of the esoteric Buddhism of the Shingon sect was adapted analogically to the native beliefs in the Inner and Outer Ise Shrines. Therefore, Watarai Shintō is not necessarily representative of the indigenous religious mentality of the Yamato race. In Chikafusa's day, however, it was one of the powerful systems of thought. The five most important works in which the shrine officials of the Watarai family recorded this synthesis are called the *Shintō Gobusho (The Five Shintō Books)*. We know that Chikafusa came into contact with one of these, the *Ruiju Shingi Hongen*

[5] Chang Heng-chü (1020-77), Ch'eng I-ch'uan (1033-1107), and Chu Hsi (1130-1200) all studied Zen, but in their great syntheses of Sung Neoconfucianism they rejected Buddhism (Haga, 1956, 46-50). [The "mandate of heaven" referred to above and below is central for Chinese imperial polity, a practical view that reconciled de facto power to de jure legitimacy.—Ed.]

(Classified Traditions Concerning the Genesis of Shintō Deities).[6] This provided an important foundation for a historical view that placed the Yamato deities and the tennō in the same line.

Chikafusa served the Southern Court during this period of constant military conflict, and his purpose in writing *Jinnō Shōtōki* was to demonstrate historically the legitimacy (correct succession) of the Southern Court. In fact, both the Jimyōin line of the Northern Court (the line of Gofukakusa), and the Daikakuji line of the Southern Court (the line of Kameyama), traced their ancestry back to Gosaga. (See Figure 17.1.) Therefore, both lines should have had an equal claim to the right of succession. Chikafusa's assertion of the legitimacy of the Southern Court was based on his belief that the succession should be determined directly by the reigning tennō himself.[7] If there were any infringement by others on this "direct" determination, the succession already could not be said to be "correct" (shō). What Chikafusa calls correct succession (shōtō) has more the character of "direct" or "straight" succession than mere legitimacy itself (Varley, 1980, 15-16).

Even if both lines had descended from the sons of Gosaga, Gosaga

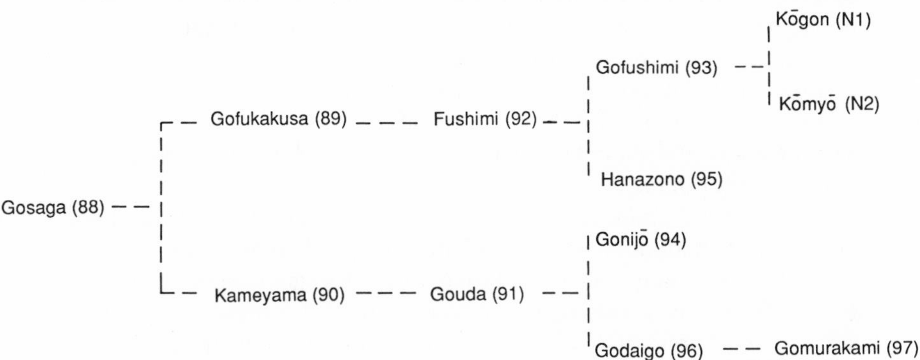

FIGURE 17.1 Succession of Sovereigns, Gosaga to Gomurakami and Kōmyō (Numbers designate the traditional succession of sovereigns, with N1 and N2 designating two in the brief Northern line; in this chart, the upper descendants of Gosaga are of the Jimyōin or Northern line, and the lower are of the Daikakuji or Southern line)

[6] Chikafusa had many opportunities to come into contact with Ise Shrine officials in connection with the management of his land holdings. Besides evidence that he borrowed a copy of the *Ruiju Shingi Hongen* from Godaigo Tennō, it is known that he received the secret sections of the text from its author Watarai Ieyuki when he made a pilgrimage to the shrine in 1336 (Varley, 1980, 13). The secret sections of the text were shown only to qualified people.

[7] "If the principles governing succession to the throne operated as I have described even in the ancient period, we must realize how much more difficult it is in this later age to sustain the tennōship unless the succession is properly maintained" (*Jinnō*, 2:125; from Varley, 1980, 175).

Tennō himself had "commanded that Kameyama's become the tennō line" (*Jinnō*, 2:165-68). Therefore the tennō line should be returned to "the correct line of Kameyama as the direct successor" (ibid., 169). Moreover, Kameyama himself, as the abdicated tennō, had gone so far as to offer a petition at the Iwashimizu Hachiman Shrine praying for the succession of Prince Takaharu (Godaigo; ibid., 171). It would have to be recognized that Kōgon, who had been installed as tennō by the Kamakura bakufu despite this petition, was an illegitimate sovereign (ibid., 189), as was his younger brother Kōmyō, who was installed by Ashikaga Takauji to succeed him.

Of course, from our point of view, such a theory cannot be accepted. It is a fact, however, that it made a deep impression on people of subsequent ages. The pre-modern figure most deeply impressed by it was perhaps Tokugawa Mitsukuni (1628-1700) who had the *Dai Nihon Shi (The History of Great Japan)* compiled as a project of the Mito han (fief). This history recognized the Southern Court as the legitimate line of succession, and the authority of this view was recognized even after the Meiji Restoration in 1868.[8] Indeed, in the mid-nineteenth century, Chikafusa's assertion that it was unwarranted for warriors to interfere in the prerogatives of the tennō gave rise to the "theory of respecting the tennō" and provided the spiritual foundation of the Meiji Restoration. The influence of this theory is due precisely to the precision with which Chikafusa propounded his concept of ri. Such precision is rare in Japanese prose; that, and the ready understandability of his prose, gave his work great persuasive power for many generations.

Although the *Taiheiki* (*The Chronicle of the Great Peace*; ca. 1372) also takes its material from history, it is a work of another kind.[9] In fact, this work is usually included among war tales (gunki monogatari). In terms of content, however, battle scenes are by no means its principal subject, and I prefer to deal with it as an example of embellished histories (kōshi). The following is from the Chinese preface:

> I will state my humble opinion. When one observes the changes in society over the full range from the distant past to the present, and considers the origins of peace or discord in the world, what covers everything without exception is the virtue of heaven. The wise sov-

[8] The present royal house is in the line of the Northern Court. In spite of that, since the reign of the Meiji Tennō (r. 1867-1912), the Southern line has been recognized as the legitimate. This is probably due to the continuing influence of factions associated with Mito historical scholarship. [Mitogaku, or Mito studies, rose in the seventeenth century, combining national studies (kokugaku), history, and Shinto.—Ed.]

[9] [For an almost complete translation, see Helen Craig McCullough, *The Taiheiki: A Chronicle of Medieval Japan* (New York: Columbia University Press, 1959). Passages quoted here, however, are not included in that work, and the translations are mine.—Trans.]

ereign makes this inclusive virtue his model and protects the country. It is the discipline of the land to provide a place for everything, excluding nothing. Excellent subjects make this their model and protect the state in order to make it safe. When that virtue is lacking, even if the sovereign reigns, he will not maintain his position. As it is often told, King Chieh of Hsia was exiled to Nan-ch'ao, and King Chou of Yin was defeated at Mu-yeh.[10] When that discipline loses its correctness (shō), even if one has authority, it will not continue for long. I have heard that Chao Kao was executed at Hsien-yang, and Lu-shan was killed by Feng-hsiang.[11] Therefore, the wise sovereigns of ancient ages were circumspect in their own behavior, and their conduct provided norms for people of future generations. Later generations may obtain admonitions from past times in order to reconsider their own conduct. (*THK*, 1:34)

These words had been anticipated by the famous opening of the *Heike Monogatari*: "At the Jetavana Temple the bell gives voice to the impermanence of all as it reverberates. That the pairs of teak trees, in the hue of their flowers, show the downfall of the splendid is a matter of reason." Instead of emphasizing the principle (ri) of the mutability of all things, however, the preface of the *Taiheiki* states clearly that its theme is that of an earnest prayer for peace under Heaven. The title, *Taiheiki (The Chronicle of the Great Peace)*, stresses this theme further. The intense yearning for peace was born from the experience of a long period of internal warfare during the period in which the *Taiheiki* was composed. When we read in it of the strong yearning for peace and of the situation that has caused it, the explanation is presented in terms of numerous battle scenes. In other words, the wars narrated offered material for explaining how a peaceful polity could be established.

How can we make this a world of peace? This question also reverberates deeply for us in the twentieth century. The problem cannot be solved by conceptual principles. There is a real possibility of achieving peace only when those responsible deal effectively with events one at a time and

[10] King Chieh was the last king of the Hsia dynasty. Because of his tyranny, he lost the support of the people and was deposed by King Tang, the first sovereign of the Yin (*Shih Chi*, Hsia Pen-chi 2). King Chou was the last king of the Yin and, again due to his tyranny, was deposed by King Wu of the Chou (ibid., Yin Pen-chi 3). Both this and the previous incident have a highly legendary quality; nor can the dates of these events be determined with any degree of accuracy.

[11] Chao Kao was the minister of Ch'in Shih Huang, the first emperor of the Chin dynasty. He killed the second emperor, but was himself killed by Ying, Shih Huang's grandson (*Shih Chi*, Shih Huang Pen-chi 6). The *Taiheiki* is mistaken in stating that Chao Kao was executed. In fact, he was assassinated—the members of his family were executed. An Lu-shan was the favorite minister of Hsüan-tsung of the T'ang dynasty. He rebelled against the emperor and was later killed by his own heir, Ch'ing-hsü.

possess correct judgment of the situation. Those responsible in politics are often pressed with the need to make urgent judgments. In such situations, historical precedents provide valuable bases for decisions. That the preface of the *Taiheiki* takes up such historical sovereigns as King Chieh of Hsia and King Chou of Yin is by no means a case of using Chinese legend or historical events for the sake of literary flourish. Rather it shows that the composer of the *Taiheiki* believed that it was precisely historical precedent that could provide guiding principles for making political judgments. It thus shares the outlook of *Jinnō Shōtōki*, an outlook that can probably be traced back to *Tzu-chih T'ung-chien*. Still, there are points on which the standpoint of the *Taiheiki* is not the same as that of *Jinnō Shōtōki*. The *Taiheiki* values historical precedents that are very particular.

This is made clear in an episode, "Kitano Tsuya Monogatari no Koto" ("Discussion During a Nightlong Vigil at the Kitano Shrine," 35:316-55). Sōsei Raii (d. 1356) makes a pilgrimage to the Temmangū Shrine at Kitano, where he intends to perform devotions throughout the night. There he meets three monks, each of whom gives him a talk on politics. These monks act as mouthpieces for the author, especially a hermit monk who speaks in the dialect of the Kantō region. As actual examples of periods of peace under heaven, the ascetics list the reign of Daigo Tennō (r. 897-930), and the shogunal regencies of Hōjō Yasutoki (regent, 1224-42) and Hōjō Tokiyori (regent, 1246-56), expounding on what superior results could be obtained when sound judgments were made in politics. The military government of the Muromachi bakufu, which officially began in 1336, was highly aware of being the successor of the Kamakura bakufu, also a warrior government, and made its ideal the performance of good administration based on the precedents established by its predecessor. This assertion is clearly recorded in the *Kemmu Shikimoku (The Kemmu Code)*, which the bakufu presented to the court in the same year.[12] For example, in the afterword to the proposed code we find the following:

> In the distant past, investigate the reigns of Engi (Daigo Tennō) and Tenryaku (Murakami Tennō), during which the sovereigns governed with virtue. In the recent past, take up the political conduct of Yoshitoki (regent 1205-24) and his son Yasutoki (regent 1224-42). If these are made the leading principles of rule, and if governors act in such a way that they win the trust and respect of the people, the foundations of a great peace under heaven will be ensured. (7)

This is consistent with the opinions expressed in the "Kitano Tsuya Monogatari no Koto," and the author of the *Taiheiki* must have been a

[12] "First, good government must be carried out according to the precedents of that time when the shogunate was at its height" (*Kemmu Shikimoku*, 3).

person with the same kind of spiritual makeup as those who participated in writing the *Kemmu Shikimoku*. Indeed, there is a strong possibility that the author was given information and materials by intellectuals of the Muromachi bakufu in the period of its establishment (Suzuki T., 1973, 293-96).

This veneration of precedent was a vital force not only for those who governed, but also for those who had to make decisions or act in a world at war. At least, to the extent that they are depicted in the *Taiheiki*, the people of this period were always conscious of historical precedent. It is for this reason that a great number of famous incidents and legends from Chinese and Japanese history alike are cited. Similarly, readers of the *Taiheiki* during this period and later discovered models for living in it that could be applied by analogy to their own times. This gave them the confidence, the enjoyment, or perhaps the comfort of saying, for example, "I am the Kusunoki Masashige of Edo"[13] (Yamazaki 1971, 254-65). The accounts of events recorded in the *Taiheiki* must have had, therefore, the quality of actual fact.

Imagawa Ryōshun's *Nan Taiheiki* (*A Chastisement of the Taiheiki*; 1402) charges that there are many mistakes in the work. But what Ryōshun attacks is precisely the fact that incidents deserving of inclusion in the *Taiheiki* were ignored—the valorous deeds of warriors, and especially warriors of the Imagawa house (Sakurai, 1954, 151-52). That Ryōshun himself, who lived when the *Taiheiki* was compiled, displayed such an attitude reflects his recognition of it as a record of historical facts. It is precisely when one is aware of the work's factual nature that it can be used as a model for one's own judgment and action. A work thought purely fictional carries far less conviction as a model.

However, in arguing for the factual nature of the *Taiheiki* as a whole I am not suggesting that it consists entirely of historical verities. For example, while a great number of battle scenes are presented descriptively, no one would believe that the compiler had actually witnessed all these engagements. Readers must have consented to the inclusion of literary embellishments in order to have the story told in an interesting manner. The degree to which such embellishments were regarded as such would differ greatly, depending on the sophistication of a given reader. The passage in which Kusunoki Masashige displays his great martial valor at Chihaya Castle provides a good example. This passage, in which Masashige executes a series of brilliant maneuvers against a huge force of the bakufu army (*THK*, 7:216-24), is overly elaborated. But if sophisticated readers would have thought it over-colored, there would also have been many people who believed that everything in it was historical fact. What was

[13] [Kusunoki Masashige (1299-1336) is one of the most heroic characters of the *Taiheiki*; writers of the Edo period frequently compared their central characters to him, and his fame has lasted into modern times.—Trans.]

certain for all readers then, however, was that Masashige did indeed do battle with Kamakura forces at Chihaya Castle, and that on this point the *Taiheiki* could be trusted to the same extent as a historical record. That is, regardless of its embellishment of events, the *Taiheiki* does record historical facts that were well known in detail to readers of the period, and it was because people knew it to be a prevailingly factual account that protests such as Ryōshun's appeared.

This kind of writing is seen in the so-called yen-i, of which the *San-kuo Chih Yen-i (The Romance of the Three Kingdoms)* is the outstanding example.[14] The events related in this work are not fundamentally different from the *San-kuo Chih*, its source.[15] In the later adaptation, however, many battle scenes are recounted with a wealth of imagined description, so reducing its factual character. The *Taiheiki* shares this emphasis. Its Chinese yen-i model differs from the *San-kuo Chih* original by its radical transformation of the work's central characters: Liu Pei, Ts'ao Ts'ao, Sun Ch'üan, Chu-ko Liang, and Kuan Yü. This is especially true of the depiction of Chu-ko Liang (or K'ung-ming), who is described as if he were a Taoist immortal or sorcerer. This characterization is quite different from the image that emerges from actual historical accounts and Chu-ko Liang's own writings.[16] Yet his making judgments and taking actions as a loyal stalwart of Szechuan is consistent with the historical character of Chu-ko Liang in the orthodox histories. Intellectuals of the period in which this yen-i was written did not care if the amount of fiction was increased for the sake of adding interest, so long as it was possible to recognize reliable historical facts in the account. And it is when this tacit understanding is established between writers and readers that a genre such as yen-i comes into being. *San-kuo Chih Yen-i*, the first yen-i, was compiled in the latter half of the fourteenth century and therefore belongs to the same period as the *Taiheiki*. The contemporaneousness of the two makes Chinese influence improbable. But it is a notable fact that a genre corresponding to yen-i was established in Japan at this time.

Yen-i were not suddenly created at this moment. They had a prototype in the embellished histories (kōshi; Ch. chiang-shih). Chiang-shih appear among the shuo-hua (J. setsuwa) that were recited in urban resorts during

[14] An abbreviation of *San-kuo Chih T'ung-su Yen-i*. The oldest printed edition is of 1494 and has twenty-four books; the popularly circulated version in the Ming and Ch'ing dynasties has one hundred and twenty kai (rounds). Lo Pen (the popular name of Kuang Chung), who is said to be the author, seems to have lived from 1328 to around 1398 (Cheng, 1957, 192). It is not clear which of the extant versions was written by Lo Pen.

[15] A history in sixty-five parts compiled by Ch'en Shou (1232-97).

[16] "Ch'u Shih Piao" ("A Memorial to the Throne on Departing for Battle," *San-kuo Chih* 35, 919-20), by Chu-ko Liang (popular name K'ung-ming) is said to be so moving that a person who reads it without shedding tears is not human, but I am struck rather by his rare wisdom, which enabled him so splendidly to combine his principles of building up the state by the actual business of administration. K'ung-ming left the "Ch'u Shih Piao" for the young second emperor, Liu Ch'an (r. 223-63), as he went off for battle in 227.

the Sung.[17] As previously observed, the most popular of the kōshi was the *Shuo-san Fen (The Tale of Three Kingdoms)*, and the p'ing-hua of the Yüan were born from the recitation of this work. The *Ch'üan-hsiang San-kuo Chih P'ing-hua (The Fully Illustrated Story of the San-kuo Chih)* was published between 1321 and 1324.[18] The fictional dimension in this is conspicuous, and there are many chapters in which "a person with a modicum of historical knowledge would recognize the fabrication at a glance" (Cheng, 1957, 193-94). The *San-kuo Chih Yen-i* reduced the number of such passages or rationalized them by "adding a number of historical facts" (ibid.).

Yen-i are, then, substantially factual in nature.[19] They appeared after the mid-fourteenth century, sharing history told in an interesting manner with the more highly fictitious embellished histories, the origins of which can be traced back at least as far as the late eleventh century. Because the *Taiheiki* also possesses this interesting manner of feeling, I would like to assign it to the class of embellished histories (kōshi). The *Baishōron* and *Gen'ishū*, which were compiled a little later, also depict battle scenes with loving description.[20] And in both—although it is neither prominent nor very rich—there is an element of fiction, placing them as well in the class of embellished histories. The fictional character of these works is not of a degree to evoke great interest. By comparison with treatises that have no fictional character, however, they too can only be called embellished histories.

Recited Narratives

MONOGATARI OF PRIVATE STRIFE

Katarimono (recited narratives) continued to be written after the beginning of the fourteenth century, the most outstanding of them being the

[17] "As entertainments in the resorts (wa-ssu) of the capital . . . [there were kōshi]. Among performers of kōshi were Li T'sao, Yang Chung-li, Chang Shih-i, Hsü Ming, Chao Shih-heng, Ku Chiu, and others. . . . Ho Ssu specialized in the *Shou-san Fen*, and Yin Ch'ang won popularity for his performances of *Wu-tai Shih*." (*Tung-ching Meng-hua Lu [A Record of Occurrences in the Eastern Capital Now Seen Only in Dreams]*, 5:132-33.)

[18] One of the five kinds of *Ch'üan-hsiang P'ing-hua* and in three books. It bears a colophon stating, "Newly published by the Yü family of Chien-an." This work does not survive in China, and the only extant text is in the Cabinet Library (Naikaku Bunko) of the National Library of Official Documents (Kokuritsu Kōmonjo Kan). *Chiu-chien (The Nine Admonitions of the Duke of Liang)*, *Wu-tai-shih P'ing-hua (The Story of Five Dynasties)*, and *Hsüan-hua I-shih (Unrecorded Stories of Occurrences in the Hsüan-hua Era)* are also embellished histories.

[19] Chang Hsüeh-ch'eng (1738-1801) said of the *San-kuo Chih Yen-i* that "it is seven parts fact and three parts fiction" (*Ping-ch'en Cha-ji [Miscellaneous Notes]*, compiled 1796). This statement has been a source of grief for scholars who wish to deal with yen-i as literature, but this kind of statistical argument has nothing to do with the literariness of a text (Li, 1977, 74).

[20] The compilation of the *Baishōron* has been dated between 1352 and 1378-88 (*Baishōron*, Introduction, 11); the *Gen'ishū* was completed between 1378 and 1388.

Soga Monogatari (The Tale of the Soga Brothers) and the *Gikeiki (The Story of Yoshitsune)*.[21] The extant popularly circulated versions of both are intended for reading, and it is hard to imagine that they were recited to musical accompaniment.[22] The popularly circulated versions date, however, from the second half of the sixteenth century or later.[23] They can hardly provide a reliable basis for judging the nature of the counterparts of these stories in the fourteenth century. We do know that stories of the Soga brothers' revenge against their father's murderer, Kudō no Saemon Suketsune, were being recited in the fourteenth century. In the *Zakki (Miscellaneous Notes)* of the temple Daigoji, for example, there is the following entry: "The matter of Soga Jūrō and Gorō. The following is based on a performance by a blind person from a rural province."[24] A detailed genealogy of the characters in the story follows.

At the beginning of the *Zakki* it is noted that "these notes were begun in the Seventh Month of 1347." Clearly, a blind performer who had come from a rural area *recited* the story of the Soga brothers sometime in the mid-fourteenth century. The temple monks must have enjoyed the performance and copied down the important human relationships in their *Zakki*. In the nō, *Mochizuki*, a woman disguises herself as a blind female performer in order to take revenge on her husband's murderer. She recites the story of the Soga brothers at a banquet.[25] In the twenty-fifth round of the *Shichijūichiban Shokuninzukushi Utaawase (The Seventy-one Round Poetry Match on All the Types of Artisans)*, there is a scene (Round 25) in which a blind female performer accompanying a biwa hōshi (player of a lute-like instrument) recites the story while beating a drum, beginning: "To the royal descendant in the eleventh generation from Uda Tennō, to this legitimate son of Itō, was born Kawazu Saburō, father of Jūrō and Gorō. . . ."[26] Considering all these facts together, we may recognize that

[21] [A complete translation of *Gikeiki* with an introduction appears in Helen Craig McCullough, *Yoshitsune: A Fifteenth-Century Japanese Chronicle* (Stanford: Stanford University Press, 1966; page numbers given with quotations from the *Gikeiki* refer to McCullough's translation).—Trans.]

[22] The rufubon or popularly circulated version of the *Soga Monogatari* has twelve books. Beginning with the oldest, an old movable wooden type edition that can be dated around 1650, there are many printed editions. There are also many printed editions of the rufubon text of the *Gikeiki*, beginning with an old movable wooden type edition from the Genna era (1596-1625). It has eight books.

[23] The Daisenji kanabon text (mostly in syllabic characters; hereafter "Japanese"), retains the form of the manabon, which also has ten books. [On manabon, see n. 28, below.] This text was completed before 1359 (Araki, 1941b, 10-11). The establishment of a twelve-book text must have occurred after the completion of the Daisenji text, and therefore in the second half of the sixteenth century or later.

[24] It is not presently known whether this text is extant. The quotation is taken from Nose, 1942b, 2-5.

[25] For the passage in *Mochizuki*, see *Yōkyokushū*, 2:401.

[26] *Shichijūichiban*, 99. Reliable evidence is lacking for establishing the date of compilation of this utaawase. However, it is said to be the work of Kanroji Chikanaga (1424-1500),

the story of the Soga brothers' revenge was being recited by blind performers, including women, before 1347, and that these performances were accompanied by drums rather than biwa. However, the fragments of the katari [narrative as a story or act] that appear in *Mochizuki* and *Shichijūichiban Shokuninzukushi Utaawase* cannot be found in any of the extant texts of *Soga Monogatari*, and we can infer from this that a different text was recited in the fourteenth century (Nose, 1942b, 289-90).

The revenge of the Soga brothers was consummated on the twenty-seventh day of the Fifth Month, 1193. Although the *Azuma Kagami (The Mirror of the Eastern Provinces)* relates these details properly, it is not grounded on official documents, for even Tora of Ōiso, Soga Sukenari's (Jūrō) beloved, appears in the account.[27] We may conclude from that that the compiler of the *Azuma Kagami* utilized pre-existing private documents in constructing the account. Since the first half of the *Azuma Kagami* was compiled between 1265 and 1273, the process of making this famous revenge into a monogatari had been going on for seventy years after it took place (Kadokawa, 1943, 403-21). This does not mean, however, that the story was simply expanded and given a more literary quality until it finally became the widely circulated (rufubon) version of the *Soga Monogatari*. The oldest extant text that is recognized as the *Soga Monogatari* is the Sinified (manabon) text in ten fascicles.[28] The date of its completion can be established as sometime in the first half of the thirteenth century.[29]

The Sinified version is very loosely ordered. With a number of stories simply piled together, it has a marked effect of randomness, even compared to the widely circulated (rufubon) text, which is itself a series of episodes strung together—and a much greater number at that. The

---

and, if that is true, it must have been completed in the second half of the fifteenth century. [As may be clear, an illustrated version with more than poems is involved.—Ed.]

[27] *Azuma Kagami*, 13:490-92. [Soga Sukenari and Soga Tokimune are the heroes of *Soga Monogatari*. They are more widely known by their childhood names of Jūrō and Gorō. Tora is romanticized in fictional versions as she would not have been in the official one, in which she does not appear in any event.—Trans., Ed.]

[28] A manabon text is one of which Chinese characters are the main kind of orthography [and are termed "Sinified" here.] However, the language of a manabon text is not Chinese and, in fact, does not have even the Chinese flavor of Japanese kambun (prose in Chinese). It is perhaps best to think of it as a style of Japanese mixed prose in which the use of kana is limited to an extreme degree. The manabon text of the *Soga Monogatari* is the ancestor of all the textual lines. The oldest extant example is the Myōhonji manuscript, a hand-copied text bearing the date 1546 (Yamagishi, 1927, 234-56).

[29] [In his note curtailed here, the author discusses one incident in versions of the *Soga Monogatari* and the Kakuichi manuscript line of the *Heike Monogatari* to give logical confirmation of a date from about the mid-fourteenth century for at least one major textual line. "There is also strong external evidence to support this view (Yamashita, 1972, 144-45)," he concludes.—Ed.]

weaker ordering of the Sinified (manabon) version testifies to the fact that the stories interpolated into the widely circulated version are always supplementary to the main plot. As a result, they do not seriously impede the progress of the story. In contrast, the stories added to the Sinified version often dwell on legends (hon'en) or miracles at this or that temple or shrine, and in particular at Hakone Gongen Shrine and Izu Gongen Shrine, dilating on their stories, conspicuously straying from Jūrō and Gorō. I believe this is because preachers engaged in reciting the legends of shrines and temples, and especially those who recited the legends of the deities (hon'en) of the Hakone and Izu shrines, participated in the establishment of the Sinified text of the *Soga Monogatari*. Even from internal evidence alone, the establishment of this text was undeniably the result of a process in which existing stories of the Soga brothers' revenge became combined with recited secularized narratives (shōdō) that were being performed in the eastern provinces.

The participation of preachers from the eastern provinces in the compilation of the Sinified text was pointed out at an early stage of research, based on its points in common with the *Shintōshū (An Anthology of Legends Concerning Deities)*.[30] Many passages in these works bear close resemblance, not only in content but also in wording.[31] This does not mean, however, that the Sinified text of *Soga Monogatari* was written with direct reference to the *Shintōshū*. Rather, the striking similarities between the two texts result because both arose from the same oral tradition: the *Shintōshū* collected recited narratives (katarimono) that were recited in secularized recited stories (shōdō) of the eastern provinces, while the Sinified text of the *Soga Monogatari* incorporated a large number of these same recited narratives (katarimono). It has been conjectured that the Sinified text was the work of the monks of the Buddhist temple complex on Mount Hakone, that this work formed the basis for the ten-part Japanese (kanabon) text compiled by priests of Mount Hiei, and that the latter was further expanded into the twenty-unit popular version.[32] It is better, however, to consider the problem of actual authorship to be unclear and to limit what can be said about the establishment of the Sinified

[30] In ten books, the *Shintōshū* is a collection of setsuwa and commentaries concerning Shinto, principally legends (hon'en) of Shinto deities enshrined in various provinces. The setsuwa that appear in the collection provided ample material for the genres of monogatari sōshi [one name for stories that appear between earlier monogatari and later sōshi] and jōruri [performances, not puppet-theater] which developed in the fifteenth and sixteenth centuries. It was compiled in the period between 1352 and 1361. The identity of the compiler is unclear, but Tsukudo Reikan has suggested that it must have been a preacher connected with the Tendai sect (Tsukudo, 1937, 83-103).

[31] Fifty-two passages have been identified in which the phrasing of the Sinified version of the *Soga Monogatari*, and the *Shintōshū* is the same or highly similar (Murakami, 1969, 259-306).

[32] Among others, Araki, 1941b, 31-35.

text to the participation, in some fashion, of preachers from the eastern provinces in compiling it (Tsukudo, 1943, 262-70).[33]

Extant texts of the *Shintōshū* are labelled, "a work from Agui."[34] This certainly suggests that the collection transmits the recited narratives by Chōken or Shōgaku. But I wonder if it is not in fact a kind of trademark? It is extremely doubtful that preachers of the legitimate Agui line bear responsibility for the sermons recorded in the *Shintōshū*. Although the Agui preachers were criticized for their worldly opportunism, the secularized recited stories (shōdō) of Agui preachers in the capital were performed according to an authentic formula that preserved the ceremonies and etiquette of well-established tradition. If this were not true, it is unlikely that Chōken and Shōgaku would have written such a large number of Buddhist petitions (gammon and hyōbyaku).

Recited secularized stories (shōdō) in the eastern provinces during the fourteenth century, however, were extremely degenerate, with the sung parts (shō, Ch. ch'ang) and the unsung parts (kō, Ch. chiang), the basic elements of sekkyō (entertainments by itinerant performers), failing to preserve the standards of previous ages. It is difficult to believe, for example, that the shō sections were performed in the strict style of Buddhist ceremonial music (shōmyō), in which hymns have prescribed numbers of syllables. Moreover, the kō sections seem not to have required the refined language previously used. At least, as far as can be determined from the evidence of the *Shintōshū*, the recitational style of these entertainments (sekkyō) was quite plain and in a popular mode.

This is not to say that the recited secularized stories (shōdō) were different in kind from the existing sermons of the Agui line. It is a fact that the stories of the Agui were transmitted to the eastern provinces.[35] The

[33] [There are likely to be verbal and taxonomic confusions in this. Katarimono are "recited narratives," i.e., were always presented orally, unlike monogatari, which were recited only sometimes (e.g., the *Genji Monogatari*) or in some textual states (e.g., the *Heike Monogatari*). Shōdō and sekkyōbushi (as distinguished from sekkyō) designate the same thing, although both terms (and sekkyō) suggest sermons. Shōdō (sekkyōbushi) seem to have originated in Muromachi preaching, but by the period when they were considered a recited art, they were delivered by outcasts whose knowledge of Buddhism was trivial. That being the case, the stories increasingly featured secular matters and outlooks (hence our translation, "recited secularized narratives"). Shōdō were lengthy and usually in five parts. Although the length varied, three parts seem often to have been recited, as all katarimono were, to accompaniment, but by the rudest of instruments—the sasara, consisting of one stick rubbed against another, serrated one. More sophisticated versions of shōdō also existed, especially in the Kyoto area. Simple explanation is difficult, given the complexity of the facts and of similar names for different things, or of different for the same.—Ed.]

[34] [Agui (a strange reading of the characters) was a satellite temple of the Chikurin'in. Chōken and Shōgaku were the most famous of the preachers at Agui, so that mention of anything connecting nominally Buddhist stories and Agui at this time would at once bring these famous preachers to mind. Especially since, as the author goes on to show, they were accused of popularizing preaching in ways that purists thought indefensible.—Ed.]

[35] Shōgaku was entrusted with the administration of the religious complexes on Mount

traditional recitational styles of the sekkyō (entertainments) would have been inappropriate, however, for attracting audiences in the eastern provinces. Even in the capital, Shōgaku's style of performance was so closely attuned to the tastes of his audiences that he was criticized by Kokan. We can easily imagine that when this style of recitation was brought into the eastern provinces it degenerated even further. Perhaps we should say that the recited secularized stories (shōdō) degenerated in one way in the capital and in another way in the eastern provinces during and after the fourteenth century. Thus, while they were quite different from the secularized stories (shōdō) of Chōken and Shōgaku, it is difficult to deny that those which existed in the background of the compilation of the *Shintōshū* were offshoots of Agui sekkyō (entertainments). And because the Agui was widely known as a leading line of reciters of the stories, the compilers of the *Shintōshū* used the phrase "a work from Agui" as a kind of trademark.

I have used the phrase "shōdō of the eastern provinces" in this discussion, but I have used it only in discussing the relationship of these stories with the *Shintōshū*. In fact, there is no doubt that the same kind of phenomenon could be discerned if the discussion were expanded to include "provincial secularized stories." It has been established that there were itinerant performers of entertainments (sekkyōshi) in every area of Japan, and performers associated with Kumano were especially prominent. Among them there even were some who were capable of writing nō.[36] There is also no doubt, however, that shōdō (recited secularized stories) were different from their predecessors in the thirteenth century, and I have called them late-period shōdō. The differences between middle-period shōdō and late-period shōdō are at once the differences between the *Heike Monogatari* and the *Soga Monogatari*, in which their respective characteristics are reflected.

The Kakuichi version of the *Heike Monogatari* represents the final stage in the development of the work.[37] It has undertones of pathos but

Izu and Mount Hakone by the Chief Priest of Shōren'in, Monzeki Jien. (Monzeki refers either to a royal prince who has entered the priesthood or to a temple that has been given an equivalent rank. In this case it refers to the latter, for Jien was not the son of a tennō.) Thus, Agui shōdō would of course have been transmitted to these areas (Kadokawa, 1969, 345-47). [Both shōdō and sekkyō had religious origins. The latter were presented around the country by performers (sekkyōshi), altering as time passed. It was accompanied by a succession of instruments, developing into jōruri in the wider sense and sometimes using smallish puppets.—Ed.]

[36] *Shii no Shōshō (The Lesser Captain of the Fourth Rank)*, which is the original version of *Kayoi Komachi (Komachi and The One Hundred Nights)*, was first composed by a shōdō performer of Yamato (see ch. 18, n. 32).

[37] [There have been many versions of the *Heike Monogatari*—longer or shorter, for reading or reciting, in Japanese or Chinese, etc. The "Kakuichi version" is taken as the standard one today. It is in a line of manuscripts originally marked with ones (ichi) by a group of reciters.—Ed.]

strongly proclaims the promise of the *Amitāyus Sūtra (Amidakyō)*: "The holy light shines on the worlds in the ten directions, enfolding forever all who call upon the sacred Name." The concluding "Initiates' Chapter" of the *Heike Monogatari* in particular stresses the theme of the whole—that while no one can escape impermanence, this reality should be linked to the expectation of being received in Amida's Western Paradise.[38] In contrast to this, the consuming grudge of the Soga brothers against their father's murderer is the central motif of the *Soga Monogatari* from beginning to end, with dark gloom the dominant strain. It is true that the end of the story in the rufubon text leaves one with a somewhat brighter impression. Ōiso no Tora and Tegoshi no Shōshō become nuns and are instructed in the Jōdo Buddhist doctrine and practice of invoking the name of Amida (nembutsu) by Hōnen. They hear heavenly music in the clouds and, wrapped in a miraculous fragrance, ascend in them to the Western Paradise, where they are welcomed by a host of bodhisattvas (*Soga*, 12:407-26). This passage does not exist in the Sinified (manabon) text of the *Soga Monogatari* and was written later in imitation of the "Kanjō no Maki" of the Kakuichi text of the *Heike Monogatari*. It would be difficult to believe that this kind of narrative, with its Jōdo Buddhist motif, existed in the original version of the *Soga Monogatari*. The performers in the background of the establishment of the Sinified text probably belonged to the Ji wing of the Jōdo sect (Kadokawa, 1969, 382-92).[39] This may be deduced from the fact that the entertainments (sekkyō) of the Ji Shū preachers was characterized by a style of relating (katari), in which appear the spirits of the dead.

This characteristic tone of Ji shōdō remains to a considerable extent in the Daisenji manuscript of the *Soga Monogatari*, and while it is much lighter, its traces may still be discerned in the popularly circulated version (rufubon). They are to be found in the sentimentality that is characteristic of all extant versions. What I mean here by sentimentality is a pervasive tone giving certain subjects an emotionalism exceeding the bounds of what one would normally expect from them. Such a tone would have been received with greater enthusiasm by people with a penchant for emotion than by more intellectual readers. Even today, lovers of the recitation (gidayū) in the puppet theater (bunraku) are strongly attracted by this kind of sentimentality. Modern bunraku traces its roots to the vari-

[38] [The "Kanjō no Maki" concluding the *Heike Monogatari* deals with the last years of Kenrei Mon'in (1155-1213), consort of Takakura (r. 1168-80). When the Minamoto were victorious in the Battle of Dannoura in 1185, she was spared from death but confined to the convent Jakkōin in Ōhara to the north of Kyoto. With the opening of the work, this close is the most Buddhist in emphasis.—Ed.]

[39] [The Ji sect of Buddhism was founded in 1276 by Ippen (1239-89) as an offshoot of the Jōdo sect. It is distinguished by affiliations with esotericism, the Zen sects, and Shinto.—Ed.]

ous types of Edo-period jōruri, whose origins may in turn be traced back to the relation (katari) of the *Soga Monogatari.* And in the background of *that* one should recognize the somber sentimentality characteristic of Ji Shū sekkyō.[40]

Yet there are also cases in which the same degree of sentimentality appears in a brighter vein. The strong man exploits of Benkei and Tadanobu in the *Gikeiki (The Story of Yoshitsune)* are good examples of this, and it would be more appropriate to call these scenes fantastic. The unreal, exaggerated quality was probably best loved by the warriors of the Sengoku period (1467-1586), and although it had been already liked, its popularity was at its peak in the fifteenth and sixteenth centuries. Audiences of this period also loved sentimentality. Indeed, it can be said that the parallel existence of the fantastic and the sentimental is the characteristic feature common to all Japanese narrative literary arts from the fifteenth century on. In general, the tendency toward the unreal and fantastic is more conspicuous in the *Gikeiki*, while the *Soga Monogatari* is the more sentimental—even if there are also fantastic scenes in the widely circulated version (rufubon) of the latter. We are reminded of the aragoto (rough, bold business) scenes in kabuki by the strong man exploits of Soga Tokimune (Gorō) in the chapters from "Ōiso no Hairon no Koto" ("The Matter of a Quarrel at a Sake Banquet") to "Benzaiten no Koto" ("The Matter of Sarasvatī") (6:242-59).[41] However, the corresponding passages of the Sinified (manabon) version have not the slightest trace of this unreal, spectacular quality (5:92-93).

Unfortunately, there is no extant version of the *Gikeiki* at a stage of completion that would correspond to the Sinified version of the *Soga Monogatari*, and it is thus unclear whether the lost early *Gikeiki* had the fantasticized Benkei and Tadanobu of the rufubon version. There is a line of texts bearing the titles of *Hōgan Monogatari (The Tale of the Lieutenant of the Military Guard)* or *Yoshitsune Monogatari.*[42] This *Hōgan* line is thought to belong to a stage of development somewhat older than the rufubon text, but it does not differ significantly from it in its degree of the fantastic.[43] Therefore, even though it is difficult to deduce the process of

[40] [Yoshitsune early and Yoshitsune late therefore represent the fantastic and the sentimental that the author speaks of.—Ed.]

[41] [Sarasvatī (J. Benzaiten) is the female deity of music (especially the biwa).—Trans.] The kabuki plays, *Ya no Ne (The Arrowhead)* and *Kusazuribiki (The Tasset-Pulling Contest)* are based on material from these episodes in the *Soga Monogatari* (Leiter, 1979, 215, 431).

[42] [Hōgan (lieutenant in the military guard) is the last official rank Yoshitsune held, but in subsequent literature it became almost synonymous with his name and his tragic fate. Indeed, in modern Japanese, the phrase "Hōgan biiki" means "siding with the underdog."—Trans.]

[43] *Shomonogatari Mokuroku (A Catalogue of Various Monogatari)*, a catalogue of the library of the Fushimi Princely Household compiled in 1420, lists *Kurō Hōgan Monogatari*, one scroll (*Kammon Shihai*, 220). However, the relationship between this no-longer-exist-

textual development of the *Gikeiki* to the same degree that we can do so for the *Soga Monogatari*, it would be impossible to deny that the extant texts of *Gikeiki* are amalgamations of a number of preexisting stories. For example, the young Yoshitsune, still bearing his childhood name of Ushiwakamaru, displays superhuman martial prowess in his duel with Benkei (3:119-28). Yet in later chapters, when he flees the capital to seek refuge in Ōshū, he is portrayed as a frail aristocrat suffering the hardships of a difficult journey. He becomes seasick on Lake Biwa, and his feet are bloodied crossing over Mount Arachi (7:317). In fact, he survives the perils of the journey and reaches Hiraizumi in Ōshū only because of the resourcefulness and resolution of the superhuman Benkei.[44]

Not only are there these contradictions in the portrayal of characters, but also many points where the events depicted are not consistent. For example, on his way to Fujiwara Hidehira's capital in Hiraizumi, Ushiwakamaru undergoes his capping ceremony at the Atsuta Shrine with the sponsorship of the chief priest, and he gives himself the adult name of Yoshitsune (2:64-65). After he has reached Hiraizumi and won the support of Hidehira, he immediately returns to the capital to visit Oniichi Hōgen, who possesses a secret military treatise (2:81-98). In this part of the chapter, however, he suddenly appears once again in the temple page's costume he had worn before his capping ceremony.

This and similar inconsistencies may be attributed to the number of preexisting stories about Yoshitsune that were clumsily and indifferently amalgamated in the *Gikeiki* (Kadokawa, 1974, 248-49). Some sections of the text, such as the story of Yoshitsune's encounter with Oniichi Hōgen, or the story of Benkei's background and his first encounter with Yoshitsune (3:100-28), could easily stand alone. And these we may certainly consider to be preexisting stories later incorporated into the *Gikeiki*.

In both the *Soga Monogatari* and the *Gikeiki* we must recognize a process in which fictional stories concerning real or nonexistent characters are created within a relatively common range of subject matter and are later brought together as a famous literary work. This thesis is supported by the similar process of compilation visible in Chinese chang-hui hsiao-shuo (J. shōkai shōsetsu), a kind of hsiao-shuo in which lengthened sto-

---

ing work and the lines of extant ones is not clear. Among extant textual lines, the texts in a line titled *Hōgan Monogatari* are the oldest. The kind of texts from this line, which are titled *Yoshitsune Monogatari*, were established second. The popularly circulated (rufubon) line of texts, titled *Gikeiki*, emerged independently of the second- from the first-kind, *Hōgan Monogatari*, texts (Yamagishi, 1966, 160-75). [As we have seen, "Hōgan" was a title held by Yoshitsune; "Gikei" is the Sinified reading of "Yoshitsune."—Ed.]

[44] [Yoshitsune is probably the favorite Japanese hero. He and his mighty aide, Benkei, are celebrated singly or together in narratives, nō, kabuki, travel writings, and popular songs. As a result, the historical Minamoto Yoshitsune is almost beyond recovery.—Ed.]

ries are separated into short units called hui or rounds. The Southern Sung sui-pi *Tsui-weng T'an-lu (Miscellaneous Notes of a Drunken Old Man)* discusses early hsiao-shuo listing (in vol. 1, part 1) the titles of one hundred and seven books.[45] The ones that require our attention are *Ching-mien Shou (The Blue-faced Beast); Hua Ho-shang (Monk Flower); Wu Hsing-che (Wu the Ascetic)*; and *Pei-chou Wang Tse (Wang Tse of Pei Prefecture)*.[46] The first three of these are the central characters in *Shui-hu Chüan* (J. *Suikoden; The Water Margin*), while Wang Tse is one of the main characters in *P'ing-yao Chuan (Subjugating Specters)*. Thus, the *Tsui-weng T'an-lu* provides important evidence that individual hsiao-shuo with these characters as their main characters were being recited, and that these hsiao-shuo were later brought together into much longer written works that incorporated them into a main plot filled out with new elements.

The *P'ing-yao Chüan* is a good example of this process of assimilation and accretion. Originally a work consisting of one or two small volumes, it was first expanded into a text of four with twenty rounds (hui) and later into six with forty rounds.[47] Among the additions in the forty-round version, fifteen offer new material explaining the backgrounds of central characters, which are often unclear in the twenty-round version. In addition, new scenes of action were added at places in the story where the main characters had not shown sufficient vitality. Moreover, in terms of attitude, the twenty-round book deals sympathetically with Wang Tse's insurgence, whereas the forty-round book emphasizes the rebellion of his army against sovereign authority.

The accretions and emendations observable in the forty-round version bring to the story a measure of unity and consistency in the actions of characters and the development of the main plot. The enlargements also add a considerable amount of detail to depictions of characters and action. On the other hand, the later and longer version loses the touch of the earlier for the feelings and the existence of common people in Sung China, as well as no little of the earlier, unsophisticated fantasy (Yokoyama, 1981, 31-39). It cannot be concluded, however, that the twenty-round version simply patched together particular preexisting stories told by shuo-hua-jen (professional storytellers), because we discover that nar-

[45] The original title of the *Tsui-weng T'an-lu* was *Hsin-pien Tsui-weng T'an-lu (The New Selection of Miscellaneous Notes of a Drunken Old Man)*. Compiled by Lo Yeh (dates unknown). Two small volumes. The only extant text is a printed edition published in Yüan that was transmitted to Japan through Korea. Originally in the private collection of the Date family, it is now in the collection of the Tenri Library.

[46] The "Blue-faced Beast" is a sobriquet for Yang Chih; "Monk Flower" is Lu Chih-shen (because he had a flower tattoo on his back); and "Wang Tse of Pei Prefecture" is Wang Sung. Pei-chou is Ching-ho Hsien in Ho-pei Sheng.

[47] [A note on other Chinese titles is omitted here.—Ed.]

rative elements suggestive of authorship by intellectuals have been inserted. For example, the story, "Tu Ch'i-sheng Cuts a Child with His Sorcery" (found in the second half of the eleventh round of the twenty-round version; forty-round version, 29, 185-87), incorporates material from the Fifth Southern T'ang text *Chung-ch'ao Ku-shih* (*Stories of the Middle T'ang*, 9-10). However, it should also be recognized that the twenty-round version retains not a few traces of stories from the oral tradition.

I consider the most conspicuous of these traces to be precisely that the backgrounds of many central characters are not clearly related. In the editor's preface to the T'ien-hsü-chai edition of the twenty-round text (published 1620), Chang Yü (dates unknown) points out that "characters enter the scene suddenly and disappear without notice," and he concludes, "I suspect this book is not a complete version" (Sun, 1953, 124-25). The reason why characters of unexplained background suddenly appear is precisely that they were already well known from preexisting, independent stories in the oral tradition. It is difficult to accept Chang Yü's theory that the text is incomplete.

The lack of integrity and consistency in the plot can also be considered due to a preexisting oral tradition. Even when a written text of a hsiao-shuo existed, illiterate people depended on oral delivery. The twenty-round version of the *P'ing-yao Chüan* would have been delivered in a series of performances spreading over several days or weeks, and interest would focus on that part of the story being recited on a particular day. The lack of tightly-knit structure or a unified theme would not have been much of a problem. Such an outlook influenced reception even after woodblock editions of the text were published, and readers of these editions probably did not pay much attention to unity or inconsistency (Ōta T., 1967, 398).

The same thing was true of those Japanese recited narratives (katari-mono), which are rooted in secularized narratives (shōdō). This is particularly clear for the *Soga Monogatari* and the *Gikeiki*, connected as they are with late-period secularized narratives. Even for works like the popularly circulated versions of the *Soga Monogatari* and the *Gikeiki*, which were of course intended to be read, it was clearly assumed that the chapter (ku) rather than the whole was the fundamental literary radical. There is manifestly a loose ordering much given to subplots, even when they impede the main plot, and an indifference to contradictions like Yoshitsune's reappearance in child's clothes well after he had had his capping ceremony. These developments in prose narrative appear to have developed naturally, contemporaneously, and independently in Japan and China.

CHAPTER 18

The Growth and Flowering of Nō

FROM SARUGAKU TO NŌ

There was in China a type of performance art called san-yüeh (J. sangaku), which included comic mime, singing and dancing, as well as acrobatics and conjuring tricks. San-yüeh was transmitted to Japan in the eighth century, both from China itself and from Korea. In order to encourage instruction in the various arts of san-yüeh, the Japanese government established the special census classification of sangakuko, under which families engaged in sangaku were exempted from taxes and labor levies. The exemption was withdrawn on the eleventh day of the Seventh Month of 782 (*SNG*, 37:486), no doubt because sangaku was flourishing so well that patronage and protection were no longer necessary. Many of the former sangakuko performers became low-ranking functionaries in the royal bodyguards or were employed by the large temples of Nara, performing whenever there was an official gathering or celebration. Not a few of them, however, chose to remain outside the census register in order to avoid tax and labor levies, making their way as professional sangaku performers. This entailed a substantial sacrifice of status, because to be outside the census register meant to be considered outcasts (semmin).

Sangaku performers attached to Buddhist temples developed an art, shushi, in which Buddhist allegories were presented in performance. For their part, professional sangaku performers developed dengaku [literally, field music], which were performed with Shintō ceremonies connected with agriculture. The mainstream of sangaku, however, was comic mime, and this aspect of the art seems to have been most loved, whether in official or in outcast sangaku. It was for this reason that sangaku came to be called sarugaku (literally, monkey entertainments).[1] By the middle of the

[1] There are many examples in classical Japanese of this shift from "n" sounds to "r" sounds: "Sunda" (place name) to "Suruga"; "Inani" (a deity) to "Inari"; "Sanki" (place name) to "Saruki"; and so on. The example of "Sanki" is found in a text of *Taketori Monogatari* recognized to be older (in terms of content) than the widely circulated (rufubon) text. In the case of sarugaku, the sound shift from sangaku to sarugaku suggested a shift from the Chinese character san ("miscellaneous") to the character saru ("monkey") (Nose, 1942a, 146). [Later, as nō assumed more and more the aspect of a ga art, the Chinese character for "saru" changed again, to one meaning "to say" or "to do." Both characters are used in Zeami's treatises.—Trans.]

eleventh century, the comic mime of sarugaku had developed into a quite realistic art, and a number of popular actors had emerged. The character of sarugaku in this period is described in detail in Fujiwara Akihira's (985?-1066) *Shin Sarugaku Ki* (*An Account of the New Sarugaku*; Nose, 1942a, 146-63).[2]

After the beginning of the thirteenth century, there was a remarkable infusion of elements of song and dance into the comic mime of sarugaku performances of the professional performers, and great emphasis seems to have been given to plot development in the mime. This new art, in which mime with a definite plot (Zeami later called this monomane) was combined with song and dance, came to be called nō only in the second half of the fourteenth century; but in terms of the actual character of performances, nō already existed in the middle of the thirteenth.[3] The new art met with great success, and dengaku performers also began to perform it. The mainstream of sarugaku performers, who before had specialized in comic mime, had shifted already to performances of the new dance theater, and there gradually developed the custom of distinguishing between dengaku nō and sarugaku nō. Given their shared origins in sangaku, a broad definition of sarugaku would include dengaku. A narrow definition of sarugaku, however, was employed when it was distinguished from dengaku, and the distinction between sarugaku nō and dengaku nō gradually became fixed.

For its part, shushi, which also falls within the broad definition of sarugaku, reached the height of its popularity in the eleventh and twelfth centuries, declining after the beginning of the thirteenth. The most important play of the shushi repertoire, however, *Shiki Samban*, was inherited by sarugaku (in the narrow sense).[4] This was not a sudden occurrence. *Shiki Samban* was a ceremonial play performed as a prayer for peace and abundant harvests of the five grains. It has three roles: Inatsumi no Okina (Old Man of the Rice Harvest); Chichi no Jō (Old Man Father); and Yotsugi no Okina (Eldest Transmitter).[5] The role of Yotsugi no Okina was traditionally played by a sarugaku performer (in the narrow sense) and was called samban sarugaku. This was probably because Yotsugi no Okina was portrayed as an old peasant, making the role more appropriate for sarugaku performers, whose social status was inferior to

[2] *SGRJ*, 6:480–87.

[3] *MGK* [8.I.1233], 325.

[4] As explained below, *Shiki Samban* is the prototype of *Okina (The Old Man)*, one of the most important plays in the current repertoire. Though it is performed now only on special occasions, it is the initial play in the standard cycle of five plays that developed during the Edo period, and on those rare occasions when a full five-play cycle is performed it would be inconceivable to omit *Okina*. [Auth., Trans.]

[5] [Yotsugi was the name of the principal dialoguist in the *Ōkagami (The Great Mirror)*, discussed in vol. two.—Ed.]

that of shushi performers. With the decline of shushi, however, all three roles came to be performed by sarugaku performers, and by the first half of the fourteenth century, the samban sarugaku role became a kyōgen role [performed by an actor of the comic interludes for nō] (Nose, 1942a, 172-80).

These facts have important implications. First, they are symptomatic of the phenomenon of ascending from zoku to ga that has been observed in other genres (see also vol. one, pp. 419-22). For example, with the help of waterfront prostitutes (asobi) and itinerant performers (kugutsu), various kinds of folk songs and provincial Shinto song ballads that had once been zoku melodies became imayō (present-style songs) in the capital style. These imayō rose in turn to become banquet songs performed by courtiers.[6] Moreover, such songs continued to have vitality in the zoku realm, providing bases for yet other new ga songs in succeeding periods (vol. two, ch. 9). Similarly, renga, which was born as a form of trivial word-play, rose to the status of a noble literature in the mid-thirteenth century. And it did not die out, flourishing instead in a ga-zoku style as haikai renga [or haikai no renga].[7] The same happened within sarugaku, defined in the broad sense.

It must also be pointed out that magical, incantatory elements permeated sarugaku in the narrow sense, because of its assumption of roles originally performed in shushi. There is much in the modern nō that has affinities with the mythological world of Shinto, and it is in communion with the vital spirit of the universe through the central image of a nō play that the most valid—the most nō-like—response to a play is experienced (vol. one, 108-109). When the performance of a master actor makes me feel that the nō stage is filled with cherry blossoms in a performance of *Tadanori*, or when moonlight fills the stage in a performance of *Izutsu*, I touch the vital energy of those blossoms or that autumn moonlight at a profound level of being, and I am physically shaken by an emotion that defies explanation. This achievement was impossible in comic mime performances. It must have been incorporated into sarugaku as sarugaku in the narrow sense assumed some of the aspects of shushi. When one considers its contact with shushi, Zeami's statement that sarugaku was born from the songs and dances (kamiasobi) performed by the myriad deities when Amaterasu shut herself within the Heavenly Rock Cave (see vol. one, 110) is extremely significant. Thus, when the modern nō play *Okina*

[6] Even the abdicated tennō sang imayō (*Towazugatari*, 1:83-84 and 3:180).

[7] [Haikai meant comic, strange, or nonstandard (mushin). Haikai no renga returned in a sense to renga's low origins, growing as an amusement from nonstandard renga (mushin renga) to become the serious art practiced by Matsuo Bashō (1644-94) and others. Today, it is simply termed haikai or renku, so differentiating it from renga and the modern, unlinked haiku.—Ed.]

(that is, *Shiki Samban*) is performed, a special gravity is required, and in various degrees this solemnity has colored ordinary nō pieces as well.[8]

Actors who performed sarugaku in the narrow sense must have taken great pride in the fact that they had the right to perform *Okina* (*Shiki Samban*), and this encouraged the development of an aspiration for solemnity. Later, it would result in the elimination of comic elements from sarugaku nō. As I have written previously, of the roughly two hundred plays in the current nō repertoire, only the unpopular *Sanshō* is the exceptional case of play that makes humor its central motif, and *Sanshō* is performed only once every several decades (vol. one, 18). Moreover, the tradition of having kyōgen actors perform roles that require a comic touch, or those that have only a slight air of gravity, is rooted in the consciousness that nō actors are heirs to the performance art of shushi.[9]

The most important outcome of the assumption into sarugaku nō of the performance art of shushi was the invention of fukushiki mugen nō [dream plays in two parts].[10] In the current repertoire, it is the plays of this kind that we feel are most typical of nō. In the first part, the waki (usually a traveling priest) enters the stage.[11] He visits a place with historical associations. There he meets a character (the maejite, the principal role, here not in true appearance). The character relates the story of what happened there in the distant past. At a given point this character exits,

[8] Even today, the actor who is to perform the shite role in a performance of *Okina* observes the custom of bekka ("separate fire"). That is, for three days before the performance, he eats separately from the other members of his family and partakes only of food prepared over a fire that has been purified in a Shinto ritual. When he steps through the stage-entrance curtain (agemaku) onto the stage, he is purified with the sparks from a flint stone (kiribi).

[9] The comic touch is exemplified by the scene in *Ataka (Yoshitsune at the Ataka Barrier)* in which the mountain guide is sent to scout the barrier station and is frightened out of his wits when he discovers the severed heads of several mountain ascetics (*Yōkyokushū* [= *YKS*], 2:172-73). [Yoshitsune and his men are disguised as mountain ascetics.—Trans.] An example of a lesser character is offered by the mistress of prostitutes at the Nogami station in *Hanjo (Lady Han) (YKS*, 1:341).

[10] Nō in two parts have two scenes or acts with an interval (nakairi) between them, with the shite playing an assumed role in the former and true role in the latter. After performing the first part, the actor playing the former shite (maejite) leaves the stage to change his mask, costume, and possibly his wig to reappear in true role as the latter shite (nochijite). During the interval between the first and second parts, a kyōgen (comic interlude actor) relates the story of the play to the audience. Pieces that do not have this nakairi are called one part nō (tanshiki nō). Fukushiki plays in which the nochijite appears as a vision to the waki's dream are called dream nō in two parts (fukushiki mugen nō). [Auth., Trans.]

[11] A number of English translations have been suggested for waki: deuteragonist, byplayer, supporting actor, sideman, and so on. All of these are unsatisfactory in some respect, and the author has decided to use the Japanese terms shite and waki. In dream plays, the waki is merely a bystander; he does not enter into the plot to the extent presumed of roles in Western drama. In the older dramatic nō (geki nō), however, the waki might play a central role. Moreover, the waki does not necessarily play the deuteragonist role of second importance to the shite in terms of the plot. In *Hanagatami (The Flower Basket)*, for example, the deuteragonist, Keitei Tennō, is performed by a child actor (kokata), while the waki is the tennō's page. [Auth., Trans.]

returning in its true form (nochijite) to appear to the waki as in a dream. Now the shite role assumes its character as in the past, the actor performs the events of that distant past, disappearing (stage exit) again at dawn. The waki's dream, and the play, are over. The former-part shite (the maejite) is the main character's specter, and the latter (the nochijite) is none other than a vision of the dead spirit of that character, who appears in the waki's dream. Fukushiki mugen nō (two-part dream pieces) are unique to nō, unparalleled in other theaters of the world.

Of course, nō is not limited to either two parts or dream pieces. There are also many one-part and many genzaimono (living figure) nō, in which persons yet living (at the time of the action) are the central characters.[12] If one ignores differences in language and music, the genzaimono cannot be said to be unique to nō, for these plays have a form that is present in the theaters of other countries. The most nō-like of nō plays, the dream nō in two parts, however, was born from the connection between sarugaku nō and Buddhist temples and Shintō shrines, and we may consider this to be a connection that resulted from the assimilation of shushi into nō as nō assumed the functions of shushi.

We know very little directly of sarugaku nō. Nō was, however, performed in ennen nō, one of the entertainments performed by Buddhist priests; and since there is good evidence that these priests learned nō from sarugaku actors, we can deduce the aspect of sarugaku nō from what is known of ennen nō.[13] Fortunately, there is a record of an ennen performance at Kōfukuji in 1247, at which a play entitled *Konron Shugakusha* (*The Ascetic of Mount Konron*) was performed. The plot of this play seems to have involved an ascetic's travel to Mount Konron where he receives the Magical Jewel of Wishes (Nose, 1938, 377).[14] This play is at a stage one hesitates to call nō, but there can be no doubt that the nō of later periods developed from this kind of dramatic performance. Therefore, we must conclude that living figure nō (genzaimono)—and, moreover, other plays that had a dramatic plot—were the mainstream of nō in its early period. Two-part dream nō emerged later, and its prototype must have been deity nō (kami nō).

[12] [Excluding the opening play *Okina*, the five standard categories of nō in the five-play cycle established in the Edo period are the following: (first category) waki no mono (or kami nō), deity plays; (second category) shuramono, plays about martial figures; (third) kazuramono (or rarely, onnamono), woman plays; (fourth) genzaimono, plays about living people; and (fifth) kiri nō, demon plays. In genzaimono, the shite appears as a person alive at the time of the imagined action of the play.—Trans., Ed.]

[13] [Ennen, or ennen no mai (ennen dances), included ennen no nō (ennen nō) as one important kind of performance.—Ed.]

[14] Mount Konron is not the same Mount K'un-lun that exists in China but an imaginary mountain that appears in Taoist tales, a dwelling place of Taoist immortals. [Auth., Trans.]

In deity nō the maejite (former-part shite) is not a specter, but the incarnation of a deity, and the nochijite (latter-part shite) is not a vision seen in the waki's dream, but an actual aspect of the deity.[15] Yet the structure of kami nō is not unlike that of dream nō in two parts; the maejite (former shite) first appears on the stage as a child or an old man and then appears again as the nochijite (later shite) in the actual form of the deity. Sarugaku performers who served temples and shrines reenacted the legends (hon'en) of the deities enshrined there in the new dramatic art of nō. These actors established a structure for their performances in which the god first entered the stage in one of the guises mentioned and subsequently in the actual form of the deity. Later they adapted this pattern to plays in which the shite were not deities. It was with this adaption that dream nō in two parts was born (Kitagawa, 1964, 164).

It had become established that there were three means by which Shinto deities and buddhas communicated with human beings. In the first, called hyōe (possession), the deity or buddha possesses a human being and speaks through that person's mouth. In the second, called kegen, the deity or buddha appears in some incarnation different from its true aspect. When this form is that of a human being, this method is called kenin. There are also cases in which the deity or buddha appears as an animal or a plant, or in some rare cases as a stone.[16] The third method is for the deity or the buddha to appear in a dream. In this case, it speaks in its actual aspect. These methods were not limited to deities and buddhas and could be employed by spirits and ghosts as well. The spirits of dead human beings also employed these methods to communicate with living human beings. I believe that the second of these methods was adopted into the role of maejite (former shite) and the third into the role of nochijite (latter shite).

In the thirteenth and fourteenth centuries, stories of keten (incarnation) and communication in dreams were recited in great numbers, especially in accounts of the origins (engi) of shrines and temples. It was by no means an original idea for sarugaku performers to have incorporated these stories as material when they created a nō for performances in the service of shrines and temples. Yet we should pay particular note that not a few stories among engi have a pattern in which deities appear first in human incarnations and then transform themselves into their actual

[15] In fact, the "actual aspect" (honsugata) of deities amounted to nothing more than the belief that each deity had a certain appearance. However, medieval audiences of nō conceived of the deity that appeared in the second scene of kami nō not as a vision but as a substantial being. [Auth., Trans.]

[16] See *Hachimangūji Jumpaiki (A Record of a Pilgrimage to Hachiman Shrine-Temples)*, 34. This travel record is thought to have been written between 1261 and 1270. [Hachiman shrine-temples, while originally Shinto, came to be associated with both the Shinto and Buddhist establishments. There are still many such temples in Japan. [Auth., Trans.]

forms in the middle of the events being recited.[17] We may recognize this type of engi as the original source for the tradition in nō of having the same actor perform both the former and latter shite roles. The original form of nō must have been that of tanshiki nō (one-part nō), and the mainstream of nō during this early period must have been geki nō (dramatic nō), in which the content of the play focuses on the surges and undulations of the story.[18] The later developments of dream nō in two parts (fukushiki mugen nō) was a result of the incorporation of the prototype first established in kami nō into nō plays such as *Tadanori* and *Izutsu* in which human beings are the main characters.

From Kannami to Zeami: The Flower and Yūgen

There can be no doubt that sarugaku performers created the art of nō, but it was in dengaku nō that the new art was refined and that it came to possess a high degree of dramatic power. Dengaku performers adopted the musical dance theater that was called nō into their own repertoires only after its creation by sarugaku actors. In the early fourteenth century, however, dengaku nō stood in a position far superior to the nō of sarugaku, perhaps because it produced a greater number of outstanding actors. The last shogunal regent (shikken) of the Kamakura bakufu, Hōjō Takatoki (1303-33), was famous for his love of dengaku (*THK*, 5:161-63), and the shōgun himself, Ashikaga Takauji (1305-58) was a no less ardent fan. The vogue for dengaku nō is well illustrated by a subscription performance (kanjin) staged in 1349.[19] The audience packed into the temporary viewing stand in such numbers that it collapsed, killing many peo-

[17] For example, in a setsuwa concerning the Suwa Shrine, Abe no Takamaro mounts a rebellion in the eastern provinces, and Sakanoue Tamuramaro is sent to put it down. On the way to the battle grounds, Tamuramaro stops at the Suwa shrine to pray for victory. When he takes his leave, a warrior riding a dapple horse joins his company. When the battle begins, this warrior splits into five identical mounted warriors, who proceed to kill Takamaro. On the way back to the capital, this warrior suddenly begins to transform himself and, as his horse rises ten feet into the air, he assumes the aspect of a deity attired in formal court dress. Rising over the company, he announces: "I am the deity of Suwa, and I have joined your company in order to protect the royal authority. But there is no need for me to go to the capital, and I shall remain in this place." So saying, the deity disappears (*Suwa Sha Engie [The Picture Book of the Miracle of Suwa Shrine]*, compiled in 1356, 19-24). If this setsuwa were to become a nō play, an interval (nakairi) would have to be added in order to allow the shite to change his mask and costume. It is from this necessity that two-part nō (fukushiki nō) was born. In dream nō in two parts (fukushiki mugen nō), this theatrical structure was developed further.

[18] Yokomichi Mario has suggested a different definition of geki nō (*YKS*, 1, Introduction, 10-12), but I do not accept it.

[19] Performances held to solicit contributions for religious purposes. These performances were important to acting troupes. For one thing, since the performances were held by, or on behalf of, temples and shrines, they provided a place for performances and a guaranteed audience. Moreover, they were an important source of income, because a troupe received a percentage of the money raised. [Auth., Trans.]

ple.[20] Itchū, who performed at this time, was an actor of such skill that Kannami Kiyotsugu (1333-84) said of him, "He is my master in the art of performance" (*Sarugaku Dangi* [=*Dangi*], 174; *Zeami, Zenchiku* [=*ZMZC*], 261).[21] Kannami also had high praise for Dōami Inuō (d. 1413), a famous actor of the Omi dengaku school, and for Kiami of the Nara dengaku school (*Dangi*, 174-78; *ZMZC*, 261-64). However, with the beginning of Kannami's own period of activity, sarugaku nō advanced quickly, and subsequently it was sarugaku that produced brilliant actors one after the other. Dengaku declined rapidly after the middle of the fifteenth century, and gradually nō came to refer only to sarugaku nō.

In the mid-fourteenth century, dengaku and sarugaku apparently developed by mutual influence and interaction. Moreover, judging from the levels they had reached in the mid-fifteenth century, both had achieved a high degree of refinement by that time. In Zeami's *Sandō (The Three Elements in Composing a Play)*, which was completed in 1423, we find the following:

> From times now past, actors of great skill and high reputation have always been able to manifest the artistry of yūgen (graceful beauty).[22] The name of the dengaku actor Itchū can be mentioned in connection with this kind of artistry in former times. More recently, I might name the late master Kannami of our own school, or Dōami of the Hie troupe of Ōmi sarugaku. All these men made the beauty of yūgen in dance and chant the basis of their performance styles and were greatly skilled at performing in all of the Three Role Types. (*Sandō*, 161; *ZMZC*, 143)

Given these remarks by Zeami, there is no doubt that performance styles partaking of the beauty of yūgen (as yūen, refined grace) existed in nō by the period of Itchū's activity and that the focus of these styles was dance

[20] *THK*, 27, 55-57. There is a good deal of fiction in the *Taiheiki*'s account of this incident, but the fact that the performance was held is substantiated by other sources, such as the *Moromori Ki* [11. VI. 1350], 44-45.

[21] [An abbreviated title for *Zeshi Rokujū Igo Sarugaku Dangi (Master Zeami's Reflections on the Art of Sarugaku after the Age of Sixty)*. The text has a colophon stating that it was completed in the Eleventh Month of 1430. *Sarugaku Dangi* consists of the written record of Zeami's oral teachings to Motoyoshi, his second son, who transcribed and edited them. It is the longest of Zeami's treatises and contains the most complete discussion of his opinions in his later period. From a period before Zeami wrote *Kakyō*, the three role types (santei) and two basic arts (nikyoku) were central to his theories. The types are old persons (rōtai), young women (nyotai), and martial figures (guntai). The two arts are dance (bu-) and chant (-ga). With minor revisions, all translations of Zeami's treatises are by J. Thomas Rimer and Yamazaki Masakazu (see Rimer-Yamazaki 1984). The first entry in citations gives the title of the individual treatise and page numbers in Rimer-Yamazaki, 1984.—Trans.]

[22] [The meaning of "yūgen" alters with the period and literary kind: cf. "nature" in English aesthetics. By Zeami's time, the element common to various usages is beauty. His usage here and often is beauty with a refined grace (yūen), as the author goes on to show.—Ed.]

and chant accompanied by music (Nose, 1938, 371). The Three Role Types are old man roles, woman roles, and warrior roles, and among these it is the nō of woman roles that aspires to refined grace (yūen).[23] It is therefore probable that Zeami means that the performers of earlier periods made woman roles the basis of their art but were also adept at the roles of old men and warriors.

I have stated previously that one of the important characteristics of Japanese literary arts is that feminine grace is given the highest esteem in nō (vol. one, General Introduction). This aspiration for feminine beauty was realized in mid-fourteenth century nō. The custom of calling this new musical dance theater "nō" became fixed after about 1360, and the motive force behind this development must have been the formation of a nō that was distinctively nō-like, essentially the two-part dream nō. Of course, it is impossible to give an exact date for the complete formation of this essential kind. It is most likely, however, that it occurred during the period of about twenty years after 1360 (Konishi, 1983c, 12-13), a period that coincides approximately with Kannami's old age.

Kannami's most important achievement was, in one sense, his taking his troupe from the province of Yamato to the capital, where he won the patronage of Shōgun Ashikaga Yoshimitsu. This gave sarugaku nō a high social status. Yoshimitsu first saw sarugaku nō when he attended a performance in the Imagumano district of Kyoto (*Dangi*, 224-25; *ZMZC*, 301).[24] Subsequently, the Kanze sarugaku troupe (za) received Yoshimitsu's patronage, and Kannami's son Fujiwakamaru (or Zeami—Zeami Motokiyo, 1363?-1443?) became one of the shōgun's favorites. So great was Yoshimitsu's fondness for Fujiwakamaru that Sanjō Kintada (1324-83), the palace minister, criticized him both for having Zeami attend him in the viewing stands at the Gion Shrine Festival and for the way powerful daimyō (warrior lords) were vying in their attempts to curry favor with the shōgun by showering Fujiwakamaru with expensive gifts. Of course, Kintada also had harsh criticism for sarugaku in general, which he considered to be "the mummery of beggars."[25] Since provincial sarugaku was most likely performed by professional actors descended from outcasts (semmin), to the eye of a courtier with the rank of palace minister, the actors in Kannami's troupe were indeed "beggars." That these actors received special patronage from Yoshimitsu is extremely significant.

At that performance at Imagumano, Yoshimitsu granted Kannami a special exception to the existing rules of sarugaku.[26] Even within troupes

[23] The concept of the three role types first appears in the *Shikadō (The True Path to the Flower)*, which was completed in 1420 (*Shikadō*, 64-66; *ZMZC*, 112-13). In the earlier treatise, however, Zeami merely uses the term for convenience in explanation.

[24] [This occurred in 1374, when Zeami was about twelve.—Trans.]

[25] *Gogumai Ki* [7.VI.1378], 267.

[26] *Dangi*, 224-25; *ZMZC*, 293.

of sarugaku performers, there had been a system of specialization of roles in which only a special group was allowed to perform *Okina.* This group did not perform nō, while the group that did never performed *Okina.* Yoshimitsu commanded Kannami, the leader of the Yamato nō group, to perform *Okina.* Originally, those who performed *Okina* had been a special group of actors within sarugaku troupes, and just as that group performed only *Okina*, the body of the troupe performed only ordinary, other nō. With Kannami's performance, at Imagumano, performance of the piece by nō actors was gradually permitted in all sarugaku troupes (Omote, 1983, 43-46). This no doubt reflects the rise in status of nō performed by sarugaku actors.[27]

The rise of sarugaku nō occurred only because it possessed a degree of interest sufficient to win Yoshimitsu's patronage. That is, a second important achievement by Kannami was his raising of the quality of nō. The most well known example of his improvements is the addition of sections performed in the style of kusemai (a popular kind of song accompanied by dance) to the music of nō, which before Kannami had been solely in the style of kouta (short songs).[28] It is yet more important that Kannami played the leading role in the formation of two-part dream nō. Among the plays recognized as works by Kannami, *Eguchi (The Lady of Eguchi)* and *Motomezuka (The Maiden's Grave)* are of this kind.[29] It is unlikely that the texts of these plays as they are performed in the current repertoire are the same as Kannami's original works. Stylistic features typical of Zeami are especially conspicuous in the extant text of *Eguchi*, almost to the extent that one would prefer to consider the play Zeami's. In this period, the modern concept of authorship did not exist. Remodeling, even outright appropriation, was done quite freely.

There were limits even to rewriting, however, and if the basic motif of an author's play had been altered, it would no longer have been recognized as his work. In Zeami's *Goon (Five Notes)*, both *"Eguchi no Yūjo"* (*ZMZC*, 210) and *"Motomezuka"* (*ZMZC*, 211) are listed as "compositions by my late father." There is no room for doubt, therefore, that they are basically the creations of Kannami. Moreover, since there is virtually no possibility that plays with this new quality could have been produced by another sarugaku actor of Kannami's period, I would like to conclude

[27] Recognition of the right of sarugaku actors to perform *Okina* meant that they had achieved the same status as shushi, who held a higher social status. Subsequently, the "Okina group," which came to be called the nennyoshu, staged special performances of torch-light sarugaku (takigi sarugaku) at Kōfukuji and performances of *Okina* at the Kasuga lower shrine festival. This group existed until 1871 (Omote, 1978, 67-90).

[28] *Dangi*, 194-95; *ZMZC*, 174-275. In modern nō, the passages that correspond to kusemai are called kuse.

[29] *Motomezuka* is often translated "the sought-for grave," and in fact the Chinese character for "to seek" is used in the title of the play in the current repertoire. Given the content of the play, however, "motome" is almost certainly a corruption of "otome" (girl, or maiden). [Auth., Trans.]

that the literary texts of these two plays are also basically the original work of Kannami. Given the content of the two plays, they could not be two-part dream nō made up from earlier one-part nō. We may conclude, therefore, that the formation of dream plays in two scenes occurred during the period of Kannami's activity and that he played the leading role in establishing the new kind.

It is not possible to argue that dream nō in two parts flourished or enjoyed great popularity in Kannami's period. In fact, they must have been nothing more than one new experiment. *Jinen Koji (The Lay Priest Jinen)* may be regarded as atypical of Kannami's work.[30] Although the extant text of this libretto is not identical to the usual work by Kannami, the central motif, the structure, and the language of the work do retain much of the flavor of nō written by various hands before Zeami. In it, Jinen saves a young girl from a slave merchant, in a succession of brilliant scene changes and a highly charged plot. Moreover, there is not a single quotation of or allusion to a court poem (waka) (Kobayashi S., 1942b, 75-80). The second half of the play contains a section in which Jinen performs various arts for the slave merchant in exchange for the return of the girl. This section is divorced from the first half of the play, and the play thus lacks unity (ibid., 61-62).

This part of the play, however, may be considered to have been expanded, or perhaps added, after the development of yūkyō nō.[31] And Kannami's original was probably a pure geki nō (dramatic nō), focusing on the conflict between the shite (Jinen) and the waki (the slave merchant). This structure of dramatic conflict may be regarded as characteristic of Kannami's dramaturgy, for it is also evident in *Komachi*, Kannami's original version of *Sotoba Komachi*, and in *Shii no Shōshō (The Lesser Captain of the Fourth Rank)*, the original version of *Kayoi Komachi*.[32] In fact, however, this same structure is present in nō texts pre-

[30] "Kannami has written the following plays: *Sotoba Komachi [Lady Komachi on the Stupa]; Jinen Koji*, and *Kayoi Komachi* [Komachi and the Hundred Nights]" (*Dangi*, 222; *ZMZC*, 291). "*Jinen Koji*, musical composition by my late father [Kannami]" (*Goon* [ZMZC], 212). "There are old and new versions of *Jinen Koji*" (*Sandō*, 161; *ZMZC*, 143). Passages of *Jinen Koji* cited in *Goon* do not appear in the libretto performed in the current repertoire. Therefore, the "old version" was composed by Kannami, while the "new version," which is the play performed today, was composed by Zeami.

[31] The difficult term "yūkyō" is made up of the Chinese character meaning "to travel" or "to play" and the character meaning "madness." The compound might be translated "to sojourn in the realm of madness," which comes close to the intention of the yūkyō plays. All nō are attempts to entertain, but the yūkyō pieces were special: more than to enjoy the play, the spectator was expected to indulge himself in it. [Auth., Trans.]

[32] "*Komachi* was written by Kannami" (*Dangi*, 222; *ZMZC*, 291). This play corresponds to *Sotoba Komachi* in the current repertoire (Kobayashi, 1942b, 37-38). "*Shii no Shōshō [Kayoi Komachi]*, composed by Kannami" (*Dangi*, 222; *ZMZC*, 291). "The original text of *Shii no Shōshō* was written by preaching monks in Yamato and was performed by Komparu Gonnokami at [the autumn festival] of Tamunomine temple. This version was later revised [by Kannami]" (ibid.). The temple Tamunomine (or Tōnomine in modern pronunciation) is now the Danzan shrine in Sakurai City, Nara prefecture.

dating Kannami, and it amounted to the basic nō of this period. It is rather Kannami's version of *Matsukaze, Matsukaze Murasame (Matsukaze and Murasame)*, which drops the structure of dramatic nō and thus led the way to a newer nō in one or two parts.[33] Thus, while it would be mistaken to suggest that Kannami's experiments with dream nō in two parts (fukushiki mugen nō) constituted the typical art of his period, it is significant that he was moving in this direction before Zeami's perfection of the genre.

Kannami's contribution to nō may also be demonstrated by his establishment of aesthetic ideals for it. While Kannami himself left no treatise stating what kind of beauty nō should aspire for, his views may be inferred from the first five chapters of Zeami's seven-chapter *Fūshi Kaden* (*Teachings on Style and the Flower* [=*Kaden*]), which Zeami wrote on the basis of his father's teachings. The transmittal can be deduced from his discussion of training for actors forty years and older in the first three chapters, which were completed by 1400 when Zeami was around thirty-eight (*Kaden*, 1:8-9; *ZMZC*, 18-20). Moreover, in chapter three, Zeami states: "I have pondered deeply over things that my late father told me, and I am recording here those major points" (*Kaden*, 3:30; *ZMZC*, 37). And at the conclusion of Chapter Five, which was completed in 1402, we find the following: "The theories I have recorded in all the various sections of this treatise are by no means theories that have emerged from my own talents or exertions. From the time I was a small child, I received guidance from my late father . . ." (*Kaden*, 5:42-43; *ZMZC*, 46).

We may therefore reconstruct Kannami's theories on the art of nō on the basis of these chapters, arriving at the following general outline.

1. Nō must captivate its audience. That nō captivates its audience is because there is the Flower (appeal) in its art.
2. Within the Flower, there are both the temporary Flower (an appeal that exists only in given periods of an actor's career) and the true Flower (an appeal that never declines). The actor should make full use of the former, but the latter is the life of nō.
3. In order to obtain the Flower, use your mind to adapt to every possible situation.
   a. Since there are many types of audiences, the actor should be able to perform roles appropriate both for the connoisseur from the capital and for the provincial spectator who is without a discerning eye. He should also be able to change the style

[33] "In the past *Matsukaze Murasame* was *Shiokumi [The Salt-Water Gatherers]*" (*Sandō*, 161; *ZMZC*, 141). "*Matsukaze*, composition by my late father" (*Goon* [*ZMZC*], 209). "*Matsukaze Murasame*, composition by master Zeami" (*Dangi*, 222; *ZMZC*, 291). Kannami rewrote *Shiokumi*, originally a play by the dengaku nō master Kiami, into a play for sarugaku nō. Zeami revised the play further, and his version is the one performed in the current repertoire as *Matsukaze* (Nose, 1938, 1358).

of his performance depending on his audience and the circumstances of the performance.

b. In performing, be able to react appropriately even when various unexpected conditions develop on the spot.

c. The performer should achieve performance styles appropriate to his own given age throughout his career.

4. There are various ideal images of the Flower, but the most important and the most basic is the beauty of yūgen (yūen, refined grace). However, though it is rarely seen, even above the beauty of yūgen is the beauty of moisture (shiore).[34]

Kannami developed these views from personal experience. They do not have a metaphysical background, and for that reason they possess all the greater persuasive power even for modern readers.

The theory of beauty presented in the fourth element of the outline above, however, is no doubt difficult for modern Japanese or foreigners to comprehend. It had become completely impossible for us in the twentieth century to experience directly the ga of the Heian court. Of course the nō actors of Kannami's period were as unable as we are to experience this ga directly. They lived, however, in a period characterized by the awareness that it was precisely this courtly ga that was the ultimate model of beauty. Nō performers therefore displayed the highest beauty in yūgen. It was for this reason that the dengaku performers Itchū and Inuō aspired to yūgen, as did Kiami.[35] Greatly influenced by these famous actors of the past, Kannami believed that sarugaku nō should also aspire to yūgen.

As may be inferred from the fact that its art was originally founded on demon roles (*Kaden*, 2:16-17; *ZMZC*, 25), the old Yamato sarugaku nō was not an art characterized by yūgen. Nonetheless, Kannami believed that his Yamato troupe could not succeed with its traditional styles, and he actively incorporated the style of yūgen into performances. This is the principal reason that his group was able to rise from its humble origins in the provinces to win the patronage of Yoshimitsu and become the most popular troupe in the capital.

Kannami's assimilation of yūgen into his nō must have been no easy undertaking. For example, Kannami performed *Shizuka*, his original version of *Yoshino Shizuka* (*Shizuka at Yoshino*), as his own specialty. The

[34] [In a comment on shiore, the author says, in English, that "shioru" means literally "become moist." See ch. 15 for further discussion.—Ed.]

[35] "In the five levels, the art of Kiami was truly that of voice. In terms of the nine levels [Kyūi], he achieved the Style of the Flower of Profundity [shōshinkafū]" (*Dangi*, 174; *ZMZC*, 261). "Inuō [Dōami] was in the upper three levels [of the nine] and never fell even so far as the top of the middle three levels" (*Dangi*, 176; *ZMZC*, 263). Since all of the "nine levels" (Kyūi) are based on yūgen, it is clear that there were also actors in the dengaku schools who aspired to it.

tense situation in which Shizuka dances for her captors in order to give Yoshitsune time to escape may be said to be an extremely dramatic setting. The focus of the performance, however, is on the shirabyōshi (female performer) dance of Shizuka, a legendary beauty, and this lends to the play a brilliance of that graceful beauty that is yūgen. The transitional quality of this play offers excellent evidence of the pains Kannami took to shift the sarugaku nō of the Yamato troupes from geki nō (dramatic nō) to nō in the style of yūgen.

The Artistic Theory of Zeami: Mushin and Ran'i

The theories presented in chapter seven of *Fūshi Kaden*, which is entitled "Besshi Kuden" ("A Separate Secret Teaching"), differ in nature from those in the first five chapters. [Ch. 6 is dealt with in n. 41.] These differences may be traced to the conception in this chapter of the basic principles of the Flower, which may be summarized as follows (*Kaden*, 7:52-63; *ZMZC*, 55-65):

1. The Flower (hana) is fascination, and fascination is born from novelty.
2. This novelty cannot be achieved by pursuing the extraordinary. Rather, it is nothing other than a novelty born from ordinary styles performed at the most suitable time. In order to make such a performance succeed, it is essential to bear in mind the following:
   a. An actor must master a rich variety of plays, and one should take care to leave a long space of time between his performances of the same play. In contests (tachiai), it is also profitable to perform in a style different from that of your opponent.[36]
   b. In selecting plays, perform at the most appropriate time a kind of play that the spectators will not be expecting. In order to do this effectively, the actor must keep absolutely secret from the audience his preparations, his thoughts, and his judgments.
3. Even when all these conditions are met to the best possible degree, there are still occasions when one does not succeed. This is due to a course of events that cannot be altered by human abilities. In-

[36] The contests involved two or more troupes matching performances of a play. These performances were similar to waka matches but, in the case of tachiai, were judged not on the basis of individual performers but on the performances of the troupes as a whole. Also unlike waka matches, they had no appointed judge. They were usually decided by the highest ranking member of the audience in consultation with other connoisseurs present. [Auth., Trans.]

> evitably, there will come a time when the course changes once more. Therefore, one must simply wait patiently.

In short, while it is the effect of novelty that arouses the interest of the audience, the effect is not evoked by some singular new stimulus. Rather, it must be something that nonetheless appeals to the spectator.

In the opening passage of "Besshi Kuden," Zeami explains his use of the image of the Flower to express the appeal of nō.[37] People admire the beauty of flowers, but the flowers themselves are nothing more than the ordinary flowers that blossom every year. They do not change from year to year in any essential way. People feel novelty in viewing them, however, because the flowers blossom only in their appointed seasons, and they seem new to a person who has not seen them for a year (*Kaden*, 7:52-53; *ZMZC*, 55). The theory that ordinary subjects and diction can produce unexpected and new interest through their treatment is the approach advocated in the waka treatises of the Nijō school (see ch. 14), and it can be traced back further to Tameie. Because this thesis is not stated in the first five chapters of *Fūshi Kaden*, we may consider it to be something added by Zeami to his father's teachings.

By the time Zeami was thirteen, Nijō Yoshimoto had said of the lad's renga, "This is no ordinary talent" (Fukuda, 1965, 792). Renga stanzas linked by Zeami to Yoshimoto's stanzas survive from the time the actor-playwright was about sixteen, and they were described as "truly outstanding" and "transcendent" (Ijichi, 1967, 39).[38] Zeami did not neglect his practice of waka and renga after his youth, and we may easily surmise that he maintained his connection with Yoshimoto in pursuing these arts. The concepts and terminology in Zeami's early theories of nō share much with Yoshimoto's renga treatises (Konishi, 1961a, 96-111), and I consider this to be a manifestation of the close relationship between the two. The assumptions of the Nijō waka school must have entered Zeami's theories through Yoshimoto.

Yoshimoto, however, by no means adopted only the positions of the Nijō school. As we have seen, he also embraced the ideals of the Reizei school, and his own theories were a synthesis of the styles of both. In

[37] ["The theme of this secret teaching is to know the Flower. In order to know the Flower, you must first observe the flowers blooming in the fields and understand well the reason I have used the metaphor of the Flower to express all matters pertaining to our art." (*Kaden*, 7, 52: *ZMZC*, 55.)—Trans.]

[38] It is clear from "A Letter Sent by the Nijō Chancellor to the Chief Priest of the temple Sonshōin" that Zeami enjoyed the good will of Yoshimoto. This letter survives in the collection of the Shōkōkan Library in Mito City. These stanzas are recorded in the *Fuchiki (Diary by an Unknown Author)*, which states that they were composed at a renga session sponsored by Yoshimoto when Zeami was fifteen. The critical notes were written by Chief Priest Sūkaku. The *Fuchiki* survives in the collection of the Higashiyama Royal Library. Ijichi has established (as cited in the text) that it is the diary of abdicated Sukō.

opposition to the Nijō school, which prized a light, clear beauty of elegant simplicity (heitan), the Reizei poets prized a number of kinds of beauty, and especially yūen (refined grace). In Yoshimoto's synthesis, he advocates the use of various kinds of beauty while making refinement or graceful beauty (yūgen) the basic element. Yet in all the kinds of beauty striven for the tone must be ordinary throughout. Novelty is to be sought in the manner of combining the ordinary with the ordinary. This is precisely Zeami's own position.

The esteem of yūgen was already prominent with Kannami, who did not appear, however, to have stated a clear opinion concerning whether roles inappropriate to yūgen, such as Buddhist priests, shura, deities, and demons, could be performed without contradicting the basic effect of yūgen.[39] Zeami himself did not refer specifically to the problem in his early period. Not until his middle period did he begin to consider it—in the treatises beginning with the *Shikadō (The True Path to the Flower)*.[40] The concept of seeking novelty in the ordinary while making yūgen the keynote of art, however, was an important impetus toward his solution. This position is consistent with Nijō theories of waka and is presented as the basic principle of the Flower in the seventh chapter ("Besshi Kuden") of *Fūshi Kaden*. This suggests two related conclusions: first, that this basic principle of the Flower must have provided the foundations for Zeami's middle-period theories of nō, in which he exploited yūgen even more profoundly, and second, that it was in the "Besshi Kuden" that Zeami's own opinions first found their way into the *Fūshi Kaden*.[41]

Zeami probably learned the concepts that he would later develop into the basic principles of the Flower from Nijō Yoshimoto, with whom he was intimate from childhood. However, Yoshimoto died in 1388, fourteen years before the completion of the fifth chapter of *Fūshi Kaden* in

[39] [Often translated "warrior roles," shura nō are explained subsequently by the author.—Trans.]

[40] [The *Shikadō* was completed in VI.1420.—Trans.]

[41] Although the theories presented in the "Besshi Kuden" differ in important respects from those in the first five chapters of *Fūshi Kaden*, the period of its completion cannot be far removed from that of the earlier chapters. Internal evidence for this view may be found in the following passage from Chapter 3: "However, the fine actor who possesses the true Flower has at his disposal both the principle of blooming and the principle of fading. Therefore, his Flower will endure. What should one do in order to master this principle? Perhaps it is discussed in the separate secret teaching" (*Kaden*, 3, 30; *ZMZC*, 36). Zeami probably designated this chapter a "separate teaching" because it contains his own opinions, as opposed to the first five, which are a record of his father's teachings. However, it is not clear whether the text of "Besshi Kuden" that existed in 1400, the date of completion of chapter three of *Fūshi Kaden*, was the same as the extant text. His sixth chapter contains a discussion of the important concept of sōō (adaptability), in which Zeami argues that even a poor play can be brought to life depending on the occasion on which it is performed. These issues are also taken up in the "Besshi Kuden," and it seems likely, therefore, that the sixth chapter is made up largely of Zeami's own opinions.

1402, and it is therefore impossible to believe that Zeami developed theories that combined Nijō and Reizei theories of waka under Yoshimoto's tutelage or with Yoshimoto's ideas particularly in mind. Rather, Zeami must have thought of the shogun, Ashikaga Yoshimitsu, as the recipient of his theories and the nō performances that were based on them. As I have stated previously, Yoshimitsu loved expression in waka and renga that combined the styles of the Reizei and Nijō schools, and it was for precisely this reason that Yoshimoto supported this style so enthusiastically. Kannami respected the quality of yūgen in nō, but in his case this meant only that he recognized it as one excellent style among a great variety of others. It did not mean that he considered it to be the ultimate beauty. In fact, the specialty of the Yamato sarugaku nō group was demon roles (*Kaden*, 2:16; *ZMZC*, 25). During his period, the nō embodying yūgen was performed by Inuō (Dōami) of the Ōmi dengaku troupe and Kiami, another dengaku nō performer (*Dangi*, 174-76; *ZMZC*, 261-64). Because the yūgen style was highly admired by the shōgun and other connoisseurs in the capital, Kannami aggressively adopted it into his own group's nō repertoire. Zeami, of course, developed yūgen even further. There is no question that Yoshimitsu's opinions and tastes were leading forces in the background of these developments. Yoshimitsu died suddenly in 1408, but Zeami must already have shifted toward yūgen before his death. It is also most likely that dream nō in two parts were transformed into a subgenre of yūgen nō (in which dance and chant are central) during the period before Yoshimitsu's death.

The *Sandō* (*The Three Elements in Composing a Play*), which was completed in 1423, lists twenty-nine plays to be used as models in composing new plays (*Sandō*, 160; *ZMZC*, 142-43). Among these, the *Sarugaku Dangi* lists the following as Zeami's work (*Dangi*, 16:221-22; *ZMZC*, 291).[42]

Yawata (The God of War): possibly an earlier title for the play *Yumiyawata (The Bow at Hachiman Shrine)*
Aioi (Twin Pines): now called *Takasago (The Twin Pines of Takasago)*
Oimatsu (The Aged Pine)
Shiogama (place name): now called *Tōru (Minamoto Tōru)*
Aridōshi (The Deity Aridōshi)
Hakozaki (The Hakozaki Hachiman Shrine)
U no Ha (The Cormorant's Wing)
Mekurauchi (Vengeance of a Blind Person): no longer extant
Matsukaze Murasame (Matsukaze and Murasame): now called *Matsukaze*

[42] When present titles are not specified for extant plays, the old title is still current.

Hyakuman (The Kusemai Performer Hyakuman)
Higaki no Onna (The Shirabyōshi Performer Higaki): now called *Higaki*
Satsuma no Kami (The Governor of Satsuma): now called *Tadanori (Taira Tadanori)*
Sanemori (Taira Sanemori)
Yorimasa (Minamoto Yorimasa)
Kiyotsune (Taira Kiyotsune)
Atsumori (Taira Atsumori)
Kōya: possibly an early title for *Kōya Monogurui (The Raving Man at Kōya)*
Ōsaka (Meeting Slope): possibly an early title for *Ōsaka Monogurui (The Raving Man at Ōsaka)*
Koi no Omoni (The Burden of Love)
Sano no Funabashi (The Floating Bridge at Sano): now called *Funabashi*
Taisanmoku (The Deity of Mount T'ai)

The list probably includes plays written after Yoshimitsu's death, but even those may be considered to have been composed under the influence of his preferences. The most important of these plays for my present discussion are those in the category of shura plays, represented for example by *Tadanori, Kiyotsune*, and *Atsumori*. Even though they are shura roles, the shite of these plays are dead warriors of the Taira clan who had steeped themselves in the elegant refinement of the court. Shura is the world to which people who have killed during their lifetimes go after death, a hell in which at least in widespread belief, they must for eternity do battle and inflict mortal wounds upon each other. Of shura roles, Zeami states: "Such dead warrior roles, even when well performed, have little of interest" (*Kaden*, 2:15; *ZMZC*, 24). But that does not say all he thought (*Kaden*, 2:15; *ZMZC*, 24-25), since he also writes,

> However, when the stories of such famous warriors as the Genji or Heike are skillfully related to the beauties of the seasons, and the play is a good one, they are more moving than any other role. In performances of these roles, it is especially desirable that there be some element of heightened spectacle.

For example, the shite role of *Yorimasa* is Minamoto Yorimasa, a famous waka poet, and the depiction of his character brings a refined, courtly elegance to the play. Taira Sanemori, the shite of *Sanemori*, was the old warrior who dyed his white hair black and donned a red robe so that he might die a glorious death in battle. Despite Sanemori's advanced age, the play has the spectacle to which Zeami refers. That Zeami incorporated this kind of courtly elegance and spectacle into shura nō reflects that the connoisseurs of the capital, among whom Yoshimitsu was the supreme arbiter of taste, prized the beauty of yūgen. Certainly, Kannami must have aspired to this kind of nō, but such a play does not survive among his extant compositions, and we may conclude that it was Zeami who first realized the aim in actual composition.

The same aspiration may be seen in Zeami's demon plays. The essence of a demon role is prodigious strength and fearsomeness. Since these effects are precisely the opposite of those that appeal, this presents a paradox. The more the actor attempts to achieve the essence of these roles, the less interest they will have for spectators. Zeami concluded that the most desirable style for such parts is not that of a fearful demon (in the terminology of the middle-period treatises, "the demon role in the style of strong movement"), but one that expresses the awful strength of the demon as the basic element of the performance while exhibiting other elements that evoke interest. In his early period, he compared this level of performance to "a flower blooming on the rocks" (*Kaden*, 2:16-17; *ZMZC*, 25-26). In less metaphorical terms, this means performing with the heart of a human being even while having the form of a demon. In such a performance the actor seeks to evoke interest by increasing his movements and making them more subtle. In his middle-period treatises, Zeami refers to this style as "the demon role in the style of delicate movement." *Koi no Omoni* and *Funabashi* are exemplary of plays in this style. *Koi no Omoni* is Zeami's adaptation of the older play *Aya no Taiko (The Large Damask Drum)*, and *Funabashi* is also considered to be an adaptation of an earlier play (*Sandō*, 161; *ZMZC*, 143). In both cases, the older play was in the style of "strong movement."

It is important that, as yūgen was incorporated in nō, dream pieces in two parts also developed steadily. If these two-part works have their prototype in deity plays, *Takasago* and *Oimatsu*, in which the former shite (maejite) are human incarnations of deities, should naturally have been included among the model plays composed by Zeami. The inclusion of shura plays, such as *Tadanori, Sanemori, Yorimasa, Atsumori, Funabashi*, and *Tōru*, in which the former shite are the spirits of dead warriors, reflects that dream plays in two parts (fukushiki mugen nō) were gradually gaining favor with audiences, and that Zeami himself had confidence in the kind. It seems strange, however, that there is no dream play with a female shite among the exemplary plays designated by Zeami.

In the *Sandō*, Zeami refers to plays with female shite (nyotai no nō) as "the precious jewels among the semiprecious," adding the actors playing female roles must be "actors of the highest sensibility in performance" (*Sandō*, 153; *ZMZC*, 137-38). These statements clearly show that Zeami had in mind specific examples. He explains that it is female roles in which the element of "madness" (kurui) was added to the intrinsically refined appeal of the role.[43] Among his own plays, *Izutsu* would be the most appropriate example. The possibility is strong, however, that this play was not composed until shortly before 1427 (Kitagawa, 1971, 187). There is also a text of *Eguchi*, which is considered to have been originally the work of Kannami, copied with revisions by Zeami and dated the Ninth Month of 1424.[44] The highly refined language of this text suggests that it is a substantially improved revision of the play by Zeami. This play, however, also is not included in the list of exemplary plays in the *Sandō*, which was completed in the Second Month of 1423. This fact must be interpreted to mean that Zeami's revisions of *Eguchi* were undertaken in the period from the Second Month of 1423 to the Ninth Month of 1424. We ought to conclude that Zeami composed his dream nō in two parts, and with shite roles for female characters, only after his shura plays.

I would like to propose that Zeami's invention of unifying imagery is another important development in his middle period. In *Takasago*, for example, the image of pines recurs again and again throughout the play and is symbolic of its theme. The twisted branches of a pine tree on the seashore are suggestive of old age, but its evergreen leaves are symbolic of eternal youth. It is this theme of eternal youth that is symbolized by the pine trees. Unity is essential to drama, and in the West, there have been many kinds of unity, from the three unities of the neoclassical theater (unity of time, place, and action) to the unity of impression seen in modern theater. None of these various kinds of unity, however, are complete in nō. Nō does possess a unity of imagery, and this has become its most salient characteristic.

Ezra Pound, who discovered this fact, pointed out, however, that this unity of imagery does not exist in all nō but can only be recognized in the "better plays."[45] Pound had no knowledge whatsoever of the authors of

[43] As Donald Keene has pointed out, this "madness" is not lunatic behavior. Rather, it refers to speech and actions resulting from some unbearable emotion that leads to violation of decorous norms for an individual of a certain kind or class (Keene, 1970, 131). A court lady, for example, was expected to speak in a quiet, calm manner befitting the refined elegance of her appearance, but the shite of *Sumidagawa* has a violent dispute with people of low rank. Therefore, she is a "mad woman." In *Hanagatami* (see below) the shite is asked to "do something crazy," to which she replies, "Very well, I shall rave." When the tennō orders her to stop her raving, she immediately does so. [Auth., Trans.]

[44] The text is in the collection of the temple Hōzanji. At the beginning of the scroll is the notation, "the nō play *Eguchi*, Komparu Dono," and at the end, "20.IX.1424, written by Zeami."

[45] Pound also suggested as examples of unity of imagery the following: the autumn leaves and the snow flurries in *Nishikigi (The Brocade Tree)*; the pines in *Takasago*; the blue-gray waves and the wave patterns in *Suma Genji (Genji at Suma)*; and the feather mantle in *Hagoromo (The Feather Mantle)* (Pound-Fenollosa, 1917, 26-27). In fact, the suggestion of

nō, but an examination of the "better plays" reveal that almost all of them are plays by Zeami or members of Zeami's group.[46] "Zeami's group" includes, besides Zeami, Motomasa, Motoyoshi, and Zenchiku. That is, it includes those who succeeded to his dramatic art (including some authors not yet identified). The aesthetic importance of this matter requires detailed specification. *Takasago* is not alone in possessing unity of imagery, as a schematic representation shows.

U no Ha: the tide, the moon
Taisanmoku: flowers
Hakozaki: pines
Oimatsu: pines, plum blossoms
Yawata Hachiman: the bow
Yōro: a fountain
Kiyotsune: dark hair, the moon
Sanemori: flowers, brocade
Atsumori: flute
Tadanori: cherry blossoms
Yorimasa: plants
Higaki: water
Izutsu: the wooden well frame, the moon
Tsuchiguruma: the barrow
Taema: lotus flowers
Hanagatami: flowers
Hanjo: fan
Kinuta: fulling blocks, the moon
Tōru: the moon.

A number of other plays unified by their imagery are Zeami's adaptations to an extent that they have been considered his own work: *Akoya no Matsu* (the pines); *Matsukaze* (the pines, the moon); *Hyakuman* (a cart); *Koi no Omoni* (the heavy burden); and *Funabashi* (floating bridge). Only three of Zeami's known works do not have unified imagery: *Ari-dōshi, Ōsaka Monogurui*, and *Kōya Monogurui*.

This is to say that during Zeami's middle period he still composed works like *Kōya Monogurui* that lacked unified imagery, which shows that such unity was not yet an aim. We should also observe that, through Pound, English poets learned of the concept of unified imagery in nō and

---

the snow flurry as a unifying image in *Nishikigi* is based on a mistaken interpretation of the play, and the unifying images of *Suma Genji* are flowers and the moon.

[46] *Takasago* is Zeami's composition, and the possibility is strong that *Nishikigi* and *Suma Genji* are his also (Omote, 1979, 493-96). I regard *Hagoromo* as a composition by Zeami's group. The term "Zeami's group" is my own. [The remainder of this note has been incorporated into the author's text, with some slight adaptation.—Ed.]

that it contributed to the development of the Imagism sponsored by Pound and to the aesthetic of W. B. Yeats (Miner, 1958, 135-55).

There are no extant nō treatises by Zeami for a period of about fifteen years after the completion of *Fūshi Kaden* in 1402. After this long silence, Zeami completed *Kashū* (*Learning the Flower*) in or before 1418, and *Kakyō* (*A Mirror Held to the Flower*) in 1424.[47] There are eight other treatises recognized as belonging to this period, but *Kakyō* is by far the most important. Zeami's theories during this period are different in many respects from those of the period of the *Fūshi Kaden*, and I would like to consider this Zeami's middle period.

Several matters of importance emerge in the middle-period treatises. One is his theory of a realm of performance that he calls the "level of perfect maturity" (taketaru kurai or ran'i).[48] This theory is developed in the *Shikadō* (*The True Path to the Flower*), which was completed in 1420. An actor who has achieved the stage of highest advancement through long years of accumulated practice and experience will on rare occasions mix into his performance some unorthodox style that in years past he has learned to exclude from his art, and by so doing he achieves a performance rich in interest for the audience.

Precisely because the nō of the master actor is perfect in every respect (Zeami calls this a "pure and orthodox style," or zefū), the audience may become completely accustomed to it, and even though the performance is in fact quite perfect, the audience may come to feel it lacks savor. In this case, the actor who has achieved the level of perfect maturity may include elements of "improper style" (hifū). This will lend novelty to his performance, and this improper style will be received by the audience as a pure and orthodox style (*Shikadō*, 67; *ZMZC*, 114–16). This "stage of perfect maturity" (taketaru kurai) may thus be understood as a "style of non-yūgen," the basic tone of which is the style of strength, or "take," which in his early period Zeami considered to be a style complementary, or opposed, to yūgen (*Kaden*, 3:46-47; *ZMZC*, 34; Konishi, 1961a, 163-70). In short, a master actor occasionally mixes in non-yūgen elements when his performance has become so suffused by yūgen that it has lost its novelty, when yūgen no longer produces the Flower. This concept partakes of Zeami's early theory that novelty is produced when the actor presents an art that the audience does not expect, and that for this reason the strat-

[47] *Kashū* is not extant. However, a fragment in Zeami's calligraphy survives in the collection of the Kanze school. This fragment bears a colophon, dated II.1418. *Kashū* was an earlier and partial version of *Kakyō*.

[48] Rimer-Yamazaki translate this term as "Perfect Freedom" (*Shikadō*, 67), emphasizing Zeami's theory that an actor who had achieved this level of performance is able to transcend technique in a performance of perfect freedom. The author wishes to emphasize, however, that this freedom is attained through long experience. It is when the mature actor transcends his own mastery that he is able to perform with perfect freedom. [Auth., Trans.]

egy of concealment is essential (*Kaden*, 7:59-60; *ZMZC*, 61-62).[49] In contrast to Zeami's early period, however, in which the yūgen style was only one of a variety of styles, this theory is one of the salient features of his middle period, in which his theories tend to be concerned solely with the achievement of yūgen.

To the extent that an improper style can become a pure and orthodox style when, by the manner in which it is employed, it produces the Flower, the distinction between an improper style and a pure and orthodox style itself is not a fixed entity. Rather, in Zen Buddhist terms, it may be thought of as Non-being (mu). But the working of the actor's mind is not necessarily that of Non-being. Indeed, the mind (kokoro) that ponders and makes judgments concerning when and in what manner to perform in an improper style exists as part of the actor's awareness.

The most characteristic assertion of Zeami's middle period, however, is his concept of abolishing the mind (kokoro), i.e., transcending cognition. In *Kakyō*, he states that the actor must use his mind while performing as if he were watching his own performance from the spectators' seats (*Kakyō*, 81-82; *ZMZC*, 88-89). When the actor's mind shifts to the spectators' seats, the actor on stage performs without mind. This is performance at the "level-of-No-mind." In fact, however, it is impossible for the actor to perform without use of mind, and he will of course perform by using discourse of thought. *This* thought, however, is not the mind that ponders and makes decisions such as "I shall perform in this way," or "I must not perform in this way." Rather, it is, so to speak, another mind that exists at the very depths of that ordinary mind and which the actor himself cannot be aware of as a mind.[50]

In the same section of *Kakyō*, Zeami states that it is precisely during those intervals when there is no physical performance by the shite—when the actor breaks off chanting, or when movement stops in the dance, or indeed in any of the intervals that occur during the performance of a role—that the audience is made to feel the greatest fascination.[51] He calls these intervals in which the actor performs no physical art (waza) "spaces in which the actor does nothing" ("senu hima"). But if these intervals were simply empty spaces in which there was nothing, they could have

[49] That the "Flower that is concealed" has very great effectiveness as a strategy can be demonstrated by modern information theory, game theory, and statistical decision-making theory (Konishi, 1980, 120-28). [It can be seen how strong throughout is the presumption that nō must move its audiences, both because Zeami was a practical man of the theater knowing audiences had to be moved and because affectivism was a major feature of the dominant waka aesthetics.—Ed.]

[50] Zeami calls this consciousness the shōne, the "fundamental mind" or, more literally, "the rock of essence" (*Kakyō*, 14, 96-97; *ZMZC*, 100). [Compare Coleridge's distinctions between the primary and secondary imaginations.—Ed.]

[51] [The kambun title of this section is "The matter of linking together all the arts of the nō in one mind" (mannō o isshin ni tsunagu; ibid.).—Trans.]

only a negative value for the spectators. Zeami explains that the discerning spectators will praise the master actor for the interest of the intervals in which he does nothing for no other reason than that he binds together the moments of physical performance before and after that interval with his mind. This thought is projected outside the actor's interior state, evoking in the discerning spectator an inexplicable response (*Kakyō*, 96-99; *ZMZC*, 100-101). The mind that links the moments before and after the interval in which the actor does nothing does not differ from that which observes the actor's own performance from the spectators' position.

When the actor is performing some physical action, he is made to move by the workings of the mind that makes decisions concerning how the action should or should not be performed—that is, by a mind at the level of awareness. When there is no action at all, however, the mind at the level of awareness has no object of intentionality upon which to work. Therefore, when the actor's mind nevertheless continues to work in intervals when there is no physical performance, it may be considered to belong not to mind at the level of awareness but to another mind that exists at a more profound level. Moreover, the profounder mind that enables the actor to link together the moments before and after intervals in which there is no physical performance must be one that hides even from the actor himself the fact that it exists:

> It would be wrong to allow an audience to observe that this inner mind [naishin] exists. If it were observed, it would be an element of physical performance. It would no longer be "not performing." The actor must achieve a state of No-mind [mushin no kurai], binding together the moments before and after the intervals in which he performs no physical art by the workings of an inner mind that his own mind conceals even from himself. This is the interior intensity of thought that links all the arts of nō through one mind. (*Kakyō*, 97; *ZMZC*, 100)

The mind that conceals works at the level of awareness; the mind that is concealed corresponds to what Jung calls "preconsciousness." This way of stating the theory may seem extremely irrational, but I have actually seen the profound beauty of this art in which the actor "does nothing" in any number of performances by the master actors of the modern nō. On a number of occasions, I have asked these actors about their performances, and they have invariably replied with something like, "I did not think about it particularly while I was performing."[52] The art of these

[52] It is by no means true that master actors achieved performances corresponding to the level of No-mind by studying Zeami's treatises. High levels of performance were achieved by obediently practicing under the direction of a senior actor in a master-disciple relation-

modern masters is by no means different from the realm Zeami designates as the "stage of No-mind" (mushin no kurai).

The "inner mind that his own mind conceals even from himself" also exists in the exploitation of a unique point of view in the expression of nō. I have designated this point of view "narration by the actor" (yakuji). In the usual narrative or dramatic text, when there is a narrative of events or the circumstances of the scene, all explanation is entrusted to a general narrator. The characters of the work never overlap with this narrator. In the case of nō, the chorus (jiutai) corresponds to this narrator. The progress and circumstances of the drama, and sometimes even the interior mental states of characters, are explained in the third person by the words of the chorus.

In Zeami's plays, however, explanations that would normally be given by the chorus are often spoken by the shite, the waki, or the various tsure [roles that may accompany a shite or waki]. An example of this may be seen in *Hanagatami (The Flower Basket)*. Before his accession to the throne, Keitei Tennō had lived in Echizen, where he had been deeply in love with Teruhi no Mae, a lady who waited on him. The play begins after his departure from Echizen. Lady Teruhi languishes in yearning for him and finally resolves to travel to the capital. Carrying a flower basket he had given her as a remembrance, she sets out. It so happens that Keitei is making an excursion to view the autumn leaves, and Lady Teruhi encounters his procession on the road. She performs the kusemai *Ri Fujin (Imperial Consort Li)*. At first Keitei does not recognize that the dancer is Lady Teruhi. But his eye is caught by the flower basket, and he orders her to bring it to him. This sets the stage for the following scene:

Waki [Attendant]. (Prose)
It is His Majesty's decree. Give His Majesty the flower basket.

Shite [Lady Teruhi]. (Verse)
(a) *So unexpected is the fact*
That her breast swells with feeling,
Her mind floats in the sky.
Embarrassing as it is,
Here is the flower basket—
She presents it.

Waki. (Verse)
(b) *His Majesty in his turn,*
Observes the proffered basket,

---

ship. The study of Zeami's treatises by nō actors did not begin until around 1947, and even then it was limited to a small group led by Kanze Hisao (1925-78).

And there is no doubt whatever
That in the province
This very flower basket
Was the one his hands had held.

(Prose)
And he gave it to you when he departed from the province.

(Verse—The Tennō's message)
"Put aside your bitterness
That I failed to write to you
And cease your wild behavior—
Then things will be as once they were,
And you will serve me as before."
His Majesty so speaks. (*YKS*, 1:355-56)

In the italicized passage (a), the interior state of the shite (Lady Teruhi) is explained in the third person. In principle, third-person relation should be narrated by the chorus from an omniscient point of view. The shite's speaking the passage in the third person makes one feel a sense of strangeness. Moreover, in the italicized passage (b), which describes the interior mental state of the tennō, content that would normally be the responsibility of the chorus is stated by the waki (the tennō's retainer). Of course, because he will shift to a mode of delivery in which he addresses the shite from his own point of view in the prose part, "And he gave it to you . . . ," the waki chants the italicized passage (b) in a style called kakaru and then shifts to prose when he addresses the shite. This serves to emphasize the differences in his points of view.

I have used the general term "narration by the actor" (yakuji) to designate all such passages in which narration that would normally be the responsibility of the chorus is instead spoken by a character in a shite or waki role. I can now establish two additional terms: "narration by the shite" (shiteji), in which the shite chants these lines; and "narration by the waki" (wakiji), in which they are chanted by the waki.

One may well ask why this extraordinary point of view—narration by the actor—was employed. Consider the example above. The shite senses that Keitei has recognized that she is indeed Lady Teruhi. The thought of Lady Teruhi at this moment, the intensity of her emotional state, could not be expressed completely, even if the shite speaks from her own point of view; that is, in the first person. Of course, the shite could appeal to the audience by exploiting a highly expressive voice, or with violent gestures, and indeed these are the usual methods of expressing emotion in theater. Such methods not only have limits, they are also inconsistent with actual psychology. When it has been confronted with ultimate joy, the mind is tangled with thoughts and feelings, so that it is no longer able to grasp consciously what is what. It is in the state described in the play: "Her mind floats in the sky (kokoro sora naru)." This phrase may also be interpreted to mean, "Her mind is void." Even if such a mental state can be depicted to some extent with modes of speaking that belong to the mental surface level, the true psychology of such a mental state can never be grasped there.

Only when this mental state is grasped precisely as the character herself cannot consciously comprehend can it become true expression. And it is precisely at this point that the shite shifts her mind completely to the point of view of the chorus (jikata). Thus, while physically it is the shite who chants, "So unexpected is the fact / That her breast swells with feeling," psychologically it is the chorus. When the mind of the shite is shifted completely to the chorus—as a third person—the shite's own mind becomes void. The mind that had become void, however, is awareness at a level that can be aware of joy, of bitterness, or of anxiety. At a deeper level is swirling a chaotic mind that can neither be depicted nor explained. For that reason, the actor performs no physical action or technique (waza) that can be grasped by the mind. This does not mean, however, that the actor is in a state of abstracted stupefication. Inexplicable thought flows violently at a much deeper level, and this is the mind that links the moments before and after the interval in which the shite "does not perform."

The same analysis may be applied to the role of the tennō. His emotions are tangled in an intricate knot: surprise when he realizes that the flower basket is the one he had given Lady Teruhi, remorse at having left her alone until now, and the feelings of love that well up when he recognizes her. These emotions are stated as narration by the waki (wakiji).[53] Interior states that one would expect to be related from a first-person point of view are instead described in the third person. This technique has a great deal in common with the technique of indirect interior monologue in stream-of-consciousness novels. In this technique, an omniscient narrator intervenes and relates matters not spoken of by the characters in the work as if they were flowing directly from the minds of individual char-

[53] In modern nō, the role of the tennō is performed by a juvenile actor (kokata). These actors usually play the roles of boys (e.g., Umewakamaru in *Sumidagawa*) or young girls (the maiden in *Jinen Koji*). In this case, however, a child actor is used because a performance of the role of Keitei by an adult would have a tendency to give the tennō's expressions of love too real an impression. However, if the child actor were to chant the tennō's lines in this scene, it would be too far removed from reality, and so the waki is made to speak these lines as a proxy. In modern performances of *Funabenkei (Benkei on the Bridge)*, a juvenile actor performs the role of Yoshitsune with quite different dramatic effects. Of course, in *Hanagatami*, this additional strategic consideration does not reduce the effectiveness of these lines as narration by the waki.

acters. The point of view is third person. The familiar example of this technique is of course the opening scene of Virginia Woolf's *Mrs. Dalloway* (London: Hogarth Press, 1980, 5; Humphrey, 1954, 29-33).

Nevertheless, there are also important differences between the technique of indirect interior monologue and that of narration by the actor. In indirect interior monologue, the omniscient narrator enters directly into the interior mental state of the character, expressing from the narrator's point of view things that the character is not aware of. In narration by the actor, the mind of the character is projected onto the position of the narrator and is expressed by the very character. Second, while mental states expressed as indirect interior monologue wander lingeringly through various levels of mind from the surface to the extreme limit of the deepest, what is expressed in narration by the actor is never separate from the surface-level context. A mind that belongs to deeper levels can be grasped when the spectator unites with the interior mind of the character. Third, in the stream-of-consciousness novel, the flowing thought of the character becomes the principal subject of the entire work, while narration by the actor is no more than a limited, local technique of point of view that enables the spectator to grasp the interior state of a character at certain moments. In order to distinguish this special technique of narration by the actor (yakuji) from both the omniscient point of view and the limited point of view, I would like to call the technique of yakuji the "projective point of view."

The use of this projective point of view is not limited only to apprehending deep levels of thought. There are many cases in which it is used merely as a proxy in passages that would normally be performed by the chorus (jiutai). Such examples are especially numerous in cases of narration by the waki and narration by the tsure. The chorus recites only in scenes with the shite on stage. In modern nō, shitekata actors perform these roles as an exclusive specialty.[54] In the fifteenth century, there was apparently no systematic specialization of roles distinguishing shite actors and waki actors. It is clear, however, that since there are no examples of the chorus chanting the waki's michiyuki (travel piece) or the machiutai (waiting piece), the chorus did not exist for waki or tsure roles.[55] Thus, passages assigned to waki or tsure would have to have been chanted by the waki or tsure themselves, even if they might be more appropriate in

[54] Shitekata are the actors that specialize in the roles of shite, shitetsure, and in the chorus (jiutai). There are five schools of shitekata: Kanze, Hōshō, Komparu, Kongō, and Kita. Wakikata actors perform only waki and wakitsure roles. The three wakikata schools are Takayasu, Jukuō, and Shimogakari Hōshō. [Auth., Trans.]

[55] The michiyuki or travel piece is related by the waki after self-identification, and tells of the places visited on the way to the scene of the play. The machiutai or waiting piece is related by the waki at the beginning of the second scene, in a two-part dream nō preceding the entrance of the nochijite. [Auth., Trans.]

terms of content for performance by the chorus. The performance by waki and tsure actors of passages more appropriate to narration by the chorus influenced the performances of shite actors and finally developed into what I have called narration by the shite. Therefore, in the early stages of this development, narration by the shite was merely a substitute for the chorus; it had not yet become a unique technique of point of view employed to make spectators susceptible to deeper levels of mind. There is the following passage in *Jinen Koji (The Lay Priest Jinen)*:

Shite (Jinen). (Prose)

In the evening rain from the Temple of the Clouds I shall deliver a sermon to amuse the assembled company as they wait for the moon; *so speaking the preacher mounts the platform and clangs a gong to signal his prayer.*

(Verse)

It is with care.
It is with reverence that I speak
To the Buddha Shakyamuni
Manifested in mundane form
To inculcate his teaching;
O buddhas of the past, now, future,
O bodhisattvas Everywhere—hear what I pray
As for the deities of this place
The *Heart Sūtra* will be my text. (*YKS*, 1:97)

The italicized passage is "narration by the shite," but here it is nothing more than a substitute for the chorus. It must have been Zeami who invented the projective point of view as a technique of expressing deeper levels of mind. Indeed, it does not occur in plays before him. The following is a list of extant plays predating Zeami.[56]

Plays Composed Principally by Kannami[57]

Fushimi (place name): *Kinsatsu (The Golden Plate)*
Furu (place name)
Matsukaze Murasame (Matsukaze and Murasame): Matsukaze
Eguchi no Yūjo (The Woman of Eguchi): Eguchi (place name)

[56] This list includes both extant plays written before Zeami and plays that Zeami substantially revised but that were originally composed before him.

[57] Plays that Kannami played the greatest role in composing. For example, as stated earlier *Matsukaze* was a revision by Kannami of the dengaku nō play *Shiokumi (The Salt Water Gatherers)*. Zeami's further revision of this play resulted in the *Matsukaze* performed in the current repertoire (*YKS*, 1:57). Motoyoshi considered the play to have been composed principally by Zeami.

Shii no Shōshō (The Lesser Captain of the Fourth Grade): *Kayoi Komachi (Komachi and the Hundred Nights)*
Komachi (Lady Komachi): Sotoba Komachi (Komachi on the Stupa)
Motomezuka (The Maiden's Grave)
Jinen Koji (The Lay Priest Jinen)
Shizuka ga Mai (Lady Shizuka's Dance): Yoshino Shizuka (Shizuka in Yoshino)

Other Plays Predating Zeami
Akoya no Matsu (The Pine of Akoya)
Michimori (Taira Michimori)
Shigehira (Taira Shigehira): Kasa Sotoba (The Bamboo Hat Stupa)
Aoi no Ue (Lady Aoi)
Ukifune (Lady Ukifune)
Kashiwazaki (The Cape of Kashiwa)
Tango Monogurui (The Raving Man at Tango)
Urin'in (The Temple Urin'in)[58]
Ama (The Woman Diver)
Moriya (Mononobe Moriya)
Kusakari (The Grass Cutter): Yokoyama
Hitsuji (The Sheep)
Ōshō Kun (Lady Wang Chao)
Ukai (The Cormorant Fisher)

In all these plays, narration by the actor does not exist or is limited to substitution for choral relation. Narration by the actor was invented by Zeami during the same period he fully grasped the performance realm of mushin, "the age of No-mind" (mushin no kurai). After Zeami, narration by the actor was exploited widely (Konishi, 1966b, 1-12).

Another important development in Zeami's dramaturgy during his middle period was the deepening of his concept of yūgen. The esteem of yūgen is an important characteristic of Zeami's treatises even in his early period, but in his middle period his conception of yūgen became even more refined. That is, he began to aspire for a kind of beauty that, while it is still yūgen, could perhaps better be called the beauty of hie (a chilled beauty).

As we have seen, the model plays he named in 1423 did not include *Izutsu (The Well Frame)* and *Kinuta (Fulling Blocks)*. That must be because they were written later. Zeami himself said of *Kinuta*, "In this decadent age, I doubt that anyone knows the true flavor of a play like this" (*Dangi*, 180; *ZMZC*, 265). Motoyoshi, the compiler of *Sarugaku Dangi*,

[58] This is not the *Urin'in* performed in the current repertoire but a nō entitled *Urin'in* in Zeami's holograph (*YKS*, 1:148-54).

adds that this kind of "unsurpassed flavor without flavor" could be comprehended only by a spectator with a high level of discernment, and he despairs of expressing it in words. For the ordinary spectator, he writes, *Ukifune* and *Matsukaze* probably seem to be the most excellent plays (*Dangi*, 180-81; *ZMZC*, 265-66). As these remarks suggest, *Kinuta* has an extremely introverted tone.[59] The central motif is the grief and bitterness of a wife whose husband has been away for a long time, and one would expect that the basic effect would be one of refined grace (yūen).

Instead, however, the play is dominated by the image of the desolate chill of a cold evening in late autumn, and yūen is present only faintly in the depths of this cold loneliness. Consider this moving passage (*YKS*, 1:335; all in verse, with the chorus speaking, as usual, for the shite).

Chorus
The voice of the wind-swept pines
Falls upon the cloth,
The voice of the wind-swept pines
Falls upon the cloth,
Telling me to heed the cold
Brought by the wind of night.

Shite (Lady)
Word from him is rare
As his infrequent visits are,
And in the autumn wind

Chorus
It is an evening that manifests
The misery I feel.

Shite
Off in that distant place of his
He must know this, too.

Chorus
The moon will not inquire of him
With whom he shares his thought.

Shite
How lovely it is,
How right is the hour.
For autumn is the season,
Twilight is the hour.

[59] [For discussion of the meaning of introversion (naikōsei), see vol. one, pp. 16-29.—Ed.]

Chorus
The mating cries of stags as well
Fill my heart with pain.
Unseen gales from the mountains
Bear down upon me.
And from which branch can it be
A last leaf has come?
In the heavens the sharp cold chills
The bright light of the moon
As it reflects upon the straw fern
Thatched upon my eaves.

Shite
And the glistening drops of dew
Jewel a curtain to my sorrow,

Chorus
Assuaging my yearning heart
As I wait out the night alone.

The shite responds to the beauty of this cold, desolate scene, and this response clearly is not simply one of lonely contemplation. This tone is what Shinkei would have called beauty of the chill (hie). Indeed, a rearrangement of the first part of this passage into renga stanzas suggests the degree to which this play partakes of the beauty of hie.[60]

Koromo ni matsu no	The voice of the wind-swept pines
koe zo otsu naru	seems to fall upon the cloth
yoi goto ni	with every evening
yosamu o kaze ya	the wind seems to bid me heed
shirasu ran	the cold of night

The stanzas are effectively linked by the association of the "robe" ("koromo") and the "cold nights" ("yosamu") of the chilly season, and the association of "pines" ("matsu") and "wind" ("kaze"). The next section could be rearranged into the following:

Otozure no	Word from him is rare
mare naru naka no	as his infrequent visits are
aki no kaze	in the autumn wind
uki o shirasuru	an evening that manifests
yūbe naramashi	the anguish that it shows me

[60] [Renga stanzas composed by the author follow, although not linked into a whole, so emphasizing Shinkei's art more than Sōgi's: see ch. 15.—Trans., Ed.]

These stanzas are linked by conception (kokorozuke). Moreover, "autumn" often becomes a pivot word (kakekotoba) for "estrangement" ("aki"). Next:

Tōzatobito ya	Those in distant places
nagameakasan	surely gaze on it till dawn
ta ga yo to wa	"whose night is it?"
utsurou tsuki no	is what the brilliant moon inquires
yomo towaji	of no one anywhere

This is an extremely profound link, based as it is on a famous honka [foundation poem for alluding to] from the *Shūishū* (3:176):

Izuko ni ka	Is there anywhere
Koyoi no tsuki no	People are unable to see
Miezaran	The moon tonight?
Akanu wa hito no	But never to be satisfied—
Kokoro narikeri.	That marks out the human heart.

Just as the honka lends depth to my stanzaic link, its presence in the background of the passage upon which my stanzas are linked suggests subtle nuances in the expression of the character's mental state.

Zeami was more than forty years older than Shinkei, and it is difficult to believe that he learned the beauty of chill from the younger man. Rather, Japanese conceptions of chill beauty were developed in both renga and nō by contact with the Sung poetry being brought into Japan by Zen priests. After Yoshimitsu's sudden death in 1408, Ashikaga Yoshimochi ruled the country as shogun for approximately twenty years until his own death in 1428. During this period, Zeami must have been highly aware of Yoshimochi's preferences, both in writing plays and in staging performances. Yoshimochi had a keen critical eye for even the most subtle details of a performance, and surely Zeami had him in mind when he wrote the following: "These days, however, their eyes are highly skilled and so audiences have come to observe even the slightest fault, so that if a presentation is not as elegant as a polished gem or a bouquet of flowers, it cannot meet the expectations of a cultured group of spectators" (*Shikadō*, 72; *ZMZC*, 118).

While Yoshimochi did not particularly shun Zeami, he seems to have been more attracted to the nō of the dengaku master Zōami, and he held a number of subscription performances for Zōami between 1413 and 1422 (Nose, 1938, 1053-55). Zeami himself praised Zōami's art as the Flower of Grace (kankafū).[61] His account of Zōami's performance in the

[61] A style of nō masks now called zō is thought to be the invention of Zōami. The refined

dengaku *Shakuhachi (The Shakuhachi Flute)* is of particular importance: "He blew a note on the shakuhachi, performed his chant with artless strength and clarity, and then left the stage, casually entering the dressing room—this was a performance of chill upon chill [hie ni hietaru]" (*Dangi*, 176; *ZMZC*, 262). The style of the Flower of Grace is the ultimate stage of yūgen. Zōami's performance "with artless strength and clarity"—an introverted, unexpressive performance—is nothing other than the art of the beauty of chill (hie). Zeami's emphatic praise of the beauty of chill reflects that he now had to compete with Zōami; ultimately, the beauty of chill had its roots in the tastes of Yoshimochi (Konishi, 1961a, 278).[62] *Izutsu* and *Kinuta* were born from Zeami's aspiration for an art of hie.

It would have been difficult, however, for Zeami to attract Yoshimochi to his own nō by striving for the same style as Zōami's. Zeami therefore invented a new type of performance in which, through the projective point of view, the interior mental states of the shite are grasped by another mind. This was performance in the realm of No-mind, in which intervals that are completely empty in terms of performance were filled by a deep level of mind ("preconsciousness"). "Another mind of which, though it is also my mind, I myself am not aware is gazing upon my mind"—this mode of apprehension is the hallmark of Kyōgoku poetics (see ch. 14). Yoshimochi had intimate connections with poets of the Reizei school (Nishi, 1965, 38-43), and he must have learned of this style through them. As we have seen, it is a mode of apprehension based on Tendai shikan, but in this matter Tendai shikan is not different from Zen. Yoshimochi, who was a fervent adherent of Zen, must have understood this kind of expression, or apprehension, in a Zen fashion.[63]

Furthermore, Zeami himself had sufficient knowledge of Zen to create the projective point of view. He had an intimate relationship with Chikusō Chigon (d. 1423) of the Fuganji Temple, and it is certain that he learned Sōtō Zen from Chikusō and his closest disciple. Indeed, from around 1420, terminology and the method of argument characteristic of Sōtō Zen became conspicuous in Zeami's treatises (Kōsai, 1958, 20-39). This is further evidence that Zeami was frantically searching for a nō that

appeal (yūen) and the graceful elegance of these masks are suggestive of what must have been Zōami's performance style.

[62] "I also call this a chilled performance. This realm of performance is not known even to connoisseurs with a substantial level of understanding and could not possibly be imagined by provincial connoisseurs. I wonder if this is a realm of performance that can be achieved only by an unsurpassed master who had also been gifted with rare natural talent? This kind of performance is called 'nō that comes out of the mind,' 'nō of No-mind,' and 'nō of No-design.' " (*Kakyō*, 16, 101; *ZMZC*, 103).

[63] Yoshimochi was the most important supporter of the Zen establishment during this period (*Gaun* [4. Intercalary X.1449], 45). Moreover, he had sufficient knowledge of Zen doctrine to debate with Genrei Richū (dates unknown) of the temple Nanzenji (ibid. [25.I.1465], 160).

would satisfy Yoshimochi's critical eye and enable him to achieve a higher artistic level in his performances than had Zōami.

From Zeami to Zenchiku: The Flower of the Return and the Stage of Essence

The period after 1427-28 or slightly earlier, when Zeami wrote the *Kyūi (The Nine Levels)*, is what I consider his later period.[64] During this period he developed the ideal of the Flower of the Return (kyaraika), and with this concept he begins to evolve a position different from those he had held earlier (Konishi, 1961a, 22-24). Kyarai is a Zen term referring to the basic teaching of Zen: for one who has achieved the state of ultimate awakening (satori) to dwell there in peace would be to vitiate the effect of awakening. Therefore, when one has truly achieved the ultimate awakening one must return once again to the state before awakening. This process of returning to one's previous self is nothing other than kyarai. In order to make clear the nature of the Flower of the Return, Zeami established nine levels of the art of nō (*Kyūi*, 121-22; *ZMZC*, 174-75).[65]

The Upper Three Flowers

1. The art of the Flower of Sublimity [myōkafū, the highest of the upper three Flowers]: "In Silla in the dead of night the sun shines brightly."
2. The art of the Flower of Profundity [chōshinkafū, the middle of the upper three Flowers]: "Snow covers a thousand mountains; why is there one peak not white?"
3. The art of the Flower of Grace [kankafū, the lowest of the upper three Flowers]: "Pile up snow in a silver bowl."[66]

The Middle Three Levels[67]

4. The level of the True Flower [shōkafū, the highest of the three middle levels]: "In the bright mist the sun sinks, and all the mountains are crimson."

[64] Zeami transmitted the *Shūgyoku Tokka (Finding Gems and Gaining the Flower)* to Zenchiku in 1428. Since the theories dealt with in this treatise take the nine levels (kyūi) as their premise, we may conclude that the *Kyūi* was completed before this date.

[65] All information in square brackets has been provided for the convenience of the reader; it is not contained in the original. A detailed analysis of the literary sources of the lines of poetry quoted in the *Kyūi*, as well as a penetrating interpretation of them, may be found in Nose, 1940, 547-72.

[66] [This is a famous line found in a number of Zen texts, e.g., *Hekigan Roku*, item 13. To feel the beauty of yūgen in white snow was part of the traditional sensibility of the Middle Ages, and it is at the level of the art of the Flower of Grace that this kind of yūgen is achieved in performance. (See *Hekigan Roku*, Shinchōsha edition, p. 166.)—Trans.]

[67] Although the upper three Flowers may also be considered "levels" in the topology of the kyūi, Zeami distinguishes them as "arts of the flower" (kafū). The middle three levels and the lower three levels are called "levels of performance" (kurai).

5. The level of Broad Mastery [kōshōfū, the middle of the three middle levels]: "Relate completely the meaning of the clouds on the mountain, the moon over the sea."[68]
6. The level of Basic Design [semmonfū, the lowest of the three middle levels]: "What the world calls the way is not the True Way."[69]

The Bottom Three Levels

7. The level of Subtle Strength [gōsaifū, the highest of the bottom three levels]: "The metal hammer's shadow moves; the blade of the sacred sword gleams cold."[70]
8. The level of Crude Strength [gōsofū, the middle of the bottom three levels]: "Three days after its birth, the tiger wants to eat an ox."
9. The level of Blunt Crudeness [soenfū, the lowest of the three bottom levels]: "The five skills of the flying squirrel." Confucius said, "The flying squirrel has five skills. It can climb trees, swim in the water, dig holes, fly, and run. Yet in all of these talents it is bound by its innate weakness."

Considered in the ordinary way, one would think that the beginning actor should begin with the lowest level of the bottom three levels and practice each level in order, finally achieving the art of the Flower of Sublimity. Zeami denies this, however, declaring that the beginning actor should begin at the lowest of the three middle levels, that is at the level of basic design (semmonfū). At this level the actor strives for yūgen as the keynote of performance, but the techniques of performance are not yet very complex. At the level of broad mastery (kōshō), the actor expands and refines his techniques. The highest of the middle three levels, the level of the True Flower, is reached when the actor achieves the beauty of yūgen in the techniques learned at the previous levels. As is suggested by the image, "In the bright mist the sun sinks, and all the mountains are crimson," the actor at this level strives for a yūgen that is bright and positive.

In contrast to this, the art of the Flower of Grace, the lowest of the

[68] [See *Hekigan Roku*, item 53. Two Zen monks, Monk Wood Cutter and Monk Fish, relate to each other everything they have learned of the significance of the clouds on the mountain peak and the moon over the sea. That is, they penetrate completely one another's essential natures. Here, the metaphor suggests a complete mastery of the techniques of performance. Zeami goes on to state that the level of broad mastery is the turning point determining whether the actor will advance to the level of the True Flower or fall to the lower three levels (*Kyūi*, 121; *ZMZC*, 174).—Trans.]

[69] Zeami has turned Lao Tzu's famous line to his own purposes: to practice the theatrical styles presently recognized as the correct way of the nō is not the True Way. [Lao Tzu's original meaning was that the way (tao; J. dō, michi) that can be pointed to and called the way is not the immutable, essential Way.—Trans.]

[70] ["The shadow of the metal hammer moving is a performance of strong movement. The sacred sword, its gleam cold, is a performance of chill" (*Kyūi*, 122; *ZMZC*, 175).—Trans.]

upper three Flowers, is symbolized by piling up snow in a silver bowl, an image that evokes a feeling of chill (hie). This art has an implicit, negative aspect, resembling the beauty also called chill and esteemed in Reizei poetics (see ch. 14). The poetic image attached to the art of the Flower of Profundity is not completely white: "Snow covers a thousand mountains; why is there one peak not white?" This is an image of the depths of a mountain range made up of line upon line of peaks. Even if the snow on one low mountain has melted early, the scene as a whole still appears completely white. This level of performance corresponds to the level of perfect maturity (ran'i), in which even though some elements of an improper style (hifū) are mixed into the performance of a master actor, the performance as a whole will still appear to be in a proper and orthodox style (zefū).

The art of the Flower of Sublimity (myōkafū), the highest level of the art of nō, is one that evokes a response that cannot be explained rationally. From the point of view of the actor, it is the realm of No-mind (mushin), in which his performance transcends his own thought. From that of the audience, it is the expression of No-design (mufū), the goodness of which cannot be directly felt. In fact, this is an instantaneous response.[71] It also exists in the arts of the Flower of Profundity and the Flower of Grace. It would be impossible to say that its totality is performed only in the style of the Flower of Sublimity, and it is therefore difficult to recognize the Flower of Sublimity as a style of performance juxtaposed against the Flower of Profundity and the Flower of Grace. It

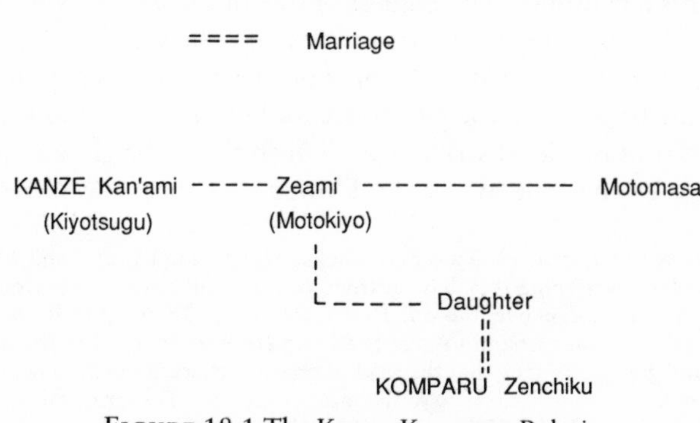

FIGURE 18.1 The Kanze-Komparu Relation

[71] Speaking from my own experience as a spectator of nō, it is in the smallest and most subtle movements that I experience a response that makes me feel as if I have been shattered physically and mentally into countless fragments—when the shite holds his fan out or stoops quietly to enter an artificially constructed mound. This response defies explanation.

may, however, be considered to be the "level" at which such an art can be performed.

The levels of accomplishment and styles of performance (ifū) discussed above all conform to Zeami's theories in his middle period and they appear for the first time there. What is new in the *Kyūi* of Zeami's late period is his assertion that an actor who has achieved one of the upper three levels can also make the audience feel interest in a performance in one of the styles of the lower three levels (*Kyūi*, 124-25; *ZMZC*, 176). Yoshimochi, who had prized only "a presentation as elegant as a polished gem or a bouquet of flowers" (*Shikadō*, 72; *ZMZC*, 118), died in 1428. His successor, Ashikaga Yoshinori (1394-1441), loved the performances of Zeami's nephew Onnami Motoshige (1398-1467). Considering this, and that Onnami was famous more for his performances in a wide variety of plays than as a theorist or a dramaturgist, we may hold with certainty that Zeami must have considered Yoshinori's tastes in developing his new theories. Far more importantly, Zeami himself became interested in Zen in his late period. Among the aphorisms attached to his nine levels of performance, at least six are clearly from Zen verse. There is no room for doubt that his concept of kyarai is based on Zen.

The Flower of the Return refers to a realm of performance in which a master actor, having achieved perfection in the art of yūgen, performs in a style that is non-yūgen. It can be easily understood even from modern performances of nō.[72] Zeami refers to the Flower of the Return in another treatise, stating that it is a "style performed only once in a lifetime," and that this one performance can only take place after one has reached the age of forty. Zeami taught this art only to Motomasa, his eldest son. Unfortunately, Motomasa died too early to have had a chance to perform in this style and never recorded his father's oral teachings (*Kyaraika*, 247). Although he referred to it frequently, Zeami never explained the Flower of the Return itself, and there is nothing in his treatises from which we may reconstruct his conception of this ideal realm of performance. The only clues we have are found in the nō treatises of Komparu Zenchiku (1405-70?).

Zenchiku was Zeami's son-in-law and was also on intimate terms with Motomasa. As we have seen, in 1428 Zeami wrote *Shūgyoku Tokka (Finding Gems and Gaining the Flower)* for Zenchiku. In this treatise, he discusses the concept of kyarai (*Shūgyoku Tokka*, 136; *ZMZC*, 189-90).[73] On the basis of this secret teaching, Zenchiku composed *Rokurin*

[72] Although Kanze Kasetsu (1886-1959) specialized in the nō characterized by yūgen, his most outstanding performances were of non-yūgen plays such as *Haku Rakuten (Po Chü-i)* or *Shōzon (The Surprise Attack by Shōzon)*.

[73] It is likely that Zenchiku married Zeami's daughter in the same year or slightly earlier. Certainly, Zeami would not have transmitted secret teachings of the Kanze school to the

Ichiro no Ki (Six Circles, One Dew). The six [ascending] circles may be summarized as follows:

1. The circle of life (jurin): the source from which yūgen is born in the chant and the dance, it has an infinite life.
2. The circle of rising (ryūrin); the level at which the basic life performance (jurin), which cannot be perceived by the senses, produces an interest that can be apprehended mentally.
3. The circle of stability (jūrin): the stage at which the various techniques of the nō come to have a stable expressive power.
4. The circle of figures (zōrin): the stage at which the actor is able to express the mental image of the performance he is attempting to perform just as he imagines it.
5. The circle of radical innovation (harin): the stage at which the actor crushes to pieces what is recognized as a pure and orthodox style (zefū) but is able nevertheless to achieve a performance rich in interest.
6. The circle of Emptiness (kūrin): the stage at which the actor transcends distinctions between pure and orthodox styles and improper styles, achieving a return (kyarai) to the basic life of performance, which expresses nothing.

These metaphysical stages in the actor's art share an essential character symbolized by the image of the circle. This is indicated by the application of the term "circle" (rin) to each of the six stages (*Rokurin Ichiro no Ki*, 197-203). This figure of the circle expresses a drop of water, and it is a symbol for the essence (shō) that forms all six stages. When this essence appears as function (yū), it is expressed by the image of a sword.

This is an extremely subjective metaphysics of nō. In terms of its content, however, it clearly succeeds to the theories developed in *Kyūi*. Why did the nine levels change to six circles? In my view, the direct cause is that, in *Shūgyoku Tokka*, Zeami had proposed a new distinction: between the Flower of Essence (shōka) and the Flower of Function (yūka). Having pursued the Flower throughout his career, Zeami now made a distinction between the Flower that exists in every case and the Flower that appears only at certain times and under certain conditions. The former he called the Flower of Essence, and the latter the Flower of Function (*Shūgyoku Tokka*, 129-33; *ZMZC*, 187). The six circles proposed by Zenchiku applied this concept of essence (shō) to Zeami's nine levels as a whole and reorganized them into a system of levels based on essence

leader of another troupe otherwise (Itō, 1969, 19-20). Zenchiku was twenty-four at this time.

(shō); that is, six "levels of essence" (shōi). This topology is the six circles (Konishi, 1961a, 260-65).

Zenchiku based this topology on a number of existing kinds of thought. Among them, one of the most important was the doctrine of Watarai Shinto of the Ise Shrine (Itō, 1962, 171-90). The basic position of Watarai Shinto, however, is the explanation of Japanese deities by linking them to the metaphysics of the esoteric Buddhism of the Shingon sect. In fact, in *Six Circles, One Dew*, Zenchiku grasps kyarai, originally a Zen concept, in terms of Shingon esoteric Buddhism. While Zenchiku's concept of the "circle of the Emptiness" is extremely subjective, it is suggestive in understanding Zeami's theory of kyarai:

> Ultimate awakening (satori) is identical with the state of not yet awakening.
>
> All things wither away, and faintly, child-like, every dance, every song returns to the place where first it sprouted. (*Rokurin Ichiro no Ki Chū* (*Notes to the Rokurin Ichiro no Ki*, 218)

The extreme limit of this negated expression, which perhaps may be called Non-being (mu), was born in the High Middle Ages, and it is one of the most important expressive forms in Japanese art. Precisely because he took up this form of expression directly, Zenchiku's theories are well worth our attention.

The subject of both Zeami's *Kyūi* and Zenchiku's *Rokurin Ichiro no Ki* is the performance of nō, and to them and their theories, the character of nō literary texts—of the words—is nothing more than the background. This is particularly true at Zeami's level of the Flower of Sublimity and the Flower of Profundity, or in Zenchiku's "circle of radical innovation" and "circle of Emptiness." That is, plays corresponding to these concepts are not actually required. Indeed, it is difficult to imagine that either Zeami in his late period or Zenchiku, his successor, produced new ways of writing plays. The plays Zeami composed in his late period must have been much the same as those composed in his middle period. The only differences were in the way they were performed. Zenchiku also succeeded to Zeami's middle-period style of composing plays.

Unlike the case for Zeami, for Zenchiku there are no primary materials indicating his authorship of plays, and one is forced to rely on lists of nō authors compiled during and after the sixteenth century.[74] According to these, Zenchiku was the author of the following five plays: *Kamo (The*

[74] Seven texts of such lists are extant from the period between 1524 and 1765. The earliest is the *Nōhon Sakusha Chūmon* (*Notes on the Authors of Nō*, 1524), and the latest is the *Nihyakujūban Utai Mokuroku* (*A List of Two Hundred and Ten Nō*, 1765). My study of these nō is based on Matsuda Tamotsu's "Sakusha Kotei Kiso Shiryō Ichiran" ("A List of Basic Materials for the Establishment of Nō Composers"; Matsuda, 1972, 215-39).

Kamo Shrine); Yōkihi (The Consort Yang); Bashō (The Spirit of the Plantain); Tamakazura (Lady Tamakazura); and *Ugetsu (Rain and Moon)*. In addition, with the exception of one list of playwrights that attributes them to Zeami, Zenchiku is listed as the author of the following three plays: *Oshio (The Hill of Oshio); Tatsuta (The Goddess of Tatsuta)*; and *Kogō (Lady Kogō)*. These eight plays can probably be recognized as the work of Zenchiku. There are two other plays for which the possibility of authorship by Zenchiku cannot be denied: *Teika (Lord Teika)* and *Saigyōzakura (Priest Saigyō and the Cherry Blossoms)*. They are listed on two lists of playwrights, one attributing them to Zeami and the other to Zenchiku.[75] These plays have some special features when compared to Zeami's attested plays, but in general their style has much in common. They are outstanding for the extent to which the genius of dream nō in two parts in two scenes has been perfected.

Had Zeami and Zenchiku not become related by marriage, it is unlikely that dream nō of this quality could have been produced by the Komparu troupe. These plays are superior to those composed by Motomasa, which can be identified with the same degree of certainty as Zeami's: *Matsugasaki* (place name); *Yoshinoyama (Mount Yoshino)*, which was later called *Yoshino Koto (Playing Koto at Yoshino); Utaura (Divination with Waka); Yoroboshi (The Tottering Boy); Morihisa (Taira Morihisa)* and *Sumidagawa (The River Sumida)*. Only *Yoshinoyama* is a dream nō in two parts.[76] All the rest are gendaimono, nō whose central figure is taken to be living at the time of the action. Motomasa seems to have returned to the styles of his grandfather (Kannami) rather than following in his father's footsteps, but Zeami's influence may be seen in the refined language of the plays. In this respect, Motomasa's plays are second only to Zeami's, and they are far superior to the plays of playwrights in other troupes. I have referred to the playwrights who composed in Zeami's style as the Zeami group.[77] The activity of this group continued until around the beginning of the devastating Ōnin War in 1467.

[75] Besides these two plays, some lists of authors attribute *Aoi no Ue (Lady Aoi)* to Zenchiku. However, there is reliable evidence that this play was originally composed by an Ōmi sarugaku actor and later revised into its form in the current repertoire by Zeami (Omote, 1979, 489).

[76] Some scholars add to this list *Tomonaga (Minamoto Tomonaga), Koremori (Taira Koremori)*, and *Tsunemori (Taira Tsunemori)* (Nishino, 1973, 60-72).

[77] As suggested above, this concept includes authors whose identities have not yet been established. It is based on the existence of plays that are in Zeami's style but cannot be recognized as his own. For example: *Tomoe* (Tomoe was Minamoto Yoshinaka's mistress): *Hagoromo (The Feather Mantle); Yuya (Yuya, Madam of Pleasure-girls)*; and *Akogi (The Fisherman at Akogi)*.

EDITOR'S APPENDIX

Some Canons of Renga

The author is one of the last living people to have been taught to compose renga. His teacher was Yamada Yoshio, whose family practiced Satomura school renga as a family art. For more detail on *One Hundred Stanzas by Three Poets at Minase*, see the discussion in his *Sōgi* (Konishi, 1971c, 186-95, 236-43), and for his precedent on topics, subtopics, and motifs, see Yamada, *Renga Gaisetsu* (Yamada Y., 1937, 233-40). Or for an English version, see Miner, 1979, 171-225.

Sheets and Formal Locations for Moon and Flower Stanzas

A normal hundred-stanza renga (hyakuin) is written on the fronts and backs of four folded sheets; it has four flower stanzas and seven moon stanzas. That is, there is one flower stanza for each sheet and one moon stanza for each side, with the exception of the nagori no ura, the back of the fourth sheet. For a stanza to be a flower stanza, only the word hana (flower) is allowed; a named flower (na no hana) like plum (ume) or chrysanthemum (kiku) does not count. "Tsuki" designates a moon stanza unless used in the sense of month or time (e.g., tsukihi). If not otherwise qualified by season (e.g., natsu no tsuki, summer moon), a moon imparts an autumn topic to a stanza. A flower stanza is always a spring stanza. Part of the interest of an individual sequence is early or late inclusion of a flower or moon stanza. Upon occasion poets include more than the four and seven required.

The formal locations and the names for sheets and sides follow.

1-22	First Sheet (sho'ori)	
	1-8	Front (sho'omote): moon 7
	9-22	Back (shoura): moon 18; flower 21
23-50	Second Sheet (ni no ori)	
	23-36	Front (ni no omote): moon 35
	37-50	Back (ni no ura): moon 46; flower 49
51-78	Third Sheet (san no ori)	
	51-64	Front (san no omote): moon 63
	65-78	Back (san no ura): moon 74; flower 77
79-100	Fourth Sheet (nagori no ori)	
	79-92	Front (nagori no omote): moon 91
	93-100	Back (nagori no ura): moon omitted; flower 99

The Jo-Ha-Kyū Pattern

This also leads to variations, chiefly those of the Jo and the Kyū continuing into the Ha section (the Jo) or beginning there one or more stanzas early (the Kyū).

Jo: Preface or Introduction; stately in tone; opening stanza refers to season and conditions of the time of composition.
Ha: Development (more literally Breaking); the most agitated and longest section.
Kyū: Fast Close; smoother than the Ha, less stately than the Jo.

The Formal Pattern for a One-Hundred Stanza Sequence (Hyakuin)

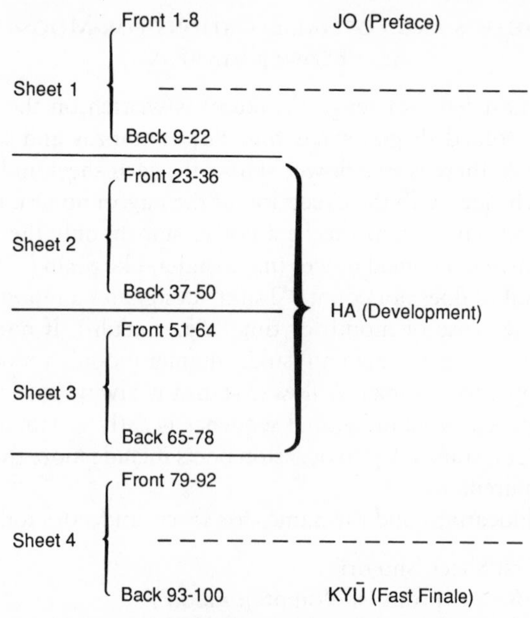

Figure A.1 The Formal Pattern for a One-Hundred-Stanza Sequence

Particular Stanzas

The author sometimes uses names for particular stanzas, and above all he refers to the double status of a given stanza. Here are names for the most important stanzas, all of which have certain requirements as to verbal termination or tone, or both.

hokku	opening stanza
waki	second stanza
daisan	third stanza
ageku	last stanza

The double status of a stanza can best be exemplified by considering, for example, stanza 17. As *a stanza added to a predecessor* (16), it is a tsukeku, added stanza. As *a stanza added to by a successor* (18), it is a maeku, preceding stanza. It follows that there is necessary semantic connection in the 16-17 and the 17-18 links. But 17 has no semantic connection with any other stanza—not even with 13, 14, and 15, if 17 is the fifth in a run of five spring stanzas.

CHRONOLOGICAL TABLE

(Events in countries other than China and Korea are marked by an asterisk.)

Christian Era	*Japan*	*China*	*Korea*	*Other Countries*
A.D. 1011	Fujiwara Nobunori dies. Jōjin born.	Sung (Northern)	Koryŏ	
1012	Jōson born.			
1013	Minamoto Tamenori dies.			
1016	Goichijō Tennō ascends the throne.			
1019				Ssu-ma Kuang born.
1020				Chang Tsai (Heng-ch'ü) born.
1021				Wang An-shih born.
1025				Chao-chüeh Ch'ang-ts'ung born.
1032				Fo-yin Liao-yüan born.
1033				Ch'eng I (I-ch'uan) born.
1036	Goichijō Tennō dies.			Su Shih (Tung-p'o) born.
1039				Su Ch'e born.
1041	Ōe no Masafusa born.			
1042	Fujiwara Morozane born.			
1045				Huang T'ing-chien (Shan-ku) born.
1049	Miyoshi Tameyasu born.			
1051	Beginning of the Mutsu rebellion.			
1052				Hsüeh-tou Ch'ung-hsien dies.
1055	Fujiwara Akisue born. Minamoto Toshiyori (Shunrai) born?			
1056	Fujiwara Mototoshi born.			Su Shih and Su Ch'e pass the national examination for officials.

Christian Era	Japan	China	Korea	Other Countries
1062	Nakamikado Munetada born. The Mutsu rebellion is suppressed. (Cf. *Mutsu Waki.*)			
1063	Fujiwara Atsumitsu born.			
1071	*Jōjin Azari Haha no Shū* begins with this year.			
1072	Shirakawa Tennō ascends the throne. Jōjin goes to China.			
1073	Fujiwara Toshitada born.	Sung (Northern)	Koryŏ	
1074	Jōson dies.			
1075	Fujiwara Tsunetada born.			Kim Pu-sik of Koryŏ born.
1077				Chang Tsai (Heng-ch'ü) dies. Yeh Meng-te born.
1078	Fujiwara Tadazane born.			
1079	Horikawa Tennō born. Sanuki no Suke born?			Wen T'ung dies.
1080				Kim Kŭn of Koryŏ is sent as an envoy to Sung China.
1081	Jōjin dies in China.			
1084				*Tzu-chih T'ung-chien* compiled. Sŏngjong of Koryŏ ascends the throne.
1086	Shirakawa Tennō abdicates. Horikawa Tennō ascends the throne. *Goshūishū* compiled.			Wang An-shih dies. Ssu-ma Kuang dies.
1090	Fujiwara Akisuke born. The new style of waka composition is implemented at about this time.			
1091				Chao-chüeh Ch'ang-ts'ung dies.
1092	The second ("sequel") part of *Eiga Monogatari* was probably written between this year and 1107.			

Christian Era	Japan	China	Korea	Other Countries
1094				Sŏngjong of Koryŏ abdicates.
1095		Sung (Northern)	Koryŏ	Pak In-liong of Koryŏ dies.
1096	*Waka Gasshō* compiled at about this time.			*The First Crusade begins.
1097	Minamoto Tsunenobu dies. Fujiwara Tadamichi born.			Su Shih exiled to Hainan Island.
1098				Fo-yin Liao-yüan dies.
1099	*Horikawa Hyakushu* compiled between this year and 1104.			
1101	Fujiwara Morozane dies. "Kobi Ki" written.			Su Shih (Tung-p'o) dies. Hui-tsung ascends the throne.
1103	Minamoto Arihito born.			
1104	Fujiwara Kiyosuke born.			
1105				Huang T'ing-chien (Shan-ku) dies.
1106	Fujiwara Michinori (Shinzei) born. Compilation of *Kokin Utaawase* is suspended.			Yejong of Koryŏ ascends the throne.
1107	Horikawa Tennō dies. (Cf. *Sanuki no Suke Nikki.*) Toba Tennō ascends the throne.			Ch'eng I (I-ch'uan) dies.
1109	*Hokke Hyakuza Hōdan* compiled.			
1111	Ōe no Masafusa dies.			
1112				Su Ch'e dies.
1114	Fujiwara Shunzei born. *Shumpishō* compiled 1114-15.	Sung (Northern)	Koryŏ	
1116	*Eikyū Hyakushu* compiled. *Ungoji Kechienkyō Kōen Utaawase* held.			
1118	Saigyō born. *Naidaijin Ke Utaawase* (judged by Toshiyori and Mototoshi) held.			
1119	*Chōshūki* mentions a picture scroll of *Genji Monogatari.*			

Christian Era	Japan	China	Korea	Other Countries
1120	*Fa-hua Hung-tsan Chuan* copied. Gen'ei MS copy of *Kokinshū* is made.			
1121	Takashina Nakayuki born. *Kampaku Naidaijin Ke Utaawase* held.			
1123	Fujiwara Akisue dies. Fujiwara Toshitada dies. Toba Tennō abdicates. *Shūi Ōjōden* compiled.	Sung (Northern)		Hung Mai born.
1124	*Yōen Narabō Utaawase* held. The first draft of *Kin'yōshū* probably compiled.			Yang Wan-li born.
1125	Second draft of *Kin'yōshū* compiled.			Lu Yu (Fang-weng) born.
1126				Hui-tsung abdicates. Fan Ch'eng-ta born. Wu K'o born?
1127	Goshirakawa Tennō born.		Koryŏ	Sung court moves south and has its capital at Linan (Hangchow).
1130				Chu Hsi born.
1133	Hōnen born.	Sung (Southern)		
1134	*Chūgū no Suke Akisuke Ke Utaawase* held. *Uchigiki Shū* copied.			
1135				Chong Ch'i-sang of Koryŏ dies. **History of the Kings of Britain* probably compiled at about this time.
1138	Shunzei becomes a pupil of Mototoshi. Fujiwara Tsunetada dies.			
1139	Miyoshi Tameyasu dies. Konoe Tennō ascends the throne. Gotokudaiji Sanesada born.			
1141	Nakamikado Munetada dies. Myōan Eisai born.			**Poema del Cid* probably composed at about this time.

Christian Era	Japan	China	Korea	Other Countries
1142	Fujiwara Mototoshi dies.			
1144	Fujiwara Atsumitsu dies. *Shikashū* compiled.			
1145				*Samguk Sagi* compiled in Koryŏ. *The Second Crusade begins.
1147	Minamoto Arihito dies.			*Tung-ching Meng-hua-lu* compiled. Yeh Ming-te dies.
1149	Kujō Kanezane born. Minamoto Michichika born.	Sung (Southern)	Koryŏ	
1150	*Kyūan Hyakushu* compiled. Cloistered Prince Shukaku born.			*Minnesang probably composed from about this time.
1151				Kim Pu-sik of Koryŏ dies.
1153	Kamo no Chōmei born.			
1155	Konoe Tennō dies. Fujiwara Akisuke dies. Jien born. Fujiwara Yorizane born.			*Temüjin of Mongolia born at about this time.
1157				T'ien-t'ung Cheng-chüeh dies.
1158	Taira Sukemori born.			**Le Chanson de Roland* probably composed between 1100 and this year.
1159	Fujiwara Michinori (Shinzei) dies. (Cf. *Heiji Monogatari.*) Minamoto Yoshitsune born.			
1162	Fujiwara Tadazane dies. Fujiwara Teika born.			
1164	Fujiwara Tadamichi dies.			
1167	Kujō Yoshimichi born. *Taira Tsunemori Ke Utaawase* held.			
1168	Takakura Tennō ascends the throne.			Yi Kyu-bo of Koryŏ born.
1169	Gokyōgoku Yoshitsune born.			
1170	Minamoto Ienaga born?			
1173	Kōben (Myōe) born. Shinran born.			Wu K'o still alive in this year.

Christian Era	Japan	China	Korea	Other Countries
1174	*Kenrei Mon'in Ukyō no Daibu Shū* begins with this year.	Sung (Southern)	Koryŏ	
1175	Sesonji Koreyuki dies.			Various kinds of storytelling flourished in the amusement quarters of the capital during the Southern Sung.
1177	Fujiwara Kiyosuke dies.			
1178	Shunzei serves as manager of the Kujō household.			
1179	Takashina Nakayuki dies.			
1180	Takakura Tennō abdicates.			
1181	Takakura Tennō dies. (Cf. *Takakura In Shōkaki.*)			
1185	Taira Sukemori dies. (Cf. *Kenrei Mon'in Ukyō no Daibu Shū.*)			
1186	Teika becomes manager of the Kujō household.			
1187	*Senzaishū* compiled.			**Lay of Igor's Campaign* probably composed at about this time.
1188	Kujō Yoshimichi dies.			
1189	Minamoto Yoshitsune dies. Keisei born. Teika composes *Sōsotsu Hyakushu.*			*The Third Crusade begins.
1190	Saigyō dies. Prior to this year, the *Shinkokinshū* style (narrow sense) is created.			Yüan Hao-wen of Chin Dynasty born.
1191	Gotokudaiji Sanesada dies. Eisai introduces Lin-chi (J. Rinzai) Zen to Japan.	Sung (Southern)	Koryŏ	*Samhansi Kugam* compiled in Koryŏ.
1192	Cloistered former tennō Goshirakawa dies. Minamoto Sanetomo born. Kinugasa Ieyoshi born.			
1193	Kujō Michiie born. Soga brothers avenge their father's death. *Roppyakuban Utaawase* held.			Fan Ch'eng-ta dies.
1194	Saionji Saneuji born.			

Christian Era	Japan	China	Korea	Other Countries
1196	Kujō Kanezane ousted from office. *Ienaga Nikki* begins with this year.			
1197	Juntoku Tennō born. Mikohidari Tameie born.			Wu-an P'u-ning born.
1198	In this year or 1199, *Shukaku Hōshinnō Ke Hyakushu* compiled. Between this year and 1202, *Takakura In Itsukushima Gokōki* written.			
1199	*Omuro Senkaawase* compiled.			
1200	Kigen Dōgen born. *Gotoba In Hyakushu* compiled. Shunzei presents his "Waji Sōjō." *Shōji Shodo Hyakushu* and *Shōji Nido Hyakushu* compiled. In this year or next, *Mumyō Sōshi* written.			Chu Hsi dies.
1201	*Gotoba In Naikū Hyakushu* and *Gotoba In Gekū Hyakushu* composed.	Sung (Southern)	Koryŏ	Around this time, Tung Chieh-yüan of Chin Dynasty composes *Hsi-hsiang-chi Chu-kung-t'iao*?
1202	Cloistered Prince Shukaku dies. Minamoto Michichika dies. Enni Ben'en born. *Minasedono Koi Jūgoshu Utaawase* held. *Minase Sakura no Miya Utaawase* held.			Hung Mai dies. *The Fourth Crusade begins.
1203	Fujiwara Mitsutoshi (Shinkan) born. Kujō Motoie born. *Sengohyakuban Utaawase* compiled.			
1204	Fujiwara Shunzei dies. From this year, Teika's activity in waka composition wanes.			*At about this time, *Nibelungenlied* composed?
1205	The first draft of *Shinkokinshū* completed.			
1206	Gokyōgoku Yoshitsune dies. From around this year, ushinmushin renga is in vogue.			Yang Wan-li dies. Irnyŏn of Koryŏ born. *Temüjin of Mongolia ascends the throne and styles himself Jenghis Khan.

Christian Era	Japan	China	Korea	Other Countries
1207	Kujō Kanezane dies. *Saishō Shitennō In Shōji Waka* compiled. *Ienaga Nikki* ends with this year.			
1209	The first draft of Teika's *Kindai Shūka* written.	Sung (Southern)	Koryŏ	
1210	Juntoku Tennō ascends the throne.			Lu Yu dies. *Around this time, *Parzival* composed?
1212	Hōnen dies. Mukan Fumon born. Chōmei's *Hōjōki* written. Teika's shih appear in his diary.			
1213				Lan-ch'i Tao-lung born.
1215	Myōan Eisai dies. *Dairi Meisho Hyakushu* compiled. Teika recovers from a period of literary stagnation. At about this time, *Teika Hachidaishō* compiled?			Ta-hsiu Cheng-nien born.
1216	Kamo no Chōmei dies. *Hyakuban Utaawase* held. Teika records the joint judgments. *Teika Hyakuban Jikaawase* written. *Shinkokinshū* revised prior to this year.			Ta-hsiu Cheng-nien born.
1217	Utaawase held on the fourth day of the Eleventh Month. Teika records the joint judgments. Second draft of *Teika Hyakuban Jikaawase* written.			
1219	Minamoto Sanetomo assassinated. *Kenshun Mon'in Chūnagon Nikki* written.			*Jenghis Khan, invading lands to the west, reaches India.
1220	Gosaga Tennō born.	Sung (Southern)	Koryŏ	
1221	Jōkyū Civil War begins. Juntoku Tennō is deposed, and former sovereigns Gotoba and Tsuchimikado are exiled.			Yi In-no of Koryŏ dies.
1222	*Kankyo no Tomo* written.			
1223	Dōgen studies in China.			
1224	Hōjō Yasutoki appointed shogunal regent.			

Christian Era	Japan	China	Korea	Other Countries
1225	Jien dies. Fujiwara Yorizane dies.			*Jenghis Khan returns to Mongolia.
1226	Mujū born.			Wu-hsüeh Tsu-yüan born.
1227	Dōgen returns from China and introduces Ts'ao-tung (J. Sōtō) Zen to Japan. Hōjo born.			*Jenghis Khan dies.
1228	Koga Masatada born.			*The Fifth Crusade begins.
1229	Taira Mitsumori dies.			
1230	Since 1229, Teika has been copying *Mo-ho Chih-kuan*, collating it, and marking it for reading according to Japanese syntax.			
1232	Kōben (Myōe) dies. *Iwashimizu Wakamiya Utaawase* held; judge is Teika. *Kōmyōbuji Sesshō Ke Utaawase* held; judge is Teika. Third draft of *Teika Hyakuban Jikaawase* written after this year. *Kenrei Mon'in Ukyō no Daibu Shū* ends around this year.	Sung (Southern)	Koryŏ	
1234	Minamoto Ienaga dies.			
1235	Nampo Shōmei born. Fair copy of *Shinchokusenshū* completed. *Kyakuhaibōki* written.			
1239	Chishin Ippen born.			
1240	*Chishō Monogatari*, in 6 vols., is mentioned in a document on the back of Teika's copy of *Hyōhanki*.			
1241	Fujiwara Teika dies. Asukai Masaari born. Kōhō Kennichi born.			Yi Kyu-bo of Koryŏ dies.
1242	Gosaga Tennō ascends the throne. Former tennō Juntoku dies. Tsumori Kunisuke born. Hōjō Yasutoki resigns as shogunal regent. *Tōkan Kikō* written around this year.			*Mongolian army invades Hungary and reaches the Adriatic Sea.

Christian Era	*Japan*	*China*	*Korea*	*Other Countries*
1243	Hananomoto renga develops at about this time.			
1244				Wei Ching-chih compiles *Shih-jen Yü-hsieh*.
1246	Gosaga Tennō abdicates. Gofukakusa Tennō ascends the throne. Hōjō Tokiyori appointed shogunal regent. Open discord between Tameie and Mitsutoshi.			
1247	Cloistered Prince Shōjo born. Mimes perform at the ennen (monks' entertainment) of Kōfukuji Temple. Kameyama Tennō born.	Sung (Southern)	Koryŏ	I-shan I-ning born.
1249	Saionji Sanekanu born.			
1250	Nijō Tameyo born.			
1252	Kujō Michiie dies. *Jikkinshō* compiled.			
1253	Kigen Dōgen dies.			
1254	Shunzei's Daughter (Koshibe Zenni) dies. Kyōgoku Tamekanu born. Nijō Morotada born. Tachibana Narisue's *Kokon Chomonjū* compiled.			*Marco Polo born.
1257	Gofukakusa In Nijō (author of *Towazugatari*) born. *Shishu Hyaku Innenshū* compiled.			Yüan Hao-wen dies.
1259	Gofukakusa Tennō abdicates. Kameyama Tennō ascends the throne.			
1260	Tettan Dōshō born.			Ch'oe Cha of Koryŏ dies. *Kublai ascends the throne and is called Great Khan.
1262	Shinran dies.			
1263	Shūkan Dōsen born.			
1264	Kinugasa Ieyoshi dies.			
1265	Fushimi Tennō born. *Shokukokinshū* compiled.	Sung (Southern)	Koryŏ	*Dante Alighieri born.

Christian Era	Japan	China	Korea	Other Countries
1266	Prince Munetaka resigns as shogun.			
1268	Keisei dies.			
1269	Saionji Saneuji dies.			Ta-hsiu Cheng-nien goes to Japan. *Chu-tzu Yü-lei* compiled. *The Eighth Crusade begins.
1271	Yōfuku Mon'in born. *Fūyōshū* compiled. *Towazugatari* begins with this year.	Yüan		Mongolia renamed "Yüan." *Around this year, Marco Polo visits Yüan.
1272	Gosaga Tennō dies. Tachibana Narisue dies. Koga Masatada dies.			
1274	Kameyama Tennō abdicates.			Yüan and Koryŏ troops invade Japan, but are driven back by a great storm.
1275	Fujiwara Tameie dies. Musō Soseki born. *Ōtaku Fuketsu Shō* written between this year and 1278.	Sung (Southern)		King Ch'ungyŏl of Koryŏ ascends the throne.
1276	Fujiwara Mitsutoshi (Shinkan) dies.			Wu-an P'u-ning dies.
1278	Kokan Shiren born.			Lan-ch'i Tao-lung dies in Japan.
1279	The nun Abutsu goes to Kamakura to lodge a lawsuit.			Wu-hsüeh Tsu-yüan goes to Japan. Fall of the Sung dynasty.
1280	Kujō Motoie dies. Enni Ben'en dies. Kyōgoku Tamekanu is appointed attendant to the Crown Prince (later Fushimi Tennō). *Shasekishū* compiled. Abutsu makes journey recorded in *Isayoi Nikki*.	Yüan	Koryŏ	
1281				Troops of Yüan and Koryŏ again invade Japan and are driven back once more by a great storm.

Christian Era	Japan	China	Korea	Other Countries
1282	Cloistered Prince Shōjo dies.			
1283	Yoshida Kenkō born.			*Ying-k'uei Lü-sui* compiled.
1284	Hōjo dies.			
1285	Nijō Tamesada born. *Tamekanu Kyō Wakashō* written between this year and 1287.			
1286				Wu-hsüeh Tsu-yüan dies in Japan.
1287				Yi Che-hyŏn of Koryŏ born.
1288	Gofushimi Tennō born.			
1289	Chishin Ippen dies. Tonna born around this year.			Ta-hsiu Cheng-nien dies in Japan. Irnyŏn of Koryŏ dies.
1290	Sesson Yūbai born.			
1291	Mukan Fumon dies.			*The Crusades are abandoned.
1292				**Vita Nuova* of Dante Alighieri written 1292-93.
1293	Kitabatake Chikafusa born. Gatsurin Dōkō born.			
1295	Nijō Tameakira born. *Kyūreishū* compiled.			
1296	Anthologies of enkyoku—*Enkyokushū*, *Shūkashū*, etc.—compiled between this year and 1306.	Yüan	Koryŏ	Ch'u-shih Fan-ch'i born.
1297	Ōgimachi Kinkage born. *Futsū Shōdō Shū* written.			
1298	Kujō Takahiro dies. Kyōgoku Tamekanu exiled to Sado.			I-shan I-ning goes to Japan. Paek I-jong of Koryŏ studies in Yüan China.
1299	Tsumori Kunisuke dies. *Goshu Utaawase* held.			
1300	Chūgan Engetsu born. *Sanjūban Utaawase* held.			*Around this time, Minnesang declines.

Christian Era	*Japan*	*China*	*Korea*	*Other Countries*
1301	Asukai Masaari dies.			In Yüan times, the tsa-chü (Chinese opera) flourished, but little is known of its chief authors, Kuan Han-ch'ing and Ma Chih-yüan.
1303	Hōjō Takatoki born. Tamekanu is pardoned and returns to the capital. *Sentō Gojūban Utaawase* held. *Sanjūban Utaawase* held. *Zōtanshū* compiled. *Shingosenshū* compiled around this year.			
1304				*Petrarch born.
1305	Cloistered former tennō Kameyama dies. Ashikaga Takauji born. Ayanokōji Shigesuke born.			
1306	Sasaki Dōyo born. *Sen'yō Mokuroku* compiled. *Towazugatari* ends with this year.	Yüan	Koryŏ	
1307				Paek I-jong returns to Koryŏ. Sung culture becomes influential in Koryŏ.
1308	Gonijō Tennō dies. Hanazono Tennō ascends the throne. Nampo Shōmei dies.			
1309	Enkei MS of *Heike Monogatari* copied 1309-10.			
1310	Petitions by Nijō Tameyo and Kyōgoku Tamekanu about the appointment of compiler for *Gyokuyōshū*; continues through 1311.			
1312	Mujū dies. Prince Muneyoshi born. *Gyokuyōshū* nominally completed.			
1313	Kōgon Tennō born. *Gyokuyōshū* actually completed. Final decree handed down in lawsuit between Nijō and Reizei families.			*Boccaccio born. **Purgatory* in the *Divine Comedy* written 1310-13.

Christian Era	Japan	China	Korea	Other Countries
1314	Anthologies of enkyoku—*Shūkashō*, *Gyokurin'en*, etc.—compiled 1314-19.			
1315	Kyōgoku Tamekanu exiled to Tosa.			
1316	Kōhō Kennichi dies.			
1317	Former tennō Fushimi dies.			I-shan I-ning dies in Japan.
1318	Hanazono Tennō abdicates. Kian Mon'in born. Bumpo MS copy of *Hōgen Monogatari* is made.	Yüan	Koryŏ	**Inferno* in the *Divine Comedy* written 1307-18.
1320	Nijō Yoshimoto born. From about this year, former tennō Hanazono devotes himself to Zen.			
1321				*Ch'üan-hsiang P'ing-hua* published ca. 1321-24. *Dante Alighieri dies.
1322	Saionji Sanekanu dies.			
1323	Shibu Kassenjō MS copy of *Heike Monogatari* made around this year.			
1324	Sanjō Kintada born.			*Marco Polo dies.
1325	Nijō Tameshige born. Gidō Shūshin born.			
1326	Imagawa Ryōshun born.			
1328				Lo Pen (Kuan-chung) born? Yi Saek of Koryŏ born.
1331	Tettan Dōshō dies. Civil war begins between Southern and Northern Courts.			
1332	Kyōgoku Tamekanu dies.			
1333	Hōjō Takatoki dies. Kannami Kiyotsugu born.			
1336	Former tennō Gofushimi dies. Zekkai Chūshin born. Muromachi shogunate established; Kemmu Code enacted.	Yüan	Koryŏ	

Christian Era	Japan	China	Korea	Other Countries
1338	Nijō Tameyo dies.			
1340	First account of Kakuichi performing heikyoku is seen in *Taiheiki.*			Ch'ü Yu born.
1341	Nijō Morotada dies.			
1342	Yōfuku Mon'in dies.			
1346	Sesson Yūbai dies. Kokan Shiren dies. *Fūgashū* nominally completed.			
1347	Blind performers recite the story of the Soga brothers prior to this year.			Yi Sung-in of Koryŏ born?
1349	Asayama Bontōan born. Stand at a dengaku performance collapses and many people killed. *Fūgashū* actually completed. Nijō Yoshimoto's *Renri Hishō* written.			
1351	Musō Soseki dies. Gatsurin Dōkō dies.			
1352	Gokōgon Tennō ascends the throne. Yoshida Kenkō dies? *Baishōron* written between this year and 1388. *Shintōshū* written ca. 1352-61.			
1353	Renga verse by Shūa first seen in this year.			**Decameron* written.
1354	Kitabatake Chikafusa dies.			
1357	Nijō Yoshimoto compiles *Tsukuba Shū.*			
1358	Kian Mon'in dies. Ashikaga Takauji dies. Hino Meishi dies. Ashikaga Yoshimitsu born.	Yüan	Koryŏ	
1359	*Shinsenzaishū* compiled.			
1360	Nijō Tamesada dies. Ōgimachi Kinkage dies. Nō perceived as genre from about this time.			
1361	Reizei Tamemasa born.			

Christian Era	Japan	China	Korea	Other Countries
1362	"Hōryūji Engi Shirabyōshi" composed.			
1363	Zeami Motokiyo born? *Shinsatsu Ōrai* written. Hananomoto renga declines at about this time.	Yüan		
1364	Former tennō Kōgon dies. Nijō Tameakira dies.			
1367				Yi Che-hyon of Koryŏ dies.
1368	Ashikaga Yoshimitsu appointed shogun.			Ming dynasty founded.
1370				Ch'u-shih Fan-ch'i dies.
1371	Gokōgon Tennō abdicates. Kakuichi dies.			
1372	Reizei Tamehide dies. Tonna dies. Nijō Yoshimoto's *Ōan Shinshiki (New Rules of Renga)* set by royal sanction.			
1373	Sasaki Dōyo dies.	Ming	Koryŏ	
1374	Kannami noticed by Ashikaga Yoshimitsu when former performs subscription nō at Imagumano.			Kao Ch'i (Ch'ing-ch'iu) dies. *Petrarch dies.
1375	Chūgan Engetsu dies.			*Boccaccio dies.
1376	Yōsō Sōi born.			
1378	Fujiwakamaru (Zeami) composes renga with Nijō Yoshimoto. Kyūsei dies.			
1381	Seigan Shōtetsu born. *Shin'yōshū* compiled.			
1383	Sanjō Kintada dies. *Shingoshūishū* compiled.			
1384	Kannami Kiyotsugu dies.			
1385	Nijō Tameshige dies.			
1386	Takayama Sōzei born?			
1387	Nankō Sōgen born. *Gen'ishū* written at about this time.		Koryŏ	

Christian Era	*Japan*	*China*	*Korea*	*Other Countries*
1388	Nijō Yoshimoto dies. Gidō Shūshin dies.			
1389	Ayanokōji Shigesuke dies. Prince Muneyoshi dies?			
1391	Gyōkō born. Nijō Tamesuke killed; Nijō waka school becomes extinct.			
1392	Gokomatsu Tennō ascends the throne. Civil war ends between Northern and Southern Courts. Zuikei Shūhō born.	Ming		Yi Sung-in of Koryŏ dies. Chosŏn (Yi dynasty) founded.
1394	Ashikaga Yoshimitsu resigns as shogun and is appointed chancellor. Ashikaga Yoshinori born. Ikkyū Sōjun born.		Chosŏn (Yi Dynasty)	
1396				Yi Saek of Chosŏn dies.
1397	Nōa born.			*Chien-teng Hsin-hua* written.
1398	Onnami Motoshige born.			Lo Pen (Kuan-chung) dies?
1400	First three books of *Fūshi Kaden* written.			*Chaucer dies. *Canterbury Tales* left unfinished.
1401	Reizei Mochitame born. Tō no Tsuneyori born?			
1402	Ichijō Kaneyoshi born. Zeami writes Books 4 and 5 of *Fūshi Kaden*.			
1403	Zekkai Chūshin dies. Gyōjo born. Komparu Zenchiku born.			
1406	Shinkei born.			
1408	Ashikaga Yoshimitsu dies. Ashikaga Yoshimochi appointed shogun.			*Yung-lo Ta-tien* compiled.
1411	Senjun born.			
1412	Gokomatsu Tennō abdicates. Shōkō Tennō ascends the throne.	Ming	Chosŏn (Yi Dynasty)	
1413	Dōami Inuō dies.			

Christian Era	*Japan*	*China*	*Korea*	*Other Countries*
1416	Asukai Masachika born.			
1417	Reizei Tamemasa dies. Imagawa Ryōshun dies? Asayama Bontōan dies after this year.			
1418	Sugihara Katamori (Sōi) born. Zeami's *Kashū* written before this year.			
1420	Zeami's *Shikadō* written.			*Chien-teng Yü-hua* written.
1421	Iio Sōgi born.			
1423	Chikusō Chigon dies. Zeami's *Sandō* written.			
1424	Kanroji Chikanaga born. Zeami copies *Eguchi*, completes *Kakyō*.			
1427	Zeami's *Kyūi* written around this year.			Ch'ü Yu dies.
1428	Shōkō Tennō dies. Gohanazono Tennō ascends the throne. Ashikaga Yoshimochi dies. Zeami's *Shūgyoku Tokka* written.			
1429	Kanze Masamori born.			
1430	Tōgen Zuisen born. *Sarugaku Dangi* (Zeami's teaching) written.			
1432	Kanze Motomasa dies. Komparu Sōin born. *Sesson Daioshō Gyōdōki* written.			
1434	Zeami exiled to Sado.	Ming	Chosŏn (Yi Dynasty)	
1435	Kanze Kojirō Nobumitsu born.			
1440	Keijo Shūrin born.			
1441	Ashikaga Yoshinori killed. Anegakōji Mototsuna born.			
1443	Zeami Motokiyo dies? Botanka Shōhaku born.			

Christian Era	*Japan*	*China*	*Korea*	*Other Countries*
1445	Reizei Masatame born.			
1446	*Gaun Jikkenroku Batsuyū* begins with this year.			
1447				Li Tung-yang born.
1448	Ninagawa Chiun dies. Saiokuken Sōchō born.			
1452	Inawashiro Kensai born.			*Leonardo da Vinci born.
1454	Reizei Mochitame dies. Komparu Zempō born.			
1455	Gyōkō dies. Takayama Sōzei dies. Sanjōnishi Sanetaka born.			
1458	Yōsō Sōi dies.			
1459	Seigan Shōtetsu dies.			
1460	Zenchiku's *Goon Sangyokushū* written.			
1463	Nankō Sōgen dies. First part of *Sasamegoto* written.	Ming	Chosŏn (Yi Dynasty)	*François Villon dies at about this time.
1464	Gohanazono Tennō abdicates. Gotsuchimikado Tennō ascends the throne.			
1465				*Erasmus born?
1466	Sōgi's *Chōrokubumi* written.			
1467	Onnami Motoshige dies. The Ōnin Civil War begins. Shinkei composes solo renga, *Yama Nani Hyakuin*. Zenchiku's *Shidō Yōshō* written.			
1468	Nōa dies.			
1469	Gyōjo dies. *Kawagoe Senku* jointly composed by Shinkei and Sōgi.			
1470	Kanze Masamori dies. Komparu Zenchiku dies at about this time.			Sŏngjong of Chosŏn ascends the throne.
1471	*Kokinshū Ryōdo Kikigaki* written. Sōgi composes solo renga, *Mishima Senku*.			

Christian Era	Japan	China	Korea	Other Countries
1472				Wang Shou-jen (Yang-ming) born.
1473	Zuikei Shūhō dies. *Gaun Jikkenroku Batsuyū* ends with this year.			
1474	Ikkyū appointed abbot of Daitokuji Temple.			
1475	Shinkei dies.			Li Meng-yang born. *Michelangelo born.
1476	Senjun dies. Sōgi compiles *Chikurinshō*.	Ming	Chosŏn (Yi Dynasty)	
1477	Ōnin Civil War ends.			
1478				*Thomas More born.
1479	Sōgi's *Oi no Susami* written.			
1480	Komparu Sōin dies. Sōgi's *Tsukushi Michi no Ki* written.			
1481	Ichijō Kaneyoshi dies. Ikkyū Sōjun dies.			
1483	Kanze Jūrō dies.			Ho Ching-ming born. *Martin Luther born. *Raphael born.
1485	Sugihara Katamori (Sōi) dies.			*Malory's *Morte D'Arthur* published.
1488	Kanze Nagatoshi born. *Minase Sangin Hyakuin* composed.			
1489	Tōgen Zuisen dies.			
1490	Asukai Masachika dies.			*François Rabelais born at about this time.
1491	*Yunoyama Sangin Hyakuin* composed.			
1492				*Columbus discovers the continent of America.
1494				Sŏngjong of Chosŏn dies.
1495	Sōgi compiles *Shinsen Tsukuba Shū*. *Yodo no Watari* written.			

Christian Era	Japan	China	Korea	Other Countries
1499	Sōgi composes solo renga, *Nanihito Hyakuin. Chikuba Kyōginshū* compiled.			
1500	Gotsuchimikado Tennō dies. Kanroji Chikanaga dies.	Ming	Chosŏn (Yi Dynasty)	
1502	Iio Sōgi dies.			
1504	Anegakōji Mototsuna dies.			
1505	Konoe Masaie dies.			
1510	Inawashiro Kensai dies.			
1516	Kanze Nobumitsu dies.			*Latin version of *Utopia* completed.
1518	Keijo Shūrin dies.			
1519	Kanze Shigeyuki dies.			*Leonardo da Vinci dies.
1520				*Raphael dies.
1521				Ho Ching-ming dies.
1522				24-volume version of *San-kuo-chih Yen-i* published.
1523	Reizei Masatame dies.			
1524	*Nōhon Sakusha Chūmon* compiled.			
1526				Wang Shih-chen born.
1527	Botanka Shōhaku dies.			
1528				Wang Yang-ming dies.
1531		Ming	Chosŏn (Yi Dynasty)	Li Meng-yang dies.
1532	Saiokuken Sōchō dies.			
1533				*Montaigne born.
1535				*Thomas More dies.
1536				*Erasmus dies.
1537	Sanjōnishi Sanetaka dies.			
1541	Kanze Nagatoshi dies.			

Christian Era	Japan	China	Korea	Other Countries
1545	Sōboku dies.			
1546	Nichijo copies Chinese-character version of *Soga Monogatari.*			*Martin Luther dies.
1553				*François Rabelais dies.

BIBLIOGRAPHY

Three sections follow. The first includes editions and collections referred to in the main text of this volume. The second includes studies published in Japanese, and the third, in languages other than Japanese. In each instance, the entry here is by the abbreviated form used in the text. Tokyo is the place of publication unless otherwise specified.

A title preceded by an asterisk designates a work that, in the text, is cited by literary unit (uta, shih, etc.) rather than by page.

An "equals" sign indicates that the first element of the "equation" is an abbreviated version of the second or an equivalent—for example, a romanizing of the Chinese rather than the Japanese pronunciation of a Chinese work.

The citation under an author's name of, for example, "1951b" without a preceding "1951a" implies the existence of another work published in 1951 that is cited as "1951a" in another volume of this history.

Abbreviations are used for three important series: *NKBT* designates *Nihon Koten Bungaku Taikei* (Iwanami Shoten, 1957-67), ed. Takagi Ichinosuke et al.; *ZGRJ* designates *Zoku Gunsho Ruijū* (Zoku Gunsho Ruijū Kanseikai, 1902-28), ed. Hanawa Hokinoichi; and *SZKT* designates *Shintei Zōho Kokushi Taikei* (Yoshikawa Kōbunkan, 1929-66), ed. Kuroita Katsumi et al.

A. Editions

**Akazome = Akazome Emon Shū. Akazome Emon; SKST*, 2:13. See *SKST*.

**Akishino = Akishino Gessei Shū. Akishino Gessei Shū to Sono Kenkyū* (Kasama Shoin, 1976). Edited by Katayama Tōru.

Ama no Karumo. Ama no Karumo; Katsura no Miyabon Sōsho, 17 (Tenri: Yōtokusha, 1956). Compiled and edited by Manuscript Division, Bureau of the Royal Household.

Ariake = Ariake no Wakare. Ariake no Wakare no Kenkyū (Ōfūsha, 1969). Edited by Ōtsuki Osamu.

Asaji. Asaji; Rengaron Shū, C, 2. See *Rengaron Shū* C.

Asaji ga Tsuyu. Asaji ga Tsuyu (Koten Bunko, 1953). Edited by Kimura Miyogo.

Asukai = Asukai Masaari Nikki. Asukai Masaari Nikki (Koten Bunko, 1949). Edited by Sasaki Nobutsuna.

Ayanokōji Toshikazu Kyō Ki. See *Toshikazu Ki*.

Azuma Kagami. Azuma Kagami; SZKT, 32-33 (1932-33).

Azuma Mondō. Azuma Mondō; Rengaron Shū B. See *Rengaron Shū* B.

Baishōron. Baishōron; SNKB, 3 (1975). Edited by Yashiro Kazuo and Kami Hiroshi. See *SNKB*.

Ban Dainagon Emaki. Ban Dainagon Ekotoba; Nihon Emakimono Zenshū, 4 (Kadokawa Shoten, 1961). With an introduction by Tanaka Ichimatsu.

Ben no Naishi Nikki. Ben no Naishi Nikki Shinchū (Taishūkan, 1958). Edited by Tamai Kōsuke.

Ben'yōshō = Ryōshun Isshiden. Ryōshun Isshiden; NKGT, 5. See *NKGT*.

Bingashū. Bingashū; GBSS, 3. See *GBSS*.

BSS = Bunka Shūreishū. See *Bunka Shūreishū*.

Bukkō = Bukkō Kokushi Goroku. Bukkō Kokushi Goroku; TSDK, 80. See *TSDK*.

*_Bunka Shūreishū [BSS]. Bunka Shūreishū; NKBT_, 69 (1964). Edited by Kojima Noriyuki.

Buntai Meiben. See _Wen-t'i Ming-pien_.

Butsu Hongyō Shukkyō. See _Hongyōkyō_.

_CE_ = _Chōshū Eisō_. See _Chōshū Eisō_.

_CG_ = _Chōya Gunsai_. See _Chōya Gunsai_.

Ch'eng-chai Shih-hua. Ch'eng-chai Chi; Ssu-pu Ts'ung-k'an, 64 (Taipei: T'ai-wan Shang-wu Yin-shu-kuan, 1975).

Chien-nan Shih-kao. Lu Fang-weng Chi, chüan 2; _Kuo-hsüeh Chi-pen Ts'ung-shu Ssu-pai-chung_, 289 (Taipei: T'ai-wan Shang-wu Yin-shu-kuan, 1975).

Chikamatsu Zenshū. Chikamatsu Zenshū (Asahi Shimbunsha, 1925-27). Edited by Fujii Shiei. 10 vols.

*_Chikuba_ = _Chikuba Kyōginshū_. "_Chikuba Kyōginshū_," _Biblia_, no. 43 (Tenri: Tenri Library, 1969). Edited by Kimura Miyogo.

Chikuenshō. Chikuenshō; NKGT, 3. See _NKGT_.

*_Chikurinshō [CRS]. Kōhon Chikurinshō_ (Iwanami Shoten, 1937). Edited by Hoshika Muneichi.

Chikurinshō no Chū. Chikurinshō Kochū; KKSK, 2 (1967). Edited by Yokoyama Shigeru. See _KKSK_.

Ching-pen T'ung-su Hsiao-shuo. Ching-pen T'ung-su Hsiao-shuo (Shanghai: Shang-hai Ku-tien Wen-hsüeh Ch'u-pan-she, 1954).

Ching-te Ch'uan-teng Lu. See _Keitoku Roku_.

Chomonjū = _Kokon Chomonjū. Kokon Chomonjū; NKBT_, 84 (1966). Edited by Nagazumi Yasuaki and Shimada Isao.

Chōrokubumi. Chōrokubumi; Rengaron Shū C, 2. See _Rengaron Shū_ C.

*_Chōshū Eisō [CE]. Heian Kamakura Shikashū; NKBT_, 80 (1964). Edited by Hisamatsu Sen'ichi.

Chōshūki. Chōshūki; Zōho Shiryō Taisei (Kyoto: Rinsen Shoten, 1965), 16-17. Edited by Yano Tarō.

Chōya Gunsai [CG]. Chōya Gunsai; SZKT, 29a (1938).

Chu Tzu Yü-lei. Chu Tzu Yü-lei Ta-ch'üan (Kyoto: Chūbun Shuppansha, 1973). 8 vols.

Ch'uan-ch'i = _T'ang Sung Ch'uan-ch'i Chi_ (Peking: Wen-hsüeh Ku-chi K'an-hsing-she, 1956); rpt. in _Lu Hsün Ch'üan-chi_, 10 (Peking: Jen-min Wen-hsüeh Ch'u-pan-she, 1973). 1973 edition used.

Ch'üan T'ang-shih [CTS]. Ch'üan T'ang-shih (Peking: Chung-hua Shu-chü, 1960). 25 vols.

Chuang Tzu. Chuang Tzu; Hsin-pien Chu-tzu Chi-ch'eng, 3 (Taipei: Shih-chieh Shu-chü, 1978).

Chūgaishō. Chūgaishō; ZGRJ, 11b.

Chung-ch'ao Ku-shih. Chung-ch'ao Ku-shih; Ts'ung-shu Chi-ch'eng, 1:274 (Shanghai: Shang-wu Yin-shu-kuan, 1936).

Chūyūki. Chūyūki; Shiryō Taisei, 8-14 (Naigai Shoseki, 1934-35). Edited by Yano Tarō. Republished in _Zōho Shiryō Taisei_, 9-15 (Kyoto: Rinsen Shoten, 1965). 1965 edition used.

Chūyū Shihai = _Chūyūki Burui Shihai Kanshishū. Heian Kamakura Mikan Kanshishū; Toshoryō Sōkan_ (Meiji Shoin, 1972). Compiled and edited by Manuscript Division, Bureau of the Royal Household.

CRS = _Chikurinshō_. See _Chikurinshō_.

CTS = _Ch'üan T'ang-shih_. See _Ch'üan T'ang-shih_.

Dai Nihon Bukkyō Zensho. See _DNBZ_.

Dai Nihon Shi. Dai Nihon Shi (Mito: Gikō Seitan Sambyakunen Kinenkai, Ibaraki Prefectural Government, 1928-29). 17 vols.

Daie Roku = Daie Fukaku Zenji Goroku = Ta-hui P'u-chüeh Ch'an-shih Yü-lu. Daie Fukaku Zenji Goroku; TSDK, 47. See *TSDK*.

Daigoji Zakki. Muromachigokoro: Chūsei Bungaku Shiryōshū (Kadokawa Shoten, 1978). Compiled by Okami Masao Kanreki Kinen Kankōkai.

Daijō Kishinron = Ta-ch'eng Ch'i-hsin Lun. Daijō Kishinron; TSDK, 32. See *TSDK*.

**Dainagon Tsunenobu Shū [DTS]. Heian Kamakura Shikashū; NKBT*, 80 (1964).

Dairi Meisho Hyakushu. Dairi Meisho Hyakushu; SGRJ, 8 (1928). Edited by Uematsu Yasushi. See *SGRJ*.

Dangi = Sarugaku Dangi. See *Zeami, Zenchiku*.

Denryaku. Denryaku; Dai Nihon Kokiroku (Iwanami Shoten, 1960-70). Edited by the Institute for the Compilation of Historical Materials, University of Tokyo. 5 vols.

Diamond Sūtra. See *Kongōkyō*.

DNBZ = Dai Nihon Bukkyō Zensho (Suzuki Academic Foundation, 1970-73). 100 vols.

DTS = Dainagon Tsunenobu Shū. See *Dainagon Tsunenobu Shū*.

Eiga Monogatari [EM]. Eiga Monogatari; NKBT, 75-76 (1964-65). Edited by Matsumura Hiroshi and Yamanaka Yutaka.

Eiga no Ittei. Eiga no Ittei; Karon Shū B, 1. See *Karon Shū* B.

Eika Taigai = Eika no Taigai. Eika no Taigai; Karon Shū A. See *Karon Shū* A.

Eikyū Hyakushu. See *Horikawa In Godo Hyakushu*.

Einin Gannen Jūgoya Utaawase. Jūgoya Utaawase; SGRJ, 9 (1931). Edited by Akiyama Kenzō. See *SGRJ*.

EM = Eiga Monogatari. See *Eiga Monogatari*.

Enkyokushū. Chūkinsei Kayōshū; NKBT, 44 (1959). Edited by Shimma Shin'ichi.

Enkyoku Shūsei. Enkyoku Shūsei (Koten Bunko, 1972-77). Reproduction of Sonkeikaku manuscript, with an introduction by Takeishi Akio. 5 vols.

Enkyoku Zenshū. Enkyoku Zenshū (Waseda University Press, 1917). Edited by Yoshida Tōgo.

Eyō = Shūmon Rentō Eyō. Rentō Eyō; ZZK, II-B-9-3. See *ZZK*.

Fa-hua Ching. See *Hokkekyō*.

FGS = Fūgashū. See *Fūgashū*.

Fo Pen-hsing Chi-ching. See *Hongyōkyō*.

**Fuboku Wakashō. Sakusha Bunrui Fuboku Wakashō* (Kazama Shobō, 1967-70; revised edition, 1981). Compiled and edited by Yamada Seiichi and Ogano Shigeji. 2 vols. 1981 edition used.

**Fūgashū. Fūga Wakashū; Chūsei no Bungaku* (Miyai Shoten, 1974). Edited by Iwasa Miyoko, with an introduction and annotation by Tsugita Kasumi.

**Fujiwara Tameie Zenkashū. Fujiwara Tameie Zenkashū* (Musashino Shoin, 1962). Edited by Yasui Hisayoshi.

Fukegatari. An edited text is contained in Masuda, 1960b. See Section B, Studies Published in Japanese.

Fukurozōshi. Fukurozōshi Chūkai. Edited by Ozawa Masao et al. (Hanawa Shobō, 1974-76). 2 vols.

Fūshi Kaden. See *Zeami, Zenchiku*.

Fushimi Ki = Fushimi Tennō Shinki. Fushimi Tennō Shinki; Shiryō Taisei Zo-

kuhen, 34 (Naigai Shoseki, 1938). Edited by Yano Tarō. Republished in *Zōho Shiryō Taisei*, 3 (Kyoto: Rinsen Shoten, 1965).

Fusō Ryakuki. Fusō Ryakuki; SZKT, 12 (1932).

Fusō Shūyōshū. Fusō Shūyōshū. Original woodblock printed copy in possession of Central Library, University of Tsukuba. 30 vols.

Futsū Shōdō Shū. "Kōkan *Futsū Shōdō Shū*," *Joshidai Bungaku, Kokubunhen*, 11-12 (Osaka: Osaka Women's College, 1960). Edited by Murayama Shūichi.

Fūyōshū. Zōtei Kōhon Fūyō Wakashū (Kyoto: Yūzan Bunko, 1970). Edited by Nakano Sōji and Fujii Takashi.

Gaun = Gaun Jikkenroku. Gaun Jikkenroku Batsuyū; Dai Nihon Kokiroku (Iwanami Shoten, 1961). Edited by The Institute for Compilation of Historical Materials, University of Tokyo.

GBSS = Gosan Bungaku Shinshū. Gosan Bungaku Shinshū (University of Tokyo Press, 1967-81). Compiled and edited with introductions to each volume by Tamamura Takeji. 8 vols.

GBZS = Gosan Bungaku Zenshū. Gosan Bungaku Zenshū. Edited by Uemura Kankō. 5 vols. (1-3: Shōkabō, 1906-08; 4: Watanabe Tamezō, 1915; 5: Teikoku Kyōikukai Shuppambu, 1936). Reprinted with supplement (Kyoto: Shibunkaku, 1973). 1973 edition used.

Gekimōshō. Gekimōshō; Rengaron Shū A, 1. See *Rengaron Shū* A.

Gempei Jōsuiki. Gempei Jōsuiki; Kōchū Nihon Bungaku Taikei, 15-16 (Kokumin Tosho, 1926). Edited by Masuko Kaiei.

Gempei Tōjō Roku. Gempei Tōjō Roku to Kenkyū (Toyohashi: Mikan Kokubun Shiryō Kankōkai, 1963). Edited by Yamashita Hiroaki.

**Gengenshū. Nōin Hōshi Shū: Gengenshū to Sono Kenkyū* (Miyai Shoten, 1979). Edited by Kawamura Teruo.

Gengo Henjishō = Shugyoku Henjishō. Shugyoku Henjishō; Genji Monogatari Kochū Shūsei, 4 (Musashino Shoin, 1980). Edited by Nakano Kōichi.

Gen'ishū. Gen'ishū; SNKB, 3 (1975). Edited by Yashiro Kazuo and Kami Hiroshi. See *SNKB*.

Genji Monogatari [GM]. Genji Monogatari; NKBT, 14-18 (1958-63). Edited by Yamagishi Tokuhei.

Genji Monogatari Emaki. Genji Monogatari Emaki; Nihon Emaki Taisei, 1 (Chūō Kōronsha, 1977). Edited by Komatsu Shigemi.

Genji Monogatari Rōkashō. Rōkashō; Genji Monogatari Kochū Shūsei, 8 (Ōfūsha, 1983). Edited by Ii Haruki.

Genkō Shakusho. Genkō Shakusho; SZKT, 31 (1930).

Genshō = Genshō Kuden = Waka Kuden. Waka Kuden; NKGT, 4. See *NKGT*.

Genzō = Shōbō Genzō. Kohon Kōtei Shōbō Genzō (Chikuma Shobō, 1971). Edited by Ōkubo Dōshū.

Gikeiki. Gikeiki; NKBT, 37 (1959). Edited by Okami Masao.

GM = Genji Monogatari. See *Genji Monogatari.*

Gō Sochi Shū. Gō Sochi Shū; SKST, 2-51. See *SKST*.

Gōdanshō. See *Kohon Gōdan, Rufubon Gōdan.*

Gogumai Ki. Gogumai Ki; Dai Nihon Kokiroku (Iwanami Shoten, 1980-84). Edited by The Institute for Compilation of Historical Materials, University of Tokyo.

Gōke Shidai. Shintei Zōho Kojitsu Sōsho 2 (Meiji Tosho and Yoshikawa Kōbunkan, 1953).

Gonsenshū. Agui Shōdōshū (Kadokawa Shoten, 1972). Edited by Nagai Yoshinori and Shimizu Yūsei.

Goon. See *Zeami, Zenchiku*.

Gosan Bungaku Shinshū. See *GBSS*.

Gosan Bungaku Zenshū. See *GBZS*.

**Gosenshū [GSS] = Gosen Wakashū. Gosen Wakashū Sōsakuin* (Ōsaka Joshi Daigaku, 1965). Edited by Katagiri Yōichi et al.

**Goshūishū [GSIS] = Goshūi Wakashū. Daisenjibon Goshūi Wakashū* (Ōfūsha, 1971). Edited by Fujimoto Kazue.

Gotoba In = Gotoba In Gokuden. Gotoba In Gokuden; Karon Shū A. See *Karon Shū* A.

Gotoba In Gyoshū. Gotoba In Gyoshū; SKST 4:1. See *SKST*.

GSIS = Goshūishū. See *Goshūishū*.

GSS = Gosenshū. See *Gosenshū*.

Guhishō. Guhishō; NKGT, 4. See *NKGT*.

Gukanshō. Gukanshō; NKBT, 86 (1967). Edited by Okami Masao and Akamatsu Toshihide.

Gumon Kenchū. Gumon Kenchū; NKGT, 5. See *NKGT*.

Gyokuyō. Gyokuyō (Kokusho Kankōkai, 1906-07). Edited by Kurokawa Mamichi and Yamada Yasue. 3 vols.

**Gyokuyōshū [GYS]. Gyokuyō Wakashū; Shimpen Kokka Taikan*, 1. See *Shimpen Kokka Taikan*.

Gyokuzui. Gyokuzui (Kyoto: Shibunkaku, 1984). Edited by Imagawa Fumio.

GYS = Gyokuyōshū. See *Gyokuyōshū*.

Hachimangūji Jumpaiki. Chūsei Shimbutsu Setsuwa (Koten Bunko, 1950). Edited by Kondō Yoshihiro.

Haku Kōzan Shishū [HKS] = Po Hsiang-shan Shih-chi. Haku Kōzan Shishū; KST, 4. See *KST*.

Hamamatsu = Hamamatsu Chūnagon Monogatari. Hamamatsu Chūnagon Monogatari; NKBT, 74 (1964). Edited by Matsuo Satoshi.

Hanazono Ki = Hanazono Tennō Shinki. Hanazono Tennō Shinki; Shiryō Taisei, Zokuhen, 33-34 (Naigai Shoseki, 1938). Edited by Yano Tarō.

Haru no Miyamaji. Haru no Miyamaji; ZGRJ, 18b.

HCUT = Heianchō Utaawase Taisei. Heianchō Utaawase Taisei (published by the editor, 1957-69; reprinted by Dōhōsha, Kyoto, 1979). Edited by Hagitani Boku. 10 vols.

Heiji = Heiji Monogatari (Kotohira manuscript). *Heiji Monogatari; NKBT*, 31 (1961). Edited by Nagazumi Yasuaki and Shimada Isao.

Heiji, Kujō = Heiji Monogatari (Kujōke manuscript). *Heiji Monogatari (Kujōkebon) to Kenkyū* (Toyohashi: Mikan Kokubun Shiryō Kankōkai, 1960). Edited by Yamagishi Tokuhei and Takahashi Teiichi.

Heike, Enkei = Heike Monogatari (Enkei manuscript). *Ōei Shosha Enkeibon Heike Monogatari* (Kaizōsha, 1935). Edited by Yoshizawa Yoshinori.

Heike Monogatari [HM] (Kakuichi manuscript). *Heike Monogatari; NKBT*, 32-33 (1959-60). Edited by Takagi Ichinosuke, Ozawa Masao, Atsumi Kaoru, and Kindaichi Haruhiko.

Heike, Nagato = Heike Monogatari (Nagato manuscript). *Heike Monogatari: Nagatobon* (Kokusho Kankōkai, 1906). Edited by Kurokawa Mamichi, Hotta Kusuzō, and Furuuchi Michiyo.

Heike, Shibu = Heike Monogatari (Shibu Kassenjō manuscript). *Shibu Kassen-*

jōbon Heike Monogatari (Daian, 1967). Reproduction of the manuscript with an introduction by Matsumoto Ryūshin. 3 vols.

Heike, Yasaka = *Heike Monogatari* (Yasaka manuscript). *Heike Monogatari* (Kokumin Bunko Kankōkai, 1911). Edited by Furuya Chishin.

Heike, Yashiro = *Heike Monogatari* (Yashiro manuscript). *Yashirobon Heike Monogatari* (Ōfūsha, 1967-73). Edited by Satō Kenzō and Haruta Sen. 3 vols.

Hekigan Roku = *P'i-yen Lu. Hekigan Roku Teihon* (Risōsha, 1963). Edited by Itō Yūten.

Hekirenshō. Hekirenshō; Yoshimoto Rengaronshū, 1. See *Yoshimoto Rengaronshū.*

Hi no Kawakami. Hi no Kawakami; NKGT, 4. See *NKGT.*

Hitorigoto. Kodai Chūsei Geijitsuronshū; Nihon Shisō Taikei, 23 (Iwanami Shoten, 1973). Edited by Shimazu Tadao.

HKS = *Haku Kōzan Shishū.* See *Haku Kōzan Shishū.*

HM = *Heike Monogatari.* See *Heike Monogatari.*

HMDS = *Honchō Mudaishi.* See *Honchō Mudaishi.*

Hōbutsushū. Hōbutsushū: Kyūsatsubon (Koten Bunko, 1969). Edited by Yoshida Kōichi and Koizumi Hiroshi.

Hōgen = *Hōgen Monogatari* (Kotohira manuscript). *Hōgen Monogatari; NKBT*, 31 (1961). Edited by Nagazumi Yasuaki and Shimada Isao.

Hōgen, Bumpo = *Hōgen Monogatari* (Bumpo manuscript). Supplement in *Kamakurabon Hōgen Monogatari.* See *Hōgen Yasutoyo.*

Hōgen, Nakarai = *Hōgen Monogatari* (Nakarai manuscript). *Hōgen Monogatari (Nakaraibon) to Kenkyū* (Toyohashi: Mikan Kokubun Shiryō Kankōkai, 1959). Edited by Yamagishi Tokuhei and Takahashi Teiichi.

Hōgen, Yasutoyo = *Hōgen Monogatari* (Yasutoyo manuscript = Kamakura manuscript). *Kamakurabon Hōgen Monogatari; Denshō Shiryō Shūsei*, 8 (Miyai Shoten, 1974). Edited by Kitagawa Tadahiko and Takegawa Fusako.

Hōjōki. Hōjōki; Nihon Koten Zensho (Asahi Shimbunsha, 1970). Edited by Hosono Tetsuo.

Hokke Hyakuza = *Hokke Hyakuza Hōdan Kikigaki Shō. Kōchū Hokke Hyakuza Kikigaki Shō* (Musashino Shoin, 1976). Edited by Kobayashi Yoshinori.

Hokke Kōsanden = *Kōsan Hokkeden. Kōsan Hokkeden; TSDK*, 51. See *TSDK.*

Hokkekyō = *Fa-hua Ching* = *Lotus Sūtra. Hokkekyō; Iwanami Bunko* (Iwanami Shoten, 1962-67). Edited by Sakamoto Yukio and Iwamoto Yutaka. 3 vols.

Honchō Bunshū. Honchō Bunshū; SZKT, 30 (1938).

Honchō Kōsōden. Honchō Kōsōden; DNBZ, 63. See *DNBZ.*

Honchō Monjū. Honchō Monjū; Kokushi Taikei (new series), 30. Yoshikawa Kōbunkan, Dec. 1938.

Honchō Monzui. Honchō Monzui; SZKT, 30 (1938).

Honchō Mudaishi [HMDS]. Honchō Mudaishi; SGRJ, 6. Edited by Hanami Sakumi. See *SGRJ.*

Honchō Reisō [HR]. Honchō Reisō; SGRJ, 6 (1931). See *SGRJ.*

Honchō Seiki. Honchō Seiki; SZKT, 9 (1933).

Honchō Shinsenden. Kohon Setsuwa Shū; Nihon Koten Zensho (Asahi Shimbunsha, 1967). Edited by Kawaguchi Hisao.

Honchō Zokumonzui [HZM]. Honchō Zokumonzui; SZKT, 29b.

Hongyōkyō = *Butsu Hongyō Shukkyō* = *Fo Pen-hsing Chi-ching*. *Butsu Hongyō Shukkyō; TSDK*, 3. See *TSDK*.

Horikawa Hyakushu = *Horikawa In no Ōntoki Hyakushu Waka*. *Kōhon Horikawa In no Ōntoki Hyakushu Waka to Sono Kenkyū* (Kasama Shoin, 1976-77). Edited by Hashimoto Fumio and Takizawa Sadao. 2 vols.

Horikawa In Godo Hyakushu = *Eikyū Hyakushu*. *Eikyū Yonen Hyakushu; SGRJ*, 8 (1928). Edited by Uematsu Yasushi. See *SGRJ*.

Hōsō Ruirin. *Hōsō Ruirin; ZGRJ*, 10a.

Hosshinshū. *Kōchū Kamo no Chōmei Zenshū* (Kazama Shobō, 1964). Edited by Yanase Kazuo.

Hosshōji Shū = *Hosshōji Kampaku Gyoshū*. *Hosshōji Kampaku Gyoshū; SGRJ*, 6 (1931). Edited by Hanami Sakumi. See *SGRJ*.

Hossokushū. *Hossokushū; Tendaishū Zensho*, 20 (Tendai Shūten Kankōkai, 1936). Edited by Iwata Kyōen.

HR = *Honchō Reisō*. See *Honchō Reisō*.

Hsi-yu Chi. *Hsi-yu Chi* (Hong Kong: Shang-wu Yin-shu-kuan, 1961). 2 vols.

Hung-chih. See *Wanshi*.

Hyakuban Utaawase. *Hyakuban Utaawase, Kempo Yonen; SGRJ*, 9 (1931). Edited by Akiyama Kenzō. See *SGRJ*.

Hyakurenshō. *Hyakurenshō; SZKT*, 11 (1929).

HZM = *Honchō Zokumonzui*. See *Honchō Zokumonzui*.

Ichigon = *Ichigon Hōdan*. *Kana Hōgoshū; NKBT*, 83 (1964). Edited by Miyasaka Yūshō.

Ienaga Ki = *Minamoto Ienaga Nikki*. *Minamoto Ienaga Nikki: Kōhon, Kenkyū, Sōsakuin* (Kazama Shobō, 1985). Edited by Gotō Shigeo et al.

IM = *Ise Monogatari*. See *Ise Monogatari*.

Imakagami. *Imakagami; Nihon Koten Zensho* (Asahi Shimbunsha, 1950). Edited by Itabashi Tomoyuki.

Isayoi Nikki. *Kōchū Abutsu Ni Zenshū* (Kazama Shobō, 1958). Edited by Yanase Kazuo.

Ise Monogatari [IM]. *Ise Monogatari; NKBT*, 9 (1957). Edited by Ōtsu Yūichi and Tsukijima Hiroshi.

Ise Monogatari Shōmonshō. *Ise Monogatari no Kenkyū: Shiryōhen* (Meiji Shoin, 1969). Edited by Katagiri Yōichi.

Iwade Shinobu. *Iwade Shinobu Monogatari: Hommon to Kenkyū* (Kasama Shoin, 1977). Edited by Ogi Takashi.

Iwashimizu Wakamiya Utaawase. *Iwashimizu Wakamiya Utaawase; SGRJ*, 9 (1931). Edited by Akiyama Kenzō. See *SGRJ*.

I-wen = *I-wen Lei-chü*. *I-wen Lei-chü* (Taipei: Hsin-hsing Shu-chü, 1973). 4 vols. Facsimile of 1146 woodblock edition.

Izumi Nikki = *Izumi Shikibu Nikki*. *Izumi Shikibu Nikki Sōsakuin* (Musashino Shoin, 1959). Edited by Tsukahara Tetsuo and Maeda Kingo.

JAHS = *Jōjin Azari Haha no Shū*. See *Jōjin Azari Haha no Shū*.

Jikaishū. See *Kyōunshū*.

Jikkinshō. *Jikkinshō: Hommon to Sakuin* (Kasama Shoin, 1982). Edited by Izumi Motohiro.

Jindaiki. *Nihon Shoki; SZKT*, 4 (1951-52). Edited by Maruyama Jirō. 2 vols.

Jinnō = *Jinnō Shōtōki*. *Jinnō Shōtōki; NKBT*, 87 (1965). Edited by Iwasa Tadashi.

Jizō Reigenki. *Jizō Reigenki; ZGRJ*, 25b.

Jōjin Azari Haha no Shū [JAHS]. Jōjin Azari Haha no Shū no Kisoteki Kenkyū. See Section B, Studies Published in Japanese (Hirabayashi Fumio, 1977).

Jōkyūki. Jōkyūki; SNKB, 1 (1974). Edited by Matsubayashi Yasuaki. See *SNKB.*

Jūmon = Jūmon Saihishō. Jūmon Saihishō; Rengaron Shū B. See *Rengaron Shū* B.

Jung-chai = Jung-chai Sui-pi. Jung-chai Sui-pi; Kuo-hsüeh Chi-pen Ts'ung-shu (Shanghai: Shang-wu Yin-shu-kuan, 1935).

Junrei Kōki = Nittō Guhō Junrei Kōki. See *Nittō Guhō Junrei Kōki.*

Kaden = Fūshi Kaden. See *Zeami, Zenchiku.*

Kagaku Taikei = Nihon Kagaku Taikei. See *NKGT.*

Kagerō = Kagerō Nikki. Kagerō Nikki Sōsakuin (Kazama Shobō, 1963; rev. ed., 1981). Edited by Saeki Umetomo and Imuda Tsunehisa. 1981 edition used.

**Kagurauta [KR]. Kodai Kayō Shū; NKBT,* 3 (1957). Edited by Konishi Jin'ichi.

Kaidōki. Kaidōki no Kenkyū: Hommon Hen (Kasama Shobō, 1979). Edited by Eguchi Masahiro.

Kakaishō. See *Shimyōshō.*

Kakyō. See *Zeami, Zenchiku.*

Kammon Shihai = Kammon Nikki Shihai Monjo. Kammon Nikki Shihai Monjo, Bekki; Toshoryō Sōkan (Nara: Yōtokusha, 1965). Edited with an introduction by Manuscript Division, Bureau of the Royal Household.

Kankyo = Kankyo no Tomo. Kankyo no Tomo; Chūsei no Bungaku (Miyai Shoten, 1974). Edited by Minobe Shigekatsu.

Kanrin Koro Shū. See *Koro.*

Kanshi Taikan [KST]. See *KST.*

Karon Shū A. *Karon Shū; NKBT,* 65 (1961). Edited by Hisamatsu Sen'ichi.

Karon Shū B. *Karon Shū,* 1; *Chūsei no Bungaku* (Miyai Shoten, 1971). Edited by Hisamatsu Sen'ichi.

Katsuragawa Jizō Ki. Katsuragawa Jizō Ki; ZGRJ, 33a.

Kaze ni Tsurenaki Monogatari. Kaze ni Tsurenaki Monogatari; Zoku Zoku Gunsho Ruijū, 15 (Kokusho Kankōkai, 1907). Edited by Hatakeyama Takeshi, Wada Hidematsu, and Yatomi Hamao.

KDSK = Kindai Shūka. See *Kindai Shūka.*

Keikandō. Rengaron Shū A, 2. See *Rengaron Shū* A.

Keitoku Roku = Keitoku Dentōroku = Ching-te Ch'uan-teng Lu. Keitoku Dentōroku; TSDK, 51. See *TSDK.*

Kemmu Shikimoku. Muromachi Bakufu Hō: Chūsei Hōsei Shiryōshū, 2 (Iwanami Shoten, 1957). Edited by Satō Shin'ichi and Ikeuchi Yoshisuke. Revised edition, 1969. 1969 edition used.

Kempō Gonen Utaawase. Utaawase, Kempō Gonen Jūichigatsu Yokka; SGRJ, 9 (1931). Edited by Akiyama Kenzō. See *SGRJ.*

Kengen Ninen Sanjūban Utaawase. Sanjūban Utaawase, Kengen Ninen Gogatsu Yokka; SGRJ, 9 (1931). See *SGRJ.*

Kenjō Chinjō. Kenjō Chinjō, supplement to *Shinkō Roppyakuban Utaawase.* See *Roppyakuban Utaawase.*

Kenrei Mon'in Ukyō no Daibu Shū. See *Ukyō.*

Kensakushū = Wakan Kensakushū. Heian Kamakura Mikan Kanshishū. See *Chūyū Shihai.*

Kenshun = Kenshun Mon'in Chūnagon Nikki = Kenju Omae Nikki. Kenju Omae Nikki; Nihon Koten Zensho (Asahi Shimbunsha, 1954). Edited by Tamai Kōsuke.

KGS = Kikigaki Shū. See *Kikigaki Shū.*

Kigoshō. *Kigoshō; NKGT*, Bekkan, 1. See *NKGT*.
Kikigaki Shū [KGS]. *Kikigaki Shū; SGZS*. See *SGZS*.
Kindai Shūka [KDSK]. *Kindai Shūka; Karon Shū* A. See *Karon Shū* A.
Kinkai Wakashū [KKWS]. *Kinkai Wakashū; NKBT*, 29 (1961). Edited by Kojima Yoshio.
Kinrai Fūteishō. *Kinrai Fūtei; NKGT*, 5. See *NKGT*.
**Kin'yōshū [KYS]*. *Kin'yō Wakashū Sōsakuin* (Osaka: Seibundō, 1976). Edited by Matsuda Shigeo et al.
Kitayama Jugō Kujūga no Ki. *Kitayama Jugō Kujūga no Ki; ZGRJ*, 33b.
**KJK, Song = Kojiki, Song*. *Kodai Kayō Shū; NKBT*, 3 (1957). Edited by Tsuchihashi Yutaka.
**KKS = Kokinshū = Kokinwakashū*; *Iwanami Bunko* (Iwanami Shoten, 1981). Edited by Saeki Umetomo.
KKSK = Kichō Kotenseki Sōkan. *Kichō Kotenseki Sōkan* (Kadokawa Shoten, 1968-77). 12 vols.
KKWS = Kinkai Wakashū. See *Kinkai Wakashū*.
KMS = Konjaku Monogatari Shū. See *Konjaku Monogatari Shū*.
Kōan Hachinen Utaawase. *Mikan Chūsei Utaawase Shū*, 2 (Koten Bunko, 1959). Edited by Taniyama Shigeru and Higuchi Yoshimaro.
Kogawadera Engi. *Jisha Engi; Nihon Shisō Taikei*, 20 (Iwanami Shoten, 1975). Edited by Sakurai Tokutarō.
Kohon Gōdan = Kohonkei Gōdanshō. *Kohonkei Gōdanshō Chūkai* (Musashino Shoin, 1978). Edited by *Gōdanshō* Kenkyūkai.
Kohon Setsuwa Shū. *Kohon Setsuwa Shū, Honchō Shinsenden*. See *Honchō Shinsenden*.
Kojiki. *Nihon Koten Zensho* (Asahi Shimbunsha, 1962-63). Edited by Kanda Hideo and Ota Yoshimaro. 2 vols.
Kokin Rokujō. *Kokin Waka Rokujō; Toshoryō Sōkan* (Tenri: Yōtokusha, 1967-69). Edited by the Library Division, Royal Household Agency of Japan. 2 vols.
Kokin Wakashū Ryōdo Kikigaki. See *Ryōdo Kikigaki*.
Kokinshū. See *KKS*.
Kokinshū Jochū. *Kokinshū Jochū; ZGRJ*, 16b.
Kokinshū Sanryūshō = Kokin Wakashū Jo Kikigaki Sanryūshō. See Section B, Studies Published in Japanese (Katagiri, 1973 [*Kokinshū Chūshakusho Kaidai*, 2]).
Kokon Chomonjū. See *Chomonjū*.
Komparu = Komparu Kodensho Shūsei. *Komparu Kodensho Shūsei* (Wan'ya Shoten, 1969). Edited by Omote Akira and Itō Masayoshi.
Kōmyōbuji Sesshō Ke Utaawase. *Kōmyōbuji Sesshō Ke Utaawase; SGRJ*, 9 (1931). Edited by Akiyama Kenzō. See *SGRJ*.
Kongōkyō = Diamond Sūtra. *Kongō Hannyakyō; Iwanami Bunko* (Iwanami Shoten, 1960). Edited by Nakamura Hajime and Kino Kazuyoshi.
Konjaku Monogatari Shū [KMS]. *Konjaku Monogatari Shū; NKBT*, 22-26 (1959-63). Edited by Yamada Yoshio, Yamada Tadao, Yamada Hideo, and Yamada Toshio.
Korai Fūtei = Korai Fūteishō. *Korai Fūteishō; NKGT*, 2. See *NKGT*. The first version is the one used.
Koro = Kanrin Koro Shū. *Kanrin Koro Shū; GBZS*, 4. See *GBZS*.
Kōsan Hokke Den. See *Hokke Kōsanden*.
Kōsōden = Liang Kao-seng Chuan. *Kōsōden; TSDK*, 50. See *TSDK*.

KR = *Kagurauta*. See *Kagurauta*.

KST = *Kanshi Taikan*. *Kanshi Taikan* (Seki Shoin, 1936–39; rpt. Ōtori Shuppan, 1974). Edited by Saku Setsu. 5 vols.

Kūgeshū. *Kūgeshū; GBZS*, 2. See *GBZS*.

KUS = *Kyōunshū*. See *Kyōunshū*.

KUSS = *Kyōun Shishū*. See *Kyōunshū*.

Kyakuhaibōki. *Myōe Shōnin Shiryō*, 2. See *Myōe Shiryō*.

Kyaraika. See *Zeami, Zenchiku*.

Kyōgoku Sōgo = *Kyōgoku Chūnagon Sōgo*. *Kyōgoku Chūnagon Sōgo; Karon Shū* B, 1. See *Karon Shū* B.

Kyōun Shishū [KUSS]. See *Kyōunshū*.

Kyōunshū [KUS]. *Kyōunshū, Kyōun Shishū, Jikaishū; SNKB*, 5 (1976). Edited by Nakamoto Tamaki. See *SNKB*.

KYS = *Kin'yōshū* = *Kin'yō Wakashū*. See *Kin'yōshū*.

Kyūei = *Shoshin Kyūeishū*. *Shoshin Kyūeishū; Rengaron Shū* A, 1. See *Rengaron Shū* A.

Kyūi. See *Zeami, Zenchiku*.

Kyūreishū. *Heian Kamakura Mikan Kanshishū*. See *Chūyū Shihai*.

Kyūshū Mondō. *Kyūshū Mondō*. See *Rengaron Shū* A, 1.

Lao Tzu. *Lao Tzu Tao-te-ching* (Taipei: Hua-lien Ch'u-pan-she, 1974).

Lin-chi Lu. See *Rinzai Roku*.

Liu-i Shih-hua. *Liu-i Shih-hua* (Peking: Jen-min Wen-hsüeh Ch'u-pan-she, 1962). Edited by Cheng Wen.

Lotus Sūtra. See *Hokkekyō*.

Lo-yang = *Lo-yang Ch'ieh-lan Chi*. *Lo-yang Ch'ieh-lan Chi* (Shanghai: Shanghai Ku-tien Wen-hsüeh Ch'u-pan-she, 1958). Edited by Fan Hsiang-yung.

Maigetsushō. *Maigetsushō*. See *Karon Shū* A.

Maka Shikan = *Mo-ho Chih-kuan*. *Maka Shikan; TSDK*, 46. See *TSDK*.

Makura no Sōshi [MSS]. *Makura no Sōshi; NKBT*, 19 (1958). Edited by Ikegami Shinji.

Manabon Soga Monogatari. See *Soga, Myōhon*.

Man'yōshū [MYS]. *Man'yōshū, Yakubunhen* (Hanawa Shobō, 1972). Edited by Satake Akihiro, Kinoshita Masatoshi, and Kojima Noriyuki.

Masahisa Kyō Ki. *Masahisa Kyō Ki*; author's holograph, in possession of Manuscript Division, Bureau of the Royal Household (no. F9-108).

Masukagami. *Masukagami; NKBT*, 87 (1965). Edited by Tokieda Motoki and Kidō Saizō.

Matsukage = *Matsukage Chūnagon Monogatari*. *Matsukage Chūnagon Monogatari* (Koten Bunko, 1971). Edited by Ōhashi Chiyoko.

Matsura no Miya = *Matsura no Miya Monogatari*. *Matsura no Miya Monogatari; Kadokawa Bunko* (Kadokawa Shoten, 1970). Edited by Hagitani Boku.

Meigetsuki [MGK]. *Meigetsuki* (Kokusho Kankōkai, 1911-12). Edited by Sakamoto Tarō. 3 vols.

Meihōki = *Ming-pao Chi*. *Meihōki; TSDK*, 51. See *TSDK*.

Meikō Ōrai. See *Unshū Shōsoku*.

Meisho Hōgakushō. *Meisho Hōgakushō*; 1666 woodblock edition in possession of Konishi Jin'ichi.

Meng Tzu. *Meng Tzu I-chu* (Taipei: Ho-t'u Lo-shu Ch'u-pan-she, 1977). Edited by Yang Po-chün.

MGK = *Meigetsuki*. See *Meigetsuki*.

Michichika Ki = *Tsuchimikado Naidaijin Ki. Chūsei Bungaku Mikan Shiryō no Kenkyū* (Hitaku Shobō, 1982). Edited by Satō Takaaki.

Michinori Shomoku = *Michinori Nyūdō Zōsho Mokuroku. Michinori Nyūdō Zōsho Mokuroku; SGRJ*, 21 (1930). Edited by Hanami Sakumi. See *SGRJ*.

Midō Kampaku Ki. Midō Kampaku Ki; Dai Nihon Kokiroku (Iwanami Shoten, 1952-54). Edited by the Institute for Compilation of Historical Materials, University of Tokyo. 3 vols.

Minamoto Ienaga Nikki. See *Ienaga Ki*.

Minase Sakura no Miya Utaawase. Minase Sakura no Miya Utaawase; SGRJ, 9 (1931). See *SGRJ*.

Minase Sangin = *Minase Sangin Hyakuin. Minase Sangin; Sōgi*. See Section B, Studies Published in Japanese (Konishi, 1971c).

Minasedono Koi Jūgoshu Utaawase. Minasedono Koi Jūgoshu Utaawase; SGRJ, 9 (1931). See *SGRJ*.

Ming-pao Chi. See *Meihōki*.

Mino = *Shinkokinshū Mino no Iezuto. Shinkokinshū Mino no Iezuto; Motoori Norinaga Zenshū*, 3 (Chikuma Shobō, 1969). Edited by Ōkubo Tadashi.

Miyakoji no Wakare. Asukai Masaari Nikki. See *Asukai*.

MMSS = *Mumyō Sōshi*. See *Mumyō Sōshi*.

Mo-ho Chih-kuan. See *Maka Shikan*.

Monzen = *Wen Hsüan*. See *Wen Hsüan*.

Moromori Ki. Moromori Ki; Shiryō Sanshū (Zoku Gunsho Ruijū Kankōkai, 1968-82). Edited by Fujii Sadafumi and Kobayashi Hanako. 11 vols.

Mototoshi Shū. Mototoshi Shū; SKST, 2:68. See *SKST*.

MSK = *Myōe Shōnin Kashū*. See *Myōe Shōnin Kashū*.

MSN = *Murasaki Shikibu Nikki*. See *Murasaki Shikibu Nikki*.

Mumonkan = *Wu-men Kuan. Mumonkan; TSDK*, 48. See *TSDK*.

Mumyōshō. See *Karon Shū* A.

Mumyō Sōshi [MMSS]. Mumyō Sōshi; Shinchō Nihon Koten Shūsei (Shinchōsha, 1976). Edited by Kuwabara Hiroshi.

Murasaki Shikibu Nikki [MSN]. Murasaki Shikibu Nikki; NKBT, 19 (1958). Edited by Ikeda Kikan and Akiyama Ken.

Mutsu Waki. Mutsu Waki (Gendai Shichōsha, 1982). Edited by Kajiwara Masaaki.

Myōe Den = *Toganoo Myōe Shōnin Denki. Toganoo Myōe Shōnin Denki*: (a) Kōzanji manuscript, copied in 1599, published in *Myōe Shōnin Shiryō*, 1. See *Myōe Shiryō*; (b) 1665 woodblock edition. Reprinted in *Kokubun Tōhō Bukkyō Sōsho, Denkibu* (Tōhō Shoin, 1925), edited by Washio Junkei and Inamura Tangen.

Myōe Shiryō = *Myōe Shōnin Shiryō. Myōe Shōnin Shiryō; Kōzanji Shiryō Sōsho* (University of Tokyo Press, 1971-78). Edited by Kōzanji Tenseki Monjo Sōgō Chōsadan. 2 vols.

Myōe Shōnin Kashū [MSK]. Gokuraku Gan'ōjō Ka, Myōe Shōnin Kashū: Hommon to Sakuin (Kasama Shoin, 1977). Edited by Yamada Iwao and Kimura Akira.

MYS = *Man'yōshū*. See *Man'yōshū*.

Nakamurabon Yowa no Nezame. Yowa no Nezame Monogatari (Koten Bunko, 1954-55). Edited by Kaneko Takeo. 2 vols.

Nakatsukasa Nikki = *Nakatsukasa Naishi Nikki. Suifu Meitokukai Shōkōkan Zōhon Nakatsukasa Naishi Nikki: Hommonhen* (Shintensha, 1982). Edited by Kokubo Takaaki.

Nīberungen no Uta = *Nibelungenlied. Nīberungen no Uta; Iwanami Bunko* (Iwanami Shoten, 1955). Translated by Sagara Morio. 2 vols.

Nihon Kagaku Taikei [NKGT]. See *NKGT*.

Nihon Meisōden. Nihon Meisōden; ZGRJ, 8b.

Nihon Ōjō Gokuraku Ki. Ōjōden; Nihon Shisō Taikei, 7 (Iwanami Shoten, 1974). Edited by Inoue Mitsusada and Ōsone Shōsuke.

Nihon Shoki [NSK]. Nihon Shoki; SZKT, 1 (1951-52). Edited by Kuroita Katsumi et al. 2 vols.

Nishidaishū. See *Teika Hachidaishō*.

Nittō Guhō Junrei Kōki. Nittō Guhō Junrei Kōki; Dai Nihon Bukkyō Zensho, 72 (Suzuki Gakujitsu Zaidan, 1972).

NKGT = *Nihon Kagaku Taikei. Nihon Kagaku Taikei* (Bummeisha and Kazama Shobō, 1940-81). Edited by Sasaki Nobutsuna, Kyūsojin Hitaku, and Higuchi Yoshimaro. 15 vols.

Nihon Ryōiki. Nihon Ryōiki; NKBT, 70 (1967). Edited by Endō Yoshimoto.

Nōin Shū. Nōin Shū; SKST, 2:20. See *SKST*.

Nōin Utamakura. Nōin Utamakura; NKGT, 1. See *NKGT*.

Nomori no Kagami. Nomori no Kagami; NKGT, 4. See *NKGT*.

**NSK, Song* = *Nihon Shoki, Song. Kodai Kayō Shū; NKBT*, 3 (1957). Edited by Tsuchihashi Yutaka.

Ochikubo = *Ochikubo Monogatari. Ochikubo Monogatari; NKBT*, 13 (1957). Edited by Matsuo Satoshi.

Ōgishō. Ōgishō; NKGT, 1. See *NKGT*.

Oi no Kurigoto. Oi no Kurigoto; Kodai Chūsei Geijitsuron. See *Hitorigoto*.

Oi no Susami. Rengaron Shū C, 2. See *Rengaron Shū* C.

Ōjō Yōshū. Genshin; Nihon Shisō Taikei, 6 (Iwanami Shoten, 1970). Edited by Ishida Mizumaro.

OK = *Ōkagami. Ōkagami; NKBT*, 21 (1960). Edited by Matsumura Hiroshi.

Omuro Senkaawase. Omuro Senkaawase; SGRJ, 9 (1931). Edited by Akiyama Kenzō. See *SGRJ*.

Ōtaku Fuketsu Shō. Ōtaku Fuketsu Shō; 1634 woodblock edition in possession of Kōyasan University Library.

P'ing-yao Chuan (B) = *San-Sui P'ing-yao Chuan. P'ing-yao Chuan* (Shanghai: Shang-hai Ku-tien Wen-hsüeh Ch'u-pan-she, 1956). This sole modern edition has not a few mistakes and omissions. They have been emended by reference to the Shu-yeh T'ang 1812 edition in Konishi Jin'ichi's possession.

P'i-yen Lu. See *Hekigan Roku*.

Po Hsiang-shan Shih-chi. See *Haku Kōzan Shishū*.

Po-shih Ch'ang-ch'ing Chi. Po-shih Ch'ang-ch'ing Chi (Peking: Wen-hsüeh Ku-chi K'an-hsing-she, 1955). 3 vols.

Rakusho = *Rakusho Roken. Rakusho Roken; NKGT*, 5. See *NKGT*.

Rangyoku Kusemaishū. Rangyoku Kusemaishū; Yōkyoku Taikan, supplementary volume (Meiji Shoin, 1931). Edited by Nogami Toyoichirō.

Renga Haikai Shū. Renga Haikai Shū; Nihon Koten Bungaku Zenshū, 32 (Shōgakkan, 1974). Edited by Kaneko Kinjirō, Teruoka Yasutaka, and Nakamura Shunjō.

Renga Haja Kenshō. Renga Haja Kenshō; 1693 woodblock edition in Wataya Collection, Tenri Library. 2 vols.

Renga Jūyō. Renga Jūyō; Rengaron Shū A, 1. See *Rengaron Shū* A.

Rengaron Shū A. *Rengaron Shū; Iwanami Bunko* (Iwanami Shoten, 1953-56). Edited by Ijichi Tetsuo. 2 vols.

Rengaron Shū B. *Rengaron Shū; NKBT*, 66 (1961). Edited by Kidō Saizō.

Rengaron Shū C. *Rengaron Shū; Chūsei no Bungaku* (Miyai Shoten, 1972-82). Edited by Kidō Saizō and Shigematsu Hiromi. 2 vols.

Rengaron Shū D. *Rengaron Shū; Nihon Koten Bungaku Zenshū*, 51 (Shōgakkan, 1973). Edited by Ijichi Tetsuo.

Renri Hishō [RRHS]. Renri Hishō; Rengaron Shū B. See *Rengaron Shū* B.

Rika = Rika Wakashū. Rikashū; SKST, 5:26. See *SKST*.

Rinzai Roku = Lin-chi Lu. Teihon Rinzai Zenji Goroku (Shunjūsha, 1971). Edited by Hirano Sōjō.

Rokudai Shōshiki. Rokudai Shōshiki; SGRJ, 2 (1929). Edited by Kawakami Tasuke. See *SGRJ*.

Rokuichi Shiwa. See *Liu-i Shih-hua*.

Rokuon = Rokuon Nichiroku. Rokuon Nichiroku (Zoku Gunsho Ruijū Kanseikai, 1934-62). Edited by Tsuji Zennosuke. 7 vols.

Rokurin Ichiro no Ki. Komparu Kodensho Shūsei. See *Komparu*.

Rokurin Ichiro no Ki Chū. See *Komparu*.

Roppyakuban Utaawase [RU]. Shinkō Roppyakuban Utaawase (Yūseidō, 1976). Edited by Konishi Jin'ichi.

Rōran no Uta = Chanson de Roland. Rōran no Uta; Iwanami Bunko (Iwanami Shoten, 1965). Translated by Arinaga Hiroto.

RRHS = Renri Hishō. See *Renri Hishō*.

RU = Roppyakuban Utaawase. See *Roppyakuban Utaawase*.

Rufubon Gōdan = Rufubonkei Gōdanshō. Gōdanshō; SGRJ, 21 (1930). Edited by Hanami Sakumi. See *SGRJ*.

Ruiju Shingi Hongen. Ruiju Shingi Hongen; Zoku Zoku Gunsho Ruijū, 1 (Kokusho Kankōkai, 1906). Edited by Inoue Yorikuni and Saeki Ariyoshi.

Ruiju Utaawase Maki. Sanshū Ruiju Utaawase to Sono Kenkyū (Bijitsu Shoin, 1945). Edited by Horibe Seiji.

RUSS = Ryōun Shinshū. See *Ryōun Shinshū*.

Ryōdo Kikigaki = Kokin Wakashū Ryōdo Kikigaki. Chūsei Kokinshū Chūshakusho Kaidai, 3b. See Section B, Studies Published in Japanese (Katagiri, 1981).

Ryōgen = Ryōgenshū. Ryōgenshū; GBZS, 3. See *GBZS*.

**Ryōjin Hishō. Ryōjin Hishō; Iwanami Bunko* (Iwanami Shoten, 1933; rev. ed., 1957). Edited by Sasaki Nobutsuna. 1957 edition used.

Ryōun Shinshū [RUSS]. Ryōun Shinshū; SGRJ, 6 (1931). Edited by Hanami Sakumi.

Saga no Kayoi. Saga no Kayoi; Asukai Masaari Nikki. See *Asukai*.

Sagoromo = Sagoromo Monogatari. Sagoromo Monogatari; NKBT, 79 (1965). Edited by Mitani Eiichi and Sekine Yoshiko.

Saigyō Monogatari. See *SGZS*.

Saigyō Monogatari Emaki. See *SGZS*.

**Saigyō Zenshū [SGZS]*. See *SGZS*.

Saihokushū [SH]. Saihokushū; GBZS, 1. See *GBZS*.

Sakumon Daitai. "Kōtei *Sakumon Daitai*," Part 2 of "*Sakumon Daitai* no Kisoteki Kenkyū." See Bibliography B, vol. 2 (Ozawa, 1963).

Samboe. Shohon Taishō Samboe Shūsei (Kasama Shoin, 1980). Edited by Koizumi Hiroshi and Takahashi Nobuyuki.

**Samboku Kikashū [SBS]. Awabon Samboku Kikashū: Hommon Kōihen* (Kazama Shobō, 1979). Edited by Sekine Yoshiko and Ōi Yōko.

Sandō. See *Zeami, Zenchiku*.

Sangoki. Sangoki; NKGT, 4. See *NKGT.*
Sangoku Denki. Sangoku Denki; Chūsei no Bungaku (Miyai Shoten, 1976-82). Edited by Ikegami Jun'ichi. 2 vols.
Sangoku Shiki = Samguk Sagi. Sangoku Shiki (Seoul: Chikazawa Shoten, 1928). Edited by Imanishi Ryū. Revised by Suematsu Yasukazu in the third edition, 1941; reprinted by Kokusho Kankōkai, 1971. 1971 edition used.
**Sankashū [SK]. Sankashū; NKBT*, 29 (1961). Edited by Kazamaki Keijirō and Kojima Yoshio.
San-kuo Chih. San-kuo Chih (Peking: Chung-hua Shu-chü, 1959). 5 vols.
San-kuo Chih P'ing-hua. San-kuo Chih P'ing-hua (Shanghai: Shang-hai Ku-tien Wen-hsüeh Ch'u-pan-she, 1955).
San-kuo Chih Yen-i = San-kuo Chih T'ung-su Yen-i. Ming Hung-chih Pan, San-kuo Chih T'ung-su Yen-i (Taipei: Hsin Wen-feng Ch'u-pan, 1979). Facsimile of 1494 woodblock edition.
San-Sui P'ing-yao Chuan. See *P'ing-yao Chuan.*
Santaishi = San-t'i Shih = T'ang-shih San-t'i Chia-fa. Zōchū Santaishi; Kambun Taikei, 2 (Fuzambō, 1910). Edited by Hattori Unokichi.
San Tendai Godaisanki. San Tendai Godaisanki no Kenkyū, Pt. 3 (Ōkura Shuppan, 1959). Edited by Shimazu Kusako.
Sanuki no Suke Nikki [SN]. Sanuki no Suke Nikki; Nihon Koten Zensho (Asahi Shimbunsha, 1953). Edited by Tamai Kōsuke.
Sarashina = Sarashina Nikki. Sarashina Nikki; NKBT, 20 (1951). Edited by Nishishita Kyōichi.
Sarugaku Dangi. See *Zeami, Zenchiku.*
Sasamegoto. Sasamegoto; Rengaron Shū B. See *Rengaron Shū* B.
Sayogoromo. Sayogoromo Kōhon (Koten Bunko, 1957). Edited by Matsuo Satoshi.
SBS = Samboku Kikashū. See *Samboku Kikashū.*
Seia = Seiashō. Seiashō; NKGT, 5. See *NKGT.*
Seiki = Honchō Seiki. Honchō Seiki; SZKT, 9 (1933).
Seireishū [SRS]. Seireishū; NKBT, 71 (1965). Edited by Watanabe Shōkō and Miyasaka Yūshō.
Sekiso Ōrai. Sekiso Ōrai; Nihon Kyōkasho Taikei, 2 (Kōdansha, 1967). Edited by Ishikawa Ken.
**Sengohyakuban Utaawase. Sengohyakuban Utaawase no Kōhon to Sono Kenkyū* (Kazama Shobō, 1968). Edited by Ariyoshi Tamotsu.
Senjūshō. Senjūshō; Iwanami Bunko (Iwanami Shoten, 1970). Edited by Nishio Kōichi.
Sentō Gojūban Utaawase. Sentō Gojūban Utaawase; SGRJ, 9 (1931). Edited by Akiyama Kenzō. See *SGRJ.*
**Senzaishū [SZS] = Senzai Wakashū. Senzai Wakashū* (Kasama Shoin, 1969). Edited by Kubota Jun and Matsuno Yōichi.
Sesson Daioshō Gyōdōki. Sesson Daioshō Gyōdōki; GBZS, 1. See *GBZS.*
SG. See *Shūi Gusō.*
SGRJ = Shinkō Gunsho Ruijū. Shinkō Gunsho Ruijū (Naigai Shoseki, 1928-37). Edited by Ueda Kazutoshi et al. 24 vols.
**SGZS = Saigyō Zenshū. Saigyō Zenshū* (Nihon Koten Bungakkai, 1982). Edited by Kubota Jun.
SH = Saihokushū. See *Saihokushū.*
Shasekishū. Shasekishū; NKBT, 85 (1966). Edited by Watanabe Tsunaya.
Shichijūichiban = Shichijūichiban Shokunin Utaawase. Shokunin Utaawase

Sōgō Sakuin (Kyoto: Akao Shōbundō, 1982). Edited by Iwasaki Kae, Hasegawa Nobuyoshi, and Yamamoto Yuiitsu.

Shichiken Jidai Renga Kushū. Shichiken Jidai Renga Kushū; KKSK, 11 (1975). Edited by Kaneko Kinjirō and Ōta Takeo. See *KKSK*.

**Shigeyuki Shū. Shigeyuki Shū; SKST*, 1:138. See *SKST*.

Shigisan Engi. Shigisan Engi; Nihon Emaki Taisei, 4 (Chūō Kōronsha, 1977). Compiled by Komatsu Shigemi.

Shih Chi. Shih Chi (Peking: Chung-hua Shu-chü, 1959). 10 vols.

Shih-jen Yü-hsieh. See *Yü-hsieh*.

Shih-lin Shih-hua. Shih-lin Shih-hua; Tseng-pu Chin-tai Mi-shu, 4 (Kyoto: Chūbun Shuppansha, 1980).

Shikadō. See *Zeami, Zenchiku*.

**Shikashū [SKS] = Shika Wakashū. Shikashū Sōsakuin* (Meiji Shoin, 1972). Edited by Takizawa Sadao.

**Shikashū Taisei [SKST]. Shikashū Taisei* (Meiji Shoin, 1973-76). Edited by the Wakashi Kenkyūkai. 7 vols.

Shiki Shō = Shiki Tōgen Shō. Shiki Shō; 16th-century manuscript in the possession of Naikaku Bunko, National Library of Official Documents. 14 fascs.

Shimpen Kokka Taikan. Shimpen Kokka Taikan (Kadokawa Shoten, 1983-87). Compiled and edited by Taniyama Shigeru et al. 10 vols.

Shimyōshō. Shimyōshō, Kakaishō (Kadokawa Shoten, 1968). Edited by Ishida Jōji.

**Shinchokusenshū = Shinchokusen Wakashū. Shinchokusen Wakashū; Shimpen Kokka Taikan*, 1 (1983). See *Shimpen Kokka Taikan*.

**Shingoshūishū = Shingoshūi Wakashū. Shingoshūi Wakashū; Shimpen Kokka Taikan*, 1 (1983). See *Shimpen Kokka Taikan*.

Shinkei Sakuhinshū. Shinkei Sakuhinshū; KKSK, 5 (1972). Edited by Yokoyama Shigeru. See *KKSK*.

Shinkei Teikin = Shinkei Sōzu Teikin. Shinkei Sōzu Teikin; ZGRJ, 17b.

Shinkō Gunsho Ruijū [SGRJ]. See *SGRJ*.

**Shinkokinshū [SKKS] = Shinkokin Wakashū. Shinkokin Wakashū; NKBT*, 28 (1958). Edited by Hisamatsu Sen'ichi, Yamazaki Toshio, and Gotō Shigeo.

Shinkokinshū Mino no Iezuto. See *Mino*.

Shinobine Monogatari. Taikō Shinobine Monogatari (Osaka: Izumi Shobō, 1985). Edited by Kokubo Takaaki and Yamada Yūji.

Shinsatsu = Shinsatsu Ōrai. Shinsatsu Ōrai; Nihon Kyōkasho Taikei, 2. See *Sekiso Ōrai*.

Shinsen Nihon Koten Bunko [SNKB] (Gendai Shichōsha, 1974-76). 5 vols.

**Shinsen Tsukuba Shū [STBS]. Shinsen Tsukuba Shū: Meiōbon*. (Kokusho Shuppan, 1945). Edited by Yokoyama Shigeru and Noguchi Eiichi. Facsimile reprint by Kazama Shobō, 1958.

**Shinsenzaishū = Shinsenzai Wakashū. Shinsenzai Wakashū; Shimpen Kokka Taikan*, 1. See *Shimpen Kokka Taikan*.

Shinsen Zuinō. See *Karon Shū* A.

**Shinshoku Goshūishū = Shinshoku Goshūi Wakashū. Shinshoku Goshūi Wakashū; Shimpen Kokka Taikan*, 1. See *Shimpen Kokka Taikan*.

**Shinshoku Kokinshū = Shinshoku Kokin Wakashū*. Same as preceding.

Shintōshū. Shintōshū; Tōyō Bunkobon (Kadokawa Shoten, 1959). Edited by Kondō Yoshihiro.

**Shin'yōshū = Shin'yō Wakashū. Shin'yō Wakashū; Shimpen Kokka Taikan*, 1. See *Shimpen Kokka Taikan*.

Shiseki Shūran. Kaitei Shiseki Shūran (Kondō Shuppambu, 1900-03). Compiled and edited by Kondō Heijō. 32 vols. *Shintei Zōho Shiseki Shūran* (Kyoto: Rinsen Shoten, 1967-68). 43 vols. First 34 vols. recompiled and edited by Tsunoda Bun'ei and Gorai Shigeru, and last 9 vols. by Kondō Heijō. 1967-68 edition used.

Shishu Hyaku Innenshū. Shishu Hyaku Innenshū (Koten Bunko, 1969). Facsimile of 1653 woodblock edition, with an introduction by Yoshida Kōichi. 3 vols.

Shittanzō. Shittan Gusho; DNBZ, 42. See *DNBZ*. Facsimile of Ryōgon In manuscript.

Shōan Gannen Goshu Utaawase. Shōan Gannen Goshu Utaawase; ZGRJ, 15b.

Shōan Ninen Sanjūban Utaawase. Shōō Ninen Sanjūban Utaawase; SGRJ, 9 (1931). Edited by Akiyama Kenzō. See *SGRJ*. "Shōō" is a scribal error for "Shōan."

Shōbō Genzō. See *Genzō*.

Shōbō Genzō Zuimonki. See *Zuimonki*.

Shōji Nido Hyakushu. Shōji Ninen Dainido Hyakushu Waka; SGRJ, 8 (1928). Edited by Uematsu Yasushi. See *SGRJ*.

Shōji Ninen Waji Sōjō. See *Waji Sōjō*.

Shōji Shodo Hyakushu = Shōji Ninen In Onhyakushu. Shōji Ninen In On'hyakushu; ZGRJ, 14b.

Shōkenkō. Shōkenkō; GBZS, 2. See *GBZS*.

Shoku Nihongi [SNG]. Shoku Nihongi; SZKT, 2 (1935).

**Shokugosenshū = Shokugosen Wakashū. Shokugosenshū Sōsakuin* (Meiji Shoin, 1983). Edited by Takizawa Sadao.

**Shokugoshūishū = Shokugoshūi Wakashū. Shokugoshūi Wakashū; Shimpen Kokka Taikan*, 1. See *Shimpen Kokka Taikan*.

**Shokushūishū = Shokushūi Wakashū*. Same as preceding.

Shōmon Ki. Shōmon Ki (Gendai Shichōsha, 1975). Edited by Hayashi Rikurō.

Shoshin Kyūeishū. See *Kyūei*.

Shōtetsu = Shōtetsu Monogatari. Shōtetsu Monogatari; Karon Shū A. See *Karon Shū* A.

Shūchūshō. Shūchūshō no Kōhon to Kenkyū (Kasama Shoin, 1985). Edited by Hashimoto Fumio and Gotō Sachiko.

Shugyoku Henjishō. See *Gengo Henjishō*.

Shūgyoku Tokka. See *Zeami, Zenchiku*.

**Shūi Gusō [SG]. Fujiwara Teika Zenkashū* (Bummeisha, 1940). Edited by Reizei Tameomi. Facsimile reprint by Kokusho Kankōkai, 1974.

Shui-hu Chuan. Shui-hu Ch'üan-chuan (Peking: Jen-min Wen-hsüeh Ch'u-pan-she, 1954). 3 vols.

Shūi Ōjōden. Shūi Ōjōden; DNBZ, 68. See *DNBZ*.

**Shūishū [SIS] = Shūi Wakashū. Shūi Wakashū no Kenkyū* (Kyoto: Daigakudō Shoten, 1970-76). Edited by Katagiri Yōichi.

Shumpishō = Shunrai Zuinō. Shunrai Zuinō; NKGT, 1. See *NKGT*.

SIS = Shūishū. See *Shūishū*.

SK = Sankashū. See *Sankashū*.

SKKS = Shinkokinshū. See *Shinkokinshū*.

SKS = Shikashū. See *Shikashū*.

**SKST*. See *Shikashū Taisei*.

SN = Sanuki no Suke Nikki. See *Sanuki no Suke Nikki*.

SNG. See *Shoku Nihongi*.

SNKB. See *Shinsen Nihon Koten Bunko*.

Soga = *Rufubon Soga Monogatari. Soga Monogatari; NKBT*, 88 (1966). Edited by Ichiko Teiji and Ōshima Tatehiko.

Soga, Daisenji manuscript = *Daisenjibon Soga Monogatari. Daisenjibon Soga Monogatari.* Edited by Araki Yoshio. See Section B, Studies Published in Japanese (Araki, 1941b).

Soga, Myōhonji manuscript = *Myōhonjibon Soga Monogatari. Myohonjibon Soga Monogatari.* Edited by Kadokawa Gen'yoshi. See Section B, Studies Published in Japanese (Kadokawa, 1969).

Sōgi Nanihito = *Sōgi Dokugin Nanihito Hyakuin. Sōgi Dokugin Nanihito Hyakuin; Renga Haikai Shū.* See *Renga Haikai Shū.*

**Sōkonshū. Sōkonshū* (Okayama: Dept. of Japanese Literature, Women's College of Notre Dame, 1967-73). Edited by Shirai Tatsuko. 4 vols.

Sompi Bummyaku. Sompi Bummyaku; SZKT (1957-64). 5 vols.

Sōtan Shū = *Sone Yoshitada Shū. Sone no Yoshitada Shū no Kōhon Sōsakuin* (Kasama Shoin, 1973). Edited by Kansaku Kōichi.

Sou-shen Chi. Sou-shen Chi; Hsüeh-chin T'ao-yüan, 12 (Taipei: Hsin-feng Ch'u-pan, 1980).

SRS = *Seireishū.* See *Seireishū.*

STBS = *Shinsen Tsukuba Shū.* See *Shinsen Tsukuba Shū.*

Su Tung-p'o Shih-chi. See *Tōba.*

Sumiyoshi Monogatari. Sumiyoshi Monogatari to Kenkyū (Toyohashi: Mikan Kokubun Shiryō Kankōkai, 1964). Edited by Kuwabara Hiroshi.

Sung Shu. Sung Shu (Peking: Chung-hua Shu-chü, 1974). 8 vols.

Suwa Sha Engie. Chūsei Shimbutsu Setsuwa, Zoku Zoku (Koten Bunko, 1971). Edited by Kondō Yoshihiro and Miyaji Takakuni.

**SZS* = *Senzaishū.* See *Senzaishū.*

Ta-ch'eng Ch'i-hsin Lun. See *Daijō Kishinron.*

Ta-hui = *Ta-hui P'u-chüeh Ch'an-shih Yü-lu.* See *Daie Roku.*

Taiheiki [THK]. Taiheiki; NKBT, 34-36 (1960-62). Edited by Gotō Tanji, Kamada Kisaburō, and Okami Masao.

Takemuki ga Ki. Utatane, Takemuki ga Ki (Kasama Shoin, 1975). Edited by Tsugita Kasumi and Watanabe Shizuko.

Taketori, Kohon = *Kohon Taketori Monogatari. Kohon Taketori Monogatari* (Taishūkan, 1968). Edited by Nakata Takanao.

Tamekanu Shō = *Tamekanu Kyō Wakashō.* See *Karon Shū* A.

T'ang Sung Ch'uan-ch'i Chi. See *Ch'uan-ch'i.*

Tannishō. Shinran Shū; NKBT, 82 (1964). Edited by Nabata Ōjun and Taya Raishun.

T'ao-shih = *T'ao Yüan-ming Shih-chi.* See *Tōshi.*

TBS = *Tsukuba Shū.* See *Tsukuba Shū.*

**Teika Hachidaishō* = *Nishidai Shū. Teika Hachidaishō to Kenkyū* (Toyohashi: Mikan Kokubun Shiryō Kankōkai, 1956-57). Edited by Higuchi Yoshimaro. 2 vols.

Teika Hyakuban Jikaawase [THJA] (second revised text). *Teika Kyō Hyakuban Jikaawase; ZGRJ*, 15a.

Teika Karyū Ryōkyō Senkaawase. Teika Karyū Ryōkyō Senkaawase; SGRJ, 10 (1929). Edited by Uematsu Yasushi. See *SGRJ.*

Tentoku = *Tentoku Utaawase.* See *Utaawase Shū.*

THJA = *Teika Hyakuban Jikaawase.* See *Teika Hyakuban Jikaawase.*

THK = *Taiheiki.* See *Taiheiki.*

Tōba = *So Tōba Shishū* = *Su Tung-p'o Shih-chi. So Tōba Shishū; KST*, 5. See *KST*.

Tōfū Renga = *Tōfū Renga Hiji; Rengaron Shū* D. See *Rengaron Shū* D.

Toganoo Myōe Shōnin Denki. See *Myōe Den*.

Tōkan = *Tōkan Kikō. Tōkan Kikō: Hommon Oyobi Sōsakuin* (Kasama Shoin, 1977). Edited by the Department of Japanese Literature, Kumamoto Women's College.

Tokorodokoro Hentō. Rengaron Shū A, 1. See *Rengaron Shū* A.

Tong Munsŏn. Tong Munsŏn (Seoul: Kyŏnghŭi Ch'ulp'ansa, 1967). 3 vols. Facsimile of early 17th-century woodblock edition.

Torikaebaya Monogatari. Matsuakibon Torikaebaya (Musashi Shobō, 1969). Edited by Suzuki Hiromichi.

Tosa = *Tosa Nikki. Tosa Nikki; NKBT*, 20 (1957). Edited by Suzuki Tomotarō.

Tōsan Roku = *Tōsan Gohon Zenji Goroku* = *Tung-shan Wu-pen Ch'an-shih Yü-lu. Tōsan Gohon Zenji Goroku; TSDK*, 43. See *TSDK*.

Tōshi = *Tō Emmei Shishū* = *T'ao Yüan-ming Shih-chi. Tō Emmei Shishū; KST*, 2. See *KST*.

Toshikazu Ki = *Ayanokōji Toshikazu Kyō Ki. Ayanokōji Toshikazu Kyō Ki; SGRJ*, 4 (1931). Edited by Matsumoto Hikojirō. See *SGRJ*.

Towazugatari. Towazugatari; Shinchō Nihon Koten Shūsei (Shinchōsha, 1978). Edited by Fukuda Hideichi.

Ts'ang-hai Shih-hua. Ts'ang-hai Shih-hua; Han-hai, 4:13. 1825 Ch'ing woodblock edition in possession of Central Library, University of Tsukuba.

Ts'ang-lang Shih-hua. Chiao-cheng Ts'ang-lang Shih-hua Chu (Taipei: Kuang-wen Shu-chü, 1972). Facsimile of 1881 Ch'ing woodblock edition.

TSDK = *Taishō Shinshū Daizōkyō. Taishō Shinshū Daizōkyō* (Taishō Issaikyō Kankōkai, 1924-32). Edited by Takakusu Junjirō and Watanabe Kaikyoku. 85 vols.

Tsuchimikado Naidaijin Nikki. See *Michichika Ki*.

Tsuika = *Keiyū Hōgen Shō. Tsuika; NKGT*, 3. See *NKGT*.

Tsui-weng T'an-lu = *Hsin-pien Tsui-weng T'an-lu. Tsui-weng T'an-lu* (Shanghai: Shin-chieh Shu-chü, 1965, 2nd printing).

Tsūken Shomoku. See *Michinori Shomoku*.

Tsukuba Mondō. See *Rengaron Shū* B.

**Tsukuba Shū [TBS]*. "Hirodaibon *Tsukuba Shū*," in *Tsukuba Shū no Kenkyū*. Edited by Kaneko Kinjirō. See Section B, Studies Published in Japanese (Kaneko Kinjirō, 1965).

Tsukushi Michi no Ki. "Tsukushi Michi no Ki" in *Sōgi Tabi no Ki Shichū*. See Section B, Studies Published in Japanese (Kaneko Kinjirō, 1970).

Ts'ung-shu Chi-ch'eng. Ts'ung-shu Chi-ch'eng (Shanghai: Shang-wu Yin-shu-kuan, 1935-37). Edited by Wang Yün-wu et al. 516 vols.

Tsurezuregusa. Tsurezuregusa; Nihon Koten Zensho (Asahi Shimbunsha, 1947). Edited by Tachibana Jun'ichi.

Tsutsumi = *Tsutsumi Chūnagon Monogatari. Tsutsumi Chūnagon Monogatari; NKBT*, 13 (1957). Edited by Teramoto Naohiko.

Tung-ching Meng-hua Lu. Tung-ching Meng-hua Lu Chu; Chung-kuo Ku-tai Tu-ch'eng Tzu-liao Hsüan-k'an (Shanghai: Shang-wu Yin-shu-kuan, 1959). Edited by Teng Chih-ch'eng. Republished by Chung-hua Shu-chü, Peking, in 1982. 1982 edition used.

Tung-shan Wu-pen Ch'an-shih Yü-lu. See *Tōsan Roku*.

UAS = *Utaawase Shū*. See *Utaawase Shū*.

Uchigiki Shū. Uchigiki Shū no Kenkyū to Kōhon (Osaka: Seibundō, 1983). Edited by Higashitsuji Yasukazu.

Uji = Uji Shūi Monogatari. Uji Shūi Monogatari; NKBT, 27 (1960). Edited by Watanabe Tsunaya and Nishio Kōichi.

Ukyō = Kenrei Mon'in Ukyō no Daibu Shū. Kōhon Kenrei Mon'in Ukyō no Daibu Shū (Tōhō Shobō, 1959). Edited by Ikari Masashi.

UM = Utsuho Monogatari. See *Utsuho Monogatari.*

Unshū Shōsoku = Meikō Ōrai. Unshū Shōsoku; SGRJ 6 (1931). Edited by Hanami Sakumi.

Unzushō. Unzushō; SGRJ, 4 (1931). Edited by Matsumoto Hikojirō. See *SGRJ.*

Utaawase Shū [UAS]. Utaawase Shū; NKBT, 74 (1965). Edited by Hagitani Boku and Taniyama Shigeru.

* *Utamakura Nayose. Kōhon Utamakura Nayose: Hommonhen* (Ōfūsha, 1977). Edited by Shibuya Torao.

Utatane no Ki. Utatane, Takemuki ga Ki. See *Takemuki ga Ki.*

Utsuho Monogatari [UM]. Utsuho Monogatari: Hommon to Sakuin (Kasama Shoin, 1973). Edited by the *Utsuho Monogatari* Kenkyūkai.

Waga Mi = Waga Mi ni Tadoru Himegimi. Waga Mi ni Tadoru Himegimi (Koten Bunko, 1956). Edited by Kaneko Takeo. 2 vols.

Waji Sōjō = Shōji Ninen Waji Sōjō. Shōji Ninen Shunzei Kyō Waji Sōjō; Karon Shū B, 1. See *Karon Shū* B.

Waka Dōmōshō. Waka Dōmōshō; NKGT, 1 and Bekkan 1. See *NKGT.*

Waka Genzai Shomokuroku. Waka Genzai Shomokuroku; ZGRJ, 17a.

Waka Kubon. Waka Kubon; Karon Shū A. See *Karon Shū* A.

Waka Kuden = Genshō Kuden. Waka Kuden; NKGT, 4. See *NKGT.*

Wakan Kensakushū. Heian Kamakura Mikan Kanshishū. See *Chūyū Shihai.*

Wakan Rōeishū. Kōi Wakan Rōeishū (Kyoto: Daigakudō Shoten, 1981). Edited by Horibe Seiji. Supplement edited by Katagiri Yōichi.

Waka Teikin. Waka Teikin; NKGT, 4. See *NKGT.*

Wakatei Jisshu. Wakatei Jisshu; NKGT, 1. See *NKGT.*

Wanshi = Wanshi Zenji Kōroku = Hung-chih Ch'an-shih Kuang-lu. Wanshi Zenji Kōroku; TSDK, 48. See *TSDK.*

Wen Hsüan [WH]. Wen Hsüan (Hong Kong: Shang-wu Yin-shu-kuan Fen-kuan, 1936).

Wen-t'i Ming-pien. Wen-t'i Ming-pien Hsü-shuo (Hong Kong: T'ai-p'ing Shu-chü, 1965). Edited by Lo Ken-tse.

WH = Wen Hsüan. See *Wen Hsüan.*

Wu-men Kuan. See *Mumonkan.*

Yaemugura. Yaemugura (Koten Bunko, 1961). Edited by Imai Gen'e.

Yakaku Teikinshō. Yakaku Teikinshō; SGRJ, 21. See *Michinori Shomoku.*

Yakumo Mishō. Yakumo Mishō; NKGT, Bekkan, 3. See *NKGT.*

Yamato Monogatari. Yamato Monogatari; NKBT, 9 (1957). Edited by Abe Toshiko and Imai Gen'e.

YKS = Yōkyokushū. See *Yōkyokushū.*

Yodo no Watari. Yodo no Watari; Rengaron Shū A, 2. See *Rengaron Shū* A.

Yōkyoku Sambyakugojūbanshū. Yōkyoku Sambyakugojūbanshū; Nihon Meicho Zenshū (Nihon Meicho Kankōkai, 1928). Edited by Nonomura Kaizō. Vol. 29.

Yōkyoku Sōshō. Kōchū Yōkyoku Sōshō (Hakubunkan, 1914). Edited by Haga Yaichi and Sasaki Nobutsuna. 3 vols.

Yōkyokushū [YKS]. Yōkyokushū; NKBT, 40-41 (1960-63). Edited by Yokomichi Mario and Omote Akira.

Yowa no Nezame [YN]. Yoru no Nezame; NKBT, 78 (1964). Edited by Sakakura Atsuyoshi.

Yoshimoto Rengaronshū. Yoshimoto Rengaronshū (Koten Bunko, 1952-55). Edited by Okami Masao. 3 vols.

Yü-hsieh = Shih-jen Yü-hsieh. Shih-jen Yü-hsieh (Shanghai: Ku-tien Wen-hsüeh Ch'u-pan-she, 1982). Edited by Wang Chung-wen. 2 vols.

Yunoyama = Yunoyama Sangin Hyakuin. Yunoyama Sangin Hyakuin; Renga Haikai Shū. See *Renga Haikai Shū*.

Zeami, Zenchiku [ZMZC]. Zeami, Zenchiku; Nihon Shisō Taikei, 24 (Iwanami Shoten, 1974). Edited by Omote Akira.

Zekkai Roku = Zekkai Oshō Goroku. Zekkai Oshō Goroku; TSDK, 80. See *TSDK*.

Zengi Gemonshū. Zengi Gemonshū; 1637 woodblock edition in possession of Central Library, University of Tsukuba. 2 vols.

ZMZC = Zeami, Zenchiku. See *Zeami, Zenchiku*.

Zōtanshū. Zōtanshū; Chūsei no Bungaku (Miyai Shoten, 1973). Edited by Yamada Shōzen and Miki Norihito.

Zuimonki = Shōbō Genzō Zuimonki; NKBT, 81 (1965). Edited by Nishio Minoru et al.

ZZK = Zoku Zōkyō. Dai Nihon Zoku Zōkyō (Kyoto: Zōkyō Shoin, 1905-12). 150 vols.

Studies Published in Japanese

AKAMATSU Toshihide

1944 "Kajin to Shite no Myōe Shōnin," *Shiseki to Bijutsu* 15, no. 10 (1944). Republished in *Myōe Shōnin to Kōzanji* (Kyoto: Dōhōsha, 1981). 1981 edition used.

1967 "*Heike Monogatari* no Gempon ni Tsuite," *Bungaku* 35, no. 2 (1967). Republished in *Heike Monogatari no Kenkyū* (Kyoto: Hōzōkan, 1980). 1980 edition used.

1970 "Kyokō to Shijitsu: Gion no Nyōgo, Seishi no Yume, *Chishō Monogatari—Heike Monogatari* no Gempon ni Tsuite Zokuron," *Shirin* 53, no. 6 (1970). Republished in *Heike Monogatari no Kenkyū* (1980). See preceding entry. 1980 edition used.

AKIYAMA Kenzō

1939 *Nisshi Kōshōshi Kenkyū* (Iwanami Shoten, 1939).

ANDŌ Toshio

1968 *Tendai Gaku: Kompon Shisō to Sono Tenkai* (Kyoto: Heirakuji Shoten, 1968).

AOKI Masaru

1929 "Dōkateki Bungei Shichō," *Iwanami Kōza: Sekai Shichō* (Iwanami Shoten, 1929). Republished as *Shina Bungaku Shisōshi* (Iwanami Shoten, 1943); republished in *Aoki Masaru Zenshū*, vol. 1 (Shunjūsha, 1969). 1969 edition used.

1935b "Shina Shisō: Bungaku Shisō," *Iwanami Kōza: Tōyō Shisō* (Iwanami Shoten, 1935). Republished in *Aoki Masaru Zenshū*, vol. 1. See preceding entry.

ARAKI Yoshio
1941a *Sōgi; Sōgen Sensho*, 70 (Sōgensha, 1941).
1941b *Daisenjibon Soga Monogatari* (Musashino Shoin, 1941).

ARIYOSHI Tamotsu
1968 *Shinkokin Wakashū no Kenkyū: Kiban to Kōsei* (Sanseidō, 1968).

ASAHARA Yoshiko
1970 "*Kankyo no Tomo* to *Heike Monogatari*: Tenkyosetsu o Megutte," *Nihon Joshi Daigaku Bungakubu Kiyō*, no. 19 (1970).

ATSUMI Kaoru
1962 *Heike Monogatari no Kisoteki Kenkyū* (Sanseidō, 1962). Republished by Kasama Shoin, 1978. 1978 edition used.

FUJI Naomoto
1949 *Chūsei Bunka Kenkyū* (Kyoto: Kawara Shoten, 1949).

FUJIHIRA Haruo
1969 *Shinkokin Kafū no Keisei* (Meiji Shoin, 1969).

FUKUDA Hideichi
1965 "Zeami to Yoshimoto," *Geinōshi Kenkyū*, no. 10 (1965). Revised and republished in *Yōkyoku Kyōgen; Nihon Bungaku Kenkyū Shiryō Sōsho* (Yūseidō, 1981) under the title "Zeami no Yōshō Jidai o Shimesu Yoshimoto no Shojō." 1981 edition used.
1972 *Chūsei Wakashi no Kenkyū* (Kadokawa Shoten, 1972).

FUKUDA-PLUTSCHOW (FUKUDA Hideichi and Herbert PLUTSCHOW)
1975 *Nihon Kikō Bungaku Binran: Kikō Bungaku Kara Mita Nihonjin no Tabi no Sokuseki* (Musashino Shoin, 1975).

GORAI Shigeru
1965 *Kōya Hijiri; Kadokawa Shinsho*, vol. 199 (Kadokawa Shoten, 1965).

HAGA Kōshirō
1945 *Higashiyama Bunka no Kenkyū* (Kawade Shobō, 1945). Republished in *Haga Kōshirō Rekishi Ronshū*, vols. 1-2 (Kyoto: Shibunkaku, 1981). 1981 edition used.
1956 *Chūsei Zenrin no Gakumon Oyobi Bungaku ni Kansuru Kenkyū* (Nihon Gakujitsu Shinkōkai, 1956). Reprinted in *Haga Kōshirō Rekishi Ronshū*, vol. 3 (Kyoto: Shibunkaku, 1981). 1981 edition used.

HASEGAWA Tadashi
1961 "Sasaki Dōyo o Megutte," *Shirin Sokai*, no. 3 (1961). Republished in *Senki Bungaku; Nihon Bungaku Kenkyū Shiryō Sōsho* (Yūseidō, 1974). 1974 edition used.

HASHIMOTO Fumio
1966 *Inzeiki no Kadanshi Kenkyū* (Musashino Shoin, 1966).

HASHIMOTO-TAKIZAWA (HASHIMOTO Fumio and TAKIZAWA Sadao)
1976-77 *Kōhon Horikawa In Ōntoki Hyakushu Waka to Sono Kenkyū* (Kasama Shoin, 1976-77). 2 vols.

HIGUCHI Yoshimaro
1953 "*Teika Kyō Hyakuban Jikaawase* Seiritsu Kō," *Kokugo to Kokubungaku* 30, no. 6 (1953).

HIRABAYASHI Fumio
1977 *Jōjin Azari Haha no Shū no Kisoteki Kenkyū* (Kasama Shoin, 1977).

HIRABAYASHI Moritoku

1968 "*Kōsan Hokkeden* Hoan Gannen Shodensetsu Songi," *Shoryōbu Kiyō*, no. 20 (1968). Republished in *Hijiri to Setsuwa no Shiteki Kenkyū* (Yoshikawa Kōbunkan, 1981). 1981 edition used.

1970 "Keisei Shōnin Denkō Hoi," *Kokugo to Kokubungaku* 47, no. 6 (1970).

HORIBE Seiji

1940 "Shinshiryō no Yoru *Sumiyoshi Monogatari* no Ichikōsatsu," *Kokugo Kokubun* 10, no. 9 (1940). Republished in *Chūko Nihon Bungaku no Kenkyū* (Kyoto: Kyōiku Tosho, 1943). 1943 edition used.

1943 "Saigyō to Kemari," *Chūko Nihon Bungaku no Kenkyū*. See preceding entry. Original publication date unknown; 1943 edition used.

1945 *Sanshū Ruiju Utaawase to Sono Kenkyū* (Bijitsu Shoin, 1945).

IJICHI Tetsuo

1943 *Sōgi; Nihon Bungakusha Hyōden Zensho* (Seigodō, 1943).

1967 "Higashiyama Gobunkobon *Fuchi Ki* o Shōkaishite Chūsei no Waka, Renga, Sarugaku no Koto ni Oyobu," *Kokubungaku*, vol. 35 (1967).

IKEDA Tomizō

1973 *Minamoto Toshiyori [Shunrai] no Kenkyū* (Ōfūsha, 1973).

IMAI Usaburō

1958 *Sōdai Ekigaku no Kenkyū* (Meiji Tosho, 1958).

INADA Toshinori

1978 *Shōtetsu no Kenkyū* (Kasama Shoin, 1978).

INOUE Muneo

1961 *Chūsei Kadanshi no Kenkyū: Muromachi Zenki* (Kazama Shobō, 1961).

1965 *Chūsei Kadanshi no Kenkyū: Nambokuchō Ki* (Meiji Shoin, 1965).

1972 *Chūsei Kadanshi no Kenkyū: Muromachi Kōki* (Meiji Shoin, 1972).

IRIYA Sensuke

1976 *Ōi Kenkyū* (Sōbunsha, 1976).

ISHII Kyōdō

1928 "Gommitsu no Shiso: Kōben," *Taishō Daigaku Gakuhō*, vol. 3 (1928). Republished in *Myōe Shōnin to Kōzanji*. See Akamatsu, 1944.

ITŌ Masayoshi

1962 "*Rokurin Ichiro* no Keisei: Komparu Zenchiku no Shisōteki Haikei o Megutte," *Kokugo Kokubun* 31, no. 12. Republished in *Komparu Zenchiku no Kenkyū* (Kyoto: Akao Shōbundō, 1970). 1970 edition used.

1969 "Komparu Zenchiku Denki Shiryō Oboegaki," *Bunrin*, no. 3 (1969). Republished in *Komparu Zenchiku no Kenkyū*. See preceding entry.

IWAHASHI Koyata

1962 *Hanazono Tennō; Jimbutsu Sōsho*, vol. 99 (Yoshikawa Kōbunkan, 1962).

IWASA Miyoko

1983 "Kyōgoku Tamekanu no Kafū Keisei to Yuishikisetsu," *Sōritsu Nijū Shūnen Kinen Tsurumi Daigaku Bungakubu Ronshū* (Tsurumi Daigaku, 1983).

KADOKAWA Gen'yoshi
1943 "*Soga Monogatari* no Hassei," *Kokugakuin Zasshi* 49, no. 1 (1943). Republished in *Katarimono Bungei no Hassei* (Tōkyōdō, 1975). 1975 edition used.
1969 "Myōhonjibon *Soga Monogatari* Kō," *Myōhonjibon Soga Monogatari; Kichō Kotenseki Sōkan*, vol. 3 (Kadokawa Shoten, 1969).
1974 "*Gikeiki* no Seiritsu," *Akagi Bunkobon Yoshitsune Monogatari; Kichō Kotenseki Sōkan*, vol. 10 (Kadokawa Shoten, 1974). Republished in *Katarimono Bungei no Hassei* (1975). See above. 1975 edition used.

KANEKO Hikojirō
1942 "*Hōjōki* to Shina Bungaku to no Kankei ni Tsuite no Kenkyū," *Teikoku Gakushiin Kiyō* 1, no. 1 (1942).

KANEKO Kinjirō
1962 *Rengashi Kensai Den Kō* (Nan'undō Ōfūsha, 1962).
1965 *Tsukuba Shū no Kenkyū* (Kazama Shobō, 1965).
1969 *Shinsen Tsukuba Shū no Kenkyū* (Kazama Shobō, 1969).
1970 *Sōgi Tabi no Ki Shichū* (Ōfūsha, 1970).
1982 *Shinkei no Seikatsu to Sakuhin* (Ōfūsha, 1982).
1983 *Sōgi no Seikatsu to Sakuhin* (Ōfūsha, 1983).

KATAGIRI Yōichi
1962 "*Reizeike Zō Sōshi Mokuroku* ni Tsuite," *Wakashi Kenkyūkai Kaihō*, no. 8 (1962).
1971-73-81 *Chūsei Kokinshū Chūshakusho Kaidai* (Kyoto: Akao Shōbundō, 1971, 1973, 1981). 3 vols.

KATAYOSE Masayoshi
1943-74 *Konjaku Monogatari Shū no Kenkyū*, 2 vols. (Vol. 1: Sanseidō, 1943. Vol. 2: Kamakura: Geirinsha, 1974).

KAWASE Kazuma
1970 *Gosamban no Kenkyū* (Antiquarian Booksellers Association of Japan, 1970). 2 vols.

KAZAMAKI Keijirō
1932 "*Shinkokin*teki Naru Mono no Han'i," *Iwanami Kōza: Nihon Bungaku* (1932). Republished in *Shinkokin Jidai; Kazamaki Keijirō Zenshū*, vol. 6 (Ōfūsha, 1970). 1970 edition used.

KEENE, Donald
1984 *Hakutai no Kakaku* (Asahi Shimbunsha, 1984). Translated by Kanaseki Hisao. 2 vols.

KIDŌ Saizō
1971-73 *Rengashi Ronkō* (Meiji Shoin, 1971, 1973). 2 vols.

KIM Sa-yŏp
1973 *Chōsen Bungakushi* (Kanazawa Bunko, 1973).

KIM Tong-uk
1974 *Chōsen Bungakushi* (Nihon Hōsō Shuppan Kyōkai, 1974).

KIMURA Miyogo
1963 "*Chikuba Kyōginshū* Kō," *Tayama Hōnan Sensei Kakō Kinen Rombunshū* (Tayama Hōnan Sensei Kakō Kinenkai, 1963).

KISHIBE Shigeo
1960-61 *Tōdai Ongaku no Rekishiteki Kenkyū: Gakuseihen* (Tokyo Daigaku Shuppankai, 1960-61).

KITAGAWA Tadahiko

1964 "Yamato Sarugaku to Fukushiki Mugen Nō no Seiritsu," *Bungaku* 33, no. 9 (1964). Republished in *Kannami no Geiryū; Miyai Sensho*, 4 (Miyai Shoten, 1978). 1978 edition used.

1971 "Zeami to Fukushiki Mugen Nō no Tenkai," *Geinōshi Kenkyū*, no. 34 (1971). Republished in *Kannami no Geiryū* (1978). See preceding. 1978 edition used.

KOBAYASHI Hideo

1942 "*Heike Monogatari*," *Bungakkai* 9, no. 7 (1942). Republished in *Shintei Kobayashi Hideo Zenshū*, 8 vols. (Shinchōsha, 1978). 1978 edition used.

KOBAYASHI Shizuo

1942b *Yōkyoku Sakusha no Kenkyū* (Maruoka Shuppansha, 1942).

KOIZUMI Hiroshi

1973 *Koshōbon Hōbutsushū: Kenkyūhen; Kichō Kotenseki Sōkan*, 8 (Kadokawa Shoten, 1973).

KONISHI Jin'ichi

1943b "Yūgen no Gen'igi," *Kokugo to Kokubungaku* 20, no. 6 (1943).

1948-51a-53e *Bunkyō Hifuron Kō*, 3 vols. (Vol. 1: Oyashima Shuppan, 1948. Vol. 2: Kōdansha, 1951. Vol. 3: Kōdansha, 1953).

1951b "Ushintei Shiken," *Nihon Gakushiin Kiyō* 9, no. 2 (1951).

1951c "Chūsei Hyōgen Ishiki to Sōdai Shiron," *Kokugo* 1, no. 1 (1951).

1952b "Shunzei no Yūgenfū to Shikan," *Bungaku* 20, no. 2 (1952).

1953b "Chūseijin no Bi: Karon o Chūshin to Shite," *Kokugo to Kokubungaku* 30, no. 4 (1953).

1953d "Yōembi: Ban Tōshi to no Kōshō," *Kokugo Kokubun* 22, no. 7 (1953).

1953eii "Hon'i Setsu to Tōdai Shiron," *Kokugo* 1, nos. 2-4 (1953).

1955a "Yoshimoto to Sōdai Shiron," *Gobun*, no. 14 (1955).

1956b "Michi no Keisei to Kairitsuteki Sekai," *Kokugakuin Zasshi* 57, no. 5 (1956).

1958b "Hie to Yase," *Bungaku Gogaku*, no. 10 (1958).

1960a "*Gyokuyōshū* Jidai to Sōshi," *Chūsei Bungaku no Sekai: Nishio Minoru Sensei Koki Kinen Rombunshū* (Iwanami Shoten, 1960).

1960c "Shōdō Bungaku," *Chūsei Bungei to Minzoku; Minzoku Bungaku Kōza*, vol. 5 (Kōbundō, 1960).

1961a *Nōgakuron Kenkyū* (Hanawa Shobō, 1961).

1962b "Nō no Keisei to Tenkai," *Nō Kyōgen Meisakushū; Koten Nihon Bungaku Zenshū*, vol. 20 (Chikuma Shobō, 1962).

1965c "Teika wa Shōchō Kajin ka?" *Gengo to Bungei* 7, no. 6 (1965).

1966b "Nō no Tokushu Shiten," *Bungaku* 34, no. 5 (1966).

1966c "Chūsei Buntai no Atarashisa," *Kokugo Tsūshin*, no. 87 (1966).

1967b "Bunjin to wa Nani ka?" *Gengo to Bungei*, 8, no. 4 (1967).

1970c "Gosanshi no Hyōgen: Sesson Yūbai to Keijijōshi," *Bungaku Gogaku*, no. 58 (1970).

1971c *Sōgi; Nihon Shijinsen*, vol. 16 (Chikuma Shobō, 1971).

1974a "*Genji Monogatari* to *Shinkokin*teki Hyōgen," *Murasaki*, no. 12 (1974).

1975a *Michi: Chūsei no Rinen; Gendai Shinsho* (Kōdansha, 1975).

1980 "*Fūshi Kaden*: Hisureba Hana," *Kokubungaku* 25, no. 1 (Gakutōsha, 1980).

1983c "Nō no Tanjō," *Geinōshi Kenkyū*, no. 81 (1983).
See Also Section C, "Studies Not Published in Japanese."

KŌSAI Tsutomu

1958 "Zeami no Zenteki Kyōyō," *Bungaku* 26, no. 12 (1958). Republished in *Zeami Shinkō* (Wan'ya Shoten, 1962). 1962 edition used.

KUBOTA Jun

1973 *Shinkokin Kajin no Kenkyū* (University of Tokyo Press, 1973).

KUNISAKI Fumimaro

1962 *Konjaku Monogatari Seiritsu Kō* (Waseda University Press, 1962). Revised edition 1978. 1978 edition used.

KUWABARA Hiroshi

1967 *Chūsei Monogatari Kenkyū: Sumiyoshi Monogatari Ronkō* (Jigensha, 1967).

KYŪSOJIN Hitaku

1960-61 *Kokin Wakashū Seiritsuron* (Kazama Shobō, 1960, 1961). 4 vols.

MANAKA Fujiko

1974 *Jichin Kashō Oyobi Shūgyokushū no Kenkyū* (Ōtsu: Enryakuji, 1974).

MASUDA Katsumi

1960a *Setsuwa Bungaku to Emaki* (San'ichi Shobō, 1960).

1960b "*Fukegatari* no Kenkyū," *Chūsei Bungaku no Sekai*. See Konishi, 1960a.

MATSUDA Takeo

1956 *Kin'yōshū no Kenkyū* (Yamada Shoin, 1956).

MATSUDA Tamotsu

1972 *Zeami to Nō no Tankyū* (Shindokushosha, 1972).

MATSUMOTO Yasushi

1971 *Towazugatari no Kenkyū* (Ōfūsha, 1971).

MATSUMURA Hiroshi

1956-60-67 *Eiga Monogatari no Kenkyū*. 3 vols. (Vol. 1: Tōkō Shoin, 1956. Vol. 2: Tōkō Shoin, 1960. Vol. 3: Ōfūsha, 1967).

MATSUNO Yōichi

1973 *Fujiwara Shunzei no Kenkyū* (Kasama Shoin, 1973).

MATSUO Satoshi

1939 "*Kakuremino no Monogatari*," *Bungei Bunka* 2, nos. 3-4 (1939). Republished in *Heian Jidai Monogatari no Kenkyū* (Tōkō Shobō, 1955). 1955 edition used.

MEZAKI Tokue

1959 "Nōin no Den ni Okeru Nisan no Mondai," *Geirin* 10, nos. 2-3 (1959). Republished in *Heian Bunkashiron* (Ōfūsha, 1968). 1968 edition used.

1960 "*Shigeyuki Shū* no Seiritsu to Sono Shiryōteki Kachi," *Nihon Rekishi*, no. 139 (1960). Republished in *Heian Bunkashiron* (1968). See preceding. 1968 edition used.

1978 *Saigyō no Shisōteki Kenkyū* (Yoshikawa Kōbunkan, 1978).

MITANI Eiichi

1952 *Monogatari Bungakushiron* (Yūseidō, 1952).

1956 "Taketori no Okina Densetsushū," *Taketori Monogatari Hyōkai* (Yūseidō, 1956).

MIZUHARA Hajime

1979 *Enkeibon Heike Monogatari Ronkō* (Katō Chūdōkan, 1979).

MIZUKAMI Kashizō

1950 "Bontōan Shu Denki Shōkō," *Nihon Bungaku Kyōshitsu*, no. 5 (1950). Republished in *Chūsei Karon to Renga* (Zentsū Kikaku Shuppan, 1977). 1977 edition used.

1969 "*Maigetsushō* Gishosetsu to Sono Hanron ni Tsuite no Hihan," *Gengo to Bungei* 11, no. 6 (1969). Republished in *Chūsei Karon to Renga* (1977). See preceding. 1977 edition used.

MORI Katsumi

1948 *Nissō Bōeki no Kenkyū* (Kunitachi Shoin, 1948). Republished in *Mori Katsumi Chosakushū*, vol. 1 (Kunitachi Shoin, 1975). 1975 edition used.

MURAKAMI Manabu

1969 "Manabon *Soga Monogatari, Shintōshū* Dōbun Ichiran," *Myōhonjibon Soga Monogatari*. See Kadokawa, 1969.

NAGAI Kazuko

1962 "*Nezame* no Kaisaku Taido ni Tsuite," *Gakushūin Daigaku Kokugo Kokubun Gakkaishi*, no. 26 (1962). Republished in *Nezame Monogatari no Kenkyū* (Kasama Shoin, 1968). 1968 edition used.

NAGAI Yoshinori

1967 "Ninnaji no Risshi wa Jōson ka?" *Taishō Daigaku Kenkyū Kiyō*, no. 52 (1967).

NARAEBON KOKUSAI KENKYŪ KAIGI (International Research Team on the Naraebon)

1982 *Otogi Sōshi no Sekai* (Sanseidō, 1982).

NISHI Kazuyoshi

1965 "Zeami Geijitsu no Haikei," *Gobun*, no. 21 (1965). Republished in *Zeami Kenkyū* (Salvia Shuppansha, 1967). 1967 edition used.

NISHINO Haruo

1973 "Motomasa no Nō," *Bungaku* 41, no. 7 (1973).

NOSE Asaji

1932 "Shirabyōshi to Kusemai: Kusemai ni Tsuite," *Kokugo Kokubun* 2, no. 1 (1932). Republished in *Nose Asaji Chosakushū*, vol. 4 (Kyoto: Shibunkaku, 1982). 1982 edition used.

1938 *Nōgaku Genryū Kō* (Iwanami Shoten, 1938).

1940-44b *Zeami Jūrokubushū Hyōshaku*, 2 vols. (Vol. 1: Iwanami Shoten, 1940; enlarged edition, 1949. Vol. 2: Iwanami Shoten, 1944).

1942a "Nō no Senkō Geijitsu," *Nō no Rekishi; Nōgaku Zensho*, vol. 2 (Sōgensha, 1942). Republished in *Nose Asaji Chosakushū*, vol. 4 (1982). See Nose, 1932. 1982 edition used.

1942b "Jōwa Jidai no *Soga Monogatari*," *Kokugo Kokubungaku Kenkyū: Ronkō to Shiryō*, no. 10 (1942). Republished in *Nose Asaji Chosakushū*, vol. 1 (Kyoto: Shibunkaku, 1985). 1985 edition used.

1944a *Yūgenron* (Kawade Shobō, 1944). Republished in *Nose Asaji Chosakushū*, vol. 2 (Kyoto: Shibunkaku, 1981). 1981 edition used.

1945 *Tsurezuregusa; Kokubungaku Koten Kōwa* (Kenkyūsha, 1945). Republished in *Nose Asaji Chosakushū*, vol. 2 (1981). See preceding. 1981 edition used.

1946-47a "Kakari no Geijitsuteki Seikaku," *Yūgen* vol. 1, nos. 3-5, through vol. 2, nos. 1-2. Republished in *Nōgaku Geidō* (Hinoki Shoten, 1954); republished in *Nose Asaji Chosakushū*, 1. See Nose, 1942b.

OKADA Masayuki

1929b *Nihon Kambungakushi* (Kyōritsusha, 1929). Revised edition by Yamagishi Tokuhei and Nagasawa Kikuya (Yoshikawa Kōbunkan, 1954). 1954 edition used.

OKAMI Masao

1947 "Shinkei Oboegaki: Ao to Keikyoku to Minu Omokage," *Kokugo Kokubun* 16, no. 5 (1947).

ŌKUBO Dōshū

1953 *Dōgen Zenji no Kenkyū* (Chikuma Shobō, 1953). Revised and enlarged edition, 1966. 1966 edition used.

OMOTE Akira

1976-77-78 "Yamato Sarugaku no 'Chō' no Seikaku no Hensen," *Nōgaku Kenkyū*, nos. 2-4 (1976-78).

1979 "Zeami Sakunō Kō," *Kanze* 27, no. 8 (1960). Revised and republished in *Nōgakushi Shinkō*, vol. 1 (Wan'ya Shoten, 1979). 1979 edition used.

1983 "Kannami Kiyotsugu to Yūzakiza," *Bungaku* 51, no. 7 (1983).

ŌTA Seikyū

1958 *Nihon Kagaku to Chūgoku Shigaku* (Kōbundō, 1958).

ŌTA Tatsuo

1967 *Heiyō Den; Chūgoku Koten Bungaku Taikei*, vol. 36 (Heibonsha, 1967).

PLUTSCHOW, Herbert E.

1983 *Tabi Suru Nihonjin: Nihon no Chūsei Kikō Bungaku o Saguru* (Musashino Shoin, 1983).

SAKURAI Yoshirō

1954 "*Taiheiki* no Shakaiteki Kiban: *Taiheiki* Ron no Josetsu to Shite," *Nihon Rekishi*, no. 75 (1954). Republished in *Senki Bungaku; Nihon Bungaku Kenkyū Shiryō Sōsho* (1974). See Hasegawa, 1961. 1974 edition used.

SATŌ Ryōō

1963 *Hyakuza Hōdan Kikigaki Shō* (Nan'undō Ōfūsha, 1963).

SATŌ Takaaki

1982 *Chūsei Bungaku Mikan Shiryō no Kenkyū* (Hitaku Shobō, 1982).

SATŌ Teruo

1973 *Rōran no Uta to Heike Monogatari* (Chūō Kōronsha, 1973). 2 vols.

SEKIYAMA Kazuo

1978 *Sekkyō no Rekishi: Bukkyō to Wagei; Iwanami Shinsho*, vol. 64 (Iwanami Shoten, 1978).

SHIBUYA, Torao

1979 *Kōhon Utamakura Nayose: Kenkyū Sakuin Hen* (Ōfūsha, 1979).

SHIMAZU, Tadao

1953 "Reizei Kafū no Yukue," *Kokugo Kokubun* 22, no. 6 (1953).

1969 *Rengashi no Kenkyū* (Kadokawa Shoten, 1969).

SHIONOYA On

1938 "Shina Bungaku to Nihon Bungaku to no Kōshō," *Kokugo to Kokubungaku* 15, no. 4 (1938).

SHIRAI Chūkō

1976 *Chūsei no Kikō Bungaku* (Bunka Shobō Hakubunsha, 1976).

SUGITA Tsuguko

1974 "*Jōkyūki* Shohon to *Azuma Kagami*," *Gunki to Katarimono*, no. 11 (1974).

SUZUKI Hiromichi

1968 *Heian Makki Monogatari Ron* (Hanawa Shobō, 1968).

SUZUKI Hisashi

1975 "*Tsurezuregusa* Mikkan: Daihyakukujūsandan-Dainihyakusanjūgodan no Raii," *Fukushima Daigaku Kyoikugakubu Ronshū*, no. 27b (1975).

SUZUKI Keizō

1960 *Shoki Emakimono no Fūzokushiteki Kenkyū* (Yoshikawa Kōbunkan, 1960).

SUZUKI Tomie

1973 "*Taiheiki* Sakusha to Gen'e Hōin," *Kokugo to Kokubungaku* 50, no. 5 (1973). Republished in *Senki Bungaku; Nihon Bungaku Kenkyū Shiryō Sōsho* (1974). See Hasegawa, 1961. 1974 edition used.

TAKAHASHI Teiichi

1978 *Zoku Heike Monogatari Shohon no Kenkyū* (Kyoto: Shibunkaku, 1978).

TAKEUCHI Yoshio

1936 *Chūgoku Shisōshi; Iwanami Zensho*, vol. 73 (Iwanami Shoten, 1936). Revised edition, 1957. 1957 edition used.

TAMAGAMI Takuya

1943 "Mukashi Monogatari no Kōsei," *Kokugo Kokubun* 13, nos. 6, 8, 9 (1943). Republished in *Genji Monogatari Kenkyū: Genji Monogatari Hyōshaku*, Supplement 1 (Kadokawa Shoten, 1966). 1966 edition used.

TAMAMURA Takeji

1955 *Gosan Bungaku: Tairiku Bunka Shōkaisha to Shite no Gosan Zensō no Katsudō; Nihon Rekishi Shinsho* (Shibundō, 1955).

TANAKA Yutaka

1965 "Kambyō Iō no Setsu," *Gobun*, no. 25 (1965). Republished in *Chūsei Bungakuron Kenkyū* (Hanawa Shobō, 1969). 1969 edition used.

TANIYAMA Shigeru

1943 *Yūgen no Kenkyū* (Kyoto: Kyōiku Tosho, 1943).

1951 "Yasashiku En: Fukugōbi ni Tsuite no Ichi Kōsatsu," *Jimbun Kenkyū* 2, no. 1 (1951). Republished in *Yūgen; Taniyama Shigeru Chosakushū*, vol. 1 (Kadokawa Shoten, 1982). 1982 edition used.

1961 *Senzai Wakashū no Kenkyū*, published privately by author (1961). Republished in *Senzai Wakashū to Sono Shūhen; Taniyama Shigeru Chosakushū*, 3 (Kadokawa Shoten, 1982). 1982 edition used.

TONOMURA Hisae
1965 *Sōga no Kenkyū* (Shibundō, 1965).

TSUGITA Kasumi
1964 "*Gyokuyōshū* no Keisei," *Nihon Gakushiin Kiyō* 22, no. 1 (1964).

TSUKUDO Reikan
1932 "Shōdō Bungaku to Shite no *Hyakuza Hōdan,*" *Bungaku*; supplement to *Iwanami Kōza: Nihon Bungaku*, no. 14 (1932). Republished in *Chūsei Geibun no Kenkyū* (Yūseidō, 1966). Republished in *Tsukudo Reikan Chosakushū*, vol. 3 (Serika Shobō, 1976). 1976 edition used.
1937 "*Shintōshū* to Kinko Shōsetsu: Honjimono Kenkyū no Gutaiteki Hōhō," *Nihon Engekishi Ronsō* (Kōgeisha, 1937). Republished in *Tsukudo Reikan Chosakushū*, vol. 4 (Serika Shobō, 1976). 1976 edition used.
1938 *Shūkyō Bungaku; Nihon Bungaku Taikei*, vol. 19 (Kawade Shobō, 1938). Republished in *Tsukudo Reikan Chosakushū*, vol. 1 (Serika Shobō, 1976). 1976 edition used.
1943 "Rekishi to Densetsu: *Soga Monogatari* Seiritsu Kō," *Kokugo to Kokubungaku* 20, no. 11 (1943). Republished in *Tsukudo Reikan Chosakushū*, vol. 4 (1976). See Tsukudo, 1937. 1976 edition used.

YAMADA Shōzen
1973 "Myōe no Waka to Bukkyō," *Kokugo to Kokubungaku* 50, no. 4 (1973). Republished in *Myōe Shōnin to Kōzanji* (1981). See Akamatsu, 1944. 1981 edition used.

YAMADA Yoshio
1911 *Heike Monogatari Kō; Kokugo Shiryō Kamakura Jidai no Bu, Heike Monogatari ni Tsukite no Kenkyū*, Pt. 1 (Kokutei Kyōkasho Kyōdō Hambaijo, 1911). Reprinted by Benseisha, 1968.
1932a "Renga Oyobi Rengashi," *Iwanami Kōza: Nihon Bungaku* (Iwanami Shoten, 1932).
1932b *Jinnō Shōtōki Jutsugi* (Min'yūsha, 1932).
1937 *Renga Gaisetsu* (Iwanami Shoten, 1937).
1938 "Hana," *Chūō Kōron* 53, no. 5 (1938). Republished in *Ōshi* (Sakura Shobō, 1941).

YAMAGISHI Tokuhei
1927 "Adauchi Bungaku to Shite no *Soga Monogatari*," *Nihon Bungaku Renkō, Chūsei* (Chūkōkan, 1927). Republished in *Rekishi Senki Monogatari Kenkyū; Yamagishi Tokuhei Chosakushū*, vol. 4 (Yūseidō, 1973). 1973 edition used.
1940 "*Towazugatari* Oboegaki," *Kokugo to Kokubungaku* 17, no. 9 (1940). Republished in *Monogatari Zuihitsu Bungaku Kenkyū; Yamagishi Tokuhei Chosakushū*, vol. 5 (Yūseidō, 1972). 1972 edition used.
1942 "Chōken to Sono Sakuhin: Sakumonshū o Chūshin to Shite," *Nihon Shogaku Shinkō Iinkai Kenkyū Hōkoku*, special issue no. 6 (1942). Republished in *Nihon Kambungaku Kenkyū; Yamagishi Tokuhei Chosakushū*, vol. 1 (Yūseidō, 1972). 1972 edition used.
1954 *Tsutsumi Chūnagon Monogatari Hyōkai* (Yūseidō, 1954).
1966 "Tachibanabon *Hōgan Monogatari* Kaidai," *Hōgan Monogatari* (Koten Kenkyūkai, 1966). Republished in *Rekishi Senki Monogatari*

Kenkyū (1973) under the title "Tachibanabon *Hōgan Monogatari* ni Tsuite." See Yamagishi, 1927. 1973 edition used.

YAMASHITA Hiroaki

1972 *Heike Monogatari Kenkyū Josetsu* (Meiji Shoin, 1972).

YAMAUCHI Masujirō

1980 *Imakagami no Kenkyū* (Ōfūsha, 1980).

YAMAZAKI Masakazu

1971 "*Taiheiki* Kara no Hakken: Shiseikatsusha no Tame no Rekishi," *Rekishi to Jimbutsu* 1, no. 3 (Chūō Kōronsha, 1971). Republished in *Senki Bungaku; Nihon Bungaku Kenkyū Shiryō Sōsho* (1974). See Hasegawa, 1961. 1974 edition used.

YANAGIDA Kunio

1940 "Ariō to Shunkan Sōzu," *Bungaku* 8, no. 1 (1940). Republished in *Teihon Yanagida Kunio Shū*, vol. 7 (Chikuma Shobō, 1968). 1968 edition used.

YANASE Kazuo

1937 "*Ise Ki* Kenkyū," *Kokubungaku Kenkyū*, vol. 8 (1937). Republished in *Kamo no Chōmei Kenkyū; Yanase Kazuo Chosakushū*, vol. 2 (Katō Chūdōkan, 1980). 1980 edition used.

1938 "*Hosshinshū* Kenkyū Josetsu," *Kamo no Chōmei no Shinkenkyū* (Chūbunkan, 1938). Revised and republished in *Hosshinshū Kenkyū; Yanase Kazuo Chosakushū*, vol. 3 (Katō Chūdōkan, 1975). 1975 edition used.

1977 *Shun'e Kenkyū; Yanase Kazuo Chosakushū*, vol. 1 (Katō Chūdōkan, 1977). 1977 edition used.

YASHIMA Chōju

1953 "*Maigetsushō* Songi: *Maigetsushō* wa Gisho ka?" *Kokugo* 2, no. 1 (1953).

YASUI Hisayoshi

1973 *Fujiwara Mitsutoshi no Kenkyū* (Kasama Shoin, 1973).

YOKOMICHI Mario

1960 "Sōga no Shinkyū," *Chūsei Bungaku no Sekai.* See Konishi, 1960a.

YOKOYAMA Hiroshi

1981 "*San Sui Heiyō Den*: Kaisetsu," *San Sui Heiyō Den; Tenri Toshokan Zempon Sōsho, Kanseki no Bu*, vol. 12 (Tenri: Tenri University Press, 1981).

YOSHIKAWA Kōjirō

1961 "So Tōba no Bungaku to Bukkyō," *Bukkyōshigaku Ronshū* (Kyoto: Tsukamoto Hakushi Shōju Kinenkai, 1961). Republished in *Yoshikawa Kōjirō Zenshū*, vol. 13 (Chikuma Shobō, 1974). 1974 edition used.

1962 *Sōshi Gaisetsu; Chūgoku Shijin Senshū Nishū*, vol. 1 (Iwanami Shoten, 1962). Republished in *Yoshikawa Kōjirō Zenshū*, vol. 13 (1974). See preceding. 1974 edition used.

1963 *Gen Min Shi Gaisetsu; Chūgoku Shijin Senshū Nishū*, vol. 2 (Iwanami Shoten, 1963). Republished in *Yoshikawa Kōjirō Zenshū*, vol. 15 (Chikuma Shobō, 1974). 1974 edition used.

Studies Not Published in Japanese

ARIÈS, Philippe

1977 *L'Homme devant la mort* (Paris: Editions du Seuil, 1977). Translated by Helen Weaver as *The Hour of Our Death* (New York: Alfred A. Knopf, 1981). English version used.

BACKUS, Robert L.

1985 *The Riverside Counselor's Stories: Vernacular Fiction of Late Heian Japan* (Stanford: Stanford University Press, 1985).

BOWRA, C. M.

1952 *Heroic Poetry* (London: Macmillan, 1952). Reprinted by St. Martin's Press, New York, 1961. 1952 edition used.

BOWRING, Richard

1982 *Murasaki Shikibu: Her Diary and Poetic Memoirs* (Princeton: Princeton University Press, 1982).

BRAZELL, Karen

1973 *The Confessions of Lady Nijō* (Garden City, N.Y.: Anchor Press/ Doubleday, 1973). Republished by Stanford University Press, Stanford, Calif., 1976. 1973 edition used.

BROWER, Robert H.

1972 "Ex-Emperor Go-Toba's Secret Teachings: *Go-Toba no In Gokuden*," *Harvard Journal of Asiatic Studies* 32 (1972).

1978 *Fujiwara Teika's Hundred-Poem Sequence of the Shōji Era, 1200; Monumenta Nipponica Monograph* no. 55 (Tokyo: Sophia University, 1978).

1981 "The Reizei Family Documents," *Monumenta Nipponica* 36, no. 4 (1981).

BROWER-MINER (BROWER, Robert H. and Earl MINER)

1961 *Japanese Court Poetry* (Stanford: Stanford University Press, 1961).

1967 *Fujiwara Teika's Superior Poems of Our Time: A Thirteenth-Century Poetic Treatise and Sequence* (Stanford: Stanford University Press, 1967).

CHENG Chen-to

1938 *Chung-kuo Su-wen-hsüeh Shih* (Shanghai: Shang-wu Yin-shu-kuan, 1938). Republished by Tso-chia Ch'u-pan-she, Peking, 1954. 1954 edition used.

1957 *Chung-kuo Wen-hsüeh Yen-chiu* (Peking: Tso-chia Ch'u-pan-she, 1957). 3 vols.

CRANE, R. S.

1953 *The Languages of Criticism and the Structure of Poetry* (Toronto: University of Toronto Press, 1953).

GATTEN, Aileen

1982 "Three Problems in the Text of 'Ukifune,' " *Ukifune*, pp. 83-111. See Pekarik, 1982.

HARRIES, Philip Tudor

1980 *The Poetic Memoirs of Lady Daibu* (Stanford: Stanford University Press, 1980).

HOCHSTEDLER, Carol
1979 *The Tale of Nezame: Part Three of Yowa no Nezame Monogatari* (Ithaca, N.Y.: Cornell University East Asia Papers 22, 1979).

HSIANG Ta
1934 "T'ang-tai Su-chiang K'ao," *Yen-ching Hsüeh-pao*, no. 16 (1934).

HU Shih-ying
1980 *Hua-pen Hsiao-shuo Kai-lun* (Peking: Chung-hua Shu-chü, 1980).

HU Wan-ch'uan
1984 *P'ing-yao Chuan Yen-chiu* (Taipei: Hua-cheng Shu-chü, 1984).

HUIZINGA, Johan
1919 *Herfsttij der Middleuwen: Studie over Lebens en Gedachtenvormen der Vertiende en Vijftiede Eeuw in Frankrijk en de Nederlanden* (Haarlem: H. D. Tjeenk Willink & Zoon N, V, 1950). Translated by F. Hopman as *The Waning of the Middle Ages: A Study of the Forms of Life, Thought and Art in France and the Netherlands in the XIVth and XVth Centuries* (London: Edward Arnold, 1924). English version used.

HUMPHREY, Robert
1954 *Stream of Consciousness in the Modern Novel* (Berkeley and Los Angeles: University of California Press, 1954); issued in paperback by the same press in 1962. 1962 edition used.

HURVITZ, Leon
1976 *Scripture of the Lotus Blossom of the Fine Dharma (The Lotus Sūtra)* (New York: Columbia University Press, 1976).

ISER, Wolfgang
1976 *Der Akt des Lesens: Theorie ästhetischer Wirkung* (Munich: Wilhelm Fink, 1976). Translated by the author as *The Act of Reading: A Theory of Aesthetic Response* (Baltimore and London: The Johns Hopkins University Press, 1978). English version used.

KEENE, Donald
1967 *Essays in Idleness: The Tsurezuregusa of Kenkō* (New York: Columbia University Press, 1967).

KEENE, Donald, ed.
1955 *Anthology of Japanese Literature* (New York: Grove Press, 1955).
1970 *Twenty Plays of the Nō Theatre* (New York and London: Columbia University Press, 1970).

KONISHI Jin'ichi
1958a "Association and Progression: Principles of Integration in Anthologies and Sequences of Japanese Court Poetry," tr. Robert H. Brower and Earl Miner, *Harvard Journal of Asiatic Studies* 21 (1958).
1975b "The Art of Renga," tr. with introduction by Karen Brazell and Lewis Cook, *Journal of Japanese Studies* 2, no. 1 (1975).

KUO Chen-i
1939 *Chung-kuo Hsiao-shuo Shih* (Ch'ang-sha: Shang-wu Yin-shu-kuan, 1939). 2 vols. Republished by Tai-wan Shang-wu Yin-shu-kuan, Taipei, 1981. 1981 edition used.

KUO Shao-yü

1934-47 *Chung-kuo Wen-hsüeh P'i-p'ing-shih* (Shanghai: Shang-wu Yin-shu-kuan: vol. 1, 1934; vol. 2, 1947). Reprinted by Tai-wan Shang-wu Yin-shu-kuan, Taipei, 1970. 1970 edition used.

LaFLEUR, William R.

1978 *Mirror for the Moon: A Selection of Poems by Saigyō, 1118-1190* (New York: New Directions, 1978).

LEITER, Samuel L.

1979 *Kabuki Encyclopedia* (London: Greenwood Press, 1979).

LI, Peter

1977 "Narrative Patterns in *San-kuo* and *Shui-hu*." In *Chinese Narrative: Critical and Theoretical Essays*, ed. Andrew H. Plaks (Princeton: Princeton University Press, 1977).

LIU, James J.-Y.

1962 *The Art of Chinese Poetry* (Chicago: The University of Chicago Press, 1962).

LIU Ling-sheng

1936 *Chung-kuo P'ien-wen-shih* (Shanghai: Shang-wu Yin-shu-kuan, 1936).

LO Tsung-t'ao

1972 *Tun-huang Chiang-ching Pien-wen Yen-chiu* (Taipei: Wen-shih-che Ch'u-pan-she, 1972).

McCULLOUGH, Helen Craig

1988 *The Tale of the Heike* (Stanford: Stanford University Press, 1988).

MALM, William P.

1975 "The Musical Characteristics and Practice of the Japanese Noh Drama in an East Asian Context." In *Chinese and Japanese Music Dramas*, ed. J. I. Crump and William P. Malm; *Michigan Papers in Chinese Studies*, no. 19 (Ann Arbor: Center for Chinese Studies, The University of Michigan, 1975).

MEECH-PEKARIK, Julia

1982 "The Artist's View of Ukifune," *Ukifune*. See Pekarik, 1982.

MILLS, D. E.

1970 *A Collection of Tales from Uji: A Study and Translation of Uji Shūi Monogatari* (Cambridge: Cambridge University Press, 1970).

MINER, Earl

1958 *The Japanese Tradition in British and American Literature* (Princeton: Princeton University Press, 1958).

1969a *The Metaphysical Mode from Donne to Cowley* (Princeton: Princeton University Press, 1969).

1979 *Japanese Linked Poetry: An Account with Translations of Renga and Haikai Sequences* (Princeton: Princeton University Press, 1979).

MINER, Earl, ed.

1985 *Principles of Classical Japanese Literature* (Princeton: Princeton University Press, 1985).

MINER-ODAGIRI-MORRELL (MINER, Earl, Hiroko ODAGIRI, and Robert E. MORRELL)

1985 *The Princeton Companion to Classical Japanese Literature* (Princeton: Princeton University Press, 1985).

MORRELL, Robert E.

1985 *Sand and Pebbles (Shasekishū): The Tales of Mujū Ichien, A Voice for Pluralism in Kamakura Buddhism* (Albany: State University of New York Press, 1985).

MORRIS, Ivan

1964 *The World of the Shining Prince: Court Life in Ancient Japan* (London: Oxford University Press, 1964).

PEKARIK, Andrew, ed.

1982 *Ukifune: Love in The Tale of Genji* (New York: Columbia University Press, 1982).

POUND-FENELLOSA (POUND, Ezra and Ernest FENELLOSA)

1917 *"Noh" or Accomplishment, A Study of the Classic Stage of Japan* (New York: Alfred A. Knopf, 1917). Republished as *The Classic Noh Theatre of Japan* (New York: James Laughlin, 1959). 1959 edition used.

RIMER-YAMAZAKI (RIMER, J. Thomas and YAMAZAKI Masakazu)

1984 *On the Art of Nō Drama: The Major Treatises of Zeami* (Princeton: Princeton University Press, 1984).

ROHLICH, Thomas H.

1983 *A Tale of Eleventh-Century Japan: Hamamatsu Chūnagon Monogatari* (Princeton: Princeton University Press, 1983).

SANSOM, George B.

1958-61-64 *A History of Japan* (Stanford: Stanford University Press, 1958, 1961, 1964; reprinted Rutland, Vt. and Tokyo: Charles E. Tuttle, 1974). 3 vols. 1974 edition used.

SCHAFER, Edward H.

1973 *The Divine Woman* (Berkeley and Los Angeles: University of California Press, 1973).

SUN K'ai-ti

1937 "T'ang-tạí Su-chiang Kuei-fan yü Ch'i Pen chih T'i-ts'ai," *Kuo-hsüeh Chi-k'an* 6, no. 2 (1937). Republished in *Su-chiang Shuo-hua yü Pai-hua Hsiao-shuo* (Peking: Tso-chia Ch'u-pan-she, 1956). 1956 edition used.

1953 *Jih-pen Tung-ching So-chien Chung-kuo Hsiao-shuo Shu-mu* (Shanghai: Shang-tsa Ch'u-pan-she, 1953).

TU Sung-pai

1976 *Ch'an-hsüeh yü T'ang-Sung Shih-hsüeh* (Taipei: Li-ming Wen-hua Shih-yeh Kung-ssu, 1976).

URY, Marian

1977 *Poems of the Five Mountains* (Mushinsha, 1977).

1979 *Tales of Times Now Past: Sixty-two Stories from a Medieval Japanese Collection* (Berkeley: University of California Press, 1979).

VARLEY, H. Paul

1980 *A Chronicle of Gods and Sovereigns: Jinnō Shōtōki of Kitabatake Chikafusa* (New York: Columbia University Press, 1980).

WALEY, Arthur
1949 *The Life and Times of Po Chü-i* (London: Allen & Unwin, 1949).

WATSON, Burton
1975-76 *Japanese Literature in Chinese* (New York: Columbia University Press, 1975-76). 2 vols.

WILLIAMSON, George
1930 *The Donne Tradition: A Study in English Poetry from Donne to the Death of Cowley* (Cambridge, Mass.: Harvard University Press, 1930).

WILLIG, Rosette F.
1983 *The Changelings: A Classical Japanese Court Tale* (Stanford: Stanford University Press, 1983).

YI Ka-wŏn
1961 *Hanguk Hanmun Haksa* (Seoul: Mingjung Sogwan, 1961).

YÜEH Heng-chün
1969 *Sung-tai Hua-pen Yen-chiu; Kuo-li Tai-wan Ta-hsüeh Wen-shih Ts'ung-k'an*, no. 29 (Taipei: National Taiwan University, 1967). Revised edition, 1969. 1969 edition used.

INDEX

Spelling (i.e., pronunciation) of names and titles follows the ideas of our author. Sovereigns are entered by royal name followed by "Tennō," priests by their best known name in religion, and other Japanese historical figures most commonly by their given name. Chinese and Koreans are listed surname first. All titles are entered in romanized versions of the Japanese (or Chinese or Korean). Whatever inconsistencies are involved, numerous cross-references are supplied and matter is added in parentheses. The Contents and Chronological Table should also be consulted. Index prepared by Aileen Gatten.

utagatari (oral waka stories), 56-57, 57n, 106, 108-9; in *Heike*, 331
utaimono (sung texts), 318
utamakura (poetic adornments, locales with poetic place names), 34n, 34-37, 228, 304-5, 358; defined, 34-35; examples of, 35; in kikō, 482-85
Utamakura Nayose (*Place Names with Poetic Associations*, early 14th c.), 36, 36n, 484
utamonogatari (waka narrative), 57n, 109, 332
Utatane no Ki, 290, 295. *See also* Abutsu
Utaura (*Divination with Waka*), 560
Utsuho Monogatari (*The Hollow Tree*, mid-10th c.), 18, 40n, 147n, 152, 168n, 172, 285n

Vairocana (J. Dainichi Nyorai), 83n
variety shows, Chinese (tsa-chi), 320, 322-23
verse-topics (kudai): defined, 46n; in shih, 186-87; in waka composition, 46, 50, 188. *See also* hon'i; waka topics
vocation, artistic. *See* michi

wabi (misery, desolation), ideal of, 144-45, 363, 435, 441
wabun (prose written in Japanese), 95, 117, 125, 136, 140, 142, 166, 168, 172, 174, 284-96, 297, 380, 471-91, 496; influence on renga, 449, see also *Genji Monogatari, Ise Monogatari*; as premier art, 290-91; in song, 350-52. *See also* mixed style; monogatari; nikki; quasi-classical prose
Waga Mi ni Tadoru Himegimi (13th c.?), quoted, 285
Waji Sōjō (*Memorial in Japanese, Dated Shōji* 2), 207. *See also* Shunzei
waka (or tanka; 31-syllable verse form), 24-94, 124-25, 130-31, 135-36, 140, 142, 148-49, 153, 158-60, 162-68, 171, 177, 179, 185-273, 329, 380, 385-424, 446n, 483-84, 488, 498; amoebic, *see* amoebic waka; background (ji), 251-53; contemplative, 185, 198-201, 209, 230-33, 238, 240, 256-58, 393-95, 397, 400-408, 413-16; critical terms in, 68-71, 185-201; design (mon), 251-53; early and high medieval distinguished, 27; emotive, 69-85, 267-69, 272, 285, 288; forenotes to, 111, 482; formal, 265, 272; fragmentation in, 241-54; ga in, *see* ga; ideals of sabi and tranquility in, 60-68; influence on renga, 274-80, 427, 429, 433, 435-36, 440n, 449, 452-53, 464n; influence of shih on, 46-50, 60-68, 181, 224-26, 242-45, 400, 402, 429; influence of, on song, 350-54; influence of Zen on, 363, 379, 392n, 395, 413-16; informal, 264, 272; innovations in, 24-94, 211; in mixed-style prose, 304; in monogatari, 103-4, 108-9; on nature, 44-54, 264, 267, 269, 272, 397-98, 404-6, 408-13; neoclassicism in, 185-201; in nikki, 110-12, 294; in nō, 530, 534-37; non-oblique expression in, 52-54; nuance (yosei) in, 211; objective portrayal in, 163; personal collections of, *see* kashū; plain style of, 255, 258, 261; prefaces to, in Chinese prose, 12; pseudo-classicism in, 255-61, 284; religious perspective in, 79-85, 265-73, 393; royal anthologies of, *see* chokusenshū; schools of, *see* Kyōgoku, Mikohidari, Nijō, Reizei, Rokujō; sequences, 135, 206-9, 247, 253-54, 278-80, 410n, 418-24, defined, 37-38; stories centered on, *see* utagatari, utamonogatari; topics, *see* waka topics; treatises, *see* karon; unconventional (hikaika), 274, 326; zoku in, *see* zoku. *See also* association; progression; Shunzei; Tamekanu; Teika; utaawase; yōen; yūgen
Waka Dōmōshō, 141n
Waka Gasshō (ca. 1096), 36n
Waka Genzaisho Mokuroku, 141n
Waka Kubon, 55n
Waka Kuden, 261. *See also* Genshō
waka matches. *See* utaawase
Waka Teikin, quoted, 423n
waka topics (dai): assigned (daiei), 37-44, 50, 191-97, 455; categories of, 37-38; composite (ketsudai), 46, 50; twelfth-century, 34-44. *See also* hon'i; utaawase; verse-topics
Wakadokoro (Bureau of Waka), 209, 227, 274
Wakan Kensakushū (late 13th c.), 179n, 180; quoted, 179-80
wakan konkōbun. *See* mixed style
Wakan Rōeishū (*Collection of Japanese and Chinese Songs*), 17, 38, 100, 155, 180
Wakatei Jisshu, 55n
waki (secondary character in nō), 358, 484-85; defined, 523n; in dramatic nō, 530; in dream nō, 523-25; narration by, 544-48. *See also* nō
wakikata, defined, 547n
Wang An-shih, 448, 497
Wang Ch'ang, 221n
Wang Ch'ang-ling, 42-43, 200, 395

This book has been composed and printed by
Princeton University Press
Designed by Jan Lilly
Typography: Linotron Sabon and Zapf Chancery
Paper: Glatfelter's Sebago